AF527041

MAGBOOK

Indian Constitution & Polity

For **UPSC, State PCS (Prelims & Mains)** and other Examinations

Manohar Pandey

Edited by
Ameebh Ranjan
Fazle Kibria

3e

ARIHANT PUBLICATIONS (INDIA) LTD.

All Rights Reserved

卐 © PUBLISHER

No part of this publication may be re-produced, stored in a retrieval system or by any means, electronic, mechanical, photocopying, recording, scanning, web or otherwise without the written permission of the publisher. Arihant has obtained all the information in this book from the sources believed to be reliable and true. However, Arihant or its editors or authors or illustrators don't take any responsibility for the absolute accuracy of any information published and the damage or loss suffered thereupon.

All disputes subject to Meerut (UP) jurisdiction only.

卐 ADMINISTRATIVE & PRODUCTION OFFICES

Regd. Office

'Ramchhaya' 4577/15, Agarwal Road, Darya Ganj, New Delhi -110002
Tele: 011- 47630600, 43518550

Head Office

Kalindi, TP Nagar, Meerut (UP) - 250002, Tel: 0121-7156203, 7156204

卐 SALES & SUPPORT OFFICES

Agra, Ahmedabad, Bengaluru, Bareilly, Chennai, Delhi, Guwahati, Hyderabad, Jaipur, Jhansi, Kolkata, Lucknow, Nagpur & Pune.

卐 PRICE ₹ 350.00

卐 **PO No.** : TXT-59-T069759-3-26

Published By Arihant Publications (India) Ltd.
For further information about the books published by Arihant, log on to www.arihantbooks.com or e-mail at info@arihantbooks.com

Follow us on    

MAGBOOK

Preface

Due to its highly unpredictable and difficult nature, Civil Services is one of the most coveted and prestigious exam in India. It tests the aspirants on the analytical and logical, subjective as well as contemporary levels in the subjects.

This book on Indian Constitution & Polity caters to this unpredictable and difficult nature of questions asked in various exams. It provides a clear conceptual clarity of the topic as well as explains the subject in a comprehensible, lucid way thus making the understanding of the subject strong and clear.

Upon the complete of this book, the candidate can easily and elaborately understand the Union Executive, Judiciary, Legislature, Local Self Government, Centre-State Relation, Special Provisions for State & UT's and Provisions for Certain Classes, etc., in a simplified manner.

The concepts and ideas of this book had been presented in such a way that an aspirant can easily solve subjective as well as objective questions after the complete analysis of the book.

The book is presented with the following features:

- Complete syllabus, facts from NCERT as well as compilation of updated facts
- Extensive coverage of Prelims oriented facts which includes the facts asked by UPSC as well as State PCS
- Compilation of self check at the end of each chapter which include questions for practice.
- Compilation of UPSC Mains Questions (2024-2015) topicwise through which aspirants can analyse the level of their understanding and preparation of the exam.

This revised edition has been developed by a team of experts who have worked diligently on the content. The project management team, including Mona Yadav (Project Manager), Himanshi Verma (Project Coordinator), Kanupriya Saini, Khushi (Proof Readers), Vinay Sharma (DTP Operator) and Bilal, Ankit Prajapati (Cover & Designers), have also made significant contributions.

We hope that the comprehensive study of this book will help aspirants preparing for the Civil Services and other competitive exams to achieve their goals and make their dreams come true. We welcome your valuable suggestions as they will assist us in improving future editions of the book.

Contents

The Constitution is the Supreme legal document of India. It is in place to uphold the Rule of Law and enjoys the ultimate supreme authority in India.

Chapter One

Constitutional Development of India

The constitutional development in India under the British rule can be divided into two phases :

- Phase 1 : Under East India Company (1773-1858)
- Phase 2 : Under British Crown (1858- 1947)

UNDER THE EAST INDIA COMPANY

East India Company ruled in India from 1773 to until the passing of Government of India Act of 1858.

Regulating Act, 1773

- This was the first step taken by the British Government to control and regulate the affairs of the East India Company in India. It recognised Political and Administrative functions of the East India Company for the first time.
- It laid the foundation of Central administration in India. It designated the Governor of Bengal as the Governor-General of Bengal.
- The first Governor-General of Bengal was Lord Warren Hastings. The Regulating Act of 1773 passed on the recommendation of the Secret Committee by the then British Prime Minister Lord North.
- The Governors in Councils at Madras and Bombay were brought under the control of Bengal, especially in matters of foreign policy.
- Now, they could not wage war against Indian states without Governor of Bengal's approval.
- An Executive Council was also created for providing assistance to Governor-General of Bengal comprising of four members.
- The executive body of East India Company known as the Court of Directors, were elected for a period of four years. They were primarily responsible to report to British Government regarding revenue, military and civil affairs of the company in India.
- The Governor-General had no veto powers. The Supreme Court was established at Fort Williams in Calcutta, 1774 comprising one Chief Justice and three other judges. Sir Elijah Impey was appointed as the first Chief Justice of this court.
- Three other judges-Robert Chambers, Stephen Caesar and John Hyde were also appointed.
- The act also prohibited the servant of the company from engaging in any private trade or accepting presents or bribes from the native Indian.

Act of Settlement, 1781

- This Act was an Amending Act, which removed the shortcomings of the Regulating Act, 1773. It is also known as the Judicature Act, 1781.
- The basic aim of the Act of Settlement, 1781 was to establish a new system of courts for removing the grievances against the Supreme Court.
- Revenue collectors and judicial officers of the company's courts were also exempted from the jurisdiction of the Supreme Court.

- It provided that appeals from provincial courts will now be directed to the Governor-General-in-Council rather than the Supreme Court.
- The Act specified that it would have jurisdiction over all inhabitants of Calcutta. It required the Supreme Court to consider and respect the religious and social customs and practices of the Indians when enforcing its decrees and processes.

> Under this Act, Governor-General and the members of his Council were exempted from the jurisdiction of the **Supreme Court**. It also provided that the public servants of the company were not to be subject to the jurisdiction of the Supreme Court for things done by them in their official capacity.

Pitt's India Act, 1784

- It was introduced to remove the drawbacks of the Regulating Act of 1773 and Act of Settlement, 1781.
- Under this Act, the company's territories in India were called the British Possessions in India for the first time.
- British Government was given the supreme control over Company's affairs and its administration in India. The Act placed the Indian affairs under the direct control of the British Government.
- The Act clearly distinguished the commercial and political functions of the Company. Thus, establishing a system of dual government.
- The Court of Directors were responsible for the commercial affairs while a Board of Control comprising of six members was appointed to look after the political affairs in India. It was named after the then British Prime Minister, William Pitt.
- It included a Secretary of State, Chancellor of Exchequer and Four Privy Councillors. The board was to directly report to the British Parliament.
- The Governor-General received Veto Rights (a Veto Right is the power to unilaterally reject a proposal, decision or resolution, even if it has been approved by a majority of members).
- This act reduced the number of members of Executive and Provincial Council from 4 to 3. One would be Commander-in-Chief of the British Crown.

The Act of 1786

- Lord Cornwallis demanded that power of the Governor-General should be enlarged to empower him to override the majority of his Council and act on his own special responsibility.
- The Act of 1786 merged the offices of Governor-General and Commander-in-Chief.
- Thus, *via* Act of 1786, Cornwallis became the first effective ruler of British India under the authority of Board of Control and the Court of Directors.

Charter Act of 1793

- According to this Act, the Charter of the Company was renewed for 20 years and it was declared that it would be allowed to continue with the possession of all territories for the next 20 years.
- A set of rules and regulations was established to effectively govern and manage the internal affairs of the British territories in Bengal.
- The regulation applied to the rights, persons and property of the Indian people and it bound the courts to regulate their decisions by the rules and regulations.
- Thus, this Act laid the foundation of government by written laws and regulations in British India in place of the personal rule of the past rulers.
- It laid down that the member's of the Board of Control and their staff were to be paid out of the Indian revenues. It mandated royal approval for appointment of Governor-General, Governors and the Commander-in-Chief.

Charter Act, 1813

- This Act renewed the company's Charter for a further 20 years. It however, deprived the company of its monopoly of trade except trade in tea and with China.
- The Charter Act of 1813 asserted constitutional position and established crown's sovereignty over British territories in India.
- It subjected the three Councils of the Governors to greater control of Parliament by requiring them to place all their regulations before the British Parliament.
- The Christian Missionaries were allowed to spread education and their religion in India.
- The company's commercial profits and territorial revenues were governed by this law. It was requested that it keep its commercial and territorial accounts separate.
- There was also a clause requiring that the company spends ₹ 1 lakh annually for education of Indians. It authorised the local government in India to impose taxes on persons.

Charter Act, 1833

- This Act was passed to renew Company's Charter. This Act was the last step towards centralisation in India under British Raj.
- It made the Governor-General of Bengal as the Governor-General of India. First Governor-General of India was Lord William Bentinck (in 1833).
- This Act for the first time created a Government of India with the Governor-General or the head, having authority over the entire territorial area possessed by the British in India.
- The Governor-General of India was given the power to legislate over the entire British India. It took away the Legislative Powers of the Governors of Bombay and Madras.
- The East India Company was now no longer a commercial body and was reduced to a purely administrative and political body. All the trade activities of the company in India came to an end.
- The Indian Council was to consist of four members one of whom one will only be acting as a member for legislative matters. A law member was added without voting right.
- The Act of 1833 also made the first attempt to codify laws of the country.
- Thus, the First Law Commission was set-up under the Chairmanship (1834) of Lord Macaulay.
- Laws made under this Act were known as Acts, earlier they were known as Regulations.
- The Act was intended to end the slave trade in India at the time.
- Slavery was abolished in the United Kingdom and all of its possessions by the British Parliament in 1833.

Charter Act, 1853

- It separated for the first time, the legislative and executive functions of the Governor-General's Council. The legislative function was to be performed by the new Legislative Council of Governor-General composed of six new members called Legislative Councillors.
- This Council came to be known as the Indian (Central) Legislative Council.
- The Act served as the foundation of the modern parliamentary form of government as the Legislative Council functioned as a mini-parliament utilising the same process of legislation as followed in the British Parliament.
- British Parliament was empowered to put Company's Governance in India to an end at any suitable time.
- The first Governor-General to assume independent charge was Lord Dalhousie.
- The law member became a full member with the right to vote.
- The number of members of Court of Directors was reduced from 24 to 18 out of which 6 people were to be nominated by the British Crown.
- It introduced an open competition system of selection and recruitment of civil servants. Accordingly, the Macaulay Committee (the committee on the Indian Civil Service) was appointed in 1854.
- Local representation was introduced for the first time in the Indian Legislative Council by appointing 4 out of the 6 members from the local (provincial) Governments of Madras, Bengal, Bombay and Agra.

UNDER BRITISH RULE

Acts passed under British Rule are as follows :

Government of India Act, 1858

- The Act was enacted in the wake of the Revolt of 1857, known as the First War of Independence or the Sepoy Mutiny.
- This Act was also known as the Act for Good Government in India and the Magna Carta of Indian independence.

Note *The Magna Carta or the Great Charter, was a document that established the rule of law and the idea that everyone, including the king, should be ruled by the law equally and fairly.*

- This Act transferred the government territories and revenues of India from the East India Company to the British Crown.
- In other words, it established the rule of the British Crown in India.
- Thus, the rule of the East India Company in India came to an end by this Act.
- The designation of the Governor-General of India was replaced with the Viceroy of India. Lord Canning was the first Viceroy of India.
- This Act abolished the office of board of control and court of directors.
- Thus, it ended the system of dual government established under the Pitt's India Act, 1784.

- Secretary of state was the new office created under the act having complete authority over the Indian administration and was supposed to exercise the powers of the British Crown in India.

Indian Councils Act, 1861

- Indian Councils Act, 1861, was passed by British Parliament on 11th August, 1861 which altered the composition of the Viceroy's Council for executive and legislative purposes.
- This Act made a beginning of representative institutions by associating Indians with the law making process.
- It provided that the Viceroys Executive Council should have some Indians as the non-official members while transacting the legislative businesses.

> The Viceroy **Lord Canning**, for the first time nominated three Indians to his Legislative Council. They were **Raja of Benaras, Maharaja of Patiala** and **Sir Dinkar Rao**.

- Without the Viceroy's approval, no bill relating to government finances, debt, the armed forces, religion or international relations could be passed. The Viceroy could also override the decisions of the Council.
- The Viceroy had absolute veto power and could issue ordinances without the consent of the Legislative Council during an emergency.
- Such ordinance would be enforceable for a period of six months. Lord Canning introduced the Portfolio System in 1859 which laid the foundation of Cabinet System in India.
- It restored the Legislative Power to Bombay and Madras Presidencies. It thus reversed the centralising tendencies that started from the Regulating Act of 1773 and reached its climax under the Charter Act of 1833.
- The Act established the new Legislative Councils for Bengal (1862), North-West frontier provinces (1866) and Punjab (1897).
- Law member was added in the Executive Council of Governor-General.

Indian Councils Act, 1892

- The Act increased the number of non-official members in the Central and Provincial Legislative Councils. However, the majority of the official members remained.
- The act introduced indirect provision of election for some of the non-official seats in Central and Provincial Legislative Councils. However ,the term 'Election' was nowhere used in the Act.
- This election was in the form of nomination of some of the non-official members to :
  - Central Legislative Council by Viceroy on recommendation of the Provincial Legislative Councils and Bengal Chamber of Commerce.
  - Provincial Legislative Council by the Governors on the recommendation of district boards, municipalities, trade associations, universities, chambers and zamindars.
- This Act also provided the power of discussing budget to the Legislative Councils.

Indian Councils Act, 1909

- The Act of 1909, is commonly known as the Morley-Minto Reforms. Morley was the Secretary of State for India in England and Minto was the Viceroy of India.
- The following were the main features of the Act of 1909 :
  - The Central Legislative Council was renamed as Imperial Legislative Council.
  - The number of members of the Legislative Council at the Centre was increased from 16 to 60.
  - The right of separate electorate was given to the Muslims introducing a system of communal representation for Muslims. According to this, only Muslim voters could elect Muslim members.
  - The Act effectively legalised communalism and Lord Minto came to be known as the Father of Communal Electorate.
  - Official members were to form the majority in Central Legislative Council, but in provinces, non-official members would be in majority.
  - The members of the Legislative Councils were permitted to discuss the budgets, suggest the amendments and even to vote on them, excluding those items that were included as non-vote items.
  - They were also entitled to ask supplementary questions during the legislative proceedings.
  - Elections were introduced in India for the first time. Indians were allowed in Executive Council of Viceroy.

- Separate representation for presidency corporations, universities, zamindars and chamber of commerce was established.

> - Two Indians were nominated to the Council of the Secretary of State for Indian affairs.
> - The Viceroy was empowered to nominate one Indian member to his Executive Council. **Satyendra Prasad Sinha** became the first Indian to join the Viceroy's Executive Council as a law member in 1909.

Government of India Act, 1919

- This Act is also known as the Montague-Chelmsford Reforms as Montague was the Secretary of State for India and Lord Chelmsford was the Viceroy of India in 1919.
- The objective of this Act was gradual introduction of responsible government in India as declared by the British Government on 20th August, 1917.
- The following were the salient features of this Act.
  - It introduced a system of dyarchy (It is a form of government where power is shared between two rulers or authorities.) in provinces.
  - It divided the provincial subjects of administration into two categories :
    —Transferred subjects These were to be administered by the Governor with the help of ministers responsible to the Legislative Council.
    —Reserved subjects These were to be administered by the Governor and the Executive Council without having any responsibility towards the Legislature.

However, this experiment was largely unsuccessful.

- This Act set the Devolution Rules, by which subjects of administration were divided into two categories namely, Central and Provincial.
  - Central category It had subjects of all India importance (like railways and finance).
  - Provincial category It had matters related to the administration of the provinces.
- It introduced bicameralism (concept of two houses) and direct elections in the country for the first time.
- Indian Legislative Council was replaced by a bicameral legislature consisting of :
  - Council of States - the upper house
  - Legislative Assembly- the lower house
- The majority of members of both houses were to be chosen by direct elections.
- The number of Indians in the Governor-General's Executive Council was raised to three (other than the Commander-in-Chief).
- The Indian members were entrusted with departments such as law, education, labour, health and industries.
- Communal representation (It is a system where only members of a particular community can vote in elections and only a representative of that community can contest the election) was extended to Sikhs, Indian Christians, Anglo-Indians, etc.
- It provided for a new office of the High Commissioner for India in London and transferred to him some of the functions of the Secretary of State for India.
- It also provided for franchise for those who were educated, paid tax and had property and granted reservation to women on 41 seats in Provincial Legislature and limited reservation in Central Legislature.
- It made provision for the establishment of a Public Service Commission, which came into being in 1926 for the recruitment of civil servants.
- It separated Provincial budgets from the Central budget and Provincial Legislatures were authorised to enact their budgets.

> **Simon Commission, 1927**
>
> - The Act of 1919, had provided for the appointment of a commission to review the provisions of the Act.
> - In 1927, the British Government announced the appointment of a Seven-Members Statutory Commission under the Chairmanship of **Sir John Simon**. All the members of the commission were British and hence all the parties of India boycotted the commission.
> - The commission submitted its report in 1930 and recommended the abolition of dyarchy, extension of responsible government in the provinces, establishment of a federation of British India and Princely States, continuation of communal electorate and so on.

Nehru Report, 1928

- The Nehru Report was memorandum outlining a proposed new Dominion Status Constitution for India.
- It was prepared by a committee of the All Parties Conference chaired by Motilal Nehru in Delhi (February, 1928). Some of the important elements of the report were as follows :
  - It contained a bill of rights (19 rights).
  - All power of government and all authority legislative, executive and judicial are derived from

the people and the same shall be exercised through organisations established by or under and in accord with this Constitution.

- There shall be no state religion, men and women shall have equal rights as citizens. There should be Federal form of government with residuary powers vested in the Centre.
- It included a suggestion that the provinces should be linguistically determined. It did not provide for separate electorates for any community or weightage for minorities.

Government of India Act, 1935

Establishment of All Indian Federation

- The Federation consists of provinces and Princely States as units.
- Distribution of power between centre and units through three lists - Federal (59 items), Provincial (54 items) and Concurrent list (36 items).
- The right to make laws on residuary subjects was given to Viceroy.
- A provision has been made for the establishment of an All India Union consisting of provinces of India, Chief Commissioners Provinces and Princely States.
- Provision to separate Burma from India.

Establishment of Public Service Commission

- Union Public Service Commission at the Centre.
- State Public Service Commission in the States.
- Joint Service Commission for two or more States.

Bicameral System was Introduced in 6 out of 11 States

Bengal, Bombay, Madras, Bihar, Assam and United Provinces.

Adoption of Dyarchy at the Centre

The federal subjects were to be divided into reserved and transferred subjects.

Responsible Government in Provinces

- The Governor had to make decisions in consultation with Ministers responsible to the Provincial Legislature.
- This provision came into effect in 1937 and discontinued in 1939.

Abolition of Dyarchy in the Provinces

Establishment of responsible government i.e., Provincial autonomy.

Extension of Franchise

Voting rights were extended to around 10% of the total population.

Establishment of Reserve Bank

For the purpose of controlling currency.

Expansion of Communal Representation

For the first time the system of election for Dalit castes, women and working class.

Abolition of Indian Council in England

Indian Secretary was provided with a team of advisors.

Provision of Federal Court in India

- Federal Court of India was a judicial body, established in India in 1937.
- The first Chief Justice was **Maurice Gwyer**.

August Offer, 1940

- On 8th August, 1940, the Viceroy of India Lord Linlithgow made the offer which is called August Offer. The following proposals of August offer were as follows:
  - Dominion status as the objective for India.
  - Expansion of the Viceroy's Executive Council, which would have a majority of Indians (who would be drawn from major political parties).
  - Setting up of a Constituent Assembly after the end of Second World War where mainly Indians would decide the Constitution.
  - No future Constitution was to be adopted without the support of consent of minorities.

Cripps Mission, 1942

- In 1942, Cripps Mission was sent to India under the leadership of Sir Stafford Cripps. Some of the proposals given by the Cripps Mission are given below :
  - Dominion status would be given to India, after the Second World War.
  - Once the Second World War ends, an elected body would be set-up in India for framing of Indian Constitution.
  - Even the Indian states would participate in the Constitution-making body.
- Almost all the parties and sections in India rejected the proposals given by the Cripps Mission.

Cabinet Mission, 1946

- The then British Prime Minister Clement Attlee formulated a Cabinet Mission to India to discuss and finalise plans for the transfer of power from the British Raj to Indian leadership.
- It will also provide India with independence under Dominion Status in the Commonwealth of the Nations.
- In March, 1946, Lord Attlee sent a Cabinet Mission to India consisting of three ministers, namely Lord Pethick Lawrence, Sir Stafford Cripps and Mr. AV Alexander.

Interim Government, 1946

- The Interim Government of India, also known as the Provisional Government of India, formed on 2nd September, 1946. In these elections, the Indian National Congress (INC) won around 69% of the seats and had a majority.
- The Congress Party won 208 seats and the Muslim League won 73 seats. Pt. Jawaharlal Nehru became the Vice-President of Interim Government and served as the de-facto Prime Minister.
- Eventhough, the Muslim League refused to be a part of the Interim Government, insisting on their demand for a separate nation, it eventually became a part of it.

Interim Government (1946)

Member	Portfolios Held
Pt. Jawaharlal Nehru	External Affairs and Commonwealth Relations
Sardar Vallabhbhai Patel	Home Affairs/Information and Broadcasting
Dr. Rajendra Prasad	Food and Agriculture
Dr. John Mathai	Industries and Supplies
Jagjivan Ram	Labour
Sardar Baldev Singh	Defence
CH Bhabha	Works, Mines and Power
Liaquat Ali Khan	Finance
Abdur Rab Nishtar	Posts and Air
Asaf Ali	Railways and Transport
C. Rajagopalachari	Education and Arts
Ibrahim Ismail Chundrigar	Commerce
Ghaznafar Ali Khan	Health
Joginder Nath Mandal	Law

The members of the Interim Government were members of the Viceroy's Executive Council. The Viceroy continued to be the head of the Council. But, Jawaharlal Nehru was designated as the Vice-President of the Council.

Mountbatten Plan, 1947

The British Government proposed a plan announced on 3rd June, 1947 which is known as Mountbatten plan or 3rd June plan which included following principles :

- Principle of Partition of India was accepted by the British Government.
- Successor governments would be given Dominion Status. Implicit right to secede from the British Commonwealth.
- The Indian Independence Act, 1947 was the implementation of 3rd June, Plan.

Indian Independence Act, 1947

- The Indian Independence Act which came into force on 18th July, 1947, divided British Indian territory into two new states i.e., India and Pakistan, which were to be dominions under the Commonwealth of Nations until their Constitutions came into effect.
- To demarcate boundary line between India and Pakistan, a commission was constituted under the Chairmanship of Sir Cyril Radcliffe.
- The office of Viceroy was abolished. Each of the two independent dominions would be provided with a Governor-General appointed by the British king on the advice of the dominion cabinet.

> **Lord Mountbatten** became the first Governor-General of dominion India. Later, the Constituent Assembly elected C. Rajagopalachari as the Governor-General of Independent India.

- By this Act, the sovereignty and responsibility of the British Crown over India were to lapse from the Appointed Day (the date India gets independence – later decided as 15th August, 1947).

First Cabinet of Free India (1947)

Minister	Portfolios Held
Pt. Jawaharlal Nehru	Prime Minister, External Affairs and Commonwealth Relations, Scientific Research
Sardar Vallabhbhai Patel	Home Affairs, Information and Broadcasting and States Reorganisation
Dr. Rajendra Prasad	Food and Agriculture
Maulana Abul Kalam Azad	Education
Dr. John Mathai	Railways and Transport
RK Shanmukham Chetty	Finance
Dr. BR Ambedkar	Law
Jagjivan Ram	Labour
Sardar Baldev Singh	Defence
Rajkumari Amrit Kaur	Health
CH Bhabha	Commerce
Dr. Shyama Prasad Mukherjee	Industries and Supplies
Rafi Ahmed Kidwai	Communications
VN Gadgil	Works, Mines and Power

The Constitution of India is the Supreme Law of India. It was drafted by the Constituent Assembly which was elected by the elected members of the Provincial Assemblies.

Chapter Two

Making of the Indian Constitution

The Constituent Assembly was formed in December, 1946. The Assembly spent next three years in framing of the most important document for a newly independent nation.

The concept of a Constituent Assembly for India first came to the forefront by the communist leader MN Roy in the year 1934. It was officially demanded for the first time by the Indian National Congress in 1935.

This demand was at last accepted in the August Offer of 1940 in which the British Government offered to set-up a representative body consisting of Indians to frame a Constitution for India.

CONSTITUENT ASSEMBLY

- August Offer, 1940 The British Government offered for the first time the setting up of a Constituent Assembly after the Second World War consisting mainly of Indian members. This offer was rejected by the Congress.
- Cripps Proposals, 1942 It made a proposal for the formation of a Constituent Assembly consisting entirely of Indians after the Second World War which would frame a new Constitution for India.
- The Cripps Proposals were rejected by the Muslim League as it wanted partition with two separate Constituent Assemblies.
- Cabinet Mission, 1946 Cabinet Mission suggested a plan for the formation of Constituent Assembly consisting of members elected by provincial assemblies by proportional representation.
- Although it rejected the formation of two Constituent Assemblies, it was most agreeable to Muslim League because some of the provisions of this scheme seemed favourable to them.

Formation of Constituent Assembly

- The Constituent Assembly was set-up in December, 1946 as per the Cabinet Mission Plan of 1946. However, the elections to the assembly were indirect in nature.
- The Assembly was to have proportional representation from existing provinces and from various Princely States.
- Bulk of these elections was completed by the end of July 1946, under the supervision of reforms office under Governor-General (Viceroy).
- Members of the Constituent Assembly included Jawaharlal Nehru, Dr. Rajendra Prasad, Sardar Vallabhbhai Patel, Maulana Azad and many more supreme leaders of the country.

- The assembly consisted of 389 members that represented :
  - British India (296 seats) - 292 members from eleven governor provinces and 4 members from four chief commissioner provinces(one from each).
  - Princely States (93 seats)
- The strength of the Constituent Assembly was reduced to 299 following the withdrawal of the Muslim League members after the partition of the country.
- Each province and Princely State or group of states were allotted seats proportional to their respective population.
- The seats in each British province were distributed among the three main communities-Muslims, Sikhs and General (except muslims and sikhs), in proportion to their respective population.
- The members of that particular community would elect their representative in the provincial legislative assembly through the method of proportional representation by means of single transferable vote.
- The heads of the Princely States would nominate the representative of their respective Princely States.
- Hence, the Constituent Assembly thus formed was a partly elected and partly nominated body.

> In July-August 1946, the elections for the Constituent Assembly (for 296 seats) were held. Seats won by different sections were as follows :
>
> - **208 seats**- Indian National Congress
> - **73 seats** - Muslim League
> - **15 seats** - small groups and independents
>
> The 93 seats allotted to the Princely States remained unfilled as they decided to stay away from the Constituent Assembly.

- Parties that represented the Constituent Assembly were the Congress Party, (which had a majority), Muslim League, Scheduled Caste Federation, the Indian Communist Party and the Union Party.

Proceeding of the Constituent Assembly

- The Constituent Assembly met for the first time on 9th December, 1946. The Muslim League boycotted the Constituent Assembly owing to their continued demand of a separate state of Pakistan.
- Thus, the strength of the assembly was reduced to 299. The meeting was attended by only 211 members. Dr. Sachchidananda Sinha was elected as the Interim President of the Assembly.
- On 11th December, 1946, Dr. Rajendra Prasad was elected as the President and HC Mukherjee and VT Krishnamachari as the Vice-President of the Constituent Assembly. BN Rau was appointed as the Constitutional Advisor.

Objective Resolution

On 13th December, 1946, Pt. Jawaharlal Nehru moved the objective resolution, which laid down the fundamentals and philosophy of the constitutional structure.

Main Points of the Objective Resolution

- India is an independent sovereign republic. It means having the highest power or being completely independent.
- India shall be a Union of erstwhile British Indian territories, Indian state and other parts outside British India and Indian states as are willing to be a part of the Union.
- Territories forming the Union shall be autonomous units and exercise all powers and functions of the government and administration, except those assigned to or vested in the Union.
- All people of India shall be guaranteed and secured social, economic and political justice; equality of status and opportunities and equality before law; and fundamental freedoms of speech, expression, belief, faith, worship, vocation, association and action, subject to law and public morality.
- The minorities, backward and tribal areas, depressed and Other Backward Classes shall be provided adequate safeguards.
- The objectives resolution was adopted unanimously by the Constituent Assembly on 22nd January, 1947.

> **Changes in the Constituent Assembly through the Indian Independence Act of 1947**
>
> - The Constituent Assembly was made a fully sovereign body which could frame any Constitution and repeal or change any law made by the British Parliament related to India.
> - The Assembly was assigned with the dual task of framing the Constitution as well as enacting the ordinary laws for the country, i.e., it also functioned as a Legislative Body. It was chaired by **Dr. Rajendra Prasad** when it met as a constituent body and it was chaired by **GV Mavalankar** when it met as a Legislative Body.

Important Personalities Related to Constituent Assembly

Persons	Responsibilities in the Constituent Assembly
Sir BN Rau	Constitutional or Legal Advisor to the Constituent Assembly
HVR Iyengar	Secretary of the Constituent Assembly
SN Mukherjee	Chief Draftman of the Constitution in the Assembly
Prem Behari Narain Raizada	Calligrapher of the English version of the Indian Constitution
Beohar Rammanohar Sinha and Nand Lal Bose	Illumination, Beautification and Ornamentation of the Constitution (Nand Lal Bose worked on the Hindi version)
Vasant Krishna Vaidya	Calligrapher for the Hindi version of the Indian Constitution

Women Participation in Constituent Assembly

- There were fifteen female members in the Constituent Assembly and all of them had been freedom fighters. These women were a part of Presidential panel and various other sub-committees.
- Some of these women were Rajkumari Amrit Kaur, Sarojini Naidu, Sucheta Kripalani, Vijya Lakshmi Pandit and Durgabai Deshmukh.

Committees of Constituent Assembly

Drafting and other important committees related to Constituent Assembly are as follows :

Drafting Committee

- The Drafting Committee was appointed on 29th August, 1947 with Dr. BR Ambedkar as the Chairman.
- Other members of committee are :
  - N. Gopalaswamy Ayyangar
  - KM Munshi
  - Alladi Krishnaswamy Ayyar
  - Syed Muhammed Saadulla
  - N. Madhava Rau (replaced BL Mitter)
  - TT Krishnamachari (replaced DP Khaitan who died in 1948)

Other Committees

Name of the Committee	Chairman
Committee on the Rules of Procedure	Dr. Rajendra Prasad
Steering Committee	Dr. Rajendra Prasad
Finance and Staff Committee	Dr. Rajendra Prasad
Adhoc Committee on the National Flag	Dr. Rajendra Prasad
Credential Committee	Alladi Krishnaswamy Ayyar
House Committee	B. Pattabhi Sitaramayya
Order of Business Committee	KM Munshi
Committee on the Functions of the Constituent Assembly	GV Mavalankar
Advisory Committee on Fundamental Rights, Minorities and Tribal and Excluded Areas	Vallabhbhai Patel
Provincial Constitution Committee	Vallabhbhai Patel
Minorities Sub-Committee	HC Mukherjee
Fundamental Rights Sub-Committee	JB Kripalani
North-East Frontier Tribal Areas and Assam Excluded and Partially Excluded Areas Sub-Committee	Gopinath Bordoloi
States Committee	Jawaharlal Nehru
Union Powers Committee	Jawaharlal Nehru
Union Constitution Committee	Jawaharlal Nehru
Excluded and Partially Excluded Areas (other than those in Assam) Sub-Committee	AV Thakkar

Sessions of the Constituent Assembly

Session	Held
First	9th-23rd December, 1946
Second	20th-25th January, 1947
Third	28th April - 2nd May, 1947
Fourth	14th-31st July, 1947
Fifth	14th-30th August, 1947
Sixth	27th January, 1948
Seventh	4th November, 1948 - 8th January, 1949
Eighth	16th May - 16th June, 1949
Ninth	30th July - 18th September, 1949
Tenth	6th-17th October, 1949
Eleventh	14th-26th November, 1949

ENACTMENT OF THE CONSTITUTION

- The Constituent Assembly took almost 3 years (2 years, 11 months and 18 days) to complete its historic task of drafting the Constitution for Independent India.
- On 26th November, 1949, the people of India through the Constituent Assembly adopted, enacted and gave themselves the Constitution of India.
- The Constitution contained a Preamble, 395 Article, 22 Parts and 8 Schedules. The Preamble was enacted after the Constitution had already been enacted.
- In all, 284 members signed the Constitution on 24th January, 1950. The date 26th November, 1949 is also mentioned in the Preamble as the date on which the people of India adopted, enacted and gave to themselves the Constitution.
- According to Article 394, provisions relating to the citizenship, elections, provisional Parliament and temporary and transitional provisions contained in 5, 6, 7, 8, 9, 60, 324, 366, 367, 379, 380, 388, 391, 392, 393 and 394 came into force on the day of adoption (i.e., 26th November, 1949) of the Constitution.
- And the remaining provisions of the Constitution came into being on the day of the commencement (i.e., 26th January, 1950) of the Constitution.
- The Constituent Assembly held its final session on 24th January, 1950. It continued to function as the provisional Parliament of India from 26th January 1950 to until the formation of a new Parliament after the first general elections in 1951-52.
- When the Constitution of India came into force on 26th January, 1950, it repealed the Indian Independence Act, 1947 and Government of India Act, 1935.
- India ceased to be dominion of the British Crown and became a sovereign, democratic and republic.

  Note *It is a system of government where the people have power and participate in the decision-making process.*
- 26th January was chosen at the date of commencement because on this day, Purna Swaraj was celebrated on 26th January, 1930 after the Lahore Session in December, 1929.
- Every year, 26th November is observed as Constitution Day since 2015.

Beyond Constitution Making : Other Key Functions Performed by the Constituent Assembly

- Ratification of India's membership of the commonwealth- May, 1949
- Adoption of National Flag- 22nd July, 1947
- Adoption of National Anthem- 24th January, 1950
- Adoption of National Song - 24th January, 1950
- Election of Dr. Rajendra Prasad as the first President of India - 24th January, 1950

Schedules and Parts of the Indian Constitution

Twelve Schedules and Twenty two parts of the Indian Constitution are :

Schedules of the Constitution

Schedules	Features
First Schedule	The States and the Union Territories of India
Second Schedule	Salaries and emoluments
Third Schedule	Oath and affirmation
Fourth Schedule	Allocation of seats in the Council of States
Fifth Schedule	Administration and Control of Scheduled Areas
Sixth Schedule	Administration of Tribal Areas in Assam, Mizoram, Tripura and Meghalaya
Seventh Schedule	Distribution of powers between Union and States (Union, State and Concurrent list)
Eighth Schedule	Languages recognised by Constitution (22)
Ninth Schedule	Acts and Regulations protected from Judicial Review
Tenth Schedule	Anti-Defection Law
Eleventh Schedule	Panchayats
Twelfth Schedule	Municipalities

Parts & Articles of the Constitution

Part	Subject Matter		Articles Covered
I	The Union and its Territory		1 to 4
II	Citizenship		5 to 11
III	Fundamental Rights		12 to 35
IV	Directive Principles of State Policy		36 to 51
IV A	Fundamental Duties		51 A
V	The Union		52 to 151
	Chapter I	The Executive	52 to 78
	Chapter II	Parliament	79 to 122
	Chapter III	Legislative Powers of the President	123
	Chapter IV	The Union Judiciary	124 to 147
	Chapter V	Comptroller and Auditor-General of India	148 to 151
VI	The States		152 to 237
	Chapter I	General	152
	Chapter II	The Executive	153 to 167
	Chapter III	The State Legislature	168 to 212
	Chapter IV	Legislative Powers of the Governors	213
	Chapter V	The High Courts	214 to 232
	Chapter VI	Subordinate Courts	233 to 237
VIII	The Union Territories		239 to 242
IX	The Panchayats		243 to 243-0
IX A	The Municipalities		243 P to 243 ZG
IX B	The Co-operative Societies		243 ZH to 243 ZT
X	The Scheduled and the Tribal Areas		244 to 244 A
XI	Relations between the Union and the States		245 to 263
	Chapter I	Legislative Relations	245 to 255
	Chapter II	Administrative Relations	256 to 263
XII	Finance, Property, Contracts and Suits		264 to 300 A
	Chapter I	Finance	264 to 291
	Chapter II	Borrowing	292 to 293

Parts & Articles of the Constitution

Part	Subject Matter		Articles Covered
	Chapter III	Property, Contracts, Rights Liabilities, Obligations and Suits	294 to 300
	Chapter IV	Right to Property	300 A
XIII	Trade, Commerce and Intercourse within the Territory of India		301 to 307
XIV	Services under the Union and the States		308 to 323
	Chapter I	Services	308 to 314
	Chapter II	Public Service Commission	315 to 323
XIVA	Tribunals		323 A to 323 B
XV	Elections		324 to 329 A
XVI	Special Provisions Relating to Certain Classes		330 to 342
XVII	Official Language		343 to 351
	Chapter I	Language of the Union	343 and 344
	Chapter II	Regional Languages	345 to 347
	Chapter III	Language of the Supreme Court, the High Courts and so on	348 and 349
	Chapter IV	Special Directives	350 to 351
XVIII	Emergency Provisions		352 to 360
XIX	Miscellaneous		361 to 367
XX	Amendments of the Constitution		368
XXI	Temporary, Transitional and Special Provisions		369 to 392
XXII	Short Title, Commencement, Authoritative Text in Hindi and Repeals		393 to 395

Part IV-A and Part XIV-A were added by 42nd Amendment Act, 1976. Part IX-A was added by the 74th Amendment Act, 1992 and Part IX-B was added by the 97th Amendment Act, 2011.

The Constitution of India is provided with a sort of basic structure that are defined as the salient features of it.

Chapter Three

Salient Features of the Indian Constitution

FEATURES OF INDIAN CONSTITUTION

The salient features of the Constitution are classified as below :

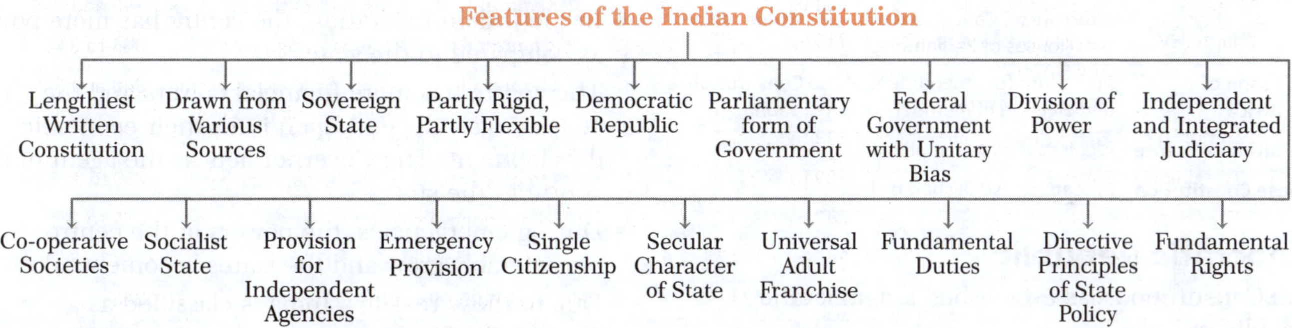

Lengthiest Written Constitution

- Generally, Constitutions can be classified into written, like the American Constitution or unwritten, like the British Constitution and most of the Constitutions are written.
- The Constitution of India is the lengthiest of all the Written Constitutions of the world. It is a very comprehensive, elaborate and detailed document.
- Originally, it had 395 Articles, 22 Parts and 8 Schedules. At present, the Constitution has 470 Articles, 25 Parts and 12 Schedules.
- As of April 2025, it has around 105 amendments have been made, adding, deleting, or modifying several articles and parts.

Sovereign State

- The Indian Constitution has been adopted by the people of India, which means that sovereignty is vested in the Indian people.
- The underlying meaning of sovereignty is that the people of India are not subject to power.

Partly Rigid and Partly Flexible

- Whether a Constitution is rigid or flexible depends on the nature of amendments that can be done to it.
- Rigidity in a Constitution suggests that making amendments to the Constitution follow a rigorous procedure as in case of the USA.
- On the other hand, a flexible constitution is one that can be amended in the same manner as ordinary laws are amended in case of Britain.
- Amendments to the Constitution are made by Indian Parliament, the procedure for which is laid down in Article 368.

Sources of Indian Constitution

Sources	Descriptions
UK Constitution	Law-making procedures, Parliamentary government, Rule of law, Single citizenship, Cabinet System and Bicameralism, Delegation of powers to Lok Sabha.
US Constitution	Fundamental Rights, Independent judiciary, Judicial Review, Procedure of President, Removal of the judges of the Supreme Court and High Courts and post of Vice-President.
Canadian Constitution	Federation with strong centre, Residuary powers in the Centre, Appointment of State Governors by Centre and advisory jurisdiction of the Supreme Court.
Irish Constitution	Directive Principles of State Policy, the method of the Presidential election, nominating 12 members of Rajya Sabha.
Weimar Constitution of Germany	Suspension of Fundamental Rights during emergency.
USSR	Fundamental Duties and the ideal of Justice (social, economic and political)
Australian Constitution	Principle of co-operative federalism, freedom of inter-state trade, commerce and intercourse, Concurrent list, joint sitting of the two Houses of Parliament.
Constitution of South Africa	Procedure for amendment of the Constitution and election of members of Rajya Sabha.
Constitution of France	Ideals of liberty, equality and fraternity.
Japanese Constitution	Procedure established by law.

Democratic Republic

- The Constitution has established a democratic republic in India.
- The term democratic is understood to mean that the source of government's power lies in the people and that the separation of powers sets the best tone for freedom in a liberal democracy.

Parliamentary form of Government

- There are two significant forms of government system in the world :
  - American Presidential form of Government which is based on the doctrine of separation of powers between the legislative and executive organs.
  - British Parliamentary form of Government which is based on the principle of co-ordination and co-operation between the legislative and executive wings of the government. Executive is responsible to the legislature in this form of government.
- Parliamentary form of Government is also known as the Westminster model of government, cabinet government and responsible government.
- The role of Prime Ministers in the Parliamentary form of Government is so significant that it is sometimes also known as the Prime Ministerial Government.

Federal Government with Unitary Bias

- The Constitution of India establishes a Federal System of Government. However, it contains both federal and unitary elements.
- That is why it is often described as 'federal in form and unitary in spirit'.
- The term 'federation' is nowhere used in the text of the Constitution, instead Article 1 describes India as a 'Union of States'.
- The phrase 'Union of States' signifies two things about the Indian federation :
  - The Indian federation is not formed due to the agreement between its individual states.
  - No state has the right to secede from the Indian federation.
- In the Indian federation, the centre has more powers as compared to the states.
- The centre has more financial powers and the states largely depend upon it for their economic development. The Governor acts as the agent of the centre in the states.
- During emergencies, the powers of the centre considerably grow and the states become weak.
- Due to these reasons, India is classified as a quasi-federal state.
- The centre is placed at a more powerful position as compared to states but the jurisdiction of powers has been clearly defined by the Constitution of India.
  - Dr. BR Ambedkar has said that "the Constitution should be given a tight structure of federalism".
  - G. Austin has called Indian federalism as co-operative federalism.
  - SR Bommai *v/s* Union of India 1994 case clearly upheld the idea of federalism, stating that state governments are not below the centre and highlighting the importance of working together through cooperative federalism.

Division of Powers

- The clear division of powers between the centre and the state enables a smooth functioning.
- This is ensured by dividing subjects under three lists which are as follows :

- Union List It consists of 100 subjects (originally 97 subjects) such as defence, international affairs, railways, etc and the centre is the only decision-making entity.
- State List States can make their decisions without Centre's direction on 61 subjects (originally 66 subjects) such as public health, police, etc.
- Concurrent List Both the centre and the state have jurisdiction over 52 subjects (originally 47 subjects) including education, economic and social planning, etc. Parliament has exclusive power to make any law with respect to any matter not enumerated in the Concurrent List or State List.

Independent and Integrated Judiciary

- The Constitution provides for an integrated judiciary with the Supreme Court at the apex of the hierarchy.
- The High Courts stand in its middle at the state level and the lower courts are placed at the bottom.

Integrated Judiciary Hierarchy of Courts in India

- Supreme Court (at National Level)
- High Court (at State Level)
- District and Subordinate Courts and Other Lower Courts (at District, Town or Local Level)

Independent Judiciary

- An independent judiciary ensures a justice system that is not controlled by the other arms of the government or any political authority.
- The judiciary in India has been made independent of the executive as well as the legislature.
- The independence of the judiciary is strengthened with the following provisions such as :
  - The Supreme Court of India is a federal court, highest court of appeal, guarantor of the Fundamental Rights of the citizens and the guardian of the Constitution.
  - The judges are appointed on the basis of their qualifications and cannot be removed easily.
  - The Supreme Court and the High Court have the power of Judicial Review.
  - They have the power to declare acts of legislatures and actions of the executive as void, if such acts or actions are found to be in conflict with the provisions of the Constitution.
- There are various other provisions to ensure its independence like-security of tenure, all the expenses of the Supreme Court charged upon the Consolidated Fund of India, fixed service conditions of judges, the conduct of judges cannot be discussed in the legislature.
- The Supreme Court has been provided with the power to punish for its contempt, ban on practice after retirement and so on.

Due Process of Law *v/s* Procedure Established by Law

- The Indian Constitution has the provision of 'procedure established by law' as against the principle of 'due process of law' contained in the American Constitution.
- That means, the power and scope of Judicial Review in India is narrower than that in the US.
- This has resulted in a blend of British Parliamentary Sovereignty and American Judicial Supremacy in India. The Supreme Court of India has the authority to use Judicial Review to declare any law enacted by Parliament **unconstitutional** while Parliament possesses the power to **amend** any significant portion of the Constitution.

Fundamental Rights

- The Fundamental Rights are guaranteed to the citizens by our Constitution. These are enumerated in Part III of the Constitution. Constitution of India guarantees six Fundamental Rights to every citizen.

- These rights are fundamental because they are basic to the moral and spiritual development of the individual and these rights cannot be easily abridged by the Parliament.

Directive Principles of State Policy

- The Directive Principles of State Policy are enumerated in Part IV from Articles 36 to 51 of the Constitution.
- Their instructions or directives mentioned in the Constitution for the State and Central Government.
- The Directive Principles of State Policy have been adopted from the Irish Constitution.
- The Directive Principles were included in our Constitution in order to provide social and economic justice to the people of India.
- American constitutionalist Grenville Austin in his book 'The Indian Constitution Cornerstone of a Nation' has called Directive Principles the Soul of the Constitution.
- The Directive Principles are not enforceable in a Court of Law, but they are nevertheless fundamental in the governance of the country.
- The Supreme Court in the Minerva Mills Case (1980) held that "the Indian Constitution is founded on the bedrock of the balance between the Fundamental Rights and the DPSPs".

Fundamental Duties

- The Fundamental Duties were not part of the Constitution originally. They were inserted in Part IVA of the Constitution by the 42nd Amendment Act, 1976 upon the recommendation of the Swaran Singh Committee.
- A new Article - Article 51A enumerates originally 10 Fundamental Duties but were increased to 11 by 86th Constitutional Amendment Act, 2002.
- These duties were inspired from the Constitution of erstwhile Union of Soviet Socialist Republics (USSR).

Universal Adult Franchise

- Article 326 of the Constitution of India provides Universal Adult Suffrage. Anybody who has completed 18 years of age, is eligible to vote in general elections.
- This is one of the most revolutionary aspects of Indian democracy. The voting age was reduced to 18 years from 21 years in 1989 by the 61st Constitutional Amendment Act, 1988.

Secular Character of State

- Secularism means that the state promotes no religion as everyone has equal rights irrespective of their religion.
- The Indian Constitution provides India to be a secular state.
- The term secular was added to the Preamble of the Indian Constitution by the 42nd Constitutional Amendment Act, 1976.
- The Western concept of secularism is separation between state and religion.
- This negative concept of secularism is inapplicable in the Indian situation where society is multi-religious. Hence, the Indian Constitution embodies the positive concept of secularism i.e., giving equal respect to all religions or protecting all religions equally.

Single Citizenship

- In India, there is only single citizenship. An Indian is a citizen of India only, he is not a citizen of any Indian state.
- Single citizenship is meant to strengthen national unity and national integration.
- In the United States of America, there is concept of dual citizenship. An American individual is a citizen of America and at the same time he is also a citizen of the state where he/she lives.
- In India, there is no distinction between citizens and they all have the same political and civil rights throughout the Territory of India regardless of their birthplace and place of residence.

Emergency Provisions

- The Constitution makers also foresaw that there could be situations when the government could not be run as in ordinary times.
- To cope with such situations, the Constitution elaborates on emergency provisions.

Three Types of Emergency		
1 Emergency caused by war, external aggression or armed rebellion (Article 352).	2 Emergency arising out of the failure of Constitutional Machinery in states (Article 356).	3 Financial Emergency on the ground of threat to the financial stability or credit of India (Article 360).

- During an Emergency, the federal structure of India is converted into unitary structure without bringing in any real Constitutional Amendments. This is a unique feature of the Indian Constitution.

Provision of Independent Agencies

- Election Commission (Article 324) to ensure free and fair elections in the country.
- Comptroller and Auditor-General (Article 148) to audit the accounts of centre and the states. CAG acts as the public purse and looks into the legality of government expenditure.
- Union and State Public Service Commissions (Article 315) to conduct examinations for recruitment in all India services, higher central services and state services.
- Various provisions in the Constitution such as the security of tenure, fixed service conditions etc, ensures the independence of these bodies.

Socialist State

- By the 42nd Constitutional Amendment Act of 1976, the word 'Socialist' has been added to the Preamble of the Constitution, which was not there in the original form of the Constitution.
- The purpose of the Constitution is to establish equality in the entire society from political, economic and social point of view.

Cooperative Societies

- The Constitution of India recognises cooperative societies as a vital aspect of the country's economic and social development.
- This is reflected in
  - 97th Constitutional Amendment Act, 2011 provided constitutional status and protection to co-operative societies.
  - Article 19(1)(C) recognise the right to form co-operative societies as a Fundamental Right.
  - Article 43 B promotion of cooperative societies.
  - Article 243 ZH to 243 ZT, Part IX B entitled as 'co-operative societies'.

NATURE OF THE INDIAN CONSTITUTION

- The nature of the Indian Constitution is unitary or federal, in its context there is no unanimity among the scholars.
- If the centre is the only user of the powers of the government and the state is subordinate to it then the government will be unitary, on the contrary, if there is division of powers between the centre and the states, then the government will be federal.

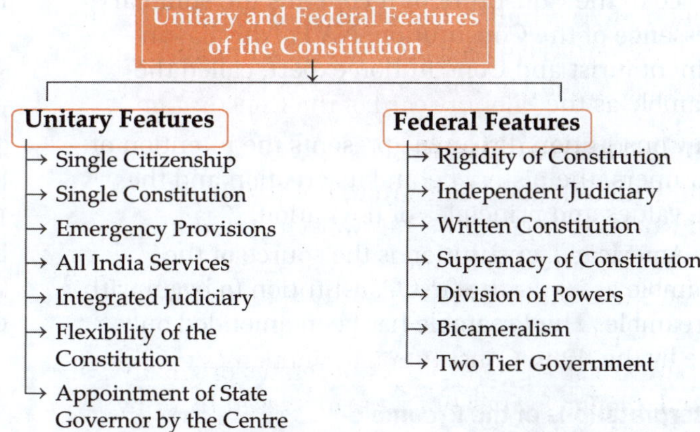

"The Preamble of the Indian Constitution constitutes the essence of the philosophy upon which the whole constitutional structure is based.

Chapter Four

The Preamble

The term 'Preamble' refers to the introduction or preface to the Constitution. It contains the summary or essence of the Constitution. NA Palkhivala, an eminent jurist and Constitution expert, called the Preamble as the 'identity card of the Constitution.'

In a Constitution, Preamble presents the intention of its framers, the history behind its creation and the core values and principles of the nation.

The American Constitution is the source of the Preamble as it was the first Constitution to begin with a Preamble. The Preamble has been amended only once by the 42nd Constitutional Amendment, 1976.

Interpretations of the Preamble

- **Alladi Krishnaswamy Iyer**, the Chairman of the Constituent Assembly (who played an important role in the making of the Constitution) said that "The Preamble of the Constitution is the idea of our long-held dreams".
- According to **KM Munshi**, "The Preamble is the future and birth certificate of our Sovereign, Democratic, Republic".

PREAMBLE OF THE INDIAN CONSTITUTION

- The Preamble is based on the Objectives Resolution, which was drafted in the Constituent Assembly by Jawaharlal Nehru on 13th December, 1946 and adopted by Constituent Assembly on 22nd January, 1947.
- The Constituent Assembly enacted the Preamble after the rest of the Constitution was already enacted to ensure that it remains in conformity with the rest of the Constitution.
- Through 42nd amendment, the words Socialist and Secular were added and the phrase unity of the nation was changed to unity and integrity of the nation.
- The Preamble is neither a source of power to the legislature nor a prohibition on power to the legislature. It is non-justiciable (means something is not capable of being decided by a court of law or legal principles) and non-enforceable (means something cannot be enforced or carried out) in nature.

THE PREAMBLE

WE, THE PEOPLE OF INDIA,

having solemnly resolved to constitute India into a SOVEREIGN, SOCIALIST, SECULAR, DEMOCRATIC REPUBLIC

and to secure to all its citizens.

JUSTICE, social, economic and political; LIBERTY, of thought, expression, belief, faith and worship;

EQUALITY, of status and of opportunity and to promote among them all

FRATERNITY, assuring the dignity of the individual and the unity and integrity of the Nation;

IN OUR CONSTITUENT ASSEMBLY

this twenty-sixth day of November, 1949, do

HEREBY ADOPT, ENACT AND GIVE TO OURSELVES THIS CONSTITUTION.

Importance and Utility of the Preamble

- The Preamble of the Constitution contains ideas that the Constitution seeks to achieve. It does not grant any power but it gives direction and purpose to the Constitution.

- It outlines the objectives of the whole Constitution. It also enshrines the grand objectives and socio-economic goals, which are to be achieved through constitutional processes.

Components of the Preamble

- The Preamble has four components which are as follows :
    - Source of Authority of the Constitution The Preamble states that the Constitution derives its authority from the people of India.
    - Nature of Indian State It declares India to be of a sovereign, socialist, secular, democratic and republican polity.
    - Objectives of the Constitution It specifies justice, liberty, equality and fraternity as the objectives.
    - Date of Adoption of the Constitution It stipulates 26th November, 1949 as the date.

Important Terms of the Preamble

Some important terms used in Preamble are as follows :

Main Keywords of Preamble

Source of Authority	Nature of State	Objectives of Constitution	Date of Adoption of the Indian Constitution
We, The People of India	Sovereign → Socialist → Secular → Democratic → Republic	Justice → Liberty → Equality → Fraternity	26th November, 1949

We, The People of India

- The phrase We, The People signifies that the Constitution rests on the authority of the people of India.
- The Constitution of India is made by representatives elected by people of India.

Sovereign

- The word sovereign means supreme or independent. India is internally and externally sovereign. It is an independent state and not a dominion of any other nation. It is a supreme authority and no authority is above it.
- This means, India is externally free from the control of any foreign power and internally, it has a free government which is directly elected by the people and makes laws that govern the people. It is free to conduct its own affairs.
- The doctrine of popular sovereignty is also one of the basic structure of Constitution of India.
- Hence, citizens of India also enjoy sovereign power to elect their representatives in elections held for Parliament, State Legislature and Local Bodies as well.
- India's membership in Commonwealth and UNO in no way constitute a limitation on its sovereignty.
- In 1949, India made an extra-constitutional declaration of continuation of her full membership of the commonwealth of nation. It also accepted the British crown as the head of the commonwealth. India became a member of the United Nations Organisation in the year 1945.

Socialist

- The word 'Socialist' was added to the Preamble by the 42nd Amendment, 1976.
- However, the Constitution already had implicitly included the socialist content even before this amendment in the form of Directive Principles of State Policy (DPSP's-Articles 36 to 51).
- In the Avadi Session (1955), the Congress party adopted a resolution to establish a 'socialistic pattern of society'.
- Socialism forms the part of basic structure of the Constitution.
- There are two forms of socialism such as Communistic socialism and Democratic socialism. India has opted for democratic socialism which upholds the principle of mixed economy.
    - Communistic socialism or 'state socialism' Nationalisation of all means of production and distribution. It involves the abolition of private property.
    - Democratic socialism It believes in the concept of 'mixed economy' where both the public and the private sectors co-exist and work together. This kind of socialism also aims to end poverty, disease, ignorance and inequality of opportunity.

- Indian socialism derives its roots from Marxism and Gandhism, leaning heavily towards Gandhian socialism. It implies social and economic equality.

Social and Economic Equality

- **Social Equality** It means the absence of discrimination on the grounds only of caste, colour, creed, sex, religion or language. Under social equality, everyone has equal status and opportunities.
- **Economic Equality** It means that the state will endeavour to make the distribution of wealth more equitable and provide a decent standard of living for all. This in effect emphasises a commitment towards the formation of a welfare state. India has adopted a socialistic and mixed economy and the state has framed many laws to achieve its aim.

Secular

- The word 'Secular' was inserted into the Preamble by the 42nd Constitutional Amendment, 1976. It implies equality of all religions and religious tolerance.
- The meaning of Secularism in the West is different from that of India. In the West, secularism implies complete separation of state with religion.
- In India, follows a positive concept of secularism which means that the state shall respect all religions equally and there will be no special provisions for any religion.
- State will give its commitment to religious freedom and worship to everyone.
- The Supreme Court in 1974 said that concept of secularism was already implicitly mentioned before the 42nd Amendment in Articles 25 to 28.
- Freedom of Religion has been protected as a Fundamental Right. The Constitution has been given supremacy over religious scriptures under Articles 25 to 28.
- All citizens, irrespective of their religious beliefs are equal in the eyes of law. No religious instruction is imparted in government schools.
- The Supreme Court in the SR Bommai v/s Union of India (1994) held that secularism was an integral part of the basic structure of the Constitution.

Democratic

- The democratic polity is based on the doctrine of popular sovereignty which indicates the possession of supreme power by the people.
- The first part of the Preamble, We, The people of India and its last part, give to ourselves this Constitution clearly indicate the democratic spirit as provided by the Constitution.
- Mainly, there are two types of democracy-direct democracy and indirect democracy.
- Indirect democracy is also called representative democracy.
- Representative democracy was adopted in the Indian Constitution and an attempt has been made to make the Constitution fully representative by providing voting rights to all the adults of the country without making criteria of education, wealth, income or gender.
- Some of the manifestations of democratic character of the Indian polity includes Universal Adult Franchise, periodic elections, absence of discrimination on various grounds, rule of law, etc.
- The purpose of the Indian Constitution is not only to establish political democracy but also establish social and economic democracy as well.
- According to Dr. BR Ambedkar, "Social and economic democracy is the real goal and ultimate objective".

"The Constitution envisions to establish an egalitarian social order rendering to every citizen social, economic and political justice in a social and economic democracy of the Bharat Republic".

—The Supreme Court of India, 1997

Republic

- A democratic republic is an entity in which the head of the state is elected, directly or indirectly, for a fixed tenure.
- As opposed to a monarchy, in which the head of state is appointed on hereditary basis for a lifetime or until he/she abdicates from the throne.
- Britain is an example of monarchical polity while USA is an example of a republican polity.
- The term republic in the Preamble implies that India has an elected head.
- The President of India is indirectly elected by an electoral college for a term of five years.
- The post of the President of India is not hereditary and is open to all citizens without any discrimination.

Justice

- The ideal of justice embodied in the Constitution is kind of integrated and holistic. It envisages political justice, social justice and economic justice.
- In Articles 14 to 18 of Part III, political justice has been ensured through various Fundamental Rights.

- Articles 36 to 51 of Part IV aims at providing social and economic justice through the Directive Principles of State Policy (DPSP's).
- Political justice means a fair and equal political system where all citizens can freely participate and influence governance without discrimination or bias.
- Social justice It means equal treatment of all citizens without any social discrimination based on caste, colour, race, religion or sex. It also denotes absence of privileges and distribution of wealth, opportunities, and privileges irrespective of religion, race, caste and creed. It promotes working towards improvement in the conditions of SCs, STs, OBCs and women.
- Economic justice It is non-discrimination on the basis of economic factors. It also includes removal of inequalities in income, wealth and property. Social and economic justice together is called as the distributive justice.
- The ideals of socio-economic and political justice have been taken from the Russian Revolution of 1917.

Liberty

- The term Liberty signifies two things :
  - Absence of restraints on the activities of the individuals.
  - Providing opportunities for the development of individual personalities.
- It means freedom or the free will of the individual to pursue his/her interests. It means that an individual cannot be arbitrarily restricted to do or profess something unless there are valid reasons to do so.
- The Preamble mentions these freedoms and rights as freedom of thought, expression, belief, faith and worship.
- These are guaranteed in the Constitution in the form of Fundamental Rights (Articles 19, 25 to 28) and are protected against the arbitrary interference by the state as they are enforceable in the court of law in case they are violated.
- Liberty as provided to the citizens through the Preamble and the Fundamental Rights is not absolute but qualified.
- That means, it has to be enjoyed within the limits of the Constitution and it does not mean the license to do what one likes.

Equality

- It means equal treatment under law irrespective of the status of the individual and absence of any special privileges (it is a special advantage or right given to a person or group that is not available to others) to any section of the society.
- The Preamble provides equality of status and opportunity to all the citizens of India.
- The following three kinds of equality (Civic, Political and Economic) is provided to Indians through the Constitution.

1. Civic Equality This kind of equality is provided through various Fundamental Rights.

Articles Related to Civic Equality under Fundamental Rights

- **Article 14** Equality before the law.
- **Article 15** Prohibition of discrimination on grounds of religion, race, caste, sex or place of birth.
- **Article 16** Equality of opportunity in matters of public employment.
- **Article 17** Abolition of untouchability.

2. Political Equality It is evident in the following two provisions of the Constitution :
   - Article 325 It states that no person is to be declared ineligible for inclusion in electoral rolls on grounds of religion, race, caste or sex.
   - Article 326 It states that the election to the Lok Sabha and the State Assemblies to be on the basis of adult suffrage.
3. Economic Equality It is provided in Article 39 which states that there is an equal right to adequate means of livelihood and equal pay for equal work to men and women.

Fraternity

- It refers to the common brotherhood of all Indians. It asserts that social divisions should be removed and the identity of belongingness of Indian Nationality is nurtured.
- Article 51 A, it shall be the duty of every citizen of India to promote harmony and the spirit of common brotherhood amongst all the people of India transcending religious, linguistic, regional or sectional diversities.
- The Preamble declares that fraternity has to assure the dignity of the individual and the unity and integrity of the nation.

- The word 'integrity' has been added to the Preamble by the 42nd Constitutional Amendment Act, 1976.
- The Fundamental Rights, Fundamental Duties and DPSPs have various provisions that strive to uphold the dignity of Individuals. Article 21 of the Constitution elaborates on the dignity of individual.
- KM Munshi, a member of the Drafting Committee of the Constituent Assembly holds the opinion that the phrase' dignity of the individual signifies that the Constitution not only ensures material betterment and maintain a democratic set-up, but that it also recognises that the personality of every individual is sacred.
- 'Unity and integrity' not only talks about the psychological dimension but also the territorial dimension of the nation's integration. That's why India is described as a 'Union of States' in Article 1 of the Constitution.

Preamble as Part of the Constitution

- The Preamble aids in the legal interpretation where the language of the Constitution is found to be ambiguous. It declares the basic type of government and policy which is sought to be established in the country.
- The Constitution being a legal document, has the date of adoption clearly mentioned in then Preamble to the Indian Constitution.

Supreme Court Judgement Related to Preamble

- Berubari Union Case (1960)
- Kesavananda Bharati Case (1973)
- Raghunath Rao Ganpatrao Case (1993)
- LIC India Case (1995)

- The question whether the Preamble is a part of the Constitution is dealt by the Supreme Courts in various court cases.

Berubari Union Case (1960)

- In legal parlance, the Preamble connotes, the preface and introductory part of any legal political doctrine and is conventionally not treated as the executive part of it.
- The executive part includes the detailed provisions, articles and clauses that have a legal effect and can be enforced with authority. The Preamble is conceived to be more of a visionary objective.
- Based upon this line of thinking the Supreme Court held in Berubari Union Advisory Opinion Case (1960), indicated that the Preamble of the Indian Constitution cannot be treated as a part of the Constitution.

Kesavananda Bharati Case (1973)

The Supreme Court reversed the opinion and pronounced that the Preamble is a part of the Constitution and the values enshrined must be the fundamental guiding principles for governance.

Raghunath Rao Case (1993)

- The Court said following regarding the Preamble
  - It is not a power source.
  - Legislature cannot be banned by this.
- It is useful to understand ambiguous provisions of the Constitution.

Union of India *v/s* LIC of India Case (1995)

The Supreme Court again held that the Preamble is an integral part of the Constitution.

- The Preamble has been amended only once so far in 1976 by the **42nd Constitutional Amendment Act**, which has added three new words **Socialist**, **Secular** and **Integrity** to the Preamble.
- The 42nd amendment is based upon the recommendations of the **Swaran Singh Committee**, an internal committee set-up by the Indian National Congress.

"

Union of India includes only states whereas Territory of India covers States and Union Territories. India came into existence in its present form after the integration of the British-Indian Territories and Princely States.

Chapter Five

The Union and its Territories

Articles 1 to 4 under Part I of the Constitution specifies the provisions related to the Union and its Territory.

India came into existence in its present form after the integration of the British-Indian territories and Princely States. At present, Union of India consist of 28 States and 8 Union Territories.

PROVISIONS OF NEW STATES

- Part 1 of the Constitution, from Articles 1 to 4 expressly deals with the Indian Union and its Territories.
- The First Schedule of the Constitution contains the names of States and Union Territories and their territorial extent.

Article 1

- The Constituent Assembly was divided on the country's name, with some members favouring the traditional name 'Bharat' and others preferring the modern name 'India'.
- To reconcile this difference, the Assembly opted for a compromise, adopting a dual name: 'India, that is, Bharat'.
- The provisions of the Constitution pertaining to the states are applicable to all the states in the same manner.

Special Provisions for Some States

- The Constitution contains special provisions under Part XXI for certain states, which override the general provisions. These special provisions apply to 12 states (Maharashtra, Gujarat, Nagaland, Assam, Manipur, Andhra Pradesh, Telangana, Sikkim, Mizoram, Arunachal Pradesh, Goa and Karnataka).
- There are also separate provisions for certain areas within the states, such as the Scheduled and Tribal Areas under the **Fifth** and **Sixth Schedules**.
- The term 'Union of States' was suggested by **Dr. BR Ambedkar**, which indicates two things; first, the Indian federation is not the result of an agreement among the states and second, the Union/states do not have right to secede from the Union. Therefore, India is called as **Indestructible Union of destructible states**.
- The country is a single, undivided unit, and its division into states is solely for the purpose of facilitating administration and governance.

- The expression Union of India needs to be distinguished from the expression Territory of India. While the Union of India includes only the states which share federal powers with the centre.
- Territory of India includes the entire territory over which India has sovereign rights and territories possibly acquired by the Government of India at any time.

Acquisition of a Foreign Territory by India

India is a sovereign state and can acquire a foreign territory through these modes recognised by the international laws

CESSION

A formal transfer of territory from one country to another, usually through a treaty or agreement. Example : India acquired the territories of Goa, Daman and Diu from Portuguese by means of Cession in 1961.

OCCUPATION

Taking control of a territory without opposition, often after the previous ruler or occupant has abandoned it or is no longer in control. Example : India occupied the territory of Azad Kashmir in 1947, which was previously part of the Princely State of Jammu and Kashmir.

CONQUEST

Forcibly taking control of a territory through military action. Example : India conquered the territory of Hyderabad in 1948, which was previously a Princely State.

SUBJUGATION

Forcing a territory or state to submit to one's control, often through military power or coercion. Example : India subjugated the territories of the Princely States of Junagadh, Jodhpur and Travancore, etc.

- The territories under this Article is classified into the following categories :
  - Territories of the states
  - Union Territories
  - Territories that may be acquired at any time by the Government of India
- In India's federal system, states are equal partners with the Central Government and share powers and responsibilities.
- However, Union Territories and acquired territories are governed directly by the Central Government, without the same level of autonomy as states.
- The government can also acquire a foreign territory without any parliamentary approval.

Article 2

- As per Article 2, Parliament may by law admit into the Union of India or establish new states on such terms and conditions as it thinks fit.
  - The power to admit new states which are already in existence.
  - The power to establish new states which are not in existence.
- Hence, Article 2 is related to admission or establishment of new states that are not a part of the Union of India.
- India passed 35th Amendment Act, 1974 which inserted new Article 2A by which Sikkim became an associate state of Indian union.
- Parliament made 36th Amendment Act, 1975 and Sikkim became 22nd state of Indian union.

Article 3

- Article 3 contains provisions related to the internal readjustment of the territories of the constituent states of the Union of India.
- In other words, it is related to the formation or re-organisation or changes in the existing states of the Union of India.
- Under Article 3, the Parliament has power to reorganise the states in following ways
  - Formation of a new states by :
    (i) separating the territory from any state
    (ii) by uniting two or more states or parts of states
    (iii) by uniting any territory to a part of any state
  - Increase the area of any state.
  - Diminish the area of any state.
  - Alter the boundaries of any state.
  - Alter the name of any state.
- Two conditions in this regard under Article 3 are as follows :

(i) A bill contemplating the above changes can be introduced in either House of Parliament only with the prior recommendation of the President.

(ii) Before recommending the bill, the President has to refer the same to the State Legislature concerned for expressing its views within a specified period.

  - These provisions were not included in the original Constitution, they are added by the Fifth Constitutional Amendment Act, 1955.

- Moreover, the power to form new states also means that the Parliament can form a new state or Union Territory by uniting a part of any state or Union Territory to any other state or Union Territory.
- The Parliament or the President is not bound by the views of the legislature and may accept or reject the proposal, even if the views were received on time.
- Parliament doesn't need to ask states for input on every amendment moved to a bill and for Union Territories, Parliament can make decisions without consulting them at all.
- Under Articles 2 and 3, the bill related to the establishment of new states or their admission and change in the name, area and boundaries of existing states, etc., can be passed by simple majority without any special procedure and like any other ordinary legislation.

- Thus, the territorial integrity or continued existence of any state is not guaranteed by the Constitution as it authorises the Parliament, the power to form a new state or alter the area, boundary or names of any states without their consent.
- This is contrary to the United States of America, where the boundary of states cannot be altered by the Federal Government without the consent of the states.
- Therefore, USA is described as 'an indestructible union of indestructile states.'

Creation of a New State

The following points describe how a new state is created

- A law has to be passed by the **Parliament** for formation of a new state or altering the area of a state or altering the names of the existing states.
- No bills for the formation of new states or alteration of the boundaries or names of the existing states shall be introduced in either House of the Parliament, except on the recommendation of the **President**.
- The President, before introducing the bill in the Parliament, shall refer it to the concerned State Legislature for its opinion within a specified time limit.
- If the State Legislature does not give its opinion within the specified time limit, the time limit may be extended.
- The bill may be introduced even if the opinion has not come. The Parliament is not bound to accept or act upon the views of the State Legislature.

Article 4

- Article 4 states that laws made for admission or establishment of new states under Article 2 and formation of new states and alteration of areas, boundaries or names of existing states under Article 3 are not to be considered as Amendment of the Constitution under Article 368.
- This implies that such laws can be passed by a simple majority and by the ordinary legislative process.
- However, Article 4 raised a very interesting and important question relating the power of the Parliament to cede (give up or grant) Indian Territory to a Foreign country.
- The Central Government's decision to cede a part of the territory known as the Berubari Union (West Bengal) to Pakistan led to the political agitation and controversy and thereby necessitated the presidential reference to Supreme Court in 1960.

Note *Political agitation is a sustained effort to influence public opinion or arouse public feeling through demonstrations, appeals or discussions.*

- In this case, the Supreme Court held that the power of Parliament to diminish the area of a state does not cover cession of the Indian Territory to a Foreign country.
- Hence, Indian Territory can be ceded to a foreign state only by amending the Constitution under Article 368.
- Consequently, the Ninth Constitutional Amendment Act, 1960 was enacted to transfer the said territory to Pakistan.
- In 1969, the Supreme Court ruled that the settlement of a boundary dispute between India and another country does not need amendment in the Constitution.
- If it does not involve cession of Indian territory to a Foreign country and hence can be done by executive action.
- Further, the 100th Constitutional Amendment Act (2015) facilitated the exchange of certain territories between India and Bangladesh.
- As part of this agreement, India transferred 111 enclaves to Bangladesh, while Bangladesh handed over 51 enclaves to India.

REORGANISATION OF STATES

- At the time of independence, India had two types of political units i.e., the British Provinces and the Princely States.
- Two independent and separate dominions of India and Pakistan were created by the Indian Independence Act, 1947.
- Three options were available to the Princely States i.e., namely to join India, to join Pakistan or remain independent.
- Of the 552 Princely States situated within the geographical boundaries of India, 549 joined India.
- Only Hyderabad, Junagadh and Kashmir refused to join India. However, later on, they were also integrated with India under different circumstances. Others were integrated soon after independence.
- Junagadh Princely State was merged with India on the basis of plebiscite.
- The Princely State of Hyderabad was annexed by military action (Operation Polo) and the ruler of the Princely State of Jammu and Kashmir Hari Singh joined Kashmir in India by signing a letter of accession with India due to the invasion of Pakistani tribals.
  - The merger of the Princely States in India was the result of the visionary policy and bold diplomatic efforts of the then Home Minister Sardar Vallabhbhai Patel.
  - After independence, the states in India were divided into four categories A, B, C and D by integrating the British Provinces and Princely States, the details of which are as follows

States and Territory of India in 1950

- The Constitution of India came into force on 26th January, 1950. It made India a **sovereign democratic republic.**
- The Republic of India was declared to be a Union of States under the new Constitution.
- The Constitution of India divided the states into four parts i.e., **Part A** (Erstwhile Governor's provinces of British India), **Part B** (Erstwhile Princely States with legislature in them), **Part C** (Consisted certain erstwhile Chief Commissioner provinces and some Princely States) and **Part D** (Andaman and Nicobar islands).
- The Part-C states were in total 10 in number and they were centrally administered.

States in Different Parts

States in Part-A	States in Part-B	States in Part-C	States in Part-D
1. Assam	1. Hyderabad	1. Ajmer	1. Andaman and Nicobar Islands
2. Bihar	2. Jammu and Kashmir	2. Bhopal	
3. Bombay	3. Madhya Bharat	3. Bilaspur	
4. Madhya Pradesh	4. Mysore	4. Cooch Behar	
5. Madras	5. Patiala and East Punjab	5. Coorg	
6. Orissa	6. Rajasthan	6. Delhi	
7. Punjab	7. Saurashtra	7. Himachal Pradesh	
8. United Provinces	8. Travancore Cochin	8. Kutch	
9. West Bengal	9. Vindhya Pradesh	9. Manipur	
—	—	10. Tripura	

COMMITTEES AND COMMISSIONS OF NEW STATE

- During the British rule, the provinces were formed according to the political and administrative facilities, not on the basis of any discretion or populist consideration. At the time of independence, the classification of Princely States as Indian states was purely temporary.
- After independence, demands arose from different parts of the country, especially from South India, that states should be re-organised on linguistic basis. In this context, the following commissions were constituted by the government from time-to-time.

Dhar Commission

- Consequently, in June 1948, the Government of India appointed the Linguistic Provinces Commission under the Chairmanship of SK Dhar to study the feasibility of organising states on linguistic basis.
- The commission rejected the linguistic basis of re-organisation of states and it recommended the re-organisation of states on the basis of administrative convenience.

JVP Committee

- The Dhar Commission's report created much resentment and led to the appointment of another Linguistic Provinces Committee in December, 1948 to examine the linguistic basis of state re-organisation.
- This committee consisted of Jawaharlal Nehru, Vallabhbhai Patel and Pattabhi Sitaramayya and hence, was popularly known as JVP Committee. JVP Committee submitted its report in April, 1949.

- This Committee also rejected language as the basis for reorganisation of states.
- The first linguistic state of India known as Andhra Pradesh was formed in October, 1953 following the hunger strike of Potti Sriramulu.

Fazl Ali Commission

- The formation of Andhra Pradesh spurred the demand from other regions for creation of states on linguistic line.
- This compelled the Government of India to appoint a three-member States Reorganisation Commission in December, 1953 to look into the question of redrawing of the boundaries of states.
- This commission was chaired by Fazl Ali with the members of Hriday Nath Kunzru and KM Panikkar, to revisit the whole question.
- It submitted its report in September, 1955 and largely accepted language as the basis of re-organisation of states. However, this committee rejected the theory of 'One language-One State'.
- It held the opinion that preserving India's unity should be the main consideration when re-organising the country's political divisions.
- Fazl Ali Commission acknowledged four major factors that can be taken into account in any scheme of re-organisation of states, which are as follows.
    - Linguistic and cultural homogeneity (it refers to a sense of pride and common background shared by individuals within a cultural or nation, often leading to a higher level of unity and identification with the national indentity).
    - Preservation and strengthening of the unity and security of the country.
    - Financial, economic and administrative considerations.
    - Planning and promotion of the welfare of the people in each state as well as of the Nation as a whole.
- The committee recommended to abolish the four fold classification of states and territories under the Original Constitution and creation of 16 states and 3 centrally administered territories.
- Fazl Ali Commission's recommendations were broadly accepted and it was followed by the States Reorganisation Act, 1956 and the Seventh Constitutional Amendment Act, 1956.
- These changes abolished the distinction between Part-A and Part-B states and Part-C states were abolished.
- Some of the states were united with the adjacent states while some of them were given the designation of Union Territories.
- On 1st November, 1956, India was reorganised into 14 States and 6 Union Territories under the State Reorganisation Act of 1956.

Linguistic Movements

- Political movements for the creation of new, linguistic based states developed around India in early 1950's.
- A fast upto death protest by **Sriramulu** stirred the regional agitation. Indeed, Sriramulu died out of fasting in cause of demanding Statehood for Telugu speaking people.
- Owing to the popular demand, 11 Telugu-speaking districts of **Madras** became the new state of **Andhra** in October, 1953 with **Kurnool** as its capital.
- In 1956, **Hyderabad** was declared state's capital. The boundaries were changed again in 2014 as the state of **Telangana** was carved out of Andhra Pradesh as per the **Andhra Pradesh Reorganisation Act, 2014**.
- **Andhra Pradesh** is the first state to be created on linguistic basis in India. Similar, movements also followed in Mysore, Bombay, Kerala regions for creation of Linguistic States.

States Reorganisation Act, 1956

- The recommendations of the States Reorganisation Commission were accepted by the Parliament with some changes and the States Reorganisation Act was passed in July, 1956.
- The new states were formed in the following manner:
    - Kerala By merging the Travancore-Cochin state with the Malabar district of Madras state and Kasaragode of South Canara.
    - Andhra Pradesh By merging Telugu speaking areas of Hyderabad state with the Andhra state.
    - Madhya Pradesh By merging Madhya Bharat state, Vindhya Pradesh state and Bhopal state into Madhya Pradesh state.
    - Bombay By merging the Saurashtra state and Kutch state into the Bombay state.
    - Mysore By merging Coorg state into Mysore state.
    - Punjab By merging the Patiala and East Punjab states union (pepsu) into Punjab state.
    - Rajasthan By merging Ajmer state into Rajasthan state.

- UT of Laccadive, Minicoy and Amindivi islands was formed by detaching territory from the Madras state.
- The following 14 States and 6 Union Territories were established under this Act.

States and UT's of India in 1956

States	
1. Andhra Pradesh	8. Madras
2. Assam	9. Mysore
3. Bihar	10. Orissa (Odisha)
4. Bombay	11. Punjab
5. Jammu and Kashmir	12. Rajasthan
6. Kerala	13. Uttar Pradesh
7. Madhya Pradesh	14. West Bengal
Union Territories	
1. Andaman and Nicobar Islands	4. Laccadive, Minicoy and Amindivi Islands
2. Delhi	5. Manipur
3. Himachal Pradesh	6. Tripura

Formation Details of States (According to year Chronology)

States	Description
Odisha	Orissa was made a separate province in 1936 by the British and in 1950 it became a state. It was renamed Odisha in 2011.
Bihar	In 1912, Bihar alongwith Orissa were separated from the Bengal Presidency. On 1st April, 1936, Bihar and Orissa became two separate provinces. Bihar was formed as a state in 1950.
Uttar Pradesh	United Province was created in the year 1937 by the British regime and post-independence it was renamed as Uttar Pradesh in 1950.
Assam	Assam became a constituent state of India in 1950.
West Bengal	Became a state in 1950.
Tamil Nadu	The erstwhile Madras Presidency was reorganised as a state in 1950 and renamed Tamil Nadu in 1969.
Andhra Pradesh	Formed by the State of Andhra Pradesh Act, 1953 by carving out some areas from the state of Madras. It is the first state, carved out on linguistic line.
Kerala	Formed by the State Reorganisation Act, 1956, it comprised Travancore and Cochin areas.
Rajasthan	Known as the Rajputana under British India, the Princely States came together in 1948, to from the United State of Rajasthan. In May 1949, it was renamed the United States of Greater Rajasthan and in 1956, the state of Rajasthan was born.
Madhya Pradesh	Central Provinces and Berar under British India were merged with Madhya Bharat, Vindhya Pradesh and Bhopal to from a state as Madhya Pradesh in 1956.
Karnataka	Formed from the Princely State of Mysore by the State Reorganisation Act, 1956. It was renamed as **Karnataka** in 1973 from Mysore.
Gujarat and Maharashtra	The State of Bombay was divided into two states namely, Maharashtra and Gujarat (15th state) by the Bombay (Reorganisation) Act, 1960.
Nagaland	State of Nagaland Act, 1962 created the state of Nagaland (16th state), which was carved out of Assam.
Haryana	It was carved out from the state of Punjab by the Punjab (Reorganisation) Act, 1966.
Punjab	Post-independence, the Princely State of Patiala was merged with eight other similar states to form Patiala and East Punjab States Union (PEPSU). In 1956, this region was merged with the rest of Punjab and in 1966, Haryana was separated as 17th independent state. Both Punjab and Haryana share Chandigarh as its capital, which is a Union Territory.
Himachal Pradesh	State of Himachal Pradesh Act, 1970 elevated the Union Territory of Himachal Pradesh to the status of state (18th state of India).
Manipur and Tripura	Both these states were elevated from the status of Union Territories by the North-Eastern Areas (Reorganisation) Act, 1971. Manipur was 19th and Tripura was formed as 20th state.
Meghalaya	First carved out as a sub-state within the state of Assam by 22nd Constitutional Amendment, 1969. Later, in 1971, it received the status of a full-fledged 21st state by the North-Eastern Areas (Reorganisation) Act, 1971.
Sikkim	Sikkim was given first the status of associate state, by the 35th Constitutional Amendment Act, 1974. 36th Amendment Act, 1975, uplifted its status to a 22nd full state in 1975. From 1947 to 1974, Sikkim was a **protectorate** of India.
Mizoram	It was uplifted to the status of a 23rd full state by the State of Mizoram Act, 1986.
Arunachal Pradesh	It received the status of a 24th full state by the State of Arunachal Pradesh Act, 1986.
Goa	It was separated from the Union Territory of Goa, Daman and Diu and it was made a 25th full-fledged state by the Goa, Daman and Diu Reorganisation Act, 1987. But, Daman and Diu remained as Union Territory till date.
Chhattisgarh	Created as 26th state of India, in 2000, by dividing Madhya Pradesh on 1st November, 2000.
Uttarakhand	Earlier known as Uttaranchal, it was formed in 2000 by dividing Uttar Pradesh on 9th November, 2000. In January 2007, the name of the state was officially changed from Uttaranchal to Uttarakhand. It is 27th state of the Union of India.
Jharkhand	Created as 28th state, in 2000, by dividing Bihar on 15th November, 2000.
Telangana	Created as 29th state on 2nd June, 2014, it was separated from Andhra Pradesh on the recommendation of Shri Krishna Committee Report.

FORMATION OF UTs

- After the States Reorganisation Act of 1956, Part-C and Part-D states were combined into a single category of Union Territory.
- The concept of the Union Territory was added by the Constitution (Seventh Amendment) Act, 1956. Union Territories (UT's) are the federal territories and are administered by the Union Government of India.
- In the Union Territories, Lieutenant Governors are appointed by the President of India who serves as their administrators.
- Puducherry, Jammu and Kashmir and Delhi were granted Partial Statehood, that's why they are the exception in this regard. They have an elected legislature and government. The description of the formation of Union Territories is as follows :
  - Delhi was earlier a state. On 27th March, 1952, the first Delhi Legislative Assembly elections were held on 48 seats. Chaudhary Brahm Prakash Yadav was the first Chief Minister of Delhi. However, after the State Reorganisation Act of 1956, Delhi lost its Statehood and became a Union Territory.
  - In 1991, Partial Statehood status was granted to the Union Territory of Delhi and it came to be known as the National Capital Territory of Delhi.

In 1954, **Puducherry** was merged into the Republic of India after attaining independence from French rule and became the Union Territory of Puducherry. In 1963, Puducherry was granted the status of Partial Statehood.

  - Chandigarh became a Union Territory in 1966.
  - Lakshadweep became a Union Territory in 1956.
  - In 1961, Daman and Diu and Goa were merged into the Republic of India, after attaining independence from Portuguese rule. In 1987, Goa was granted the status of Statehood and became the first Union Territory to receive such status.
  - In 2019, Jammu and Kashmir Reorganisation Act, 2019 was passed by the Indian Parliament and it reconstituted the state of Jammu and Kashmir into two Union Territories- UT of Jammu and Kashmir and UT of Ladakh.
  - In 2020, Dadra and Nagar Haveli and Daman and Diu were merged into a single Union Territory known as Dadra and Nagar Haveli and Daman and Diu.
  - Andaman and Nicobar Islands is a Union Territory of India consisting of 572 islands, of which 38 are inhabited, at the junction of the Bay of Bengal and the Andaman Sea.
- Articles 239 to 241 are related to Union Territories under Part-VIII of the Constitution. All Union Territories belong to the same category but there is no uniformity in their administrative system.

Union Territories and their Year of Formation

Union Territories	Year of Formation
1. Andaman and Nicobar Islands	1956
2. Delhi (National Capital Territory)	1956
3. Lakshadweep	1956
4. Puducherry	1962
5. Chandigarh	1966
6. Jammu and Kashmir	2019
7. Ladakh	2019
8. Dadra and Nagar Haveli and Daman and Diu	2020

Change of Names of Some States and Union Territories

Years	Changes
1950	The United Provinces was the first state to have a new name i.e., 'Uttar Pradesh'.
1969	Madras was renamed as 'Tamil Nadu' by the Madras State (Alteration of Name) Act, 1968.
1973	Mysore was renamed as 'Karnataka', by the Mysore State (Alteration of Name) Act, 1973. Laccadive, Minicoy and Amindivi islands were renamed 'Lakshadweep', by the Laccadive, Minicoy and Amindivi islands (Alteration of Name) Act, 1973.
1992	The Union Territory of Delhi was redesignated as the National Territory of Delhi, by the 69th Constitutional Amendment Act, 1991.
2006	Pondicherry was renamed as 'Puducherry'.
2006	Uttaranchal was renamed as 'Uttarakhand'.
2011	Orissa was renamed as 'Odisha' by the Orissa (Alteration of Name) Act, 2011.

A citizen is a person who enjoys full membership of the political community or state in which he ordinarily lives. However, citizenship is the status of being a citizen.

Chapter Six

Citizenship

RIGHTS AND PRIVILEGES

- Citizenship is one of the most commonly used term in a democracy.
- It is used at all levels of politics, in formal legal documents, in laws, in Constitution, in party manifesto and in speeches.
- This definition was given by the English Sociologist TH Marshall in his work 'Citizenship and Social Class' written in 1949.
- The concept of citizenship is particularly related to the concept of a republic as the elected head of the state is the first citizen of a country.

There are two principles of citizenship:

(i) Jus Soli It confers citizenship on the basis of place of birth.

(ii) Jus Sanguinis It confers citizenship on the basis of blood ties.

Citizens and Aliens

- Citizens are different from aliens. While citizens enjoy all the civil and political rights that are provided for being the full members of the Indian state, on the other hand, aliens do not enjoy such rights because they are the citizens of some other state.
- There are two kinds of aliens :

(i) Friendly Aliens These are subjects of those countries with whom India has friendly or cordial relationships.

(ii) Enemy Aliens These are subjects of those countries that share a hostile relationship with India.

- Enemy aliens enjoy lesser rights in India as compared to friendly aliens. For example, Benefits of Article 22 are not available to enemy aliens.

Privileges Exclusive to Indian Citizens

The Constitution confers the following rights and privileges to the citizens of India (and denies the same to aliens) :

- Right against discrimination on grounds of religion, race, caste, sex or place of birth (Article 15).
- Right to equality of opportunity in the matter of public employment (Article 16).
- Right to freedom of speech and expression, assembly, association, movement, residence and profession (Article 19).
- Cultural and educational rights (Articles 29 and 30).
- Right to vote in elections to the Lok Sabha and State Legislative Assembly.
- Right to contest for the membership of the Parliament and the State Legislature.
- Eligibility to hold certain public offices such as President of India, Vice-President of India, Judges of the Supreme Court and the High Courts, Governor of States, Attorney-General of India and Advocate- General of States.

- Alongwith the above mentioned rights, residents also have obligations to the Indian state, such as paying taxes, upholding the national anthem and flag and so forth.

Rights and Duties of Citizens

- Rights under Articles 15, 16, 19, 29 and 30.
- Right to vote, contest elections and hold public office.
- **Articles 16** and **326** are not available to even **Overseas Citizens of India (OCI)**. Recently, the Government of India gave Non-Residents of India (NRI's) the Right to vote. However, voting through postal ballots is not allowed. An NRI has to be present in the constituency, where he is registered as a voter, on the day of polling.
- Overseas Citizens of India (OCI) is an immigration status that allows foreign citizens of Indian origin to live and work in India indefinitely
- Constitutional posts can only be held by citizens of India and neither foreigners nor OCI/PIO are eligible.
- Duties of citizens but not of aliens are to pay tax, respect national symbols, defend the country, etc.
- In India, both citizens by birth and naturalisation are eligible for the office of President. In the USA, only citizens by birth are eligible.
- Enemy aliens do not enjoy protection against arrest and detentions (**Article 22**).

Fundamental Rights to Foreigners

- Article 14 Equality before law.
- Article 20 Protection in respect of conviction for offences.
- Article 21 Protection of personal life and liberty.
- Article 21(A) Right to elementary education.
- Article 22 Protection against arrest and detention in certain cases.
- Article 23 Prohibition of human trafficking and forced labour.
- Article 24 Prohibition of employment of children in factories.
- Article 25 Freedom of conscience and free profession, practice and propagation of religion.
- Article 26 Freedom to manage religious affairs.
- Article 27 Freedom from payment of taxes for promotion of any religion.
- Article 28 Freedom from attending religious instructions or worship in certain educational institutions.

TYPES OF CITIZENSHIP

- There are two kinds of citizenships, single citizenship and dual citizenship.
- In India, there is a single citizenship i.e., citizenship of the Union of India.
- The Constitution (under Articles 5 to 8) provides for citizenship at the commencement of the Constitution i.e., from 26th January, 1950.
- Despite having a federal structure with dual polity at the central and state level, the Indian Constitution provides for only a single citizenship.
- Citizens in India are provided only the citizenship of the Indian union and they owe allegiance to it. They are not entitled to a separate state citizenship.
- India has borrowed the idea of single citizenship from the British Constitution. (The dual citizenship system has been adopted by several federal states, including the United States and Switzerland).
- This system of single citizenship avoids the problem of discrimination as all the Indian citizens enjoy the same civil and political rights throughout the nation, regardless of where they were born or where they currently reside.
- They are not discriminated against. However this rule has some exceptions too :
  - Article 15 It prohibits discrimination against any citizens only on grounds of religion, race, caste, sex or place of birth but not on the ground of residence.
  - Article 16 The Parliament can prescribe residence within a state or Union Territory as a condition for certain employment in that state or Union Territory.
  - Article 19 The right to freedom of movement and residence available to citizens is subject to the protection of the interests of any Scheduled Tribe.
  - Article 35(A) Until 2019, the Legislature of the State of Jammu and Kashmir was given the power to define the permanent residents of the state and to confer them any special rights and privileges.
  - Article 35A was inserted in the Constitution of India by "the Constitution (Application to Jammu and Kashmir) Order, 1954". This order was issued under Article 370 of the Constitution by the President. Article 370 conferred special status to the status of Jammu and Kashmir. However, this article was abolished in the year 2019 by the presidential order "the Constitution (Application to Jammu and Kashmir) Order, 2019".

Dual Citizenship

- In dual citizenship, a person has citizenship of both the union and the states.
- For example, in the USA, an individual is both the citizens of the USA as well as the citizens of the particular state to which he belongs.
- Thus, persons having dual citizenship enjoy dual sets of rights and also they pay allegiance to both the National and the State Governments. However, this system is prone to discrimination as the states in that country may favour the citizens of their state in matters related to right to hold public offices, right to vote, etc.
- The Constitution of India does not entitle any Indian citizen to be a citizen of any two states. If a person voluntarily acquires citizenship of other country, his Indian citizenship automatically ends.
- The Indian Citizenship (Amendment) Act, 2005 amends the Citizenship Act, 1955. Under this Act, the Central Government may, on the basis of an application submitted to any person, can assign status if
  - the person is a citizen of a particular country and is of Indian origin.
  - if the person acquired the citizenship of a particular country after the passing of the Citizenship (Amendment) Act, 2003, but was a citizen of India before that.
  - a person who has been registered as an overseas Indian citizen shall, from the date of registration, have the rights of an overseas Indian citizen.

Other Provisions Related to Citizenship

Apart from the above provisions, our Constitution also contains some other provisions related to citizenship as mentioned below:

- According to Article 9, No person shall be a citizen of India by virtue of Article 5 or be deemed to be a citizen of India by virtue of Article 6 or Article 8, if he has voluntarily acquired the citizenship of any Foreign state.
- According to Article 10, Every person who is deemed to be a citizen of India under any of the foregoing provisions of this part shall, subject to the provisions of any law that may be made by Parliament, continue to be such citizen.
- According to Article 11, Nothing in the foregoing provisions of this part shall derogate from the power of Parliament to make any provision with respect to the acquisition and termination of citizenship and all other matters relating to citizenship.

Constitutional Provisions Related to Citizenship

Provisions	Categories of Persons to Become the Citizen of India
Person Domiciled in India (Article 5)	• A person who was born in the Territory of India. Either of whose parents was born in the Territory of India irrespective of the nationality of parents or place of birth. • Who has been ordinarily resident in the territory of India for not less than five years immediately preceding such commencement of the Constitution shall be a citizen of India.
Person Migrated from Pakistan (Article 6)	• A person who has migrated to the Territory of India from the territory now included in Pakistan shall deemed to be a citizen of India at the commencement of this Constitution if – He or either of his parents or any of his grand-parents was born in undivided India. – In the case, where such person has so migrated before the 19th day of July, 1948, he has been ordinarily resident in the territory of India since, the date of his migration or – In the case, where such person has so migrated on or after the 19th day of July, 1948, he has been registered as a citizen of India on an application made by him. The article provides that no person shall be so registered unless he has been resident in the territory of India for atleast six months immediately preceding the date of his application.
Persons Migrated to Pakistan but later Returned to India (Article 7)	• A person who migrated to Pakistan from India after 1st March, 1947, but later returned to India for resettlement could become an Indian citizen. For this, He had to be resident of India for six months preceding the date of his application for registration.
Person of Indian Origin Residing Outside India (Article 8)	• The article states that any person who or either of whose parents or grandparents was born in India and who is ordinarily residing in any other country. • They shall be deemed to be a citizen of India if he has been registered as a citizen of India by the diplomatic or consular representative of India.

CITIZENSHIP ACT, 1955

- The Citizenship Act of 1955 provides for acquisition and loss of citizenship after the commencement of the Constitution.
- This Act has been amended so far multiple times in 1957, 1960, 1986, 1992, 2003, 2005, 2015 and 2019.
- The Citizenship Act of 1955 initially included provisions for Commonwealth Citizenship, but this aspect was removed through the Citizenship (Amendment) Act of 2003.
- The process of acquisition of citizenship and loss of citizenship are described below :

Acquisition of Citizenship

The Act provides for the acquisition of Indian citizenship after the commencement of the Constitution in five ways, i.e., by birth, by descent, by registration, by naturalisation and by incorporation of territory.

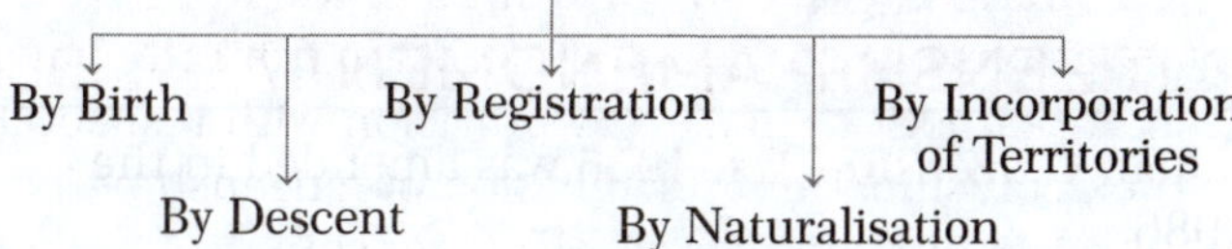

By Birth

- Every person born in India on or after 26th January, 1950, but before 1st July, 1987, shall be a citizen of India by birth.
- A person born in India after 1st July 1987, but before 3rd December, 2004 is considered a citizen of India only if either of their parents is an Indian citizen at the time of their birth.
- A person born in India after 3rd December, 2004 shall be citizen of India, if both parents are citizen of India or if one is citizen of India and other is not illegal migrant.

Note *An illegal migrant is someone who violates a country's immigration laws by entering or living in the country without proper authorisation or documentation.*

- As an exception, the children of foreign diplomats and enemy foreigners will not be included in this.

By Descent

- Broadly, a person born outside India on or after 26th January, 1950, but before 10th December, 1992 a citizen of India by descent if his father was a citizen of India at the time of that person's birth. If any person is born on or after 10th December, 1992, but before 3rd December, 2004 are considered as the citizens of India.
- From 3rd December, 2004 onwards, a person born outside India will not be considered a citizen of India by descent, unless their birth is registered at an Indian consulate within one year of birth or with the permission of the Central Government after the expiry of this period.
- The provision of granting citizenship to a person born abroad on the basis of mother's citizenship is made by the Citizenship Amendment Act, 1992.

By Registration

- The prescribed authority may, on application, register as a citizen of India, any person who is not an illegal migrant by virtue of Constitution or the provisions of the Citizenship Act.
- This mode of acquiring citizenship is available to any of the following categories :
  - Persons of Indian origin who are ordinarily resident in India for 7 years immediately before making an application for registration.
  - Persons of Indian origin who are ordinarily resident in any country or place outside undivided India.
  - Spouses of Indian citizens who have lived in India for 7 years. Minor children of Indian citizens.
  - A person of full age and capacity whose parents are Indian citizens.
  - A person of full age and capacity who were previously citizens of independent India or whose parents had Indian citizenship , and have lived in India for 12 months immediately before making an application for registration.
  - A person of full age and capacity who is registered as an Overseas Citizen of India cardholder who has lived in India for 12 months before making an application for registration and holding the card for 5 years.

Indian Origin

A person is considered of Indian origin if

- They were born in undivided India.
- Their parents were born in undivided India.
- They were born in a territory that became part of India after 15th August, 1947.
- Their parents were born in a territory that became part of India after 15th August, 1947.

Oath of Allegiance

All eligible individuals must take an oath of allegiance before being registered as citizens of India.

By Naturalisation

- Citizenship by naturalisation can be acquired by making an application in the prescribed manner.
- The Central Government can grant Indian citizenship through naturalisation to individuals who meet the following criteria :
  - They are not citizens of a country that prohibits Indians from becoming naturalised citizens.
  - If they are already citizens of another country, they agree to renounce that citizenship if their Indian citizenship application is approved.
  - They have lived in India or worked for the Indian Government (or a combination of both) for the 12 months preceding their application.
  - Spent at least 11 years in India or in service to the Indian Government (or a combination of both) during the 14 years preceding the 12 months before their application.

The Citizenship (Amendment) Act, 2019, provides an exception for individuals from Afghanistan, Bangladesh or Pakistan who belong to certain religious communities (Hindu, Sikh, Buddhist, Jain, Parsi or Christian). For these individuals, the required period of residence or service is reduced to at least 5 years.

  - He has an adequate knowledge of a language recognised by the Constitution in the Eighth Schedule.
  - Intend to live in India or work for the Indian Government, an international organisation that India is a part of, or an Indian-based organisation in case a certificate of naturalisation is granted.
- However, the Government of India can exempt certain individuals from these conditions if they have made significant contributions to Science, philosophy, art, literature, world peace and human progress.
- Additionally, all naturalised citizens must take an oath of allegiance to the Constitution of India.

By Incorporation of Territories

- If any new territory becomes a part of India, after a popular verdict, the Government of India shall specify the persons of that territory to be the citizen of India.
- For example, The Citizenship (Pondicherry) Order (1962) was issued under the Citizenship Act (1955), when Pondicherry became a part of India.

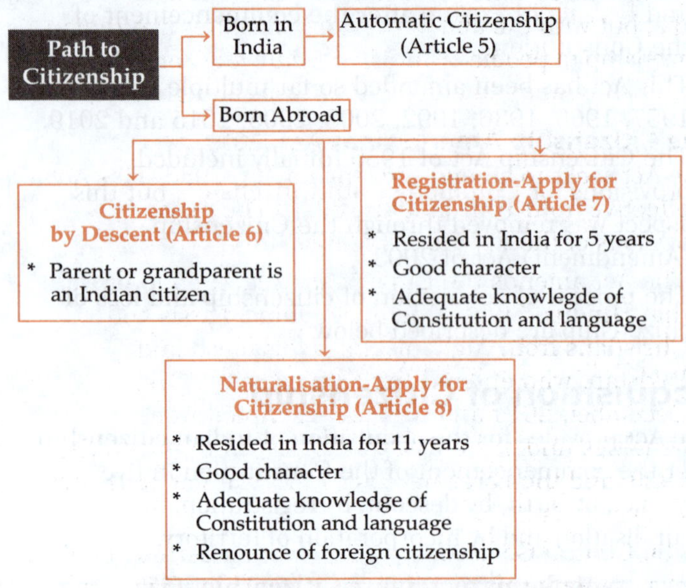

THE CITIZENSHIP AMENDMENT ACT, 1986

- The Indian Citizenship Act, 1955 was amended in the year 1986.
- It deals with the situation arising out of large numbers of people coming to India illegally from Bangladesh, Sri Lanka and some African countries.

Special Provisions of Citizenship for Persons Covered Under the Assam Accord

- The Citizenship (Amendment) Act, 1985, made special provisions for individuals covered by the Assam Accord, which addressed the issue of foreigners in Assam. According to these provisions
- Individuals who entered illegally in Assam from Bangladesh before 1st January, 1966 and have been living there continuously since their arrival, are considered Indian citizens starting from 1st January, 1966.
- Individuals who moved to Assam from Bangladesh between 1st January, 1966, and 25th March, 1971, and have been living there continuously since their arrival, must register themselves if they have been identified as foreigners. Once registered
  - They will be considered Indian citizens after 10 years from the date of detection as a foreigner.
  - During the 10 years period, they will have the same rights and responsibilities as Indian citizens, except for the right to vote.

The Citizenship Amendment Bill, 2015

The bill was passed by the Parliament in March, 2015. Although there is no provision for dual citizenship in India, but with the aim of providing facilities like Indian citizenship to people of Indian origin living abroad, Citizenship Amendment Bill, 2015 was brought into.

The Citizenship Amendment Act, 2019

The Act seeks to amend Citizenship Act, 1955. This Act is effective from 10th January, 2020. The major provisions of the Act are as follows :

- The Act amends the Citizenship Act, 1955 to provide that Hindus, Sikhs, Buddhists, Jains, Parsis and Christians from Afghanistan, Bangladesh and Pakistan, who entered India on or before 31st December, 2014 and who are exempted from penalties under the Passport (Entry into India) Act, 1920, and the Foreigners Act 1946 will not be treated as illegal migrants.
- The Central Government may award a certificate of registration or naturalisation to eligible individuals who meet the specified conditions.
- Upon receiving this certificate, they will be considered Indian citizens from the date of their entry into India.
- Any ongoing legal proceedings against these individuals related to illegal migration or citizenship will be dismissed once they are granted citizenship.
- These provisions do not apply to :
    - Tribal areas in Assam, Meghalaya, Mizoram or Tripura (as listed in the Sixth Schedule of the Constitution).
    - Areas under 'The Inner Line' (notified under the Bengal Eastern Frontier Regulation, 1873).
- Before the Citizenship (Amendment) Act, 2019, migrants from Afghanistan, Bangladesh or Pakistan belonging to certain religious communities (Hindu, Sikh, Buddhist, Jain, Parsis or Christian) who entered India without valid documents or with expired documents were considered illegal migrants and ineligible for Indian citizenship.
- However, in 2015, the Central Government exempted them from penalties under the Passport (Entry into India) Act, 1920 and the Foreigners Act, 1946.
- In 2016, they were also made eligible for long-term visas to stay in India.
- Finally, with the enactment of the Citizenship (Amendment) Act, 2019, these migrants became eligible for Indian citizenship.
- For regarding acquiring citizenship by naturalisation for these communities, the 11 years requirement has been reduced to 5 years.
- The Act also provided that registration of Overseas Citizen of India can be cancelled by the Central Government, if they had violated the provisions of the Act or any other law notified by the Central Government.

Loss of Citizenship

Article 10 states that, the right of citizenship of a citizen cannot be taken away except under law made by the Parliament. The Citizenship Act, 1955 also lays down three modes by which an Indian citizen may lose his/ her citizenship. These are as follows :

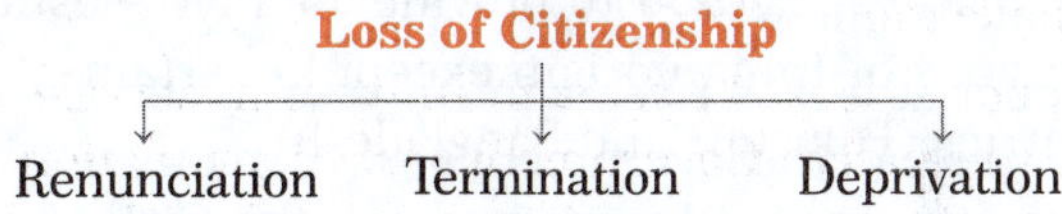

Renunciation

- It is a voluntary act by which a person, after acquiring the citizenship of another country, gives up his Indian citizenship. This provision is subject to certain conditions.
- However, if a person renounces his citizenship during a war in which India is a participant, the Central Government can withhold its registration.
- When a person renounces his Indian citizenship, every minor child of that person also loses Indian citizenship. Although the child may acquire Indian citizenship on attaining the age of 18 years.

Termination

It takes place by operation of law when an Indian citizen voluntarily acquires the citizenship of another country. He automatically ceases to be an Indian citizen (Article 9).

Deprivation

- Central Government can terminate a person's Indian citizenship under the following conditions:
    - The citizen has shown disloyalty to the Constitution of India.
    - The citizen has unlawfully communicated with enemy during war.
    - Citizen has within five years after registration or naturalisation been imprisoned in any country for two years.
    - The citizen has been ordinarily resident out of India for seven years continuously.

- Apart from this, Indian citizenship is lost in the event of a man or a woman marrying a woman or man from another country, getting citizenship there, going abroad to do a government job and in the event of insanity, beggar hood, retirement, etc.

INDIAN CITIZENSHIP FOR FOREIGN NATIONALS

- In the year 2000, under the Chairmanship of LM Singhvi, a comprehensive study of the Indian Diaspora and making recommendations for making constructive relations with them was entrusted.
- The committee submitted its report in the year 2002 and the recommended amendment in the Citizenship Act, 1955 to provide dual citizenship to citizens of Indian origin except in certain countries (Pakistan and Bangladesh).
- Thereafter, several amendments to the Citizenship Act were done :
  - The Citizenship Amendment Act, 2003 It included provision for the grant of Overseas Citizenship of India (OCI) to the PIO's of 16 specified countries except Pakistan and Bangladesh.
  - The Citizenship Amendment Act, 2005 It broadened the eligibility criteria for Persons of Indian Origin (PIO's) from all countries, except Pakistan and Bangladesh, to obtain OCI status. However, this is subject to their home country allowing dual citizenship under their laws. OCI is not equivalent to dual citizenship, as the Indian Constitution prohibits holding dual citizenship or nationality under Article 9.
  - The Citizenship Amendment Act, 2015 This amendment introduced a new "Overseas Citizen of India Cardholder" scheme, which combines the earlier Person of Indian Origin (PIO) card scheme and OCI card scheme into a single category.
- The PIO card scheme was launched on 19th August, 2002, followed by the OCI card scheme on 2nd December, 2005.
- Although the OCI scheme gained more popularity, both schemes ran concurrently, causing confusion among applicants.
- To address these issues and provide better facilities, the Government of India decided to merge the two schemes into a single one, combining their benefits.
- The Citizenship (Amendment) Act, 2015, was enacted to achieve this goal. As a result, the PIO scheme was discontinued on 9th January, 2015 and existing PIO cardholders were automatically converted to OCI cardholders from the same date.

Overseas Citizens of India

- The Central Government can register the following individuals as Overseas Citizen of India (OCI) cardholders :
  - A person of full age and capacity who
  - Were Indian citizens at the time of the commencement of the Constitution or later.
  - Were eligible to become Indian citizens at the time of the commencement of the Constitution.
  - Belonged to a territory that became part of India after 15th August, 1947.
  - Are children, grandchildren or great- grandchildren of such citizens.
- Minor children of individuals mentioned in Clause (a).
- Minor children with both parents as Indian citizens or one parent as an Indian citizen.
- Foreign-born spouses of Indian citizens or OCI cardholders, with a registered marriage subsisting for at least two years before the application.
- However, individuals who have themselves or their parents, grandparents or great grandparents held citizenship of Pakistan, Bangladesh or other specified countries are not eligible for OCI registration.

OCI, also known as **dual citizenship**, has been in force since December, 2005. It includes a foreign citizen who is eligible to become a citizen of India on 26th January, 1950 or who was a citizen of India on or after 26th January, 1950 or a citizen of any part of India acceding to India after 15th August, 1947 can get this card.

Rights and Restrictions of Overseas Citizen of India (OCI) Cardholders

- Entitlements OCI cardholders are entitled to specific rights, as specified by the Central Government.
- Restrictions OCI cardholders do not have the same rights as Indian citizens and are excluded from :
  - Equal opportunities in public employment (Article 16)
  - Election as President (Article 58)
  - Election as Vice-President (Article 66)
  - Appointment as a Supreme Court Judge (Article 124)

- Appointment as a High Court Judge (Article 217)
- Voter registration
- Membership in the House of the People or Council of States
- Membership in State Legislative Assembly or Council
- Appointment to public services and posts in the Union or State Governments, except for specified positions by the Central Government.

Benefits to OCI Cardholders

- OCI cardholders can enter India multiple times, get a multipurpose life-long visa to visit India and are exempted from registering with **Foreigners Regional Registration Office** (FRRO).
- If an individual is registered as an OCI for a period of five years, he/she is eligible to apply for Indian citizenship. At all Indian international airports, OCI cardholders are provided with special immigration counters.
- OCI cardholders can open special bank accounts in India, buy the **non-farm property** (it refers to real estate that is not primarily used for agricultural purposes, including residential, commercial and industrial properties) and exercise ownership rights and can also apply for a **Permanent Account Number** (PAN) card.

Renunciation of Overseas Citizen of India (OCI) Cardholder Status

- An OCI cardholder can voluntarily renounce their status by making a declaration. Once the Central Government registers this declaration, the individual will no longer be an OCI cardholder.
- When an OCI cardholder renounces their status :
  - Their spouse of foreign origin (who also holds an OCI card) will also lose their OCI status.
  - All minor children of the individual (who are registered as OCI cardholders) will also cease to be OCI cardholders.

Grounds for Cancellation of Overseas Citizen of India (OCI) Cardholder Status

- The Central Government may cancel an OCI cardholder's registration if
  - The registration was obtained through fraud, false representation or concealment of material facts.
  - The OCI cardholder has shown disaffection towards the Indian Constitution.
  - The OCI cardholder has engaged in unlawful trade or communication with an enemy during a war involving India.
  - The OCI cardholder has been sentenced to imprisonment for at least two years within five years of registration.
  - The OCI cardholder has violated the Citizenship Act (1955) or other specified laws added by the Citizenship (Amendment) Act, 2019.
  - Cancellation is necessary for India's sovereignty, integrity, security, friendly foreign relations or public interest.
  - The OCI cardholder's marriage has been dissolved or they have solemnised a new marriage without dissolving the previous one.
- Before cancellation, the OCI cardholder will be given a reasonable opportunity to be heard (added by the Citizenship (Amendment) Act, 2019).

Non-Resident Indians (NRI)

- NRI's are those who have not acquired foreign citizenship but are ordinarily living in foreign countries and having Indian passport.
- A person is considered as NRI if he/she is not residing in India for 182 days or more in a financial year.
- Any other person deported on the United Nations Organisation and any other appointments by Government of India are also placed under this category. They enjoy all the rights that are available to Indian citizens.

Voting Rights to NRI

- In year 2012, on occasion of 10th Pravasi Bharatiya Diwas (PBD), Indian Government allowed Non-Resident Indians (NRI's) to vote and participate in election process, after registration of overseas electors under Representation of People Act, 1950.
- In January, 2015, government accepted the recommendations of Election Commission's empowered committee to allow e-ballots for NRIs.

National Population Register (NPR)

- NPR is a record of usual residents of the country. It is a register consisting of people who has been residing in a local area for at least the last six months or intends to stay in a particular location for the next six months.
- The NPR is being prepared under provisions of the Citizenship Act, 1955 and the Citizenship (Registration of Citizens and Issue of National Identity Cards) Rules, 2003. It is mandatory for every usual resident of India to register in the NPR.

- The data for the NPR was first collected in 2010 alongwith the house listing phase of Census 2011. The NPR exercise is conducted at the local, sub-district, district, state and national levels.
- The NPR will collect both demographic data and biometric data. Biometric data will be updated through Aadhar details.

National Register of Citizen (NRC)

- The National Register of Citizens (NRC) is a register containing names of all genuine Indian citizens' residing in India. The register was first prepared and its updation process was put into action after the 1951 Census of India.
- The NRC is now being updated in Assam to include the names of those residents (or other descendants) who appear in the NRC, 1951 or in any of the Electoral Rolls up to the midnight of 24th March, 1971 or in one of the other admissible documents issued up to mid-night of 24th March, 1971, which would prove their presence in Assam or in any part of India on or before 24th March, 1971.
- Assam witnessed large-scale illegal migration from erstwhile East Pakistan and after 1971, from present-day Bangladesh.
- This led to the six-year-long Assam Movement from 1979 to 1985, for deporting illegal migrants. The All Assam Students' Union (AASU) led the movement that demanded the updating of the NRC and the deportation of all illegal migrants who had entered Assam after 1951.
- The Assam Movement against illegal immigration eventually led to the historic Assam Accord of 1985, signed by the movement leaders and the Rajiv Gandhi Government.
- The updation process of NRC started in the year 2013 under the strict monitoring and supervision of the Supreme Court of India.
- On mid-night of 31st December, 2017, Draft NRC was released and subsequently on 30th July, 2018, the complete draft of NRC was released.

Indian Diaspora

- The Indian Diaspora is a generic term to describe the people who migrated from territories that are correctly within the borders of the **Republic of India**. It also refers to their descendants.
- According to the Ministry of Overseas Indian Affairs, India has the second largest diaspora in the world after China.

Pravasi Bharatiya Divas (PBD)

- Pravasi Bharatiya Divas (PBD) is celebrated on 9th January once in every two years in India, to mark the contribution of overseas Indian community in the development of India.
- The day commemorates the arrival of Mahatma Gandhi in India from South Africa in 1915. Started in 2003, Pravasi Bharatiya Conference is sponsored by the Ministry of External Affairs.

Different Classes of Persons on Legal Grounds

Classes of Persons	Description
Citizen	Full members of India, they enjoy Fundamental Rights and Duties bearing full allegiance to the State and Constitution.
Alien Foreigner	They do not get all these rights, which are available to the citizens of India. They have 'Right to Life' under Article 21 but not the 'Right to Freedom of Speech' under Article 19. These Alien Foreigners can be enemies or friends.
Stateless Person	Illegal migrants are included in this category, who are declared illegal due to lack of documents related to citizenship.
Refugee	Persons who have taken refugee in India due to discrimination and fear of discrimination on grounds of class, race, language, nationality, social oppression from their country of origin; like-Rohingya.

Part III (Articles 12 to 35) of the Constitution of India contains a comprehensive list of 'Justiciable' Fundamental Rights, which has been described as the 'Magna Carta' of the Indian Constitution.

Chapter Seven

Fundamental Rights

India's Constitution has the most detailed Fundamental Rights compared to any other country, including the USA. The Fundamental Rights are defined as the basic Human Rights of all citizens. They are deemed essential to protect the rights and liberties of the people against the encroachment of the power by the government. Fundamental Rights safeguard against abuse of power, promoting a rule of law where governance is based on principles, not personal discretion. The concept of Fundamental Rights is inspired from the American Constitution's Bill of Rights.

CONSTITUTIONAL PROVISIONS

- Fundamental Rights enshrined in the US Constitution are affected by Bill of Rights, 1791.
- Fundamental Rights provide protection to the citizens to maintain public order in the country and against the harsh rules of the states.
- Rights have been given this name, since they have obtained the judicially protection by the Constitution, which is Fundamental Law of land.
- Fundamental Rights are crucial and 'fundamental' for the complete development of individuals in all aspects of life including the moral, intellectual, material and spiritual development.
- Originally, the Constitution of India provided for seven Fundamental Rights. However, the Right to Property (Article 31) was deleted from the list of Fundamental Rights by the 44th Amendment Act, 1978. It is a legally protected right under Article 300(A) in Part-XII of the Constitution. So, at present there are only six Fundamental Rights.

Features of Fundamental Rights

- The Fundamental Rights are guaranteed by the Constitution to all persons without any discrimination.
- They uphold the equality and dignity of all individuals in the larger public interest and unity of the nation.
- Fundamental Rights are regarded as fundamental because they are basic laws of a country.
- These are guaranteed by the Constitution and they are most essential for the attainment of intellectual, moral and spiritual status by the individual.
- Fundamental Rights are inalienable rights because they cannot be taken away from citizens in normal times.
- Fundamental Rights include individual as well as group rights such as equality before law, freedom of speech, freedom of association, etc.
- The objective behind the inclusion of the Fundamental Rights in the Indian Constitution is to establish a government of laws and not of men.
- Some of them are available only to the citizens (Articles 15, 16, 19, 29 and 30) while others are available to all persons whether citizens or foreigners or legal persons like corporation or companies.
- All of them are available against the arbitrary action of the state. However, some of them are also available against the action of private individuals (Articles 15(2), 17, 23 and 24).
- Some of the Fundamental Rights place limitations on the state's authority (negative in character) while some of them confer certain privileges on the persons (positive in nature).

- They are not sacrosanct (it means something in treated as if it is holy and kept free from violation or criticism.) or permanent.
- The Parliament can curtail or repeal them but only by a Constitutional Amendment Act and not by an ordinary act.
- Fundamental Rights are not absolute or unlimited rights, they are restricted rights. The Constitution itself imposes certain restrictions on the individuals in the enjoyment of Fundamental Rights.
- The Parliament is authorised to impose reasonable restrictions on these Fundamental Rights.
- The grounds on which the Fundamental Rights can be restricted, include the following :
  - In the interest of sovereignty and security of India. In the interest of public order, morality and decency.
  - In the promotion of the well-being of weaker sections in society including women, children, SCs, STs and OBCs. In maintaining friendly relationships with other foreign nations.
- They can be suspended during the operation of a National Emergency except the rights guaranteed by Articles 20 and 21.
- Further, the six rights guaranteed by Article 19 can be suspended only when emergency is declared on the grounds of war or external aggression (i.e., external emergency).
- They are justiciable that means in case of violation of these rights individuals can approach the Supreme Court and High Court directly.
- Any aggrieved person can directly go to the Supreme Court as it is the defender of these rights.
- The Fundamental Rights are limited by three exceptions :
  - Article 31(A) Allows for saving laws providing for acquisition of estates.
  - Article 31(B) Validates certain acts and regulations (listed in the Ninth Schedule).
  - Article 31C Supports laws that implement specific Directive Principles.
- Parliament has the power to limit or withdraw Fundamental Rights from the members of :
  - Armed forces
  - Paramilitary forces
  - Police forces
  - Intelligence agencies
  - Similar services (Article 33)

Difference between Fundamental Rights and Ordinary Legal Rights

- Ordinary laws are used to protect and enforce ordinary legal rights, while Fundamental Rights are guaranteed and protected by Constitution itself. Ordinary legal rights can be changed by making a law by the Parliament, but to change the Fundamental Rights, the Constitution has to be amended.
- No part of the government can do anything against the Fundamental Rights.

HISTORICAL ASPECTS OF FRs

- Fundamental Rights were first developed in Britain in 1215, King John was compelled by the people of Britain to sign the Magna Carta to recognise the ancient liberties.
- After this, in 1689, the British people forced the emperor to sign the Bill of Rights, which were given to the public from time to time by their emperors.
- In 1789, the constitutional recognition of Human Rights was started in the Constitution of France. In 1791, the Charter of Rights was announced in the Constitution of America.
- In the year 1925, Annie Besant's 'Common Wealth of India Bill' and the Nehru Report of the year 1928, also had provision for Fundamental Rights.
- In the Karachi Session of 1931 (President-Vallabhbhai Patel), the Indian National Congress had demanded Fundamental Rights in its Menifesto.
- The Sapru Committee (1944-45) pleaded for two types of Fundamental Rights i.e., justiciable and non-justiciable.

Declaration of Human Rights in General Assembly of the United Nations

The comprehensive declaration of Human Rights was approved by the United Nations General Assembly on 10th December, 1948. There are total 30 Articles in it. Right to education is mentioned in **Article 26**, Right to get public service with equality in **Article 21** and Right to food is mentioned in Article 25.

Origin of Fundamental Rights

- **1215 Magna Carta** Issued by King John of England, 1st formal recognition of rights
- **1689 Bill of Rights** Issued in England
- **1776 US Declaration of Independence** Rights asserted by Americans as a result of American Revolution
- **1789 French Declaration of Rights** Resulting from French Revolution
- **1948** Universal Declaration of Human Rights
- **1950** Indian Constitution adopts Fundamental Rights from the US Constitution

Definition of State (Article 12)

- Article 12 defines the term state for the purposes of Part III. According to it, the state includes Government and Parliament of India, Government and Legislature of States, all local authorities and all other authorities under the control of the Government of India.
- Thus, all public authorities including the elected representatives, judges and judicial officials, bureaucrats, autonomous institutions, public corporations, private bodies and trusts, government universities and educational bodies etc., come under the definition of state.
- The State includes all its agencies and any actions by these agencies that violate Fundamental Rights can be challenged in court.

Definition of Laws (Article 13)

- Under Article 13, all laws in force in the Territory of India immediately before the commencement of this Constitution, in so far as they are inconsistent with the provisions of this part, shall to the extent of such inconsistency, be declared as void.
- The state shall not make any law which takes away or abridges the rights conferred by this part. If any law is made in contravention of this clause it shall to the extent of the contravention be declared as void.
- Article 13 broadly defines 'law' to encompass various forms of legislation and legal instruments, including :
    - permanent laws enacted by Parliament or State Legislatures.
    - temporary laws like ordinances issued by the President and Governor.
    - delegated legislation (executive legislation) such as orders, bye-laws, rules, regulations or notifications.
    - non-legislative sources like customs or usages with the force of law.
- As a result, any of these can be challenged in court for violating a Fundamental Right and potentially declared void.
- The Supreme Court judgement, brought 24th Constitutional Amendment Act and inserted the phrase "Nothing in this article shall apply to any amendment of this Constitution made under Article 368."
- Article 13 declares that a Constitutional Amendment is not a law and hence, cannot be challenged. However, the Supreme Court held in the Kesavananda Bharati Case (1973) that a Constitutional Amendment can be challenged on the ground that it violates a Fundamental Right that forms a part of the basic structure of the Constitution and hence, can be declared as void.

Judicial Review and Fundamental Rights

- Judicial review is the power conferred on the Supreme Court and High Courts of India to declare a law unconstitutional, if it is inconsistent with any of the provisions of Part III of the Constitution, to the extent of the contravention.
- Article 13 provides for the judicial review of all the Legislations in India, if it is in contravention with and any of the Fundamental Rights given under Part III of the Constitution.
- The principle of judicial review has been adopted from the United States of America.

Courts Decisions Regarding Articles 13 and 368

- The Supreme Court in the Shankari Prasad Case (1951), held that the Parliament can amend any of the provisions of the Constitution including Fundamental Rights by its amending power under Article 368.
- In the Sajjan Singh Case (1965), the Supreme Court defended its above verdict that Parliament can amend any part of Fundamental Rights by its amending power under Article 368.
- In the Golaknath Case (1967), the Supreme Court, however, reversed its earlier position and declared that Fundamental Rights are transcendental and cannot be subjected to amendment.
- In the Kesavananda Bharati Case (1973), the Supreme Court came up with a balanced approach and mooted a basic structure doctrine as per which Fundamental Rights can be amended by the Parliament, but without disturbing the basic structure of the Constitution.

- The provision made by the 42nd Constitutional Amendment was struck down by the courts decision of Minerva Mills *vs* Federation of India, 1980.
- In this decision, the court said that the basic goals of the Constitution will be protected by the court and on the basis of this, the court can review any amendment.

CLASSIFICATION OF FRs

- Originally Constitution of India provided for the 7 Fundamental Rights, but at present there are 6 Fundamental Rights provided to the citizens.
- Earlier there was also a provision for the right to property under Article 31 but by 44th Amendment Act of 1978, it was removed.
- The Constitution of India classifies the Fundamental Rights under six groups as follows :

Classification of Fundamental Rights

Category	Consists of
Right to Equality **(Articles 14-18)**	• Equality before law and equal protection of laws **(Article 14)**. • Prohibition of discrimination on grounds of religion, race, caste, sex or place of birth **(Article 15)**. • Equality of opportunity in matters of public employment **(Article 16)**. • Abolition of untouchability and prohibition of its practice **(Article 17)**. • Abolition of titles except military and academic **(Article 18)**.
Right to Freedom **(Articles 19-22)**	• Protection of six rights regarding freedom of: (i) speech and expression, (ii) assembly, (iii) association, (iv) movement, (v) residence and (vi) profession **(Article 19)**. • Protection in respect of conviction for offences **(Article 20)**. • Protection of life and personal liberty **(Article 21)**. • Right to elementary education **(Article 21A)**. • Protection against arrest and detention in certain cases **(Article 22)**.
Right Against Exploitation **(Articles 23 and 24)**	• Prohibition of traffic in human beings and forced labour **(Article 23)**. • Prohibition of employment of children in factories, etc. **(Article 24)**.
Right to Freedom of Religion **(Articles 25-28)**	• Freedom of conscience and free profession, practice and propagation of religion **(Article 25)**. • Freedom to manage religious affairs **(Article 26)**. • Freedom from payment of taxes for promotion of any religion **(Article 27)**. • Freedom from attending religious instruction of worship in certain education institutions **(Article 28)**.
Cultural and Education Rights **(Articles 29 and 30)**	• Protection of language, script and culture of minorities **(Article 29)**. • Right of minorities to establish and administer educational institutions **(Article 30)**.
Right to Constitutional Remedies **(Article 32)**	• Right to move the Supreme Court for the enforcement of Fundamental Rights including the writs of : (i) habeas corpus, (ii) mandamus, (iii) prohibition, (iv) certiorari and (v) quo warranto **(Article 32)**.

Fundamental Rights Available to Foreigners and Indian Citizens

Fundamental Rights Available Only to Citizens and Not to Foreigners	Fundamental Rights Available to Both Citizens and Foreigners (except enemy aliens)
• Prohibition of discrimination on grounds of religions, race, caste, sex or place of birth **(Article 15)**. • Equality of opportunity in matters of public employment **(Article 16)**. • Protection of six rights regarding freedom of; (i) speech and expression, (ii) assembly, (iii) association, (iv) movement, (v) residence and (vi) profession **(Article 19)**. • Protection of language, script and culture of minorities **(Article 29)**. • Right of minorities to establish and administer educational institutions **(Article 30)**.	• Equality before law and equal protection of laws **(Article 14)**. • Protection in respect of conviction for offences **(Article 20)**. • Protection of life and personal liberty **(Article 21)**. • Right to elementary education **(Article 21(A))**. • Protection against arrest and detention in certain cases **(Article 22)**. • Prohibition of traffic in human beings and forced labour **(Article 23)**. • Prohibition of employment of children in factories etc., **(Article 24)**. • Freedom of conscience and free profession, practice and propagation of religion **(Article 25)**. • Freedom to manage religious affairs **(Article 26)**. • Freedom from payment of taxes for promotion of any religion **(Article 27)**. • Freedom from attending religious instruction or worship in certain educational institutions **(Article 28)**.

Right to Equality (Articles 14-18)

- The Right to Equality is extremely important for our society with social and economic inequalities.
- All humans are equal by birth, so they should be treated equally. The Constitution has accepted this principle.
- Articles 14 to 18 deals with the Right to Equality. The detailed description is given below :

Equality Before the Law and Equal Protection of Law (Article 14)

- The state shall not deny to any person equality before the law or equal protection of the laws within the territory of India.
- The word person has wider meaning which includes constitutional corporations, companies, registered societies, etc.

Difference between Equality before Laws and Equal Protection of Laws

Equality before Laws	Equal Protection of Laws
The concept of equality before law is a **British concept.**	The concept of equal protection of law is an **American concept.**
The concept connotes the absence of any special privileges in favour of any person.	The concept connotes the equality of treatment under equal circumstances, both in the privileges conferred and liabilities imposed by the laws.
It defines the equal subjection of all persons to the ordinary law of the land administered by ordinary law courts.	It defines the similar application of the same laws to all persons who are similarly situated.
It says that whether rich or poor, high or low, official or non-official persons are not above the law.	It says that the like should be treated alike without any discrimination.

Exceptions

- Under Article 361(1), the President or the Governor of a state, shall not be answerable to any court for the exercise and performance of the powers and duties of his office or for any act done or purporting to be done by him in the exercise and performance of those powers and duties.
- No criminal proceedings shall be initiated or continued against the President or the Governor of a state in any court during his term of office.
- No process for the arrest or imprisonment of the President, or the Governor of a state, shall be issued from any court during his term of office.
- No civil proceedings in which relief is claimed against the President or the Governor of a state, shall be initiated during his term of office in any court in respect of any act done or purporting to be done by him in his personal capacity,
    - whether before or after he entered his office as President or as Governor of a state, until the expiry of 2 months after the notice in writing has been delivered to the President or the Governor, as the case may be,
    - or left at his office stating the nature of the proceedings, the cause of action therefore, the name, description and place of residence of the party by whom such proceedings are to be instituted and the relief which it claims.
- Article 361 A grants immunity from civil or criminal proceedings in any court for publishing or broadcasting a substantially accurate report in a newspaper, radio or television regarding proceedings in :
    - Either House of Parliament
    - Either House of the State Legislature
- Article 105 Members of Parliament are granted immunity from court proceedings for :
    - statements made in Parliament or its committees.
    - votes cast in Parliament or its committees.
- Article 194 State Legislators are protected from court proceedings for :
    - statements made in the State Legislature or its committees.
    - votes cast in the State Legislature or its committees.
- Article 31C is an exception to Article 14 that exempts laws enacted by states to implement specific Directive Principles (Article 39, Clauses b and c) from being challenged under Article 14. The Supreme Court has ruled that when Article 31-C applies, Article 14 does not.
- Under international law, the visiting head of government and foreign diplomats posted in the country are not subject to the jurisdiction of local courts.
- The United Nations Organisation (UNO) and its agencies are granted diplomatic immunity.

Rule of Law

- Rule of Law was propounded by AV Dicey, the British jurist. His concept has the following three elements or aspects :

  (i) Absence of arbitrary power, that is, no man can be punished except for the breach of law.

(ii) Equality before the law, that is, equal subjection of all citizens.

(iii) The primacy of the rights of the individual, that is, the Constitution is the result of the rights of the individual rather the Constitution being the source of individual rights.

- The first and the second elements are applicable to the Indian system and not the third one. In the Indian system, the Constitution is the source of the individual rights.
- According to John Locke, 'where there is no law, there is no liberty'.
- Therefore, the existence of law is necessary for the existence of liberty. It is by law that liberty is protected.

Prohibition of Discrimination on Certain Grounds (Article 15)

- Article 15 directs that state shall not discriminate against a citizen on the grounds only of race, caste, religion, sex or place of birth.
- The word only indicates that the discrimination on other ground is not prohibited.
- Under Article 15, the right guaranteed is available only to the citizens.
- Article 15(2) provides that no citizen shall be subjected to any disability, liability, restriction or condition on grounds only of religion, race, caste, sex or place of birth with regard to :
    - access to shops, public restaurants, hotels and places of public entertainment or
    - the use of wells, tanks, bathing ghats, roads and places of public resort maintained wholly or partly by state funds.
    - This provision prohibits discrimination both by the state and private individuals.

Exceptions

- Article 15(3), empowers the state to make special provisions for the protection of women and children.
- Article 15(4), which was added by the 1st Constitutional Amendment Act, 1951, enables the state to make special provisions for protection of the interests of the backward classes including SCs and STs.
- Article 15(5), the state can make any special provisions for the advancement of any socially and educationally backwards classes or for the STs or SCs. This provision was added by the 93rd Constitutional Amendment Act, 2005.
- Article 15(6), the state can
    - Make any special provisions for the advancement of any economically weaker sections.
    - reservation of upto 10% seats in admission to educational institutions including private educational institutions whether or not they are aided by the state other than the minority educational institutions.
- It was added by the 103rd Constitutional Amendment Act, 2019.

27% Reservation for the OBCs

The Central Government enacted the Central Educational Institutions (Reservation in Admission Act, 2006), reserving 27% of seats in central higher educational institutions, including IITs and IIMs, for Other Backward Classes (OBCs). The Supreme Court upheld this act in 2008 but excluded the **creamy layer** (advantaged sections) among OBCs from benefiting from this quota.

10% Reservation to Economically Weaker Sections (EWS)

In 2019, the Central Government introduced a 10% reservation for Economically Weaker Sections (EWS) in educational institutions to give effect to Article 15(6). This benefit is available to individuals who meet the following eligibility criteria

- Gross annual family income below ₹ 8 lakh from all sources (salary, agriculture, business, etc.) in the preeceding financial year.
- Exclusion criteria: Families owning or possessing any of the following assets, regardless of income:
    - 5 acres or more of agricultural land
    - Residential flats of 1000 sq.ft or larger
    - Residential plots of 100 sq.yards or larger in notified municipalities
    - Residential plots of 200 sq.yards or larger in non-notified areas
- Property owned by a family in multiple locations will be combined to determine EWS status.

Equality of Opportunity in Matters of Public Employment (Article 16)

- As per the Article 16(1) all citizens have the right to equal opportunities in employment and appointments to public offices.
- Article 16(2) states that no citizen shall be discriminated on grounds only of religion, race, caste, sex, descent, place of birth or residence for any employment or office under the state i.e., Constitution guarantees equality of opportunity.

- The state is free to specify the qualifications. There can be any other ground for non-eligibility.
- There are four exceptions to this general rule of equality of opportunity in public employment which are as follows :
    - Article 16(3) Parliament can prescribe residence as a condition for certain employment or appointment in a State or Union Territory or local authority or other authority.
    - Article 16(4) The state can provide for reservation of appointments or posts in favour of any backward class that is not adequately represented in the state services.
    - Article 16(5) A law can provide that the incumbent of an office related to religious or denominational institution should belong to the particular religion.
    - Article 16(6) The state is permitted to make a provision for the reservation of upto 10% of appointments or posts in favour of any Economically Weaker Sections of citizens.
- The Supreme Court in the Indra Sawhney's Case (popularly known as Mandal Commission Case, 1992), laid down the following points, which summarise the law on the issue of reservation are as follows :
- In the year 1990, VP Singh's Government announced 27% reservation for OBCs in the government jobs.
- The Supreme Court upheld the constitutional validity of 27% reservation for the OBCs with certain conditions :
    - The particular class should not be adequately represented in the services under the state.
    - No benefit of reservation to creamy layer among the OBCs.
    - Total reservation should not exceed 50% except in some extraordinary situations.
    - No reservation in Promotion.
    - The carry forward rule in case of backlog vacancies is valid withing 50% limit.
    - A permanent statutory body to be established to examine complaints of over-inclusion and under-inclusion in the list of OBCs. National Commission for Backward Classes was established in 1993.
    - Maintenance of efficiency in administration.
    - Concept of Creamy Layer (it term used to describe members of a backward class who are more advanced socially economically and educationally than others in their class) introduced income and post criteria to prevent advanced sections within the backward classes to take benefit of the Other Backward Classes (OBCs) quota.
    - The 76th Amendment Act, 1994 granted immunity to the Tamil Nadu Reservations Act of 1993 by placing it in the Ninth Schedule, thereby insulating its controversial 69% reservation quota from judicial review.

Mandal Commission and Creamy Layer

- In 1979, the Morarji Desai-led government established the Second Backward Classes Commission, chaired by **MP BP Mandal**, as per Article 340 of the Constitution.
- The commission's mandate was to examine the socio-economic status of backward classes and recommend measures for their upliftment.
- The commission submitted its report in 1980 in which it identified 3743 castes as socially and educationally backward.
- Mandal Commission recommended the 27% reservation in government jobs for OBCs (Non-Creamy Layer).
- The Creamy Layer in OBC should be excluded from the list of beneficiaries of reservation. In 1993, National Commission for Backward Class (NCBC) was established by an act of Parliament.
- It was formed as an initiative for investigating the conditions and difficulties of the socially and educationally backward classes and thus making appropriate recommendations.
- Currently, the NCBC has given a constitutional status by the Constitutional **102nd Amendment Act, 2018**.
- The court has placed under the Creamy Layer person belonging to backward classes who are highly affluent. They cannot be given the benefit of reservation.

- By the 77th Constitutional Amendment Act, 1995, Article 16 (4(a)) was added, making provision for reservation in promotion for Scheduled Castes, Scheduled Tribes.
- The Constitution 81st Amendment Act, 2000 has added a new Clause (4-B) in Article 16 of the Constitution, which seeks to end the 50% limit for the SCs/STs in backlog vacancies, which could not be filled up due to the non-availability of eligible candidates of these categories.
- The 82nd Amendment Act, 2000 overturned a previous ruling by introducing a new clause to

Article 335. It grants the state the authority to relax qualifying marks or lower evaluation standards for Scheduled Castes (SCs) and Scheduled Tribes (STs) in promotion reservations, thereby allowing for more flexible promotion policies.

- The 85th Constitutional Amendment Act, 2001 added provision for consequential seniority for Scheduled Castes and Scheduled Tribes in case of reservation in promotion.
- Under Article 16, the guarantee against discrimination is limited to employment and appointment under the state.
- According to M. Nagarayan *v/s* Union of India decision, 2006, the 77th and 85th Constitutional Amendment Act was challenged by the general caste employees in the Supreme Court, but the court continued the reservation of promotion and made it mandatory to fulfill the following three condition before reservation of promotion.
  - To prove the authenticity of backwardness.
  - There is inadequate representation of that class.
  - Reservation should not affect the overall efficiency of the administration.
- By 103rd Constitutional Amendment Act, 2019, Article 16 was amended to permit the government to reserve upto 10% of all posts for the Economically Weaker Section of Society.
- The 104th Constitutional Amendment Act, 2019, extended the reservation of seats for members from Scheduled Caste and Scheduled Tribe in the Lok Sabha and State Legislative Assemblies by a period of 10 years.

Abolition of Untouchability (Article 17)

- Untouchability and its practice in any form is forbidden. The enforcement of any disability arising out of untouchability shall be an offence, punishable in accordance with the law.
- Constitution does not prescribe any punishment for the practice of untouchability, but it empowers the Parliament under Article 17 and Article 35 to prescribe punishment by law.
- In this regard, the Parliament enacted the Untouchability (Offences) Act, 1955, which prescribes the punishment for the practice of untouchability. This Act was amended by the Untouchability (Offences) Act, 1976 to widen its scope and provide for more stringent penal provisions and renamed as Protection of Civil Right Act, 1955.
- A special law for the protection of SCs and STs was enacted named as Scheduled Castes and Scheduled Tribes, Prevention of Atrocities Act, 1989 to provide for strong punitive measures, which could serve as a deterrence against brutalities. However, the Act does not define Untouchability.
- Although the term 'untouchability' is not explicitly defined in the Constitution or the Act, the Mysore High Court has interpreted it as the historical practice of imposing social disabilities on certain individuals based on their birth specific castes.
- This interpretation excludes instances of social boycott or exclusion from religious services against specific individuals.
- Furthermore, the Supreme Court has established in the People's Union for Democratic Rights Case (1982) that the right protected under Article 17 can be enforced against private individuals, and it is the State's constitutional responsibility to ensure that this right is upheld and protected from violation.

According to the Supreme Court, **Untouchability** should not be understood in its literal or grammatical sense. It is to be understood as the practice as it had developed historically; like,

- preventing Dalits from using public resources, including common water resources.
- preventing Dalits from entering into places of worship which the ordinary people do.
- calling Dalits by denigrating names.
- A person convicted of this offence is also disqualified for the election of Union or State Legislature.

Abolition of Titles (Article 18)

This Article abolishes titles and make four provisions in that regard :

- Article 18(1) No title, except a military or academic distinction, shall be conferred by the state.
- Article 18(2) No citizen of India shall accept any title from any foreign state.
- Article 18(3) No person who is not a citizen of India shall, while he holds any office of profit or trust under the state, accept without the consent of the President, any title from any foreign state.
- Article 18(4) No person holding any office of profit or trust under the state shall, without the consent of the President accept any present emolument or office of any kind from or under any foreign state.
- National Awards like Bharat Ratna, Padma Vibhushan, Padma Bhushan and Padma Shri do not come under

the purview of Article 18 and thus, the state can accord such awards to eminent personalities. Nevertheless, the British Knighthood i.e., sir is deemed to be a title and thus, no Indian citizen can accept it.

- From the above, it is clear that the hereditary titles of nobility like Maharaja, Raj Bahadur, Rai Bahadur, Rai Saheb, Dewan Bahadur, etc, which were conferred by colonial states are banned by Article 18 as these are against the principle of equal status of all.
- Article 51(A) of Constitution lays down Fundamental Duties for every citizen. It was believed that there should by honours and decorations for the recognition of excellence in performance of these duties. Thus, they are not violative of provisions under Article (18).
- In the 1995 Balaji Raghavan Case, the Supreme Court upheld the constitutional validity of India's National Awards, including the Bharat Ratna, Padma Vibhushan, Padma Bhushan and Padma Shri.
- The court ruled that these awards do not constitute 'titles' as defined in Article 18, which only prohibits hereditary titles of nobility but the awardees should not use these honours as suffixes or prefixes to their names.
- India's National Awards were established in 1954 but were briefly discontinued by the Janata Party Government in 1977.
- The Indira Gandhi Government revived them in 1980. Since then, the Padma Awards have been announced annually on Republic Day, with exceptions in 1978 to 1979 and 1993 to 1997.
- The government limits the number of Padma Awards to 120 per year, excluding posthumous awards and those given to non-resident Indians, foreigners, and overseas citizens.
- Additionally, the Bharat Ratna Award is restricted to a maximum of three recipients per year.

Right to Freedom (Articles 19 to 22)

Personal liberty is the most important of all the Fundamental Rights. These articles taken together from 19 to 22 on personal liberties, provide the backbone of the chapter on the Fundamental Rights.

The Six Freedom Rights (Article 19)

- Article 19 (1) of the Constitution guarantees to the citizens of India the following Six Freedom Rights
- Article 19(1) (a) Right to freedom of speech and expression. It includes rights to express one's own ideas, beliefs and convictions without restraint either verbally or in any other form.
- The Supreme Court held that the freedom of speech and expression includes the following :
    - Right to propagate one's views as well as views of others.
    - Freedom of the press.
    - Freedom of commercial advertisements.
    - Right against tapping of telephonic conversation.
    - Right to telecast, i.e., government has no monopoly on electronic media.
    - Right against bundh called by a political party or organisation.
    - Right to know about government activities.
    - Freedom of silence.
    - Right against imposition of pre-censorship on a newspaper.
    - Right to demonstration or picketing but not right to strike.
- The government can restrict free speech and expression in certain situations, such as protecting national security, maintaining public order, or preventing defamation, as long as the restrictions are reasonable.
- Article 19(1)(b) Right to assemble peaceably and without arms It includes the freedom to hold public gatherings, hold protests and participate in processions, all of which are only permitted on public property. It does not offer protection from disruptive, violent or destructive gatherings.
- Under Section 144 of Criminal Procedure Code (1973), a Magistrate can restrain an assembly, meeting or procession if there is a risk of obstruction, annoyance or danger to human life, health or safety or a disturbance of the public tranquility or a riot or any affray.
- Article 19(1)(c) Right to form associations or unions or co-operative societies It involves the freedom to form (and not form) organisations such as trade unions, businesses, partnerships, societies, clubs and political parties.
- The right to form associations and unions encompasses both the freedom to establish and continue them, as well as the freedom not to join or form one.
- However, the State can impose reasonable restrictions on this right to protect India's sovereignty, public order and morality. The right to official recognition of an association is not a Fundamental Right.

- Article 19(1)(d) Right to move freely throughout, the Territory of India The freedom of movement has two dimensions, *viz*, internal right to move inside the country (Article 19) and external right to move out of the country and right to come back to the country (Article 21).
- The state can impose reasonable restrictions on the exercise of any of the rights either in the interests of the general public or for the protection of the interests of any Scheduled Tribe.
- Access to tribal areas is limited to preserve the unique culture, language and traditions of Scheduled Tribes. This restriction also aims to protect tribal communities from exploitation and safeguard their traditional way of life and properties.
- Similarly, the Supreme Court has ruled that the movement of sex workers can be restricted to protect public health and maintain public morals.
- Additionally, the Bombay High Court has upheld restrictions on the movement of individuals with AIDS, citing public health concerns.
- Article 19(1) (e) Right to reside and settle in any part of the Territory of India This right consists of two components :
  (i) the freedom to temporarily reside anywhere in the country, and
  (ii) the freedom to permanently settle anywhere in the country, establishing a home or domicile.
- The purpose of this right is to eliminate internal barriers and divisions within the country, fostering a sense of nationalism and broad-mindedness.
- The right of outsiders to reside and settle in tribal areas is restricted to protect the distinctive culture and customs of Scheduled Tribes and to safeguard their traditional vocation and properties against exploitation. The state can impose reasonable restrictions on the exercise of any of the rights either in the interests of the general public or for the protection of the interests of any Scheduled Tribe.
- Article 19(1) (f) Right to practice any profession or to carry on any occupation, trade or business It doesn't include the right to carry on a profession that is immoral or dangerous.
- The state can impose restrictions in the interests of the general public. Also state can make laws with respect to making the professional or technical qualifications necessary for practicing any profession or carrying on any occupation, trade or business as well as directly engage in any trade, business, industry, or service, either exclusively or in competition with citizens.
- In the Anuradha Bhasin Case (2020), the Supreme Court ruled that the right to conduct business or profession online is protected under Article 19(1)(g).
- Any restrictions on this right must meet the conditions outlined in Article 19(6), including the principle of proportionality. Additionally, the Court held that an indefinite internet shutdown is unlawful under the Temporary Suspension of Telecom Services (Public Emergency or Public Safety) Rules, 2017.
- These six rights are protected against only state action and not private individuals. Moreover, these rights are available only to the citizens and to shareholders of a company. The state can impose reasonable restrictions on the enjoyment of these six rights.
- A new Article 361 (a) was added to the Constitution by the 44th Constitutional Amendment Act, 1978, under which newspapers were given full freedom to publish proceedings of Parliament and Legislatures.

Protection in Respect of Conviction for Offences (Article 20)

- Protection under Article 20 is available against the following three types of convictions :
  - Under Ex-post Facto Legislation No person shall be convicted of any offence except for violation of a law in force at the time of the commission of the Act. It can not be subjected to a penalty greater than that, which might have been inflicted under the law in force at the time of the commission of the offence.

> - A law that imposes penalties or increases punishment for actions already done is known as an **ex-post-facto law**.
> - **Article 20** prohibits such laws from being enacted, but only in the case of criminal laws, not civil or tax laws.

  - Double Jeopardy No person shall be prosecuted and punished for the same offence more than once. It is applicable only in case of judicial proceedings and not departmental authorities.
  - Prohibition Against self-incrimination No person accused of any offence shall be compelled to be a witness against himself.
- However, self-incrimination does not give the accused privilege of absolute silence. The accused is expected to co-operate to the investigating agencies by revealing certain details of evidences and information

relating to crime or offence that took place. Thus, the accused cannot disallow authorities from taking his/her fingerprints, search of his/her residence, etc.

- The right against self-incrimination protects individuals from being forced to provide oral and documentary evidence.

  However, it does not extend to :
  - Producing physical evidence
  - Providing biometric samples (e.g., fingerprints, blood)
  - compulsory exhibition of one's body
- Additionally, this protection only applies in criminal proceedings, not in civil or non-criminal cases.
- By 44th Amendment of the Constitution, it was provided that the right conferred under Article 20 cannot be suspended by an order under Article 359 during an emergency.
- Under certain laws like the Unlawful Activities Prevention Act, (UAPA), the onus of proving the innocence lies on the accused rather than the prosecution proving the crime.

Protection of Life and Personal Liberty
(Article 21)

- According to Article 21, no person shall be deprived of his/her life and personal liberty except according to the procedure established by law.
- This right is available to both citizens as well as non-citizens.
- Article 21 cannot be suspended during an emergency.
- The Supreme Court, through a liberal interpretation of the article has derived a number of inferred rights. The Article 21 stands not merely for the right to life and personal liberty, but also for the right to dignity and all other attributes of human personality that are essential for the full development of a person.
- In the landmark Gopalan Case (1950), the Supreme Court interpreted Article 21 narrowly, ruling that it only protects against arbitrary actions by the executive, not the legislature.
- This means that the state can limit an individual's right to life and personal liberty through legislation.
- The Court based its decision on the phrase 'procedure established by law' in Article 21, which differs from the 'due process of law' in the US Constitution.
- According to Article 21, use of 3rd degree method by police is violative of Article 21.
- Prevention of sexual harassment of working women comes under Article 21. The Supreme Court in the Vishaka Case held the above ruling.
- Euthanasia and the Supreme Court (with reference to Article 21): For the first time in the year 1994, in the case of P. Rathinam *v/s* Union of India, the Supreme Court accepted the right of a person to die.

The Supreme Court overruled Gopalan Case judgement in the Maneka Gandhi Case and in the subsequent cases. It has declared the following rights as part of Article 21 :

- Right to dignified life
- Right to free education upto 14 years of age
- Right against cruel punishment
- Right to free legal aid and Right to speedy trial
- Right to health of workers
- Right against denial of wages
- Right to healthy and livable environment
- Right to shelter for the workers
- Right to travel abroad
- Right to privacy
- Right to marry the person of one's choice
- Right to livelihood
- Right against solitary confinement
- Right against handcuffing
- Right against inhuman treatment
- Right against delayed execution
- Right against bonded labour
- Right against custodial harassment
- Right to emergency medical aid (Right to Doctor's assistance)
- Right to timely medical treatment in government hospitals
- Right not to be driven out of a state
- Right to fair trial
- Right of prisoners to have necessities of life
- Right of women to be treated with decency and dignity
- Right against public hanging
- Right to road in hilly areas
- Right to information
- Right to social and economic justice and empowerment
- Right to sleep
- Right to freedom from noise pollution
- Right to sustainable development

- In the year 1996, the Supreme Court changed its complete decision and said that the right to die is not a Fundamental Right under Article 21 (right to life) of the Constitution. In March 2011, the Supreme Court allowed passive euthanasia in the Aruna Shanbaug Case.
- The Supreme Court allowed passive euthanasia in March 2018 while hearing a petition by a voluntary organisation called Common Cause. Thus, the court has included the right to death in Article 21 of the Constitution.
- In KS Puttaswamy Case (2017) the Supreme Court declared that the right to life and personal liberty guaranteed in Article 21 also implicitly includes the right to privacy.

Other Important Judgements

- The Supreme Court decriminalised homosexuality by striking off parts of Section 377 of the Indian Penal Code (IPC) that were held violative of Fundamental Rights of LGBTQ Community.
- The Supreme Court has struck down as unconstitutional, the 158 year old Section 497 of the Indian Penal Code, which criminalises adultery. The law was violative of Article 21 (Right to life and personal liberty) and Article 14 (Right to equality).
- The Supreme Court in Shayara Bano Case (2017) had declared the practice of Triple Talaq (talaq-e-biddat) as unconstitutional. The Triple Talaq was held to be violative of Article 14 (the right to equality), Article 15, Article 21 (Right to privacy) and Article 25 (Religious right).

Even Animals have Rights Against Torture

- The Supreme Court observed on May, 2014, that even bulls have rights against torture and it banned **Jallikattu** (bull fighting) and bullock cart racing in Tamil Nadu. The court also banned bullock cart racing in Maharashtra.
- The word life has been given an expanded definition and any disturbance from the basic environment which includes all forms of life, including animal life that fall within the meaning of **Article 21** of the Constitution.

Difference between Procedure Established by Law and Due Process of Law

Procedure Established by Law	Due Process of Law
Inspired by British Constitution	Inspired by American Constitution
Upheld the supremacy of the Parliament.	The supremacy of the judiciary and the proper method are considered.
Judiciary does not have the power to interpret the reasonableness of laws.	In America, the judiciary can declare such laws as unconstitutional, which have been made by the Legislature but violates the principle of **natural justice**.

Right to Education *(Article 21 A)*

- Under Article 21A, the state shall provide free and compulsory education to all children of the age of 6 to 14 years in such manner as the state by law may determine. Article 21A was inserted by the 86th Constitutional Amendment Act, 2002.
- Before this amendment, the Constitution included a provision for free and compulsory education for children under Article 45 in the Directive Principles of State Policy. But it was not legally enforceable. However, with the amendment, the courts can now intervene to ensure its implementation.
- This amendment added a Fundamental Duties under Article 51A (k), to provide opportunities for education to his/her child or ward between the age of 6 to 14 years.
- The Supreme Court, in the Unni Krishnan Case (1993), established a Fundamental Right to primary education as part of the right to life under Article 21.
- This judgement overturned the Court's earlier decision in the Mohini Jain Case (1992), which had recognised a Fundamental Right to education at all levels, including professional education like medicine and engineering.

Right to Education Act, 2009

- Parliament passed the Right of Children to Free and Compulsory Education (RTE) Act in 2009 to implement Article 21A. This law ensures every child receives full-time, high-quality elementary education in a formal school that meets essential standards.
- The legislation aims to promote equality, social justice, and democracy by providing inclusive education to all, thereby creating a just and humane society. Both the Constitutional Amendment Act (2002) and the RTE Act (2009) came into effect on 1st April, 2010.

Protection Against Arrest and Detention in Certain Cases *(Article 22)*

- Article 22 grants protection to persons who are arrested or detained.
- The first part of Article 22 confers following rights on a person, who is arrested or detained under an ordinary law :
  - Right to be informed on grounds of arrest.

- Right to consult and be defended by a legal practitioner.
- Right to be produced before a Magistrate within 24 hours of arrest.
- Right to be released after 24 hours unless the magistrate authorises further detention.

- The Supreme Court clarified that Article 22's protection against arrest and detention only applies to criminal or quasi-criminal cases, or activities harmful to public interest. It does not cover :
  - Arrests ordered by a court
  - Civil arrests
  - Arrests for failing to pay income tax
  - Deportation of foreigners
- As per Article 22(3) safeguards are not available to foreigners and citizens detained under the Preventive Detention Act.
- The second part of Article 22 grants protection to persons arrested or detained under a preventive detention law :
  - Rights not to be detained beyond three months.
  - Right to be communicated of the grounds of detention.
  - Right to make a representation against the detention order.
- The 44th Amendment Act of 1978 reduced the detention period without opinion from advisory board from three to two months, but this change is not in force yet hence there is still three month period.
- Judicial custody means that accused will held in prison and not in lock-up. During judicial custody, the police officer incharge of the case is not allowed to interrogate the suspect without the approval of the court. State Governments have their own rules releasing prisoners on parole.

Preventive Detention

Preventive detention means detention of a person without trial and conviction by a court. Its purpose is not to punish a person for a past offence but to prevent him from committing an offence in the near future. Thus, preventive detention is only a precautionary measure and based on suspicion. The preventive detention laws made by the Parliament are :

- Preventive Detention Act, 1950, expired in 1969.
- Maintenance of Internal Security Act (MISA), 1971, repealed in 1978.
- National Security Act (NSA), 1980.
- Terrorist and Disruptive Activities (Prevention) Act (TADA), 1985. It was repealed in 1995.

Right Against Exploitation (Articles 23 and 24)

Rights against exploitation are explained under Articles 23 and 24.

Prohibition of Traffic in Human Beings and Forced Labour (Article 23)

- According to Article 23, traffic in human beings, beggar and other similar forms of forced labour are prohibited. Any contravention of this provision shall be an offence, punishable in accordance with law.
- Traffic in human beings means selling and buying men and women like goods and includes immoral traffic in women and children for immoral and other purposes.
- Article 23 prohibits 'begar', a system where local landlords forced tenants to work without pay, as well as other forms of forced labour like bonded labour.
- Forced labour means compelling someone to work against their will, using physical, legal, or economic coercion, including paying less than the minimum wage. The Parliament has enacted Immoral Traffic (Prevention) Act, 1956 and the Bonded Labour System (Abolition) Act, 1976 to punish for offences of exploitation.
- Article 23 permits the state to impose compulsory service for public purposes, for example, military service or social service.

Supreme Court Judgements Enlarging the Dignity of the Individual

- After Bandhua Mukti Morcha *v/s* Union of India (1984), the Supreme Court decided that the government should take necessary steps to abolish bonded labour.
- In the case of Ranjit Rai *v/s* State of Rajasthan (1983), the Supreme Court ruled that in times of famine, minimum paying wages less than wages is more or less similar to forced labour.

Prohibition of Employment of Children in Factories, etc (Article 24)

- The essence of Article 24 is the prohibition of employment of children below 14 years of age in hazardous jobs. This provision is in the interest of public health and safety of the lives of children.
- In MC Mehta *vs* State of Tamil Nadu Case, the Supreme Court held that the state authorities should protect economic, social and humanitarian rights of children, working illegally in the public and private sectors.

- The government has passed the Child Labour (Prohibition and Regulation) Act, 1986 which seeks to eliminate child labour.
- In 1996, the Supreme Court ordered the creation of a Child Labour Rehabilitation Welfare Fund, requiring employers who hire child labour to pay a fine of ₹ 20,000 per child.
- The Commissions for Protection of Child Rights Act, 2005 established a national and state-level framework to safeguard child rights.
- This includes setting up a National Commission and State Commission for child rights and specialised Children's Courts to ensure speedy justice for crimes against children and violations of their rights.
- In 2006, the government banned the employment of children as domestic servants or workers in business establishments like hotels, dhabas, etc.
- In 2016, government enacted the Child Labour (Prohibition and Regulation) Amendment Act, which completely prohibited the employment of children below 14 years. It also prohibits the employment of adolescents in the age group of 14 to 18 years in hazardous occupations.
- The Act declared child labour as a cognizable offence. There is a penalty of ₹ 50,000 and a jail term of upto two years.

  Note *Cognizable offence is a criminal offence in which a police officer can arrest someone without a warrant and begin an investigation without a court order*

Right to Freedom of Religion (Articles 25 to 28)

India is a secular state, not an atheist state. The state protects all the religions; but interferes with none. It believes in the ancient Indian doctrine of Sarva Dharma Sambhava.

Freedom of Conscience and Free Profession and Practice of Religion (Article 25)

- Under Article 25, all persons are equally entitled to the freedom of conscience and the right to profess practice and propagate religion. The right to propagate does not mean alluring a person to join any religion.
- Article 25(1) does not give the right to convert, but only the right to spread the tenets of ones own religion.
- Freedom of Conscience Absolute inner freedom of an individual to mould his/her own relation with God or Creatures in whatever manner he/she likes.
- Right to Profess To declare freely and openly one's faith and belief.
- Right to Practice To perform the prescribed religious duties, rites and rituals and to exhibit his religious beliefs.
- Right to Propagate Spread and publicise his/her religious views for the edification of others. It only indicates persuasion and exposition without any element of coercion. The rights are available to both citizens and non-citizens.
- The two explanations mentioned in Article 25 :
  - Being considered a part of Sikh religion, permission to wear and carry a sword.
  - Sikh, Jain and Buddhist religions are also included under Hindu.

Freedom to Manage Religious Affairs (Article 26)

- The Article 26 grants freedom to manage religious affairs subject to public order, morality and health and every religious denomination or any section thereof shall have the following right :
  - To establish and maintain institutions for religious and charitable purposes. To manage its own affairs in the matters of religion.
  - To own and acquire movable and immovable property and to administer such property in accordance with law.
  - Article 25 protects individual religious freedom, while Article 26 protects the freedom of religious groups. Similar to Article 25, the rights granted by Article 26 are subject to public order, morality and health, but are not subject to other Fundamental Rights restrictions.
  - The court has the right to decide whether a particular ritual or method of worship is necessary according to the beliefs of that religion or not and if a particular practice is against public health or morality or is not an integral part of religious practice and if it violates the law regulating social, economic or political, the court can intervene.

- State regulations cannot interfere with matters that are essentially religious.

> - The Supreme Court established three criteria to define a religious denomination :
>   - —A shared system of beliefs (doctrines) that promote spiritual well-being
>   - —A unified organisation —A distinctive name
> - Applying these criteria, the Court recognised 'Ramakrishna Mission' and 'Ananda Marga' as religious denominations within Hinduism. However, it did not consider Aurobindo Society a religious denomination.

Freedom as to Payment of Taxes for Promotion of any Particular Religion (Article 27)

- Article 27 says that individuals cannot be forced to pay taxes that specifically support or promote a particular religion or religious group.
- This means the government cannot use public funds collected through taxes to favour one religion over another. Instead, taxes can be used to support all religions equally.
- It is Article 27 that spells out the secular character of a state. It means the state does not recognise any religion as the official religion. It regards religion as the personal affairs of the individuals and does not interfere in religious belief and faith.
- The provision prohibits only levy of a tax and not a fee. This is because the purpose of a fee is to control secular administration of religious institution and not to promote or maintain religion.

Freedom from Attending Religious Instruction (Article 28)

- Article 28 grants freedom as to the attendance at religious instruction or religious worship in certain educational institutions.
- Article 28 divides educational institutions into four categories :
  - Wholly maintained by the state.
  - Recognised by the state.
  - Receiving aids out of the state funds.
  - Administered by state, but established under a religious endowment.
- In the first case, there can be no religious instructions, whatsoever in the second and third case, the religious instructions can be permitted, but the pupils cannot be compelled to attend such instructions. In the fourth case, there is no restriction whatsoever, as far as religious instructions are concerned.

Cultural and Educational Rights (Articles 29 and 30)

Articles 29 and 30 of the Indian Constitution deals with the Cultural and Educational Rights.

Protection of Interests of Minorities (Article 29)

- Under Article 29, any section of the citizens residing in the territory of India or any part there of having a distinct language, script or culture of its own and shall have the right to conserve the same.
- No citizen shall be denied admission into any educational institution maintained by the state or receiving aid out of state funds on grounds only of religion, race, caste, language or any of them.
- The Supreme Court has observed that the right to administration is not the right to maladministration. The university can put basic qualifications for the selection of teachers.
- Article 29 protects the rights of both religious and linguistic minorities. The Supreme Court has ruled that the protection under this article extends to all citizens, not just minorities due to the phrase 'section of citizens' which refers to both minority and majority groups.
- Minority is that group, which has its own language or religion and on the basis of number in any part of the country or in the whole country, it is smaller than any other group, such minority groups have the right to preserve and develop their own language, script and culture.

Right of Minorities to Establish and Administer Educational Institutions (Article 30)

- All minorities, whether based on religion or language, shall have the right to establish and administer educational institutions of their choice.
- It provides to religious, educational and cultural institutions, the right to own, possess and dispose immovable property.
- The compensation given by the government for taking over property of a minority educational institution cannot limit their rights. This protection was added by the 44th Constitutional Amendment Act, 1978. Through this act the

right to property was removed as a Fundamental Right.

- The government cannot discriminate against schools run by minorities when granting aid.
- This article also includes the right of minorities to impart education to their children in its mother language.
- Minority educational institutions are of three types :
  - Those seeking state recognition and aid (subject to state regulations).
  - Those seeking only state recognition (subject to state regulations).
  - Those seeking neither recognition nor aid (free to administer, but must follow general laws like contract, labour and tax laws).

The Supreme Court in the **Secretary of Malankara Syrian Catholic College Case (2006)** outlined key principles for the establishment and administration of minority educational institutions.

- The provisions under article are applicable only on minorities i.e. religious or linguistic and not on any section of citizen.

Right to Constitutional Remedies (Article 32)

- Article 32 provides institutional framework for the enforcement of the Fundamental Rights by the Supreme Court.
- Dr. BR Ambedkar called this article as The fundamental of the Fundamental Rights and The heart and soul of the Constitution.
- To enforce the Fundamental Rights, the Supreme Court is empowered under Article 32, to issue writs of various forms. The concept of issuing writs is taken from the UK.

Writ

- A writ means an order. Anything that is issued under an authority is a writ.
- In this sense, using the power conferred by Article 32, the Supreme Court issues directions, orders or writs.
- Article 32 (3) confers the power to Parliament to make law empowering any court to issue these writs. But this power has not been used. Therefore, only Supreme Court under Article 32 (2) and High Courts under Article 226 can issue writs.

Forms of Writs

Writs	Meaning	Description
Habeas Corpus	To have the body i.e., to be produced before the court	The court can examine legality of arrest or detention. This kind of writ is issued to protect personal liberty of an individual against the arbitrary action of both the state and private individuals.
Mandamus	We command	This kind of writ is issued against a public authority or an officer and inferior courts for compelling the authority to do a particular work that it ought to do but has not done. Private rights cannot be enforced by the writ of the Mandamus.
Prohibition	To forbid	This kind of writ is issued by the higher courts to the lower courts or the quasi-judicial bodies when the latter exceed their judicial authority. The objective is to keep the lower courts or the quasi-judicial bodies within the limits of their respective jurisdiction. The difference between Mandamus and Prohibition is that while the former can be issued against judicial as well as administrative authorities, the latter is issued only against the judicial or quasi-judicial authorities.
Certiorari	To be certified	This writ is issued to quash the order of a lower court or the decision of a tribunal in excess of its jurisdiction. The purpose of this writ is to secure that the jurisdiction of an inferior court or tribunal is properly exercised and that it does not usurp the jurisdiction, it does not possess.
Quo Warranto	By what authority	This kind of writ is issued to ensure that the person holding a public office is qualified to hold the office. Besides the normal writs issued on violation of Fundamental Rights, there has been a progressive strengthening of the Fundamental Rights by the judiciary. The principle of **Locus Standi** applies only to the writs of Mandamus, Prohibition, Certiorari.

Martial Law and Fundamental Rights

- Article 34 provides for the restrictions on Fundamental Rights while martial law is in force in any area within the territory of India. The term martial law has not been defined in the Constitution. There are no grounds mentioned for the imposition of martial law. It is imposed under the extraordinary circumstances like war, invasion, insurrection, rebellion, riot or any violent resistance to law.
- Martial law (also known as the 'military rule's refers to a situation where the military takes control of civil administration and rules with their own regulations, outside of ordinary law. This means :
  - Ordinary law is suspended
  - Military tribunals govern
  - Different from military law that applies only to armed forces
- During the operation of martial law, the military authorities are vested with abnormal powers to take all necessary steps. However, the SC held Habeas Corpus is not suspended when martial law is in force.

Legislation Effecting Certain Fundamental Rights

- Article 35 lays down that the power to make laws, to give effect to certain specified Fundamental Rights shall vest only in the Parliament and not in the State Legislatures. These rights are :
  - prescribing residence as a condition for certain employments or appointments in a Union Territory or local authority or other authority (Article 16).
  - empowers courts other than Supreme Court and High Courts to issue directions, orders and all kinds of writs (Article 32).
  - restricting or abrogating the application of Fundamental Rights to members of armed forces, police forces, etc (Article 33).
  - indemnifying any government or any other person for any act done during the operation of martial law in any area (Article 34).
  - punishment for acts involving untouchability (Article 17).
  - traffic in human beings and forced labour (Article 23).

Suspension of Fundamental Rights

- The Constitution contains provisions for automatic suspension of the Fundamental Rights under certain circumstances, e.g., during the National Emergency under Article 352 (i.e., war or external aggression).
- Under Article 358, when National Emergency is proclaimed on the grounds of war or external aggression (and not armed rebellion), the Fundamental Rights under Article 19 are automatically suspended.
- The Constitution empowers the President, under Article 359 to suspend any or all the Fundamental Rights by issuing a separate proclamation during a National Emergency. The 44th Amendment Act, 1978 prohibits the suspension of Articles 20 and 21 (protection in respect of conviction for offences and protection of life and personal liberty, respectively) even during a National Emergency.

Right Outside Part III in the Constitution

These rights are also known as Constitutional, Legal and Non-Fundamental Rights. These are as follows:

- **Article 265 No Tax shall be levied or collected except by authority of law**
- **Article 300** A right to property
- **Article 301** Freedom of trade, commerce and intercourse
- **Article 326** Right to vote

The Directive Principles of State Policy are in the nature of general directions to the state, where the state is expected to incorporate them in policies framing and laws.

Chapter Eight

Directive Principles of State Policy

CONSTITUTIONAL PROVISIONS

- The Directive Principles of State Policy are enumerated in Part IV of the Constitution from Articles 36 to 51.
- Article 36 clearly directs the state to secure and protect a social order which stands for the welfare of the people.
- Article 37 says that Directive Principles are not justiciable, but these are Fundamental to the Governance of the country and it shall be duty of the state to apply these principles in making laws.

Features of Directive Principles

- Directive Principles of State Policy (DPSP's) contain the ideals that should guide the formulation of policies and laws by the government.

This concept is remarked as a novel feature by **Dr. BR Ambedkar** in the Constitutional Governments throughout the world, with the growing acceptance of a **Welfare State**.

- The Directive Principles resemble the Instrument of Instructions enumerated in the Government of India Act of 1935. In the words of Dr. BR Ambedkar, the Directive Principles are like the Instrument of Instructions, which were issued to the Governor-General and to the Governors of the colonies of India by the British Government under the Government of India Act of 1935.
- The framers of the Constitution borrowed this novel feature of the Constitution from the Constitution of Ireland which had itself copied it from the Spanish Constitution.
- They are non-justiciable in nature but they impose a moral obligation on the state authorities for their application.
- They aim to establish a welfare state instead of Police state. They are supplementary to the Fundamental Rights. DPSPs supplement the political democracy established by the Fundamental Rights by establishing social and economic democracy.

The Supreme Court in various judgements has established that any law framed for implementing DPSPs should be reasonable in relation to **Article 14** (equality before law) and **Article 19** (right to six freedoms).

- They realise the ideals enshrined in the Preamble, which solemnly resolves to secure to all citizens of India values of justice, liberty, equality and fraternity.
- They have served as useful beacon-lights to courts in exercising their power of judicial review and determining constitutional validity of law.
- The Directive Principles are meant to be the Fundamental Principles, which should necessarily be made the basis of all executive and legislative action that may be taken in the governance of the country.

Views about DPSPs

Personalities	Views
KC Hier	'Directive Principles promote the conflicts in Parliament and Judiciary'.
Ivor Jennings	The Directive Principles have been given names such as 'Virtuous moral aspiration and Fabian socialism'.
Dr. BR Ambedkar	Directive Principles establish the economic democracy. DPSP and Fundamental Rights together are the soul of the Constitution and its philosophy.
Austin	"Directive Principles and Fundamental Rights have been called the Basic Soul of the Constitution". DPSP and Fundamental Rights together are the conscience of the Constitution.

CLASSIFICATION OF DPSPs

Directive Principles have not been classified in the Constitution. However, the Directive Principles are a unique blend of socialist, Gandhian and liberal-intellectual principles and the ideals of the Indian Freedom Movement. Hence, they have been classified as :

Socialist Principles

These principles lay down the framework of a democratic socialist state, which aims at providing social and economic justice and set the path towards welfare state.

These principles direct the State in following ways :

- Article 38 The State shall strive to promote the welfare of the people by securing and protecting as effectively as it may, a social order, in which justice – social, economic and political, shall inform all the institutions of the national life.
- The state shall, in particular, strive to minimise the inequalities in income and endeavour to eliminate the inequalities in status, facilities and opportunities, not only amongst individuals, but also among groups of people residing in different areas and engaged in different vocations (44th Constitutional Amendment Act, 1978).
- Article 39 The State shall, in particular, direct its policy towards securing :
    - that the citizens, men and women equally have the right to an adequate means of livelihood.
    - that the ownership and control of the material resources of the community are so distributed as best to subserve the common good.
    - that the operation of the economic system does not result in the concentration of wealth and means of production to the common detriment.
    - that there is equal pay for equal work for both men and women.
    - that the health and strength of workers, men and women and the tender age of children are not abused and that citizens are not forced by economic necessity to enter into a profession unsuited to their age or strength.
    - that children are given opportunities and facilities to develop in a healthy manner (42nd Constitutional Amendment Act, 1976) and in conditions of freedom and dignity and that childhood and youth are protected against exploitation and against moral and material abandonment.
- Article 39(A) To promote equal justice and to provide free legal aid to the poor.
- Article 41 The State shall, within the limits of its economic capacity and development, make effective provisions for securing the right to work, to education and to public assistance in cases of unemployment, old age, sickness and disablement and in other cases of undeserved wants.
- Article 42 The State shall make provision for securing just and humane conditions of work and for maternity relief.
- The Maternity Benefit (Amendment) Act, 2017 has made amendments to the Maternity Benefits Act, 1961.
- As per the Amendment, 2017, the duration of paid maternity leaves available for women employees increased to 26 weeks from 12 weeks. However, for those women who are expecting their second child, the duration of the leave remains at 12 weeks.
- Article 43 To secure a living wage, a decent standard of life and social and cultural opportunities, for all workers.

Living Wage The amount a person needs to earn to meet their basic needs and maintain a decent standard of living, considering factors like housing, food, healthcare and education.

Living wage, Minimum wage and Fair wage

Minimum Wage The lowest legal wage an employer can pay their employees, set by government regulations to protect workers from exploitation and ensure a basic level of income.

Fair Wage A wage that reflects the worker's skill, effort and contribution to the organisation, ensuring equal pay for equal work and considering industry standards.

- Article 43(A) The State shall take steps by suitable legislation or in any other way, to secure the participation of workers in the management of undertakings, establishments or other organisations engaged in any industry.
- Article 47 To raise the level of nutrition and the standard of living of people and to improve the public health.

Gandhian Principles

These principles are based on Gandhian ideology and represent the programme of reconstruction enunciated by Gandhi during the national movement. Gandhiji promoted the concept stateless society, this idea was also promoted by the Karl Marx.

Some of his ideas were included as Directive Principles. They direct the State in following ways :

- Article 40 The state shall take steps to organise Village Panchayats and endow them with such powers and authority as may be necessary to enable them to function as units of self-government.
- Article 43 The State shall endeavour to promote cottage industries on an individual or cooperative basis in rural areas.
- Article 43 (B) To promote voluntary formation, autonomous functioning, democratic control and professional management of cooperative societies (97th Constitutional Amendment Act, 2011).
- Article 46 The State shall promote with special care, the educational and economic interests of the weaker sections of the people and in particular, of the Scheduled Castes and the Scheduled Tribes and shall protect them from social injustice and all forms of exploitation.
- Article 47 Prohibition of toxic drugs and drinks which are injurious to health.
- Article 48 Taking steps for preserving and improving the breeds and prohibiting the slaughter of cows and calves and other milch and draught cattle.

Liberal-Intellectual Principles

These liberal-intellectual principles direct the State in following ways:

- Article 44 The State shall endeavour to secure for the citizens a Uniform Civil Code throughout the territory of India.

Uniform Civil Code (UCC)

Article 44 of **Part IV** of the Constitution (Directive Principles of State Policy) directs the State to frame a Uniform Civil Code for all citizens.

- The Government of India passed the **Hindu Marriage Act**, the Hindu Succession Act to reform Hindu laws to bring change in this direction, but not much effort was made by the government in this direction.
- **After Shah Bano** (1989), the Supreme Court directed the Government of India to introduce a Uniform Civil Code, but the government led by **Rajiv Gandhi** did not implement it under the pressure of minorities.
- **Sarla Mudgal** *v/s* **Union of India** (1995) and after hearing the writ of Christian priests in the year 2005, the Supreme Court directed the government to implement Uniform Civil Code, but due to the lack of determination of the government, Uniform Civil Code could not be implemented. At present, Uniform Civil Code is applicable in state of **Goa** and **Uttarakhand**.

- Article 45 To provide early childhood care and education for all children until they complete the age of six years.
- Article 48 The state shall endeavour to organise agriculture and animal husbandry on modern and scientific lines.
- Article 48(A) To protect and improve the environment and to safeguard the forests and wildlife of the country (42nd Constitutional Amendment Act, 1976).
- Article 49 It shall be the obligation of the state to protect every monument or place or object of artistic or historic interest (declared by or under law made by Parliament), of national importance, from spoilation, disfigurement (A lasting change to a person's appearance or functionality that is caused by a medical condition.), destruction, removal, disposal or export, as the case may be.
- Article 50 The State shall take steps to separate the Judiciary from the Executive in the public services of the state.
- Article 51 The state shall endeavour to :
  - promote international peace and security.
  - maintain just and honourable relations between nations.
  - foster respect for international law and treaty obligations in the dealings of organised peoples with one another.
  - encourage settlement of international disputes by arbitration.

DPSP Outside Part IV

- Article 335 says that the claims of SCs and STs shall be taken into consideration, consistently with the maintenance of efficiency of administration, in the making of appointments to services and posts in connection with affairs of the Union or a State.
- Article 350(A) enjoins every state and every local authority within the state to provide adequate facilities for the instructions in the mother tongue at the primary stage to children of linguistic minority areas.
- Article 351 enjoins the Union to promote the spread of Hindi language so that it may serve as a medium of expression of all the elements of the composite culture of India.

AMENDMENTS MADE IN DPSPs

Important amendments related to Directive Principles of State Policy are as follows :

42nd Amendment Act, 1976

- Article 39(f) To secure opportunities for healthy development of children.
- Article 39(a) Provision for equal justice and free legal aid to the poor.
- Article 43(a) Making provision for participation of workers in management of industries.
- Article 48(a) Protection of environment and wildlife.

44th Amendment Act, 1978

Article 38(2) It provides that the state shall strive to minimise the inequalities in income and endeavour to eliminate inequalities in status, facilities and opportunities.

86th Amendment Act, 2002

Article 45 It provides that the State shall endeavour to provide early childhood care and education for all children until they complete the age of six years. The subject matter or Article 45 was changed and the elementary education was made a Fundamental Right under Article 21(A).

97th Amendment Act, 2011

Article 43(B) The State shall endeavour to promote voluntary formation and management of cooperative societies.

Journey of Conflict Between Fundamental Rights and Directive

Champakam Dorairajan Case (1951) In this case, Supreme Court held that Directive Principles have to conform to and run as subsidiary to Fundamental Rights.

Golaknath's Case (1967) In this case, the Supreme Court rules that Parliament has no power to take away the Fundamental Rights which are sacrosanct in Fundamental Rights cannot be amended for the implementation of the Directive Principles.

24th Constitutional Amendment Act (1971) This Act made it clear that the Parliament has power to amend any provision of the Constitution, including the Fundamental Rights.

25th Constitutional Amendment Act (1971) This Act introduced Article 31(c) which provides that in case of implementing Article 39 (b) and (c) if there is a conflict with Fundamental Rights, (Articles 14, 19 and 31) the law shall not be declared 'null and void'.

Kesavananda Bharati Case (1973) Supreme Court in this case overruled the Golaknath's Case, but made it clear that courts retained the power to Judicial Review in case of law giving effect to Directives under Article 39 (b) and (c). One of the crucial implications of this judgement was 'basic structure' which cannot be altered.

42nd Amendment Act, 1976 During the period of Emergency, Parliament passed the 42nd Amendment Act, 1976 which provided for implementation of any of the Directive Principles and not just those specified in Article 39 (b) and (c).

Minerva Mill's Case (1980) It made the provision of supremacy of Directive Principles over Fundamental Rights as held in the 42nd Amendment Act, 1976 as unconstitutional. However, Fundamental Rights in Article 14 and 19 were accepted as subordinate or DPSP's specified in Article 39 (b) and (c).
The Supreme Court also held that 'the Indian Constitution is founded on the bedrock of the balance between the Fundamental Rights and the Directive Principles.

Present Position Currently, Fundamental Rights take precedence over Directive Principles. However, this does not mean that the Directive Principles can not be implemented. Parliament can modify Fundamental Rights to enforce Directive Principles, as long as the changes do not compromise with the basic structure of the Constitution.

IMPLEMENTATION OF DPSPs

Since, the commencement of the Constitution, there have been a number of legislations to implement the DPSP.

- Land Reforms Almost all the states have passed land reform laws to bring changes in the agrarian society and to improve the conditions of the rural masses. Under this, Agriculture Ceiling Act was passed to give effect to Article 39(B).
- Labour Reforms The following Acts were enacted to protect the interests of the labour section of the society and to give effect to Articles 41, 42, 43(A).
  - The Minimum Wages Act (1948) (code on wages, 2020).
  - The Child Labour Prohibition and Regulation Act (1986).
  - The Maternity Benefit Act (1961) and the Equal Remuneration Act (1976) have been made to protect the interests of women workers.
- Panchayati Raj System Through 73rd Constitutional Amendment Act, 1992, Government fulfilled constitutional obligation stated in Article 40.
- Cottage Industries To promote cottage industries as per Article 43, the Government has established several boards such as Village Industries Board, Khadi and Village Industries Commission etc., which provide essential help to cottage industries in finance and marketing.
- Education Government has implemented provisions related to free and compulsory education as provided in Article 45.
- After 86th Constitutional Amendment Act, 2002 accept the provision of Article 45 for free and compulsory education to children between age of 6 to 14 years.
- Rural Area Development Programmes such as the Community Development Programme (1952), Integrate Rural Development Programme (1978-79) and Mahatma Gandhi National Rural Employment Guarantee Act (MGNREGA-2006) were launched to raise the standard of living particularly in rural areas, as stated in the Article 47 of the Constitution.
- Health Central Government sponsored schemes like Pradhan Mantri Gram Swasthya Yojana (PMGSY) and National Rural Health Mission (NRHM) are being implemented to fulfill the social sector responsibility of the Indian State.
- Environment The Wildlife (Protection) Act, 1972, the Forest (Conservation) Act, 1980 and the Environment (Protection) Act, 1986 have been enacted to safeguard the wildlife and the forests respectively and fulfill Clause under Article 48(A).
- Welfare of Women Reservation of one-third of seats through 73rd and 74th Amendment Act has been made in Panchayats and Municipalities.
- India has set up national commissions to safeguard the interests of weaker sections, including :
  - Backward Classes (1993, now constitutionally recognised)
  - Minorities (1993)
  - Women (1992)
  - Child Rights (2007)
- India has taken steps to empower SCs, STs and weaker sections, including :
  - Reserving seats in education, government and representative bodies
  - Enacting laws to prevent social injustice and exploitation (1955, 1976 and 1989)
  - Establishing National Commissions to protect their interests (1990, split into two separate commissions in 2003).
- In 2019, the Central Government introduced a 10% reservation for Economically Weaker Sections (EWSs) in education and government jobs, benefiting individuals not already covered under SC, ST or OBC reservations.
- This was enabled by the 103rd Constitutional Amendment Act, 2019.

Legal Services Authorities Act, 1987

Free legal services (under Section 12 of the Legal Services Authorities Act) are available to :

- Women, children and vulnerable groups
- SC/ST members (but not OBCs)
- Industrial workers, disaster victims *and* disabled persons
- Those in custody or with low income (₹ 1 lakh, or as prescribed by the state)
- Trafficking victims, beggars *and* transgender individuals (with an income ceiling of ₹ 2,00,000)
- Senior citizens (subject to state-specific income limits)

- In spite of the above steps by the Central and State Governments, the Directive Principles have not been implemented fully and effectively due to several reasons like inadequate financial resources, unfavourable socio-economic conditions, population explosion, strained Centre-State relations and so on.

> Fundamental Duties are an important part of Indian Constitution. They stressed that the citizens should become conscious that in addition to the enjoyment of rights.

Chapter Nine

Fundamental Duties

Fundamental Duties are a set of ideals that emphasise the duty of every citizen of the country towards the Indian state, its Constitution, values and institutions.

No duties of the citizen were incorporated in the original Constitution of India at the time of its commencement in 1950. However, the duties of the state in the form of Directive Principles were present.

A set of 10 duties were added later in 1976. One more Fundamental Duty was added in the year 2002. The Fundamental Duties not only guide the citizens but also guide the Legislative and Executive action of elected or non-elected institutions.

> The legal utility of **Fundamental Duties** and **Directive Principle** is the same. Fundamental Duties are addressed to the citizens and there is **no legal sanction** in the case of their violation.

The success of this provision will solely depend upon the manner and person against whom these duties would be enforced. If the duties are not known to all, then there would not be proper enforcement of these duties.

CONSTITUTIONAL PROVISIONS

- Fundamental Duties are incorporated under Article 51A (Part IVA) of the Indian Constitution.
- The Original Constitution did not contain provisions related to Fundamental Duties. This Article was inserted by the 42nd Constitutional Amendment Act, 1976.
- The Fundamental Duties in the Indian Constitution are inspired by Constitution of erstwhile USSR. It declared that the citizens' exercise of their rights and freedom was inseparable from the performance of their duties and obligations.
- Notably, none of the Constitutions of major democratic countries like USA, Canada, France, Germany, Australia and so on specifically contain a list of duties of citizens. Japanese Constitution is perhaps, the only democratic Constitution in the world which contains a list of duties of citizens.
- The Fundamental Duties were incorporated in the Constitution on the basis of the recommendation of the Sardar Swaran Singh Committee.
- Eight Fundamental Duties were recommended by this committee, but 10 Fundamental Duties were added by the 42nd Amendment. A new Fundamental Duty was added by the 86th Constitutional Amendment, 2002 i.e., at present the number of Fundamental Duties in the Indian Constitution is 11.

11 Fundamental Duties for Citizens

Article 51A provides that it shall be the duty of every citizen of India

To abide by the Constitution and respect its ideals and institutions, the National Flag and National Anthem.

To uphold and protect the sovereignty, unity and integrity of India.

To promote harmony and the spirit of common brotherhood amongst all the people of India and to renounce practices derogatory to the dignity of women.

To protect and improve the **natural environment.**

To safeguard **public property.**

To cherish and follow the noble **ideals** that inspired the freedom struggle.

Duty of every parent or guardian to provide opportunities for education of his child or ward between the age of 6 to 14 years (86th Constitutional Amendment Act, 2002).

To defend the country and render **national service** when called upon to do so.

To preserve the **rich heritage** of our composite culture.

To develop the **scientific temper** and spirit of inquiry.

To strive towards excellence in all spheres of individual and collective activity.

Swaran Singh Committee

- This committee was set up in 1976 by the Congress Government when the need for it was felt, when the internal emergency was in force during 1975 to 1977.
- It was set up to make recommendations about Fundamental Duties.
- The committee recommended adding a new chapter in the Constitution that emphasises the responsibilities of the citizens along with their rights.
- The government accepted this recommendation and enacted the 42nd Constitutional Amendment Act, 1976 which added a new Article 51(A), which lists 10 Fundamental Duties. The Congress Party saw this step as correcting a historical mistake and addressing a gap in the original Constitution.
- Interestingly, certain recommendations of the Sardar Swaran Singh Committee were not accepted by the Congress Party and hence, not incorporated in the Constitution. These include :
  - The Parliament may provide for the imposition of such penalty or punishment as may be considered appropriate for any non-compliance with or refusal to observe any of the duties.
  - No law imposing such penalty or punishment shall be called in question in any court on the ground of infringement of any Fundamental Rights or on the ground of repugnancy to any other provision of the Constitution.
  - Duty to pay taxes should also be a Fundamental Duty to the citizens.

Significance of Fundamental Duties

- Fundamental Duties are a reminder to the citizens that while enjoying privileges, they also have duties to follow.
- The main purpose of including the Fundamental Duties in the Constitution is to make the citizens aware of their social and economic responsibilities and they warn them to do or not to do something in the interest of their country, fellow citizens and themselves.
- Article 51A talks about respect for the National Flag. Instructions related to this are included in the Indian Flag Code-2002.
- If more than one interpretation of a law is possible, then while interpreting it, the court can certainly keep in mind the Fundamental Duties.
- Article 51A(a)(c) related to the protection of the environment has been specially taken cognizance of by the court.
- The Fundamental Duties assist courts in assessing the constitutionality of laws.
- The Supreme Court has established that :
  - Article 51A (Fundamental Duties) can aid in interpreting ambiguous laws to determine their validity (Mohan Kumar Singhania Case, 1991).

- A unified approach is necessary when interpreting laws, considering the interconnection between Fundamental Rights (Part III), principles of governance (Part IV), and duties of the citizens (Part IVA) (Ramlila Maidan Incident Case, 2012).
- Fundamental Duties are legally enforceable (i.e they can be enforced through laws), allowing Parliament to establish penalties or punishments for non-compliance, ensuring citizens fulfill their constitutional obligations.

Report of Verma Committee

Verma Committee (1999) identified the existence of following legal provisions :

- The prevention of insults to **National Honour Act, 1971**.
- The various criminal laws provide for punishment for encouraging enmity and discrimination.
- The **Indian Penal Code** declares the imputations and assertions prejudicial to national integration as punishable offences.
- The **Wildlife Protection Act, 1972** and **Forest Conservation Act, 1980** recommended reorienting approaches to school curriculum and teacher's education programmes and professional education.
- **The Protection of Civil Rights Act (1955)** imposes penalties for crimes related to caste-based or religious discrimination, protecting individuals from such offenses.
- **The Unlawful Activities (Prevention) Act (1967)** allows the government to ban communal organisations.
- **The Representation of People Act (1951)** disqualifies politicians from office if they engage in corrupt practices, such as seeking votes based on religion or stirring up hatred between different groups based on caste, race, language, religion, etc.
- **National Commission to Review the Working of the Constitution** (NCRWC), 2002 and Supreme Court in 2003 directed to implement recommendations of Justice Verma Committee.

Criticism of Fundamental Duties

- The lists of duties are not exhaustive as it does not cover duties like casting vote, paying taxes, family planning, etc. Some of the duties are vague, ambiguous and difficult to understand by the common man.
- They have been described as a code of moral precepts due to their non-justifiable character.
- Their addition in Part IV of the Constitution has reduced their value and significance. Instead, they should have been kept under Part III to give them equal value as the Fundamental Rights.
- Critics argued that adding Fundamental Duties to the Constitution was unnecessary, as citizens would have performed these duties anyway, even if they were not explicitly stated in the Constitution.

Relation between Fundamental Rights and Fundamental Duties

- The Constitution of India not only provide with the Fundamental Rights but also with the Fundamental Duties. Although, the Fundamental Rights were introduced in the Constitution much before the Fundamental Duties and are enforced by the court.
- Fundamental Duties are not enforceable. These are the moral duties of responsible citizen.
- The Fundamental Duties complements to the Fundamental Rights.
- Article 21 of the Constitution of India provides for Right to Education and Article 51A(k) provides that all parents and guardians must provide their children with free and compulsory education during the age group of 6 to 14 years.

Difference between Fundamental Rights and Duties

Fundamental Rights	Fundamental Duties
These are mentioned in Part III of the Indian Constitution in **Articles 12-35**.	These are mentioned in Part IV A of the Indian Constitution in the **Article 51A**.
They were taken from the Constitution of the **USA**.	They were borrowed from the Constitution of the former Soviet Union or USSR.
These can be controlled in conditions that are subject to basic nature.	They can be controlled in any condition.
They are **political** and **social in nature**.	These are political, social and **economic in nature**.
Fundamental Rights can be **enforced by the courts**.	Fundamental Duties **cannot be enforced by the courts**.
Not all citizens have the liberty to enjoy Fundamental Rights, for example, the Indian Army.	Fundamental Duties are extended to all citizens of the nation.

The basic structure of a Constitution includes a preamble outlining national goals, Fundamental Rights for citizens principles guiding government policies etc.

Chapter Ten

Basic Structure of the Constitution

EVOLUTION OF THE BASIC STRUCTURE

- The concept of basic structure has emerged and reinforced through the various Supreme Court judgements.
- The Parliament passed various constitutional amendment acts during the course of these judgements that also contributed in shaping the basic structure of the Constitution.

Shankari Prasad Case (1951)

- This case dealt with the issue of whether Parliament has the power to curtail Fundamental Rights under Article 368.
- The First Constitutional Amendment Act, 1951 which curtailed the right to property was challenged.
- The Supreme Court upheld this amendment act and ruled that the Parliament's power to amend the Constitution under Article 368 also extends to amending the Fundamental Rights.
- The constitutional amendment acts do not come under the definition of 'law' in Article 13.
- Hence, the constitutional amendment acts that abridge or take away any Fundamental Rights cannot be held unconstitutional or void under Article 13.
- First and Fourth Amendment Acts The Parliament of India passed the First Amendment to the Constitution in 1951 followed by the Fourth Amendment in 1955 to protect its authority to implement land re-distribution.
- The First Amendment Act curtailed the Right to Property.

Sajjan Singh Case (1964)

- The Supreme Court reaffirmed its stand in the Shankari Prasad Case and held that a constitutional amendment act under Article 368 is not a law as defined in Article 13.
- 17th Amendment Act This amendment act inserted certain state laws in the Ninth Schedule to protect them from judicial scrutiny.

Golaknath Case (1967)

- The Supreme Court reversed its earlier stand and ruled that Fundamental Rights have 'transcendental and immutable' position and thus, the Parliament does not have the power to abridge or take away any of these rights including the provisions on private property.
- The constitutional amendment act can be declared void if they violate any Fundamental Rights as they come within the meaning of 'law' under Article 13.
- 24th Amendment Act Parliament passed the 24th Amendment in 1971 to abrogate the Supreme Court ruling in the Golaknath Case.
- It amended the Constitution to provide expressly that Parliament has the power to amend any part of the Constitution under Article 368 including the provisions relating to Fundamental Rights. Such acts would not amount to 'law' under Article 13.

Kesavananda Bharati Case (1973)

- In this case, the Supreme Court reviewed the decision in Golaknath *v/s* State of Punjab and considered the validity of the 24th Constitutional Amendment Act.
- The court outlined the 'basic structure doctrine' in this case.
- The court held that although no part of the Constitution including Fundamental Rights, was beyond the amending power of the Parliament, the basic structure of the Constitution could not be abrogated even by a Constitutional Amendment.
- Hence, the Parliament cannot abridge or take away those Fundamental Rights that form the 'basic structure' of the Constitution.
- 39th Amendment Act Its provision kept the disputes involving election of the Prime Minister and the Speaker of the Lok Sabha outside the jurisdiction of all courts.

Indira Nehru Gandhi Case (1975)

- In Indira Gandhi *v/s* Raj Narain, the Supreme Court referred to Kesavananda Bharati Case and accepted the doctrine of basic structure of framework of Constitution.
- The Supreme Court struck down a provision in the 39th Amendment Act (1975) that kept the election disputes involving the Prime Minister and Speaker of Lok Sabha outside the scope of judicial review.
- The Court held that this provision violated the basic structure of the Constitution.

42nd Constitutional Amendment Act, 1976

- To neutralise the effect of doctrine of the basic structure, the government enacted the Constitution (42nd Amendment) in 1976 and added **Clauses (4) and (5) to Article 368**, which provided for exclusion of judicial review of Amendments of the Constitution made before or after the 42nd Amendment.
- It also declared that there shall be no limitation on the amending power of the Parliament under Article 368.

Minerva Mills Case (1980)

- In Minerva Mills *v/s* Union of India 1980, the Supreme Court struck down Clauses (4) and (5) of Article 368 inserted by the 42nd Amendment.
- These clauses destroyed the essential features of the basic structure of the Constitution.

Waman Rao Case (1980)

- In this case, the Supreme Court reaffirmed the basic structure doctrine and ruled that any constitutional amendments made after 24th April, 1973 (the date of the Kesavananda Bharati judgement).
- This case would be subject to scrutiny to ensure they do not alter the fundamental framework or the basic structure of the Constitution.

IR Coelho *v/s* State of Tamil Nadu (2007)

In this case, the Supreme Court held that any law, including those protected by the Ninth Schedule, can be subject to judicial review and can be struck down if it is found to violate the basic structure of the Constitution.

LEGITIMACY OF THE BASIC STRUCTURE

- Currently, Parliament has the power to amend any part of the Constitution, including Fundamental Rights, under Article 368, but with one limitation: it cannot alter the Constitution's 'basic structure'.
- However, the Supreme Court has not yet explicitly defined what constitutes the 'basic structure'.
- Some of the elements of the 'basic structure' has been established during the course of various judgements and debates.

Elements of the Basic Structure

- Sovereignity, unity and integrity of India
- Supremacy of the Constitution
- Parliamentary system
- Democratic and republican government
- Separation of powers
- Rule of law
- Free and fair elections
- Judicial rewiew
- Welfare state
- Secularism
- Federalism
- Freedom and dignity of individual

A Constitutional Amendment is a formal change to the text of the written Constitution of a nation or a state.

Chapter Eleven

Amendments of the Constitution

CONSTITUTIONAL PROVISIONS

- Article 368 in Part XX of the Constitution deals with the powers of the Parliament to amend the Constitution and its procedure.
- The process of amending the Indian Constitution is neither as rigid as in the US nor as flexible as in the UK, but a synthesis of both. It is based on the pattern of amendment process of the South African Constitution.
- Using its Legislative Power, the Parliament can amend any part, provision of the Constitution in the form of variation, addition or repeal.

> As ruled by Supreme Court in **Kesavananda Bharati Case** in 1973, the Parliament cannot amend those provisions which form the basic structure of the Constitution.

Kinds of Amendment

- Two kinds of amendments have been included under Article 368 :
  - (i) That requires special majority of the Parliament.
  - (ii) That requires a special majority of Parliament as well as the ratification by half of the State Legislatures by simple majority.
- Some provisions of the Constitution can also be amended by a simple majority of the Parliament in the same way as the ordinary legislative process. However, such amendments do not come under Article 368.
- Hence, the Constitution can be amended by following manner :
  - Simple majority of the Parliament
  - Special majority of the Parliament
  - Special majority of the Parliament and ratification by states

Amendments by Simple Majority

- It is an amendment by majority of the Members of each House of Parliament present and voting (similar to the ordinary legislative process).
- These amendments are kept outside the scope of Article 368. These provisions include :
  - Admission or establishment of new states
  - Formation of new states and alteration of areas, boundaries or names of existing states
  - Abolition or creation of Legislative Councils in States (Article 169)
  - Second Schedule–emoluments, allowances, privileges and so on of the President, the Governors, the Speakers, Judges, etc.
  - Quorum in Parliament
  - Salaries and allowances of the Members of Parliament
  - Rules of procedure in Parliament
  - Privileges of the Parliament, its members and its committees

- Use of English language in Parliament
- Number of puisne judges in the Supreme Court
- Conferment of more jurisdictions on the Supreme Court
- Use of official language
- Citizenship–acquisition and termination
- Elections to Parliament and State Legislatures
- Delimitation of Constituencies
- Union Territories
- Fifth Schedule administration of Scheduled Areas and Scheduled Tribes
- Sixth Schedule administration of tribal areas

Amendments by Special Majority

- It is done by majority of the total membership of each House and a majority of two-third of the Members of each House of Parliament present and voting.

> The term 'total membership' refers to the full strength of the House, including all seats, regardless of whether some seats are vacant or members are absent.

- Technically, a special majority is only necessary for the third reading of a bill, but as a precautionary measure, the rules of the Houses require a special majority at all crucial stages of the passage of the bill and not just the third reading.
- The main provisions that can be amended under special majority are as follows :
  - Fundamental Rights (Part III).
  - Directive Principles of State Policy (Part IV).
  - All other provisions which are not covered by the first and third categories.

Amendments by Special Majority and Ratification by States

- There are certain provisions which are related to the federal structure, can be amended by special majority of the Parliament and also by simple majority i.e., consent of half of the State Legislatures.
- The consent of at least half of the states is required for the bill to pass, regardless of whether the remaining states take action or not. Additionally, there is no time limit for the states to provide their consent.
- The provisions that can be amended under this includes :
  - Election of the President and its manner.
  - Extent of the Executive Power of the Union and the States.
  - Supreme Court and High Courts.
  - Distribution of Legislative Powers between the Union and the States.
  - Goods and Services Tax Council.
  - Any of the lists in the Seventh Schedule.
  - Representation of states in Parliament.
  - Power of Parliament to amend the Constitution and its procedure (under Article 368 itself).

AMENDMENT PROCEDURE

- According to the Article 368, the process of amendment can be initiated only by the introduction of a Bill for the purpose in either House of Parliament. The amendment cannot be initiated by the State Legislature.
- The Bill for this purpose can be introduced by both government and the private member. Permission of the President is not required in this regard.
- A Bill introduced by Member of Parliament who is not a Minister is known as Private Member Bill. The member must give atleast a month's notice before the Bill can be listed for introduction.
- After its introduction, the Bill is passed in each House by special majority i.e., a majority of not less than two-third of the members of that House present and voting and not less than 50% of the total membership of the House.
- The bill must be passed by each house separately.
- There is no provision of joint sitting in case of a deadlock between the two Houses over the Bill.
- If Constitutional Amendment Bill wants to amend any of the following provisions of Constitution Bill, it must also be ratified by the Legislature of half of the States.
  - Article 54, Article 55, Article 73, Article 162 or Article 241.
  - Chapter IV of Part V, Chapter V of Part VI or Chapter I of Part XI.
  - Any of the lists in the Seventh Schedule.
  - The representation of states in the Parliament.
  - The provisions in Article 368.
- Once, the Bill is passed by both the Houses of Parliament, then it is presented before the President for his/her assent.

- After the President assent a Bill becomes an Act and Constitution stands amended in accordance with the terms of the Act. As per the 24th Constitutional Amendment Act, 1971, the President must give his assent to the Constitutional Amendment Bill. He cannot return it or withold his assent.

Constitutional Amendments

Number	Amendment made	Date of Commencement	Objectives
First	15, 19, 85, 87, 174, 176, 341, 342, 372 and 376, Inserted Articles 31A, 31B and Ninth Schedule	18th June, 1951	To overcome certain practical difficulties related to Fundamental Rights. It made provision for special treatment of educationally and socially Backward Classes and added Ninth Schedule to the Constitution.
Second	Article 81 (I) (b)	1st May, 1953	Representation of states in the Parliament.
Third	Seventh Schedule	22nd February, 1955	It substituted entry 33 of List III (Concurrent List) of the Seventh Schedule to make it correspond to Article 369.
Fourth	Articles 31, 31A, 35B,305 and Ninth Schedule	27th April, 1955	Restrictions on property rights and inclusion of related bills in Ninth Schedule of the Constitution.
Fifth	Article 3	24th December, 1955	Provide for a consultation mechanism with concerned states in matters relating to the amendments to the territorial matters and in the re-naming of the state.
Sixth	269, 286 and Seventh Schedule	11th September, 1956	Amend the Union and State lists with respect to raising of taxes.
Seventh	1, 3, 49, 80, 81, 82, 131, 153, 158, 168, 170, 171, 216, 217, 220, 222, 224, 230, 231 and 232, Insert Amendment 258A, 290A, 298, 350A, 350B, 371, 372A and 378A Part VIII and Schedules First, Second, Fourth and Seventh	1st November, 1956	Re-organisation of states on linguistic lines, abolition of Class A, B, C and D States and introduction of Union Territories.
Eighth	Article 334	5th January, 1960	Clarify State's power of compulsory acquisition and requisitioning of private property and include Zamindari abolition laws in Ninth Schedule of the Constitution.
Ninth	First Schedule	28th December, 1960	Minor adjustments to Territory of Indian Union consequent to agreement with Pakistan for settlement of disputes by demarcation of border, villages, etc.
Tenth	Article 240 First Schedule	11th August, 1961	Incorporation of Dadra and Nagar Haveli as a Union Territory, consequent to acquisition from Portugal.
Eleventh	Articles 66 and 71	19th December, 1961	Election of Vice-President by Electoral College consisting of members of both Houses of Parliament, instead of election by a Joint Sitting of Parliament. Indemnify the President and Vice-President, Election procedure from challenge on grounds of existence of any vacancies in the electoral college.
Twelfth	Article 240, First Schedule	20th December, 1961	Incorporation of Goa, Daman and Diu as a Union Territory, consequent to acquisition from Portugal.
Thirteenth	371A, and 170	1st December, 1963	Formation of State of Nagaland, with special protection under Article 371A.
Fourteenth	81, 240, Insert 239A First and Fourth Schedule	28th December, 1962	Incorporation of Pondicherry into the Union of India and creation of Legislative Assemblies for Himachal Pradesh, Tripura, Manipur and Goa.
Fifteenth	124, 128, 217, 222, 224, 224A, 226, 297, 311, 316, Entry of Article 78, List I and Seventh Schedule	5th October, 1963	Raising of retirement age of judges from 60 to 62 and other minor amendments for rationalising interpretation of rules regarding judges, etc.
Sixteenth	19, 84, 173 Third Schedule	5th October, 1963	Make it obligatory for seekers of public office to swear their allegiance to the Indian Republic and prescribe the various obligatory templates.
Seventeenth	Article 31A Ninth Schedule	20th June, 1964	To secure the constitutional validity of acquisition of estates and place, land acquisition laws in Ninth Schedule of the Constitution.

Number	Amendment made	Date of Commencement	Objectives
Eighteenth	Article 3	27th August, 1966	Provision was made for the formation of two states i.e. Punjab and Haryana.
Nineteenth	Article 324	11th December, 1966	To clarify the duties of the Election Commission.
Twentieth	Article 233A	22nd December, 1966	Indemnify and validate judgements, decrees, orders and sentences passed by judges and to validate the appointment, posting, promotion and transfer the judges barring a few who were not eligible for appointment under Article 233. Amendment needed to overcome the effect of judgement invalidating appointments of certain judges in the State of Uttar Pradesh.
Twenty First	Eighth Schedule	10th April, 1967	Includes Sindhi in the list of Languages in Eight Schedule.
Twenty Second	Article 275, Insert 244A and 371B	25th September, 1969	Provision to form Autonomous States within the State of Assam.
Twenty Third	Articles 330, 332, 333 and 334	23rd January, 1970	Extend reservation for SC / ST and nomination of Anglo-Indian members in Parliament and State Assemblies for another 10 years i.e. upto 1980.
Twenty Fourth	Articles 13 and 368	5th November, 1971	Enable Parliament to dilute Fundamental Rights through amendments to the Constitution.
Twenty Fifth	Articles 31 and 31C	20th April, 1972	Restrict Property Rights and compensation in case the state takes over private property.
Twenty Sixth	Articles 366 and 363A Removes Articles 291 and 362	28th December, 1971	Abolition of privy purse paid to former rulers of Princely States which were incorporated into the Indian Republic.
Twenty Seventh	Amendment 239A, 240 Insert 239B and 371C	15th February, 1972	Reorganisation of Mizoram and Arunachal Pradesh into a Union Territory with a Legislature and Council of Ministers.
Twenty Eighth	Insert Article 312A, Removes Article 314	29th August, 1972	Rationalise Civil Service rules to make it uniform across those appointed prior to independence and Post-Independence.
Twenty Ninth	Ninth Schedule	9th June, 1972	Place Land Reform Acts and amendments to these Acts under Ninth Schedule of the Constitution.
Thirtieth	Article 133	27th February, 1973	Change the basis for appeals in Supreme Court of India in case of civil suits from value criteria to one involving substantial question of law.
Thirty First	Articles 81, 330 and 332	17th October, 1973	Increase size of Parliament from 525 to 545 seats. Increased seats going to the new states formed in North-East India and minor adjustment consequent to 1971 Delimitation exercise.
Thirty Second	Inserted 371, 371D and 371E and Amendment Seventh Schedule	1st July, 1974	Protection of regional rights in Telangana and Andhra regions of State of Andhra Pradesh.
Thirty Third	Articles 101 and 190	19th May, 1974	Prescribes procedure for resignation by Members of Parliament and State Legislatures and the procedure for verification and acceptance of resignation by House Speaker.
Thirty Fourth	Ninth Schedule	7th September, 1974	Place Land Reform Acts and amendments to these Act under Ninth Schedule of the Constitution.
Thirty Fifth	80, 81, Insert 2A and Tenth Schedule	1st March, 1975	Terms and conditions for the Incorporation of Sikkim into the Union of India.
Thirty Sixth	80, 81, 371F Amendment Removes Article 2A First Removed, Fourth of Tenth Schedule	26th April, 1975	Formation of Sikkim as a State within the Indian Union.
Thirty Seventh	239A and 240	3rd May, 1975	Formation of Arunachal Pradesh Legislative Assembly.
Thirty Eighth	Articles 123, 213, 239B, 352, 356, 359 and 360	1st August, 1975	Enhance the powers of President and Governors to pass ordinances.
Thirty Ninth	Articles 71, 329 Insert 329A Ninth Schedule	10th August, 1975	Question regarding election of President, Vice- President, Prime Minister and Speaker of Lok Sabha taken out of the purview of the Judiciary.

Number	Amendment made	Date of Commencement	Objectives
Fourtieth	Article 297 Ninth Schedule	27th May, 1976	Enable Parliament to make laws with respect to Exclusive Economic Zone and vest the mineral wealth with Union of India. Place Land Reform and other Acts and amendments to these Acts under Ninth Schedule of the Constitution.
Forty First	Article 316	7th September, 1976	Raise Retirement Age, Limit of Chairman and Members of Union and State Public Commissions from 60 to 62 .
Fourty Second	31, 31C, 39, 55, 74, 77, 81, 82, 83, 100, 102, 103, 105, 118, 145, 150, 166, 170, 172, 189, 191, 194, 208, 217, 225, 227, 228, 311, 312, 330, 352, 353, 356, 357, 358, 359, 366, 368, 371F, 31D, 32A, 39A, 43A, 48A, 131A, 139A, 144A, 226A, 228A and 257A Insert Parts 4A and 14A Amendment Preamble and Seventh Schedule	1st April, 1977	Amendment passed during internal emergency by Indira Gandhi. Provides for curtailment of Fundamental Rights, imposes Fundamental Duties and changes the basic structure of the Constitution by making India a **Socialist, Secular** and **Republic.** Shifted 5 items from State List to Concurrent List-education, forests, protection of wild animals and birds, weights, measures and administration of justice.
Fourty Third	145, 226, 228 and 366 Remove Articles 31D, 32A, 131A, 144A, 226A and 228A	13th April, 1978	Amendment passed after revocation of internal emergency in the country. Repeals some of the more Anti-Freedom Amendments enacted through Amendment Bill 42.
Fourty Fourth	19, 22, 30, 31A, 31C, 38, 71, 74, 83, 103, 105, 123, 132, 133, 134, 139A, 172, 192, 194, 217, 225, 226, 227, 329, 352, 356, 358, 359, 360 and 371F, 361 134A, 361A Removes 31, 257A and 329A. Part XII, Ninth Schedule	6th September, 1978	Amendment passed after revocation of internal emergency in the country. Provides for Human Rights, safeguards and mechanisms to prevent abuse of Executive and Legislative Authority. Annuls some amendments enacted in Amendment Bill 42.
Fourty Fifth	Article 334	25th January, 1980	Extend reservation for SCs/STs and nomination of Anglo-Indian members in the Parliament and State Assemblies for another 10 years i.e. upto 1990.
Fourty Sixth	269, 286 and 366 Seventh Schedule	2nd February, 1983	Amendment to negate judicial pronouncements on scope and applicability on Sales Tax.
Fourty Seventh	Ninth Schedule	26th August, 1984	Place Land Reform Acts and amendments to these Act under Ninth Schedule of the Constitution.
Fourty Eighth	Article 356	26th August, 1984	Article 356 amended to permit President's rule upto 2 years in the State of Punjab.
Fourty Ninth	Article 244 Schedules Fifth and Sixth	1st April, 1985	Sixth Schedule was applicable to Tripura.
Fiftieth	Article 33	11th September, 1984	Technical Amendment to curtailment of Fundamental Rights as per Part III as prescribed in Article 33 to cover security personnel protecting property and communication infrastructure.
Fifty First	Articles 330 and 332	16th June, 1986	Provide reservation to Scheduled Tribes in Nagaland, Meghalaya, Mizoram and Arunachal Pradesh Legislative Assemblies.
Fifty Second	101, 102, 190, 191 and Tenth Schedule	1st March, 1985	*Anti Defection Law* provide disqualification of members from Parliament and Assembly in case of defection from one party to other.
Fifty Third	Article 371(G)	14th August, 1986	Special provision with respect to the State of Mizoram.
Fifty Fourth	125, 221 and Second Schedule	1st April, 1986	Increase the salary of Chief Justice of India and other Judges and to provide for determining future increases without the need for Constitutional Amendment.
Fifty Fifth	Article 371(H)	20th February, 1987	Special powers to Governor consequent to formation of State of Arunachal Pradesh.
Fifty Sixth	Article 371(I)	30th May, 1987	Transition provision to enable formation of State of Goa.
Fifty Seventh	Article 332	21st September, 1987	Provide reservation to Scheduled Tribes in Nagaland, Meghalaya, Mizoram and Arunachal Pradesh Legislative Assemblies.
Fifty Eighth	Article 394A Part XXII	9th December, 1987	Provision to publish authentic Hindi translation of Constitution as on date and provision to publish authentic Hindi translation of future amendments.

Number	Amendment made	Date of Commencement	Objectives
Fifty Ninth	Article 356 Article 359A	30th March, 1988	Article 356 amended to permit President's rule upto 3 years in the State of Punjab, Article 352 and Article 359A amended to permit imposing emergency in the State of Punjab or in specific districts of the State of Punjab.
Sixtieth	Article 276	20th December, 1988	Profession Tax increased from a maximum of ₹ 250 to a maximum of ₹ 2500.
Sixty First	Article 326	28th March, 1989	Reduce age for voting rights from 21 to 18.
Sixty Second	Article 334	20th December, 1989	Extend reservation for SCs/STs and nomination of Anglo-Indian members in Parliament and State Assemblies for another 10 years i.e. upto 2000.
Sixty Third	Article 356 Removes Article 359A	6th January, 1990	Emergency powers applicable to State of Punjab, accorded in Article 359A as per Amendment 59 repealed.
Sixty Fourth	Article 356	16th April, 1990	Article 356 amended to permit President's Rule up to 3 years and 6 months in the State of Punjab.
Sixty Fifth	Article 338	12th March, 1990	National Commission for Scheduled Castes and Scheduled Tribes formed and its statutory powers specified in the Constitution.
Sixty Sixth	Ninth Schedule	7th June, 1990	Place land reform acts and amendments to these act under Ninth Schedule of the Constitution.
Sixty Seventh	Article 356	4th October, 1990	Article 356 amended to permit President's Rule upto 4 years in the State of Punjab.
Sixty Eighth	Article 356	12th March, 1991	Article 356 amended to permit President's Rule upto 5 years in the State of Punjab.
Sixty Ninth	239AA and 239AB	1st February, 1992	To provide for a Legislative Assembly and Council of Ministers for Federal National Capital of Delhi. Delhi continues to be a Union Territory.
Seventieth	54 and 239AA	21st December, 1991 retrospectively	Includes National Capital of Delhi and Union Territory of Pondicherry in electoral college for Presidential Election.
Seventy First	Eighth Schedule	31st August, 1992	Include Konkani, Manipuri and Nepali in official language of Eighth Schedule.
Seventy Second	Article 332	5th December, 1992	Provide reservation to Scheduled Tribes in Tripura State Legislative Assembly.
Seventy Third	Part IX	24th April, 1993	Statutory provisions for Panchayat Raj as third level of administration in villages.
Seventy Fourth	Part IXA	1st June, 1993	Statutory provisions for Local Administrative bodies as third level of administration in urban areas such as towns and cities.
Seventy Fifth	Article 323B	15th May, 1994	Provisions for setting up Rent Control Tribunals.
Seventy Sixth	Ninth Schedule	31st August, 1994	Enable continuance of 69% reservation in Tamil Nadu by including the relevant Tamil Nadu Act under Ninth Schedule of the Constitution.
Seventy Seventh	Article 16	17th June, 1995	A technical amendment to protect reservation to SCs/STs employees in promotions.
Seventy Eighth	Ninth Schedule	30th August, 1995	Place Land Reform Acts and amendments to these act under Ninth Schedule of the Constitution.
Seventy Ninth	Article 334	25th January, 2000	Extend reservation for SCs/STs and nomination of Anglo-Indian members in the Parliament and State Assemblies for another 10 years i.e. upto 2010.
Eightieth	269, 270 and Removes Article 272	9th June, 2000	Implement Tenth Finance Commission recommendation to simplify the tax structures by pooling and sharing all taxes between States and the Centre.
Eighty First	Article 16	9th June, 2000	Protect SCs/STs reservation in filing backlog of vacancies.
Eighty Second	Article 335	8th September, 2000	Permit relaxation of qualifying marks and other criteria in reservation in promotion for SCs/STs candidates.
Eighty Third	Article 243M	8th September, 2000	Exempt Arunachal Pradesh from reservation for Scheduled Castes in Panchayati Raj Institutions.
Eighty Fourth	55, 81, 82, 170, 330 and 332	21st February, 2002	Extend the usage of 1971 National Census Population figures for statewise distribution of Parliamentary seats.
Eighty Fifth	Article 16	4th January, 2002	A technical amendment to protect seniority in case of promotions of SCs/STs employees.

Number	Amendment made	Date of Commencement	Objectives
Eighty Sixth	45, 51A and Article 21A	12th December, 2002	Provides Right to Education until the age of fourteen and early childhood care until the age of six.
Eighty Seventh	81, 82, 170 and 330	22nd June, 2003	Extend the usage of 1971 National Census Population figures for statewise distribution of Parliamentary seats.
Eighty Eighth	270, 268A and Seventh Schedule	15th January, 2004	To extend statutory cover for levy and utilisation of Service Tax.
Eighty Ninth	Article 338 Article 338A	28th September, 2003	The National Commission for Scheduled Castes and Scheduled Tribes was bifurcated into the National Commission for Scheduled Castes and the National Commission for Scheduled Tribes.
Ninetieth	Article 332	28th September, 2003	Reservation in Assam Assembly relating to Bodoland Territory Area.
Ninety First	75, 164, Article 361B and Tenth Schedule	1st January, 2004	Restrict the size of Council of Ministers to 15% of Legislative Members and to strengthen Anti-Defection Laws.
Ninety Second	Eighth Schedule	7th January, 2004	Enable Levy of Service Tax and include Bodo, Dogri, Maithali and Santhali as National languages.
Ninety Third	Article 15	20th January, 2006	To enable provision of reservation for Other Backward Classes (OBCs) in Government as well as private educational institutions.
Ninety Fourth	Article 164	12th June, 2006	To provide for a Minister of Tribal Welfare in newly created Jharkhand and Chhattisgarh States and deletion of Bihar's name.
Ninety Fifth	Article 334	25th January, 2010	To extend the reservation of seats for SCs and STs in the Lok Sabha and State Assemblies from 60 to 70 years.
Ninety Sixth	Eighth Schedule	23rd September, 2011	Substituted Odia for Oriya.
Ninety Seventh	Article 19 (1) (c) Article 43 B, Part IXB (Articles 243 ZH-ZT)	13th January, 2012	To give right to form cooperative societies and give a framework for their working.
Ninety Eighth	371J	2nd January, 2013	To empower the Governor of Karnataka to take steps to develop the Hyderabad-Karnataka region.
Ninety Ninth	New Articles. 124A, 124B and 124C Amended Articles. 124, 127, 128, 217, 222, 224A, 231.	31st December, 2014	To regulate the procedure to be followed by the National Judicial Appointments commission for recommending persons for appointment as the Chief Justice of India and other judges of the Supreme Court and Chief Justices and other Judges of High Courts and for their transfer and for matter connected therewith.
One Hundred	Amendment of First Schedule to Constitution	28th May, 2015	To the acquiring of territories by India and transfer of certain territories to Bangladesh in pursuance of the agreements and its protocol between India and Bangladesh.
One Hundred One	Amendment of Articles 248, 249, 250, 268, 269, 270, 271, 286, 366, 368 Sixth and Seventh Schedule	8th September, 2016	Introduced the Goods and Sevices Tax (GST).
One Hundred Two	Amendment of Articles 338, 342 and 366	11th August, 2018	Constitutional status to National Commission for Backward Classes.
One Hundred Three	Amendment of Articles 15 and 16	12th January, 2019	10% reservation to economically weaker section in educational institution and government job.
One Hundred Four	Amendment of Article 334	22nd January, 2020	Removal of reservation of Anglo-Indian community in Lok Sabha and State Assemblies and extension of reservation for SCs and STs in Lok Sabha and State Assemblies.
One Hundred Five	Amended Articles 338 B, 342A and 336	18th August, 2021	To restore state's power of states to make their own OBC lists.
One Hundred Six	Amended Articles 330 A, 332 A, 239 A and 334 A	28th September, 2023	Also known as Women Reservation Act, 2023 (Nari Shakti Vandan Adhiniyam). It reserves one-third of all seats for women in the Lok Sabha and State Legislative Assemblies and the Legislative Assembly of the National Capital Territory of Delhi.

"India adopted the parliamentary form of democracy in the year 1947 since India has been familiar with its working during the times of British rule.

Chapter Twelve

Parliamentary Form of Government

PARLIAMENTARY SYSTEM

The Constitution of India establishes a parliamentary system of government at both the central and state levels. The provisions for this system are outlined in Articles 74 and 75 for the Central Government and Articles 163 and 164 for the State Governments.

Features of the Parliamentary Form of Government

- The President is the nominal executive (Head of State), while the Prime Minister is the real executive (Head of Government). The Prime Minister leads a council of Ministers that advises the President and their advice is binding on the President.
- The part with the majority in the Lok Sabha forms the government and its leader becomes the Prime Minister. If no party has a majority, the President may invite a coalition to from the government.
- Ministers are collectively responsible to Parliament, especially the Lok Sabha (Article 75). If the Lok Sabha passes a vote of no confidence, the entire Council of Ministers, headed by the Prime Minister, must resign.
- Ministers must be memebrs of Parliament. If a minister is not a memebr for six consecutive months, they lose their position.
- Parliamentary form of government runs under the leadership of the Prime Minister. Apart from being the leader of the party, he/she is also the leader of the Council of Ministers and leader of the Parliament.
- Dissolution of the Lok Sabha can happen before the expiry of its term by the President on the recommendation of the Prime Minister.

Features of the Presidential Government

- The American President holds a ceremonial position and leads the executive branch, serving as both the head of state and the head of government.
- The President cannot be removed before an expiry of the fixed term of four years except by an impeachment for an unconstitutional activity.
- A non-elected body of departmental secretaries called the '**Kitchen Cabinet**' helps the President.
- The President does not possess the power to dissolve the lower house of the Congress (the house of representatives).

Reasons for Adopting Parliamentary System in India

- India was familiar with the Parliamentary system as it was followed during British rule.
- India preferred to choose more responsibility but less stability provided by the parliamentary system.
- The Constitution framers did not want the conflict between the legislative and executive organs.
- The presidential system is prone to such conflicts. The diverse nature of Indian society encouraged Constitution-makers to choose a parliamentary system as this system allows for representation of various groups, interests, and regions, fostering national unity and a United India.
- India has debated whether to replace its parliamentary system with a presidential system since the 1970s.

"

A federation is a political system created when smaller units, like states or provinces, agree to work together under a single government.

Chapter Thirteen

Federalism and Federal Structure

HISTORICAL BACKGROUND

- Government of India Act, 1935, for the first time introduced the federal concept and used the expression Federation of India in a Constitution Act relating to India.
- Though in every respect the distribution of legislative power between the Union and the States as envisaged in the 1935 Act has not been adopted in the Constitution, but the basic framework is the same.
- Under this system, the provinces derived their authority directly from the crown and exercised legislative and executive powers, broadly free from Central control, within a defined sphere.
- Nevertheless, the centre retained control through the Governor's special responsibilities and his obligation to exercise his individual judgement and discretion in certain matters.

The Constitution of India provides for a federal structure of governance. However, Article 1 does not identify India as a Federation of States but a Union of States. As per Dr. BR Ambedkar, it is indicative of two things :

- the Indian Federation is not the result of an agreement among the states like the American Federation, and
- the states have no right to secede from the federation.

- The Indian model is based on the Canadian model with a strong union.
- Both countries term their federation as Union and have similar formation by the way of disintegration.
- India's federal structure has a unitary bias as the Constitution provides for provisions which convert the federal nature into a unitary one during emergencies.
- Indian Constitution has been referred as being federal in form but un7itary in spirit.

Theorist **KC Wheare** has argued that the nature of Indian Constitution is **quasi-federal** stating that "Indian Union is a unitary state with subsidiary federal features rather than a federal state with subsidiary unitary features".

- In SR Bommai *v/s* Union of India in 1994, the Supreme Court established that federalism as Constitution's basic feature.
- It further added that federalism was a matter of principle in Indian Constitution and not administrative convenience.

FEDERAL FEATURES

Various federal features of the Indian Constitution are :

1. Dual Polity The Indian Constitution established the system of dual polity in the country with Union Government at the Centre and State Government in states.
2. Written Constitution The Constitution of India is one of the lengthiest written document in the world. Originally, it had 395 Articles, 22 Parts and 8 Schedules.

Today, the Constitution has 470 Articles, 25 Parts and 12 Schedules.

3. Division of Powers The Seventh Schedule of the Constitution provides clear division of powers between the Centre and the states to enable a smooth functioning. This is ensured by dividing subjects under three lists– Union, State and Concurrent Lists.
4. Supremacy of the Constitution All the organs of the government execute their functions within the jurisdictions set by the Constitution. Thus, the Constitution is the Supreme Law of the land and all laws enacted by both Union and State must be in compliance with its provisions. The courts have the power to rule any law unconstitutional and declare them void and invalid by means of judicial review.
5. Rigid Constitution Rigidity in a Constitution suggests that making amendments to the Constitution follow a rigorous procedure. The Indian Constitution has continued to remain relevant through the way of amendments.
6. Bicameralism The Constitution provides for a Bicameral Legislature that consists of Rajya Sabha and Lok Sabha. The Upper House (Rajya Sabha) represents the states of Indian Federation. On the other hand, the Lower House (Lok Sabha) represents the people of India as a whole. The Upper House maintains the federal equilibrium by protecting the interests of the States against union pressure.
7. Independent Judiciary The Constitution establishes an Independent Judiciary for two primary purposes.
   - Firstly, to protect the supremacy of the Constitution by the means of judicial review.
   - Secondly, to settle disputes between States and Union or between States.

   Provisions such as fixed salary and tenures have been put in place in order to ensure the independence of judiciary headed by the Supreme Court of India.

UNITARY FEATURES

Various unitary features of the Indian Constitution are:

1. Strong Union The Constitution has provided for a strong Union in order to ensure that the federation remains intact. The Union has residuary powers as compared to the states on the matter of division of subjects.
2. Parliamentary Supremacy The Parliament is empowered to make laws on any subject from State List if Rajya Sabha passes a resolution which places the matter with respect to matter of national interest. The legislative powers of Parliament are overarching without any amendments and limits state's exclusive authority. This step can be taken even under normal circumstances when no state of emergency is declared.
3. Indestructible Union As per the Constitution, India is an indestructible union of destructible states. In other words, states in India do not have right to territorial integrity. By a way of unilateral decision and simple majority, the Parliament has the power to change territorial boundaries and names of states.

In opposition to India's union, the **United States of America** forms a destructible union of indestructible states.

4. Single Constitution Usually in a federation, the states have the right to frame their own Constitution separate from that of centre. India does not extend this power to the states and therefore both Union and States operate within the framework of a Single Constitution.
5. Flexible Constitution As compared to other federations, the India has simpler laws concerning amendments. In most cases laws can be amended by the way of simple majority and unilateral action of Parliament with a few exceptions as discussed before.
6. Unequal State Representation Seats in Rajya Sabha are divided among States and Union Territories on the basis of population. Therefore, states with larger population have more representation as compared to smaller states.

Emergency Provisions

- The Constitution mentions three kinds of emergencies. These include **National, State** and **Financial**. When any of the emergencies has been declared the **Central Government** becomes all powerful and exercises control over states.
- The federal structure is transformed into the unitary system. This transformation is unique to Indian federation wherein without any amendment the nature of **Union-State relations** undergoes structural changes.

7. Single Citizenship In India, there is only single citizenship. An Indian is a citizen of India only. He/she is not a citizen of any Indian state. Single citizenship is meant to strengthen national unity and national integration.
8. Integrated Judiciary The Indian Judiciary enjoys independence but in its own structure, it is an integrated institution. The Supreme Court is the apex court at topmost level. It is followed by the High Courts at the state level. The lower and district courts are at the bottom levels. The single system of judiciary enforces both Union and State laws.
9. All India Services Although, India has public services both at Centre and State level, All India Services (IAS, IPS and IFS) is common to both Centre and the State. These officers are recruited and trained by the union and they possess complete control over them.
10. Integrated Audit Controls The Comptroller this also Auditor-General of India audits both Central and State Government's accounts. This restricts the financial autonomy of states. In addition, the States hold no say or power in the decision of the President in appointment or removal of the CAG.
11. Integrated Election Machinery As in the case with Comptroller and Auditor-General, the Election Commission conducts election both at Central and State level. The body is constituted by the President and States have no role in the appointment or removal of members of the Election Commission.
12. Appointment of Governors Following the Canadian model, the Governor of a state is not elected but rather appointed by the President. He/she is the head of the state and holds office till the pleasure of the President. He/she acts as an agent of the Union and through him/ her Central exercises control over states.

Veto Power over State Bills

- Unlike with Union Government, the President enjoys **absolute veto** over state bills.
- The Governor has the power to reserve certain bills for President's assent. In this case, the President can withhold assent not just once but twice.

EVOLUTION OF FEDERALISM

- Indian federalism is a balanced compromise which enables States and Centre work independently and together, pertaining to subjects in concern.
- By achieving this balance, the country has been able to resolve territorial disputes, water disputes between states, creation of new states and more.
- Federalism in India has been evolved through following phases :
  - During first phase i.e., 1950-1967, the political party system has heavily influenced the working of federalism in India.
  - There was dominance of a single party. Institutions like the Planning Commission and the National Development Council became instruments of domination over the States by the Centre.
  - In the next phase i.e., during 1967-1977 there was a dilution of the single party dominance and emergence of regional parties.
  - As a result, there were additional stress introduced into the Centre-State relationship, which greatly politicised it.
  - There was also introduction of unethical practices such as defections and the abuse of the Governor's position which led to aggressive centralisation.
  - The third phase of federalism began in 1977-1989. There was political misuse of Article 356.
  - This exercise of emergency power by the Centre has led to increased antagonism and mistrust therefore the Sarkaria Commission in 1983 was appointed to look into Centre-State relations.
  - Post 1989, several changes have heavily influenced the working of the federal system like multi-party system and coalition government.
  - This has placed unprecedented power in the hands of the regional parties to influence national and regional policy. In 1990, the economic reforms were introduced.
  - This opened the gates for globalisation, which imposed new responsibilities and roles for the states.
  - The latest phase in federalism had begun in 2014. During this period, two opposing and parallel phenomena might be seen.
  - First off, the new administration has made a number of decisions that demonstrate its enthusiasm for cooperative federalism.
  - Parallel to this shift towards cooperative federalism, another trend has been noted of competitive federalism.

COOPERATIVE AND COMPETITIVE FEDERALISM

- According to Dr. BR Ambedkar, the federal nature of the Constitution is established by the existence of dual polity.
- The Union and States are created and derive power from the Constitution.
- The nature of Union-State relations has been interpreted in various ways by many Constitutional experts and political theorists.
- While some have identified the nature as quasi-federal, others have the opinion that India is extremely federal.
- Federalism can be classified as either cooperative or competitive based on its nature and relationship between Central and State Governments.

Difference between Cooperative and Competitive Federalism

Cooperative Federalism	Competitive Federalism
In Cooperative federalism, the Centre and States share a horizontal relationship, where they 'cooperate' in the larger public interest.	In Competitive federalism, the relationship between the Central and State Governments is vertical and between State Governments it is horizontal.
It is an important tool to enable states' participation in the formulation and implementation of national policies.	States compete with each other to attract funds and investment, which facilitates efficiency in administration and enhances developmental activities.
Union and the States are Constitutionally obliged to cooperate with each other on the matters specified in **Schedule VII** of the Constitution.	While the Union and States adhere to constitutional provisions, competitive elements are executive decisions and not constitutionally mandated.
This entails cooperation amongst Centre and Federal units and even local bodies which act collectively to achieve a common goal.	This entails states compete with each other at various social and development indicators in a healthy manner.
Cooperative federalism is part of the basic structure of Indian Constitution.	Competitive federalism is not part of the basic structure of Indian Constitution.

Reviews of Federalism by Constitutional Experts

Constitutional Experts	Description of Indian Federal Structure and Constitution
KC Wheare	Quasi Federal
K Santhanam	Reasons for increased unitary bias – (i) Supremacy of Centre in finances and (ii) Strong Planning Commission controlling development across states
Paul Appleby	Extremely federal
Morris Jones	Bargaining federalism
Ivor Jennings	Federation with a strong centralising tendency
Alexandrowicz	India is a case *sui generis* (i.e., unique in character)
Granville Austin	Cooperative federalism; a new kind of federation to meet India's peculiar needs

Centre-State Relations constitute the core of federalism in India and play a vital role in the political sphere of India.

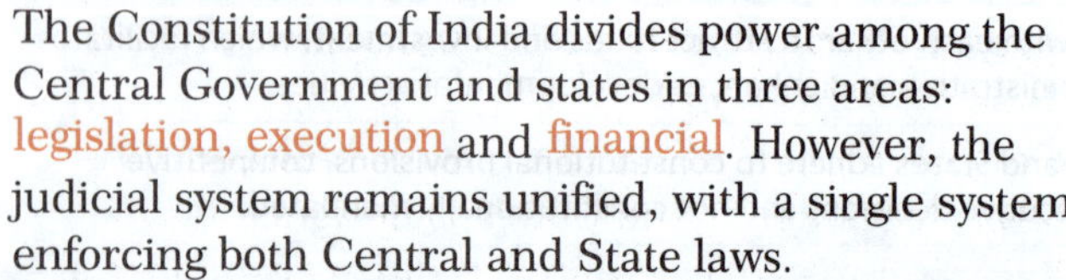

Chapter Fourteen

Centre-State Relations

The Constitution of India divides power among the Central Government and states in three areas: legislation, execution and financial. However, the judicial system remains unified, with a single system enforcing both Central and State laws.

The co-operation and harmony between the Centre and States are crucial for the success of the federal system. To facilitate this, the Constitution outlines detailed provisions governing the complex relationships between the Central Government and States. The Centre-State Relations can be broadly studied under three heads :

- Legislative relations
- Administrative relations
- Financial relations

LEGISLATIVE RELATIONS

- The legislative relations between the Centre and the States Governments are discussed in Part XI from Articles 245 to 255 of the Constitution of India.
- As Indian Constitution provides for federal structure, it divides the legislative powers between the Centre and the States with respect to both the territory and the subjects of legislation.
- The legislative relations between the Centre and States are divided into four categories :

Territorial Extent of Central and State Legislation

- The Constitution sets clear boundaries on the areas where the Central Government and states have the power to make laws.
- The ability to pass legislation that covers all or a portion of India's territory belongs to Parliament (territory includes Union, State, Union Territory) under Article 245(1) of the Constitution.
- As per Article 245(1), laws can be passed by the State Legislature that is applicable to the entire state or only a portion of it. State laws are not applicable outside of the state unless there is a sufficient relationship between the state and the item.
- Under Article 245(2), the only body with the power to pass 'extra territorial' (means something is outside the laws or boundaries of a country, state or region.) legislation is Parliament. Hence, the Indian laws enacted by Parliament apply to Indian citizens and their properties across any part of the world.
- However, there are certain restrictions to their legislative powers. They are as follows :
  - The President has the authority to enact rules that have the same force and effect as laws passed by Parliament for the Andaman and Nicobar islands, Dadra and Nagar Haveli, Daman and Diu, Lakshadweep and Ladakh.
  - An Act of Parliament may be made to apply with specific modifications and exceptions to a specified state area by the Governor, or it may be made to apply to all of the state.
  - The Governor of Assam may also instruct an Act of Parliament to not apply or to apply with particular adjustments in a tribal area or autonomous district.
  - The same authority belongs to the President for the States of Meghalaya, Tripura and Mizoram.

Distribution of Legislative Subjects

- The distribution of items of legislation are given under Article 246.
- Constitution provides for a three-fold distribution of legislative subjects between Centre and States *viz*, List I Union List and List II State List and List III Concurrent List in the Seventh Schedule.
- Parliament has exclusive power to make laws with respect to any of the matters enumerated in Union List.
- This list at present has 98 subjects including defense, currency, foreign affairs, communication, foreign affairs and other matters of national interest.
- However, Parliament has power to make laws with respect to any matter for any part of the territory of India notwithstanding that such matter is a matter enumerated in the State List in 'normal circumstance'.
- This list at present has 59 subjects including police, public order, sanitation, public health, local government, etc.
- The Legislature of any state has exclusive power to make laws for such state or any part thereof with respect to any of the matters enumerated in State List.
- Parliament and State Legislature have power to make laws with respect to any of the matters enumerated in Concurrent List.
- This list at present has 52 subjects including matters related to marriage and divorce, criminal law, civil procedure, population control and family planning, newspaper, books, etc.

> The **42nd Amendment Act of 1976** transferred 5 subjects to Concurrent List from State List i.e. education, forests, weights and measures, protection of wild animals and birds and organisation of all court except the Supreme Court and the High Courts.

- The Parliament has the authority to legislate on any matter, even if it falls under the State List, for areas within India that are not part of any state, such as Union Territories or acquired territories.
- Article 248 of the Constitution States that Parliament has exclusive power to make any law with respect to any matter not enumerated in the Concurrent List or State List.
- This is the residuary power of legislation of Parliament. When there is a conflict between laws, the order of priority is
  - Union List takes precedence over State List
  - Union List takes precedence over Concurrent List
  - Concurrent List takes precedence over State List
- When both the Central Government and a State Government make laws on the same subject in the Concurrent List, the Central Law takes priority and overrides the state law.
- On the other hand, the State Legislation will take precedence in the state, if it has been reserved for the President's consideration and has gained his approval.
- But, the Central Government can still override the State law by passing a new law on the same topic.

Powers of Parliament to Legislate on State List Matters

- The distribution of legislative powers between the Central Government and States is designed for normal circumstances. However, during exceptional times, this distribution can be modified or suspended.
- In such cases, the Constitution grants authority to the Parliament to enact laws on matters that are typically reserved for the states under five special circumstances:

1. When Rajya Sabha Passes a Resolution

- According to Article 249, if the Rajya Sabha approves a resolution with the support of two-third of the members present and voting, it will provide Parliament the authority to enact legislation on a State List. Such a resolution remains in force for one year.
- A resolution like this can be renewed as many times as desired but not for more than a year at a time.
- The laws passed in accordance with the resolution cease to be in force six months after the resolution has ceased to be in force. In the event of a disagreement between State and Union Legislation on that subject matter, the latter prevails.

2. During National Emergency

- As per Article 250, the Parliament may pass laws on any matter covered by the State List when a declaration of a National Emergency is in force.
- The legislation passed under this is only valid for six months after the emergency has ceased to operate.

- State law may also enact legislation on the matter, but in the event of a conflict, union law will take precedence.

3. **To Legislate for Two or More States**

- Under Article -252, If two or more State Legislatures request Parliament to legislate on a matter typically under state jurisdiction, Parliament can enact a law on that matter.
- This law will only apply to the states that made the request, but other states can choose to adopt it later by passing a resolution in their legislature.
- However, any changes to this law can only be made by Parliament, not by the individual State Legislatures.
- Once this resolution is passed, the states abandon all rights to legislate on that matter.
- The Wildlife Protection Act (1972), Water (Prevention and Control of Pollution) Act (1974), Prize Competition Act (1995), etc are some of the laws passed under this provision.

4. **To Implement International Treaties**

- According to Article 253, the Parliament can make laws on any matter in the State List for implementing the international treaties, agreements or conventions.
- Geneva Convention Act (1960), United Nations (Privileges and Immunities) Act (1947), etc are some of the laws enacted under this provision.

5. **During President's Rule**

- When the President's rule is imposed in a state, the Parliament becomes empowered to make laws with respect to any matter in the State List in relation to that state.
- Such a law continues to be operative even after the President's rule ends. But such a law can be repealed and altered by the State Legislature.
- Under Article 213, the Governor requires prior instructions from the President before issuing an ordinance in specific circumstances.

Centre's Control Over the State Legislation

- In addition to the Parliament's power to legislate directly on the state subjects the Constitution also provides for the Centre's consent before a bill passed by a State Legislature can become a law.
- Although, the state enjoys authority to legislate on the subjects of the State List, the Centre has power to direct the State Legislature to have conformity with the Union Laws.
- According to the Constitution, the Central Government is authorised to exercise the following influence over State Legislative affairs.
  - The Governor has the authority to reserve certain types of bills passed by the State Legislature for presidential consideration. The President has complete control over them.
  - Bills on specified subjects such as inter-state trade and commerce listed in the State List can only be introduced in the State Legislature with the President's prior consent.
  - The President may ask a state to lay aside money bills and other financial bills for his consideration in the case of a financial emergency (Article 360).

Articles Related to Legislative Relations

Articles	Subject Matters
Article 245	Extent of laws made by Parliament and by the Legislatures of States.
Article 246	Subject-matter of laws made by Parliament and by the Legislatures of States.
Article 246(A)	Special provision with goods and services tax.
Article 247	Power of Parliament to provide for the establishment of certain additional courts.
Article 248	Residuary powers of legislation.
Article 249	Power of Parliament to legislate with respect to a matter in the States List in the national interest.
Article 250	Power of Parliament to legislate with respect to any matter in the State List, if a Proclamation of Emergency is in operation.
Article 251	Inconsistency between laws made by Parliament under Articles 249 and 250 and laws made by the Legislatures of States.
Article 252	Power of Parliament to legislate for two or more states by consent and adoption of such legislation by any other state.
Article 253	Legislation for giving effect to international agreements.
Article 254	Inconsistency between laws made by Parliament and laws made by the Legislatures of States.
Article 255	Requirements as to recommendations and previous sanctions to be regarded as matters of procedure only.

ADMINISTRATIVE RELATIONS

- Articles 256 to 263 in Part XI of the Constitution deal with the administrative relations between the Centre and the States.
- The administrative relations corresponds to co-ordination aspects between the States and the Centre.
- The Constitution directs the states to oblige by the directions given by the Centre.
- This includes actions that should be taken for implementation of Union Laws and policies as determined by the Union Government.
- If the states refuse to comply with the directions given so, the President may declare a situation has arisen in the state of breakdown of constitutional machinery and may invoke President's rule in that state.

Power of the Union to Entrust Some Responsibilities to the State Governments

- According to Article 256, the Executive Power of the Governments of States is to be exercised as to ensure compliance with the Laws of the Union.
- Under Article 365, the Union Government is empowered to issue directions to the State Governments to ensure such compliance.
- Non- compliance of Central Directives by the State Governments is tantamount to the failure of constitutional machinery in the concerned state and may invite imposition of President's rule under Article 356.

Power of the Union to Issue Directions to the State Governments

- Under Article 258, the Union Government has the power to issue directions to the states with respect to construction and maintenance of means of communication of national and military importance and the protection of railways within the state.
- The cost incurred in performing these functions is borne by the Union Government. Union can give directions in matters related to the following as well.
  - Designing and implementing schemes for the welfare of the tribals.
  - Primary education to the linguistic minorities in their mother tongue under Article 351(A).
  - Promotion of Hindi under Article 351.

Mutual Delegation of Functions

- To avoid any kind of rigidity in the executive sphere, our Constitution has certain provisions, which allow for mutual delegation of executive functions by Centre and States.

> - As per **Article 258(1)**, the President may assign the executive duties of the Union to the State Government with the permission of the State Government.
> - With the agreement of the Central Government, the Governor may assign the State's Executive functions to the union. This agreement to share authority may be either conditional or unconditional.

- The Constitution also permits the state to provide the Union executive authority without the state's consent.
- However, such delegations are made by Parliament rather than the President. The executive authority of a state, however cannot be transferred in the same manner.

Obligation of States and the Centre

- Article 257 considers the Union's authority over States in specific circumstances. It provides that the executive power of every state shall be so exercised as not to impede or prejudice the exercise of the executive power of the Union and the executive power of the Union shall extend to giving of such directions to a state as may appear to the Government of India to be necessary for that purpose.
- In both cases, the Central Government has the authority to issue necessary directions to states, sanctioned by coercive power.
- If a state fails to comply with or implement these directions, Article 365 allows the President to declare that the State Government is unable to function in accordance with the Constitution. This enables the President to impose President's rule in the state under Article 356.
- Even with regard to the issues listed in the State List, the Union Government may give instructions to the State Government.
- As per Article 258(A) of the Constitution, the Governor of a State may, with the consent of the Government of India, entrust either conditionally or unconditionally to that Government or to its officers functions in relation to any matter to which the executive power of the State extends.

Provisions of All India Services

- Article 312, of the Constitution makes provision for the establishment of All India Services like IAS, IPS and IFS (Indian Forest Service).
- The members of the All India Services are recruited by the UPSC and their service conditions are regulated by the Union Government.

> In 1947, the Indian Civil Service (ICS) and Indian Police (IP) were replaced by the Indian Administrative Service (IAS) and Indian Police Service (IPS), respectively, and were established as All-India Services under the Constitution. Later, in 1966, the Indian Forest Service (IFoS) was created as the third All India Service.

- Members of these services occupy highest posts in the State Government Administration. Their ultimate control rests with the Union Government.
- Article 312, also empowers Parliament to create new All India Services if Rajya Sabha passes a resolution to this effect.
- The Rajya Sabha passes a resolution supported by two-third majority of its member for its creation. These officers are recruited and trained by the Union and they possess complete control over them.

Integrated Judiciary

- India has an Integrated Judicial System with Supreme Court at the top and State High Courts below it.
- The Single Integrated Judicial set-up enforces both the Central Laws as well as State Laws. Appointment, removal and transfer of State High Court Judges is done by the Central Government.
- Apart from that establishment of a common High Court, for two or more states, is also vested in the Central Governments.
- The President appoints the judges of the State High Court in consultation with the Chief Justice of India and the Governor of that state.

Relations Through Public Service Commission

- Centre and State Administrative relations are also strengthened through the Public Service Commissions.
- Though, the appointment of the Chairman and Members of State Public Service Commission are done by the State Governor but they can be removed by the President only.
- Parliament of our country has been authorised to create a Joint Public Service Commission (JPSC) for two or more states on request of concerned State Legislature.
- Also, Union Public Service Commission (UPSC) can serve the needs of the state on the request of Governor and approval by the President.

Centre-State Administrative Relations during Emergencies

- During National Emergency under Article 352, the centre becomes empowered to give directions to the state on any matter.
- During State Emergency under Article 356, the President assumes to himself the functions vested in the State Governments.
- Also, during Financial Emergency under Article 360, President can give directions regarding the reductions of salaries of persons serving in the state including High Court Judges.

Articles Related to Administrative Relations

Articles	Subject Matters
Article 256	Obligation of States and the Union.
Article 257	Control of the Union over States in certain cases.
Article 258	Power of the Union to confer powers, etc. on states in certain cases.
Article 258(A)	Power of the states to entrust functions to the Union.
Article 260	Jurisdiction of the Union in relation to territories outside India.
Article 261	Public acts, records and judicial proceedings.
Article 262	Adjudication of disputes relating to waters of inter-state rivers or river valleys.
Article 263	Provisions for the Inter-State Council.

FINANCIAL RELATIONS

- The financial relations between the Union Government and the states are discussed in Part XII from Articles 268 to 293 of the Constitution of India. In a federation, the Centre and the units are given their separate sources of revenues, so that they can stand on their feet.
- The Constitution provides the distribution of finances between the Centre and states. These provisions have undergone several amendments with the latest being the Alternative Scheme of Devolution developed by the 88th Constitutional Amendment Act.
- The recent initiative of goods and services tax is further expected to refine the financial relations between the centre and the states.

Distribution of Taxing Powers

- Parliament has the exclusive power to levy taxes on subjects enumerated in the Union List. State Legislature has the exclusive power to levy taxes on subjects enumerated in the State List.
- Both Union and State can levy taxes on matters enumerated in the Concurrent List. Residuary power of taxation is vested in the Parliament.
- There are no tax-related entries in the Concurrent List. However, the 101st Amendment Act of 2016 introduced an exception by granting both Parliament and State Legislatures the power to legislate on Goods and Services Tax (GST).
- This means that, for the first time, the Central Government and states have concurrent jurisdiction over taxation, specifically for GST.
- The Union List contained 97 subjects is now at 98 subjects, the State List contained 66 subjects is now at 59 subjects and Concurrent List is now increased to 52 subjects from 47.

Union List

- The Union List consists of a range of subjects in which only the Parliament of India has power to enact law.
- Defence sector
- Arms/Firearms/Explosive
- Atomic Energy
- War and Peace
- Citizenship
- Railways/shipping/Inland Waterways
- Post Telegraph
- Inter-State trade and Commerce
- Currency/Coinage
- Banking and Insurance

State List

Only the StateLegislature has the power to make laws.

- Education • Forest
- Weights and Measurement
- Administration of Justice
- Wildlife Protection
- Agriculture
- Police/Railway Police
- Public Health and Sanitation
- Taxes on lands and buildings
- Local Government

Subjects Mention in Various Lists

Concurrent List

In this list, both the Centre and the State have power to make laws.

- Criminal Law and Criminal Procedure
- Banking and Insolvency
- Prevention of Cruelty
- Civil Procedure, including all matters included in the Code of Civil Procedure
- Economic and Social Planning
- Control of Price • Trade Unions
- Trust and Trustees
- Archaeological Sites

Residual List

The subjects which are not included in any of the three lists, comes under the Residual List. Article 248 of the Constitution has given power to only Parliament to enact laws. Subject such as space technology cyber laws, etc comes under the Residual List.

- The Constitution separates two key aspects of taxation:
  - (i) Power to levy and collect taxes (levying and collecting)
  - (ii) Power to appropriate the proceeds of the tax (allocating and utilising)
- For instance, the Central Government has the authority to levy and collect income tax, but the proceeds are shared between the Central Government and the States.
- Taxing powers of the state are restricted by the following provisions in the Constitution :
- State Legislatures have the authority to levy taxes on professions, trades, callings and employments. However, there's a ceiling that no individual can be taxed more than 2,500 per year for these categories.
  - No tax can be imposed on the sale or purchase taking place outside the states.
  - No tax can be imposed on the sale or purchase taking place in the course of import or export. No tax can be imposed on the sale or purchase taking place in the course of inter-state trade and commerce.
  - A tax imposed on the sale or purchase of goods declared by the Parliament to be of special importance in inter-state trade and commerce is subject to the restrictions and conditions specified by the Parliament.
  - State cannot impose tax on sale of electricity in the following circumstances-consumed by the Centre or sold to the centre, consumed in the construction, maintenance or operation of any railway by the centre or sold to the railway company for the same purpose.
- A state can impose tax on sale of water or electricity sold to an authority established by Parliament for regulating or developing inter-state river.

Goods and Services Tax (GST)

- The **101st Amendment Act of 2016** provide for the establishment of a Goods and Services Tax Council (GST Council).
- The **GST** is an **indirect tax** that would replace existing levies such as excise duty, service tax and **Value Added Tax (VAT)**. The States and the Union Government will impose the tax on almost all goods and services produced in India or imported.
- Producers will receive credits for tax paid earlier, which will eliminate multiple taxation on the same product or service. **Direct taxes**, such as income tax, corporate tax and capital gains tax will not be affected.
- Eliminating a multiplicity of existing indirect taxes will simplify the tax structure, broaden the tax base and create a common market across states and federally administered districts.
- For the implementation of the GST, **Goods and Services Tax Council** has been established under the **Article 279(A)**. Union Finance Minister is Chairperson of this Council.

Distributions of Tax Revenue

- The 80th Amendment Act of 2000 and the 101st Amendment Act of 2016 have significantly altered the framework for sharing tax revenues between the Central Government and States, introducing major changes to the distribution scheme.
- The 80th Amendment was enacted to implement the 10th Finance Commission's recommendations, which suggested allocating 29% of certain central taxes and duties to states.
- This 'Alternative Scheme of Devolution' took effect retroactively from 1st April, 1996.
- As a result, central taxes like Corporation Tax and Customs Duties are now on par with Income Tax (non-agricultural income) in terms of mandatory sharing with states.
- The 101st Amendment has enabled the introduction of a new tax system, Goods and Services Tax (GST), by granting both Parliament and State Legislatures the power to levy GST on all transactions involving goods and services.

Following the 80th and 101st Amendments, the current framework for the distribution of tax revenues between the Central Government and States is as follows :

- Duties levied by the Centre, but collected and appropriated by the states (Article 268).
  - The stamp duties and such duties of excise on medicinal and toilet preparations as are mentioned in the Union List shall be levied by the Government of India, but shall be collected by the states.
  - The proceeds in any financial year of any such duty leviable within any state shall not form part of the Consolidated Fund of India, but shall be assigned to that state.
- Taxes levied and collected by the Centre, but assigned to the states (Article 269). The following duties and taxes concerned states in accordance with such principles of distribution as may be formulated by Parliament by law.
  - Taxes on the sale or purchase of goods other than newspapers, where such sale or purchase takes place in the course of inter-state trade or commerce.
  - Taxes on the consignment of goods in the course of inter-state trade or commerce.
  - The revenue generated from these taxes does not go into the Consolidated Fund of India.
  - Instead, principles determined by the Parliament guide the allocation of these taxes to the respective states.
- Levy and collection of Goods and Services Tax (GST) on inter-state trade and commerce (Article 269 A).
  - Article 269(A) (1) mainly deals with the Taxation and collection of tax on Goods and Services (GST). This is applicable in the case of inter-state trade or commerce.
  - The collected taxes will be distributed between the States and the Union. Parliament has the power to pass legislation on the distribution of taxes levied in accordance with this article, in accordance with the recommendations of the GST Council.
- Taxes levied and collected by the Union and distributed between the Union and the States (Article 270).
  - It says that taxes on incomes, other than agricultural incomes, shall be levied and collected by the Government of India and distributed between the Union and the States in the manner prescribed by the President, after considering the recommendations of the Finance Commission.
  - The following taxes and duties are not included in this category :

    (i) Duties and taxes mentioned in Articles 268, 269 and 269-A

    (ii) Surcharges on taxes and duties as per Article 271

    (iii) Cess for a specific purpose (a type of tax)
- Surcharge on certain taxes and duties for purposes of the centre (Article 271).
  - Surcharge on certain duties and taxes for purposes of the Union notwithstanding anything in Articles 269 and 270.
  - Parliament may at any time increase any of the duties or taxes referred in those articles by a surcharge for purposes of the Union and the proceeds of any such surcharge shall form part of the Consolidated Fund of India.
  - The Goods and Services Tax (GST) is kept outside the scope of this surcharge. Hence, this surcharge cannot be levied on GST.
- Taxes levied and collected and retained by the states. These are the taxes belonging to the states exclusively. They are enumerated in the State List. e.g., Taxes on agriculture income, excise duties on alcohol, taxes on professions, ceilings, etc.

Distribution of Non-tax Revenues

The main sources of non-tax revenues are as follows :

- For the Centre Postal and telegraph services,railways, banking, broadcasting, coinage and currency, escheat and lapse, central public sector enterprises and others.
- For the States Irrigation, forests, fisheries, state public sector enterprise and escheat and lapse.

Grants-in-Aid to the States

- The Constitution allows the state to receive grants-in-aid from the Central Government. These are the two forms of grants-in-aid.
- Statutory Grants Article 275 empowers the Parliament to make grants to the states which are in need of financial assistance. The amount may differ for each state and they are charged on Consolidated Fund of India. The Constitution also provides for particular funds to be made to states like Assam for promoting welfare of the Scheduled Tribes.
- Discretionary Grants Article 282 empowers the centre and the states authority to award grants for any public purpose, even if it falls outside the purview of their respective legislative purviews. The centre awards grants to the states in accordance with this clause.

Mutual Immunity from Taxes

- Under Article 285(1) the property of the union is exempted from all taxes imposed by a state. Parliament has the authority to lift this restriction.
  - The term 'property' encompasses Lands and buildings. Movable assets (chattels), Intangible assets (shares, debts), Tangible and intangible properties, Properties used for Sovereign purposes (e.g., armed forces) or Commercial purpose.
  - The corporations and companies created by the Central Government are not exempt from state or local taxation as they are a distinct legal entity.
- Similarly, the property and income of state are exempt from union taxation under Article 289(1).

Borrowing Powers

- Article 292 says that Union Parliament can regulate the borrowing of the Union Government on the security of the Consolidated Fund of India.
- Article 293 says that states cannot borrow from outside the country. States can borrow from within the country, but if a loan given by the centre to the state is not paid back, then centre's permission is required for any further borrowing.

Financial Relations During Emergencies

During emergencies, Centre-state financial relations change as follows :

- **National Emergency** (Article 352) The President can modify revenue distribution, reducing or cancelling Centre-to-state transfers (tax sharing and grants-in-aid) until the end of the financial year after the emergency ends.
- **Financial Emergency** (Article 360) During the operation of financial emergency, the centre can direct states to:
  - Follow specified financial principles
  - Reduce salaries and allowances
  - Submit money bills and financial bills for Presidential approval

Sources of Union-State Revenue

- GST (Goods and Services Tax)
- Currency, coinage and legal tender, foreign exchange.
- Duties of customs including export duties.
- Duties of excise on tobacco and certain goods manufactured or produced in India.
- Estate duty in respect of property other than agricultural land.
- Fees in respect of any of the matters in the Union List, but not including any fees taken in any court.
- Foreign loans–Lotteries organised by the Government of India or the Government of a State.
- Post Office Savings Bank.
- Post and telegraphs, telephones, wireless broadcasting and other like forms of communications.
- Property of the Union, public debt of the Union and railways.
- Rates of stamp duty in respect of bills of exchange, cheques, promissory notes (a promise by one party to make a payment of money at a date in the future) etc.
- Reserve Bank of India.
- Taxes on income-other than agricultural income.
- Taxes on the capital value of the assets exclusive of agricultural land of individuals and companies.
- Taxes other than stamp duties on transactions in stock exchanges and future markets.
- Taxes on the sale or purchase of newspapers and on advertisements published therein.
- Terminal taxes on goods or passengers, carried by railways, sea or rail.

Articles Related to Financial Relations

Articles	Subject Matters
Article 268	Duties levied by the Union but collected and appropriated by the states
Article 269	Taxes levied and collected by the Union but assigned to the states
Article 269(A)	Levy and collection of goods and services tax in course of inter-state trade or commerce
Article 270	Taxes levied and distributed between the Union and the states
Article 271	Surcharge on certain duties and taxes for purposes of the Union
Article 274	Prior recommendation of President required to bills affecting taxation in which states are interested.
Article 275	Grants from the Union to certain states.
Article 276	Taxes on professions, trades, callings and employments
Article 277	Savings
Article 279	Calculation of 'net proceeds' etc
Article 279(A)	Goods and Services Tax Council
Article 280	Finance Commission
Article 281	Recommendation of Finance Commission
Article 282	Expenditure defrayable by the Union or a state out of its revenues
Article 283	Custody, etc., of Consolidated Funds, Contingency Funds and money credited to the public accounts
Article 284	Custody of suitors' deposits and other money received by public servants and courts
Article 285	Exemption of property of the Union from state taxation
Article 286	Restrictions as to imposition of tax on the sale or purchase of goods
Article 287	Exemptions from taxes on electricity
Article 289	Exemption of property and income of a state from Union taxation
Article 292	Borrowing by the Government of India
Article 293	Borrowing by states

Important Sources of State Revenue

- Land revenue, including the assessment and collection of revenue, the maintenance of land records, survey for revenue purposes and records of rights, and alienation of revenues etc.
- Taxes on agricultural income
- Duties in respect of succession to agricultural land.
- Estate Duty in respect of agricultural land
- Taxes on lands and buildings.
- Taxes on mineral rights.
- Duties of excise for following goods manufactured or produced within the State (i) alcoholic liquors for human consumption and (ii) opium, Indian hemp and other narcotic drugs and narcotics.
- Electricity Duty:Taxes on the consumption or sale of electricity.
- Taxes on sale of petroleum crude, high speed diesel, motor spirit (commonly known as petrol), Natural gas aviation turbine fuel and alcohol liquor for human consumption but not including sale in the course of inter state or commerce or sale in the source of international trade or commerce such goods.
- Taxes on goods and passengers carried by roads or on inland waterways.
- Taxes on vehicles suitable for use on roads.
- Taxes on animals and boats.
- Tolls
- Taxes on profession, trades, callings and employments.
- Capitation taxes
- Taxes on entertainment and amusements to be extent levied and collected by a panchayat or Municipality or a regional council or a district council.
- Stamp duty

Commissions and Committees of Centre-State Relations

There have been several efforts for the improvements of Centre-State relations. Central Government has set-up many commissions to review and examine the federal relations from time-to-time, leading among them are.

Administrative Reform Commission (ARC)

- It was established in 1966 under the Chairmanship of **Morarji Desai** (followed by **K Hanumanthayya**) by Central Government. In order to examine thoroughly the various issues in Centre-State relations, the ARC constituted a study team under **MC Setalvad**.
- On the basis of its report, the ARC finalised its own report in 1969 and made **22 recommendations**. The important recommendations are :
  - Establishment of an Inter-State Council under **Article 263**.
  - Transferring of more financial resources to the states to reduce their dependency upon the centre.
  - Powers should be delegated to the maximum extent possible to the states to promote autonomy and efficiency.

Rajamannar Committee (1969)

- The Rajamannar Commission was a three member committee set-up by the Tamil Nadu Government in 1969 to examine all aspects of Centre-State relations under the rule of the DMK. It was formed by Dr. P.V. Rajamannar.
- The main recommendations of this committee are:
  - Residuary powers should be allocated to the states.
  - Planning Commission should be disbanded and its place should be taken by a statutory body.
  - Set up an Inter-State Council to facilitate cooperation and resolve disputes between states.
  - Make the Finance Commission a permanent body to ensure consistent and fair financial distribution.
  - Completely omit Articles 356, 357 and 365, which deal with President's rule, to prevent centralised interference.
  - Remove the provision requiring state ministries to hold office at the Governor's pleasure, ensuring more autonomy.
  - Transfer certain subjects from the Union List and Concurrent List to the State List, giving states more control.
  - Abolish All India services like IAS, IPS and IFOS to promote more localised governance.
  - The Central Government chose to ignore these recommendations, which were submitted in 1971.

Anandpur Sahib Resolution

- The Anandpur Sahib Resolution was adopted by the Akali Dal in 1973. It was a comprehensive document outlining both political and religious demands.
- The resolution sought to redefine the relationship between the Central Government and States and advocated for a more federal system. Key demands :
  - Restrict Centre's Jurisdiction Limit the Central Government's authority to defense, foreign affairs, communications and currency.
  - State Autonomy Vest all residuary powers in the states, granting them greater autonomy.
  - Federal Constitution Make the Constitution truly federal, ensuring equal authority and representation for all states at the centre.

West Bengal Memorandum

- In 1977, the West Bengal Government (led by the Communists) published a memorandum on centre-state relations and sent it to the Central Government.
- The memorandum made the following suggestions :
  - Replace 'union' with 'federal' in the Constitution to reflect a more decentralised system (a system where there is no single point of control or authority).
  - Limit the Centre's authority to defense, foreign affairs, currency, communications and economic co-ordination.
  - Give states control over all other subjects, including residuary powers.
  - Repeal Articles 356, 357 and 360, which relate to President's rule and financial emergencies.
  - Require the consent of the states for forming new states or reorganising existing ones.
  - Allocate 75% of the Centre's revenue to states.
  - Grant Rajya Sabha equal powers to Lok Sabha.
  - Abolish All India Services and maintain only central and state services.
- The Central Government did not accept these proposals.

Sarkaria Commission

- Sarkaria Commission was set-up in June, 1983 by the Central Government of India.
- The Sarkaria Commission's charter was to examine the relationship and balance of power between State and Central Governments in the country and suggest changes within the framework of Constitution of India.
- The Commission was so named as it was headed by Justice Rajinder Singh Sarkaria, a retired Judge of the Supreme Court of India and other two members of the committee were Shri B. Sivaraman and Dr. SR Sen.
- The committee submitted its report in 1988.
- The report contains 247 recommendations spreading over 19 Chapters.
- Some of the recommendations given by this commission are given below :
  - The Union Government should consult the State Governments before enacting any law related to a subject included in the Concurrent List.

- As provided in Article 263, an Inter-State Council should be constituted to resolve differences between the Union and the States. The Chief Ministers of all the States should be Ex-officio members of the Council.
- The states should be given right to amend the subjects included in State List, this requires an amendment to the Article 252 of the Constitution. An Expenditure Commission should be set-up at the Union level.
- The Corporation Tax should be distributed between Centre and the States.

> - The **Chief Minister** of the concerned state should be consulted by the Union Government before appointing the Governor in that state.
> - The persons, who are appointed to the post of Governor, should be individuals of social and administrative repute and credentials.
> - The person, who occupies the post of **Governor** should not be eligible for any appointment to a government post except the post of the President and the Vice-President.

- The assent of the President on the Bills passed by Legislatures of the States and reserved for the assent of the President, should not be delayed.
- Also, the appointment of the judges against the vacant posts in the High Court, should be made by the Central Government without any delay.

MM Punchhi Commission

- A commission on centre-state relations was set-up by the Government of India in April, 2007 under the Chairmanship of Madan Mohan Punchhi, Former Chief Justice of India.
- This Commission look into the issues of centre-state relations keeping in view the sea changes that have taken place in the polity and economy of India since, the Sarkaria Commission had last looked at the issue of Centre-State relations over two decades ago.
- The commission submitted its report in 2010.
- The commission made around 310 recommendations in total. Some of the recommendations given in its various reports are as below :
  - It recommended higher central transfers to backward states to enable them to improve their physical and human infrastructure.

> The Commission recommended a comprehensive review of all transfers to states with a view to minimising the component of discretionary transfers, particularly those channelled through **Centrally Sponsored Schemes** (CSS).

  - All future Central Legislations involving state's involvement should provide for cost sharing as in the case of the Right to Education (RTE) Act.
  - The proposed enactment for providing food security to the poor should clearly delineate the responsibilities of the Central and State Government in meeting the additional cost of implementing the provisions of the act.
  - The royalty rates on major minerals should be revised at least every three years without any delay.
  - States should be properly compensated for any delay in the revision of royalty beyond three years.
  - A part of the sale proceeds of spectrum should be devolved to states for expenditure on infrastructure projects.
  - It endorsed fully the recommendation of 12th Finance Commission with regards to the sharing of proceeds of service tax in the event of the notification of the 88th Amendment to the Constitution.
  - A Commission be constituted in the year 2015 and thereafter regularly after every five years to report on the status of local government devolution of powers. For this requisite provision be made in Parts IX and IX(A) on the same lines as Articles 339 and 340.
  - The collector is overburdened and hence, there should be a separate administrative structure for the District Panchayat.

"

Inter-State Relations encompass the dynamic interactions and connections among the various federal units, which include both States and Union Territories.

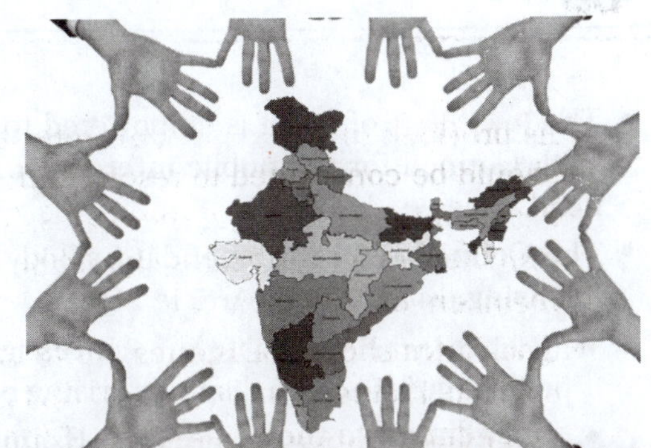

Chapter Fifteen

Inter-State Relations

INTER-STATE RIVER WATER DISPUTES

- In order to further streamline the adjudication of inter-state river water disputes, the Inter-State River Water Disputes (Amendment) Bill, 2019 was proposed.
- In the Bill, there is a provision for establishment of a Dispute Resolution Committee (DRC) by the Central Government for resolving amicably, the inter-state water disputes within a maximum period of one year and six months.
- Any dispute which cannot be settled by negotiations shall be referred to tribunal for its adjudication.
- The decision of tribunal is final and binding on the parties to the dispute.
- Under the 1956 Act, a State Government may request the Central Government to refer an inter-state river dispute to a tribunal for adjudication.
- If the Central Government believes that the dispute cannot be resolved through negotiations, it is required to establish a water disputes tribunal for adjudication within one year of receiving the complaint.
- The 2019 Bill seeks to replace this mechanism. Central Government will set-up a Disputes Resolution Committee (DRC), to resolve the dispute amicably after it receives a request from a state regarding any water dispute.

Inter-State Water Disputes

- Under Article 262, Parliament may by law provide for the adjudication of any dispute or complaint with respect to the use, distribution or control of the waters in inter-state rivers or river valleys.
- Parliament may by law provide that neither the Supreme Court nor any other court shall exercise jurisdiction in respect of any such dispute or complaint.
- Under this provision, the Parliament has enacted two laws i.e., the River Boards Act, 1956 and Inter-State Water Disputes Act, 1956.

Inter-State Water Dispute Tribunals

Names	Set-up in	States Involved
Krishna Water Disputes Tribunal	1969	Maharashtra, Karnataka and Andhra Pradesh
Godavari Water Disputes Tribunal	1969	Maharashtra, Karnataka, Andhra Pradesh, Madhya Pradesh and Odisha
Narmada Water Disputes Tribunal	1969	Rajasthan, Gujarat, Madhya Pradesh and Maharashtra
Ravi and Beas Water Disputes Tribunal	1986	Punjab, Haryana and Rajasthan
Cauvery Water Disputes Tribunal	1990	Karnataka, Kerala, Tamil Nadu and Puducherry
Second Krishna Water Disputes Tribunal	2004	Maharashtra, Karnataka, Telangana and Andhra Pradesh
Vansadhara Water Disputes Tribunal	2010	Odisha and Andhra Pradesh
Mahaday Water Disputes Tribunal	2010	Goa, Karnataka and Maharashtra
Mahanadi Water Disputes Tribunal	2018	Odisha and Chhattisgarh

INTER-STATE COUNCIL

- Article 263 provides for the establishment of an Inter-State Council to ensure coordination between the states and between Centre and States.
- It was constituted after the recommendation of the Sarkaria Commission.

- The President of India is empowered to establish such Council for the public interest and when the need arises.
- The Council is a recommendatory body with the following duties under Article 263 :
  - Resolve Inter-State Disputes Investigate and provide guidance on disputes arising between states.
  - Foster Cooperative Governance Examine and discuss matters of common interest to states and the Centre, promoting collaborative decision-making.
  - Enhance Policy Coordination Make recommendations to improve policy alignment and action between States and the Centre, ensuring cohesive governance.
- The Inter-State Council plays a crucial role in resolving disputes between states in India.
- Its primary function is to inquire into and advise on Inter-State disputes, which complements the Supreme Court's jurisdiction under Article 131 to decide legal controversies between governments.
- While the Council can address any controversy, whether legal or non-legal, its recommendations are advisory in nature, unlike the Supreme Court's binding decisions.
- This means that the Council provides guidance and recommendations to help resolve disputes, but ultimately, the decision-making power rests with the governments involved.
- It is the primary Council for Inter-State coordination that facilitates dialogue and cooperation between States and the Centre.
- The Inter-State Council was established in 1990 by the Janata Dal Government, led by VP Singh, to promote cooperative federalism in India.
- This Council is a vital platform for discussing and resolving issues between States and the Central Government.

Members of the Inter-State Council

- Chairman The Prime Minister of India
- Members
  - Chief Ministers of all States
  - Chief Ministers of Union Territories with Legislative Assemblies
  - Lieutenant-Governors and Administrators of Union Territories without Legislative Assemblies
  - Governors of States under President's Rule
  - Nine Union Cabinet Ministers nominated by the Prime Minister as members
- The Inter-State Council is a vital platform for fostering cooperation and coordination between the Central Government and States in India.
- The Inter-State Council meets at least three times a year, with all meetings held privately and decisions made unanimously.

Recommendations of Different Commissions

- **Sarkaria Commission** In its report, Sarkaria Commission made strong recommendations for establishment of a permanent Inter-State Council under **Article 263** of the Constitution. However, it recommended renaming the Council as an inter-governmental Council to differentiate it from other bodies established under the same **Article 263**.
- **Punchhi Commission** It also recommended that there should be a continuing role for the Inter-State Council in the management of matters in Concurrent List or overlapping jurisdiction.

Inter-State Trade and Commerce

- Articles 301 to 307 in Part XIII of the Indian Constitution ensure the free flow of trade, commerce and intercourse throughout the country's territory.
- Article 301 specifically states that trade, commerce and intercourse should be free from restrictions, aiming to break down border barriers between states and create a unified economic unit.
- The objective is to promote economic unity and integration, recognising that a single economic entity is essential for the country's political and cultural unity.
- This freedom isn't limited to Inter-State trade but also applies to intra-state trade, commerce and intercourse.
- In essence, Article 301 seeks to prevent any restrictions that could hinder the movement of goods, services and commercial transactions within India.
- Article 301 of the Indian Constitution guarantees freedom from restrictions but with some exceptions. These exceptions are outlined in Articles 302 to 305 of Part XIII.
- Parliament can restrict trade and commerce between states or within a state in the public interest, but cannot favour one state over another, except in cases of scarcity.

- A state can impose reasonable restrictions on trade within or with other states, but needs the President's approval. It also cannot favour one state over another.
- States can impose the same taxes on goods from other States or Union Territories as they do on locally manufactured goods, preventing discrimination.
- Trade freedom is subject to laws that allow the government to control certain industries or services, sometimes excluding private participation.

ZONAL COUNCILS

- Zonal Councils were set-up to supplement the coordination among regional states.
- Zonal Councils are statutory bodies that are established by State Reorganisation Act of 1956, made by Parliament.
- The members of each Zonal Council includes the Home Minister of the Central Government, Chief Ministers of all the states in the zone, two other Ministers from each state in the zone and administrators of each Union Territory in the zone.
- Apart from these, some other members are also associated with the Council as advisors :
  - A person nominated by the NITI Aayog.
  - Chief Secretary of the government of each state in the zone.
  - Development Commissioner of each state in the zone.
- The Central Home Minister acts as the common chairman of all the five Zonal Councils.
- Each Chief Minister in the Council serves as the Vice-Chairman of the Council by rotation. They hold the office for one year at a time.
- Five Zonal Councils have been set-up till now.

The Present Composition of Zonal Councils

- The Northern Zonal Council, comprising the States of Haryana, Himachal Pradesh, Punjab, Rajasthan, National Capital Territory of Delhi and Union Territory of Jammu and Kashmir, Ladakh and Chandigarh; HQ – New Delhi.
- The Central Zonal Council, comprising the States of Chhattisgarh, Uttarakhand, Uttar Pradesh and Madhya Pradesh; HQ – Prayagraj.
- The Eastern Zonal Council, comprising the States of Bihar, Jharkhand, Odisha and West Bengal, HQ – Kolkata.
- The Western Zonal Council, comprising the States of Goa, Gujarat, Maharashtra and the Union Territory of Daman and Diu and Dadra and Nagar Haveli, HQ – Mumbai.
- The Southern Zonal Council, comprising the States of Andhra Pradesh, Telangana, Karnataka, Kerala, Tamil Nadu and the Union Territory of Puducherry, HQ – Chennai.

North-Eastern Council

- **Establishment** The Council was created by the North- Eastern Council Act of 1971, a separate Act of Parliament.
- **Objectives** The Council aims to secure balanced development of all sectors in the North-Eastern region and promote economic growth.
- **Members** The North-Eastern Council comprises eight states, Assam, Manipur, Mizoram, Arunachal Pradesh, Nagaland, Meghalaya, Tripura and Sikkim.
- **Functions** The Council's functions are similar to those of the Zonal Councils, with some additional responsibilities, including
  - Formulating a unified and coordinated regional plan covering matters of common importance.
  - Reviewing measures taken by member states for maintaining security and public order in the region.
  - Discussing any matter of common interest in the field of economic and social planning.
  - Recommending actions on inter-state transport and communications, power and flood-control projects.

Articles Related to Inter-State Relations

Articles	Descriptions
Article 261	Mutual recognition of Public Acts, records and judicial proceedings
Article 262	Adjudication of disputes related to water distribution of inter-state rivers
Article 263	Provisions related to Inter-State Council
Article 301	Freedom of trade, commerce and intercourse
Article 302	Power of the Parliament to impose restrictions on trade, commerce and intercourse
Article 303	Restrictions on legislative powers of the Union and States with regards to trade and commerce
Article 304	Restrictions on trade, commerce and intercourse among states
Article 305	Saving of existing laws and laws providing for state monopolies
Article 307	Appointment of authority for carrying out the purposes of Articles 301 to 304

Emergency provision is a feature that is distinct in the Indian Constitution, which converts a Federal Government to a Unitary Government as per the circumstances.

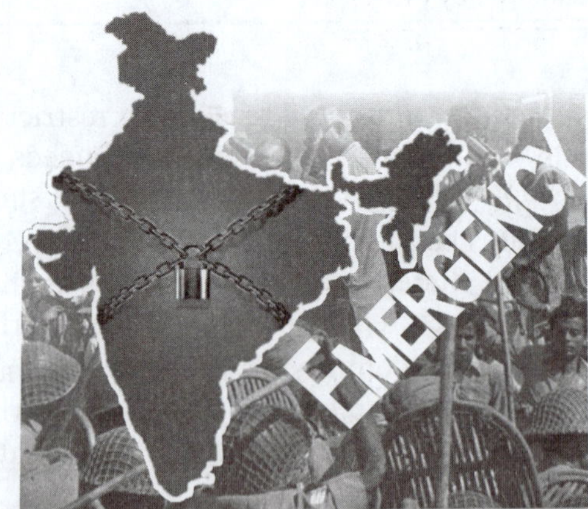

Chapter Sixteen

Emergency Provisions

The Emergency Provisions are contained in Part XVIII from Articles 352 to 360 of the Indian Constitution. The emergency powers are vested in the Union Executive. These provisions enable the Central Government to meet any abnormal situation effectively. The President is empowered to promulgate three kinds of emergencies which are as follows :

- Under Article 352, the President can declare a National Emergency when the security of India or a part of it, is threatened by war or external aggression or armed rebellion. It is known as National Emergency.
- The Constitution contains the expression 'proclamation of emergency' to indicate this kind of emergency.
- Under the Article 356, an emergency due to the failure of constitutional machinery in the states this is known as the President's Rule or State Emergency or Constitutional Emergency.
- The Constitution however, does not mention the term 'emergency' to denote this kind of situation.
- Under Article 360, an emergency due to the financial stability or credit of India or any part of the territory, known as Financial Emergency.

NATIONAL EMERGENCY

- An emergency due to war, external aggression or armed rebellion is known as National Emergency.
- The President may proclaim a state of emergency for the whole of India or part of the territory thereof.
- A proclamation of emergency made by the President, even before the actual occurrence of war, external aggression or armed rebellion if he/she is satisfied that there is inevitable danger.
- The President of India has the authority to issue multiple proclamations based on various grounds, including war, external aggression or armed rebellion even the imminent threat of these situations, regardless of whether a previous proclamation is already in effect.
- This provision was added by the 38th Amendment Act of 1975. It enables the President to respond effectively to different emergencies.
- When a National Emergency is declared on the ground of war or external aggression it is known as External Emergency. On the other hand, when it is declared on the ground of armed rebellion, it is known as Internal Emergency.
- Such a proclamation of emergency can be revoked by the President subsequently. A proclamation of National Emergency may be applicable to the entire country or only a part of it. This provision was added by 42nd Amendment Act, 1976.

> Prior to the **44th Constitutional Amendment Act, 1978**, a proclamation of emergency could be issued on the grounds of war or external aggression or internal disturbances. The expression **internal disturbances** is a vague term and could be misused by the executive. Thus, the Act has introduced the expression armed rebellion replacing internal disturbances.

- Earlier, the President could proclaim an emergency on the oral advice tendered by the Prime Minister, as it happened in 1975.

- Now, the President can declare an emergency only on the written advice of the Cabinet.
- This provision was added by 44th Amendment Act, 1978 as an additional safeguard against abuse or misuse of power.
- The 38th Amendment Act of 1975 made the declaration of a National Emergency immune from the judicial review. But, this provision was subsequently deleted by the 44th Amendment Act of 1978.
- The proclamation of emergency made by the President under Article 352, is subjected to the judicial review and its constitutionality can be questioned in a Court of Law on grounds of malafide. This judgement came after the Minerva Mills Case in 1980.

Parliamentary Approval and Duration

- Every proclamation except the previous revoking proclamation should be approved by both the Houses of the Parliament within one month from the date of its issue.
- Originally, Parliament had two months to approve a proclamation, but the 44th Amendment Act of 1978 shortened this approval period.
- It should be passed by a majority of the total membership of that House and by a majority of not less than two-third of the members of that House present and voting, i.e., special majority.
- If the Parliament fails to approve such a proclamation, it ceases to be in operation on the expiry of one month after the proclamation is made.
- If the Parliament approves such a proclamation, it will be in force, unless revoked earlier, for six months from the date on which it was approved by the Parliament.
- If the Lok Sabha is dissolved, the Rajya Sabha might approve the proclamation or extend its term. The proclamation remains in effect for 30 days following the first Lok Sabha session after its reconstitution.
- It can be approved by the Parliament any number of times, but not beyond six months at a time.
- This provision for periodical Parliamentary approval was also added by the 44th Amendment Act of 1978.
- Before this amendment, an emergency declared by the Executive and approved by Parliament had no time limit, allowing it to remain in effect indefinitely at the discretion of the Cabinet.

Revocation of the Proclamation

- The President may revoke the proclamation by issuing subsequent proclamation during the emergency.
- Parliament is not required to ratify such a proclamation.
- Before the amendment, the President had sole authority to revoke a proclamation, without the need of approval or oversight from the Lok Sabha.
- If the Lok Sabha approves a resolution of disapproval with a simple majority, the President must revoke the emergency. It was introduced by the 44th Amendment Act.

> Lok Sabha has the power to disapprove the National Emergency at any time, if not less than **1/10th members** of Lok Sabha issue a notice to the speaker or to the President. As per 44th Amendment Act, if there is no session, a special sitting of the Lok Sabha shall be held within **14 days** for the purpose of considering such a resolution.

- A resolution of disapproval and a resolution approving the continuation of a proclamation have two key differences :
  - A resolution of disapproval only needs to be passed by the Lok Sabha, whereas a resolution approving the continuation of a proclamation must be passed by both Houses of Parliament.
  - A resolution of disapproval can be adopted by a simple majority, whereas a resolution approving the continuation of a proclamation requires a special majority.

Effects of the Proclamation of Emergency

The effect of a proclamation of emergency can be studied under the following heads :

Effect on Union-State Relations

Proclamation of emergency on Union-State relations is based on following relations :

Executive Relations

- While a proclamation is in operation, the centre is empowered to issue directions to the states as to the manner in which their executive power is to be exercised.
- In normal times, the centre has the power to give directions to the states only on certain matters like maintenance of communication, protection of railways, etc.
- But during the emergency, he/she can issue directions to the states on all the matters.

- Therefore, the administration will be converted into a unitary system i.e., State Governments are under complete control of centre.

Legislative Relations

- While a proclamation of emergency is in operation, the Parliament can enact laws even on the subjects enumerated under the State List.
- The Legislatures of the State are not suspended, but it is subjected to the overriding powers of Parliament.
- Thus, the Federal Structure in the Constitution changes into unitary.
- The laws made by Parliament on the state subjects during a National Emergency become inoperative six months after the emergency has ceased to operate.
- President can issue ordinances on the state subjects also, if the Parliament is not in session.
- As per 42nd Constitutional Amendment Act, 1976, these laws may be applicable to any other state as well and not just to the state where emergency is declared.

Financial Relations

- While a proclamation of National Emergency is in operation, the President may modify the provisions of the Constitution relating to the distribution of the financial resources between the Centre and the States.
- Such as order of the President shall not have effect beyond the financial year in which the proclamation of emergency ceases to be in operation. The order of the President is subject to the approval of the Parliament.

Effect on Lok Sabha and State Assembly

- While a proclamation of National Emergency is in effect, the Lok Sabha's term may be extended by a law of Parliament for one year at a time (for any length of time) beyond its normal term of five years.
- This extension, however, cannot last longer than six months after the emergency has ended.
- Similarly, during a National Emergency, the Parliament may extend the normal tenure of a State Legislative Assembly (five years) by one year each time (for any length of time), subject to a maximum period of six months after the emergency has ended.

National Emergency Declared so Far in India

Emergency proclamation has been used in India three times so far (1962, 1971 and 1975).

- The **First National Emergency** was declared on 26th October, 1962 at the time of Chinese aggression and it was withdrawn on 10th January, 1968.
- The **Second National Emergency** proclamation was made at the time of Pakistan invasion on 3rd December, 1971 and it was withdrawn on March, 1977.
- The **Third National Emergency** was proclaimed on 26th June, 1975 on the grounds of internal disturbance and it was withdrawn on 21st March, 1977, the harsh action taken at the time of third emergency was criticised.

Effect on Fundamental Rights

- Article 358 states that as soon as a proclamation of emergency is issued on the grounds of a war or an external aggression (but not on the ground of an armed rebellion), the six Fundamental Rights enumerated under Article 19 are automatically suspended.
- Under Article 359 the President, may order to suspend the operation of any of the other Fundamental Rights except Articles 20 and 21 when an emergency declared on the basis of a war or an external aggression or in armed rebellion is in force.

Effect on Suspension of Fundamental Rights

- During a proclamation of emergency, there are no restrictions imposed on states by Article 19. States can make laws or take away Fundamental Rights mentioned under Article 19.
- These laws cannot be challenged in the courts on the basis of inconsistency. During this, only laws that are related with the emergency are protected from being challenged and not any other laws.
- When the National Emergency expires then Article 19 is automatically reinforced.
- Under Article 358, after the 44th Amendment Act came into force Article 19 is automatically suspended only when an emergency is declared on the basis of a war or an external aggression and not on the basis of an armed rebellion.
- As per 44th Amendment Act, 1978, no remedy lies for anything done during the emergency even after the emergency expires (only those laws which are related with the emergency, not other laws).
- Under Article 359, the President is authorised to suspend, the right to move any court for the enforcement of Fundamental Rights during a National Emergency. These are applicable on rights that are mentioned in the President's order.

- The duration of suspension could be for a shorter period or during the entire operation of emergency as mentioned in President's order.
- These could be extended to whole or any part of the country. The order should be laid before each house of the Parliament to get approval.
- While a Presidential order is in force, the state can make any law or can take any executive action abridging or taking away the specified Fundamental Rights. No remedy lies for anything done during the operation of the order even after the order ceases to operate.
- Following provisions were added by the 44th Amendment Act, 1978 :
  - President cannot suspend the right to move the court for the enforcement of Fundamental Rights under Articles 20 to 21 (remain enforceable even during emergency).
  - Only those laws which are related with the emergency are protected from being challenged and not other laws and the executive action taken only under such a law, is protected.

PRESIDENT'S RULE

- The President's Rule or State Emergency can be proclaimed under Articles 355, 356 and 365. It is also known as the constitutional emergency or State emergency.
- Article 355 says, it shall be the duty of the Union to protect every state against external aggression and internal disturbance.
- The Union shall ensure that the government of every state is carried on in accordance with the provision of the Constitution.
- In case of failure of Constitutional machinery, Centre can take over the Government of State.

> **Article 356** says that, if the President is satisfied that a situation has arisen in which the Government of the State cannot be carried on in accordance with the provisions of this Constitution, he/she may issue a proclamation.

- Article 365 says that whenever a state fails to comply with or give effect to any direction from the centre, it will be lawful for the President to hold that a situation has arisen in which the Government of the State cannot be carried on in accordance with the provisions of the Constitution.

Parliamentary Approval and Duration

- Within two months after the date of its issuance, a proclamation imposing President's Rule must be ratified by both Houses of Parliament.
- If the proclamation is issued at a time when the Lok Sabha has been dissolved without approving the proclamation, the proclamation will remain in effect until 30 days from the first Lok Sabha sitting following its reconstitution meanwhile, Rajya Sabha gave it its approval.
- The President's Rule is in effect for another six months if both Houses of Parliament approve it. With the consent of the Parliament, it may be prolonged for a maximum of three years every six months.
- If the dissolution of the Lok Sabha takes place during the period of six months without approving the President's Rule, then the proclamation survives until 30 days from the first sitting of the Lok Sabha after its reconstitution. Only a simple majority is required for any resolution in either House of Parliament to be approved or continued.
- Any such proclamation may be revoked or varied by a subsequent proclamation. It can be revoked by the President only.
- The 44th Amendment Act of 1978 limited Parliament's power to extend President's Rule beyond one year.
- It can only be extended for six months at a time beyond one year if two conditions are met :
  - A proclamation of emergency under Article 352 is in operation in the whole of India or in the whole or any part of the state at the time of passing of such resolution.
  - The Election Commission certifies that the continuance in force of the proclamation beyond the one year period is necessary on account of the difficulties in holding the general elections to the Legislative Assembly of the concerned state.

Effects of Imposition of the President's Rule

- During State Emergency, the President of India assumes all executive power of the state to himself/herself.
- The state administration is run directly by him/her or through a person designated for the purpose by him/her. It is the Governor of State who runs the state administration on behalf of the President.

- During the President's Rule, the State Assembly is either dissolved or kept under suspension. During this period, the MLAs do not lose their membership of the Assembly, nor there is election held to the Assembly. The President cannot suspend the operation of any provisions of the Constitution relating to the High Court.
- The Parliament can confer the power to make laws for the state. The Parliament may also authorise the President to delegate such power to any other authority as specified by him/herself.
- The Parliament makes laws and all items included in the State List. It also passes the State Budget. However, if the Lok Sabha is not in session, the President may authorise any expenditure from the Consolidated Fund of State.
- During the State Emergency, the High Court of the State, functions independently without any of its powers being curtailed. The President has also power to proclaim ordinances in the state.
- During State Emergency, the Union Government assumes absolute control over state administration except the judiciary. As the state administration is mostly run in the name of the President, the state emergency is known as President's Rule .
- A legislation passed by the President, the Parliament or any other designated authority continues to be operative even after the President's Rule and is not limited to the time period covered by the proclamation. The State Legislature has the authority to repeal ,amend or alter it.

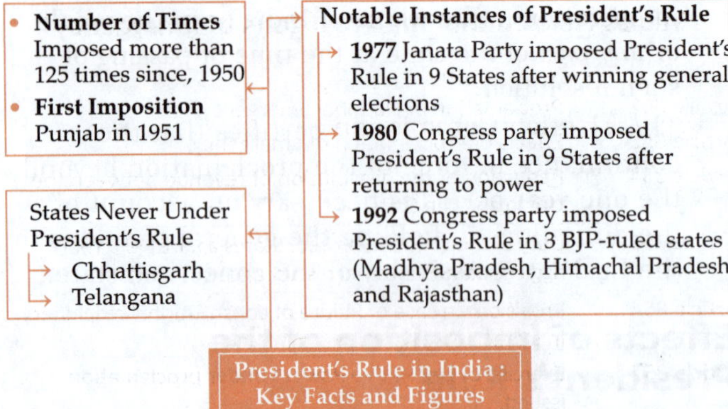

Difference between Articles 352 and 356

Article 352	Article 356
Article 352 restricts central intervention to a situation of war, external aggression or armed rebellion.	Article 356 applies to situation of failure of constitutional machinery in a state.
During this operation, the state executive and legislature continue to function and exercise the powers assigned to them under the Constitution.	During its operation, the State Executive is dismissed and the State Legislature is either suspended or dissolved. The executive and legislative powers of the state are assumed by the centre.
Under Article 352, the relationship of all the states with the centre undergoes a change.	Under Article 356, the relationship of only one state (where the President's Rule is imposed) with the centre is affected.
The proclamation under Article 352 has to be approved initially within a month with there being no upper limit provided.	The proclamation under Article 356 is to be approved by the Parliament first within two months and thereafter every six months, period for which it can remain in force is three years.
It affects Fundamental Rights of the citizens.	It has no effect on Fundamental Rights of the citizens.
The Parliament can make laws on the subjects mentioned in the State List and cannot delegate this task to any other body.	The Parliament can delegate this function of making laws for the state to the President or any other authority specified by him.
No maximum period is prescribed for its operation and it can continue indefinitely with the approval of Parliament every six months.	The maximum period prescribed for its operation is three years.
Special majority is required for the passage of every parliamentary resolution approving its proclamation or continuation.	Only a simple majority is required.

Article 356 and Judicial Review

- In SR Bommai Case (1994) , the Supreme Court held that the power of the President in issuing a proclamation of emergency is subject to judicial review to the extent of court's power.
- The satisfaction of the President must be based on relevant material. It is the responsibility of the centre to prove the justification behind the imposition of the President's Rule.
- The court cannot comment on the accuracy or sufficiency of the evidence, but it can determine whether it is pertinent to the case.
- The State Government can be reinstated alongwith the State Legislative Assembly, if it was suspended or dissolved, if the court rules that the Presidential proclamation is unlawful and unconstitutional.

- Only once the Presidential proclamation has been authorised by the Parliament should the State Legislative Assembly be dissolved.
- Under Article 356, a State Government is liable to action if it pursues any anti-secular politics as secularism is one of the 'Basic Features' of the Constitution.
- The question of the State Government losing the confidence of the Legislative Assembly should be decided on the floor of the House.
- If a new political party wins the majority at the federal level, it won't have the right to dismiss ministries created by other parties.
- The power under Article 356 is an exceptional power and should be used only occasionally to meet the requirements of special situations.

FINANCIAL EMERGENCY

- Article 360 provides that, if the President is satisfied that a situation has arisen due to which the financial stability of India or the credit of India or any part of India is threatened, he/she may make a declaration to that effect.
- Under such situation, the executive and legislative powers will go to the centre. This article has never been invoked till date.
- As per 38th Constitutional Amendment Act of 1975, the President is empowered in declaring financial emergency. It is final and conclusive and cannot be questionable in any court.
- However, the 44th Constitutional Amendment Act of 1978 deleted the provision implying that the satisfaction of the President is not beyond judicial review.

Parliamentary Approval and Duration of Operation

- The proclamation of Financial Emergency must be approved by both the Houses of the Parliament within two months from the date of issue.
- If, at the time of proclamation of Financial Emergency, the Lok Sabha stands dissolved, the proclamation needs to be approved by the Lok Sabha within 30 days of its meeting after its reconstitution, provided the Rajya Sabha has in the meantime approved it.
- Once approved by both the Houses of Parliament, the Financial Emergency continues indefinitely till it is revoked. No repeated Parliamentary approval is required for its continuation.
- A resolution approving the proclamation of Financial Emergency can be passed by either House of the Parliament only by a simple majority (a majority of the members of that House present and voting).

Effects of Financial Emergency

- The executive authority of the centre extends to giving directions to any state as the President may deem necessary and adequate for the purpose.
- It may include a provision requiring the reduction of salaries and allowances of public servant in the state and the reservation of all Money Bills or other financial bills for the consideration of the President, after they are passed by State Legislative.
- The President may issue direction for the reduction of salaries and allowance of Union servants or the Judge of Supreme Court and High Court .
- Thus, during Financial Emergency, the Centre acquires full control over the States in financial matters.

Punchhi Commission on Emergency Provisions

- The Punchhi Commission strongly came out in favour of amending **Articles 356** and **365** to enable the centre to bring specific troubled areas under its rule for a limited period.
- To check its misuse by centre, it has proposed localising emergency provisions. Under both these articles contending that localised areas either a district or parts of a district be brought under Governors Rule instead of the whole state and its duration must not be more than three months.

Articles Related with the Provisions of Emergency

Articles	Descriptions
Article 352	Proclamation of National Emergency.
Article 353	Effects of Proclamation of Emergency.
Article 354	Reduction of the distribution of revenue between the Union and the State.
Article 355	Duty of the Union to protect States against external aggression and internal disturbance.
Article 356	Provisions in case of failure of constitutional machinery in states.
Article 357	Exercise of Legislative Powers under proclamation issued.
Article 358	Suspension of provisions of Article 19 during an emergency.
Article 359	Suspension of the enforcement of the right conferred by Part III.
Article 359 1 (A)	Clause 1(A) inserted to limit the state to make law or executive to take steps for countering the crisis.
Article 360	Provisions as to Financial Emergency.

"The executive power of the Union Government lies in the President. He is the Supreme Commander of the Defence forces of the Union.

Chapter Seventeen

The President

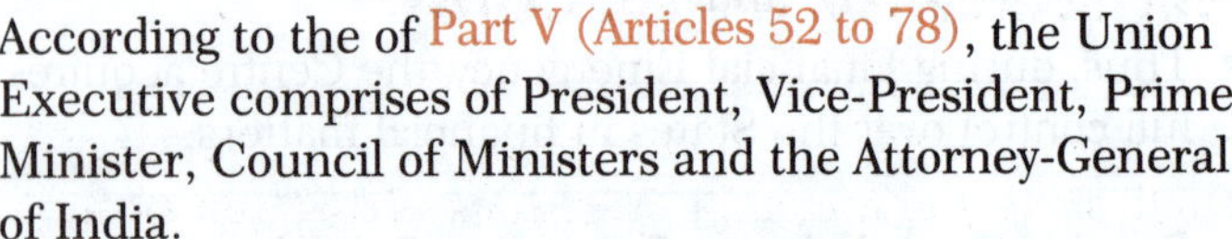

According to the of Part V (Articles 52 to 78), the Union Executive comprises of President, Vice-President, Prime Minister, Council of Ministers and the Attorney-General of India.

Article 52 states that there shall be a President of India. According to Article 53(1), the executive power of the Union vests with the President. However, the President can exercise his/her powers either directly or through officers subordinate to him/her in accordance with the Constitution.

The President of India is the nominal head of the state. He symbolises the entire nation as one political community and he is the first citizen of India. All the executive decisions are taken in the name of the President. Also, he is the Supreme Commander of the Defence Forces of the Union.

The President always comes first in the order of precedence in the official warrant of precedence.

PROCESS OF ELECTION

- Article 54 deals with the election of the President and Article 55 provides the method of the President's election.
- The President is elected by proportional representation with Single Transferable Vote System and the voting is by secret ballot.
- This system guarantees that the winning candidate is elected by receiving more than 50% of the total votes cast (absolute majority), ensuring they have the support of the majority of voters.
- Proportional representation means that in order to get elected, the candidate must get a fixed quota of votes.
- Indirect election was chosen by the Constitution makers for the election of President due to the following reasons :
    - President is only a nominal head and real power lies in the hands of the Council of Ministers headed by the Prime Minister.
    - Direct election is a very costly and time consuming process and it is not feasible for the election of a symbolic head.
- The number of votes needed to win is one more than 50% of valid votes. Under the Single Transferable Vote System, an elector can indicate more than one preference on his ballot paper.
- The nomination of a candidate for the post of President has to be proposed by 50 members and seconded by another 50 members of the Electoral College. Every candidate has to make a security deposit of ₹ 15,000 in Reserve Bank of India.
- The security deposit is liable to be forfeited in case the candidate fails to secure 1/6th of the votes polled.
- The Constitution ensures uniformity in the representation scale across states and maintains parity between states and the Union in the electoral process for the President.
- Hence, the number of votes which each elected member of the Legislative Assembly of each state and the Parliament is entitled to cast at such election shall be determined in the following manner.

- Every elected member of the Legislative Assembly of a state shall have as many votes as there are multiples of one thousand in the quotient obtained by dividing the population of the state by the total number of the elected members of the assembly.

Value of Vote of an MLA

It shows that the value of votes of each MLA from two different states is not same.

Value of the vote of MLA

$$= \frac{\text{Total population of state}}{\text{Total number of elected members in the State Legislative Assembly}} \times \frac{1}{1000}$$

- Every elected member of either House of Parliament shall have such number of votes as may be obtained by dividing the total number of votes assigned to members of the Legislative Assemblies of the states by the total number of the elected members of both the Houses of Parliament.

Value of Vote of an MP

This can be expressed as; Value of the vote of an MP

$$= \frac{\text{Total value of votes of all MLAs of all states}}{\text{Total number of elected Members of Parliament}}$$

Then, the quota of votes a candidate needs to win the elections, is determined in the following manners

Electoral Quota

$$= \frac{\text{Total number of valid votes polled}}{1+1=2} + 1$$

DISPUTES RELATING TO ELECTION

- Article 71 deals with, matters relating to the election of President i.e. all doubts and disputes arising in connection with the election of a President or Vice-President shall be required into and decided by the Supreme Court whose decision shall be final.
- The election of a person as President cannot be challenged on the ground that the Electoral College was incomplete.
- However, if the Supreme Court does declare a Presidential election void, any actions taken by the President before the such declaration remain valid and continue to be in force.

Term of Office

- According to Article 56(1), the President shall hold office for a tenure of 5 years from the date on which he/she enters the office. Even after the President completes his/her term, he/she shall occupy the office unless a successor assumes charge.
- The President can be removed by the process of impeachment or by addressing his resignation letter to the Vice-President of India. Then, it shall forthwith be communicated by him/her to the Speaker of the Lok Sabha.
- The President is eligible for re-election and may be elected for any number of term in India.
- On a contrary as per the American Constitution, a person can be elected only twice as the President.

Eligibility for Re-election

Article 57 deals with the eligibility for re-election i.e. a person who holds or who has held, office as President shall, subject to the other provisions of this Constitution be eligible for re-election to that office.

Eligibility Criteria and Oath

- Article 58 of the Constitution sets the principle qualifications one must meet to be eligible to the office of the President. A President must be
  - a citizen of India;
  - of 35 years of age or above;
  - qualified to become a Member of the Lok Sabha.
- A person shall not be eligible for election as President, if he holds any office of profit under the Government of India or the government of any state or under any local or other authority subject to the control of any of the said governments.
- Article 60 says that the oath or affirmation of office to the President is administered by the Chief Justice of India and in his absence, the seniormost Judge of the Supreme Court available.
- If any other person is acting as the President or discharging the functions of the office of the President, he should undertake a similar oath.
- In his oath, the President swears :
  - to faithfully execute the office;
  - to preserve, protect and defend the Constitution and the law and
  - to devote himself to the service and well-being of the people of India.

Salary and Emoluments

- The salary of the President of India is ₹ 5 lakh/month (non-taxable). Apart from this, the President of India also gets several allowances.
- The President of India will get ₹ 2.5 lakh/month as a pension. In addition, former Presidents are entitled to furnished rent free bungalow, two free landlines and a mobile phone and office expenses of ₹ 1 lakh per annum.

Conditions and Privileges of President's Office

- The Constitution lays down the following conditions of the President's office :
  - Article 59(1) says, President shall not be a member of either House of Parliament or a House of the State Legislature. If any such person is elected as President, he is deemed to have vacated his seat in that House on the date on which he enters upon his office as President.
  - The President should not hold any office of profit.
  - The President is entitled to use his official residence (Rashtrapati Bhawan) without payment of rent.
  - He is entitled to such emoluments, allowances and privileges as may be determined by Parliament. His emoluments and allowances cannot be diminished during his term of office.
  - He enjoys personal immunity from legal liability of his official acts. During his term of office, he is immune from any criminal proceedings, even in respect of his personal acts. However, after giving 2 months notice, civil proceedings can be instituted against him.

Articles Related to the President

Articles	Descriptions
Article 52	The President of India
Article 53	Executive power of the Union
Article 54	Election of the President
Article 55	Manner of election of the President
Article 56	Term of office of President
Article 57	Eligibility for re-election
Article 58	Qualification for election of President
Article 59	Conditions of President's office
Article 60	Oath or affirmation by President
Article 61	Procedure for impeachment
Article 62	Time of holding election and term of office of person elected

Vacancy in Office

- In case of a vacancy that is going to be caused due to the expiration of the term of the office of the President, an election to replace the outgoing President must be held before their term expires to prevent an interregnum (a period where the country is without a President).
- If there is any delay in the election process, the current President will continue to serve beyond their five-years term until a successor takes office. In such cases, the Vice-President doesn't get the opportunity to discharge the functions of the President.
- In the event of a vacancy-created for the President's post due to death, resignation, removal, etc., Article 65 of the Indian Constitution says that the Vice-President acts as the President till the new person in the office is elected.
- The election shall be conducted within 6 months of the vacancy.
- The newly elected President remains in office for a full term of five years from the day of assuming charge.
- The Vice-President reverts to his/her office when a new President is elected and enters upon his office.
- When the President is unable to act owing to his/her absence, illness or any other cause, the Vice-President discharges the President's functions for a temporary period until the President resumes his duties.
- In case both President and Vice-President are not available to perform the duties of President, the Chief Justice of Supreme Court discharges the duties of President and in his absence the next seniormost Judge of the Supreme Court performs the functions of the President.
- Justice M Hidayat-ullah, Chief Justice of India discharged the duties of President from 20th July to 24th August, 1969. He is the only Chief Justice of India to perform the functions of President.

Impeachment of the President

- Articles 56(1) (b) and 61 provide for Impeachment of the President.
- The President can be removed from office by a process of impeachment for violation of the Constitution. However, the Constitution does not define the meaning of the phrase violation of the Constitution.
- According to Article 61, when a President is to be impeached for violation of the Constitution, the

charge shall be initiated by either House of the Parliament.

- No such charge shall be initiated unless the proposal to prefer such charge is contained in a resolution which has been moved after at least 14 days notice in writing.
- It has to be signed by not less than one-fourth of the total number of members of the House.
- Once the resolution has been adopted, it has to be passed by a majority of not less than two-third of the total membership of the House.
- When a charge has been so preferred by either House of Parliament, the other House shall investigate the charge or cause the charge to be investigated and the President shall have the right to appear and to be represented at such investigation.
- If as a result of the investigation a resolution is passed by a majority of not less than two-third of the total membership of the House by which the charge was investigated or caused to be investigated, declaring that the charge preferred against the President has been sustained.
- Such resolution shall have the effect of removing the President from his office as from the date on which the resolution is so passed.
- No President has faced impeachment proceedings so far. Impeachment is a quasi-judicial process of Parliament.

> The elected members of the **Legislative Assemblies of States** and the **Union Territories** of **Delhi, Puducherry** and **Jammu** and **Kashmir** do not participate in the impeachment of the President though they participate in his/her election.

- The nominated members of either House of Parliament can participate in the impeachment (the process followed in deciding the removal of a person in a position from exercising all the powers and responsibilities that the position demands) of President though they do not participate in the election of the Presidential post.

POWERS AND FUNCTIONS

The role of President is that of a Ceremonial Head in whose name the decisions of the government are carried out. Various powers and functions related to President are as follows :

Executive Powers

- As per Article 53, all executive actions of the Government of India are formally taken in his name.
- The President can make rules specifying the manner in which the orders and other instruments made and executed in his name shall be authenticated.
- As per Article 74(1), the President appoints the Prime Minister and the other ministers. They hold office during his pleasure.
- As per Article 77(3), the President can make rules for more convenient transaction of business of the Union Government and for allocation of the said business among the ministers.
- According to Article 78(b), the President can seek any information relating to the administration of affairs of the Union and proposals for legislation from the Prime Minister.
- The President appoints the Attorney-General of India and determines his remuneration. The Attorney-General holds office during the pleasure of the President.
- The President appoints the Comptroller and Auditor-General of India, the Chief Election Commissioner and other Election Commissioners, the Chairman and Members of the Union Public Service Commission, the Governors of States, the Chairman and Members of Finance Commission and so on.
- The President can require the Prime Minister to submit, for consideration of the Council of Ministers, any matter on which a decision has been taken by a minister but, which has not been considered by the Council.
- The President can appoint a Commission to investigate into the conditions of SCs, STs and other Backward Classes.
- The President can appoint an Inter-State Council to promote Centre-State and Inter-State co-operation.
- The President directly administers the Union Territories through administrators appointed by him.
- The President can declare any area as Scheduled Area and has powers with respect to the administration of Scheduled Areas and tribal areas.

Legislative Powers

- As per Article 85, the President summons both the Houses of the Parliament and prorogues them. He or she can even dissolve the Lok Sabha.

- The President exercises these powers according to the advice of the Council of Ministers headed by the Prime Minister.
- The President inaugurates the Parliament by addressing it after every general elections and also at the beginning of the first session each year. Presidential address on these occasions is generally meant to outline the new policies of the government.
- The President can summon a joint sitting of both the Houses of Parliament, presided over by the speaker of the Lok Sabha.
- The President can send messages to both the Houses of the Parliament with respect to a pending bill or otherwise.
- When the offices of both the Speaker and Deputy Speaker in Lok Sabha and offices of both Chairman and Deputy Chairman in Rajya Sabha falls vacant, the President can appoint any member of the Lok Sabha and Rajya Sabha respectively to preside over its proceedings.
- All bills passed by the Parliament can become laws only after receiving the assent of the President.
- The President can return a bill to the Parliament, (if it is not a Money Bill) for reconsideration.
- When after reconsideration, the Bill is passed and presented to the president, with or without amendments, the President is obliged to give assent to it.
- The President nominates 12 members of the Rajya Sabha from amongst persons having special knowledge or practical experience in literature, science, art and social service.
- The President decides on questions as to disqualifications of Members of the Parliament, in consultation with the Election Commission.
- The President lays the reports of the Comptroller and Auditor-General, Union Public Service Commission, Finance Commission and others, before the Parliament.
- In the event of a Hung Parliament, where no Party has absolute majority in the Lok Sabha, the President invites parties to command the required support and form the government.
- If the majority is still not achieved, President can call for a new election.
- The President can make regulations for the peace, progress and good government in case of Andaman and Nicobar islands, Lakshadweep, Dadra and Nagar Haveli and Daman and Diu and Ladakh.
- The President can also make regulations for Puducherry but only when the Legislative Assembly is suspended or dissolved.

Nomination of Anglo-Indians

- Under **Article 331**, the President can nominate two members to the Lok Sabha from the **Anglo-Indian Community**, if the community is not adequately represented.
- However, the Anglo-Indian reserved seats in the Parliament and State Legislatures of India were discontinued by the **126th Constitutional Amendment Bill of 2019**, when enacted as the **104th Constitutional Amendment Act, 2019**.

Ordinance Making Power of President

- Article 123 empowers the President to promulgate ordinances during the recess of Parliament.
- These ordinances have the same force and effect as an Act of Parliament, but they are temporary in nature.
- The President can promulgate an ordinance only when both the Houses of Parliament are not in session or when either of the houses is not in session. That means the ordinance can only be issued at a time when a law cannot be passed. Thus, the ordinance making power of President is not a parallel power of legislation.
- Ordinances remain valid for a maximum of six weeks from the date Parliament reassembles after a recess, unless they are approved by both Houses earlier.
- It can also cease to operate before the period of six weeks if both the Houses of Parliament pass resolutions disapproving it.
  - The maximum life of an ordinance is 6 months and six weeks.
  - If the ordinance lapses without being placed before the Parliament then all acts done under it remain fully valid.
- The ordinance-making power is envisaged in the Constitution to deal with unforeseen or urgent matters. President's power of ordinance-making is not a discretionary power and he can promulgate or withdraw an ordinance only on the advice of the Council of Ministers headed by the Prime Minister.

- The ordinance making power in India is unique and it is not found in most of other democratic countries of the world like Britain and USA.

Ordinance Power and Judicial Review

- The Supreme Court of India ruled in RC Cooper *v/s* **Union of India (1970)** that the President's decision could be challenged on the grounds that immediate action was not necessary and that the ordinance had primarily been passed to avoid debate and discussion in the legislature.
- The **apex court** has established that judicial intervention is absolutely necessary. So, when the executive abuses its power to issue ordinances, the judiciary could intervene.
- As per the **38th Constitutional Amendment Act, 1975**, it made the promulgation of ordinances by the President, non-justiciable and beyond judicial review.
- **44th Constitutional Amendment** has reiterated that the satisfaction of the President to promulgate ordinance could be challenged in case an **immediate action** was not required.

Financial Powers

- No demand for a grant can be made except on his/her recommendation. Money Bill can be introduced in the Parliament only with the President's prior recommendation.
- The President can make advances out of the Contingency Fund of India to meet any unforeseen expenditure.
- The President constitutes a Finance Commission after every five years to recommend the distribution of the taxes between the Centre and the States.
- The President laid annual financial statement i.e., budget before the Parliament.

Diplomatic Powers

- The international treaties and agreements are negotiated and concluded on behalf of the President.
- However, they ultimately depend on the Approval of the Parliament.
- The President represents India in international forums and affairs.
- The President sends and receives diplomats like Ambassadors, High Commissioners and so on.

Military Powers

- As per Article 53(2), the President of India is the Supreme Commander of the Defence Forces of India.
- He/she appoints the Chiefs of the Army, the Navy and the Air Force.
- He/she can declare war or conclude peace, subject to the approval of the Parliament.

Emergency Powers

- National Emergency can be declared on grounds of war, external aggression or armed rebellion (Article 352). The President can proclaim this emergency only after receiving a written recommendation from the Cabinet.
- Powers acquired by the President during a National Emergency :
  - He can change the manner of distribution of financial resources between the Centre and the States.
  - He can suspend the Fundamental Rights of the citizens (except the rights under Articles 20 and 21).
- President's rule can be proclaimed in a state on grounds of failure of the Constitutional Machinery in the state (Article 356) or failure to comply with or to give effect to the directions given by the Union (Article 365).
- The President can proclaim Financial Emergency (Article 360), if he is satisfied that the financial stability or credit of India or any part there of is threatened.
- When a Financial Emergency is proclaimed, the President can give directions to the states to observe the canons of financial propriety.

Judicial Powers

- The President appoints the Chief Justice and the Judges of Supreme Court and High Courts.
- He can seek advice from the Supreme Court under Article 143 on any question of law or fact. However, the advice tendered by the Supreme Court is not binding on the President.
- He can grant pardon, reprieve, respite and remission of punishment or suspend, remit or commute the sentence of any person convicted of any offence including the punishment by a court martial punishment for an offence against a Union Law and death sentence.

Pardoning Power of President

- The President can issue the following orders of mercy to the convicted citizens of India under Article 72 :
  - Pardon It means absolving the convict of all guilt and punishment.
  - Commutation It is substitution of one form of punishment for a lighter form e.g. reduction of punishment from death sentence to life imprisonment.
  - Remission It is quantitative reduction of punishment without affecting nature of punishment, e.g. rigorous punishment for 2 years may be reduced for 1 year.
  - Respite It means reduction of punishment in view of a special fact such as disability of a person or pregnancy of woman.
  - Reprieve It implies a stay of death sentence or life imprisonment pending an appeal for pardon or commutation.

Comparison between Pardoning Powers of the President and the Governor

- The scope of pardoning power of the President under **Article 72** is wider than the Pardoning Power of the Governor under **Article 161**.
- Their powers differ in the following two ways:
  - The power of the President to grant pardon extends to cases where the punishment or sentence is by a **Court Martial**. But, **Article 161** does not provide any such power to the Governor.
  - The President can grant pardon in **all cases** where the sentence given is a sentence of death, but pardoning power of the Governor does not extend to death sentence cases. However, the Governor can suspend, remit or commute a death sentence.

Discretionary Powers

- The President of India almost always acts on the aid and advice of the Council of Ministers except under the following circumstances where he/she acts on his/her discretion :
  - In appointing the Prime Minister from among the contenders when no single party attains majority after elections to the Lok Sabha.
  - A Council of Ministers is voted out and after resigning advices the President to dissolve, the Lok Sabha and hold fresh elections (or resigns and advices so without being voted out).
  - The President is expected to exercise his discretion in such circumstances as much of the Lok Sabha's life may still be intact and it is worthwhile to explore the possibility of forming an alternative government.
  - President can refer a decision of an individual minister for the collective consideration of Council of Ministers.
  - When the Houses of the Parliament do not meet regularly, the President may act in his/her discretion and summon both the Houses of the Parliament.
  - While exercising a Pocket Veto, he can return the advice of the Council of Ministers once for its reconsideration or can return the bill passed by the Parliament once for its reconsideration.

Veto Powers

Under Article 111, a bill passed by the Parliament can become an act only if it receives the assent of the President. When such a bill is presented to the President for his assent, he has three alternatives:

(i) He may give his assent to the bill.

(ii) He may withhold his assent to the bill.

(iii) He may return the bill (if it is not a Money Bill) for reconsideration of the Parliament. However, if the bill is passed again by the Parliament with or without amendments and again presented to the President, the President must give his assent to the bill.

Types of Veto

- **Absolute Veto** The President does not give his assent to the bill
- **Suspensive Veto** The President's power to return a bill to Parliament with or without deliberation. (except money bill)
- **Qualified Veto** It can be overriden by the Legislature with a higher majority
- **Pocket Veto** An indirect veto that can be used by taking no actions on a bill

Veto Power of President with Respect to Bills Passed by State Legislature

- The Governor is empowered to reserve certain types of bills passed by the State Legislature for the consideration of the President.
- Then, the Governor will not have any further role in the enactment of the bill.
- The President can :
  - Give assent to the bill
  - Withhold his assent to the bill

- Direct the Governor to return the bill for reconsideration of the State Legislature. It is not mandatory for the President to give his assent if the bill is again passed by the State Legislature and sent again to him.

- The President can withhold his assent to such bills not only in the first instance but also in the second instance.
- Thus, the President enjoys absolute veto (and not suspensive veto) over state bills. Further, the President can exercise pocket veto in respect of State Legislation also.

Bills that Require Prior Recommendation of the President

- There are certain bills which can be introduced in the Parliament only on the recommendation of the President such as:
  - According to **Article 3**, a bill to alter the boundaries of the states or to change the names of the states.
  - A Money Bill as detailed in **Article 110**.
  - A Financial Bill (I) involving, **Article 110** but containing other provisions as well.
  - A Financial Bill (II) which is an Ordinary Bill but seeking to draw money from the Consolidated Fund of India can be taken up for **consideration** that is **reading two** in the process of passage of a bill.
- Legislation involving **Article 31A**. Any legislation involving items of taxation in which the states are interested or one that seeks to redefine agricultural income, etc.
- Additionally, the state bills that impose restrictions on the freedom of trade, commerce and intercourse within that state or with other states can only be introduced in the State Legislature on the prior recommendation of the President.

Constitutional Position of the President

- According to Article 53, the executive power of the union shall be vested in the President and shall be exercised by him either directly or through officers subordinate to him in accordance with the Constitution.
- As per Article 74, the President has to exercise his powers and functions with the aid and advice of the Council of Ministers headed by the Prime Minister.
- The 42nd Constitutional Amendment Act of 1976, has made the President bound by the advice of the Council of Ministers headed by the Prime Minister.
- The 44th Constitutional Amendment Act of 1978 has authorised the President to require the Council of Ministers to reconsider such advice either generally or otherwise. However, he/she shall act in accordance with the advice rendered after such reconsideration.

Presidents of India

Name	Tenure From-To	Important Facts
Dr. Rajendra Prasad	26th January, 1950 to 13th May, 1962	First President and also had the longest tenure (12 years).
Dr. S Radhakrishnan	13th May, 1962 to 13th May, 1967	Was also the first Vice-President of India.
Dr. Zakir Hussain	13th May, 1967 to 3rd May, 1969	Shortest tenure; First Muslim President; First President to die in office.
VV Giri (Vice-President)	3rd May, 1969 to 20th July, 1969	First Acting President of India
Justice M Hidayat-ullah (Acting)	20th July, 1969 to 24th August, 1969	Was also the Chief Justice of India and Second Acting President.
VV Giri	24th August, 1969 to 24th August, 1974	—
F. Ali Ahmed	24th August, 1974 to 11th February, 1977	Died in Office
BD Jatti (Acting)	11th February, 1977 to 25th July, 1977	Acting President
N. Sanjeeva Reddy	25th July, 1977 to 25th July, 1982	Youngest President (64 years)
Giani Zail Singh	25th July, 1982 to 25th July, 1987	First Sikh President
R Venkataraman	25th July, 1987 to 25th July, 1992	Oldest President (76 years)
Dr. SD. Sharma	25th July, 1992 to 25th July, 1997	—
KR Narayanan	25th July, 1997 to 25th July, 2002	First Dalit President
Dr. APJ Abdul Kalam	25th July, 2002 to 25th July, 2007	First scientist to become President
Mrs. Pratibha Patil	25th July, 2007 to 25th July, 2012	First woman to become President
Pranab Mukherjee	25th July, 2012 to 25 July, 2017	—
Ram Nath Kovind	25th July, 2017 to 21st July, 2022	Second Dalit President
Droupadi Murmu	21st July, 2022 to till date.	First Tribal woman President

****As on March, 2025***

> The Vice-President of India is the second highest Constitutional Office in India. He is accorded a rank next to the President in the Official Warrant of Precedence.

Chapter Eighteen

Vice-President

Article 63 of the Constitution provides for the Vice-President of India.

This office of Vice-President is taken from the American Constitution. According to Article 64, the Vice-President is the Ex-Officio Chairman of the Rajya Sabha.

ELECTION PROCES

- According to Article 66(1), the Vice-President is elected by an Electoral College consisting of members of both Houses of Parliament, in accordance with the system of proportional representation by means of the Single Transferable Vote and the voting in such election is by Secret Ballot.
- The Electoral College to elect a person to the office of the Vice-President consists of both elected and nominated members of the Parliament. It does not include the Members of the State Legislative Assemblies.
- The elections are held within 60 days after the expiry of term of existing Vice-President. Election to the office of the Vice-President is conducted by the Election Commission of India.
- As per Article 71(1), any disputes related to the election of the Vice-President are inquired into and decided by the Supreme Court whose decision is final.
- The election of a person as Vice-President cannot be challenged on the ground that the Electoral College was incomplete due to vacancy.
- If the election of a person as the Vice-President is declared void by the Supreme Court, acts done by him before the date of such declaration of the Supreme Court are not invalidated.
- As per Article 66(2), the Vice-President is not a member of either House of Parliament or of a House of a Legislature of any state. If a member of either House of Parliament or of a House of a Legislature of any state is elected as Vice-President, he/she is deemed to have vacated his seat in that House on the date he/she enters his office as Vice-President.

Vice-President

- **Qualifications/Eligibility** → Vice-President should be
  - A **citizen of India**
  - At least **35 years** of age
  - Qualified for election as members of **Rajya Sabha**
  - Not holding any office of profit under Government of India or State Government
- **Term of Office** → 5 years
- **Powers and Functions**
  - Ex-officio Chairman of Rajya Sabha
  - Discharge functions of President in his absence
- **Removal**
  - Can be removed from the office before the completion of his term.
  - No ground has been mentioned in the constitution
  - Resolution only in Rajya Sabha

Articles Related to Vice-President

Articles	Subject Matter
Article 63	Vice-President of India
Article 64	Vice-President as Ex-officio Chairman of the Council of States/Rajya Sabha
Article 65	Vice-President to discharge duties of President during absence or casual vacancy
Article 66	Election of Vice-President
Article 67	Term of the office of Vice-President
Article 68	Time of holding election to fill vacancy in office of Vice-President and term of office of person elected to fill casual vacancy
Article 69	Oath and affirmation of Vice-President
Article 70	Discharge of President's function in other contingencies
Article 71	Matters related to election of Vice-President

Vice-President's of India

Vice-Presidents	Tenures	Important Facts
Dr. Sarvepalli Radhakrishnan	13th May, 1952 to 12th May, 1962	First Vice-President, Longest Tenure (10 years)
Zakir Husain	13th May, 1962 to 12th May, 1967	Founder of Jamia Millia Islamia
Varahagiri Venkata Giri	13th May, 1967 to 3rd May, 1969	Shortest Tenure (2 year). First Vice-President who resigned first
Gopal Swarup Pathak	31st August, 1969 to 30th August, 1974	—
Basappa Danappa Jatti	31st August, 1974 to 30th August, 1979	—
Muhammad Hidayat-ullah	31st August, 1979 to 30th August, 1984	First Vice-President, who was Supreme Court Judge
Ramaswamy Venkataraman	31st August, 1984 to 24th July, 1987	—
Shankar Dayal Sharma	3rd September, 1987 to 24th July, 1992	The only Vice-President, who had been Chief Minister, Cabinet Minister and Congress President
Kocheril Raman Narayanan	21st August, 1992 to 24th July, 1997	—
Krishan Kant	21st August, 1997 to 27th July, 2002 (Died)	Died in office
Bhairon Singh Shekhawat	19th August, 2002 to 21st July, 2007	—
Muhammad Hamid Ansari	10th August, 2007 to 10th August, 2017	For two terms
Muppavarapu Venkaiah Naidu	11th August, 2017 to 10th August, 2022	—
Jagdeep Dhankhar	11th August, 2022 to Till Date	

***As on March, 2025**

The Prime Minister of India is the leader of Lok Sabha and real head of its government. The Council of Ministers headed by Prime Minister.

Chapter Nineteen

Prime Minister and Council of Ministers

CONSTITUTIONAL PROVISIONS

- In the scheme of the Parliamentary System of Government provided by the Constitution, the President is the nominal executive (de-jure) authority and the Prime Minister is the real executive (de-facto) authority He is the leader of ruling party and head of the government.
- Article 74 of the Constitution mentions the Prime Minister as the head of the Council of Ministers

Appointment of Prime Minister

- The procedure for the selection and appointment of the Prime Minister is not specified in the Constitution.
- Article 75 says that Prime Minister shall be appointed only by the President. However, this does not imply that the President is free to appoint anyone as the Prime Minister.
- Under normal circumstances, the President has to appoint the leader of the majority party in the Lok Sabha as the Prime Minister. But when no party has a clear majority in the Lok Sabha, then the President may exercise his/her personal discretion in the selection and appointment of the Prime Minister.
- This discretionary power was first exercised by President in 1979 when leader of coalition party Chaudhary Charan Singh was appointed as the Prime Minister.
- The President usually appoints the leader of the largest party or coalition in the Lok Sabha as the Prime Minister and asks him to seek a vote of confidence in the House within a month.
- The President may also exercise his discretion when the Prime Minister in office dies suddenly and there is no obvious successor.
- President Zail Singh exercised this discretion in 1984 when then Prime Minister Indira Gandhi was assassinated by appointing Rajiv Gandhi as the Prime Minister ignoring the precedent of appointing a caretaker Prime Minister.
- But in cases where after the death of the Prime Minister, the ruling party elects a new leader then the President is bound to appoint that person as the Prime Minister.
- The ruling of the Delhi High Court in 1980 held that the Constitution of India does not require a Prime Minister to prove their majority in the Lok Sabha before being appointed as the Prime Minister.
- Instead, the President may first appoint him and then ask him to prove majority within a reasonable timeframe. E.g. This appointment of VP Singh in 1989 and AB Vajpayee in 1996 and 1998.
- Constitutionally, Prime Minister is the leader of majority party in Lok Sabha and belongs to Lok Sabha only.
- But in history three Prime Ministers have been from Rajya Sabha e.g. IK Gujral (1997), Indira Gandhi (1966), Dr. Manmohan Singh (2004). In Britain, the Prime Minister should mandatorily belong to the Lower house or the house of commons only.

- A person who is not a member of either House of Parliament can be appointed as Prime Minister for six months, within which he should become a member of either House of Parliament.

Articles Related to Prime Minister Council of Ministers

Articles	Subject Matter
Article 74	Council of Ministers to aid and advice President
Article 75	Other provisions as to ministers
Article 77	Conduct of business of the Government of India
Article 78	Duties of Prime Minister with respect to furnishing of information to the President etc
Article 88	Rights of ministers with respect to the Houses

Qualifications

- He must be a citizen of India. He must be a member of either Rajya Sabha or Lok Sabha at the time of taking an oath or should be a member of any House within six months.
- He should have completed his 30 years if he is a member of the Rajya Sabha or can be 25 yearsof age, if he is a member of the Lok Sabha.

Oath or Affirmation

Before entering his office, the Prime Minister has to make and subscribe to an oath or affirmation. The President of India administers the oath of office to the Prime Minister.

Terms of Office

- The term of office of the Prime Minister is not fixed. He holds office during the pleasure of the President.
- President can't dismiss the Prime Minister, he can hold the position till he enjoys the majority in the Lok Sabha.
- He must resign, if he loses the confidence in Lok Sabha.

Salary And Allowances

- The Parliament determines the salary and allowances of the Prime Minister from time to time.
- He receives the same salary as given to a member of the Parliament.
- Also he gets other facilities such as medical facilities, free accommodation, travelling allowance, etc.
- The Parliament increased the sumptuary allowance in 2001 from ₹ 1,500 to ₹ 3,000 per month.

POWERS AND FUNCTIONS

Powers and functions of Prime Minister can be described as :

In Relation to the Council of Ministers

- The Prime Minister recommends to the President, those persons who are to be appointed as Ministers.
- The Prime Minister allocates and reshuffles various portfolios among the Ministers.
- The Prime Minister can ask a Minister to resign or advice the President to dismiss him/her.
- The Prime Minister presides over the meetings of the Council of Ministers and influences its decisions.
- The Prime Minister guides, directs, controls and co-ordinates the activities of all the ministers.
- The Prime Minister can cause the fall of the Council of Ministers by resigning from office.
- The resignation or death of a Prime Minister leads to the dissolution of the entire Council of Ministers.
- On the other hand, the resignation or death of any other minister only creates a vacancy which may or may not be filled.

In Relation to the President

- The Prime Minister advices the President with regard to the appointment of important officials like the Attorney-General of India, the Comptroller and Auditor-General of India, the Chairman and the Members of the Union Public Service Commission (UPSC), the Election Commissioners and so on.
- As per Article 78 he/she is the principal channel of communication between the President and the Council of Ministers.
- He communicates to the President all the decisions of the Council of Ministers relating to the administration of the affairs of the Union and proposals for Legislation.
- The Prime Minister furnishes such information relating to administration of the affairs of the Union and proposals for Legislation as the President may call for.
- The Prime Minister may also submit for the consideration of the Council of Ministers any matter on which a decision has been taken by a Minister but which has not been considered by the Council if the President says so.

In Relation to the Parliament

- The Prime Minister is the leader of the Lower House of the Parliament.
- The Speaker of Lok Sabha decides the agenda of the House in consultation with the Prime Minister.
- The Prime Minister advices the President with regard to the summoning and proroguing of the sessions of the Parliament.
- He can recommend dissolution of the Lok Sabha to the President at any time.
- The Prime Minister announces the government policies on the floor of the House. He/she has the right to intervene in any debate in the Parliament.

Prime Ministers of India

Names	Tenure From- To	Important Facts
Jawaharlal Nehru	15th August, 1947 to 27th May, 1964	First Prime Minister of India, died in office; also had the longest tenure (17 years).
Gulzari Lal Nanda (Acting)	27th May, 1964 to 9th June, 1964	First Acting Prime Minister.
Lal Bahadur Shastri	9th June, 1964 to 11th January, 1966	Only Prime Minister to die abroad during an official tour.
Gulzari Lal Nanda (Acting)	11th January, 1966 to 24th January, 1966	First to become Acting Prime Minister twice.
Indira Gandhi	24th January, 1966 to 24th March, 1977	First woman Prime Minister of India; First Prime Minister to lose an election. First member of Rajya Sabha who became Prime Minister.
Morarji Desai	24th March, 1977 to 28th July, 1979	Oldest Prime Minister (81 years) and the first to resign from office. First Chief Minister who became Prime Minister.
Chaudhary Charan Singh	28th July, 1979 to 14th January, 1980	Only Prime Minister who did not face the Parliament; also Chief Minister.
Indira Gandhi	14th January, 1980 to 31st October, 1984	First Prime Minister to be assassinated.
Rajiv Gandhi	31st October, 1984 to 2nd December, 1989	Youngest Prime Minister (40 years).
VP Singh	2nd December, 1989 to 10th November, 1990	First Prime Minister to step down after vote of no-confidence was passed.
Chandra Shekhar	10th November, 1990 to 21st June, 1991	He was also known as Jan-nayak.
PV Narasimha Rao	21st June, 1991 to 16th May, 1996	First Prime Minister from Southern India; he was not a member of either House of Parliament.
Atal Bihari Vajpayee	16th May, 1996 to 1st June, 1996	Shortest tenure of a Prime Minister.
HD Deve Gowda	1st June, 1996 to 21st April, 1997	Member of Rajya Sabha; also Chief Minister.
IK Gujral	21st April, 1997 to 19th March, 1998	He was the Minister of Information and broadcasting during the emergency.
Atal Bihari Vajpayee	19th March, 1998 to 29th April, 1999	He was the First non-Congress Prime Minister to serve a full term in the office.
Atal Bihari Vajpayee	3rd October, 1999 to 10th May, 2004	Vajpayee was one of the co-founders and a senior leader of the Bharatiya Janata Party.
Dr. Manmohan Singh	22nd May, 2004 to 26th May, 2014	First Sikh Prime Minister, Member of Rajya Sabha, longest tenure after Jawaharlal Nehru.
Narendra Modi	26th May, 2014 to till date	First Prime Minister, who was born after Independence.

******As on March, 2025***

Other Powers and Functions

- Prime Minister is the Chairman of NITI Aayog, National Development Council, National Integration Council, Inter-State Council and National Water Resources Council. He is the chief spokesperson of the Central Government.
- The decisions related to acceptance of titles like Bharat Ratna, Padma Vibhushan, Padma Bhushan and Padma Shri, etc are also taken by the Prime Minister. The Prime Minister is the Political Head of Armies. He plays a special role in strengthening the country's foreign policy.

- The National Disaster Management Authority (the appex statutory body for disaster management) is headed by the Prime Minister.

> **Deputy Prime Minister**
> There is no mention of Deputy Prime Minister in the Constitution. Deputy Prime Minister is appointed mostly due to political compulsion. Sardar Vallabhbhai Patel was the first Deputy Prime Minister during Prime Minister Nehru's time. Morarji Desai, Chaudhary Charan Singh, Jagjivan Ram, YB Charan, Devilal and LK Advani also worked as Deputy Prime Minister during the period of various Prime Ministers.

COUNCIL OF MINISTERS

- Article 74 and Article 75 deals with the provision regarding Council of Ministers.
- There shall be a Council of Ministers with the Prime Minister as a head to aid and advice the President, who shall in the exercise of his functions, act in accordance with such advice.
- Provided that the President may require the Council of Ministers to reconsider such advice, either generally or otherwise and the President shall act in accordance with the advice tendered after such reconsideration.
- The advice tendered by the Council of Ministers is bound to be accepted by the President including the suggestion of dissolution of Lok Sabha.
- The advice tendered to the President is confidential and no question can be raised on the advice, tendered in a Court of Law.
- The Prime Minister shall be appointed by the President and the other Ministers shall be appointed by the President on the advice of the Prime Minister.
- The Council of Ministers shall be collectively responsible to the lower house of the Parliament (Lok Sabha). The oaths of office and secrecy to a Minister shall be administered by the President.
- Parliament determines the salaries and allowances of the Ministers.
- The total number of Ministers, including the Prime Minister, in the Council of Ministers shall not exceed 15% of the total strength of the Lok Sabha. This provision was inserted in Article 75(1A) added by 91st Amendment Act of 2003.
- According to Article 75(5), every member of the Council of Ministers must be a member of the Lok Sabha or the Rajya Sabha or must be elected as a member of either House within six months after his appointment as a Minister; otherwise he may resign from the Council of Ministers.
- A member of either House of Parliament belonging to any political party, who is disqualified for being a member of that House under 10th Schedule shall also be disqualified to be appointed as a Minister.
- The Ministers shall hold office during the pleasure of the President.
- This means that the Ministers can be removed by the President at his/her will. However, all this is in practice used at the behest of the Prime Minister.
- There shall always be a Council of Ministers and there can arise no situation, where there can be no Prime Minister or no Council of Ministers.

Other Constitutional Provisions Related to Council of Ministers

Article 77
Conduct of Business of the Government of India
- This article says that all the executive actions of the government shall be taken in the name of the President.
- The President shall make rules for the more convenient transaction of the Government of India and for the allocation of the business to the Ministers.

Article 78
Duties of the Prime Minister
- It shall be the duty of the Prime Minister to convey all decisions of the Council of Ministers to the President.
- He shall also submit for the consideration of the Council of Ministers any matter on which a decision has been taken by a Minister but has not been taken up by the Council, if the President requires.

Article 88
Rights of Ministers as Respects the Houses
A Minister who is a member of one House of Parliament has the right to speak and to take part in the proceedings of the other House also as well as any joint sitting of the houses and any committee of Parliament in which the Minister may be named a member, but he can vote only in the House of which he is a member.

Appointment and Qualifications of Ministers

- The Ministers are appointed by the President on the advice of the Prime Minister.
- Generally, the members of Parliament (Lok Sabha and Rajya Sabha) are appointed as Ministers.
- A person who is not a member of Parliament can also be appointed as a minister but he has to become a member within 6 months otherwise he ceases to be a Minister.

Oath and Salary of Ministers

- The President administers the oath of office and secrecy to a Minister.
- The Minister swears to bear faith and allegiance to the Constitution of India, uphold the integrity and sovereignty of India, to faithfully and consciously discharge the duties of his office.
- To do right to all manner of people in accordance with the Constitution and Law.
- The salaries and allowances of Ministers are determined by the Parliament from time-to-time.
- The Ministers get salary equivalent to that of a Member of Parliament (MP).

Composition of the Council of Ministers

- The Constitution of India does not categorise the Ministers.
- But by convention the Council of Ministers consists of the three categories of Ministers.
- Sometimes, due to political reasons the Council of Ministers may also include a Deputy Prime Minister.

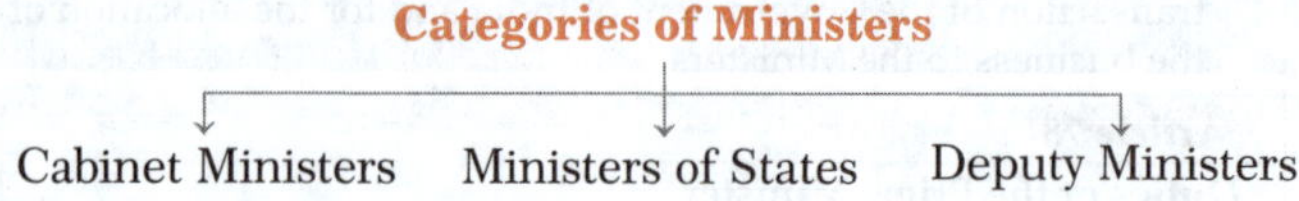

Cabinet Ministers

- They are seniormost members of Council of Ministers, who act as head of important Ministries of the Central Government. e.g., Defence Ministry, Home Ministry, Finance Ministry, etc.
- They are the integral part of Cabinet, as a result of which, they play a very important role in framing policies.
- The Constitution originally did not indicate the word Cabinet. However, this word was inserted by the 44th Constitutional Amendment Act with regard to emergency provisions.
- The Cabinet refers to an elite group within the Council of Ministers who hold powerful portfolios like defence, home, finance, etc.
- The rest of the Council of Ministers attend Cabinet meetings only when they are called to do so.
- Cabinet meetings are usually held every week to take stock of the state affairs.
- A new precedent of Group of Ministers (GoMs) has been established to scrutinise complex issues that requires the expertise of academicians and think-tanks also. Only Cabinet Ministers occupy the GoM's.

Ministers of State

- Second in rank and they can be given independent charge of Ministries or can be attached to the Cabinet Ministers.
- When attached to the Cabinet Ministers, they work under the guidance of Cabinet Ministers.
- The difference from the Cabinet Ministers lie in the fact that, they do not attend the Cabinet meetings as they are not the part of Cabinet (unless specially invited when something related to their Ministry is being considered by the Cabinet).

Deputy Ministers

- Juniormost and they are never given independent charge of Ministry (unlike Ministers of State) and always remain attached to the Cabinet Ministers or Ministers of State. They assist to discharge the political, administrative and Parliamentary duties effectively. They are neither part of Cabinet nor attend the Cabinet meetings.
- The Parliamentary secretaries are also a kind of Ministers but they are not the members of the Council of Ministers and they have no department.
- They are appointed by the Prime Minister, unlike the Council of Ministers who are appointed by the President.

Kitchen Cabinet

- The Cabinet, a small body consisting of the Prime Minister as its head and some 15 to 20 most important Ministers is the highest decision-making body in the formal sense.
- However, in practice, a still smaller body called the inner Cabinet or kitchen Cabinet has become the real centre of power.
- The Kitchen Cabinet consists of the Prime Minister and a few influential persons.
- These persons can be Cabinet Ministers and also outsiders like friends, family members, etc.
- In India, every prime minister has had his 'Inner Cabinet'. E.g. Indira Gandhi had a very powerful 'kitchen cabinet'.
- Kitchen cabinet has several advantages over a large cabinet as its smaller size makes it more efficient and helps the Prime Minister to maintain secrecy.

- In the USA and Britain, the kitchen cabinet is a very powerful body and influences the decisions of the government.

> **Care Taker Government**
>
> It is the government in the interregnum which comes into existence as soon as the Council of Ministers resign or lose confidence or the Prime Minister dies. It lasts till the next Council of Ministers is formed. It is the constitutional necessity under Article 74.

- No legal responsibility of Ministers as :
  - The Constitution does not have any provision for the legal responsibility of a Minister.
  - A Minister is not required to countersign an order of the President.
  - Also the courts cannot inquire into the nature of advice given to the President by the Ministers.

CABINET COMMITTEES

- The Cabinet Committee is institutional arrangements to reduce the workload of the Cabinet.
- These committees are extra-constitutional in nature and are nowhere mentioned in the Constitution.
- The executive works under the Government of India, Transaction of Business Rules of 1961.
- There are two types of Cabinet Committees i.e., Standing and Ad-hoc.
- Standing Committees are permanent in nature and are various types namely; Political Affairs Committee, Economic Affairs Committee, Appointment Committee and Parliamentary Affairs Committee while Adhoc Committees are temporary in nature and constituted from time-to-time, to deal with special problems.
- The Prime Minister constitutes Standing Committees of the Cabinet and sets out the specific functions assigned to them.
- The strength of each committee varies from three to eight members. It usually includes Cabinet Ministers but non-Cabinet members are not debarred.
- At present, there are Eight Cabinet Committees :
  (i) Cabinet Committee on Political Affairs.
  (ii) Cabinet Committee on Economic Affairs.
  (iii) Appointments Committee of the Cabinet.
  (iv) Cabinet Committee on Security.
  (v) Cabinet Committee on Parliamentary Affairs.
  (vi) Cabinet Committee on Accommodation.
  (vii) Cabinet Committee on Investment and Growth.
  (viii) Cabinet Committee on Employment and Skill Development.
- All committees except Cabinet Committee on Accommodation and Cabinet Committee on Parliamentary Affairs are headed by the Prime Minister.

CABINET SECRETARIAT

- The Cabinet Secretariat supervises and co-ordinates the function of Cabinet Ministers which constitutes the Cabinet Secretariat.
- The Cabinet Secretariat functions directly under the Prime Ministers. Its administrative head is the Cabinet Secretary who is also the Ex-Officio Chairman of the civil services board.
- It conveys the directives of the Cabinet or the Prime Minister on administration and allied matters. It co-ordinates among the Cabinet Committee.
- It is essentially a Secretariat to aid and advice the Cabinet and through it to the Prime Minister, President, Parliament and various Ministers of the Central Secretariat.
- It is the successor of the Secretariat of the Executive Council of Viceroy.

> **The Prime Minister's Secretariat**
>
> - It is an extra constitutional body created to assist the Prime Minister in discharging his ever growing functions.
> - It came into being on **15th August, 1947**. Since June, 1977, it is known as **Prime Minister's Office** (PMO). It is head by the Principal Secretary to the Prime Minister.
> - In this, Prime Minister takes the aid and advice from his personal secretarial experts and staff members.
> - It is meant to objectively analyse and legally process the advice rendered by the Prime Minister.
> - It occupies the status of a department of the Government of India under the allocation of **Business Rule of 1961** and has no attached sub-ordinate officer under it.
> - So far the question, as to which body is more important, it has shifted from one secretariat to the other depending on the style of working of the Prime Minister over the years.

"In the Parliament of India, a bicameral system has been adopted under the Parliamentary system. The Parliament comprises the President, the Rajya Sabha (Upper House) and the Lok Sabha (Lower House).

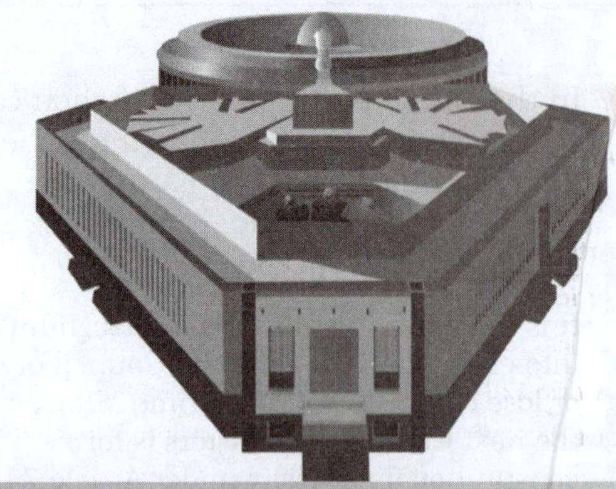

Chapter Twenty

Parliament

The Parliament is the Supreme Legislative Institution of India. It occupies a central position in the Indian democratic political system due to adoption of the Parliamentary form of government. It is also known as West minster Model of Government. The first general elections under the new Constitution were held during the year 1951-1952 and first elected Parliament came into being in April, 1952.

Articles 79 to 122 in Part V of the Constitution deal with the organisation, composition, duration officers, procedures, privileges, powers and so on of the Parliament.

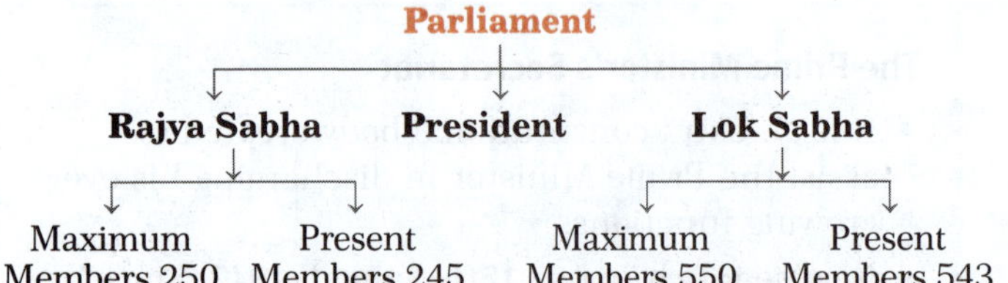

COMPOSITION OF PARLIAMENT

- According to Article 79, Parliament consists of the President and the two Houses, the Council of States and the House of the People.
- In 1954, the Hindi names Rajya Sabha and Lok Sabha were adopted by the Parliament for the Council of States and the House of the People respectively.
- Rajya Sabha represents the States and Union Territories of the country while Lok Sabha represents the people of India.
- Article 87(1) of the Constitution provides for the Presidential address at the commencement of the first session after each general election to the House of the people and at the commencement of the first session of each year.
- The President shall address both the Houses of Parliament assembled together and inform Parliament of the cause of its summons.
- The President is neither the member of Lok Sabha nor the Rajya Sabha but he is an integral part of the Parliament.
- This is in line with the Parliamentary form of government followed in Britain where the Parliament consists of the Crown (King or queen) , house of lords (upper house) and the house of commons (lower house).
- In the USA, the legislature (known as Congress) consists of the senate (upper house) and the House of representatives (lower house).
- The American President is not an integral part of the Congress.

Important Articles Related to Parliament

Articles	Subject Matters
Article 79	Constitution of Parliament
Article 80	Composition of the Council of States/Rajya Sabha
Article 81	Composition of the House of People/Lok Sabha
Article 83	Duration of the Houses of Parliament
Article 84	Qualification for membership of Parliament
Article 85	Sessions, Prorogation and Dissolution
Article 89	Chairman and Deputy Chairman of Council of States
Article 93	Speaker and Deputy Speaker of the House of People
Article 102	Disqualification for membership
Article 105	Powers and Privileges of the House of Parliament
Article 108	Joint Sitting of the Houses
Article 110	Definition of Money Bills

Articles	Subject Matters
Article 111	Assent to Bills
Article 112	Annual Financial Statement
Article 114	Appropriation Bills
Article 116	Votes on account
Article 117	Finance Bills
Article 120	Language used in Parliament
Article 122	Courts not to inquire into Parliamentary proceedings

Qualifications of the Members of Parliament

- Members of Parliament should be a citizen of India and at least 25 years of age in case of Lok Sabha and 30 years of age in case of Rajya Sabha.
- He/she should make an oath or affirmation stating that he will bear true faith and obedience to the Constitution of India and uphold the sovereignty and integrity of India.
- Elections are to be conducted through an open voting system in case of Rajya sabha and secret ballot system in case of Lok Sabha.
- He/she must possess such other qualifications as may be laid down by the Parliament by law.
- There are two more qualifications for the members of Parliament as specified in the Representation of People Act (1951)
    - The candidate must be registered as a voter in any parliamentary constituency. Any Indian citizen can contest the Rajya Sabha elections irrespective of the state in which he resides.
    - The candidate who wants to contest a reserved seat for SC's and ST's must be a member of these communities.

Salaries and Emoluments of Members

- According to Article 106, each member of the House gets salary and emoluments as established by law.
- In this regard, the salary, allowances and pension of Members of Parliament Act, 1954 has been formed.
- The Constitution did not contain the provision of pension. However, the Parliament in 1976 provided the pension to the members.

RAJYA SABHA

- Rajya Sabha is the Upper House of India's bicameral legislature. The Rajya Sabha was designed by the framers of the Indian Constitution as a check on the power of the Lok Sabha.
- The elected members of the State's Legislative Assemblies elect the members of the Rajya Sabha on the basis of proportional representation through the Single Transferable Vote System.

Structure of the Rajya Sabha

- Article 80 of the Constitution provides for the composition of Council of States/Rajya Sabha.
- The Rajya Sabha or Council of States consists of not more than 250 members. It is a permanent body as it cannot be dissolved.
- Out of 250 members, the President nominates 12 members on the basis of their excellence in the field of literature, science, art and social service and the rest are elected.
- All the states do not send an equal number of members to the Rajya Sabha. Their representation is decided on the basis of the population of respective states. Thus, the bigger state gets bigger representation and the smaller ones have lesser representation.

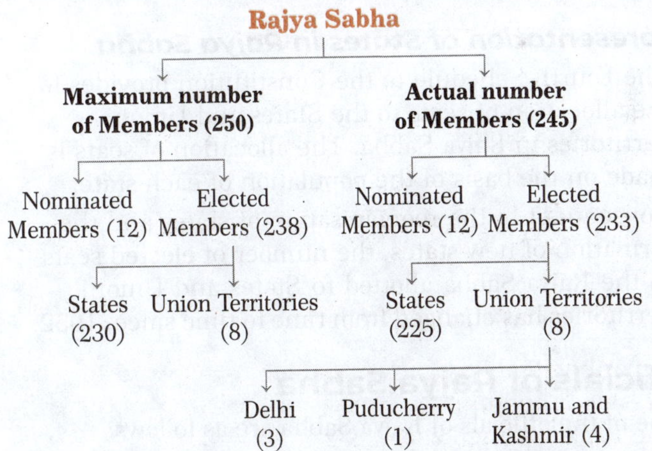

Election Procedure in Rajya Sabha

- The members of the Rajya Sabha are elected by the elected members of the respective State Legislative Assembly in accordance with the principle of proportional representation by the means of single transferable vote.

Formula for required votes in Election to Rajya Sabha

$$= \left(\frac{\text{Total number of votes}}{\text{Number of Rajya Sabha seats}}\right) + 1$$

e.g., Rajasthan Legislative Assembly has a strength of 200.

- If there are 4 seats for Rajya Sabha in Rajasthan, then a candidate has to get at least 41 votes to be elected.
- The Rajya Sabha members from Union territories are indirectly elected by an electoral college which is especially formed for this purpose.
- This election is also held in accordance with a system of proportional representation by means of single transferable vote.
- Rajya Sabha has the representation of UT's of Delhi, Puducherry and Jammu and Kashmir. Other UT's don't have a significant population to have representation in the house.

Tenure of Rajya Sabha

- As per Article 83(1), Rajya Sabha is a permanent House and is not subject to dissolution.
- There is no fixed term provided in the Constitution for the members of the Rajya Sabha.
- Parliament in the Representation of the People Act (1951) has specified the tenure of six years for the Rajya Sabha members.
- One-third of its members retire after every two years. They are entitled to contest again for membership.
- Mid-term elections take place to fill vacancies at the beginning of ever third year.

Representation of States in Rajya Sabha

- The Fourth Schedule to the Constitution provides for the allocation of seats to the States and Union Territories in Rajya Sabha. The allocation of seats is made on the basis of the population of each state.
- Consequent to the reorganisation of states and the formation of new states, the number of elected seats in the Rajya Sabha allotted to States and Union Territories has changed from time to time since, 1952.

Officials of Rajya Sabha

Some of the officials of Rajya Sabha are as follows:

Presiding Officers of Rajya Sabha

- As per Article 89, the Vice-President of India is the Ex-Officio Chairman of Rajya Sabha.
- Rajya Sabha also elects one of its members to be the Deputy Chairman.
- When the Chairman acts as the President of India, duties of the Office of the Chairman shall be performed by the Deputy Chairman.
- Deputy Chairman also acts as a Chairman when the latter is absent from the sitting of the house. He has all the powers of the Chairman while performing these duties.
- He is not subordinate to the Chairman and is directly responsible to the Rajya Sabha.
- The function of the Chairman are similar to the Speaker in so far to conduct the orderly business of the House.

Rajya Sabha Secretariat

- The Secretariat of Rajya Sabha was set-up pursuant to the provisions contained in Article 98 of the Constitution.
- Parliament may by law regulate the recruitment and the conditions of service of persons appointed to the secretarial staff of either House of Parliament.
- The Rajya Sabha Secretariat functions under the overall guidance and control of the Chairman, Rajya Sabha.
- It is headed by a Secretary-General who is a permanent officer appointed by the presiding officer of the house.
- The main activities of the Secretariat are to provide secretarial assistance and support to the effective functioning of the Council of States (Rajya Sabha).

Panel of Vice-Chairman of Rajya Sabha

- The Chairman of Rajya Sabha, from time to time, nominates from amongst the members of the House.
- They cannot preside over the house when the office of Chairman and Deputy Chairman is vacant.
- In this case the duties of the Chairman are performed by the member of the house which the president may appoint for the purpose.
- In the absence of the Chairman and the Deputy Chairman, one of them presides over the House.
- In nominating members to the panel of Vice-Chairman, the Chairman gives consideration to the strength of various parties in the House and as per convention selects some members from the opposition parties/groups for nomination to the panel.
- The Chairman may also consult the leaders of political parties/groups for the purpose before making a final choice.

LOK SABHA

- The Lower House or the House of the people is popularly known as Lok Sabha.
- Its member are directly elected by the people on the basis of a Universal Adult Franchise.

Structure of Lok Sabha

- The maximum permissible membership of Lok Sabha is 550 out of which 530 are directly elected from the states while 20 members are elected from the Union Territories.
- The distribution of seats among the states is based on the principle of territorial representation which means each state is allotted seats on the basis of its population in proportion to the total population of all the states.
- Each state is divided into territorial units called constituencies which are more or less of the same size with regard to the population.
- Every Indian citizen who has attained 18 years of age and is not disqualified under the provisions of the Constitution or any law is eligible to vote in Lok Sabha elections.
- The 61st Constitutional Amendment Act, 1988 reduced the voting age from 21 to 18 years.

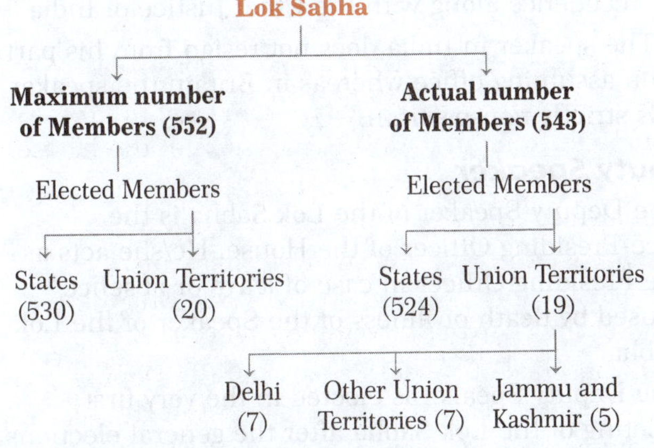

Tenure of Lok Sabha

- The normal term of Lok Sabha is five years. But the President, on the advice of the Council of Ministers, may dissolve it before the expiry of five years.
- In the case of a National Emergency, its term can be extended for one year at a time. But it will not exceed six months after the emergency is over.

Allocation of Seats to States

- Every state in India, is allocated seats in Lok Sabha according to proportion to their population. This provision is made in Article 81(2) of the Indian Constitution.
- This provision is only applicable if the state's population exceeds 60 lakhs.

Reservation in Lok Sabha

- According to **Article 330**, there is a provision of reservation of seats in Lok Sabha for Scheduled Tribes and Scheduled Castes on the basis of proportion of their population.
- At present, **84 seats** for Scheduled Castes and **47 seats** for Scheduled Tribes are reserved in Lok Sabha.

Election to the Lok Sabha

- For the purpose of holding direct elections to the Lok Sabha, each state is divided into territorial constituencies for uniformity of representation in following two respects :
  - Between the different states.
  - Between the different constituencies in the same state.
- Readjustment is made in allocation of seats in the Lok Sabha and division of each state into territorial constituencies after every census.
- This manner of this readjustment is to be decided by the Parliament. Hence, the Parliament enacted the delimitation commission acts in 1952, 1962, 1972 and 2002.
- The 42nd Amendment Act of 1976, froze allocation constitutional of seats in the Lok Sabha to the States and the Territorial Constituencies till the year 2000 at the 1971 level.
- This ban on readjustment was extended upto year 2026 by the 84th Amendment Act of 2001.
- The Constitution has adopted the first-past-the-post system (or the system of territorial representation) for the election of the members to the Lok Sabha.

Presiding Officers of the Lok Sabha

Some of officials of the Lok Sabha are as follows :

- Speaker is the Presiding Officer of Lok Sabha.
- The members of the House elect him. He/she remains in position even after Lok Sabha is dissolved till the election of a new Speaker is done in his place by next Lok Sabha.
- The term of the office of the speaker is 5 years however, he may vacate his seat earlier if he ceases to be a member of the Lok Sabha, if he resigns by writing to Deputy

Speaker or when he is removed by passing a resolution with effective majority of the Lok Sabha.

Speakers of Lok Sabha

Speakers	Tenure
Ganesh Vasudev Mavalankar (Died)	1952-1956
M. Ananthasayanam Ayyangar	1956-1962
Hukam Singh	1962-1967
Neelam Sanjiva Reddy (Resigned)	1967-1969
Gurdial Singh Dhillon	1969-1975
Bali Ram Bhagat	1976-1977
Neelam Sanjiva Reddy (Resigned)	1977-1977
KS Hegde	1977-1980
Balram Jakhar	1980-1989
Rabi Ray	1989-1991
Shivraj V Patil	1991-1996
PA Sangma	1996-1998
GMC Balayogi (Died)	1998-2002
Manohar Gajanan Joshi	2002-2004
Somnath Chatterjee	2004-2009
Ms. Meira Kumar	2009-2014
Ms. Sumitra Mahajan	2014-2019
Om Birla	2019-Till Date

(As on March, 2025)

Powers and Functions of Speaker

- The Speaker has extensive function to perform in matters of administrative and parliamentary business nature. His/her decision are final and binding. Under the Constitution, the Speaker enjoys a special position :
  - He/she certifies a bill to be a Money Bill under Article 110 and his/her decision is final.
  - He/she presides over joint sittings called for the resolution of a disagreement between the two Houses.
  - Decides whether cut motion, no-confidence motion etc., to be admitted or not.
  - Decides the disqualification of members under the Tenth Schedule.
  - Maintains the orderly conduct of business and decorum of the House.
  - Appoints the Chairman of different parliamentary committees.
  - The Speaker chairs, the Business Advisory committee, Rules committee and General Purpose committee.
  - When the Lok Sabha is dissolved, all the Members of the Lok Sabha cease to be the Member of the Lok Sabha. However, the Speaker continues in there office till the next Lok Sabha is constituted.
  - The Speaker is the final interpreter of the provisions of (a) Constitution (b) Rules of Procedure and Conduct of Business of Lok Sabha (c) The Parliamentary Precedents in the House.
  - She or he holds the casting vote (a vote that someone may exercise to resolve a tied vote in a deliberative body) in case of a tie between both the Houses.
  - She or he adjourns the House or suspends the meeting in the absence of a Quorum.
  - She or he acts as the Ex-officio Chairman of Indian Parliamentary Group and Conference of Presiding Officers of Legislative Bodies in the country.
  - She or he can allow secret meeting of the House at the request of Leader of the House.
  - She or he has security of tenure, salary is fixed by Parliament and their powers of regulation are not subject to jurisdiction of any court.
  - The work and conduct of the speaker cannot be discussed in the Lok Sabha unless a substantive motion is passed.
  - The speaker is ranked seventh in the order of precedence along with the Chief Justice of India.
  - The speaker in India does not resign from his party on assuming office whereas in Britain the speaker is strictly non-partisan.

Deputy Speaker

- The Deputy Speaker of the Lok Sabha is the Vice-Presiding Officer of the House. He/she acts as the Presiding Officer in case of leave or absence caused by death or illness of the Speaker of the Lok Sabha.
- The Deputy Speaker is elected in the very first meeting of the Lok Sabha after the general elections for a term of Five years from amongst the Members of the Lok Sabha.
- He/she holds office till either he/she ceases to be a Member of the Lok Sabha or they themselves resign from the Lok Sabha.
- He/she can be removed from office by a resolution passed in the Lok Sabha by effective majority its members.
- The Deputy Speaker is not subordinate to the Speaker. She/he is directly responsible to the House.

The Deputy Speaker also presides over the joint sitting of both the Houses of Parliament when the speaker is absent.

- When the Deputy Speaker is appointed as a member of a Parliamentary Committee he automatically becomes its Chairman.

Secretary of Lok Sabha

He is the permanent official of Lok Sabha and he is accountable to the Speaker. He invites members of Lok Sabha to its proceedings on behalf of the President.

Pro-tem Speaker

- Pro-tem Speaker is chosen for the conduct of the house when the Lok Sabha has been elected and the vote for the Speaker and Deputy Speaker has not taken place.
- Pro-tem Speaker is the temporary Speaker who presides over the first meeting of the Lower House of Parliament after the general elections besides presiding over the sitting in which the Speaker and Deputy Speaker are elected if it is a newly constituted House.
- Usually, the seniormost member of the House is selected for the post.

Panel of Chairpersons of Lok Sabha

- According to Lok Sabha rules, the Speaker appoints a panel of not more than 10 chairpersons from among the members.
- Any of them has the same authority as the Speaker when presiding over the House in the absence of the Speaker or the Deputy Speaker. He or she serves in that capacity until a new panel of chairpersons is proposed.
- However, when the position of Speaker or Deputy Speaker is vacant, a member of the panel of chairpersons cannot preside over the House. The President may designate some members of the House to fill the Speaker's position during that period.

Powers and Functions of the Parliament

Legislative Powers

- Parliament plays the primary role as a law-making body from the country.
- It has the exclusive power to make laws on the subjects enumerated in the Union list and the residuary subjects. It also has overriding powers over subjects in Concurrent Lists.
- Parliament can also make laws on state list when Rajya Sabha passes a resolution to that effect, during national emergency or President's rule, when two or more states request the Parliament or to give effect to international agreements, treaties and conventions.
- An ordinance issued by the President during the recess of the Parliament ceases to have effect if it is not approved by the Parliament within six weeks after it re-assembles.

Executive Powers

- The executive organ of the government is responsible to the Parliament for its policies and actions.
- Parliament can move and adopt several types of resolutions and motions such as adjournment motion, call attention motion, censure motion and no-confidence motion and Parliamentary procedures such as question hour, zero hour etc to exercise control over the executive.
- Several committees of the Parliament supervise the activities of the executive. e.g., the committee on government assurances, committee on petitions, etc.
- The Ministers have collective responsibility to the Parliament and there is also an individual responsibility of the Ministers.
- The Ministers remain in office so long as they enjoy the confidence of the majority in the Lok Sabha. The Lok Sabha can remove the Council of Ministry by passing a vote of no-confidence against it.

Financial Powers

- The executive cannot levy or collect any tax and cannot incur any expenditure without the approval of the Parliament. Hence, the budget is laid before the Parliament for its approval and enactment.
- The financial committees of the Parliament scrutinise government spending and financial performance and report about improper and unauthorised public expenditure.

Judicial Powers

- Parliament takes part in the impeachment process of the President for the violation of the Constitution.
- The Parliament can also remove the Vice-President from his office.
- The Parliament recommends the President regarding the removal of Judges of the Supreme Court and High Court, Chief Election Commissioner, State Election Commissioner and Comptroller Auditor-General (CAG).

- The Parliament can punish any person whether its members or outsiders for the breach of privileges or its contempt.

Amendment Powers

Rajya Sabha and Lok Sabha can together amend the Constitution by passing an Amendment Bill with two-third majority in each House.

Electoral Powers

- The Parliament also performs some electoral functions. The elected members of the Lok Sabha and Rajya Sabha take part in the election of the President.
- Members of the Lok Sabha and the Rajya Sabha together elect the Vice-President of India according to Article 66of Indian Constitution.
- The Members of the Lok Sabha elect a Speaker and a Deputy Speaker and the members of the Rajya Sabha elect a Deputy Chairman from amongst themselves.

Comparison between Lok Sabha and Rajya Sabha

- Under Article 75(3)of the Constitution, the Council of Ministers is collectively responsible to Lok Sabha, which means Rajya Sabha cannot make or unmake the government. It can, however, exercise control over the government and this function becomes quite prominent, particularly when the government does not enjoy majority in Rajya Sabha.
- Ministers may belong to either House of Parliament. has the right to speak and take part in the proceedings of either House, but he/she is entitled to vote only in the House of which, he is a member.
- Similarly, with regard to powers, privileges and immunities of the Houses of Parliament, their members and committees thereof, the two Houses are placed absolutely on equal footing by the Constitution.

Equal Powers of Rajya Sabha and Lok Sabha

- Rajya Sabha and the Lok Sabha enjoys equal powers in the introduction and passage of ordinary bills, constitutional amendment bills and financial bills involving expenditure from the Consolidated Fund of India.
- As per Articles 54and 61, equal right with the Lok Sabha in the election and impeachment of the President.
- As per Article 66equal right with the Lok Sabhain the election and removal of the Vice-President. However, Rajya Sabhaalone can initiate the removal of the Vice-President.
- He is removed by a resolution passed by the Rajya Sabha by a special majority and agreed by the Lok Sabha by a simple majority.
- As per Article 105 equal right with the Lok Sabha to make law defining Parliamentary privileges and also to punish for contempt.
- Equal right with the Lok Sabha to approve the Proclamation of Emergency (issued under Article 352), proclamations regarding failure of the constitutional machinery in states (issued under Article 356) and even a sole right in certain circumstances.
- Enlargement of the jurisdiction of the Supreme Court and the UPSC
- Equal rights in making recommendations to the President for the removal of Chief Justice of Indiaand other Judges of Supreme Court and High Courts, Chief Election Commissioner and Comptroller and Auditor-General.
- Approval of ordinances issued by the President.

Special Powers of Lok Sabha

Lok Sabha has superior powers regarding Money Bills (introduction, passage and amendments) and Financial Bills, not containing solely the matters of Article 110

- The Lok Sabha has vast financial powers. A Money Bill can be introduced only in the Lok Sabha as per the provisions given under Article 109
- After having been passed by it, the Money Bill goes to the Rajya Sabha.
- In case of any dispute as to whether a particular bill is a Money Bill or not, the Speaker of the Lok Sabha gives the decision.
- His decision is final and it cannot be challenged in any court or even in the Rajya Sabha or the Lok Sabha.
- The Speaker of Lok Sabha presides over the joint sitting of both the Houses.
- The Lok Sabha with greater number wins the battle in a joint sitting except when the combined strength of the ruling party in both Houses in less than that of opposition parties.
- Rajya Sabha can only discuss the budget, but cannot vote on the demands for grants.

- A resolution for the discontinuance of the National Emergencycan be passed only by the Lok Sabha and not by the Rajya Sabha.
- The Rajya Sabha cannot remove the Council of Ministers by Passing a no-confidence motion.
- This is because the Council of Ministers is collectively responsible only to the Lok Sabha.

Sovereignty of Parliament

- The doctrine of Sovereignty of Parliament comes from the British Parliament which translates into an understanding that the supreme power lies within the state.
- The Indian Parliament is not regarded as a sovereign body since there are legal restrictions on its authority and jurisdiction. Factors which limit Parliament's sovereignty are :
  - Written Nature of Constitution
  - Federal System of Government
  - System of Judicial Review

Special Powers of Rajya Sabha with Respect to Lok Sabha

Legislation on State Matters

- As a federal chamber, it can initiate Central intervention in the State Legislative Field.
- Article 249of the Constitution provides that the Rajya Sabha may pass resolution, by a majority or not less than two-third of the memberspresent and voting, to the effect that it is necessary or expedient in the national interest that Parliament should make laws with respect to any matter enumerated in the State List
- If such a resolution is adopted, Parliament will be authorised, to make laws on the subject specified in the resolution, for the whole or any part of the Territory of India
- Such a resolution will remain in force for such period, not exceeding one year, as may be specified therein, but this period can be extended by one year at a time by passing further resolution.

Creation of All India Services

- Another exclusive power of the Rajya Sabha is contained in Article 312 of the Constitution wherein if the Rajya Sabha passes a resolution by a majority of not less than two-third of the members present and voting declaring that it's necessary or expedient in the national interest to create one or more.
- All India Services common to the Union and the States, Parliament will have the power to create by law such services.

Approval of Proclamation

- The provision to Clause (4)of the Article 352of the Constitution, inter-alia(means 'among other things'), provides that if a Proclamation of Emergency is issued when the House of the People remains dissolved and a resolution approving the proclamation is passed by the Council of States.
- The proclamation would be legally effective up to a maximum period of 30 daysfrom the date on which the House of the People first sits after its reconstitution.
- This provision, therefore, appears to suggest that there might be an occasion when the Council of States could be called into a session at a time when the House of People stands dissolved.
- The provision to Clause (3)of the Article 356of the Constitution which relates to the proclamation to be issued by the President in case of failure of constitutional machinery in a state, contains a similar stipulation.

Disqualifications for Membership of Parliament

Disqualifications for Membership of Parliament are defined as :

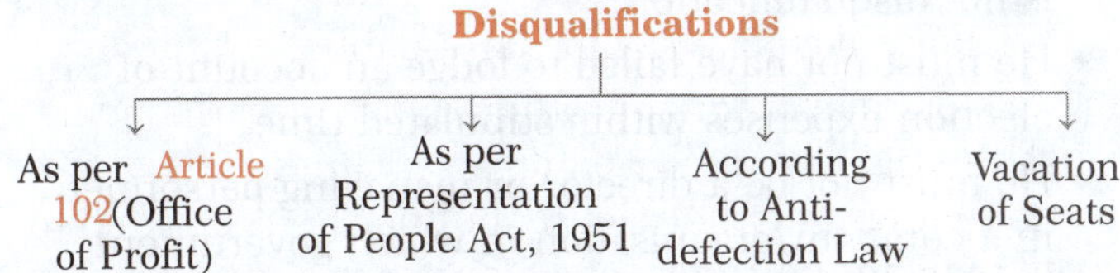

- According to Article 102 A person shall be disqualified from being a member of House of the Parliament :
  - if he or she holds an office of profit under the Government of India or the government of any state other than the office declared by the Parliament by law not disqualify its holder;
  - if he or she is of unsound mind and stand so declared by a competent court;
  - if he or she is an undischarged insolvent;
  - if he or she is not a citizen of India or has voluntarily acquired the citizenship of foreign state.
  - if he or she is so disqualified by or under any law made by Parliament.

Office of Profit

- The term is used in Article 102(1)(a) and 191(1)(a) of the Indian Constitution which bars a member of the Indian Parliament and State Legislatures from holding an office that would give its occupant the opportunity to gain a financial advantage or benefit.
- It refers to a post under Central/State Government which yields salaries, perks and other benefits.
- The actual amount of profit gained during the violation has no bearing on its classification.
- India had the **Parliament (Prevention of Disqualification) Act, 1950, 1951** and **1953** exempting certain posts from being recorded as offices of profit.
- All these Acts were replaced by the Parliament **(Prevention of Disqualification) Act, 1959**. By virtue of **Section 3** of the said Act, certain offices did not disqualify their holders from being members of Parliament. The law was again amended in 2006.

Representation of People Act, 1951

- Some additional conditions for disqualification as per the Representation of People Act, 1951 are :
  - He must not have been found guilty of certain election offences and corrupt practices.
  - He must not have been convicted for any offence that results in imprisonment for two or more years. However, detention under preventive detention law is not disqualification.
  - He must not have failed to lodge an account of election expenses within stipulated time.
  - He must not be a director or managing personnel in a company/organisation in which government has atleast 25% share.
  - He must not have been dismissed from government service due to corruption or disloyalty to state.
  - He must not be interested in government contracts, works and services.

Disqualification According to Anti-Defection Law

- The Anti-Defection Law was passed in 1985 by the 52nd Constitutional Amendment, which added the Tenth Schedule to the Constitution.
- The main objective of the law was to abolish the evils of political defection.
- The 91st Constitutional Amendment Act, 2003 provided disqualification on the ground of defection not to apply in case of split.
- The power to disqualify a member rests with the Chairman or the Speaker of the House.
- A person shall not be disqualified if his/her original political party merges with another and he and other members of the political party welcome members of the new political party.
- Under the Tenth Schedule, the grounds of disqualification as per Articles 102(2) and 191(2) of the Constitution are as follows:
  - If a member of the House belonging to a political party voluntarily gives up his or her membership of that political party.
  - If he/she abstains from voting or votes contrary to the direction issued by the political party to which he or she belongs.
  - An independent member who joins a political party after his or her election.
  - If one-third of the members of the party split from the parent party and join another party, they are disqualified, however, if two-third of the members of the party merge with another party then they are not disqualified.
  - When any nominated member joins any political party after the expiry of six months.

Vacation of Seats

- According to the Indian Constitution, an individual cannot simultaneously be a member of both Houses of Parliament. A member may have to vacate his seat
  - If the election is declared void by the court.
  - If he is elected to the Office of President, Vice-President or the Governor of a State.
  - If he is expelled from the House.
- The Chairman or Speaker can declare the seat vacated if a member has remained absent from all its meetings for a period of 60 days without permission.
- A Member of Parliament can resign from his seat. The resignation letter is addressed to Chairman of Rajya Sabha (Vice-President) or Speaker of Lok Sabha.
- A person cannot be an Member of Legislative Assembly (MLA) and Member of Parliament (MP) at the same time. If it happens that a person is both an MLA and MP, his MP seat will vacate.
- As per the RPA Act, 1951, a person may vacate his seat under following provisions:
  - If a person is elected to both the Houses of Parliament, he must intimate within 10 days in which House he desires to serve. In default of such

intimation, his seat in the Rajya Sabha becomes vacant.

- If a sitting memebr of one House is alos elected to the other House, his seat in the firsat House becomes vacant.
- It a person is elected to two seats in a House, he should exercise his option for one. Otherwise, both seats become vacant.

- Similarly, a person cannot be a memebr of both the parliament and the state legistture at the same time. If a person is so elected, his seat in Parliament becomes, vacant if he does not resign his seat in the state legislature within 14 days.

LEADERS IN PARLIAMENT

There are important functionaries in the Parliament to ensure its smooth functioning such as:

The Constitution has adopted the first-past-the-post system (or the system of territorial representation) for the election of the members to the Lok Sabha.

Leader of the House

- Generally, the Prime Minister (if she/he is a Member of Lok Sabha) or Minister nominated by the Prime Minister (has to be Member of Lok Sabha) functions as leader of the House.
- There is a Leader of House in Rajya Sabha as well who has to be a Member of Rajya Sabha and is nominated by Prime Minister.

Leader of Opposition

- The leader of the largest opposition party having no less than one-tenth seats of the total strength of the House is designated as the Leader of Opposition in both Lok Sabha and Rajya Sabha. (The official recognition in 1977).
- The main function of opposition leaders is to provide constructive criticism to the government and provide an alternative government.

Whip

- Every political party-ruling or in opposition, has its own whip appointed by party to serve as an assistant floor leader. The members of parties are expected to follow the instruction given by the whip.
- This office is based on conventions of the Parliamentary Government. It is neither mentioned in the Constitution nor in the rules of the house.

Allocation of Seats in Parliament

States	In Rajya Sabha	In Lok Sabha	States	In Rajya Sabha	In Lok Sabha
Andhra Pradesh	11	25	Manipur	1	2
Arunachal Pradesh	1	2	Meghalaya	1	2
Assam	7	14	Mizoram	1	1
Bihar	16	40	Nagaland	1	1
Chhattisgarh	5	11	Odisha	10	21
Goa	1	2	Punjab	7	13
Gujarat	11	26	Rajasthan	10	25
Haryana	5	10	Sikkim	1	1
Himachal Pradesh	3	4	Tamil Nadu	18	39
Jharkhand	6	14	Telangana	7	17
Karnataka	12	28	Tripura	1	2
Kerala	9	20	Uttarakhand	3	5
Madhya Pradesh	11	29	Uttar Pradesh	31	80
Maharashtra	19	48	West Bengal	16	42

Union Territories

States	In Rajya Sabha	In Lok Sabha
Andaman and Nicobar Islands	—	1
Chandigarh	—	1
Delhi (The National Capital Territory of Delhi)	3	7
Lakshadweep	—	1
Puducherry	1	1
Jammu and Kashmir	4	5
Ladakh	—	1
Dadra and Nagar Haveli and Daman and Diu	—	2
Nominated Members	12	—
Total	245	543

SESSIONS OF THE PARLIAMENT

Parliamentary session is the time period in which the House conducts and completes Parliamentary work by meeting continuously everyday. Sessions of Parliament are discussed below :

Summoning

- The period between the first sitting of the House and its prorogation or dissolution in case of Lok Sabha, is known as session. The period between prorogation of House and its re-assembly is known as recess.

- The Constitution only states that there should not be a gap of more than six months between two consecutive sittings of Parliament.
- Normally, three sessions of the Lok Sabha are held in a year, *viz* :

	Sessions	Months
(i)	Budget Session	February–May
(ii)	Autumn or Monsoon Session	July–September
(iii)	Winter Session	November–December

- One-tenth of the total members in each House including the Presiding Officer to be present for transacting any business are required.
- It means that there must be at least 55 members present in the Lok Sabha and 25 members present in the Rajya Sabha.
- The President from time-to-time summons each House of Parliament.
- The special session of Parliament is summoned by the President in order to transact a special business by the Parliament.
- In the special session, only the specified business is taken up. It can be held within or outside a regular session.

Adjournment

- Adjournment is a postponement of the sitting or proceedings of the House from one time to another specified for the reassembling of the House.
- During the course of a session, the Parliament may be adjourned from day-to-day or for more than a day. It may also be adjourned sine-die, which means the termination of a sitting of the House without any definite date being fixed for its next sitting.
- The Presiding Officer has the power to adjourn the House sine-die. Once, the House is adjourned sine-die, she/he is empowered to call it again anytime before or after adjourning sine-die.

Prorogation

- Prorogation means the termination of a session of the House by an order made by the President under Article 85(2)(a) of the Constitution.
- The prorogation of the House may take place any time, even while the House is sitting. However, usually, prorogation follows the adjournment of the sitting of the House sine-die.
- Prorogation does not affect the bills or any other pending work.
- Other than the notices on introducing bills, all other pending notices lapse and fresh notices have to be issued for the next session.

Dissolution

- Dissolution of the House means the end of the life of the Lok Sabha either by an order made by the President under **Article 85(2)(b)** of the Constitution or on the expiration of the period of five years from the date appointed for its first meeting.
- Dissolution puts an end to the representative character of the individuals who at the time compose the Lok Sabha. Dissolution is irrevocable.
- Under **Article 107**, following bills lapse after dissolution of Lok Sabha :
  - Bill pending in Lok Sabha and
  - Bill passed by Lok Sabha, but pending in Rajya Sabha.

Quorum

- The minimum number of members required to be present in the House before any business can take place is known as the Quorum.
- It is taken to be one-tenth of the total number of members in each House including Presiding Officer.
- The Presiding Officer is responsible to either adjourn the House or suspend the meeting until there is Quorum.
- Lame-Duck Session The last-session of the existing Lok Sabha after a new Lok Sabha has been elected. The members who do not get re-elected are known as Lame-Ducks.

Joint Sitting of Houses

- Article 108(1) of the Constitution provides the joint sitting of the Parliament to resolve a deadlock between the two Houses, in case of an ordinary legislation, the Constitution provides for the joint sitting of both Houses. It takes place under following conditions.
  - When a bill passed by one House is rejected by the other House or
  - the Houses have finally disagreed as to the amendments made in the bill or
  - more than six months lapse from the date of the receipt of the bill by the other House without the bill being passed by it, the President may, unless the bill has lapsed by reason of dissolution of Lok Sabha, notify to the Houses by message.

- Matters in joint sitting are decided by a majority of the total number of members of both Houses present and voting.

The joint sitting is presided over by the Speaker of the Lok Sabha and held according to its norms. However, in the case of a Money Bill, there is no provision in the Constitution for a joint sitting of both Houses as Lok Sabha clearly enjoys pre-eminence over Rajya Sabha in financial matters.

- As regards a Constitution Amendment Bill, it has been provided in the Constitution that such a bill has to be passed by the specific majority, as prescribed under Article 368 of the Constitution, by both Houses.
- Therefore, there is no provision for resolving a deadlock between the two Houses in regard to a Constitution Amendment Bill.
- So far joint sittings have been held thrice in 1961, 1978 and 2002. They are as follows:
  - The First Joint Sitting was held on 6th May, 1961 to consider amendments to the Dowry Prohibition Bill, 1960,
  - The Second Joint Sitting was held on 16th May, 1978 for the passage of Banking Service Commission (Repeal) Bill, 1977.
  - The Third Joint Sitting was held on 26th March, 2002 for the passage of Prevention of Terrorism Bill, 2002.

DEVICES OF PARLIAMENTARY PROCEEDINGS

Some devices of Parliamentary proceedings are:

- Question Hour Generally, the first hour of a sitting of the house is devoted to questions and that hour is called the Question Hour.
- It has a special significance in the proceedings of Parliament. Asking of questions is an inherent and unfettered parliamentary right of members.
- During the Question Hour, the members can ask questions on every aspect of administration and governmental activity.

  Questions are of three types which are as follows:
  - Starred Question It is one to which a member desires an oral answer in the House and which is distinguished by an asterisk mark. When a question is answered orally, supplementary questions can be asked thereon. Only 20 questions can be listed for oral answer on a day (as per Lok Sabha document on Question Hour, 2014).
  - Unstarred Question It is one which is not called for oral answer in the House and on which no supplementary questions can consequently be asked. To such a question, a written answer is deemed to have been laid on the table after the Question Hour by the Minister to whom it is addressed. Only 230 questions can be listed for written answer on a day.
  - Short Notice Question It is one which relates to a matter of urgent public importance and can be asked with shorter notice of less than 10 days. It is answered orally followed by supplementary questions.
- Short Duration Discussion In order to provide opportunities to members to discuss matters of urgent public importance, a convention was established in March, 1953, which was incorporated later into the rules of Procedure and Conduct of Business in Lok Sabha under Rule 193 as Short Duration Discussion.
- Under this rule, members can raise discussion for short duration without a formal motion or vote thereon.
- It is also known as Two-Hour Discussion. The Speaker can allot any two days in week for Short Duration Discussion.
- Half-an-Hour Discussion Where answer to a question whether starred or unstarred needs elucidation on a matter of fact, any member can table a notice for raising half-an-hour discussion thereon. If the notice is admitted and gets priority in ballot such a discussion may be allowed by the Speaker Who can allot three days in a week for Half-an-Hour Discussion.
- Zero Hour It is an Indian Parliamentary Innovation of discussion in the Parliament which is of urgent public importance. It is neither mentioned in the Constitution nor in the Rules of Procedure of the Houses. It has been into existence since 1962. It is an informal device used by the Member of Parliament to raise questions without mandatory notice of 10 days by informing the Speaker.
- The Presiding Officers in the Parliament regulate the zero hour by setting rules to streamline the process. It starts immediately after the Question Hour. It is the time gap between the question hour and the agenda for the day.

MOTIONS

- The term motion in parliamentary parlance means any proposal made for the purpose of obtaining a decision of the House. It is phrased in such a way that, if passed, it will intend to express the will of the House. Motions may be classified as:
  - Substantive motion It is a self-contained independent proposal made in reference to a subject which the mover wishes to bring forward.
  - Substitute motion It is moved in substitution of an original motion and proposes an alternative to it.
  - Subsidiary motion It has no meaning and cannot state the decision of the House without reference to the original motion or proceedings of the House.

Types of Motion

Different types are motions are given below :

- Calling Attention Motion Under this procedural device, a member may, with the prior permission of the Speaker, call the attention of a minister to any matter of urgent public importance and the minister may make a brief statement or ask for time to make a statement later.
- The calling attention procedure is an Indian innovation which combines asking a question with supplementaries and making brief comments; the government also gets adequate opportunity to state its case. It has been in existence since, 1954.
- Adjournment Motion Adjournment motion (Rule 56) is the procedure for adjournment of the business of the House for the purpose of discussing a definite matter of urgent public importance, which can be moved with the consent of the Speaker.
- The adjournment motion, if admitted, leads to setting aside of the normal business of the House for discussing the matter mentioned in the motion. It requires the support of 50 members to be admitted.
- It involves an element of censure against the government. The purpose is to take the government to task for a recent act of omission or commission having serious consequence.
- The adjournment motion is voted upon after the discussion. Rajya Sabha does not have this power to raise an adjournment motion.

No-Confidence Motion

- As per Article 75 of the Indian Constitution, the Council of Ministers are collectively responsible to Lok Sabha, thus they stay in office as long as they enjoy confidence of Lok Sabha.
- The government must always enjoy majority support in the popular House to remain in power. If needed, it has to demonstrate its strength on the floor of the House by moving a motion of confidence and winning the confidence of the House.
- A no-confidence motion is allowed only in Lok Sabha and in order to be admitted, it needs support of 50 members.
- The first no-confidence motion in the Indian Parliamentary tradition was moved in August, 1963 by Acharya JB Kapalani. It was presented against Jawaharlal Nehru Government but it could not be passed. So far a total of 27 no-confidence motions have been presented in Lok Sabha.

Censure Motion

- Censure motion can be moved only in Lok Sabha under Rule 184.
- A censure motion is moved against an individual minister or whole of the Council of Ministers for a negligence of duties or breach of privilege.
- The grounds for moving a censure have to be tabled before the Speaker. Speaker can also disallow a censure motion. The motion is voted upon after a debate.
- If the censure motion is passed the Council of Ministers shall pass a confidence motion to regain the trust of the House.

Types of Closure Motion

- **Simple Closure** If the matter is sufficiently discussed then the member might move a simple closure motion.
- **Closure by Compartments** For discussion, the bill or a resolution is grouped together into compartments. Therefore, a particular section or group of sections in a bill can be put to vote.
- **Kangaroo Closure** When this type of closure motion is passed, only the important clauses of a bill are discussed and voted. The remaining clauses are deemed to be passed.
- **Guillotine Closure** When the time allocated for discussion of a particular bill or resolution is over, all undiscussed clauses are put to vote along with the discussed ones on the Guillotine.

Closure Motion

- A motion that is moved by member to cut short the debate on a matter before the House is known as closure motion.

- If approved by the House, the debate is stopped and the matter is put to vote.

Privilege Motion

- This motion is taken up when (and if) Parliamentary privileges have been breached by a minister.
- It serves the purpose of censuring the concerned minister.

No-Day-Yet-Named Motion

In this, a motion has been admitted by the Speaker but no date gets fixed for discussion.

Motion of Thanks

- The President addresses the first session after every general election and every fiscal year.
- The speech of the President is discussed in both Houses on motion known as motion of thanks.
- This motion is put to vote and it must be passed otherwise it amounts to defeat of the government.

Special Mention

- A matter that cannot be raised during question hour, half an hour or short duration discussion can be raised under special mention in Rajya Sabha.
- It is equivalent to Lok Sabha device of Notice (Mention) under Rule 377.

Point of Order

- Point of order can be raised when the normal rules of procedure are not being followed by proceedings in the House.
- It suspends the proceedings and no debate allowed on a point of order thus it is an extraordinary device. Usually raised by opposition to control government functioning.

Resolutions

- Resolutions can be moved in order to draw attention of government or House on a matter of interest of general public. It can be classified into three categories:
    - Private Member's Resolution discussed on alternate Fridays and afternoon sitting.
    - Government Resolution moved by minister and can be taken up any day between Monday and Thursday.
    - Statutory Resolution can be moved by either private member or minister. Always tabled in pursuance of an Act of Parliament or a Provision of Constitution.
- All resolutions are a particular type of motion but *vice-versa* is not true. Unlike motions, all resolutions are required to be voted upon.

Youth Parliament

- On the recommendations of the Fourth All India Whips Conference, Youth Parliament was started in 2016.
- The Ministry of Parliamentary Affairs facilitates necessary training and assistance states to ensure introduction of the scheme. Its main objectives are:
    - To familiarise younger generation with practices and procedures of Parliament.
    - To imbibe the spirit of discipline, tolerance and character among the youth.
    - To enable students to acquire a proper perspec- tive on functioning of democratic institutions.

LEGISLATIVE PROCEEDINGS

All legislative proposals are initiated in the Parliament in the terms of bills. The bill is a proposed legislation. It becomes a law when it is asserted by the President. The bill can broadly be categorised as :

Ordinary Bills

- All the bills other than Financial Bills are Ordinary bills.
- Such bills can be introduced in either House of the Parliament (in Lok Sabha or the Rajya Sabha) without the recommendation of the President, except those bills under Article 3 (i.e. bills related to reorganisation of the territory of a state).
- These bills are passed by a simple majority by both the Houses. Both the Houses enjoy equal jurisdiction over such bills and in case of a deadlock due to any reason, the tie is resolved by a joint sitting.

Types of Reading

- **First Reading** The bill is introduced and printed is gazette in the House. At this stage, no discussion takes place. Second Reading This is the consideration stage when the bill is discussed clause-by-clause.
- **Second reading** has three sub-stages :
    - Stage of general discussion Provisions of the bill are discussed generally but there is no discussion on the details.
    - Committee stage The bill is referred to a select committee for **scrutiny**.
    - Consideration stage The provisions of the bill are discussed clause-by-clause in detail and amendments are moved.
- **Third Reading** During this stage, a brief general discussion of the bill takes place and the bill is finally passed. When the bill is passed by one House, it is sent to the other House for its consideration.

- Each House has laid down a procedure for the passage of a bill. According to the procedure of the House, a bill has to pass through three stages commonly known as Readings.

Money Bill

- According to Article 110, a bill shall be deemed to be a Money Bill if it contains only provisions dealing with all or any of the following matters, namely :
  - The imposition, abolition, remission, alteration or regulation of any tax;
  - The regulation of the borrowing of money or the giving of any guarantee by the Government of India or the amendment of the law with respect to any financial obligations undertaken or to be undertaken by the Government of India;
  - The custody of the Consolidated Fund or the Contingency Fund of India, the payment of money into or the withdrawal of money from any such fund;
  - The appropriation of money out of the Consolidated Fund of India;
  - The declaring of any expenditure to be charged on the Consolidated Fund of India or the increasing of the amount of any such expenditure;
  - The receipt of money on account of the Consolidated Fund of India or the public account of India or the custody or issue of such money or the audit of the accounts of the Union or of a State or
  - Any matter incidental to any of the matters specified above.
- If any question arises whether a bill is a Money Bill or not, the decision of the Speaker of the Lok Sabha thereon shall be final. Money Bills can be introduced only in Lok Sabha. Rajya Sabha cannot make amendments in a Money Bill passed by Lok Sabha.
- However, it can recommend amendments in a Money Bill, but must return all Money Bills to Lok Sabha within 14 days from the date of their receipt.
- It is open to Lok Sabha to accept or reject any or all of the recommendations of Rajya Sabha with regard to a Money Bill.
- If Lok Sabha accepts any of the recommendations of Rajya Sabha, the Money Bill is deemed to have been passed by both Houses with amendments recommended by Rajya Sabha and accepted by Lok Sabha. If the Lok Sabha does not accept any of the recommendations of Rajya Sabha, Money Bill is deemed to have been passed by both Houses in the form, in which it was earlier passed by Lok Sabha.
- If a Money Bill passed by Lok Sabha and transmitted to Rajya Sabha for its recommendations and it is not returned to Lok Sabha within the said period of 14 days, it is deemed to have been passed by both the Houses of Parliament.

Financial Bill

- While a Money Bill deals solely with matters specified in Article 110(1) (a) to (g) of the Constitution, a Financial Bill does not exclusively deal with all or any of the matters specified in the said article.
- Financial Bills can be divided into two categories:
  - In the first category, bills are which inter-alia (among other things) contain provisions attracting Article 110(1) (a) to (f) of the Constitution. They are categorised as Financial Bills under Article 117(1) of the Constitution. Like Money Bills, they can be introduced only in Lok Sabha on the recommendation of the President.
  - In the second category, those bills that contain provisions, which would on enactment involve expenditure from the Consolidated Fund of India, such bills are categorised as Financial Bills under Article 117 (3) of the Constitution. Such bills can be introduced in House of Parliament like any other Ordinary Bill. However, recommendation of the President is essential for consideration of these bills by either House.

Constitution Amendment Bill

- The Constitution vests in Parliament the power to amend the Constitution. Constitution Amendment Bill can be introduced in either House of Parliament.
- The Constitution Amendment Bill affecting vital issues as enlisted in the provision of Article 368(2) of the Constitution after having been passed by both the Houses of Parliament, have to be ratified by not less than one half of the State Legislatures.
- While motions for introduction of Constitution Amendment Bills are adopted by simple majority, a majority of the total membership of the House and a majority of not less than two-third of the members present and voting is required for adoption of effective clauses and motions for consideration and passing of these bills.
- In the case of Constitutional Amendment Bill, there is no provision for joint sitting of both the Houses to resolve the deadlock in the passage of bill. If one House rejects the bill or suggests amendments that are not acceptable to the original House the bill comes to an end.

Types of Majority

Simple Majority

Also known as ordinary majority, working majority or functional majority. It means a majority of the members of the house present and voting.

Effective Majority

It means a majority of the total membership of the house excluding the number of vacant seats. The Constitution describes this majority as "a majority of all the then members of the house".

Absolute Majority

It is simply a majority of the total membership of the house without taking into account the vacant seats and absent members.

Special Majority

A majority of the total membership of each house and a two-thirds majority of the members present and voting.

President Assent to the Bills

- After a bill has been passed by both the Houses of Parliament, it is presented to the President for his/her assent.
- The President may either give his assent to the bill, withhold his/her assent or return the bill, if it is not a Money Bill.
- The President may either give or withhold his/her assent to a Money Bill. A Money Bill can not be returned to the House by the President for reconsideration.

BUDGET IN PARLIAMENT

- The budget known as Annual Financial Statement in the Constitution has been dealt with under Article 112. According to this Article:
    - The President shall in respect of every financial year cause to be laid before both the Houses of Parliament, a statement of the estimated receipts and expenditure of the Government of India for that year.
    - The estimates of expenditure are submitted to the Parliament of India in the form of demands for grants.
    - The demand for the grant includes the estimate of expenditure from the Consolidated Fund, which is included in the annual financial statement.
- The following expenditure shall be expenditure charged on the Consolidated Fund of India :
    - The emoluments and allowances of the President and other expenditure relating to his office;
    - The salaries and allowances of the Chairman and the Deputy Chairman of the Council of States and the Speaker and the Deputy Speaker of the House of the People;
    - Debt charges for which the Government of India is liable including interest, sinking fund charges and redemption charges and other expenditure relating to the raising of loans and the service and redemption of debt; the salary, allowances and pension payable to or in respect of the Comptroller and Auditor-General of India;
    - Any sums required to satisfy any judgement, decree or award of any court or arbitral tribunal;
    - Any other expenditure declared by this Constitution or by Parliament by law to be so charged.
- The Constitution of India provides three kinds of funds:
    - Consolidated Fund of India (Article 266(1)
    - Public Account of India (Article 266(2)
    - Contingency Fund of India (Article 267)

Government Accounts

There are three types of Government Accounts namely:

Consolidated Fund of India

- This is the fund established under Article 266(1) of the Constitution and into this all receipts, revenues and loans flow.
- All expenditure from the Consolidated Fund has to be passed by Parliament through an Appropriation Bill.

Public Account of India

- It includes all those moneys where the government acts as a banker. e.g., provident fund, small savings etc. It is established under Article 266(2).
- These funds do not belong to the government and have to be paid back sometime to their rightful owners.
- Expenditure from public account is not required to be approved by Parliament.

Contingency Fund of India

- Parliament has established a Contingency Fund under Article 267 to be placed at the disposal of President to meet unforeseen expenditures pending authorisation of such expenditure by Parliament.
- This fund is held by the Finance Secretary on behalf of the President of India.
- Money can be taken out of Contingency Fund during emergency but approval from Parliament has to be taken later on.

Budget

- In India, the budget is presented to Parliament on such date as is fixed by the President.
- The Budget Speech of the Finance Minister is usually in two parts.
- Part A deals with general economic survey of the country while Part B relates to taxation proposals.
- General Budget was earlier being presented at 5 pm on the last working day of February, but since, 1999 the General Budget is being presented at 11 am on the last working day of February, i.e., about a month before the commencement of the financial year except in the year when general elections to Lok Sabha are held.

Presentation of Budget

- In an election year, budget may be presented twice– first to secure vote on account for a few months and later in full. The General Budget is presented in Lok Sabha by the Minister of Finance.
- He makes a speech introducing the budget and it is only in the concluding part of his speech that the proposals for fresh taxation or for variations in the existing taxes are disclosed by him.
- The Annual Financial Statement is laid on the table of Rajya Sabha at the conclusion of the speech of the Finance Minister in Lok Sabha.

Enactment of the Budget

The budget passes through the following six stages in Parliament :

1. Budget Presentation

- In 2017, the NDA Government decided to present the Union Budget on 1st February departing from the colonial-era tradition of presenting the budget on last working day of February.
- It is done so that the legislative approval for annual spending plans and tax proposals could be completed before the beginning of new financial year on 1st April.
- Apart from it, the other two significant changes were the merger of Railway Budget with Union Budget and abolishing the classification of plan and non-plan expenditure.

2. General Discussion on Budget

- The discussion on the budget begins a few days after its presentation. In a democratic set-up, government is anxious to give Parliament full opportunity to discuss the budgetary provisions and the various proposals for taxation.
- Since, Parliament is not able to vote the entire budget before the commencement of the new financial year, the necessity to keep enough finance at the disposal of government in order to allow it to run the administration of the country remains unmet.
- A special provision is, therefore, made for Vote-on-Account by which government obtains the Vote of Parliament for a sum sufficient to incur expenditure on various items for a part of the year. Normally, the Vote-on-Account is taken for two months only.

Methods of Voting

Voice Vote

Method through which a question is determined by the 'Ayes' or the 'Noes' by the members

Secret Ballot

Similar to open voting except that instead of using different colours for different types of votes (i.e., Green for 'Ages' and Red for 'Noes', the LED on individual result display panel flashes only white light to confirm the recording of the vote.

Division

It involves recording of votes through

- Automatic vote Recording equipment
- Distribution of 'Ayes' and 'Noes' slips in the house
- Members going into the lobbies

3. Scrutiny by Departmental Committees

- After the general discussion on the General Budget is over, the House is adjourned for a fixed period.
- During this period, the demands for grants of various ministries or departments including railways are considered by concerned Departmental Standing Committees.
- These committees are required to make their reports to the House within specified period without asking for more time.

4. Voting on Demands of Grants

- After the reports of the Standing Committees are presented to the House, the House proceeds to the discussion and voting on demands for grants, ministry-wise.
- On the last day of the allotted days, the Speaker puts all the outstanding demands to the vote of the House. This device is popularly known as Guillotine.
- Lok Sabha has the power to give assent or refuse to give assent to any demand or even to reduce the amount of grant sought by government.

- In Rajya Sabha, there is only a general discussion on the budget. It does not vote on the demands for grants.
- Only those amount is subject to the vote of Lok Sabha which is not a charged expenditure on the Consolidated Fund of India.
- Discussion in Lok Sabha on charged expenditure is permissible, but such expenditure is not voted by the House.
- Members have full opportunity to criticise the budgetary provisions during the course of discussion and make suggestions for improving the financial position of the country.

Cut Motions

- Motions for reduction to various demands for grants are made in the form of cut motions seeking to reduce the sums sought by government on grounds of economy or difference of opinion on matters of policy or just in order to voice a grievance.
- If a cut motion is adopted and passed, a no-confidence motion can be proceeded against government.
- Three types of cut motion are permitted in Lok Sabha. They are as follows:
  - **Economy Cut** It signals that the government has done undue spending and asks the government to undertake cost-cutting measures to improve efficiency.
  - **Policy Cut** It signals the complete disapproval of the budget by the House and recommends that the amount of the grant be reduce to ₹ 1.
  - **Token Cut** It signals disapproval in the overall allocation of budgetary items and asks the House to cut the amount by ₹ 100. Token cut is of symbolic nature. So far, no cut motions have been passed.

5. Appropriation Bill

- After the general discussion on the budget proposals and voting on demands for grants have been completed, government introduces the Appropriation Bill.
- The Appropriation Bill is intended to give authority to government to incur expenditure from and out of the Consolidated Fund of India.
- The procedure for passing this bill is the same as in the case of other Money Bills.

6. Finance Bill

- The Finance Bill seeking to give effect to the government's taxation proposals, which is introduced in Lok Sabha immediately after the presentation of the General Budget, is taken up for consideration after passing the Appropriation Bill.
- However, certain provisions in the bill relating to levy and collection of fresh duties or variations in the existing duties come into effect immediately on the expiry of the day on which the bill is introduced by virtue of a declaration under the Provisional Collection of Taxes Act, 1931.
- Parliament has to pass the Finance Bill within 75 days of its introduction.

Other Grants

- Supplementary Grants No expenditure in excess of the sums authorised by Parliament can be incurred without the sanction of Parliament.
- Whenever a need arises to incur extra expenditure, a supplementary estimate is laid before Parliament.
- Excess Grants If any money has been spent on any service during a financial year in excess of the amounts granted for that service and for that year, the Minister of Finance or Railways presents a demand for excess grant.
- Additional Grants It is granted when a need has arisen during the current financial year for additional expenditure upon some new service not mentioned in the budget for that year.
- Vote of Credit It is given in cases where an unforeseen demand on resources of India arises on account of the magnitude or the indefinite character of the service. The demand cannot be stated with the details ordinarily given in a budget.
- Exceptional Grants It is not part of the current service of any financial year. It is given for a certain objective.
- Token Grants It is granted when funds to meet the proposed expenditure on a new service can be made available by reappropriation, a demand for the grant of a token sum may be submitted to the vote of the House and, if the House assents to the demand, funds may be so made available.

PARLIAMENTARY PRIVILEGES

- The term Parliamentary privilege refers to certain rights and immunities enjoyed by each House of Parliament and committees of each House collectively and by members of each House individually, without which they cannot discharge their functions efficiently and effectively .
- The objective of Parliamentary privileges is to safeguard the freedom, the authority and the dignity of Parliament.
- The powers, privileges and immunities of either House of Parliament and of its committees and members have been laid down in Article 105 of the Constitution.

Types of Parliamentary Privileges

Collective Privileges	Individual Privileges
The privileges belonging to each House of Parliament collectively are the ability to publish reports, debates and proceedings, as well as the ability to prevent others from doing so.	During the session of Parliament, from 40 days before the beginning to 40 days after the finish, no member may be arrested. This privilege is only granted in civil matters; it is not granted in criminal or preventive detention situations.
Without the consent of the Presiding Officer, no one (whether a member or an outsider) can be arrested, and no legal process (civil or criminal) can be served within the House's boundaries.	In Parliament, members have the right to free expression. No member of Parliament or its committees is accountable in any court for anything said or voted in Parliament or its committees. This independence is limited by the Constitution's provisions as well as the norms and standing orders that govern Parliament's functioning.
Make rules to govern its own procedure and commercial activity, as well as to adjudicate on such issues.	Members of Parliament are exempt from jury duty when Parliament is in session. They have the right to decline to give evidence and testify in court.

Language in Parliament

- According to the Constitution, **Hindi and English** are the languages used in the Parliament for transaction of business. However, a member may address the House with permission from the Presiding Officer in his native language. There are arrangements made in both Houses for simultaneous translation.
- Though English was to be discontinued as a floor language after the expiration of fifteen years from the commencement of the Constitution, the Official Languages Act (1963) allowed English to be continued along with Hindi.

Difference between Breach of Privilege and Contempt of the House

- When any of the privileges, either of the members individually or of the House in its collective capacity , are disregarded or attacked by any individual or authority, the offence is called a breach of privilege .
- Contempt of the House may be defined generally as any act or omission which obstructs or impedes either House of Parliament in the performance of its functions or which obstructs or impedes any member or officers of such House in the discharge of his or her duty or which has a tendency, directly or indirectly, to produce such results even though there is no precedent of the offence.
- Whereas all breaches of privilege are contempts of the House whose privileges are violated, a person may be guilty of a contempt of the House eventhough she/he does not violate any of the privilege of the House, e.g., when she/he disobeys an order to attend a committee or publishes reflections on the character or conduct of a member in his capacity as a member.

PARLIAMENTARY COMMITTEES

Parliamentary Committee means a committee, which is appointed or elected by the House or nominated by the Speaker and which works under the direction of the Speaker and presents its report to the House or to the Speaker and the Secretariat for which is provided by the Lok Sabha Secretariat . Broadly, the Parliamentary Committees may be classified into the two categories which are as follows :

(i) Ad-Hoc Committees
(ii) Standing Committees

Ad-Hoc Committees

- Ad-Hoc Committees are constituted by the House or by the Presiding Officers, singly or jointly, for a specific purpose and cease to exist when they finish the task assigned to them and submit a report.
- The usual Ad-Hoc Committees are the select or joint committees on bills and others like the Railway Convention Committee , setup to review the rate of dividend payable by railways to the general revenues and those constituted to enquire into and report on specific subjects. Ad-Hoc Committees are further divided into two types :

- Inquiry Committee are constituted from time-to-time. These are constituted either by the two Houses on a motion adopted in that behalf or by the Presiding Officer to inquire into and report specific subjects.
- Advisory Committee include select or joint committees on bills appointed to consider and report on particular bills.

Joint Parliamentary Committees

- Joint Parliamentary Committee (JPC) is constituted either through a motion adopted by one House and concurred by the other or through communication between the Presiding Officers of the two Houses.
- The members are either elected by the Houses or nominated by the Presiding Officers .
- The strength of a JPC may vary. The terms of reference of a JPC are decided by the Parliament itself. JPC have overarching powers of summoning any authority including the Prime Minister and seeking attendance.

Standing Committees

- Standing Committees are those committees, which are either elected by the House or nominated by the Presiding Officer(s) (i.e., the Speaker in the case of the Lok Sabha and the Chairman in the case of the Rajya Sabha) periodically and are permanent in nature.
- Some important Standing Committees of the Lok Sabha are as follows :
  - The Business Advisory Committee
  - Committee of Privileges
  - Committee on Government Assurances
  - Estimates Committee
  - Rules Committee
  - Committee on Empowerment of Women
  - Committee on Public Undertakings
  - Committee on the Welfare of Scheduled Castes and Scheduled Tribes
  - Public Accounts Committee

Financial Committees

Some Financial Committees are as follows :

Estimates Committee

- The Estimates Committee constituted for the first time in 1950 on the recommendation of John Mathai , is a Parliamentary Committee consisting of 30 members selected every year by the Lok Sabha amongst its members in proportion of party strength .
- It has no representation from the Rajya Sabha. A Minister cannot be elected as a member of the committee. It is the largest committee of the Parliament.
- The term of office of the committee is one year .
- The Chairman of this committee is appointed by the Speaker from amongst its members. He is invariably from the ruling party.

Public Accounts Committee

- It is the oldest committee in existence from 1921. The committee consists of 22 members (at present) including 15 members of Lok Sabha and 7 members of Rajya Sabha.
- The members are elected by their respective Houses.
- A Minister cannot be elected as a member of the committee.
- The Chairman is appointed by the Speaker and is usually from the opposition party.
- The term of the office of the members is one year. Functions of the committee are as follows :
  - The main function of Public Accounts Committee (PAC) is to examine the annual audit reports of the Comptroller and Auditor-General (CAG) , which are laid before the Parliament by the President.
  - The CAG submits three audit report namely Audit report on appropriation accounts, Audit report on finance accounts and Audit report on public undertakings.
  - To scrutinize the accounts of the government so that the money dispersed were legally available for and applicable to the purpose to which they have been granted.
  - The expenditure confirms to the authority which governs it.
  - That every re-appropriation has been made in accordance with the provisions made by competence authority.
  - The PAC examines cases involving losses, nugatory expenditure and financial irregularities. It scrutinizes the reports of the CAG.
  - The CAG assists this committee in fulfillment of its responsibilities as a friend, guide and philosopher .

Committee on Public Undertakings

- This committee was created on the recommendations on Krishna Menon Committee in 1964, consists of 22 members in which 15 elected by Lok Sabha and 7 elected by Rajya Sabha. The term of the committee is one year.
- A Minister cannot be elected as a member of this committee.
- The Speaker appoints the Chairman of this committee from amongst its members who are drawn from the Lok Sabha only.
- Functions of committee on Public Undertakings are as follows :
    - To examine the reports and accounts of public undertakings.
    - To examine the reports of CAG on public undertakings.
    - To ascertain whether the affairs of the public undertaking are being managed in accordance with the sound commercial principles.

Department Related Standing Committees (*DRSC's*)

- DRSC's were setup in 1993 to scrutinize the functioning of the various Ministries. Departments of the Union Government assigned to them in order to further strengthen the accountability of the Government to Parliament.
- 24 DRSC's have been constituted consisting of not more than 31 members, out of which 21 members are nominated by the Speaker, Lok Sabha and 10 members are nominated by the Chairman, Rajya Sabha.
- 8 DRSC's function under the control and direction of the Chairman, Rajya Sabha, while 16 such committees function under the control and direction of the Speaker, Lok Sabha. No Minister can be part of the Standing Committees.
- The term of the office of each department related Standing Committees is one year from the date of its Constitution.
- One of the important functions of these committees is to examine such bills introduced in either House as are referred to them by the Chairman, Rajya Sabha or the Speaker, Lok Sabha, as the case may be and make report thereon.
- The reports of the Standing Committees have persuasive value.
- In case, the government accepts any of the recommendations of the committee, it may bring forward official amendments at the consideration stage of the bill or may withdraw the bill reported by the Standing Committee and bring forward a new bill after incorporating the recommendations of the Standing Committee.

Functions of the DRSC's

- To consider the demands for grants and the annual reports of the related ministries or departments and report thereon.
- To examine bills, pertaining to the related ministries or departments, referred to the committee and report thereon.
- To consider national basic long-term policy documents and report thereon.

Other Parliamentary Committees

- Business Advisory Committee This committee regulates the programme and time table of the House. It allocates time for the transaction of legislative and other business brought before the house by the government.
- The committee in Lok Sabha consists of 15 members including the Speaker who acts as its Chairman while in Rajya Sabha, it has 11 members including the Chairman acting as its Ex-Officio Chairman.
- Committee on Government Assurances This committee examines the assurances, promises and undertakings given by ministers from time-to-time on the floor of the House and reports on the extent to which they have been carried through.
- Committee on Subordinate Legislation This committee examines and reports to the House whether the powers to make regulations, rules sub-rules and bye-laws delegated by the Parliament or conferred by the Constitution to the executive are properly being exercised by it.
- Committee on Private Member's Bill and Resolutions This is a special committee of Lok Sabha and consists of 15 members including the Deputy Speaker as its Chairman.

  This committee classifies bills and allocates time for the discussion on bills and resolutions introduced by private members.

PARLIAMENTARY FORUMS

- Parliamentary forums are established to provide a platform to the members to interact with concerned ministers experts and key officials from nodal ministeries.
- It is also a platform to sensitise members about key issues both on macro and micro level. The first Parliamentary Forum on Water Conservation and Management was constituted in 2005.
- Some of the Parliamentary Forums are as follows :
  - Water Conservation and Management (2005)
  - Youth (2006)
  - Children (2006)
  - Population and Public Health (2006)
  - Global Warming and Climate Change (2008)
  - Artisans and Craftspeople (2013)
  - Disaster Management (2011)
  - Millennium Development Goals (2013)
- Lok Sabha Speaker is Ex-Officio President for all forums except the Parliamentary forum on Population and Public Health.
- The Chairman of Rajya Sabha is the Ex-Officio President for these two forums while Speaker is Ex-Offices Co-President.

Parliament Reform

- For Parliament, it is the most important to constantly review and refurbish its structural-functional requirements and from time-to-time to consider renewing and reforming the entire gamut of its operational procedures to guard against decay.
- Parliamentary reforms includes the following :
  - Building a better image of Parliament.
  - Improving the quality and conduct of members.
  - By law, it must be provided that Parliament should be working for at least 100-120 days.
  - Improving information supply to Parliament and efficacy of committee scrutiny.
  - Legislative planning and improving the quality of laws, including the codification of Parliamentary Privileges.
  - Improving working of Parliamentary parties, floor management, Parliamentary time-table.
  - Rationalising and modernising rules of procedure to meet today's needs.

New Parliament

- On 28th May, 2023, Prime Minister inaugurated the new Parliament building, developed as a part of Central Vista Re-development Project.
- It is part of the Central Vista Project– the ongoing re-development project to revamp India's Central Administrative Area (designed by Sir Edwin Lutyens and Sir Herbert Baker during British colonial rule) located near Raisina Hill, New Delhi.
- It is designed by Ahmedabad-based HCP Design, Planning and Management under architect **Bimal Patel** and has been built by Tata Projects Ltd. The Prime Minister was inaugurated the Parliament and placed 'Sengol', the symbol of power transfer to India from the British.
- The new Parliament building, standing alongside the existing one, encompasses a built-up area of approximately 65,000 sq m.
- Its triangular shape ensures efficient utilisation of space, accommodating the evolving needs of a growing nation. The new building includes a larger Lok Sabha Hall with a capacity of up to 888 seats and a larger Rajya Sabha hall with up to 384 seats.
- Joint sessions of Parliament can now accommodate up to 1,272 seats, facilitating inclusive and robust democratic proceedings. A state-of-the-art Constitutional Hall serves as the heart of Indian democracy, placing citizens at the center of governance.
- Recognising the importance of accessibility, the new Parliament building prioritises divyang (differently-abled) individuals. It ensures that people with disabilities can move freely within the premises, fostering inclusivity and equal participation.
- Reflecting the cultural diversity of India in line with the 'Made in India' initiative Tripura's epitome bamboo wood flooring and carpets from UP's Mirzapur embellished the new Parliament.
- As with the current structure, Dholpur stone will serve as the main building material. Red granite might take the place of red sandstone in various interior spaces.

> Usually, there is a Governor for each state, but the 7th Constitutional Amendment Act of 1956, facilitated the appointment of the same person as a Governor for two or more states.

Chapter Twenty One

The Governor

As per Article 154, Governor is the Chief Executive and the Head of the State, similar to the President he/she is a nominal Executive Head. The real Executive Power remains with the Council of Ministers headed by the Chief Minister. When a Governor discharges the responsibilities of more than one state, he/she acts on the advice of the Council of Ministers of the respective states.

APPOINTMENT, QUALIFICATIONS, OATH AND CONDITIONS

- Article 155 says, the Governor of a State shall be appointed by the President of India by warrant under his/her hand and seal.
- In America, the Governor of a State is directly elected. India has adopted the Canadian model where the Governor of a province is appointed by the Governor-General.
- The Governor in this way is a nominee of the Central Government but the office of a Governor is not subordinate to the Central Government. It is an independent constitutional office.
- His/her usual term of office is 5 years and he/she holds office during the pleasure of the President.
- The Governor can also be transferred from one state to another by the President.
- The Governor can also resign any time by addressing his resignation to the President.
- The Legislature of a State or a High Court has no role in the removal of a Governor.

Qualifications

- Under Article 157, the Constitution of India lays down two qualifications for appointment of person as a Governor,
  - The Governor should be a citizen of India.
  - The Governor should have completed the age of 35 years.
- Over the year following conventions have been adopted based on Sarkaria Commission report :
  - The Governor should be an outsider who does not reside in the state where he will be appointed.
  - When appointing the Governor of a State, the President must consult with the state's Chief Minister.

Conditions for Governor's Office

- The Governor should not be a member of either Houses of Parliament or of a House of the State Legislature. The Governor should not hold any other office of profit.
- His/her emoluments allowances and privileges are determined by the Parliament by law.

- His/her emoluments and allowances should not be diminished during his office.

Terms of Office

- According to Article 156, the Governor serves for a term of 5 years from the date he assumed office.
- His term is subject to the pleasure of President. Governors whose terms have expired may be reappointed in the same or a different state.
- The Constitution has not laid down any grounds for the removal of the Governor by President.
- A Governor can also hold office beyond his term until his successor assumes charge. Further, the Governor can resign at any time by addressing a resignation letter to the President.
- The President has the authority to transfer a Governor from one state to another for the remainder of his tenure. Governor can serve over his 5 year term until the next appointment is made.

- He is entitled to the use of his office residence (Raj Bhawan) without payment of rent.
- If he is appointed as the Governor of two or more states, his salary and allowances payable to him are shared by the states in such proportion as determined by the President.

Oath and Affirmations

Article 159 provides that the Governor shall make and subscribe an oath or affirmation. The oath of Governor is administered by the Chief Justice of the concerned State's High Court and in his/her absence, the seniormost judge of that court available.

POWERS AND FUNCTIONS

- A Governor possesses executive, legislative, financial and judicial powers. The Governor has no diplomatic, military or emergency powers like the President.
- The Governor has also been given certain discretionary powers.

Executive Powers

- All executive actions of the Government of a State are formally taken in the name of the Governor.
- The Governor appoints the Chief Minister and other Ministers on the advice of the Chief Minister. They hold office during the pleasure of the Governor.
- There should be a Tribal Welfare Minister in the states of Jharkhand, Chhattisgarh, Madhya Pradesh and Odisha appointed by the Governor.
- The Governor appoints the Advocate-General of a State and determines his remuneration.
- The Advocate-General holds office during the pleasure of the Governor.
- The Governor appoints the State Election Commissioner and determines the conditions of service and tenure of the office.
- He/she also appoints the Chief Secretary in a State. The term of Chief Secretary is not fixed.
- The Governor also makes rules for transaction of business of a State Government and for allocation among the Ministers of the said business.
- Article 333 deals with power of Governor to nominate one member of Anglo-Indian Community in State Assemblies. However, by 104th Amendment Act the provision has been abolished.
- The Governor appoints the Chairman and the members of the State Public Service Commission. However, they can be removed only by the President of India and not by the Governor.
- The Governor can ask the Chief Minister to submit for the consideration of the Council of Ministers any matter on which a decision has been taken by a Minister, but which has not been considered by the Council of Ministers.
- The Governor of State can seek any information relating to the administration of the affairs of the State and proposals for legislations from the Chief Minister. He acts as Chancellor of universities in the state and also appoints Vice-Chancellors.

Legislative Powers

- A Governor is an integral part of the State Legislature Article 168. The Governor has the right of summoning or proroguing the State Legislature and dissolving the State Legislative Assembly.
- The Governor addresses the State Legislature at the commencement of the first session after each general election and the first session of each year.
- The Governor can send message to the Houses of Parliament or the Houses of the State Legislature, with respect to a bill pending in the Legislature or otherwise.
- The Governor can appoint any member of the State Legislative Assembly to preside over its proceedings, when the offices of both the Speaker and the Deputy Speaker fall vacant simultaneously.
- The Governor decides on the question of disqualification of the members of the State

Legislature in consultation with the Election Commission.

- As per Article 202, the Governor lays the reports of the State Public Service Commission, State Finance Commission and the Comptroller and Auditor-General relating to the accounts of the state, before the State Legislature.

Ordinance Making Power of Governor

- Article 213 states that the Governor of the State may issue ordinances when the State Legislative Assembly (or either of the two Houses in states with bicameral legislatures) is not in session. He can roll-out an ordinance for only those matters on which State Legislature can make laws.
- These ordinances must be approved by State Legislatures within six weeks from its reassembly in the house.
- The ordinance introduced by him can be withdrawn anytime :
  - It was argued in DC Wadhwa *v/s* the State of Bihar (1987) that the Legislative Power of the executive to promulgate ordinances is to be used in exceptional circumstances and not as a substitute for the law-making power of the Legislature.
  - Supreme Court in Krishna Kumar Singh *v/s* the State of Bihar held that the authority to issue ordinances is not an absolute entrustment, but is 'conditional upon satisfaction that circumstances exist rendering it necessary to take immediate action'.

Governor's Assent to Bill

- When a bill is sent to the Governor after it is passed by the State Legislature, he has the following options:
  - He gives his/her assent to the bill.
  - He may withhold his/her assent to the bill.
  - He may return the bill (if it is not a Money bill) for reconsideration of the State Legislature. If the State Legislature again passes the bill with or without amendments, a Governor has to give his assent to the bill.
- He must reserve for the consideration of the President, any bill passed by the State Legislature, which endangers the position of the State High Court. In addition, the Governor can also reserve the bill if it is of the following nature
  - ultra vires, i.e., against the provisions of Constitution.
  - opposed to the Directive Principles of State Policy.
  - that bill is inconsistent to union laws.

Financial Powers

- Money Bill can be introduced in the State Legislature only with the prior recommendation of the Governor. No demands for a grant can be made except on his/her recommendation. The Governor can make advances out of the Contingency Fund of the State to meet any unforeseen expenditure state.
- The Governor constitutes State Finance Commission after every 5 years to review the financial position of the Panchayats and the Municipalities. The Constitution confers on the Governor, to introduce the annual budget and also the supplementary budgets, before State Legislature.

Judicial Powers

- As per Article 161 the Governor can grant pardons, reprieves, respites and remissions of punishment or suspend, remit and commute the sentence of any person convicted of any offence against any law relating to a matter to which the executive power of the state extends.
- He is consulted by the President while appointing the judges of the concerned State High Court.
- Under Article 233, he makes appointment, postings and promotions of the District Judges in consultation with the State High Court.
- He also appoints persons to the Judicial Services of the State (other than District Judges) in consultation with the State High Court and the State Public Service Commission.

Discretionary Powers

- Reserve a bill for the reconsideration of the President. Recommend the imposition of President'a rule in the state. While exercising his/her function as the administrator of an adjoining Union Territory (in case of additional charge).
- Appointment of the Chief Minister when no party has clear cut majority in the State Legislature.
- Seeking information from the Chief Minister with regard to the administrative and legislative matters of the state. Dismissal of the Council of Ministers when it cannot prove the confidence of the State Legislative Assembly.
- Dissolution of the State Legislative Assembly, if the Council of Ministers has lost its majority. Determining the amount payable by the State of Assam, Meghalaya, Tripura and Mizoram to the autonomous Tribal District Council as royalty accruing from licenses for mineral exploration.

Veto Powers of the President and the Governor

Bill Types	President	Governor
Ordinary Bill	• When a bill is presented to him for his assent after passed by the Parliament, he has 3 alternatives : – To give his assent – To withhold his assent – To return the bill for reconsideration of the Parliament, if the bill is passed by the Parliament again with or without amendments then he must give his assent to the bill. (Suspensive veto), • **In case of State Legislature Bills** • The President has 3 alternatives – To give his assent – To withhold his assent – To return the bill for reconsideration of the State Legislature • The State Legislature must consider it within 6 months. If the bill is passed by the State Legislature again with or without amendments then he is not bound to give his assent to the bill.	• When a bill is presented to him for his assent after passed by the State Legislature, he has 4 alternatives : – To give his assent – To withhold his assent – To return the bill for reconsideration of the State Legislature, if the bill in passed by the State Legislature again with or without amendments then he must give his assent to the bill. (Suspensive veto), – To reserve the bill for the consideration of the President. • The Governor does not have any role and the assent of the Governor is not needed.
Money Bill	• He has 2 alternatives when a bill is passed by the Parliament and is presented before him – To give his assent – To withhold his assent – He cannot return the bill in this case and enjoys absolute veto only. He usually gives his assent as it is introduced in the Parliament with his prior permission. • **With respect to State Legislature Bills, he has 2 alternatives** – To give his assent – Withhold his assent • He cannot return the bill for the reconsideration of the State Legislature.	• He has 3 alternatives with a bill is passed by the State Legislature and is presented before him – To give his assent – To withhold his assent – To reserve the bill for the consideration of the President. – He cannot return the bill in this case. He usually gives his assent as it is introduced in the State Legislature with his prior permission. • The Governor does not have any role and the assent of the Governor is not needed.

Powers During President's Rule

- If the Governor thinks that the Government of the State cannot be carried on in accordance with the provisions of the Constitution, he/she may under Article 356 recommend to the President to impose the President's rule in that state.
- As soon as the President rule is imposed, the administration of the state is carried on by the Governor acting as the representative of the President.
- SR Bommai *v/s* Union of India (1994) was a landmark judgement of the Supreme Court of India in which the court considered at length provisions of Article 356 of the Indian Constitution and associated concerns.
- The judgement tried to put a stop to the systematic misuse of Article 356 of the Indian Constitution, which allows the President to impose his rule over State Governments.
- The floor of the Assembly is the only forum that should test the majority of the government of the day and not the subjective opinion of the Governor.

Comparision between Powers of President and Governor

President	Governor
• He can pardon, reprieve, respite, remit, suspend or commute a death sentence. He is the only authority to pardon a death sentence as well as sentence by a court martial.	• He cannot pardon a death sentence. Even if a state law prescribes for death sentence, the power to grant pardon lies with the President and not the Governor. But, the Governor can suspend, remit or commute a death sentence.
• He needs no instruction for making an ordinance.	• He cannot make an ordinance without the instructions from the President in three cases: – If a bill containing the same provisions would have required the previous sanction of the President. – If he would have deemed it necessary to reserve a bill containing the same provisions for the consideration of the President.
• The President does not possess any constitutional discretion however he may exercise certain situational discretion.	• His discretionary powers are wider than the President as he possesses both situational and constitutional discretion.

The Chief Ministers and the council of Ministers, as outlined in part IV of the Indian constitution, for a key part of the state executive, alongside the Governor and Advocate General of State.

Chapter Twenty Two

Chief Minister and Council of Ministers

CHIEF MINISTER

The Chief Minister is the real executive and is the Head of the Government of a state. The position of the Chief Minister at the state level is similar to the position of the Prime Minister at the Centre.

Qualifications

A Chief Minister must be a citizen of India, should be a member of the State Legislature, 25 years of age or more.

Appointment

- Article 164 of the Constitution envisages that the Chief Minister shall be appointed by the Governor.
- The Governor appoints the leader of the largest party of the House or leader chosen by the largest coalition to become the Chief Minister.
- If no party has a clear majority, the Governor may use situational discretion.
- He may appoint a leader as Chief Minister and then ask him to demonstrate his majority on the floor of the Parliament.
- If the Chief Minister dies without a successor, the Governor may pick one at his discretion, however if the ruling party nominates someone, the Governor has no choice but to appoint that person.
- A person who is not a member of the State Legislature can be appointed as Chief Minister for six months, within this time, he should be elected to the State Legislature, failing which he ceases to be the Chief Minister.
- A Chief Minister may be a member of any one of the two houses of State Legislature.

Term of the Office

- The term of the Chief Minister is not fixed and he holds office during the pleasure of the Governor. He cannot be dismissed by the Governor as long as he enjoys the majority support in the **Legislative Assembly**.
- The State Legislative Assembly can also remove him by passing a vote of no-confidence against him.

Oath and Affirmation

- Before the Chief Minister enters his office, the Governor administers to him the oaths of office and secrecy. In his oath of office, the Chief Minister swears :
  - to bear true faith and allegiance to the Constitution of India
  - to uphold the sovereignty and integrity of India
  - to faithfully and conscientiously discharge the duties of his office and
  - to do right to all manner of people in accordance with the Constitution and the law, without fear or favour, affection or ill-will.

Salary and Allowances

- As per Article 164(5), the State Legislature determines the Chief Minister's salary and allowance by law.
- He is entitled to salary and sumptuary allowance. He also receives free housing, allowances for travel, free medical care and other perk.

Powers and Functions

Various powers and functions related to Chief Minister are as follows :

In Relation to the Council of Ministers

- The Chief Minister, recommends persons to be appointed as the Ministers by the Governor. Allocates and reshuffles the portfolios among the Ministers.
- Can ask a Minister to resign or advise the Governor to dismiss the Minister in case of difference of the opinion.
- Presides over the meetings of the Council of Ministers and influences its decisions. Guides, directs, controls and co-ordinates the activities of all the Ministers. They can dissolve the Council of Ministers by resigning from the office.

In Relation to the Governor

- According to Article 167, Chief Minister is the principal channel of communication between the Governor and the Council of Ministers.
- In this capacity, he performs the following functions :
  - the Chief Minister communicates to the Governor of all decisions of the Council of Ministers relating to the administration of the state affairs and proposals for legislation.
  - the Chief Minister furnishes such information relating to the administration of the affairs of the state and proposals for legislation as the Governor may call for.
  - if the Governor so requires, to submit for the consideration of the Council of Ministers any matter on which a decision has been taken by a Minister but which has not been considered by the Council.
  - the Chief Minister advises the Governor with regard to the appointment of important officials like Advocate-General, the Chairman and the Members of the State Public Service Commission, the State Election Commissioner, etc.

In Relation to the State Legislature

- The Chief Minister advises the Governor with regard to the summoning and proroguing of the sessions of the State Legislature.
- The Chief Minister can recommend the dissolution of the Legislative Assembly to the Governor at any time.
- The Chief Minister announces the government policies on the floor of the house. He has the right to intervene in any debate in the State Legislature.

STATE COUNCIL OF MINISTERS

- State Council of Ministers is similar to Central Council of Ministers. The Council comprises Ministers appointed by the Governor on the recommendation of the Chief Minister.
- The Governor also appoints a Tribal Affairs Minister for the following states :
  - Chhattisgarh
  - Jharkhand
  - Madhya Pradesh
  - Odisha
- According to Article 163, every state shall have a Council of Ministers headed by the Chief Minister to aid and advise the Governor in the exercise of his/her powers and functions except the discretionary ones.
- Article 164 deals with the appointment, tenure, responsibility, qualifications, oath, salary and allowances of the Ministers.

Qualifications and Appointment of Council of Ministers

- A Minister Incharge of a State Council must be a member of the State Legislature.
- If he is not a member of Legislative Assembly when he joins the Council of Ministers, he must become one in six months.
- Further, the qualifications needed to be a Member of the State Legislature are :
  - he must be a citizen of India. He must bear true faith and allegiance to the Constitution of India.
  - he must be not less than 30 years of age in the case of the Legislative Council.
  - he must not be less than 25 years of age in the case of the Legislative Assembly.
- The Council of Ministers shall be collectively responsible to the State Legislature Assembly. The term of Council of Ministers headed by Chief Minister is not fixed and they hold their office during the pleasure of Governor.

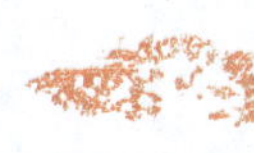

- A Minister who is not a member of the State Legislature for any period of 6 consecutive months shall cease to be a Minister.

The **91st Amendment Act of 2003** has added the following two provisions :

- The total number of ministers, including the Chief Minister in the Council of Ministers in a state shall not exceed **15% of the total strength** of the Legislative Assembly of that state. But, the number of Ministers including the Chief Minister in a state shall not be less than 12.
- For states like Sikkim, Mizoram and Goa, the strength of Assembly is less than 40. In case of Union Territory of Delhi, the strength of Council of Ministers cannot exceed 10% of strength of Assembly.

Salary and Allowances

- The salaries and allowances of Ministers are determined by the State Legislature from time-to-time.
- A Minister gets the salary and allowances which are payable to a Member of the State Legislature.

Composition of Council of Ministers

- The size of the Council is not mentioned in the Indian Constitution. Chief Minister decides the size and the rank of the Ministers as per the requirement in the State Legislature. There are four categories of Council of Ministers :
    - Cabinet Ministers They are experienced Ministers who oversee crucial departments like Home, Finance, Defence, Agriculture, Foreign Affairs, etc. A Cabinet Minister always serves as the Head of a Ministry and is given independent control of it. He attends the cabinet meeting on his own behalf, usually with the help of a Minister of State, Deputy Minister or both.
    - Ministers of State A Minister of State may be given independent charge of a ministry. He cannot attend the meetings of the Cabinet on his own right but can attend if invited.
    - Deputy Ministers A Deputy Minister is a junior member of the Council of Minister and not given independent charge of any department. He is put under the charge of either Minister of the cabinet rank or that of the Minister of State so that he gets proper training.
    - Deputy Chief Minister He has been appointed for political reasons. It is non-constitutional office. Portfolio like finance or home are usually held by him.

Responsibilities of Council of Ministers

- **Collective Responsibility**
  Article 164-Council of Minister is collectively responsible to the Legislative Assembly of the State for all their acts of omission and commission
- **Individual Responsibility**
  – The ministers hold office during the pleasure of the Governor
  – Governor can remove a minister only on the advice of the Chief Minister

Cabinet Committees

- The cabinet works through various committees called Cabinet Committees. They are of two types–**Standing** and **Ad-hoc**.
- The former are of a permanent nature while the latter are of a temporary nature.
- They are set-up by the Chief Minister according to the exigencies of the time and requirements of the situation. Hence, their number, nomenclature and composition varies from time-to-time.

ADVOCATE-GENERAL

- Article 165 in the Indian Constitution deals with the Advocate-General for the State.
- The Advocate- General is the first Law Officer of the State.
- The Advocate-General office and functions are comparable to that of the Attorney-General of India.
- The Advocate-General appointed by the Governor and holds the office during his/her pleasure.
- The Advocate-General remunerations are also determined by the Governor.
- To be appointed to the office of the Advocate-General, he/she must be qualified to be a Judge of the High Court.
- The Advocate-General has the right to attend and speak in the proceedings of either Houses of the State Legislature without any right to vote.
- The Advocate-General has the right of audience in any court in the state.

"The Constitution has given the states the option of setting up a unicameral legislature or a bicameral legislature.

Chapter Twenty Three

State Legislature

Articles 168 to 212 in Part VI of the Constitution deals with the organisation, composition, duration, officers, procedures, privileges and powers of the State Legislature.

According to Article 168 of the Indian Constitution, there shall be a legislature in every state and it shall consist of the Governor, one or two Houses of the Legislature.

- In Article 168 of the Constitution, provision has been made for a legislature for each state.
- In the states where there is unicameral system, there is only one House, that is Vidhan Sabha and in the states where there is bicameral system, there is both Vidhan Sabha and Vidhan Parishad.
- The Legislative Assembly is the lower house while the Legislative Council is the upper house of the State Legislature.
- Andhra Pradesh, Telangana, Uttar Pradesh, Bihar, Maharashtra and Karnataka are the six states that have a Legislative Council.
- The Jammu and Kashmir Legislative Council was abolished in 2019 as a result of the Jammu and Kashmir Reorganisation Bill, which reduced the State of Jammu and Kashmir to the Union Territories of Jammu and Kashmir and Ladakh.

LEGISLATIVE COUNCIL

- The position of the Legislative Council in a state is similar to that of the Rajya Sabha at the Union level.
- This applies in the matter of privileges and immunities of legislatures, disqualification of members, relation between the two Houses, legislative procedure, origin of Money Bills, etc.
- Article 169 provides for the abolition and creation of the Legislative Councils in the state by the Parliament.

Composition of the Council

- The maximum strength of the Council is fixed at one-third of the total strength of the assembly and the minimum strength is fixed at 40.
- The members of a Legislative Council are elected in accordance with the system of proportional representation by means of the Single Transferable Vote.

- The Council is constituted as provided in Clause (3) of Article 171.

Composition of Council

Article 171(3) states that the total number of members of the Legislative Council of a state consists of

- **Local Body Represntation** 1/3rd of the members are elected by the members of local bodies like muncipalities and panchayats.
- **Legislative Assembly Representation** 1/3rd are elected by the members of state assembly from among those who are not members of the assembly.
- **Graduate Representation** 1/12th are elected by graduates of three years standing in the state.
- **Teacher Representation** 1/12th are elected by teaches in educational institutions within the state.
- **Governor's Nomination** 1/6th are nominated by the Governor, including persons with expertise in areas like literature, science and social service.

LEGISLATIVE ASSEMBLY

- Legislative Assembly (Vidhan Sabha) is the lower house of the Legislature of the state as in the case of the Parliament i.e., Lok Sabha.
- It represents the will of the people of the state. Members of this House are directly elected by the people.

Composition of the Assembly

- Article 170(1) holds that the Legislative Assembly of each state shall consist of not more than 500 and not less than 60, members chosen by direct election from territorial constituencies in the state.
- However, in case of Arunachal Pradesh, Sikkim and Goa, the minimum number is fixed at 30 and in case of Mizoram it is 40 and in case of Nagaland it is 46.
- After each census, a readjustment is to be made in the total number of seats in the assembly of each state and the division of each state into territorial constituencies. Accordingly, Parliament has enacted the Delimitation Commission Acts in 1952, 1962, 1972 and 2002 for this purpose.
- By 84th Constitutional Amendment made in the year 2001, a provision has been made not to change the number of seats in the Lok Sabha and Legislative Assemblies till the year 2026.
- The Constitution provided for the reservation of seats for Scheduled Castes and Scheduled Tribes in the assembly of each state on the basis of population ration of the state.

Legislative Assemblies and Legislative Councils in States/UT's

States/UTs	Legislative Assemblies	Legislative Councils
Andhra Pradesh	175	58
Arunachal Pradesh	60	
Assam	126	–
Bihar	243	75
Chhattisgarh	90	–
Delhi	70	–
Goa	40	–
Gujarat	182	–
Haryana	90	–
Himachal Pradesh	68	–
Jammu and Kashmir	90	–
Jharkhand	81	–
Karnataka	224	75
Kerala	140	–
Madhya Pradesh	230	–
Maharashtra	288	78
Manipur	60	–
Meghalaya	60	–
Mizoram	40	–
Nagaland	60	–
Odisha	147	–
Puducherry	30	–
Punjab	117	–
Rajasthan	200	–
Sikkim	32	–
Tamil Nadu	234	–
Tripura	60	–
Uttar Pradesh	403	100
Uttarakhand	70	–
West Bengal	294	–
Telangana	119	40

Qualifications for the Houses

- According to Article 173, a person shall be qualified to be chosen to fill a seat in the Legislature of a state if he :
  - is a citizen of India and makes and subscribes before some person authorised on that behalf by the Election Commission an oath or affirmation

according to the form set out for the purpose in the Third Schedule.

- is, in the case of a seat in the Legislative Assembly, not less than 25 years of age and in the case of a seat in the Legislative Council, not less than 30 years of age.
- possesses such other qualifications as may be prescribed in that behalf by or under any law made by Parliament.

Additional Qualifications in the Representation of People's Act, 1951

- A person must be an elector for an assembly constituency in the concerned state to be elected in the Legislative Council and for Governor's nomination, the person must be a resident in the concerned state.
- A person must be an elector for an assembly constituency in the concerned state if he wishes to be elected in the Legislative Assembly.
- To contest a seat reserved for SC's and ST's, a person must be a member of SC and ST.

Disqualifications of the Houses

- Under the Constitution, a person shall be disqualified for being chosen as for being a member of the Legislative Assembly or Legislative Council of a State:
  - if he holds any office of profit under the Union or State Government (except that of a Minister or any other office exempted by State Legislature).
  - if he is of unsound mind and stands so declared by a court.
  - if he is an undischarged insolvent.
  - if he is not a citizen of India or has voluntarily acquired the citizenship of a Foreign state or is under any acknowledgement of allegiance to a Foreign state.
  - if he is so disqualified under any law made by Parliament.

Additional Disqualifications in the Representation of People's Act, 1951

- The person must not have been guilty of certain electoral offences or corrupt practices in the elections. The person must not have been convicted for any offense resulting in imprisonment for two or more years.
- The person must not have failed to lodge an account of his election expenses within time.
- The person must not have any interest in government contracts, works or services.
- The person must not hold any office of profit in a corporation where the government has atleast 25% share. The person must not have been dismissed from government service for corruption or disloyalty to the state.
- The person must not have been convicted for promoting enmity between different groups.
- The person must not have been punished for practicing or preaching social crimes such as untouchability, dowry and sati.
- According to Article 191(2), a person shall be disqualified for being a member of the Legislative Assembly or Legislative Council of a State if he is, so disqualified under the Anti-Defection Law of the Tenth Schedule.

Duration of State Legislature

Duration of Assembly

- According to Article 172(1), Legislative Assembly of every state, unless sooner dissolved, shall continue for five years from the date appointed for its first meeting and no longer.
- If a proclamation of National Emergency is in operation, the term of the assembly can be extended by Parliament by law for a period not exceeding one year at a time and not extending in any case beyond a period of six months after the **proclamation** has ceased to operate.

Duration of Council

- Like Rajya Sabha, the Legislative Council is a continuing chamber, i.e., it is a permanent body and is not subject to dissolution. But, **one-third** of its members retire on the expiration of every second year. So, a member continues as such for six years.
- The vacant seats are filled up by fresh elections and nominations at every **third year**. The retiring members are also eligible for next term.

Oath, Affirmation and Salaries

- Every member of either House of State Legislature, before taking his seat in the House has to make and subscribe an oath or affirmation before the Governor.
- In this oath, a member of the State Legislature swears:
  - to bear true faith and allegiance to the Constitution of India.
  - to uphold the sovereignty and integrity of India.
  - to faithfully discharge the duty of his office. Unless a member takes the oath, he cannot vote and participate in the proceedings of the House and

does not become eligible to the privileges and immunities of the State Legislature.

- The salaries and allowances of the members of the State Legislature are determined by the State Legislature.

Vacation of Assembly Seat

Under Article 190, Constitution mentioned about vacation of seats :

- No Double membership A person can't become a member of both Houses of the Legislature of a State and Legislature of the State by law can make a provision for the vacation of a seat by a person who is chosen as member of both Houses of the State Legislature.
- No membership of two State Legislatures If a person is chosen as a member of the Legislatures of two or more states, then he has to choose a State Legislature within a fixed time period in which he wants to continue as a member. Failing to do so, his seat in all the legislatures became vacant.
- Resignation a seat becomes vacant when a member resigns by writing to the speaker of the Legislative Assembly or chairman of the Legislative Council.
- Absence If a member remains absent from all the meetings of the house of State Legislature for a period of sixty days without its permission then the house can declare the seat of that member vacant.

Conditions for Vacancies outside Article 191

Outside Article 191, there are other cases as well related to the vacancy of seats :

- If the election of a member of the State Legislature is declared void. If a member of the State Legislature is expelled from the House.
- If the member of the State Legislature gets elected to the office of President, Vice-President or Governor of the State.

PRESIDING OFFICERS OF THE STATE LEGISLATURE

Presiding Officers of the State Legislature are as follows :

Chairman of the Council

- According to Article 182, the Legislative Council elects two of its members as Chairman and Deputy Chairman respectively.
- The Chairman is elected by the Council itself from amongst its members. He may vacate his office by resigning by writing to the Deputy Chairman or if he ceases to be a member of the Council.
- His powers and functions are comparable to the Speaker of the Assembly with few exceptions. Such as the Speaker has one special power which is not enjoyed by the Chairman.
- The Speaker decides whether a bill is a Money Bill or not and his decision on this question is final.

Deputy Chairman of Council

- Like the Chairman, the Deputy Chairman is also elected by the Council itself from amongst its members.
- The Deputy Chairman performs the duties of the Chairman's office when it is vacant.
- He also acts as the Chairman, when the latter is absent from the sitting of the Council. In both the cases, he has all the powers of the Chairman.

Speaker of Assembly

According to Article 178, the Speaker is elected by the assembly itself from amongst its members and remains in office during the life of the assembly.

Duration of the Office and Vacancy of Seat

- Article 179 says that, the Speaker holds the office from the date of his election till the first meeting of the Legislative Assembly after the dissolution of the one to which he was elected unless:
  - he ceases to be a Member of the House or
  - he resigns by writing to the Deputy Speaker or
  - if a resolution for his removal is passed by the House by absolute majority.
  - Such a resolution can only be moved after giving a notice of 14 days.

Powers and Duties of Speaker

- His duties are similar to those of the Speaker of the Lok Sabha.
- He adjourns the assembly or suspends the meeting in the absence of a quorum and maintains order and decorum in the assembly for conducting its business and regulating its proceedings.
- He exercises a casting vote in case of a tie and is the final authority to decide whether a bill is a money bill or not.
- He can allow a secret sitting of the House at the request of the leader of the House.

- He decides the questions of disqualification of a member of the assembly, arising on the ground of defection under the provisions of the Tenth Schedule of the Constitution.
- He appoints the Chairman of all the committees of the assembly and supervises their functioning.
- He himself is the Chairman of the Business Advisory Committee, the Rules Committee and the General Purpose Committee.

Deputy Speaker of Assembly

- Like the Speaker, the Deputy Speaker is also elected by the assembly itself from amongst its members.
- He is elected after the election of the Speaker has taken place.
- The Deputy Speaker performs the duties of the Speaker's office when it is vacant.
- He also acts as the Speaker when the latter is absent from the sitting of assembly. In both the cases, he has all the powers of the Speaker.

Comparison of Legislative Council and Legislative Assembly

- In the passage of an **Ordinary Bill**, both the Houses enjoy equal status but in case of disagreement, the will of the assembly prevails over that of the Council and there is no provision of joint sitting in this regard.
- A Money Bill can be introduced only in assembly not in Council. The Council has no participation in the election of the President.
- It also has no effective say in the ratification of the **Constitutional Amendment Bill**. Also, the existence of the Council depends on the will of the assembly.

Sessions of the State Legislature

- Summoning The Governor from time-to-time summons each House of State Legislature to meet. The minimum gap between the two sessions of the legislature cannot be more than 6 months.
- Adjournment It suspends the work in a sitting for a specified time which may be hours, days or weeks.
- Prorogation The Governor can also prorogue House which is in session. The Presiding Officer (Speaker or Chairman) declares the House adjourned sine die, when business of the session is completed.
- Dissolution A dissolution ends the life of the existing House and a new House is constituted after the general elections are held.
- Governor's Address Under Article 176, the Governor shall address the Legislative Assembly at the beginning of the first session after the election to the Legislative Assemblies and at the beginning of each financial year.

LEGISLATIVE PROCEDURES

The procedure followed in both the Houses to pass bills into act is the same. The bills go through the same stages in both the Houses.

Ordinary Bill

- According to Article 196, an Ordinary Bill is that bill, which is neither a Money Bill nor a bill involving expenditure from the Consolidated Fund of the State.
- It is a bill relating to matters of ordinary legislation. It can be introduced in either House of the State Legislature if it has a Legislative Council. The bill has to be passed by both the Houses of Legislature.
- Article 197 provides the following cases of conflict in the two Houses of a State Legislature :
  - A bill having been passed by the Legislative Assembly and sent to the Legislative Council is not returned within three months by the Council.
  - A bill having been passed by the Legislative Assembly is rejected by the Legislative Council.
  - If the Legislative Assembly does not accept the recommendation or the amendment proposed by the Legislative Council.
- And after all these phases, if the Legislative Assembly passes the bill again with or without the amendments proposed by the Legislative Council, it shall be deemed to be passed by both the Houses.
- It is important to note that there is no provision for holding a joint sitting of the two Houses of the State Legislature for resolving a deadlock on a Non-Money Bill. As it is in Union Bill in the Parliament.
- The above provisions show that the position of the Council with respect to the assembly is very weak and the assembly can pass any bill it wants even if the Council disagrees.

Passage of Bill in State Legislature

Step 1 Introduction of the Bill

A minister or member introduces the bill in either house of the state Legislature, outlining its title and objective.

Step 2 First Reading

The bill is published in the state gazette, and no discussions take place at this stage.

Step 3 Second Reading

General discussion of the bill takes place, with four possible actions :

- Immediate consideration
- Referral to a select committee
- Referral to a joint committee
- Public opinion solicitation

Step 4 Third Reading

The bill is voted on, with two possible outcomes :

- Acceptance (majority vote required)
- Rejection

Step 5 Passage in the Second House

The bill goes through the same three stages (First Reading, Second Reading, Third Reading) in the second house, with possible actions :

- Passage without changes
- Passage with amendments
- Rejection
- No action

Step 6 Assent of the Governor

The Governor reviews the bill and decides to :

- Give assent (becoming an act)
- Withhold assent
- Return for reconsideration
- Reserve the bill for President

Money Bill

- According to Article 199, Money Bill is a bill, which exclusively deals with taxation matters. It can only be introduced in the Legislative Assembly.
- A Money Bill is considered to be a government bill and it can only be introduced by a Minister.
- It can not be introduced in the assembly except with prior recommendation of the Governor and if any question arises whether a bill is a Money Bill or not, the decision of the Speaker of the Legislative Assembly shall be final.
- As per Article 198, if the Legislative Assembly accepts any of the recommendations of the Legislative Council, the Money Bill shall be deemed to have been passed by both Houses with the amendments recommended by the Legislative Council and accepted by the Legislative Assembly.
- The Legislative Council has to return the Money Bill within 14 days from the date of receipt with or without any amendments and the Legislative Assembly may or may not agree with the amendments, as in the case of Money Bill in the Parliament.

Assent on Bills by Governor and President

- Assent of the Governor (Article 200) deals with the procedures regarding the assent to the bills passed by the State Legislature. It holds that, when a bill has been passed by the Legislative Assembly of a State or, in the case of having a Legislative Council, has been passed by both Houses of the Legislature of the State, it shall be presented to the Governor and the Governor shall declare either that he assents to the bill or that he withholds assent there from or that he reserves the bill for the consideration of the President.
- In case of Money Bills, the Governor may either give his assent to the bill, withhold his assent to the bill or reserve the bill for the assent of the President but cannot return the bill for the reconsideration of the State Legislature.
- Assent of the President (Article 201), when a bill is reserved by the Governor for the consideration of the President, the President shall declare either that he assents to the bill or that he withholds assent to the bill or return the bill for reconsideration of the Houses of the State Legislature.
- After passing from the State Legislature again with or without recommendation or amendments, the President is not bound to give his/her assent.
- In case of a money bill reserved for the President, he may either give his assent to the bill or withhold his assent but cannot return the bill for reconsideration of the State Legislature.

State Funds

- Consolidated Fund of the State According to Article 266(1), all revenues received by the government and money received from the recovery of loans given by the government are deposited in the Consolidated Fund. After the approval of the State Legislature, the government bears all its expenses from this fund.
- State Public Account According to Article 266(2), all other public moneys received by or on behalf of the State Government are deposited in the public accounts of the state.
- State Contingency Fund Under Article 267, there is a fund established for contingency expenditure. The Contingency Fund is under the control of the Governor and permission of the Governor is mandatory to withdraw money from this fund.

PRIVILEGES OF STATE LEGISLATURE

- The privileges of the State Legislature are also extended to those persons who are entitled to speak and take part in the proceedings of a house of the State Legislature or any of its committees. Eg- the Advocate-General.

- These privileges are not available to the Governor despite being an integral part of the State Legislature.
- Each of the House has the right to publish its reports, debates and proceedings.
- It can make rules to regulate its own procedure and the conduct of its business and to adjudicate (to make a formal decision about something or to act as a judge in an argument or competition) upon such manners.
- The courts are prohibited to enquire into the proceedings of the House and its proceedings.

There are two kinds of privileges of State Legislature. They are :

1. Collective Privileges

The privileges belonging to each House of the State Legislature collectively are as follows :

- It has the right to publish its reports, debates and proceedings and also the right to prohibit others from publishing the same. It can exclude strangers from its proceedings and hold secret sittings to discuss some important matters.
- It can make rules to regulate its own procedure and the conduct of its business and to adjudicate upon such matters.
- It can punish members as well as outsiders for breach of its privileges.
- It has the right to receive immediate information of the arrest, detention, conviction, imprisonment and release of a member.
- It can institute inquiries and order the attendance of witnesses and send for relevant papers and records.
- The courts are prohibited to inquire into the proceedings of a House or its committees.
- No person (either a member or outsider) can be arrested and no legal process (civil or criminal) can be served within the precincts of the House without the permission of the Presiding Officer.

2. Individual Privileges

The privileges belonging to the members individually are as follows :

- They cannot be arrested during the session of the State Legislature and 40 days before the beginning and 40 days after the end of such session.
- This privilege is available only in civil cases and not in criminal cases or Preventive Detention cases. They have freedom of speech in the State Legislature.
- No member is liable to any proceedings in any court for anything said or any vote given by him in the State Legislature or its committees.
- They are exempted from jury service. They can refuse to give evidence and appear as a witness in a case pending in a court when the State Legislature is in session.

LAPSING OF BILLS

The position with respect to lapsing of bills on the dissolution of the assembly is mentioned below :

- A bill pending in the assembly lapses.
- A bill passed by the assembly but pending in the Council lapses.
- A bill pending in the Council but not passed by the assembly does not lapse.
- A bill passed by the assembly or passed by both the Houses but without the assent of the Governor or the President does not lapse.
- A bill passed by the assembly or passed by both the Houses, but returned by the President for reconsideration of House(s) does not lapse.

Quorum

- It is mentioned under the Article 189 (3) of the Indian Constitution. It refers to the minimum number of legislators required in the House to conduct the proceedings and hold the sitting of the House.
- It requires atleast ten members or one-tenth of the total number of members of the House, whichever is greater to hold the sitting of the House.
- The Presiding Officer adjourns or suspends the meeting until there is a quorum.

Language in State Legislature

- The Constitution has declared the official language(s) of the state is Hindi or English, to be the languages for transacting business in the State Legislature. However, the Presiding Officer can permit a member to address the House in his mother-tongue.
- The State Legislature is authorised to decide whether to continue or discontinue English as a floor language after the completion of 15 years from the commencement of the Constitution (i.e., from 1965).
- In case of Himachal Pradesh, Manipur, Meghalaya and Tripura, this time limit is 25 years and that of Arunachal Pradesh, Goa and Mizoram, it is 40 years.

Important Articles Related with State Legislature

Articles	Subject Matter
Article 168	Constitution of legislatures in states
Article 169	Abolition or creation of Legislative Councils in states
Article 170	Composition of the Legislative Assemblies
Article 171	Composition of the Legislative Councils
Article 172	Duration of State Legislatures
Article 173	Qualification for membership of the State Legislature
Article 174	Sessions of the State Legislature, prorogation and dissolution
Article 175	Right of Governor to address and send messages to the House of Houses
Article 176	Special address by the Governor
Article 177	Rights of Ministers and Advocate-General as respects the Houses
Article 178	The Speaker and Deputy Speaker of the Legislative Assembly
Article 179	Vacation and resignation of and removal from, the offices of Speaker and Deputy Speaker
Article 180	Power of the Deputy Speaker or other person to perform the duties of the office of or to act as, Speaker
Article 181	The Speaker or the Deputy Speaker not to preside while a resolution for his removal from office is under consideration
Article 182	The Chairman and Deputy Chairman of the Legislative Council
Article 183	Vacation and resignation of and removal from, the offices of Chairman and Deputy Chairman
Article 184	Power of the Deputy Chairman or other person to perform the duties of the office of or to act as, Chairman
Article 185	The Chairman or the Deputy Chairman not to preside while a resolution for his removal from office is under consideration
Article 186	Salaries and allowances of the Speaker and Deputy Speaker and the Chairman and Deputy Chairman

Articles	Subject Matter
Article 187	Secretariat of State Legislature
Article 188	Oath or affirmation by members
Article 189	Voting in Houses, power of Houses to act notwithstanding vacancies and quorum
Article 190	Vacation of seats
Article 191	Disqualifications for membership
Article 192	Decision on questions as to disqualifications of members
Article 193	Penalty for sitting and voting before making oath or when not qualified or when disqualified
Article 194	Powers, privileges, etc, of the House of Legislatures and of the members and committees thereof
Article 195	Salaries and allowances of members
Article 196	Provisions as to introduction and passing of bills
Article 197	Restriction on powers of Legislative Council as to bills other than Money Bills
Article 198	Special procedure in respect of Money Bills
Article 199	Definition of 'Money Bills'
Article 200	Assent to bills
Article 201	Bills reserved for consideration
Article 202	Annual financial statement
Article 203	Procedure in legislature with respect to estimates
Article 204	Appropriation Bills
Article 205	Supplementary, additional or excess grants
Article 206	Votes on account, votes of credit and exceptional grants
Article 207	Special provisions as to Financial Bills
Article 208	Rules of procedure
Article 209	Regulation by law of procedure in the legislature of the state in relation to financial business
Article 210	Language to be used in the legislature
Article 211	Restriction on discussion in the legislature
Article 212	Courts not to inquire into proceedings of the legislature

“

Article 124 (1) of the Indian Constitution provides that there must be a Supreme Court of India. It is the Supreme Judicial Authority and the highest Court of India.

Chapter Twenty Four

Supreme Court

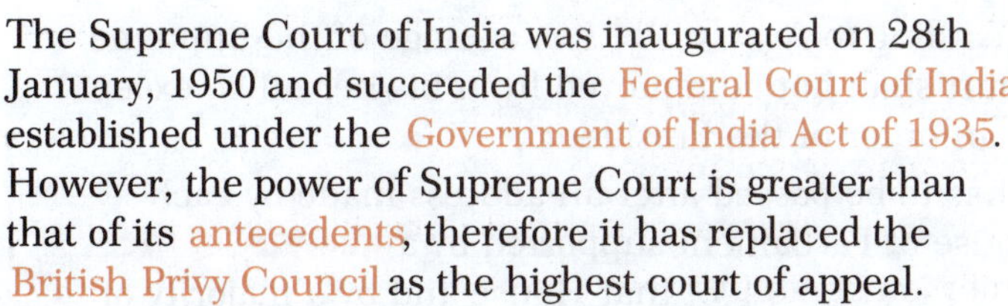

The Supreme Court of India was inaugurated on 28th January, 1950 and succeeded the Federal Court of India, established under the Government of India Act of 1935. However, the power of Supreme Court is greater than that of its antecedents, therefore it has replaced the British Privy Council as the highest court of appeal.

The Constitutional provisions related to the Supreme Court are contained in Part V from Articles 124 to 147. These articles deal with the organisation, independence, jurisdiction, powers, procedures and so on of the Supreme Court. Supreme Court is the Apex-Court or the head of entire judicial system.

Composition of Supreme Court

- As of February 2023, the Supreme Court has 34 judges including the Chief Justice of India (CJI).
- In 1950, when it was established, it had 8 judges including the Chief Justice of India. They can be regulated by the Parliament through Legislation.

Appointment of Supreme Court Judges

- The Judges of the Supreme Court are appointed by the President Article 124(2).
- The Chief Justice is appointed by the President after consultation with such Judges of the Supreme Court and High Court as he/she deems necessary.
- The other judges are appointed by the President after consultation with the Chief Justice and such other Judges of the Supreme Court and High Courts as he/she deems necessary.
- The consultation with the Chief Justice is obligatory in the case of appointment of a Judge other than Chief Justice.
- Earlier during the period from 1950-1973, the convention was to appoint the seniormost judge of the Supreme Court as the Chief Justice of India. But, this system was violated two times
  - When AN Ray was appointed as CJI in 1973.
  - When MU Beg was appointed as CJI in 1977.
- In the Second Judges Case (1993), the Supreme Court ruled that only the seniormost judge of the Supreme Court should be appointed to the office of the Chief Justice of India.

Collegium System

- Collegium system was evolved during the 'three judges case' and it is in practice, since 1998. It is used for appointments and transfers of judges in High Courts and Supreme Court.
- The Supreme Court collegium is headed by the Chief Justice of India and comprises four other seniormost judges of the court. Judges of the higher judiciary are appointed only through the collegium system.
- The collegium recommends the names of lawyers or judges to the Central Government. Similarly, the Central Government also sends some of its proposed names to the collegium.
- Through, the 99th Constitutional Amendment Act of 2014, the National Judicial Commission Act (NJAC) was established to replace the collegium system for the appointment of judges.

- However, the Supreme Court upheld the collegium system and struck down the NJAC as unconstitutional in the Fourth Judges Case (2015).

Three Judges Cases over Consultation of Collegium System

- First Judges Case (1982) The court held that consultation does not mean concurrence and it only implies exchange of views.
- Second Judges Case (1993) The court reversed its earlier ruling changed the meaning of the word consultation to concurrence. Hence, it ruled that the advice tendered by the Chief Justice of India is binding on the President in matters of appointment of Supreme Court Judges. But any such advice would be tendered after Chief Justice of India consults with two of his most senior judges.

Qualifications and Oath/Affirmations

- A person shall not be qualified for appointment as a Judge of the Supreme Court unless he/she :
    - is a citizen of India and
    - has been for atleast five years a Judge of a High Court or two such courts in succession or has been for atleast ten years an Advocate of a High Court or two or more such courts in succession and
    - is in the opinion of the President, a distinguished jurist.
- The Constitution does not prescribe minimum age limit for a judge to occupy his/her office.
- Every person appointed to be a Judge of the Supreme Court, before entering upon his/her office, make and subscribe before the President an oath or affirmation according to the form set out in the third Schedule of the Constitution.

Term of Office

- A Judge of the Supreme Court continues to hold the office till he/she attains the age of 65 years.
- A Judge of the Supreme Court can be removed from his office by the President on the recommendation of the Parliament.
- A Judge of Supreme Court, after retirement shall not do legal practice in any court in the Territory of India and shall not plead before any authority under the government.

Salaries and Allowances of Supreme Court Judges

- The Parliament has the power to regulate the salaries, allowances, privileges, leave and pension of the judges during his/her term of office.
- The only exception is that during financial emergency (Article 360), the salaries and other allowances of the judges can be reduced.
- The salaries and other allowances of the judges are charged upon the Consolidated Fund of India.
- The Chief Justice of India draw a monthly salary of ₹ 2.8 lakh per month, as oppossed to ₹ 1 lakh earlier. Similarly, the Judges of Supreme Court draws a monthly salary of ₹ 2.50 lakh.

Removal of a Supreme Court Judge

- According to Article 124 (4), a Judge of the Supreme Court shall not be removed from his/her office except by an order of the President.
- It has to be passed after an address made by each House of Parliament supported by a majority of the total membership of that House and by a majority of not less than two-third of the members of that House present and voting.
- It has been presented to the President in the same session for such removal on the ground of proved misbehaviour or incapacity.

Process of Impeachment

- The Judges Inquiry Act of 1968, regulates the procedure relating to the removal of a Judge of the Supreme Court by the process of impeachment.
- A motion for removal must be signed by atleast 100 members in Lok Sabha or 50 members in Rajya Sabha for admission of motion for removal of the judge.
- The Presiding officer of Lok Sabha or Rajya Sabha constitutes a inquiry committee to verify the charges of accusation. The inquiry committee consists of:
    - Chief Justice or Judge of Supreme Court
    - Chief Justice of High Court
    - a distinguished Jurist
- If the inquiry committee is satisfied that the judge has been guilty, it may recommend for removal of that judge.
- Both the Houses shall have to pass a resolution to this effect by a special majority in the same session.
- The judge stands evicted by an order of the President.

- No case of removal of Supreme Court Judge has happened so far.
- The case of Justice V. Ramaswami in (1991 to 1993) was not passed because of absence of majority in Lok Sabha when Congress Member of Parliaments abstained from voting.

Officials of the Supreme Court

The other officials of the Supreme Court are as follows :

Chief Justice of India

- The Chief Justice of India is the highest judicial officer of the country.
- The post is one of esteem and dignity, requires consummate jurisprudential calibre as well as personal stature to occupy the office.
- The nature of work of Chief Justice of India is largely administrative and that includes allocating work amongst the Judges of the Supreme Court.

Acting Chief Justice of India

- The President can appoint a Judge of the Supreme Court as an acting Chief Justice of India when
- the office of Chief Justice of India is vacant,
- the Chief Justice of India is unable to perform the duties of his office or
- the Chief Justice of India is temporarily absent

Adhoc Judges

- Article 127 says, when there is a lack of a quorum of the permanent judges to hold or continue any session of the Supreme Court, the Chief Justice of India can appoint a Judge of a High Court as an Adhoc Judge of the Supreme Court for a temporary period.
- He can do so only with the previous consent of the President and after consultation with the Chief Justice of the High Court concerned.
- The appointed judge should be qualified for appointment as a Judge of the Supreme Court. It is the duty of the appointed Judge, to attend the sittings of the Supreme Court.
- While, so attending he enjoys all the jurisdiction, powers and privileges, (discharge the duties) of a Judge of the Supreme Court.

Retired Judges

- Article 128 says that the Chief Justice of India can request a retired Judge of the Supreme Court or a retired Judge of High Court (who is duly qualified for appointment as a Judge of the Supreme Court), to act as a Judge of the Supreme Court for a temporary period.
- Such judge while so sitting and acting be entitled to such allowances as the President may determine and has all the jurisdiction, powers and privileges of a Judge of Supreme Court. But he/she will not otherwise be deemed to be a Judge of the Supreme Court.

Seat and Benches of the Supreme Court

- Article 130 of the Constitution of India states that the Supreme Court of India can sit in Delhi or other places as the Chief Justice of India (CJI) may decide, with the approval of the President.
- The bail applications in appeals are heard by single judge. Most of the matters are decided by division benches of the Supreme Court consisting of two judges. If the two judges disagree, the view of the senior judge prevails. Priority matters are placed before three judges bench.
- All cases involving Constitutional interpretation and presidential references are placed before a five judges bench, popularly known as a Constitutional Bench.
- The largest bench so far was the 13 judges bench that delivered the Kesavananda Bharati Case verdict in 1973.

Amicus Curiae

- Amicus Curiae means friend of the court. Amicus Curiae is someone who is not a party to a case who assists a court by offering information, expertise or insight that has a bearing on the issues in the case.
- The decision on whether to consider an Amicus brief lies within the discretion of the court.
- In civil matters, also the court can appoint an advocate as Amicus Curiae, if it thinks it is necessary in case of an unrepresented party.
- The court can also appoint Amicus Curiae in any matter of general public importance or in which the interest of the public at large is involved.

Judicial Independence

- The Constitution seeks to ensure the independence of Supreme Court Judges in various ways. Judges are generally appointed on the basis of seniority and not on political preference.

- A Judge of the Supreme Court cannot be removed from office except by an order of the President. It is passed after an address in each House of Parliament supported by a majority of the total membership of that House and by a majority of not less than two-third of the members present and voting.
- It is presented to the President in the same session for such removal on the ground of proved misbehaviour or incapacity.
- The Chief Justice of India is free to appoint and decide the conditions of service of the officers and servants of the Supreme Court without any interference from the Executive.
- The Supreme Court can punish any person for its contempt. Thus, its actions and decisions cannot be criticised and opposed by anybody.
- All the administrative expenses of Supreme Court, salaries and allowances are charged upon the Consolidated Fund of India. They are not subject to vote by the Parliament.

JURISDICTION OF THE SUPREME COURT

The Jurisdiction of the Supreme Court are four fold which are as follows :

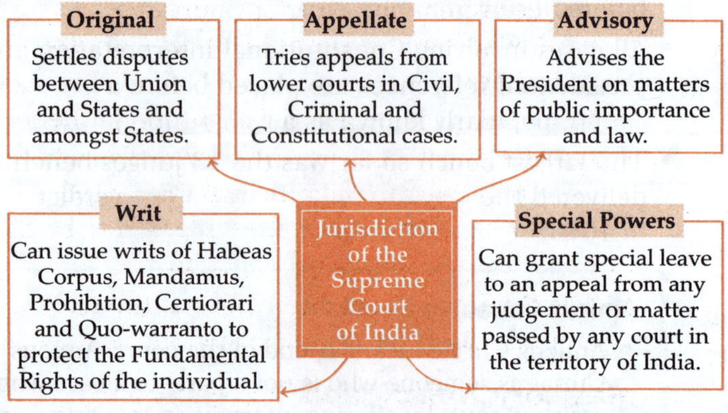

Original Jurisdiction

- According to Article 131, subject to the provisions of this Constitution, the Supreme Court shall to the exclusion of any other court have original jurisdiction in any dispute:
  - between the Government of India and one or more states
  - between the Government of India and any state or states on one side and one or more other states on the other or
  - between two or more states, if and in so far as the dispute involves any question (whether of law or fact) on which the existence or extent of a legal right depends.
- Original Jurisdiction means that the Supreme Court has the power to hear such a dispute in the first instance and not by way of appeal.
- There are certain provisions in the Constitution which exclude from the Original Jurisdiction of the Supreme Court, disputes specified in the provision to Article 363(1).
  - Complaints as to interference with inter-state water supplies, referred to the statutory tribunal mentioned in Article 262 (since the Parliament has enacted the Inter-State Water Disputes Act, 1956).
  - Matters referred to the Finance Commission Article 280.
  - Adjustment of certain expenses between the Union and the State Article 290.

Writ Jurisdiction

- Article 32 imposes duty on the Supreme Court to enforce the Fundamental Rights.
- Under this Article, every individual has a right to move the Supreme Court provided there has been any infringement on his/her Fundamental Rights.
- The Writ Jurisdiction sometimes is referred to as the Original Jurisdiction of the Supreme Court, but in the strict sense, Original Jurisdiction relates to the federal character of the Constitution.
- The Writ Jurisdiction of the Supreme Court is original but not exclusive because the High Courts are also empowered to issue writs for the enforcement of Fundamental Rights.
- The Supreme Court is empowered to issue writs, including Habeas Corpus, Mandamus, Prohibition, Quo-Warranto and Certiorari to enforce Fundamental Rights.

Appellate Jurisdiction

The Appellate Jurisdiction of the Supreme Court can be invoked by a certificate granted by the High Court concerned under Articles 132(1), 133(1) or 134 of the Constitution, in respect of any judgement, decree (a decree is an official order or decision made by a person or government with authority) or final order of a High Court in both civil and criminal cases involving substantial questions of law as to the interpretation of the Constitution.

Constitutional Appeals

- In the Constitutional matters, an appeal lies to the Supreme Court, if the High Court certifies that the case involves a substantial question of law as to the interpretation of the Constitution.
- If the High Court refuses to give the certificate, the Supreme Court may grant special leave for appeal, if it is satisfied that the case does involve such a question.

Civil Appeals

- In civil cases, an appeal lies to the Supreme Court, if a High Court certifies that the case involves a substantial question of law and further the case is fit for appeal to the Supreme Court.
- The Appellate Jurisdiction of the court in civil cases can be enlarged, if the Parliament passes a law to that effect.

Criminal Appeals

- In the criminal cases, an appeal lies to the Supreme Court, if the High Court :
  - has on appeal, reversed the order of acquittal of an accused and sentenced him to death or
  - has withdrawn for trial before itself any case from any subordinate and has in such trial convicted the accused and sentenced him to death or
  - certifies that the case is fit for appeal to the Supreme Court.
- In 1970, the criminal appeal of the Supreme Court was enlarged by adding two more cases :
  - If the High Court has reversed an order of acquittal of a person and sentenced him to life imprisonment or for ten years.
  - If the High Court has taken before itself any case from any Subordinate Court and convicted the accused person and gave him life imprisonment or 10 years sentence.

Appeal by Special Leave

The Supreme Court under Article 136 enjoys the power of granting special leave to appeal from any judgement, decree, order or sentence in any case or matter passed by any court or tribunal except court martial.

- Under the Arbitration and Conciliation Act, 1996, International Commercial Arbitration can also be initiated in the Supreme Court.
- Parliament is authorised to confer on the Supreme Court any further powers to entertain and hear appeals from any judgement, final order or sentence in a criminal proceeding of a High Court.

Advisory Jurisdiction

- According to Article 143, one of the salient features of the Supreme Court is its consultative role.
- The President can refer to the court either a question of law or a question of fact, provided that it is of public importance. However, it is not compulsory for the court to give its advice.
- The President is empowered to refer to the Supreme Court for its opinion, disputes arising out of any treaty, agreement, etc., which had been entered into or executed before the commencement of the Constitution.
- The opinion of Supreme Court is only advisory and not binding on the President.

Power of Supreme Court

Transfer Petitions

- The Supreme Court has the power to transfer the cases from one High Court to another and even from one District Court of a particular state to another District Court of the other state.
- In such transfer cases, the Supreme Court transfer only those cases, if they really lack appropriate territorial jurisdiction and those cases which were otherwise supposed to be filed under the transferred jurisdiction.
- The Supreme Court often looks at the real ground/reason for such transfer.

Revisory Jurisdiction

The Supreme Court under Article 137 is empowered to review any judgement or order made by it with a view to remove any mistake or error that might have crept in the judgement or order.

Power of Judicial Review

- The Supreme Court has the power to examine the constitutionality of the laws, acts and executive orders of both the Central and State Governments. They can be declared unconstitutional if they are found to be violating the Constitution.
- The term 'Judicial Review' is nowhere mentioned in the Constitution.
- This power has been conferred to the Supreme Court and the High Courts based on the provisions of several articles.

- The following are the three grounds based on which the constitutional validity of a law can be challenged :
    - If it violated the Fundamental Rights.
    - If it is outside the competence of the authority which has framed it.
    - If it is in conflict with the Constitutional Provisions.

Judicial Review : History and Types

Origin

- The American Supreme Court invented the Judicial Review doctrine.
- It was proposed by Chief Justice **Marshall** in the crucial 1803 Case Marbury *v/s* Madison.

Meaning

- It is a type of court proceeding in which a judge reviews the lawfulness of a decision or action made by a public body. Judicial Review is also called the interpretational and observer roles of the Indian judiciary.
- The courts have the authority to review decisions made by the legislative, executive and administrative branches of government. It tries to guarantee that governmental acts adhere to the Constitution's rules.

Stance of the Supreme Court

- Judicial Review is considered a basic structure of the Constitution Indira Gandhi *v/s* Raj Narain Case, 1975.
- The idea of basic structure has allowed Judicial Review to be applied to constitutional revisions involving Fundamental Rights as well. In the 1973, Case of Kesavananda Bharati, this doctrine was developed.
- The Supreme Court confirmed the Principle of Judicial Review in the Minerva Mill Case of 1980.

Types of Judicial Review

- **Reviews of Legislative** Actions implies the power to ensure that laws passed by the legislature are in compliance with the provisions of the Constitution.
- **Review of Administrative** Actions is a tool for enforcing constitutional discipline over administrative agencies while exercising their powers.
- **Review of Judicial Decisions** It is used to correct or make any change in previous decisions by the judiciary itself.

Constitutional Interpretation

- The Supreme Court is the final interpreter of the Constitution. It interprets the meanings of the terms used in the Constitution and shed light on the spirit and content of the provisions of the Constitution.
- Various doctrines help the court in interpreting the Constitution:
    - Doctrine of Double jeopardy
    - Doctrine of Liberal interpretation
    - Doctrine of Pith and substance
    - Doctrine of Progressive interpretation
    - Doctrine of Severability
    - Doctrine of Prospective overruling
    - Doctrine of Eclipse
    - Doctrine of Implied power
    - Doctrine of Colourable legislation

Other Powers

- Election petitions with respect to the elections of President and Vice-President are directly filed with the Supreme Court.
- Supreme Court also has special powers to enquire into the misconduct of Chairman and members of the Union Public Service Commission.
- The decree and order of the Supreme Court is enforceable throughout the country.
- All the courts and tribunals function in the Territory of India under the judicial superintendence of the Supreme Court.

A Court of Record

Article 129 states that the Supreme Court of India shall be a Court of Record. As a Court of Records, the Supreme Court has two powers. These are as follows :

- The judgements proceedings and acts of the Supreme Court are recorded for perpetual memory and testimony. These are recognised as legal precedents and legal references.
- The Supreme Court has power to punish for contempt of court, either with simple imprisonment for a term upto six months or with fine up to ₹ 2000 or with both.

Supreme Court as the Guardian of the Constitution

- The Supreme Court has been called as the Guardian of the Constitution, as it ensures that the legislature and the executive works and function as per the provisions of Constitution and not in its derogation.
- It also ensures that any Amendment of the Constitution does not violate the basic structure.

Contempt of Court

Contempt of Court may be of two types i.e., Civil Contempt and Criminal contempt under the Contempt of Courts Act (1971).

Contempt of Court Act , 1971

This act was enacted by the Parliament based on the recommendations of the special committee that was appointed in 1961 under the chairmanship of HN Sanyal, the then additional Solicitor-General of India.

Civil Contempt

It means wilful disobedience to any judgement, order, writ or other process of a court or wilful breach of an undertaking given to a court.

Criminal Contempt

It means the publication of any matter or doing an Act which :

- scandalises or lowers the authority of a court or,
- prejudices or interferes with the due course of a judicial proceeding or,
- interferes or obstructs the administration of justice in any other manner.

Curative Petition

- A curative petition is a last and final option available for persons seeking justice through the judicial system.
- A curative petition is a petition which requests the court to review its own decision even after a review petition is dismissed.
- In the case of Rupa Ashok Hurra *v/s* Ashok Hurra (2002), the Supreme Court of India established the idea of a curative petition.
- The Supreme Court declared that it may revisit its judgements in the exercise of its inherent powers in order to prevent misuse of its process and to correct severe miscarriages of justice.

Important Supreme Court Cases

Cases	Descriptions
AK Gopalan Case, 1950	The case corresponds to the charges of violation of Fundamental Right to freedom under the **Preventive Detention Act.** The court was approached over the validity of the Act. The Supreme Court held that the Constitutional validity of a law cannot be verified by the judiciary and the judiciary has only the capacity to verify whether the 'procedure according to the law' has been followed.
Champakam Dorairajan Case, 1951	The case challenged the reservations given to Backward Classes in educational institutions in Tamil Nadu. The Supreme Court overruled the caste based reservation as unconstitutional citing right against discrimination as given in Article 15.
Shankari Prasad Case, 1952	The first Constitution Amendment Act, providing for reservations, was challenged that it violated Fundamental Rights. The court held that Parliament has power to amend the Constitution.
Berubari Case, 1960	While ceding a part of Indian Territory to an alien state the court in an advisory opinion held that such process cannot take place unless a Constitution Amendment to that effect is made.
Golaknath Case, 1967	The Supreme Court while reversing the ruling made in **Shankari Prasad** and **Sajjan Singh case** held that Constitutional amendment cannot be extended to infringement of Fundamental Rights.
Kesavananda Bharati Case, 1973	For the first time, the Supreme Court propounded the Basic Structure Doctrine and held that certain basic features of the Constitution cannot be amended while others can be done so without having a sweeping change in the Constitution.
Minerva Mills Case, 1980	The Supreme Court held that Fundamental Rights and Directive Principles of State Policy are complementary to each other and if any law enacted to implement the Directive Principles not totally contravening the Fundamental Rights is valid.
Indira Sawhney Case, 1993	The Supreme Court upheld the 27% reservation made for OBCs in public employment but subjected to a cap of 50% of reservations. The Supreme Court also mooted the Creamy Layer concept to identify the well off groups within the Backward Classes.
Bommai Case, 1995	The Supreme Court held that federalism is a part of basic structure and State Governments cannot be arbitrarily dismissed by a Governor and any such test of confidence of the executive must be done on the floor of the Assembly.
Aruna Shanbaug Case (2011)	The Supreme Court has given legal sanction to passive euthanasia in a landmark verdict permitted **living will** by patients on withdrawing medical support if they slip into irreversible coma. The Supreme Court in 2011, recognised passive euthanasia in **Aruna Shanbaug Case** for which it had permitted withdrawal of life-sustaining treatment from patients who are not in a position to make an informed decision.
Transgender as 'Third Gender' 2014	The Supreme Court created the **Third Gender** status for hijras or transgenders.
Triple Talaq Case, 2017	The Supreme Court of India has declared the practice of Triple Talaq as unconstitutional by 3:2 majority and hereby direct the **Union of India** to consider appropriate legislation, particularly with reference to Talaq-e-biddat (three pronouncements of Talaq at one and the same time). In this verdict, the Supreme Court also declared that this form of Talaq is violative of the Article 14 of the Indian Constitution.
Shayara Bano Case, 2017	The Supreme Court declared that practice of Triple Talaq is unconstitutional besides affirming that is derogatory and discriminatory for women.
Internet and Mobile Association v/s RBI, 2020	In this judgement, Supreme Court declared the Circular issued by the RBI regarding ban on the trading of Crypto Currencies as unfair and unviable. However, this judgement have only structure down the circular issued by the RBI but have not declared virtual currencies as legal or illegal.

JUDICIAL ACTIVISM

- Judicial activism is phenomena wherein the judiciary assumes an extraordinary position of directing the executive to undertake such policies and measures as the judiciary deem fit citing insufficient policies or administrative lacuna.
- The foundation of judicial activism in India was laid down by Justice VR Krishna Iyer, Justice PN Bhagwati, Justice O Chinnappa Reddy and Justice DA Desai.
- It lays up a system of checks and balances for the other governmental branches.
- Judicial Activism gives judges the discretion to exercise their own judgement in situations where the law is unable to create a balance.
- It develops confidence in judges and offers understanding of the problems. Judicial activism has no bearing on the judges' commitment to uphold the rule of law in the nation.
- The Indian Judiciary has two primary approaches to Judicial Activism.
- Protecting Citizens' Rights The first approach involves courts issuing directions to government authorities to safeguard citizens' rights and promote public interest.
- Interpreting Fundamental Rights The second approach focuses on interpreting Fundamental Rights, Specifically :
  - Right to Equality (Article 14)
  - Right to Freedom (Article 19)
  - Right to Life and Personal Liberty (Article 21)

Public Interest Litigation

- Public Interest Litigation (PIL) is a legal action brought in a court to preserve Public Interest such as the prevention of pollution, terrorism, traffic accidents, construction site hazards, etc.
- It can be brought in a court of law to address any issue where the general public's interests are at stake.
- An NGO or socially concerned individual might advance a public cause by filing a PIL to seek legal remedies for a public illegal activities.
- There are no laws or statutes that specify it. It was established in India by the judiciary when it decided to address concerns about violations of Human Rights in the 1970s and 1980s.
- The concept of PIL emerged for the first time in the Mumbai Kamgar Sabha Case where Justice Krishna Iyer allowed the petition even, if the litigant had no locus standi in the case.
- Justice Bhagwati later gives much momentum to the PIL movement.
- The first reported case of PIL was Hussainara Khatoon *v/s* State of Bihar (1979) that focused on the inhuman conditions of prisons and under trial prisoners.
- A Public Interest Litigation can be filed against a State/Central Government Municipal Authorities and not any private party.

  The Supreme Court evolved the following principles in regard to PIL :
  - the court in exercise of powers under Articles 32 and 226 of the Constitution can entertain a petition filed by any interested person in the welfare of the people.
  - the court will not hold back from intervening whenever a large number of individuals are subjected to injustice in order to uphold Articles 14 and 21 of the Indian Constitution as well as the International Covenants on Human Rights.
- The following are the cases in which PIL's are filed :
  - violation of the basic Human Rights of the poor (litigations for protection of Fundamental Rights, mainly in Article 21)
  - content and conduct of the government and its policy making
  - labour exploitation issues
  - women rights
  - caste and religious issues
  - governance issues and the working of public bodies, local, state and the union
  - environmental issues
  - the issues of culture and heritage
  - other matters of public importance

Locus Standi

- 'Locus Standi' means that a person whose rights are infringed alone can move the court and no one else to seek a remedy.
- It was a traditional rule followed by Indian judiciary until the introduction of the concept of Public Interest Litigation.

Articles Related to Supreme Court

Articles	Descriptions	Articles	Descriptions
Article 124	Establishment and Constitution of the Supreme Court	**Article 136**	Special leave to appeal by the Supreme Court
Article 125	Salaries, etc of judges	**Article 137**	Review of judgements or orders by the Supreme Court
Article 126	Appointment of acting Chief Justice	**Article 138**	Enlargement of the jurisdiction of the Supreme Court
Article 127	Appointment of Adhoc judges	**Article 139**	Conferment on the Supreme Court of powers to issue certain writs
Article 128	Attendance of retired judges at sittings of the Supreme Court	**Article 139(A)**	Transfer of certain cases
Article 129	Supreme Court to be a court of record	**Article 140**	Ancillary powers of the Supreme Court
Article 130	Seat of Supreme Court	**Article 141**	Law declared by Supreme Court to be binding on all courts
Article 131	Original Jurisdiction of the Supreme Court	**Article 142**	Enforcement of decrees and orders of the Supreme Court
Article 132	Appellate Jurisdiction of the Supreme Court in appeals from High Courts in certain cases	**Article 143**	Power of the President to consult the Supreme Court
Article 133	Appellate jurisdiction of the Supreme Court in appeals from High Courts in regard to civil matters	**Article 144**	Civil and judicial authorities to act in aid of the Supreme Court
Article 134	Appellate jurisdiction of the Supreme Court in regard to criminal matters	**Article 145**	Rules of court, etc
Article 134A	Certificate for appeal to the Supreme Court	**Article 146**	Officers and servants and the expenses of the Supreme Court
Article 135	Jurisdiction and powers of the federal court under existing law to be exercisable by the Supreme Court	**Article 147**	Interpretation

Female Judges in Supreme Court of India

Names	Appointment	Retirement	Remarks
Fathima Beevi	6th October, 1989	29th April, 1992	First woman judge of the Supreme Court of India.
Sujata Manohar	8th November, 1994	27th August, 1999	—
Ruma Pal	28th January, 2000	2nd June, 2006	Longest-serving female judge of the Supreme Court of India.
Gyan Sudha Misra	30th April, 2010	27th April, 2014	—
Ranjana Desai	13th September, 2011	29th October, 2014	—
R. Banumathi	13th August, 2014	19th July, 2020	—
Indu Malhotra	27th April, 2018	13th March, 2021	The first woman judge who was elevated directly from the Bar Council of India.
Indira Banerjee	7th August, 2018	23rd September, 2022	—
Hima Kohli	31st August, 2021	1st September, 2024	—
BV Nagarathna	31st August, 2021	29th October, 2027	To be the first female Chief Justice of India in September, 2027.
Bela Trivedi	31st August, 2021	9th June, 2025	—

Chief Justice of India and their Tenure

S.N.	Chief Justice	Tenure
1.	HJ Kania	26th January, 1950 – 6th November, 1951
2.	M. Patanjali Sastri	7th November, 1951 – 3rd January, 1954
3.	Mehr Chand Mahajan	4th January, 1954 – 22nd December, 1954
4.	Bijan Kumar Mukherjea	23rd December, 1954 – 31st January, 1956
5.	Sudhi Ranjan Das	1st February, 1956 – 30th September, 1959
6.	Bhuvaneshwar Prasad Sinha	1st October, 1959 – 31st January, 1964
7.	PB Gajendragadkar	1st February, 1964 – 15th March, 1966
8.	Amal Kumar Sarkar	16th March, 1966 – 29th June, 1966
9.	Koka Subba Rao	30th June, 1966 – 11th April, 1967
10.	Kailas Nath Wanchoo	12th April, 1967 – 24th February, 1968
11.	Muhammad Hidayatullah	25th February, 1968 – 16th December, 1970
12.	Jayantilal Chhotalal Shah	17th December, 1970 – 21st January, 1971
13.	Sarv Mittra Sikri	22nd January, 1971 – 25th April, 1973
14.	AN Ray	26th April, 1973 – 27th January, 1977
15.	Mirza Hameedullah Beg	29th January, 1977 – 21st February, 1978
16.	YV Chandrachud	22nd February, 1978 – 11th July, 1985
17.	PN Bhagwati	12th July, 1985 – 20th December, 1986
18.	Raghunandan Swarup Pathak	21st December, 1986 – 18th June, 1989
19.	Engalaguppe Seetharamaiah Venkataramiah	19th June, 1989 – 17th December, 1989
20.	Sabyasachi Mukharji	18th December, 1989 – 25th September, 1990
21.	Ranganath Misra	26th September, 1990 – 24th November, 1991
22.	Kamal Narain Singh	25th November, 1991 – 12th December, 1991
23.	Madhukar Hiralal Kania	13th December, 1991 – 17th November, 1992
24.	Lalit Mohan Sharma	18th November, 1992 – 11th February, 1993
25.	MN Venkatachaliah	12th February, 1993 – 24th October, 1994
26.	Aziz Mushabber Ahmadi	25th October, 1994 – 24th March, 1997
27.	JS Verma	25th March, 1997 – 17th January, 1998
28.	Madan Mohan Punchhi	18th January, 1998 – 9th October, 1998
29.	Adarsh Sein Anand	10th October, 1998 – 31st October, 2001
30.	Sam Piroj Bharucha	1st November, 2001 – 5th May, 2002
31.	Bhupinder Nath Kirpal	6th May, 2002 – 7th November, 2002
32.	Gopal Ballav Pattanaik	8th November, 2002 – 18th December, 2002
33.	VN Khare	19th December, 2002 – 1st May, 2004
34.	S. Rajendra Babu	2nd May, 2004 – 31st May, 2004
35.	Ramesh Chandra Lahoti	1st June, 2004 – 31st October, 2005
36.	Yogesh Kumar Sabharwal	1st November, 2005 – 13th January, 2007
37.	KG Balakrishnan	14th January, 2007 – 12th May, 2010
38.	SH Kapadia	12th May, 2010 – 28th September, 2012
39.	Altamas Kabir	29th September, 2012 – 18th July, 2013
40.	P. Sathasivam	19th July, 2013 – 26th April, 2014
41.	Rajendra Mal Lodha	27th April, 2014 – 27th September, 2014
42.	HL Dattu	28th September, 2014 – 2nd December, 2015
43.	TS Thakur	3rd December, 2015 – 3rd January, 2017
44.	Jagdish Singh Khehar	4th January, 2017 – 27th August, 2017
45.	Dipak Misra	28th August, 2017 – 2nd October, 2018
46.	Ranjan Gogoi	3rd October, 2018 – 17th November, 2019
47.	Sharad Arvind Bobde	18th November, 2019 – 23rd April, 2021
48.	NV Ramana	24th April, 2021 – 26th August, 2022
49.	UU Lalit	27th August, 2022 – 8th November, 2022
50.	DY Chandrachud	9th November, 2022 – 10th November, 2024
51.	Sanjiv Khanna	11th November, 2024 – 13th May, 2025
52.	BR Gavai	14th May, 2025-Incumbent

Chief Justice of India and their Tenure

***As on March, 2025**

“

The institution of High Courts originated in India in 1862, when the High Courts were set-up at Calcutta, Bombay and Madras.

Chapter Twenty Five

High Court and Sub-ordinate Courts

HIGH COURT

- Article 214 says that the High Courts stands at the head of the judiciary in a state. There shall be a High Court for each state. The judiciary in the states consists of a High Court and the sub-ordinate courts.
- The Parliament can, however, establish by law, a common High Court for one or more States and one or more Union Territory as per Article 231 and Seventh Amendment Act, 1956.
- The territorial jurisdiction of each High Court extends over the territory of that state and in case of a common High Court the jurisdiction extends to the territory of the concerned States and Union Territories.
- Every High Court shall be a Court of Record under Article 215. As of May 2023, there are 25 High Courts in the country.
- Out of these three High Courts have jurisdiction over more than one state. In case of Union Territories, only Delhi has a separate High Court. The organisation, independence, powers, jurisdiction , procedures, etc of the High Courts are dealt with in Articles 214 to 231 in Part VI of the Constitution.

Qualifications for Judges

- The following qualifications required under the Constitution for a person to be appointed as a Judge of a High Court :
    - must be a citizen of India and
    - must have held a judicial office in the Territory of India for at least ten years or
    - must have been an Advocate of a High Court or two or more such courts in succession for at least ten years
- The Constitution has no provision for appointment of a distinguished jurist as a judge of a High Court as in the Supreme Court.
- Also, the Constitution does not prescribe a minimum age for appointment as a judge of a High Court.

Appointment of the Judges

- According to Article 216, every High Court consists of a Chief Justice and such other Judges as appointed by the President from time-to-time.
- The Constitution does not specify the strength of the High Courts.
- The Constitution, unlike in the case of the Supreme Court, does not fix any maximum number of Judges for a High Court.

- As per Article 217, every Judge of High Court is appointed by the President after consultation with Chief Justice of India and Governor of the State.
- Apart from appointing the Judges of the High Courts, the President has the power to appoint :
  - Additional judges for a temporary period, not exceeding two years, for the clearance of arrears of work in a High Court.
  - An acting judge, when a permanent Judge of a High Court (other than a Chief Justice) is temporarily absent or unable to perform his duties.
  - Apppointed to act temporarily as Chief Justice of that High Court. An acting judge holds office until the permanent judge resumes his office. Neither an additional nor an acting judge can hold office beyond the age of 62 years (now 64 years).

Retired Judges

- Chief Justice of High Court can request a retired Judge of the High Court to act as a Judge of the High Court for a temporary period. He can take this step after getting consent from the President of India and also of the person to be so appointed.
- The appointed person in this case will receive such salary and allowances as determined by the President of India.

- While appointing a Judge of a High Court, the President is to consult the Chief Justice of India, the Governor of the State and the Chief Justice of that High Court in the matter of appointment of a judge other than the Chief Justice.
- In case of a common High Court, the Governors of all the concerned states are consulted by the President.

Appointment of Chief Justice of the High Courts

The Chief Justice of the High Court is appointed by the President in consultation with the Chief Justice of India and the Governor of the concerned state.

Acting Chief Justice

The President can appoint an Acting Chief Justice of the High Court when his office is vacant or when he is temporarily absent or when he is unable to perform the duties of his office.

Tenure and Oath of Judges of High Courts

- The tenure of a judge of the High Court is not fixed in the Constitution.
- A permanent judge of the High Court serves until he or she reaches the age of 62.
- Any disputes over the age of judges are resolved by the President in consultation with the Chief Justice of India, with the President's decision being final.
- A judge does not hold office during the pleasure of the President. A judge can resign from his office by writing a resignation letter addressed to the President.
- A judge can be removed from his office by the President on the recommendation of the Parliament.
- A judge vacates his office when he is appointed as a judge of the Supreme Court or when he is transferred to another High Court.
- Under Article 219, a person appointed as a High Court Judge must take and swear an oath or affirmation before the Governor of the State or some person appointed by him before taking office.

Salaries of Judges of a High Court

Under Article 221, a Judge of the High Court is entitled to such allowances and rights as Parliament may decide from time-to-time in terms of leave of absence and pension.

Removal of Judges

- Removal of a High Court judge is governed by Articles 217 (1) (b) and 218 of the Constitution on the ground of proven misbehaviour or incapacity.
- The words misbehaviour or incapacity have neither been defined nor mentioned in the Constitution.
- The complaint about misbehaviour or incapacity against a judge has to be probed under the Judges (Inquiry) Act, 1968. It is similar to the judges of Supreme Court.

Transfer of Judges

- The President has the power to transfer a judge from one High Court to another in consultation with the Chief Justice of India.
- Article 222 of the Indian Constitution marks provisions for the transfer of a judge including Chief Justices from one High Court to any other court.
- In 1977, the Supreme Court ruled that the transfer of High Court Judge could be restore to only as an exceptional measure and only in public interest and not by way of punishment.

- In the Third Case (1998), the Supreme Court opined that in case of the transfer of High Court Judges :
  - The Chief Justice of India should consult, in addition to the collegium of four seniormost Judges of the Supreme Court, the Chief Justice of the two High Courts (one from which the judge is being transferred and the other receiving him).
  - Thus, the sole opinion of the Chief Justice of India does not constitute the Consultation process.

JURISDICTION OF THE HCs

The jurisdiction of the High Courts are described below :

Original Jurisdiction

- Original Jurisdiction means the power of a High Court to hear disputes in the first instance.
- High Courts have been given Original Jurisdiction over cases arising out of Parliament or State Legislature Elections.
- Like Supreme Court they also have Original Jurisdiction in matters of enforcement of Fundamental Rights. The High Courts have Original Jurisdiction regarding revenue matters or an act ordered or done in revenue collection.
- Over cases ordered to be transferred from a sub-ordinate court to itself which involves the interpretation of the Constitution. The four High Courts of Calcutta, Bombay, Madras and Delhi have original civil jurisdiction in cases of higher value.

Appellate Jurisdiction

- As courts of appeal, all High Courts entertain appeals in civil and criminal cases from their sub-ordinate courts as well as on their own.
- They have, however, no jurisdiction over tribunals established under the laws relating to the Armed Forces of the country.
- In civil cases, its jurisdiction extends to cases tried by Courts of Munsifs and District Judges.
- In the criminal cases, it extends to cases decided by Sessions and Additional Sessions Judges.
- It should also be noted here that a death sentence awarded by a session court or additional sessions court should be confirmed by the High Court before it can be executed, whether there is an appeal by the convicted person or not.

Writ Jurisdiction

- Under Article 226 of the Constitution, the High Courts are given powers of issuing writs not only for the enforcement of the Fundamental Rights, but also for other purposes. Hence Writ jurisdiction of High Court is more than the Supreme Court.
- In exercise of this power, a court may issue the same type of writs, orders or directions which the Supreme Court is empowered to issue under Article 32.
- The Writ Jurisdiction of High Court is in concurrent with that of Supreme Court. It means that any aggrieved individual has both options to move High Court as well as Supreme Court.

L. Chandra Kumar Case Judgement

The court held that the power of Judicial Review vested in the Supreme Court and High Courts by **Articles 32** and **226** respectively. It is the basic structure of Constitution. Hence, it cannot be excluded even by amendment to the Constitution.

Court of Record

- As per Article 215, every High Court shall be a Court of Record. As a Court of Record, a High Court has two powers such as :
  - The judgements, proceedings and Acts of the High Courts are recorded for perpetual memory and testimony.
  - These records are admitted to be of evidentiary value and cannot be questioned when produced before any sub-ordinate court.
  - It has power to punish for contempt of court, either with simple imprisonment or with fine or with both.

Supervisory Jurisdiction

- The High Courts control and supervise the working of the courts subordinate to them and frame rules and regulations for the transaction of their business.
- Under Article 227, every High Court has the power of superintendence over all the courts and tribunals except those dealing with the Armed Forces functioning within its territorial jurisdiction.
- In exercise of this power, the High Court may :
  - call for returns from such courts,
  - make and issue general rules and prescribe forms for regulating the practice and proceedings of such courts,

- prescribe forms in which books and accounts shall be kept by the offices of any such courts and
- transfer cases from one court to another.

- Under Article 235, the High Courts exercise control over the District Courts and the sub-ordinate courts in matters of posting, promotion, etc.
- According to Article 229 of the Constitution, every High Court has been ensured a complete control over the members of its staff.
- The Chief Justice of the High Court is empowered to appoint officers and servants of the court.

Control Over Sub-ordinate Courts

- Apart from above jurisdiction the High Court also enjoys administrative jurisdiction over the sub-ordinate courts. These includes followings :
- Governor in consultation with High Courts appoints the District Judges.
- The administrative control of the High Courts over the District Courts and other lower courts is full in as much as postings, promotions and grant of leave, etc., to any person belonging to the judicial service of a state and holding any post inferior to the post of judges is vested in High Court.
- The High Courts have the power to withdraw a case pending in a Sub-ordinate Court if it involves a substantial question of law that requires interpretation of the Constitution.
- Article 236 is the interpretation clause and explains terms like District Judge, Judicial Service, etc.
- The High Court's law is binding on all subordinate courts functioning within its territorial jurisdiction.

Power of Judicial Review

- The High Courts have the power of judicial review in case the laws or orders of both the Central and State Government violate the provisions of the Constitution.
- This power is similar to the power of judicial review of the Supreme Court.

Plea Bargaining

- It was introduced in India by the **Criminal Law (Amendment) Act, 2005**. Under Plea Bargain, criminal defendant and prosecutor reach an agreement subject to approval by court.
- The accused admits guilt without a trail and in return is given a lighter punishment.
- This is allowed for cases where maximum imprisonment is seven years.

INDEPENDENCE OF THE HC

The Constitution seeks to secure the independence of Judges of the High Courts in the following ways :

- A Judge of a High Court can only be removed by the President on an address of each House of the Parliament, passed by not less than two-third of the members present and voting and by a majority of that House only on the ground of proved misbehaviour or incapacity.
- After retirement, a Judge of a High Court cannot serve in any court or before any authority in India except in the Supreme Court and a High Court other than the High Court in which he had held the office.
- Their salaries and allowances cannot be changed to their disadvantage after their appointment except during a Financial Emergency.
- Their salaries and allowances are charged on the Consolidated Fund of State and are not subject to vote in the State Legislature.
- A High Court in India has the power to review its own judgement just like the Supreme Court.
- The conduct of the judges cannot be discussed in the Parliament or in a State Legislature.
- The permanent judges of the High Courts are barred from pleading or acting in any court or other authority in India except the Supreme Court and the other High Courts.
- The High Courts have the power to punish any person for its contempt.
- The jurisdiction and powers of a High Court cannot be curtailed both by the Parliament and the State Legislature.

High Courts of State/Union Territory

Court Names	Jurisdictions	Seats	Benches
Allahabad High Court	Uttar Pradesh	Prayagraj	Lucknow
Andhra Pradesh High Court	Andhra Pradesh	Amravati	
Bombay High Court	Maharashtra, Goa, Dadra and Nagar Haveliand Daman and Diu	Mumbai	Nagpur, Panaji, Aurangabad
Calcutta High Court	West Bengal, Andaman and Nicobar Islands	Kolkata	Port Blair (Circuit Bench)
Chhattisgarh High Court	Chhattisgarh	Bilaspur	

Court Names	Jurisdictions	Seats	Benches
Gauhati High Court	Arunachal Pradesh, Assam, Nagaland, Mizoram	Guwahati	Kohima, Aizawl and Itanagar
Gujarat High Court	Gujarat	Ahmedabad	
Delhi High Court	National Capital Territory of Delhi	Delhi	
Himachal Pradesh High Court	Himachal Pradesh	Shimla	
Jammu and Kashmir and Ladakh High Court	Jammu and Kashmir and Ladakh	Srinagar/ Jammu	
Jharkhand High Court	Jharkhand	Ranchi	
Karnataka High Court	Karnataka	Bengaluru	Kalaburagi, Dharwal
Kerala High Court	Kerala, Lakshadweep	Kochi/ Emakulam	
Madhya Pradesh High Court	Madhya Pradesh	Jabalpur	Gwalior, Indore
Madras High Court	Tamil Nadu, Puducherry	Chennai	Madurai
Manipur High Court	Manipur	Imphal	
Meghalaya High Court	Meghalaya	Shillong	
Orissa High Court	Odisha	Cuttack	
Patna High Court	Bihar	Patna	
Punjab and Haryana High Court	Punjab, Haryana, Chandigarh	Chandigarh	
Rajasthan High Court	Rajasthan	Jodhpur	Jaipur
Sikkim High Court	Sikkim	Gangtok	
Tripura High Court	Tripura	Agartala	
Uttarakhand High Court	Uttarakhand	Nainital	
Telangana High Court	Telangana	Hyderabad	

SUB-ORDINATE COURTS

- Articles 233 to 237 in Part IV of the Constitution deals with the organisation of the sub-ordinate courts.
- Under Article 235 of the Constitution of India, administrative control over members of the Sub-ordinate Judicial Service rests with the concerned High Courts.
- Further, in exercise of powers conferred under provision to Article 309 read with Articles 233 and 234 of the Constitution, State Government frames rules and regulations in consultation with the High Court in their state to administer sub-ordinate courts.
- Members of the State Judicial Service are governed by these rules and regulations.

District Court / Session Court in District

District Court
- Headed by a District Judge
- Deals with Civil Cases
- Appeal lies in High Court
- Has Original and Appellate Jurisdiction

Sub-ordinate Judge Court
- Exercise unlimited pecuniary jurisdiction over Civil Cases

Munsiff Court
- Exercise cases of lesser amount

Session Court
- Headed by a Session Judge Deals with Criminal Cases
- Can give any punishment including life imprisonment and capital punishment.
- Capital punishment is subject to High Court's confirmation
- Has Original and Appellate Jurisdiction

Chief Judicial Magistrate Court
- Can hear criminal cases in which sentence lies upto seven years imprisonment

Judicial Magistrate's Court
- Can hear cases upto three years sentence

Comparison between Supreme Court and High Court

Supreme Court	High Court
The Supreme Court is a Federal Court. Its only seat is located at Delhi.	There is a provision for a High Court in each State and Union Territories or one or more States or Union Territories may establish a High Court.
The Supreme Court is not bound to abide by the decision of the High Courts.	The High Courts are bound to abide by the decisions of the Supreme Court.
The Judges of Supreme Court cannot be transferred nor can they be demoted in office.	The Judges of the High Court can be transferred from one court to other High Court and may be promoted as the Judges of the Supreme Court.
The salaries and the allowances of the Judges of the Supreme Court are charged upon the Consolidated Fund of India.	Salaries and allowances of the Judges of the High Court are charged upon the Consolidated Fund of the States.
The cases involving the interpretation of the Constitution are decided only by the Supreme Court.	The cases involving the interpretator of the Constitution are not decided by the High Court.
The Supreme Court can issue writs only for the enforcement of Fundamental Rights.	High Court can issue writs not only for the enforcement of Fundamental Rights, but also for any other purpose.
A remedy under Article 32 is in itself a Fundamental Right and hence, the Supreme Court may not refuse to exercise its Writ Jurisdiction.	A remedy under **Article 226** is discretionary and hence, a High Court may refuse to exercise its Writ Jurisdiction.

> The term 'Lok Adalat' means 'People's Court' and is based on Gandhian principles. NALSA along with other Legal Services Institutions conduct Lok Adalats.

Chapter Twenty Six

Lok Adalat and Other Courts

LOK ADALAT

- A Lok Adalat shall have jurisdiction to determine and to arrive at a compromise or settlement between the parties in respect of :
  - any case pending before any court or
  - any matter which is falling within the jurisdiction of any court and not brought before such court
- The first Lok Adalat was held on 14th March, 1982, at Junagarh in Gujarat.
- They follow their own procedure. They have the power of Civil Court in respect of summoning of evidence, examination of witnesses, requisitioning of public records, etc.
- No lawyers are involved in the process. The awards passed have to be complied within a month.
- Thus, the Lok Adalat can deal with not only the cases pending before a court but also with the disputes at pre-litigation stage.
- The various matters such as matrimonial/family disputes, criminal cases, land acquisition cases, labour disputes, workmen's compensation cases, bank recovery cases, pension cases, housing board and slum clearance cases, housing finance cases, consumer grievance cases, electricity matters, municipal matters including house tax cases, etc., are being taken up in the Lok Adalats.
- The Lok Adalat shall have no jurisdiction in respect of any case or matter relating to an offence not compoundable under any law.
- Any case pending before the court can be referred to the Lok Adalat for settlement if the parties agree or if one of the parties makes an application to the court in this regard or if the court is satisfied that it is appropriate for this matter to be resolved in the Lok Adalat.
- The Lok Adalat shall have the same powers as are vested in the Civil Court under the Code of Civil Procedure (1908) with respect to the summoning and enforcing the attendance of any witness, the discovery and production of any witness, reception of evidence on affidavits, etc.
- A Lok Adalat persuades the parties to come to an understanding and settlement in terms of the compromise or settlement.
- These awards are final as there does not lay any appeal against the awards passed by a Lok Adalat.

Types of Lok Adalat

- **National Lok Adalat** Held at regular intervals on a specific subject
- **Permanent Lok Adalat** Deals with cases related to the public utility services
- **Types of Lok Adalat**
  - **Continuous Lok Adalat** A number of days are set for a Lok Adalat bench to sit continuously to facilitate settlements
  - **Daily Lok Adalat** Organised on daily basis
  - **Mobile Lok Adalat** Set-up in a multi-utility van and take Lok Adalat to different areas
  - **Mega Lok Adalat** Organised in a single day in all courts of the state

Permanent Lok Adalats

- In 2002, Permanent Lok Adalats were established by National Legal Service Authority (NALSA) or the State Legal Service Authority (SLSA) to settle public utility disputes quickly through compromise.
- It is one of the most effective Alternative Dispute Resolution (ADR) tools in India.
- It consists of a Chairman, who is a District Judge or additional District Judge and two other persons having adequate experience in public utility services.

Jurisdiction

The **Permanent Lok Adalat** shall exercise jurisdiction in respect of one or more public utility services such as transport services of passengers or goods by air, road and water; postal, telegraph or telephone services; supply of power, light or water to the public by any establishment; services in hospitals or dispensaries and insurance services.

- The Permanent Lok Adalat has no jurisdiction over any matter relating to an offense that is not compoundable under any law.
- The Permanent Lok Adalats' monetary jurisdiction shall be limited up to ₹ 1 crore.
- Before the dispute, any party may make an application to the Permanent Lok Adalat for settlement of the dispute.
- After an application is made to the Permanent Lok Adalat, no party shall invoke jurisdiction of any court in the same dispute.
- In case when parties fail to reach an agreement, the Permanent Lok Adalat shall decide the dispute on merits.
- Every award made by the Permanent Lok Adalat shall be final and binding on all the parties constituting.
- The Permanent Lok Adalat shall have the same powers as a Civil Court under the Code of Civil Procedure, 1908 for the purpose of holding any determination. They do not charge a fee for resolving disputes.

FAMILY COURTS

- The Family Courts Act was enacted in 1984, which provided for the establishment of family courts with the goal of providing conciliation and ensuring the prompt resolution of marriage and family disputes.
- These courts aim to protect individuals' Legal Rights and helps the families to deal with problems and restore family harmony.
- The Act provides for the establishment of Family Courts by the State Governments in consultation with the High Courts.
- It also makes it obligatory on the State Governments to set up a Family Court in every city or town with a population exceeding one million.
- Matters relating to the following are exclusively placed within the jurisdiction of the Family Courts:
  - matrimonial relief, including nullity of marriage, judicial separation, divorce, restitution of conjugal rights or declaration as to the validity of a marriage or the matrimonial status of any person;
  - the property of the spouses or either of them;
  - a declaration with regards to the legitimacy of a person;
  - guardianship of a person or custody of any minor and,
  - maintenance of wife, children and parents.
- Family Courts have the authority to adopt their own settlement procedures through regulations created in consultation with the High Courts.
- There is only one right of appeal and that lies with the High Courts. Moreover, it aimed to create a flexible and informal atmosphere during the course of the procedures, as well as to offer an inexpensive remedy to the victims.

OTHER COURTS

National Green Tribunal (NGT)

- National Green Tribunal (NGT) was established on 18th October, 2010 under the NGT Act of 2010 as a specialised body for handling any environmental disputes that involve multi-disciplinary issues.
- It was formed by replacing the National Environment Appellate Authority. It also draws inspiration from Article 21 of the Indian Constitution which assures to provide a healthy environment to the citizens of India.
- India has become the third country in the world after Australia and New Zealand, for setting up a specialised environmental tribunal and also the first developing country to do so.

Children's and Juvenile Court

- It has been constituted for the special psychological needs and conditions of children and adolescents.
- Juvenile Justice Committees have been formed in the High Court for its proper operation. These committees are headed by a sitting judge of the High Court.
- A three-member Juvenile Justice Board will be constituted by the State Government for a district or more districts, in which one member will be a psychologist or child welfare expert.
- Two members will be social workers (for children atleast 7 years related to education, medical or welfare work). Also, these one of the two must be female. Juveniles are generally not punished, but are placed in special homes after being ordered to do community service or for serious offences.
- Against the decisions of the Juvenile Justice Board, appeal can also be made against the district in the High Court.
- Some of the provisions of the Juvenile Justice (Care and Protection of Children Act, 2015) related to children and adolescents are mentioned below :
  - In this, the word teenager was changed from the word child.
  - Juveniles aged 16 to 18 years to be tried and punished as adults in case of heinous crime.
  - 3 to 7 years imprisonment for serious offences.
  - Juvenile Justice Board, Child Welfare Committee established for the protection of children in each district. Registration of centres is mandatory.

Court Martial

- Action related to military crimes is taken under court martial. In these courts, the judges are the highest officers of the army, so that there can be no external interference.
- Under Article 136(2) and Article 227, proceedings in the Indian Judiciary/Supreme and High Court are prohibited on the offences covered under the Army Act, 1950, Air Force Act, 1950 and Navy Act, 1957.
- The provisions of the Indian Penal Code and the Code of Criminal Procedure also do not apply to military personnel. As per Article 136(2) and 227(4), there is no Appellate Jurisdiction against Court Martial (in Supreme Court and High Court).
- Under Article 32 only Writ Jurisdiction against these and appeal can be made under 226.
- Armed Forces Tribunal was established in Delhi for appeals on the decisions of military courts.

Fast Track Court

- Fast Track Courts are similar to District Courts. They are constituted for speedy disposal of pending cases, mainly pending cases of criminal nature. In the year 2000, the 11th Finance Commission recommended their establishment. Initially they were constituted for 5 years, after that this tenure was extended.
- In these, especially 2 years or more old cases were chosen to deal with those who are on bail.
- Due to the establishment of these courts, proper justice has been done to many innocent accused and persons convicted of minor crimes in jail.

Fast Track Special Courts (FTSC's)

- In 2019, the Union Government set-up 1023 Fast-Track Courts for expeditious trial and disposal of pending cases of rape and offences against children under the Protection of Children from Sexual Offences Act (POCSO), 2012.
- Fast Track Special Courts are being set-up as a part of the National Mission for Safety of Women (NMSW). The scheme was started in October, 2019.

Commercial Courts

- The Commercial Courts Act, 2015 established specialised courts to efficiently resolve high-value commercial disputes. These courts include :
  - Commercial Courts

- Commercial Appellate Courts
- Commercial Divisions in High Courts
- Commercial Appellate Divisions in High Courts
- The Act defines 'commercial dispute' broadly, encompassing various areas such as :
  - Mercantile documents (e.g., bills of exchange, checks)
  - Joint ventures and partnership agreements
  - Intellectual property rights (e.g., patents, trademarks, copyrights)
  - Insurance disputes
  - Other commercial transactions involving merchants, bankers, financiers and traders
- The key features of the Commercial Courts Act, 2015 are as follows :
  - State Governments can establish commercial courts at the district level to handle commercial disputes of a specified value.
  - State Governments can designate commercial appellate courts at the district judge level to oversee commercial courts below that level.
  - In High Courts with ordinary original civil jurisdiction, the Chief Justice can establish commercial divisions and appellate divisions to handle commercial disputes and appeals.
  - The minimum value of commercial disputes is set at ₹ 3 lakh, but this can be increased by the Central Government.
  - Parties must undergo mediation before filing a suit, unless urgent interim relief is required.
  - Pre-Institution Mediation and Settlement Mechanism has been introduced to facilitate mediation and authorities under the Legal Services Authorities Act, 1987. It may be empowered by the Central Government to conduct pre-institution mediation.

e-Lok Adalat

- During the covid pandemic, the Legal Services Authorities under the aegis of National Legal Services Authority (NALSA) ingeniously integrated technology to move Lok Adalat on to the virtual platform, better known as e-Lok Adalats.
- Since e-Lok Adalats are organised simultaneously with regular Lok Adalats, benches are constituted on the basis of volume of cases referred by various courts or tribunals and institutions for pre-litigation cases.
- The first e-Lok Adalat was held in Madhya Pradesh on 27th June, 2020.

Gram Nyayalayas Act, 2008

- This Act came into force from 2nd October, 2009 to provide for the establishment of Gram Nyayalayas at the grass roots level for the purpose of providing access to justice at the doorsteps of citizens.
- It aims to ensure that the justice is not denied to any citizen of India due to their social and economic conditions.
- The Central Government will meet the non-recurring expenditure of the establishment of courts. More than 5000 Gram Nyayalayas are expected to be setup.
- They are expected to reduce by 50% the pendency of cases in subordinate courts. Some salient features of this Act are as follows :
  - It aims at providing inexpensive justice to people residing in rural areas.
  - It shall be a Court of the Judicial Magistrate of First Class and the Presiding Officer (Nyayadhikari) will be appointed by the State Government in consultation with the High Court.
  - It shall be established for every Panchayat at intermediate level Nyayadhikaris are the Presiding Officers of Gram Nyayalayas.
  - They are judicial officers and have similar powers as First Class Magistrates working under High Courts.
  - Gram Nyayalayas shall exercise the powers of both criminal and civil courts.
  - Appeals in criminal matter can be made to the Sessions Court in the respective jurisdiction and in civil matters to the District Court within a period of one month from the date of judgement.
  - Criminal cases, civil lawsuits, claims or disputes that are included in the First Schedule and Second Schedule to the Act must be tried by the Gram Nyayalayas. It will try to settle disputes as far as possible by bringing about conciliation between the parties.
  - It will not be bound by Rules of Evidence in Indian Evidence Act, 1872, but it will be bound by principles of natural justice.
  - A person accused of an offence may file an application for plea bargaining.

Alternative Dispute Resolution Mechanism (ADR)

- Alternative Dispute Resolution (ADR) is a way of settling disputes and disagreements between parties *via* negotiation and discussion.
- It is an effort to develop a system that is distinct from the conventional methods of dispute resolution.
- The goal of the Alternative Dispute Resolution mechanism is to help resolve commercial disputes and other conflicts in which no attempt has been made to reach a consensus through negotiation or other means.
- In India, Alternative Dispute Resolution is enshrined in Article 14 (Equality before the law) and Article 21 (Right to life and personal liberty) of the Indian Constitution.
- The Directive Principles of State Policy (DPSP) of equal justice and free legal aid are enshrined in Article 39(A) of the Indian Constitution and it can also be accomplished through ADR.
- It can help the courts to reduce the burden of litigation even while providing a well-rounded and gratifying experience for the parties involved.
- Methods of ADR includes Negotiation, Mediation, Conciliation, Arbitration.

Dispute Resolution Mechanism Under Indian Legal System

- The Indian Constitution under Article 39(A), provides for equal justice for all people by offering free legal assistance to the impoverished and weaker groups of the society.
- The Constitution under Articles 14 and 22(1) requires the state to guarantee of equality before the law and a legal system that based on advance justice for all.
- Therefore, the Legal Services Authorities Act of 1987 established.
- The National Legal Services Authority (NALSA) of legal aid programmes and to establish the policies and guidelines for providing legal services in accordance with the Act.

National Legal Services Authorities (NALSA), 1987

- In the year 1987, the Legal Services Authorities Act was enacted by the Parliament.
- It aims to secure the free and comprehensive legal services to the weaker sections of the society and to organise Lok Adalats for amicable settlement of disputes. Also, it aims to provide free legal aid to the eligible person.
- This Act comes up with the composition of the Supreme Court Legal Service Committees, the High Court Legal Service Committees, State Legal Service Committees, the District Legal Service Committees and the Taluka Legal Service Committees.
- As per the Act, every person whose annual income is less than the amount prescribed by the respective State Government, (if the case is before any court other than the Supreme Court and less than ₹ 5 lakh, if the case is before the Supreme Court) is eligible for free legal aid.
- The above limits don't apply in the cases relating to SC's/ST's, women, children, handicapped, etc. This limit can be increased by State Governments.
- NALSA monitors and evaluates the implementation of the Legal Aid schemes and programmes. And, it also takes necessary steps for followings :
  - Promoting legal itinerary.
  - Setting up of legal aid clinics in universities and law colleges.
- Training of para-legal personnel and holding legal aid camps and the Lok Adalats/Permanent Lok Adalat.

> "The term 'Tribunal' is derived from the word Tribunes, which means 'Magistrates of the Classical Roman Public'.

Chapter Twenty Seven

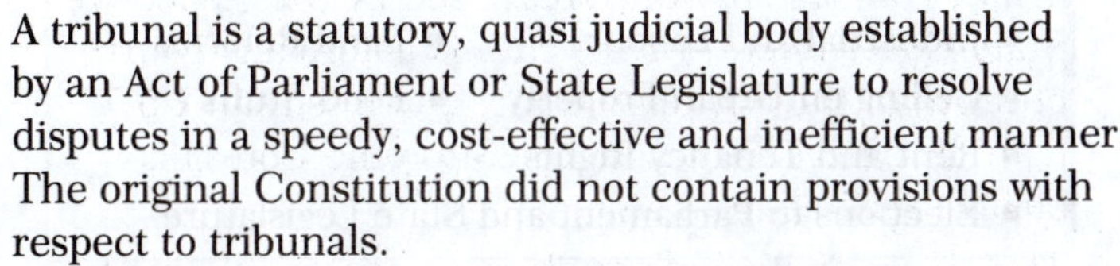

Various Tribunals and Authorities

A tribunal is a statutory, quasi judicial body established by an Act of Parliament or State Legislature to resolve disputes in a speedy, cost-effective and inefficient manner. The original Constitution did not contain provisions with respect to tribunals.

The 42nd Amendment Act of 1976 added a new Part XIV(A) to the Constitution. This part is entitled as tribunals and consists of only two Articles: Article 323(A) dealing with administrative tribunals and Article 323(B) dealing with tribunals for other matters.

ADMINISTRATIVE TRIBUNALS

- Article 323(A) empowers the Parliament to provide for the establishment of administrative tribunals.
- It empowers the Parliament for the adjudication of disputes relating to recruitment and conditions of service of persons appointed to public services corporations and other public authorities.
- In other words, Article 323(A) enables the Parliament to take out the adjudication of disputes relating to service matters from the civil courts and the High Courts and place it before the administrative tribunals.
- In pursuance of Article 323(A), the Parliament has passed the Administrative Tribunals Act in 1985.
- The Act authorises the Central Government to establish one Central Administrative Tribunal and the State Administrative Tribunals.
- The tribunals are meant to relieve the courts of overload and expedite the process of justice. According to the 42nd Amendment Act, only the Supreme Court can entertain cases relating to service matters.
- The President appoints the Chairman and other Members of the CAT and the SAT's after consulting the Chief Justice of India.
- The Chairman must be a Judge of the High Court or one who served for atleast two years as the High Court Judge or the Vice-Chairman of Tribunal.
- The Chairman and the Vice-Chairman of the Tribunal enjoys the status of a High Court Judge and his/her retirement age is 65 years.
- The retirement age for other members drawn from the administration is 62 years.

Central Administrative Tribunals (CAT's)

- It was established in 1985 under the Administrative Tribunals Act (1985) of the Parliament. Hence, it is a statutory body. It deals with the disputes relating to the recruitment and all service matters.
- The principal bench of the tribunal was established at New Delhi and additional benches in different states. Presently, 17 out of the total 19 regular benches of the tribunal operate at the

principal seats of High Courts and the remaining two at Jaipur and Lucknow.

- Its objective is to provide speedy and inexpensive justice to the aggrieved civil servants.
- It is a multi-member body consisting of a Chairman and 69 Members. The term of the Chairman and the Vice-Chairman is five years or until they attain the age of 65 years, whichever is earlier.
- The term of the members is five years or until they attain the age of 62 years, whichever is earlier. They are not eligible for re-appointment and are appointed by the President.
- They are drawn from both the judicial and the administrative streams. It is not bound by the procedure laid down in the Civil Procedure Code (1908) rather works on the principle of natural justice. Its jurisdiction extends to the members of the All India Services, Central Service and Posts.
- The chairman and the members in the CAT are appointed by the Central Government on the basis of the recommendations of the search-cum-selection committee.
- This committee is chaired by the Chief Justice of India or the judge of the Supreme Court, who is nominated by the Chief Justice of India.
- It works under the administrative control of the Department of Personnel and Training one of the three departments of Ministry of Personnel, Public Grievances and Pensions. The following categories of employees are exempted from the purview of the Administrative Tribunals (AT's) :
    - The employees of the Supreme Court and the High Court
    - Armed Forces personnel and employees of the Secretariat of the Lok Sabha and the Rajya Sabha.
- In Chandra Kumar Case (1997), Supreme Court declared that appeals against the orders of the CAT shall lie before the division bench of the concerned High Courts and later on in the Supreme Court.

State Administrative Tribunals (SAT's)

- The Administrative Tribunals Act of 1985 empowers the Central Government to establish the State Administrative Tribunals (SAT's) on specific request of the concerned State Governments.
- The Chairman and Members of the SAT's are appointed by the President after consultation with the Governor of the State concerned.
- On the basis of the recommendations of a search-cum-selection committee chaired by the Chief Justice of the High Court of the concerned state.
- The Act also makes a provision for setting up of Joint Administrative Tribunal (JAT) for two or more states. A JAT exercise all the jurisdiction and powers exercisable by the administrative tribunals for such states.

Tribunals for Other Matters

Under Article 323(B), the Parliament and the State Legislature are authorised to provide for the establishment of tribunals for the adjudication of disputes relating to the following matters:

- Taxation
- Foreign Exchange, Import and Export
- Industrial and Labour
- Land Reforms
- Ceiling on Urban Property
- Food Stuffs
- Rent and Tenancy Rights
- Elections to Parliament and State Legislature

Difference Between Articles 323(A) and 323(B)

- These articles differs in the following three aspects:
    - While Article 323(A) contemplates establishment of tribunals for public service matters only, Article 323(B) contemplates establishment of tribunals for certain other matters.
    - While tribunals under Article 323(A) can be established only by Parliament, tribunals under Article 323(B) can be established both the Parliament and State Legislatures with respect to matters falling within their legislative competence.
    - Under Article 323(A), only one tribunal for the Centre and one for each State or two or more states may be established. There is no question of hierarchy of tribunals, whereas under Article 323(B) a hierarchy of tribunals may be created.

"The Constitutional Provisions for the Local Government are given by 73rd and 74th Amendment Acts of 1992 and 1993.

Chapter Twenty Eight

Local Government (Panchayats and Municipalities)

- The Local Self-Government includes both Rural and Urban government. It is the third level of the government, constitutionalised through the 73rd and 74th Amendment Acts of 1992 and 1992.
- There are two types of Local Government in operation- Panchayats in rural areas and Municipalities in urban areas.
- It is the third level of government apart from the State and Central Government.
- The idea of Panchayati Raj forms a basic tenet of the Gandhian philosophy that envisions Village Panchayats as the units of self-government.
- Panchayati Raj Institutions (PRIs) serve as steering instruments for people's empowerment to bring tangible progress in their socio-economic life through direct participation in routine administration.
- Local government is a state subject under the Seventh Schedule.

PANCHAYATI RAJ INSTITUTIONS

- Article 40 (DPSP) of the Indian Constitution says that, the state shall take steps to organise Village Panchayats and provide them powers and authority to function as unit of self-government.
- Traditionally, Panchayats have been headed by five elderly wise men whose acumen in administration served a useful purpose in local administration.
- First state to establish Panchayati Raj is (Nagaur district) Rajasthan (by PM Jawaharlal Nehru on 2nd October, 1959) followed by Andhra Pradesh.
- During the colonial period, few notable British authorities like Lord Mayo and Lord Ripon emphasised the role of Panchayats for efficient local administration and they did try to delegate certain functions to them.
- Therefore, Lord Ripon is known as the Father of Local Self-Government.

Recommendation of Committees

Recommendations of important committees are as follows :

Balwant Rai Mehta Committee

- In 1957, the Government of India appointed a Committee to examine the functioning of the Community Development Programme (1952) and the National Extension Service (1953) and to suggest measures for their better performance.
- The Chairman of this committee was Balwant Rai G Mehta. The Committee submitted its report in November, 1957 and recommended a scheme for democratic decentralisation which ultimately came to be known as the Panchayati Raj.
- A three-tier Panchayati Raj System which includes Zila Parishad at the district level, Panchayat Samiti

at the block level and Gram Panchayat at the village level.

- These tiers should be organically linked together through a device of indirect elections.
- Members of Panchayats at each level i.e., village, intermediate and district levels are directly elected.
- All the planning and developmental activities should be entrusted to these bodies.
- The Panchayat Samiti should be the executive body, while the Zila Parishad should be the advisory, co-ordinating and supervisory body.
- The District Collector should be the Chairman of the Zila Parishad. There should be a genuine transfer of power and responsibility to these democratic bodies.
- A system should be evolved to effect further devolution of authority in future.
- These recommendations were accepted by National Development Council (NDC) in January, 1958 and the Council also left it to states to evolve their own patterns suitable to the local conditions.

K. Santhanam Committee

- In 1963, the K Santhanam Committee was appointed to look solely at the issue of PRI finance.
- The committee was asked to determine issues related to sanctioning of grants to PRIs by the State Government, evolving mutual financial relations between the three-tiers of PRIs, gifts and donation, handing over revenue in full or part to PRIs.

Ashok Mehta Committee

- In December 1977, the Janata Government appointed a Committee on Panchayati Raj Institutions under the Chairmanship of Ashok Mehta.
- It submitted its report in August, 1978 and made 132 recommendations to revive and strengthen the declining Panchayati Raj System in the country.
- The three-tier system of the Panchayati Raj should be replaced by two-tier system, i.e. the Zila Parishad at the district level and below it, the Mandal Panchayat consisting of a group of villages comprising a population of 15,000 to 20,000. A district should be the first point for the decentralisation under the popular supervision below the state level.
- The Zila Parishad should be the executive body and be made responsible for planning at the district level.
- There should be an official participation of political parties at all levels of Panchayat elections.
- The Panchayati Raj Institutions should have compulsory powers for taxation to mobilise their own financial resources.
- There should be a regular social audit by a district level agency and by a Committee of Legislators to check the funds allotted for the vulnerable social and economic groups.
- The State Government should not supersede the Panchayati Raj Institutions. In case of imperative super session, election should be held within six months from the time of super session.
- The Nyaya Panchayats should be kept as separate bodies from that of development Panchayats. They should be presided over by a qualified judge.
- The Chief Electoral officer of a state in consultation with the Chief Election Commissioner should organise and conduct the Panchayati Raj elections.
- Development functions should be transferred to the Zila Parishad and all the development staff should work under its control and supervision.
- The voluntary agencies should play an important role in mobilising the support of the people for the Panchayati Raj.
- A Minister for the Panchayati Raj should be appointed in the State Council of Ministers to look after the affairs of the Panchayati Raj Institutions.
- Seats for the SCs and the STs should be reserved on the basis of their population.
- A constitutional recognition should be accorded to the Panchayati Raj Institutions.
- This would give them the requisite status (Sanctity and Stature) and an assurance of continuous functioning.

Note *Sanctity means the quality of being holy or sacred. Stature means a person's standing in society, especially their importance or reputation.*

Due to the collapse of the Janata Government before the completion of its term, no action could be taken on the recommendations of the Ashok Mehta Committee at the Central level. But the three states **Karnataka, West Bengal** and **Andhra Pradesh** took steps to revitalise the Panchayati Raj, keeping in view some of the recommendations of the Ashok Mehta Committee.

Dantawala Committee

- The Dantawala Committee Report on Block Level Planning was constituted in the year 1977. It was constituted to suggest the institutional and conceptual framework for block planning.
- It submitted its report in 1978. As per its recommendation, block level planning should be the right sub-state planning level for proper comprehension of the actual needs of the people.

Hanumantha Rao Committee

- Hanumantha Rao Committee Report on District Planning was submitted in the year 1984.
- The Committee advocated separate district planning bodies under either the District Collector or a Minister.
- The committee recommended that the collector should be the co-ordinator at the district level, of all developmental and planning activities.

GVK Rao Committee

- The Planning Commission created the Committee to review the existing Administrative Arrangements for Rural Development and Poverty Alleviation Programme in 1985, which was chaired by GVK Rao.
- The Committee concluded that the development process had become increasingly bureaucratised and decoupled from the Panchayati Raj.
- It recognised that development was not seen at the grassroot level due to bureaucratisation resulting in Panchayati Raj Institutions being addressed as 'grass without roots'.
- Hence, it made some key recommendations which are as follows :
  - Zila Parishad to be the most important body in the scheme of democratic decentralisation.
  - It stated that the district is the proper unit for planning and development and the Zila Parishad should become the principal body for management of all development programmes which can be handled at that level.
  - The district and the lower levels of the Panchayati Raj System to be assigned with specific planning, implementation and monitoring of the rural developmental programmes.
  - Some of the planning functions at the state level should be transferred to the district level planning units for effective decentralised district planning.
  - Post of District Development Commissioner to be created. He will be the Chief Executive Officer of the Zila Parishad. Elections at the levels of Panchayats should be held regularly.

LM Singhvi Committee

- In 1986, Rajiv Gandhi Government appointed a Committee on the Revitalisation of the Panchayati Raj Institutions for Democracy and Development under the Chairmanship of LM Singhvi.
- The Panchayati Raj Institutions should be constitutionally recognised, protected and preserved. For this purpose, a new chapter should be added in the Constitution of India.
- This will make their identity and integrity reasonably and substantially inviolate. It also suggested constitutional provisions to ensure regular, free and fair elections to the Panchayati Raj bodies.
- Nyaya Panchayats should be established for a cluster of villages. The villages should be organised to make the Gram Panchayats more viable. It also emphasised the importance of the Gram Sabha and called it as the embodiment of direct democracy.
- The Village Panchayats should have more financial resources. The Judicial tribunals should be established in each state to eradicate controversies about election to the Panchayats.

Thungon Committee

- In 1988, a sub-committee of the Consultative Committee of Parliament was constituted under the leadership of PK Thungon to investigate the political and administrative structure in the district for the purpose of district planning.
- It made the following recommendations :
  - The Panchayati Raj bodies should be constitutionally recognised.
  - A three-tier system of Panchayati Raj with Panchayats at the village, block and district levels.
  - Zila Parishad should be the Pivot of the Panchayati Raj system, it should act as the planning and development agency in the district.
  - The Panchayati Raj bodies should have a fixed tenure of five years.
  - The maximum period of super session of a body should be six months.
  - A detailed list of subjects for Panchayati Raj should be prepared and incorporated in the Constitution.

- There should be reservation for women and the reservation of seats in all the three-tiers should be on the basis of population.
- A State Finance Commission should be set-up in each state. The district collector should be the Chief Executive Officer of the Zila Parishad.

Gadgil Committee

- The committee was set up in 1988 under the Chairmanship of VN Gadgil to look after policy and programmes on Panchayats. This committee discussed on 'how best Panchayati Raj Institutions could be made effective'. Its key recommendations are :
  - A constitutional status should be bestowed on the Panchayati Raj Institutions.
  - A three-tier system of Panchayati Raj with Panchayats at the village, block and district levels.
  - Panchayati Raj Institutions should be given a five year term.
  - At all three levels, Members of the Panchayats should be directly elected. Reservation should be given to SC's, ST's and women.
  - The preparation and implementation of socio-economic development plans should be the duty of Panchayati Raj authorities. A list of subjects should be established in the Constitution for this purpose.
  - Taxation and duties should be levied, collected and appropriated by Panchayati Raj entities.
  - The creation of a State Finance Commission to oversee the distribution of funds to the Panchayats.
  - Establishment of a State Election Commission to oversee the conduct of Panchayat elections.

Constitutionalisation of Panchayati Raj Institutions

- The Rajiv Gandhi Government introduced the 64th Constitutional Amendment Bill in the Lok Sabha in July 1989 to constitutionalise Panchayati Raj Institutions and make them more powerful and broad base but not passed by Parliament, second time by VP Singh Government in November, 1989, but it lapsed due to the fall of government.
- The Narasimha Rao Government introduced the Constitutional Amendment Bill in the Lok Sabha in September, 1991.
- It was passed by the Lok Sabha on 22nd December, 1992 and by the Rajya Sabha on 23rd December.
- Thus, it emerged as the 73rd Constitutional Amendment Act, 1992 and came into force on 24th April, 1993.

73rd Constitutional Amendment Act, 1992

- The Act provides for a three-tier system of the Panchayati Raj in the states, i.e., Panchayats at the village, the intermediate and the district level. The Act defines all the terms in the following manners :
  - Panchayat means an institution (by whatever name called) of local self-government for rural areas.
  - Village means, a village specified by the Governor through a public notification to be a village for this purpose and includes a group of villages so specified.
  - Intermediate level between the village and the district specified by the Governor through a public notification for this purpose.

Constitutional Provisions

Schedule 11; 29 functions; Part IX; Article 243-243(O).

Important Articles

- **Article 243 (G)** Power, authority and responsibilities of Panchayats.
- **Article 243 (H)** Power to impose taxes by and funds of the Panchayats.
- **Article 243 (I)** Constitution of Finance Commission to review financial position.

Provisions of the Act

There are some provisions of the act :

Gram Sabha

- According to Article 243(A), Gram Sabha is a body consisting of persons registered in the electoral rolls of the village comprised within the area of the Panchayat at the village level.
- It is a Village Assembly consisting of all the registered voters in the area of a Panchayat.
- It shall exercise powers and perform functions at the village level as the State Legislature determines.
- It exercises powers and functions determined by State Legislature a Gram Sabha shall meet at least twice every year.
- The quorum for Gram Sabha meetings shall be fixed at one-tenth of total members.

Three-tier System

As per **Article 243 (B)**, the Act provides for a three-tier system of Panchayats at village, intermediate block and district levels except in States with population is below 20 lakhs.

Election of the Members and the Chairpersons

- Under Article 243 (C), all members of the Panchayats at the village, the intermediate and the district levels shall be elected directly by the people.
- The Chairperson of the Panchayats at the intermediate and district levels shall be elected indirectly by and from amongst the elected members thereof.
- The Chairperson of a Panchayat at the village level shall be elected in such a manner as determined by the State Legislature. The chairperson of a Panchayat elected directly or indirectly shall have the right to vote in the meetings of the Panchayats.

Reservation of Seats

- As per Article 243 (D), the Act provided for the reservation of seats for the Scheduled Castes and the Scheduled Tribes in every Panchayat (at all the levels) in proportion of their population in the Panchayat area.
- Further, the State Legislature shall provide for the reservation of offices of chairperson in the Panchayat at the village or any other level for the SC's and ST's.
- The Act provides for the reservation of not less than one-third of the total number of seats for women (including the number of seats reserved for women belonging to the SC's and the ST's).
- The Act authorises the Legislature of a State to make any provision for reservation of seats in any Panchayat or offices of the Chairperson in the Panchayat at any level in favour of the backward classes.
- It must be noted here that the above provision relating to the reservation of seats in Panchayats (both members and chairpersons) for the Scheduled Castes is not applicable to the state of Arunachal Pradesh because the state is inhabited fully by indigenous tribal people and there are no Scheduled Castes.
- This provision was added later by the 83rd Constitutional Amendment Act of 2000.

Duration of Panchayats

- Article 243 (E) states that the tenure of Panchayats at all levels is five years. However, it can be dissolved before the completion of its term. Fresh election to constitute a Panchayat shall be completed.
  - before the expiry of its term, of five years.
  - in case of dissolution, before the expiry of a period of six months from the date of its dissolution.
- Where the remainder of the period (for which the dissolved Panchayat would have continued) is less than six months, it shall not be necessary to hold any election for constituting the new Panchayat for such period.
- A Panchayat reconstituted after premature dissolution does not enjoy the full period of five years but remains in office only for the remainder of the period.

Disqualifications

- Under Article 243 (F), a person shall be disqualified for being chosen as a member of the Panchayat, if he/she is so disqualified as follows:
  - Under any law for the time being in force for the purposes of elections to the Legislature of the state concerned.
  - Under any law made by the State Legislature.
  - No person shall be disqualified on the grounds that he is less than 25 years of age, if he/she had attained the age of 21 years.
  - All questions of disqualifications shall be referred to such authority as the State Legislature determined.

Powers and Functions

- According to Article 243 (G), the State Legislature may endow the Panchayats, with such powers and authority as may be necessary to enable them to function as institutions of self-government.
- Such a scheme may contain provisions for the devolution of powers and responsibilities upon Panchayats at the appropriate level with respect to preparation of plans for economic development and social justice.
- The implementation of schemes for the economic development and social justice as may be entrusted to them, including those in relation to the **29 matters** listed in the Eleventh Schedule.

Financial Provisions

- According to Articles 243 (H) and 243 (I), the State Legislature may, by law authorise a Panchayat to levy, collect and appropriate taxes, duties, tolls and fees.

- It can assign to a Panchayat taxes, duties, tolls and fees levied and collected by the State Government.
- It may also provides for making grant-in-aid to the Panchayats from the Consolidated Fund of the State and (provide for Constitution of funds for crediting all the financial requirements of the Panchayats).

State Finance Commission

- Under, Article 243 (I) , Governor of a State shall constitute a Finance Commission to review the financial position of the Panchayats after every five years. The commission makes the following recommendations to the Governor :
  - the principles which should govern the distribution between the States and the Panchayats of the net proceeds of taxes, duties, tolls and fees levied by the State.
  - the principles which should govern the determination of taxes, duties, tolls and fees which may be assigned to the Panchayats.
  - the principles which should govern the grants in aid to the Panchayats from the Consolidated Fund of State. The measures needed to improve the financial position of the Panchayats.
- The Central Finance Commission shall also suggest the measures needed to augment the Consolidated Fund of State to supplement the resources of the Panchayats in the States.
- The Governor laid the recommendations of State Finance Commission to be laid before the State Legislature.
- Audit of Accounts of the Panchayat As per Article 243 (J) , the State Legislature may make provisions with respect to the maintenance of the accounts by the Panchayats and the auditing of such accounts.

State Election Commission

- According to Article 243(K) the superintendence, direction and control of the preparation of electoral rolls and the conduct of all elections to the Panchayats shall be vested in the State Election Commission.
- It consists of a State Election Commissioner, who is appointed by the Governor.
- His/her conditions of service and tenure of office shall be determined by the Governor.
- He/she shall not be removed from the office except in the manner and on the grounds prescribed for the removal of a Judge of the State High Court.
- His/her conditions of service shall not be varied to his disadvantage after his appointment.

The Eleventh Schedule

As per **Article 243 (G)**, the **Eleventh Schedule** contains the following 29 functional items placed within the purview of Panchayats :

1. Agriculture, including agricultural extension
2. Land improvement, implementation of land reforms, land consolidation and soil conservation
3. Minor irrigation, water management and watershed development
4. Animal husbandry, dairying and poultry
5. Fisheries
6. Social forestry and farm forestry
7. Minor forest produce
8. Small-scale industries, including food processing industries
9. Khadi, village and cottage industries
10. Rural housing
11. Drinking water
12. Fuel and fodder
13. Roads, culverts, bridges, ferries, waterways and other means of communication
14. Rural electrification, including distribution of electricity
15. Non-conventional energy sources
16. Poverty alleviation programme
17. Education, including primary and secondary schools
18. Technical training and vocational education
19. Adult and non-formal education
20. Libraries
21. Cultural activities
22. Markets and fairs
23. Health and sanitation including hospitals primary health centres and dispensaries
24. Family welfare
25. Women and child development
26. Social welfare, including welfare of the handicapped and mentally retarded
27. Welfare of the weaker sections and in particular of the Scheduled Castes and the Scheduled Tribes
28. Public distribution system
29. Maintenance of community assets

Compulsory Provisions

- Organisation of Gram Sabha in a village.
- Establishment of a three-tier Panchayati Raj System at the District, Block and Village levels.
- Direct elections to all seats in Panchayats at the village, intermediate and district levels.
- Indirect elections to the post of chairperson of Panchayats at the intermediate and district levels.

- Minimum age for contesting elections to the Panchayats is 21 years.
- There should be reservation of seats for Scheduled Castes/ Scheduled Tribes in Panchayats, in proportion to their population and one-third seats for women.
- State Election Commission to be set up in each State to conduct elections to Panchayats.
- The tenure of Panchayats at all level is five years, if dissolved earlier, fresh elections to be held within six months.
- A State Finance Commission is set up in each state every five years.

Voluntary Provisions

- Endowing the Gram Sabha with powers and functions at the village level.
- Determining the manner of election of the chairperson of the Village Panchayat.
- Giving representation to Members of the Parliament (both the Houses) and the State Legislature (both the Houses) in the Panchayats at different levels falling within their constituencies.
- Providing reservation of seats (both members and chairpersons) for backward classes in Panchayats at any level.
- Granting powers and authority to the Panchayats to make them autonomous bodies (it is a government organisation that is established by a State Legislature or Parliament to serve the public).
- Devolution of powers and responsibilities upon Panchayats to prepare plans for economic development and social justice under Eleventh Schedule.
- Assigning to a Panchayat the taxes, duties, tolls and fees levied and collected by the State Government.
- Making the grants in aid to the Panchayats from the Consolidated Fund of the State.

Panchayats Extension to Scheduled Areas Act, 1996 (PESA)

- The 73rd Amendment Act, 1992 was not applicable to fifth Schedule and six areas.
- Therefore, PESA Act, 1996 was enacted on the basis of the report of the Bhuria Committee and came into operation on 24th December, 1996.
- The Ministry of Panchayati Raj is the nodal ministry for implementing its provisions in states.
- This Act extends Panchayats to the tribal areas of ten states, namely; Andhra Pradesh, Telangana, Chhattisgarh, Gujarat, Himachal Pradesh, Jharkhand, Maharashtra, Madhya Pradesh, Odisha and Rajasthan. It intends to provide self rule to the tribal people and govern themselves as well as their resources.
- All the State Governments have enacted their State Legislations in pursuance with the PESA Act, 1996. The Act gives radical governance powers to the tribal community and recognises its traditional community rights over local natural resources.
- It not only accepts the validity of customary law, social and religious practices and traditional management practices of community resources, but also directs the State Government not to make any law which is inconsistent with these.

Objectives of the PESA Act

The objectives of the PESA Act are as follows :

- To extend the provisions of Part IX of the Constitution relating to the Panchayats to the Scheduled Areas with certain modifications. To provide self-rule for the bulk of the tribal population.
- To have village governance with participatory democracy and to make the Gram Sabha a nucleus of all activities. To evolve a suitable administrative framework consistent with traditional practices. To safeguard and to preserve the traditions and customs of tribal communities.
- To empower Panchayats at the appropriate levels with specific powers conducive to tribal requirements.
- To prevent Panchayats at the higher level from assuming the powers and authority of Panchayats at the lower level of the Gram Sabha.

URBAN GOVERNMENT

- In urban areas, the local self-government units are known as municipalities. In India, the phrase urban local government refers to the process by which the people, acting through their elected officials, govern an urban region.
- The system of urban Government was constitutionalised through the 74th Constitutional Amendment Act of 1992.
- Urban local governments can only regulate certain urban areas that the State Government has set aside for this purpose.
- The urban local government is dealt by following three ministries :
  - The Ministry of Housing and Urban Affairs (States).
  - Ministry of Defence (Cantonment Boards).
  - Ministry of Home Affairs (Union Territories).

Evolution of Urban Local Bodies in India

- In India, Municipal organisations have a long history.
- The first such Municipal Corporation was set up in the former Presidency Town of Madras in 1688.
- Similarly, corporations were later established in Bombay and Calcutta in 1726.
- The establishment of local self-government institutions was envisioned in Lord Mayo's Resolution on financial decentralisation from 1870.
- The Resolution of Lord Ripon of 1882 has been recognised as the 'Magna Carta' of local Self-Government. In India, he is known to be the founding father of Local Self-Government.
- First urban local government in India was Municipal Corporation at Madras by a charter granted in 1687.
- The Royal Commission on decentralisation was appointed in 1907 and submitted its report in 1909 and Hobhouse served as its Chairman.
- According to the Government of India Act, 1919 under the dyarchical system, local self-government was transferred to the purview of an Indian Minister with appropriate authority.
- Local self-government was recognised as a provincial subject under the Government of India Act of 1935 provincial autonomy scheme.
- The protection of democracy in Parliament and State Legislatures is explicitly provided for in the Indian Constitution. However, local self-government in metropolitan areas was not explicitly mandated by the Constitution.

74th Constitutional Amendment Act, 1992

- Constitutional status for municipalities emerged as the 74th Constitutional Amendment Act of 1992 came into force on 1st June, 1993.
- This Act contains Part IX (A) of the Constitution of India. It also added the Twelfth Schedule to the Constitution.
- The Act contains 18 functional items of the municipalities and consists of provisions from Articles 243(P) to 243(ZG).
- The Act brought them under the purview of justifiable part of the Constitution.
- It aims to establish a uniform framework for urban local bodies and enhancing their capacity to serve as effective democratic units of self-government.

Constitution of Municipalities

- According to Article 243(Q), the following shall be constituted in every state
- A Nagar Panchayat for a transitional area, that is to say, an area in transition from a rural area to an urban area.
- A Municipal Council for a smaller urban area.
- A Municipal Corporation for a larger urban area in accordance with the provisions of this part.

- The 74th Amendment Act (1992) provides for the Constitution of the following three types of municipalities in every state :

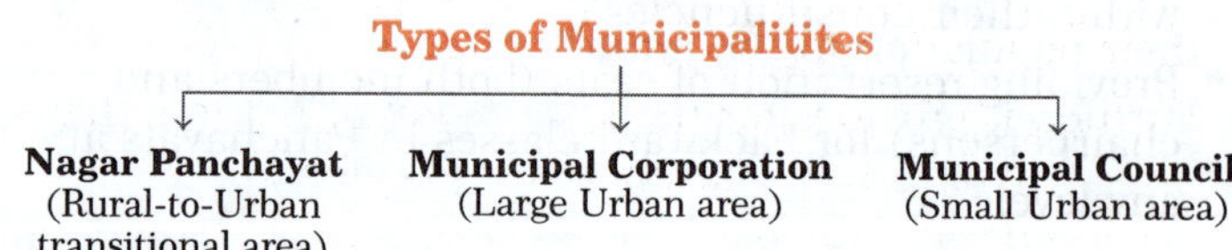

Composition of Municipalities

- According to Article 243(R), all the seats in a municipality shall be filled by persons chosen by direct election from the territorial constituencies in the municipal area.
- For this purpose, each municipal area shall be divided into territorial constituencies to be known as Wards.
- The Legislature of a State may by law provide for the representation in a municipality of
  - persons having special knowledge or experience in Municipal administration.
  - the members of the House of the People and the members of the Legislative Assembly of the State representing constituencies which comprise wholly or partly the municipal area.
  - the members of the Council of States and the members of the Legislative Council of the State registered as electors within the municipal area.

- the Chairpersons of the Committees constituted under Clause (5) of Article 243 (S).

Wards Committees

- As per Article 243(S), the Act provides a Wards Committee, constituted of one or more wards, within the territorial area of a municipality having a population of 3 lakhs or more.
- The Legislature of a State may make provision with respect to:
  - the composition and the territorial area of a Wards Committee.
  - the manner in which the seats in a Wards Committee shall be filled.
- A member of a municipality representing a ward within the territorial area of the Wards Committee shall be a member of that Committee.

Reservation of Seats

- As per Article 243(T), the Act provides for the reservation of seats for the Scheduled Castes and the Scheduled Tribes in every municipality in proportion of their population in the municipal area.
- Further, it provides for the reservation of not less than one-third of the total number of seats for women (including the number of seats reserved for women belonging to SC's and ST's).
- The State Legislature may make provisions for reservation of seats to the offices of the chairpersons in municipalities for SC's, ST's and women.

Duration of Municipalities

- As per Article 243(U), every municipality has five year tenure and before it is dissolved, it is provided a fair opportunity to be heard.
- If a municipality is dissolved earlier than the required five years, elections must be held within six months of the dissolution in order to constitute the municipality.
- A municipality constituted upon the dissolution of a municipality before the expiration of its duration.
- It shall be continue only for the remainder of the period for which the dissolved municipality would have continued had it not been so dissolved.

Disqualification of Members

- According to Article 243(V), a person shall be disqualified for being chosen as a member of a municipality
  - If he is so disqualified by or under any law currently in effect for the purpose of election to the Legislature of the State concerned.
  - It also provides that no person shall be disqualified on the basis that he is under 25 years of age, if he has attained the age of 21 years.
  - If a State law passed by the Legislature of the State disqualifies him in this manner.
  - If there is any doubt as to whether a member of a municipality has become subject to disqualifications the matter shall be referred for the judgement of such authority as the State Legislature may by law provide.

State Election Commission

- The superintendence, direction and control of the preparation of electoral rolls, and the conduct of all elections to the municipalities shall be vested in the State Election Commission.
- The State Legislature may make provision with respect to all matters relating to elections to the municipalities.

Powers and Functions of Municipalities

- According to Article 243(W), the municipalities with such powers and authorities as may be necessary to enable them to function as institutions of self-government.
- The law also contains provisions for the devolution of powers and responsibilities upon municipalities, to such conditions as may be specified, with respect to
  - the preparation of plans for economic development and social justice.
  - the performance of functions and the implementation of schemes as may be entrusted to them including those in relation to the matters listed in the Twelfth Schedule.
- The Committees with such powers and authorities as may be necessary to enable them to carry out the responsibilities conferred upon them including those in relation to the matters listed in the Twelfth Schedule.

Financial Provisions

- As per Article 243(X), the State Legislature may authorise a municipality to levy, collect and appropriate such taxes, duties, tolls and fees in accordance with such procedure and subject to such limits.
- The State Legislature may assign to a municipality for such taxes, duties, tolls and fees levied and collected by the State Government for such purposes, conditions and limits.

- The State Legislature may provide for making such grants-in-aid to the municipalities from the Consolidated Fund of the State.
- The State Legislature may provide for Constitution of such funds for crediting all moneys received respectively, by or on behalf of the municipalities and also for the withdrawal of such moneys as may be specified in the law.

Finance Commission

- As per Article 243(Y), the Finance Commission (which is constituted for the Panchayats) shall also, review the financial position of municipalities and make recommendation to the Governor for every five years.
- The principles that govern the distribution between the states and the municipalities of the net proceeds of taxes, duties, tolls and fees levied by the state.
- The principles that govern the determination of taxes, duties, tolls and fees which may be assigned to the municipalities.
- The principles which should govern the grants in aid to the municipalities from the **Consolidated Fund** (it is a central financial account that holds all government receipts and outlays, including taxes, fees and other income.) of the State.
- The State Legislature may provide for the composition of the commission, the required qualifications of its members and the manner of their selection.
- The Governor shall place the recommendations of the Commission along with the action taken report before the State Legislature.
- The **Central Finance Commission** shall also suggest the measures needed to augment the Consolidated Fund of State to supplement the resources of the municipalities in the states (on the basis of the recommendations made by the Finance Commission of the State).

Audit of Accounts

Under Article 243(Z), the State Legislature may make provisions with respect to the maintenance of accounts by Municipalities and the auditing of such accounts.

Application to Union Territories

As per Article 243(ZB), the provisions of this part are applicable to the Union Territories. But, the President may direct that they would apply to a Union Territory to such exceptions and modifications as he may specify.

Exempted Areas

- As per Article 243(ZC), the Act does not apply to scheduled areas and tribal areas in the states. It shall also not affect the functions and powers of the Darjeeling Gorkha Hill Council of the West Bengal.
- However, the Parliament may extend the provisions of this part to the Scheduled Areas and Tribal Areas subject to such exceptions and modifications as it may specify.
- The 74th Amendment Act provided for the Compulsory and Voluntary Provisions for the Municipalities as follows

Committee for District Planning

- As per Article 243(ZD), there shall be constituted a District Planning Committee in every state at the district level to consolidate the plans prepared by the Panchayats and the Municipalities in the district and to prepare a Draft Development plan for the district as a whole.
- The Legislature of a State may make provision with respect to
  - the composition of the District Planning Committees.
  - the Act provides that four-fifth of total members of such a committee shall be elected by the elected members of the District Panchayat and the Municipalities in the district.
  - the functions relating to district planning which may be assigned to such committees.
  - the manner in which the Chairpersons of such committees shall be chosen.
- Every District Planning Committee prepares the draft development plan regard to the matters of common interest between the Panchayats and Municipalities including spatial planning, sharing of water and other physical and natural resources, the integrated development of infrastructure and environmental conservation.
- The committee makes draft development plan with regard to the extent and type of available resources whether financial or otherwise. Committees consult such institutions and organisations as the Governor may by order specify.
- The Chairperson of every District Planning Committee shall forward the development plan, as recommended by such committee, to the Government of the State.

Committee for Metropolitan Planning

- As per Article 243(ZE), there shall be constituted a Metropolitan Planning Committee in every metropolitan area, to prepare a draft development plan for the metropolitan area as a whole.
- The Legislature of a State may, make provision with respect to:
  - the composition of the Metropolitan Planning Committees.
  - the manner in which the seats in such committees shall be filled. It provides that not less than two-third of the members of committee shall be the elected members of the Municipalities in the metropolitan area.
  - the representation in such committees of the Government of India and the Government of the State and such organisations and institutions.
  - the functions relating to planning and co-ordination for the metropolitan area which may be assigned to such committees.
  - the manner in which the Chairpersons of such committees shall be chosen.
- Every Metropolitan Planning Committee shall, in preparing the draft development plan :
  - have regard to the plans prepared by the Municipalities and the Panchayats in the metropolitan area.
  - in respect to matters of common interest between the Municipalities and the Panchayats, including co-ordinated spatial planning of the area, sharing of water and other physical and natural resources, the integrated development of infrastructure and environmental conservation.
  - in respect to the overall objectives and priorities set by the Government of India and the Government of the State.
  - in respect to the extent and nature of investments likely to be made in the metropolitan area by agencies of the Government of India and of the Government of the State and other available resources whether financial or otherwise.
  - Metropolitan Planning Commission shall consult such institutions and organisations as the Governor may by order specify.
  - The Chairperson of every Metropolitan Planning Committee shall forward the development plan, as recommended by such committee, to the Government of the State.

Continuance of Existing Laws and Municipalities

- Under Article 243(ZF), all the state laws relating to Municipalities shall continue to be in force until the expiry of one year from the commencement of this act.
- All Municipalities existing immediately before the commencement of this act shall continue till the expiry of their term, unless dissolved by the State Legislature.

The Twelfth Schedule

The Twelfth Schedule Under Article 243(W), contains the following 18 functional items placed within the purview of municipalities:

1. Urban planning including town planning.
2. Regulation of land-use and construction of buildings.
3. Planning for economic and social development.
4. Roads and bridges.
5. Water supply for domestic, industrial and commercial purposes.
6. Public health, sanitation, conservancy and solid waste management.
7. Fire services.
8. Urban forestry, protection of the environment and promotion of ecological aspects.
9. Safeguarding the interests of weaker sections of society including the handicapped and mentally retarded.
10. Slum improvement and upgradation.
11. Urban poverty alleviation.
12. Provision of urban amenities and facilities such as parks, gardens, playgrounds.
13. Promotion of cultural, educational and aesthetic aspects.
14. Burials and burial grounds; cremations, cremation grounds and electric crematoriums.
15. Cattle pounds, prevention of cruelty to animals.
16. Vital statistics including registration of births and deaths.
17. Public amenities including street lighting, parking lots, bus stops and public conveniences.
18. Regulation of slaughter houses and tanneries.

Interference in Electoral Matters of the Courts

- According to Article 243(ZG), the validity of any law relating to the delimitation of constituencies or the allotment of seats made or purporting to be made under Article 243(ZA) shall not be called in question in any court.

- There is no election to any Municipality shall be called in question except by an election petition presented to such authority and in such manner as is provided for by or under any law made by the Legislature of a State.

TYPES OF URBAN-LOCAL GOVERNMENTS

The following urban local government are created in India for the administration of urban areas :

Municipal Corporation

- The Municipal Corporation is the top-most urban local government. It is created for the administration of big cities such as, Delhi, Mumbai, Kolkata, Hyderabad, Bangalore, etc.
- Municipal Corporation is established in the states by the acts of concerned State Legislatures and in the Union Territories by the acts of the Parliament of India.
- A Municipal Corporation has three authorities, namely the Council, the Standing Committees and the Commissioner. The Council is the deliberative and legislative wing of the corporation.
- It consists of the councillors who are directly elected by the people as well as nominated members with knowledge and experience of municipal administration.
- The Council is headed by a Mayor elected for a term of one year. Mayor is assisted by a Deputy Mayor and he presides over the meetings of the Council. The Standing Committees are created to facilitate the working of the council.
- There is also a Municipal Commissioner, who is Chief-Executive authority of the corporation. He/she is appointed by the State Government and is generally a member of the IAS.

Municipality

- The Municipalities are established for the administration of towns and smaller cities.
- It is also set-up in the states by the acts of the concerned State Legislatures and in the Union Territory by the acts of the Parliament of India.
- Like Municipal Corporation, a Municipality also has three authorities, namely, the Council, the Standing Committees and the Chief-Executive Officer.
- The Council is deliberative and legislative wing of the Municipality. It consists of the councillors directly elected by the people. The Council is headed by a President or Chairman.
- The Standing Committees are created to facilitate the working of the Council. The Chief-Executive Officer is responsible for day-to-day general administration of the Municipality. He/she is appointed by the State Government.

Notified Area Committee

- It is set-up by government notification and not a legislation. All its members and chairman are appointed by the State Government and not elected.
- It is established to take care of administration of an area which is either a fast developing town from industrialisation or a town not yet developed to fulfill all the conditions to create a municipality.
- It is neither an elected body nor a statutory body.

Town Area Committee

- A town area committee is set-up for the administration of a small town.
- It is set-up by an Act of State Legislature and can have both elected and nominated members.
- It is quasi-municipality with limited number of municipal functions like street lighting, sanitation, etc. It may be wholly or partly elected and nominated by State Government.

Cantonment Board

- They are autonomous bodies functioning under the overall control of the Ministry of Defence. It was established by the Central Government under the provisions of the Cantonment Act, 2006.
- It is a partially elected and partly nominated body whose ex-officio President is the military officer commanding the station.
- The Vice-President is chosen from among the board's elected members. The President of India appoints the executive officer of the cantonment board.
- The elected members hold office for a term of five years while the nominated members continue so long as they hold the office in that station.

- At present, there are 62 cantonment boards in the country. The resources of these boards are limited as the bulk of the property is owned by government on which no tax can be levied.
- The Central Government provides financial assistance by way of grants in aid.
- The boards are responsible for discharging the mandatory duties like provision of public health, sanitation, primary education and street lighting, etc.

Classification of Cantonment Boards

Categories	Civil Populations
I	above 50000
II	10000 to 50000
III	2500 to 10000
IV	Below 2500

Township

- It is established to provide civic amenities to its staffs and workers living in the colonies near the plant by large public enterprises.
- It is headed by the town administrator appointed by the enterprises.

Port Trust

- It is established by an Act of Parliament to manage and protect the ports alongwith to provide civic amenities in the port areas.
- It has both elected and nominated members and its chairman is an officer. Its civic functions are more or less similar to those of municipality.

Special Purpose Agency

- It is established for single or specific purpose as statutory bodies by an Act of State Legislature or as department by an executive resolution: like Housing Boards, Pollution Control Boards, Urban Development Authorities, Town Improvement Trust, etc.
- These are function-based and not area based. These functional local bodies are established as statutory bodies by an act of state legislature or as departments by an executive resolution.
- They function as autonomous bodies and deal with the functions allotted to them independently of the local urban governments, that is, municipal corporations or municipalities and so forth.
- They are not subordinate agencies of the local municipal bodies.

CENTRAL COUNCIL OF LOCAL GOVERNMENT

- The Central Council of Local Government was set-up in 1954. It was constituted under Article 263 of the Constitution of India by an order of the President of India.
- The Council is an advisory body consists of the Union's Minister of Urban Development and the State's Minister of Local Self-Government.
- The Union Minister serves as the Council's Chairman. The Council has following functions
  - considering and recommending the policy matters.
  - making proposals for legislation.
  - drawing up a common programme of action.
  - examining the possibility of co-operation between the Centre and the States.
  - recommending Central Financial Assistance.
  - reviewing the work done by the local bodies with the Central Financial Assistance.

A Union Territory is a type of administrative unit in Republic of India. These are directly administered by Union Government. Currently, there are 8 Union Territories in India.

Chapter Twenty Nine

Constitutional Provisions of Union Territories

UNION TERRITORIES (UTs)

- Under Part-I (Article 1) of the Constitution, the Territory of India comprises three categories of territories :
  - Territories of the states
  - Union Territories
  - Territories that may be acquired by the Government of India at any time.
- The Union Territories are those areas which are under the direct control and administration of the Central Government. They are also known as centrally administered territories. At present, there are 8 Union Territories and no acquired territories.
- Initially, the territories were divided into four different categories (Part-A) Former British Indian Provinces, (Part-B) Princely States, (Part-C) Provinces under the Chief Commissioner and (Part-D) Andaman and Nicobar Islands.
- The States of Categories (Part-C) and (Part-D) were included as Union Territories by the Seventh Constitutional Amendment Act, 1956. 14 States and 6 Union Territories were established by the State Reorganisation Commission in 1956.
- Some Union Territories were made full-fledged states and some were included in other territories; For example, acquired territories Puducherry, Dadra and Nagar Haveli and Daman and Diu and Chandigarh were made Union Territories.
- At present, India has 28 States and 8 Union Territories, but there is no acquired territory.
- Dadra and Nagar Haveli and Daman and Diu Act, 2019 merged these two to form a Union Territory.

Union Territories of India and their Years of Creation

Union Territories		Year of Formations
Andaman and Nicobar Islands	–	1956
National Capital Territory of Delhi (NCT)	–	1956
Lakshadweep	–	1956
Puducherry	–	1962
Chandigarh	–	1966
Jammu and Kashmir	–	2019
Ladakh	–	2019
Dadra and Nagar Haveli and Daman and Diu	–	2019

Articles Related to Constitutional Provisions of Union Territories

Articles	Description
Article 239	Administration of Union Territories
Article 239(A)	Creation of local legislatures or Council of both for certain Union Territories
Article 239(AA)	Special provisions with respect to Delhi
Article 239(AB)	Provision in case of failure of Constitution
Article 239(B)	Power of administrator to promulgate ordinate recess of Legislature
Article 240	Power of President to make regulations for Territories
Article 241	High Courts for Union Territories

Historical Development of Union Territories

- During British rule, the Indian Territory was divided into four fold classification of Part A, B, C and D for administrative purposes.
- After independence the territories placed under Part C and Part D were combined into single category known as the Union Territory.
- The special feature of these Part C States was that they were administered by the President through a Chief Commissioner or a Lieutenant-Governor, acting as his/her agent.
- Parliament had Legislative Power relating to any subject with respect to Part C States, but the Constitution empowered Parliament to create a Legislature as well as a Council of Advisors or Ministers for Part C State.
- By the Seventh Constitutional Amendment, Act 1956, the classification of the states into A, B, C and D was abolished.
- The whole Territory of India was categorised into the states, the Union Territories and acquired territories, if any.
- Himachal Pradesh, Manipur, Tripura, Mizoram, Arunachal Pradesh and Goa, which are states today, were formerly Union Territories under Part C and Part D.
- The states or the provinces are the Constitutional Units of the Union of India enjoying federal relationship with the centre.
- The status of the Union Territories has subtle difference from that of the states in two respects:
  - they are not part of the federal structure of the Constitution and hence, do not participate in the division of power.
  - they are directly administered by the centre through the Lieutenant-Governors or Chief Commissioners, appointed by the President.

Difference Between States and Union Territories

States	Union Territories
A state is an independent body administered either by a unicameral or bicameral State Legislature.	Union Territory is not an autonomous unit, but is managed by administrators appointed by India's President.
The constitutional and executive head of the state is the Governor of the State.	The President is the executive authority for the Union Territories. The administrator is an agent of the President.
States are administered by the Chief Ministers elected by the people of India.	Union Territory is administered by the administrator who is appointed by the President.
Parliament cannot make laws on the subjects of the State list in relation to the states except under extraordinary circumstances.	Parliament can make laws on any subject of the three lists the State list in relation to the states except under in relation to the Union Territories.
State enjoys autonomous powers.	Union Territories do not have autonomous powers.

ADMINISTRATION OF UTs

- Articles 239 to 241 under Part VIII of the Constitution deals with the administration of Union Territories.
- According to Article 239(1), every Union Territory shall be administered by the President acting, to such an extent as he thinks fit, through an administrator appointed by him.
- The President has right to assign any designation to the administrator of the Union Territories as per his wish.
- The administrator is usually called the Lieutenant-Governor in the case of Delhi, Puducherry, Andaman and Nicobar Islands, Jammu and Kashmir and Ladakh and Administrator in the case of Chandigarh, Dadra and Nagar Haveli and Daman and Diu and Lakshadweep.
- Under Article 239 (2), instead of appointing an administrator from outside, the President may appoint the Governor of a State as the administrator of an adjoining Union Territory. The appointed Governor so exercises his/ her functions as such administrator independently of his/her Council of Ministers.
- The Union Territories of Puducherry (in 1963), Delhi (in 1992) and Jammu and Kashmir (in 2019) are provided with a Legislative Assembly and a Council of Ministers headed by a Chief Minister.
- The Constitution does not contain any separate provisions for the administration of acquired territories.

LEGISLATURE IN UTs

- By the 14th Constitutional Amendment Act 1962, provisions was made by adding Article 239(A) of the Constitution. Under this :
  - Parliament may by law create for any territory a Legislature and a Council of Ministers or both.
  - The Legislative and Executive Powers related to public order, police and land retain by the union to be handled through the Lieutenant-Governor of Delhi.

- Under Article 239(A), the Union Territory of Andaman and Nicobar Islands has a nominated body in place of a Legislature.
- Under Articles 239(A) and 240, the administrator of a Union Territory enjoys powers of promulgating ordinances like the Governors of States.
- Under Article 246(4), Parliament has exclusive Legislative Power over a Union Territory, including matters which are enumerated in the State list.
- The Parliament can make laws on any subject of the three lists (including the State list) for the Union Territories. This power of Parliament also extends to Puducherry, Delhi and Jammu and Kashmir, which have their own local legislatures.
- This means that, the Legislative Power of Parliament for the Union Territories on subjects of the State list remains unaffected even after establishing a local legislature for them.
- Parliament can establish a High Court for a Union Territory or put it under the jurisdiction of the High Court of adjacent state.
- Delhi is the only Union Territory that has a High Court of its own (since 1966).
- The President can make regulations for the peace, progress and good government of the Andaman and Nicobar Islands, Lakshadweep, Dadra and Nagar Haveli, Daman and Diu and Ladakh.
- Laws made by the President in relation to Union Territories have same force and effect as the Act of Parliament.
- In the case of Puducherry also, the President can legislate by making regulations but only when the assembly is suspended or dissolved.
- A regulation made by the President has the same force and effect as an act of Parliament and can also repeal or amend any act of Parliament in relation to these Union Territories.
- According to Article 240(2), these territories may repeal or amend any Act of Parliament which is for the time being applicable to the Union Territory. Apart from that the President's power to make regulations shall remain suspended while the Legislature is functioning in any of these states, to be revived as soon as such legislature is dissolved or suspended.

National Capital Territory of Delhi (NCT)

- For the first time in the year 1952, the Legislative Assembly was formed in Delhi.
- The Legislative Assembly was abolished in the year 1956 during the reorganisation of states from the States Reorganisation Act, 1956. Sarkaria Commission was established to consider the issues related to the administrative reorganisation of Delhi.
- The Constitution (69th Amendment) Act, 1991 declared the Union Territory of Delhi to be formally known as the National Capital Territory of Delhi.
- The Act gave Delhi its own Legislative Assembly, though with limited powers. The National Capital Territory of Delhi has its own Legislative Assembly, Lieutenant-Governor, Council of Ministers and Chief Minister.
- Members of the Legislative Assembly are directly elected from territorial constituencies in the NCT.
- The Legislative Assembly was abolished in 1956, after which direct federal control was implemented until it was re-established in 1993.
- The Municipal Corporation of Delhi (MCD) handles Civil Administration for the city as part of the Panchayati Raj Act. The Government of India and the Government of National Capital Territory of Delhi jointly administer New Delhi.
- The Parliament of India, the Rashtrapati Bhavan (Presidential Palace), Cabinet Secretariat and the Supreme Court of India are located in New Delhi. There are 70 members in assembly constituencies and 7 members in Lok Sabha (Indian Parliament's Lower House) constituencies in Delhi. Delhi is the only Union Territory, which has its own High Court.
- The strength of the Council of Ministers is fixed at 10% of the total strength of the assembly i.e. seven—1 Chief Minister and 6 other Ministers.
- The Chief Minister is appointed by President (not by the Lieutenant-Governor) and the other Ministers are appointed by the President on the advice of Chief Minister. All Ministers will hold office only during the pleasure of the President. Council of Ministers will be collectively responsible to the Legislative Assembly.
- In case of difference of opinion between Lt. Governor and Chief Minister, the Lt. Governor refers the matter to the President.
- When a situation arises in which the administration of the territory cannot be carried on in accordance with

above provision, the President can suspend the above provisions and make the necessary incidental or consequential provisions for administering the territory resembling Article 356.

- The Lt. Governor is empowered to promulgate ordinances during recess of the assembly. An ordinance has the same force as an act of the assembly. Every such ordinance must be approved by the assembly within six weeks from its reassembly. He can also withdraw an ordinance at any time.
- But he cannot promulgate an ordinance when the assembly is dissolved or suspended. Also, no such ordinance can be promulgated or withdrawn without the prior permission of the President.
- In the case of difference of opinion between the Lt. Governor and his Ministers, the Lt. Governor refers the matter to the President for decision and acts accordingly.
- Reservation of seats for the Scheduled Castes in the Delhi Legislative Assembly shall be made in accordance with the law made by the Parliament. (Due to non-availability of Scheduled Tribe population in Delhi, seats have not been allotted for them).
- The assembly can make laws on all matters of the State list and the Concurrent list except the three matters of the State list i.e. Public order, Land and Police.

The 7th Constitutional Amendment Act 1956, led to the creation of Zonal Councils in India to advise on matters of common interest.

- The Lieutenant-Governor is appointed by the President and is responsible to him only. Along with the constitutional head of the National Capital Territory of Delhi, the Lieutenant Governor is also the head of the executive.

Andaman and Nicobar

- The Andaman and Nicobar are the groups of islands at the juncture of the Bay of Bengal and Union of Territory of India. The Andamanese town of Port Blair is the territory's capital.
- They are linked administratively by the British to the Nicobar islands. The two sets of islands become a Union Territory of the Republic of India in 1956. Lieutenant Governor is the Executive Head of this Union Territory.
- The Union Territory of Andaman and Nicobar comes under the jurisdiction of the Calcutta High Court.

Chandigarh

- Chandigarh is a city and Union Territory of India that serves as the capital of two states, Haryana and Punjab.
- Chandigarh administration is under the control of the Administrator, who is appointed under the provisions of Article 239 of the Constitution of India.
- As per Section 29 of the Punjab Reorganisation Act, 1966, the Punjab and Haryana High Court has been conferred jurisdiction over Chandigarh Union Territory.

Dadra and Nagar Haveli and Daman and Diu

- The 10th Amendment of the Constitution of India was passed to incorporate Dadra and Nagar Haveli as a Union Territory with effect from 11th August, 1961.
- The Territory of Goa, Daman and Diu was administered as a single Union Territory until 30th May, 1987 when Goa was granted statehood.
- In December 2019, the Parliament of India passed legislation to merge Dadra and Nagar Haveli with the nearby Union Territory of Daman and Diu. On 26th January, 2020, Dadra and Nagar Haveli and Daman and Diu became a single Union Territory.
- The Union Territory of Dadra and Nagar Haveli and Daman and Diu is under the control of the Administrator and falls under the jurisdiction of Bombay High Court.

Puducherry

- Puducherry is an Union Territory of India formed out of four enclaves of former French colonies and named after the largest enclave, Puducherry. By 14th Amendment Act, Puducherry was made Union Territory of Indian Union.
- Puducherry is one of the two Union Territories in India which are entitled by special Constitutional Amendments to have an elected Legislative Assembly and a Cabinet of Ministers, thereby, enjoying partial statehood powers.
- Under the special provision, the State Government is permitted to make laws with respect to specific matters. In many cases, such legislation may require the ratification from the Union Government or the assent of the President of India.
- The centre is represented by the Lieutenant Governor, who resides at the Raj Nivas (Le Palais du Gouverneur) at the Park, the former palace of the French Governor.

- The executive arm of Union Territory of Puducherry includes the Lieutenant-Governor, Chief Minister and Council of Ministers.

Lakshadweep

- The Lakshadweep is a set of small islands situated near each other.
- The location is near the Kerala coast and falls under the jurisdiction of Kerala High Court.
- Kavaratti is its capital and it is considered one of the most beautiful places in the Indian sub-continent. The Union Territory was formed on 1st November, 1956.
- Under the Government of India (Allocation of Business) Rules 1961, Ministry of Home Affairs is the Nodal Ministry for all matters of Union Territories relating to legislation, finance and budget, services and appointment of Lieutenant Governors and administrators.
- The languages spoken here are Malayalam, Hindi, Mahl and English. Executive head is designated as administrator. The Union Territory of Lakshadweep falls under the jurisdiction of Kerala High Court.

Jammu and Kashmir

- Jammu and Kashmir's Maharaja Hari Singh signed an instrument of Accession on 26th October, 1947 with India. It was included under Indian Constitution under Article 370.
- The Article 370 was abolished in August, 2019 and state was transformed into a Union Territory. It consists of two divisions i.e., Jammu and Kashmir division.
- It is administered under the provision of Article 239 of the Indian Constitution. Lieutenant-Governor will administer the Union Territory with the help of Council of Ministers led by a Chief Minister.
- Union Territory will also have Parliamentary seats for both the houses.

Ladakh

- Till August, 2019 Ladakh was a part of Jammu and Kashmir. It was declared as a Union Territory after being separated from Jammu and Kashmir.
- It will be administered without a Legislative Assembly. The head of Union Territory will be Lieutenant-Governor and he will be assisted by the civil servant of the Indian Administrative Service. Jammu and Kashmir High Court will serve as a High Court for Ladakh.

Home Minister's Advisory Committees for Union Territories

- Under the Government of India (Allocation of Business) Rules, 1961, the Ministry of Home Affairs is the nodal agency for all matters relating to financial services and appointment of Lieutenant-Governors and administrators in Union Territories.
- Union Territories (Andaman and Nicobar Islands, Ladakh, Chandigarh, Daman and Diu and Dadra and Nagar Haveli, Lakshadweep) which do not have legislature in all the five, there Home Minister's Advisory Committee, Administrator's Advisory Committee (Administrator Advisory Committee) is the forum.

HIGH COURTS FOR UTs

- Article 241 of the Constitution provides for High Courts for Union Territories.
- Parliament by law may establish a High Court for a Union Territory or declare any court in any such territory to be a High Court for all or any of the purposes of the Constitution.
- The Lakshadweep is under the jurisdiction of the Kerala High Court.
- The Calcutta High Court has got jurisdiction over the Andaman and Nicobar Islands.
- The Madras High Court has jurisdiction over Puducherry. The Bombay High Court over Dadra and Nagar Haveli. The Guwahati High Court (Assam) over Mizoram and Arunachal Pradesh.
- The Territory of Goa, Daman and Diu had a Judicial Commissioner but recently the Jurisdiction of the Bombay High Court has been extended to this territory. Delhi has a separate High Court of its own since, 1966.

Acquired Territories

- There are no separate provisions in the Constitution relating to the administration of acquired territories but the provisions relating to Union Territories will extend by virtue.
- According to **Article 366(30)** "any other territory comprised within the Territory of India but not specified in that schedule". Parliament has plenary power of legislation regarding such territory as in the case of the Union Territories.

"

Article 244(1) of the Indian Constitution has mentioned scheduled areas. The tribal area was mentioned in the Article 244(2) of the Indian constitution.

Chapter Thirty

Administration of Scheduled and Tribal Areas

CONSTITUTIONAL PROVISIONS

- Tribal societies are traditionally governed by customary laws of different tribes and have been historically isolated from mainstream societies and thus, they require special provisions for governance. The Constitution provides Provisions under Article 244 to protect the interest of these tribal societies.
- Under Indian Constitution Part X, Article 244 deals with the Scheduled Areas and Tribal Areas.
- The Fifth Schedule of Constitution and Article 244(1) provides for the administration of the Scheduled Areas and Scheduled Tribes in any state except Assam, Meghalaya, Tripura and Mizoram. These four states are dealt under Sixth Schedule of the Constitution and Article 244(2).
- Scheduled Areas are such areas inhabited by the tribes specified as Scheduled Tribes.
- Article 244(A) of the Constitution empowers Parliament that allows the creation of an autonomous state within Assam in certain tribal areas. It was inserted into the Constitution by 22nd Constitutional Amendment Act of 1969.
- The Scheduled Areas have been given autonomy in the affairs of marriage, law, property transfer, inheritance, etc., and such others for the tribal welfare.
- The State Governments have few restrictions with regard to the control over tribal areas.

Administration and Control

The Fifth Schedule makes the following provisions for administration and control of scheduled and tribal areas :

Declaration of Scheduled Area

- The President of India can declare any area as a Scheduled Area after consulting the Governor of the concerned state and can direct the area to be reduced or increased, renamed or cancelled, but they can do so only under the law passed by the Parliament.
- The criteria for declaring any area as a Scheduled Area is as follows :
  - Preponderance of tribal population;
  - Compactness and reasonable size of the area;
  - A viable administrative entity such as a District, Block or Taluk; and
  - Economic backwardness of the area as compared to the neighbouring areas.
- The above criteria for declaration of Scheduled Areas is as such not spelt out in the Constitution, but has become well established.
- New orders may be issued from time to time defining the Scheduled Areas.
- The responsibility of such areas lies with the Governor of the concerned state and the Executive Power of the State extends to the Scheduled Areas
- The Governor in his annual report regarding the administration of these areas submits the report to the President and informs the state about these areas.

- Parliament can amend the Fifth Schedule by making general legislation. Such an amendment is not deemed to be an amendment of the Constitution, and therefore does not require a special majority, as the amendment so made is directed to this list.

States and their Scheduled Areas in Fifth Schedule

States	Scheduled Areas
Andhra Pradesh	Visakhapatnam, East Godavari, West Godavari, Adilabad, Srikakulam, Vizianagaram, Mahbubnagar, Prakasam (only some mandals are Scheduled Mandals).
Jharkhand	Dumka, Godda, Deoghar, Sahibganj, Pakur, Ranchi, Singhbhum (East and West), Gumla, Simdega, Lohardaga, Palamu, Garhwa, (some districts are only partly tribal blocks).
Chhattisgarh	Surguja, Bastar, Raigarh, Raipur, Rajnandgaon, Durg, Bilaspur, Kanker.
Himachal Pradesh	Lahaul and Spiti districts, Kinnaur, Pangi teshsil and Bharmaur Sub-tehsil in Chamba district.
Madhya Pradesh	Jhabua, Mandla, Dhar, Khargone, East Nimar (Khandwa), Sailana tehsil in Ratlam district, Betul, Seoni, Balaghat, Morena, Shandol.
Gujarat	Surat, Bharuch, Dang, Valsad, Panchmahal, Sadodar, Sabarkantha (parts of these districts only).
Maharashtra	Thane, Nasik, Dhule, Ahmednagar, Pune, Nanded, Amravati, Yavatmal, Gadchiroli, Chandrapur (parts of these districts only).
Odisha	Mayurbhanj, Sundargarh, Koraput (fully Scheduled Area in these three districts), Rayagada, Keonjhar, Sambalpur, Boudhkondmals, Ganjam, Kalahandi, Bolangir, Balasore (parts of these districts only).
Rajasthan	Banswara, Dungarpur (fully tribal districts), Udaipur, Chittaurgarh, Sirohi (partly tribal areas).
Telangana	Adilabad, Komrambeen Asifabad, Mancherial, Mulug, Warangal (Rural), Mahbubabad, Bhadradri- Kothagudens, Khammam, Nagar Kurnool.

Executive Power of Union and State in Scheduled Areas

- The Executive Power of a state extends to the Scheduled Areas.
- The Governor has a special responsibility for these areas and he submits a report to the President with respect to the conditions and administration of these areas annually or whenever so required by the President.
- The Executive Power of the centre extends to giving instructions to the states regarding the administration of these areas.

Tribal Advisory Council (TAC)

- In accordance with the provisions of Article 4 of the Constitution of India, a Tribal Advisory Council shall be established in every state having Scheduled Areas under Article 244(1) of the Fifth Schedule and, if the President so directs, also in those states having Scheduled Areas. Tribes reside in, but not Scheduled Area.
- Tribal Advisory Council shall consists of 20 members out of which three-fourth are to be representatives of the Scheduled Tribes in the State Legislative Assembly.
- Similarly, this Council can be established in a state having Scheduled Tribes but not Scheduled Areas only with the permission of President.
- Tribal Advisory Councils have been constituted in 10 states having Scheduled Areas namely Andhra Pradesh, Telangana, Chhattisgarh, Gujarat, Himachal Pradesh, Jharkhand, Madhya Pradesh, Maharashtra, Odisha and Rajasthan. Apart from this, Tribal Advisory Councils have been constituted in West Bengal, Tamil Nadu, Uttarakhand eventhough there are no Scheduled Areas.

Laws Applicable to Scheduled Areas

- The Governor has the power to make or not to make any particular Act of Parliament or the Legislature of the State applicable to a Scheduled Area or apply with the specified exceptions and modifications.
- The Governor can make regulations for the peace and good governance in Scheduled Areas. (after consulting with the Tribal Advisory Council).
- These regulations prohibit or limit the transfer of land in such areas.
- It also controls the business of moneylenders and regulates allotment of land.
- In making any such regulation, the Governor may repeal or amend any Act of Parliament or of the Legislature which is to be applied to that area.
- The Governor shall not make any regulation without consulting Tribal Advisory Council.
- Parliament has the power to make changes or repeal any provision of Fifth Schedule. This is not regarded as Amendment under Article 368.
- The Constitution provides for the formation of a commission to report on the welfare of the Scheduled Tribes in the states and the administration of the Scheduled Lands.

- Under Article 339(1), such commission shall be constituted within 10 years from the commencement of the Constitution.
- The first Commission was established in 1960 under the Chairmanship of UN Dhebar. It submitted its report in 1961.
- The committee reported on the administration of the Scheduled Areas and welfare of Scheduled Tribes in the states. The Second Commission was setup in 2002 under Dilip Singh Bhuria. It submitted its report in 2004.

Administration of Tribal Areas under Sixth Schedule

- The **Sixth Schedule** allows the formation of Autonomous District Councils in Assam, Meghalaya, Tripura and Mizoram. This provision is provided under **Articles 244(2)** and **275(1)** of the Indian Constitution.
- The special provision has been made because the tribal people of these areas have not yet adopted the mainstream lifestyle.
- By 22nd Constitutional Amendment, 1969, **Article 244** authorised Parliament Power to establish an autonomous state by merging some tribal states of Assam.

Special Provisions under Sixth Schedule

States	Provisions
Assam	• The Dima Hasao Autonomous District Council • The Karbi Anglong District • The Bodoland Territorial Region
Meghalaya	• The Khasi Hills District • The Jaintia Hills District • The Garo Hills District
Tripura	• Tripura, Tribal Areas Autonomous District Council
Mizoram	• The Chakma District • The Mara District • The Lai District

Constitution of District and Regional Councils

- The tribal areas of these states are considered as autonomous districts, but they do not fall outside the executive authority of the state concerned.
- Governor has the authority to organise and reorganise these districts, increase or decrease the boundaries, delimitation of areas, elections, qualifications, terms of office, etc.
- If there are different tribes in an autonomous district, the Governor can divide the district into several autonomous regions.
- Each Autonomous District and Regional Council has a maximum of 30 members, four of them are appointed by the Governor and the rest 26 are elected on the basis of Adult Franchise.
- The elected members shall hold office for a term of five years. On the other hand, nominated members hold office during the pleasure of the Governor. Each autonomous region has separate Regional Council.

Powers and Functions of the District Councils and Regional Councils to Make Laws

- District and Regional Councils administer the areas under their jurisdiction; can make laws on certain matters: land, forests, canal water, but such laws require Governor assent.
- District and Regional Council can constitute Village Councils/ courts for trial of suits, and cases between tribes. Jurisdiction of High Courts over such suits and cases is specified by the Governor.
- The District Council can establish: primary schools, dispensaries, markets, ferries, and roads in the district. It can also make regulations for control of money lending and trading by non-Tribals. But such regulations require the assent of the Governor.
- They are empowered to assess and collect land revenue, and to impose certain specified taxes.
- Central or State Acts do not apply to autonomous districts and autonomous regions or apply with specified modifications, and exceptions.
- Governor directs: in case of Assam for both Central and State Acts.
- President directs: in case of Meghalaya, Tripura and Mizoram for Central Acts, and Governor in respect of State Acts.
- The Governor may also direct by order that the laws passed by the State Legislature may not apply or shall apply with modifications to the territories of District Councils and Regional Councils.
- The Governor has right to suspend District Council, if any act or resolution passed by it affect the security and public order in India.
- The same applies to laws passed by the Parliament, but the Governor here has to act in consultation with the President.

Functions of District/Regional Councils

Legislative Functions

- Inheritance of Property, Marriage, Social customs.
- Management of forests (except Reserved Forests).
- Canal water, shifting cultivation, fisheries.
- Construction and management of primary schools.
- Trade and Commerce in certain products such as food, cattle, fodder, raw cotton, raw jute, etc.
- Power to assess and collect land revenue, and certain taxes.

Judicial Functions

- Judicial powers of the council are subjected to the jurisdiction of the High Court as specified by the Governor.
- Regional and district councils can constitute village councils/courts for the trial of suits and cases for people belonging to Scheduled Tribes with in such areas.
- It can also appoint suitable persons to be members of such village councils or presiding officers of these courts.
- District/Regional Councils with the previous assent of the governor make rules regulating the Constitution of village councils and courts and power to be exercised by them and procedures to be followed.

Particularly Vulnerable Tribal Groups

- Particularly Vulnerable Tribal Groups (PVTGs) are more vulnerable among the tribal groups.
- They have declining or stagnant population, low level of literacy, pre-agricultural level of technology and are economically backward.
- In 1973, the Dhebar Commission created Primitive Tribal Groups (PTGs) as a separate category, who are less developed among the tribal groups. Consequently, on the basis of the Dhebar Commission report, a criterion for identifying Particularly Vulnerable Tribal Groups was established as :
  - Pre-agricultural level of technology,
  - Low level of literacy,
  - Economic backwardness,
  - A declining or stagnant population.
- PVTGs were formerly known as Primitive tribal groups.
- In 1975, the Government of India initiated to identify the most Vulnerable Tribal Groups as a separate category called PVTGs.
- As per Census 2011, there are 75 PVTGs, spread over 18 States and 1 Union Territory (Andaman and Nicobar Islands) in the country.
- The Ministry of Tribal Affairs implements the Scheme of 'Development of Particularly Vulnerable Tribal Groups (PVTGs)' exclusively for them.
- Under the scheme, Conservation-cum- Development (CCD)/Annual Plans are to be prepared by each State/Union Territory for their PVTGs based on their need assessment, which are then appraised and approved by the Project Appraisal Committee of the Ministry.

Distribution of Particularly Vulnerable Tribal Groups

States	Tribes Found
Andhra Pradesh and Telangana	Bodo Gadaba, Bondo Poroja, Chenchu, Dongria Khond, Gutob Gadaba, Khond Poroja, Kolam, Kondareddis, Konda Savaras, Kutia Khond, Parengi Poroja, Thodi
Bihar and Jharkhand	Asurs, Birhor, Birjia, Hill Kharia, Konvas, Mal Paharia, Parhaiyas, Sauda Paharia, Savar
Gujarat	Kathodi, Kohvalia, Padhar, Siddi, Kolgha
Karnataka	Jenu Kuruba, Koraga
Kerala	Cholanaikayan (a section of Kattunaickans), Kadar, Kattunayakan, Kurumbas, Koraga
Madhya Pradesh and Chhattisgarh	Abujh Macias, Baigas, Bharias, Hill Korbas, Kamars, Saharias, Birhor
Maharashtra	Katkaria (Kathodia), Kolam, Maria Gond
Manipur	Marram Nagas
Odisha	Birhor, Bondo, Didayi, Dongria-khond, Juangs, Kharias, Kutia Kondh, Lanjila Sauras Lodhas, Mankidias, Paudi Bhuyans, Soura, Chukta Bhunjija
Rajasthan	Seharias
Tamil Nadu	Kattua Nayakans, Kotas, Kurumbas, Irulas, Paniyans, Todas
Tripura	Reangs
Uttar Pradesh and Uttarakhand	Buxas, Rajis
West Bengal	Birhor, Lodas, Totos
Andaman and Nicobar Islands	Great Andamanese, Jarawas, Onges, Sentinelese, Shorn, Pens

A Constitutional Bodies in India is an institution that derives its authority directly from the Constitution, with its composition, powers and duties explicity outlined within it.

Chapter Thirty One

Constitutional Bodies

The bodies which are mentioned in various articles in the Indian Constitution are called constitutional bodies. They directly get power from the Constitution. Constitutional Amendment is required to change the power of these bodies. Constitutional bodies are special because they are set-up and given functions and powers by the Constitution itself.

COMPTROLLER AND AUDITOR-GENERAL

- The Comptroller and Auditor-General (CAG) is an important official of the Union Government, his office has been created by the Constitution. He is appointed by the President.
- Article 148 of Constitution of India provides for an independent office of the Comptroller and Auditor General of India (CAG). He/she is the head of the Indian Audit and Accounts Department.
- His/her duty is to uphold the Constitution of India and laws of Parliament in the field of financial administration.

> **B.R. Ambedkar** rightly observed **CAG** as the guardian of the public purse and controls the entire financial system of the country at both the levels i.e., the **Centre and the States**.

- CAG is concerned only at the stage of audit after the expenditure has already taken place. He is called as the Eyes and Ears of the Public Accounts Committee. Articles 148 to 151 of the Constitution of India deals with the office of the CAG.

Qualifications

- The Constitution does not provide for specific qualifcations for the office of CAG. Since 1978, IAS officers have been appointed as CAG.
- An expert in finance, accounts and audit should be appointed as CAG.
- The CAG must be given the power to recover the loss of government money by the civil servants.
- In India, the CAG is neither a part of the executive nor the legislature. As prevalent in United Kingdom, the CAG must be made an integral part of the Parliament. Since, the executive is responsible to the legislature, on that basis, CAG must be a part of the Parliament in India.
- He/she holds office for a period of six years or up to the age of 65 years, whichever is earlier.
- He/she can resign any time from his/her office by addressing the resignation letter to the President.
- He/she can also be removed by the President on same grounds and in the same manner as a judge of the Supreme Court.

Oath and Affirmation

- Every person appointed to be the Comptroller and Auditor-General of India shall, before he enters upon his office, make and subscribe before the President or some person appointed on that behalf by him, an oath or affirmation as follows :
    - He shall uphold the sovereignty and integrity of India.
    - To bear true faith and the allegiance to the Constitution of India.

- To duly and faithfully perform his duties with his best abilities, knowledge and judgement.
- To perform the duties of office without fear or favour affection or ill will.
- To uphold the Constitution and laws.

Independence of CAG

- Under **Article 148**, he is provided with the security of tenure. He can be removed by the President only in accordance with the procedure mentioned in the Constitution.
- Thus, he does not hold his office till the pleasure of the President, though he is appointed by him.
- He is not eligible for further office, after he ceases to hold his office.
- His/ her salary and other service conditions are determined by the **Parliament**.
- According to the Act made by the Parliament, his/her salary is equal to that of a judge of the Supreme Court.
- By charging his salary and other expenses for the maintenance of his office upon the Consolidated Fund of India.
- By providing that, the salary and other service conditions of the CAG shall not be changed to his disadvantage during his tenure.
- By giving him complete control over administrative staff.
- Also, CAG cannot be represented by any minister in both the Houses of the Parliament and no minister can be called upon to take any responsibility for any actions done by the CAG.

Duties, Responsibilities and Powers

- According to Article 149, Parliament enacted CAG's Duties, Powers and Condition of Service Act, 1971 that lays down following duties of CAG.
  - Audit of receipts and expenditures of Consolidated Funds of the Union and the States and Union Territories having a Legislative Assembly.
  - Audit of the Contingency Fund of India and the public accounts of India.
  - Audit of the transactions related to authorities, developmental bodies, welfare boards, etc., substantially funded by the government.
  - Audit of all trading, manufacturing, profit and loss accounts, balance sheets and other subsidiary accounts kept by any department of the Central Government and State Governments.
  - Audit of the receipts and expenditure of all bodies and authorities substantially financed from the central or state revenues.
  - Audit of the accounts of all bodies and authorities receiving grants and loans from the Central and State Government for specific purposes.
  - Audit of all receipts of the centre and states and ensures that the rules and procedures in this regard are designed to secure an effective check on the assessment, collection and proper allocation of revenue.
  - Audit of the accounts of all stores and stock kept in all the offices and departments of the Central and State Governments.
  - Audit of the accounts of all Government Companies in accordance with the provisions of the Companies Act.
  - Audit of the accounts of all Corporations whose statutes provide for audit by him/her.
  - Audit the accounts of any other body or authority when requested by the President or Governor. For example, the audit of local bodies.
  - Audit of stocks, shares of government organisations and corporations as enacted in the statues constituting them.
  - Submits his audit reports relating to the accounts of the Centre and of a States to the President and Governor respectively.
- As per Article 150, he advises the President with regard to the prescription of the form in which the accounts of the Centre and the States shall be kept.
- Submit audit reports relating to the accounts of the Centre to President, who shall, in turn, place them before both the Houses of Parliament (Article 151).
- Submit the audit reports relating to the accounts of a state to governor, who shall, in turn, place them before the state legislature (Article 151).
- Ascertain and certify the net proceeds of any tax or duty (Article 279).
- According to the Sixth Schedule, the accounts of the District Council or Regional Council should be kept in such form as CAG, with the approval of the President, prescribes.
- In addition, these bodies' accounts are audited in such a manner as CAG may think fit and the reports relating to such accounts shall be submitted to the Governor, who shall cause them to be laid before the Council.

- Regulatory agencies like Telecom Regulatory Authority of India (TRAI), Public-Private Partnerships (PPPs), Panchayats and Municipalities should be audited by the Comptroller and Auditor-General of India.

Nature of Audit

The audit done by CAG, can be classified into following categories :

- **Regulatory Audit** This type of audit is done to see that the expenditure incurred was in conformity with the laws, rules and regulations framed to regulate the procedure for expanding public money.
- **Propriety Audit** While conducting the audit, the CAG satisfies himself that the rules and procedure ensure that assessment, collection and allocation of revenue are done in accordance with the law and there is no leakage of revenue which legally should come to government.
- **Performance Audit** This type of audit sees that government programmes have achieved that desired objectives at lowest cost and given the intended benefits.

Report of CAG

- The CAG submits three audit reports to the President :
  - Audit report on appropriation accounts
  - Audit report on finance accounts
  - Audit report on public undertakings
- The President lays these reports before both the Houses of Parliament. After this, the Public Accounts Committee examines them and reports its findings to the Parliament.

Articles Related to CAG

Article No.	Subject matter
Article-148	Comptroller and Auditor-General of India
Article-149	Duties and Powers of the Comptroller and Auditor-General
Article-150	Types of Accounts of the Union and of the States
Article-151	Audit Reports

UNION PUBLIC SERVICE COMMISSION

- The Union Public Service Commission (UPSC) is the central recruiting agency in India. It is an independent constitutional body in the sense that it has been directly created by the Constitution.
- Articles 315 to 323 in Part XIV of the Constitution contain elaborate provisions regarding the composition, appointment and removal of members along with the independence, power and functions of the UPSC.

Appointment and Tenure

- The UPSC consists of a chairman and other members appointed by the President of India. Strength is not specified in the Constitution and left at the discretion of the President.
- Further, no qualifications are prescribed for the Commission's membership except that one-half of the members of the Commission should be such persons who have held office for at least ten years either under the Government of India or under the government of a state.
- The chairman and members of the Commission hold office for a term of six years or until they attain the age of 65 years, whichever is earlier.
- The President can appoint one of the members of the UPSC as an acting chairman in the following two circumstances :
  - When the office of the chairman falls vacant; or
  - When the chairman is unable to perform his/her functions due to absence or some other reason.
  - Condition of Service The Constitution authorises the President to determine the conditions of service of the chairman and other members of the Commission.

Removal

- The President can remove the chairman or any other member of UPSC from the office under the following circumstances :
  - If he/she is adjudged an insolvent (that is, has gone bankrupt);
  - If he/she engages, during his/her term of office, in any paid employment outside the duties of his/her office;
  - If he/she is, in the opinion of the President, unfit to continue in office by reason of infirmity of mind or body.

The President can also remove the chairman or any other member of UPSC **for misbehaviour**. However, in this case, the President has to refer the matter to the Supreme Court for an enquiry.

- If the SC, after the enquiry, upholds the cause of removal and advises so, the President can remove the chairman or a member. Advice tendered by the SC in this regard is binding on the President.

Independence

- Salary and pension are charged on Consolidated Fund of India (CFI).
- Conditions of service of the chairman or a member cannot be varied to disadvantage.
- Chairman/member of the UPSC can be removed from office by the President only in the manner and on the grounds mentioned in the Constitution.
- The chairman of the UPSC (on ceasing to hold office) is not eligible for further employment in the Government of India or a state.
- A member of the UPSC (on ceasing to hold office) is eligible for appointment as the chairman of UPSC or a State Public Service Commission (SPSC), but not for any other employment in the Government of India or a state.
- The chairman or a member of UPSC is (after having completed his/her first term) not eligible for re-appointment to that office (i.e., not eligible for second term).

Functions and Other Aspects

- Watchdog of the 'Merit System' in India.
- It conducts examinations for appointments to the All-India services, Central services and Public services of the centrally administered territories.
- It assists the states (if requested by two or more states to do so) in framing and operating schemes of joint recruitment for any services for which candidates possessing-special qualifications are required.
- Recommendations made by it are only of advisory nature and not binding on the government.
- The President can exclude posts, services and matters from the purview of the UPSC.
- It serves all or any of the needs of a state on the request of the State Governor and with the approval of the President of India. UPSC is consulted on the following matters relating to :
    - Methods of recruitment to civil service and civil posts
    - Principles to be followed in making appointments
    - Suitability of candidates for appointments
    - All disciplinary matters
    - Matters of temporary appointments
    - Matters related to grant of extension of service
- Supreme Court has held that if the government fails to consult UPSC in the above-mentioned matters, the aggrieved public servant has no remedy in a court. Above provisions are not mandatory.
- Court held that a selection by the UPSC does not confer any right (not matter of right) to the post upon the candidate.
- UPSC presents a report to the President annually. The President places this report before both the Houses of Parliament.
- All cases of non-acceptance must be approved by the Appointments Committee of the Union Cabinet. An individual ministry or department has no power to reject the advice of the UPSC.
- Additional functions relating to the services of the Union can be conferred on UPSC by the Parliament.

> - **Jurisdiction of UPSC** can be extended by an act made by the Parliament.
> - **UPSC** only a central recruiting agency.
> - **Department of Personnel and Training** the central personnel agency in India.

STATE PUBLIC SERVICE COMMISSION

- Parallel to the Union Public Service Commission (UPSC) at the Centre, there is a State Public Service Commission (SPSC) in each state.
- Articles 315 to 323 in Part XIV of the Constitution deals with the composition , appointment and removal of members, power and functions and independence of a SPSC.

Appointment and Tenure

- A State Public Service Commission consists of a chairman and other members appointed by the Governor of the state.
- The Constitution does not specify the strength of the Commission but has left the matter to the discretion of the Governor.
- Further, no qualifications are prescribed for the commission's membership except that one-half of the members of the commission should be such persons who have held office for at least ten years either under the Government of India or under the Government of a State.
- The chairman and members of the Commission hold office for a term of six years or until they attain the age of 62 years, whichever is earlier.

- The Governor can appoint one of the members of the SPSC as an acting chairman in the following two circumstances:
  - When the office of the chairman falls vacant; or
  - When the chairman is unable to perform his/her functions due to absence or some other reason.
- Condition of Service The Constitution authorises the Governor to determine the conditions of service of the chairman and members of the Commission.

Removal

- Although the chairman and members of a SPSC are appointed by the Governor, they can be removed only by the President. He can remove them on the same grounds and in the same manner as he can remove a Chairman or a member of the UPSC.
- The President can remove the chairman or any other member of SPSC from the office under the following circumstances :
  - If he/she is adjudged an insolvent (that is, has gone bankrupt);
  - If he/she engages, during his/her term of office, in any paid employment outside the duties of his/ her office;
  - If he/ she is, in the opinion of the President, unfit to continue in office by reason of infirmity of mind or body.

  Note *It means a person, who has a mental disorder and was not an unsound mind.*
- The President can also remove the chairman or any other member of SPSC for misbehaviour. However, in this case, the President has to refer the matter to the Supreme Court for an enquiry.
- If the SC, after the enquiry, upholds the cause of removal and advises so, the President can remove the chairman or a member. Advice tendered by the SC in this regard is binding on the President.

Functions and Other Aspects

- Watchdog of the 'Merit System' in states.
- Consulted by Governor while framing rules for appointment to judicial service of the state other than district judge. Recommendations made by it are only of advisory nature and not binding on the government.
- Governors can exclude posts, services and matters from the purview of the SPSC.
- SPSC performs all those functions in respect of the state services as the UPSC does in relation to the Central services :
  - Methods of recruitment to civil service and civil posts.
  - Principles to be followed in making appointments.
  - Suitability of candidates for appointments.
  - All disciplinary matters.
  - Matters of temporary appointments.
  - Matters related to grant of extension of service.
- Supreme Court If the government fails to consult SPSC in the above-mentioned matters, the aggrieved public servant has no remedy in a court. Above provisions are not mandatory.
- Court held that a selection by the SPSC does not confer any right (not matter of right) to the post upon the candidate.
- SPSC presents a report to the Governor annually. Governor places this report before both the Houses of State Legislature.
- Additional functions relating to the services of the state can be conferred on SPSC by the State Legislature.
- SPSC only a central recruiting agency in the state.
- Department of Personnel central personnel agency in the state.

NATIONAL COMMISSION FOR SCs AND STs

- The National Commission for Scheduled Castes (SCs) is a constitutional body in the sense that it is directly established by Article 338 of the Constitution.
- Like the National Commission for Scheduled Castes (SCs), the National Commission for Scheduled Tribes (STs) is also a constitutional body in the sense that it is directly established by Article 338(A) of the Constitution.

> - **1978** Non-statutory multi-member commission (through resolution).
> - **1987** Commission renamed as National Commission for SCs and STs.
> - **65th CAA 1990** multi-member National Commission for SCs and STs with constitutional status.
> - **89th CAA 2003** The 89th Constitutional Amendment Act of 2003 bifurcated the combined National Commission for SCs and STs in to two separate bodies, namely, **National Commission for Scheduled Castes** (under Article 338) and **National Commission for Scheduled Tribes** (under Article 338-A).

- The separate National Commissions for SC's and ST's came into existence in 2004.

Members of National Commission for SC's and ST's

- Both the NCSC and NCST consist of a chairperson, a vice-chairperson and three other members.
- They are appointed by the President by warrant under his hand and seal.
- Their conditions of service and tenure of office are also determined by the President.
- Under the Rules made by the President, they hold office for a term of three years.
- They are not eligible for appointment for more than two terms.

Functions of NCSC and NCST

National Commission for SC's	• To investigate and monitor all matters relating to the constitutional and other legal safeguards for the SCs and to evaluate their working. To inquire into specific complaints with respect to the deprivation of rights and safeguards of the SCs. • To participate and advise on the planning process of socio-economic development of the SCs and to evaluate the progress of their development under the Union or a state. To present to the President, annually and at such other times as it may deem fit, reports upon the working of those safeguards. • To make recommendations as to the measures that should be taken by the Union or a state for the effective implementation of those safeguards and other measures for the protection, welfare and socio-economic development of the SCs. • To discharge such other functions in relation to the protection, welfare and development and advancement of the SCs as the President may specify.
National Commission for ST's	• To investigate and monitor all matters relating to the constitutional and other legal safeguards for the STs and to evaluate their working. • To inquire into specific complaints with respect to the deprivation of rights and safeguards of the STs. • To participate and advise on the planning process of socio-economic development of the STs and to evaluate the progress of their development under the Union or a state; • To present to the President, annually and at such other times as it may deem fit, reports upon the working of those safeguards; • To make recommendations as to the measures that should be taken by the Union or a state for the effective implementation of those safeguards and other measures for the protection, welfare and socio-economic development of the STs. • **Other Functions** Measures for the implementation of the PESA Act, 1996. Measures to be taken to : — Reduce and ultimately eliminate the shifting cultivation practice by tribals. — Improve the efficacy of relief and rehabilitation measures. — To prevent alienation of tribal people. — Conferring ownership rights in respect of MFPs.

Powers of NCSC and NCST

Powers of NCSC

- The Commission is vested with the power to regulate its own procedure.
- The Commission, while investigating any matter or inquiring into any complaint, has all the powers of a civil court trying a suit and in particular in respect of the following matters :
  - summoning and enforcing the attendance of any person from any part of India and examining him/her on oath;
  - requiring the discovery and production of any document;
  - receiving evidence on affidavits;
  - requisitioning any public record from any court or office;
  - issuing summons for the examination of witnesses and documents; and
  - any other matter which the President may determine.
- The Central Government and the State Governments are required to consult the Commission on all major policy matters affecting the SCs. Discharge similar functions regarding the Anglo Indian community.
- Till 2018, the commission was also required to discharge similar functions with regard to OBCs. It was relieved by the creation of NCBC (Article 338 B).

Powers of NCST

- The Commission is vested with the power to regulate its own procedure.
- The Commission, while investigating any matter or inquiring into any complaint, has all the powers of a civil court trying a suit and in particular in respect of the following matters :
  - summoning and enforcing the attendence of any person from any part of India and examining him/her on oath,

- requiring the discovery and production of any document,
- receiving evidence on affidavits,
- requisitioning any public record from any court or office,
- issuing summons for the examination of witnesses and documents, any other matter.
- which the president may determine.

NATIONAL COMMISSION FOR BCs

Establishment of National Commission for BCs

- In the Mandal Case Judgement (1992), the Supreme Court directed the Central Government to constitute a permanent statutory body to examine the complaints of under inclusion, over-inclusion or non-inclusion of any class of citizens in the list of backward classes. Accordingly, the National Commission for Backward Classes (NCBC) was set up in 1993.
- The Commission was later granted constitutional status by the 102nd Amendment Act of 2018. The amendment added a new Article 338-B to the Constitution for this reason. As a result, the Commission became a constitutional body rather than a statutory one.

Members of National Commission for BCs

- National Commission for BCs consist of a chairperson, a vice-chairperson and three other members.
- They are appointed by the President by warrant under his hand and seal.
- Their conditions of service and tenure of office are also determined by the President.
- Under the Rules made by the President, they hold office for a term of three years. They are not eligible for appointment for more than two terms.

Functions of National Commission for BCs

The functions of the Commission are the following :

- To investigate and monitor all matters relating to the constitutional and other legal safeguards for the socially and educationally backward classes and to evaluate their work.
- To inquire into specific complaints with respect to the deprivation of rights and safeguards of the socially and educationally backward classes.
- To participate and advise on the socio-economic development of the socially and educationally backward classes and to evaluate the progress of their development under the Union or a state.
- To present to the President, annually and at such other times as it may deem fit, reports upon the working of those safeguards.

Powers of NCBC

- The Commission is vested with the power to regulate its own procedure.
- The Commission, while investigating any matter or enquiring into any complaint, has all the powers of a civil court trying a suit and in particular in respect of the following matters :
  - Summoning and enforcing the attendance of any person from any part of India and examining him/her on oath.
  - Requiring the discovery and production of any document.
  - Receiving evidence on affidavits.
  - Requisitioning any public record from any court or office.
  - Issuing summons for the examination of witnesses and documents.
  - Any other matter which the President may determine.

SPECIAL OFFICER FOR LINGUISTIC MINORITIES

Constitutional Provisions

- The Seventh Constitutional Amendment Act of 1956 inserted a new Article 350(B) in Part XVII of the Constitution.
- This article contains the following provisions :
  - There should be a Special Officer for Linguistic Minorities. He is to be appointed by the President of India.
  - It would be the duty of the Special Officer to investigate all matters relating to the safeguards provided for linguistic minorities under the Constitution.
  - He would report to the President upon those matters at such intervals as the President may direct.

- The President should place all such reports before each House of Parliament and send to the governments of the states concerned.
- It must be noted here that the Constitution does not specify the qualifications, tenure, salaries and allowances, service conditions and procedure for removal of the Special Officer for Linguistic Minorities.

Commissioner for Linguistic Minorities

- The office of the Special Officer for Linguistic Minorities was created in 1957 in pursuance of the provision of Article 350-B in Part XVII of the Constitution. He/she is designated as the Commissioner for Linguistic Minorities (CLM).
- The headquarters of CLM is in New Delhi. He/she has three regional offices at Belgaum (Karnataka), Chennai (Tamil Nadu) and Kolkata (West Bengal). Each is headed by an Assistant Commissioner.
- At the Central level, the CLM falls under the Ministry of Minority Affairs. Hence, he/she submits the annual reports or other reports to the President through the Union Minority Affairs Minister.

FINANCE COMMISSION

- The Finance Commission is constituted by the President under Article 280 of the Constitution. It is a Quasi Judicial Body.
- It mainly gives its recommendations on distribution of tax revenues between the Centre and the States and amongst the States themselves. Two distinctive features of the commission's work involve :
  - Redressing the vertical imbalances between the taxation powers and expenditure responsibilities of the Centre and the States respectively.
  - Equalisation of all public services across the states.
- The qualification and tenure for the appointment of its members is determined by the Parliament. It is constituted by the President every fifth year or earlier as required.

Composition and Qualification

- Parliament may determine the qualifications which shall be requisite for appointment as members of the commission and the manner in which they shall be selected.
- The Chairman of the commission is selected from among persons who have experience in public affairs and the four other members are selected from among persons who are as follows :
  - They have been or are qualified to be appointed as Judges of the High Court.
  - They have special knowledge in the finances and accounts of the government.
  - They have wide experience in financial matters and in administration.
  - They have special knowledge of economics.

15th Finance Commission

In November, 2017, the President of India appointed the 15th **Finance Commission**, under the Chairmanship of **NK Singh**. It will make suggestions for a five-year period, from 2021-2022 to 2025-2026. Key recommendations made by the commission are

- **Vertical Devolution** (Devolution of Taxes of the Union to States): It has recommended maintaining the vertical devolution at 41% - the same as in its interim report for 2020-2021.
- **Horizontal Devolution** (Allocation between the States): For horizontal devolution, it has suggested 12.5% weightage to demographic performance, 45% to income, 15% each to population and area, 10% to forest and ecology and 2.5% to tax and fiscal efforts.
- **Revenue Deficit Grants to States** Revenue deficit grants emanate from the requirement to meet the fiscal needs of the states on their revenue accounts that remain to be met, even after considering their own tax and non-tax resources and tax devolution to them.
- **Performance Based Incentives and Grants to States** These grants revolve around four main themes namely social sector, rural economy, governance and administrative reforms and performance-based incentive system for the power sector.

16th Finance Commission

The 16th **Finance Commission** of India, established under **Article 280** of the Constitution, is mandated to recommend the distribution of tax revenues between the Central and State Governments for five years commencing 1st April, 2026. It is chaired by **Dr. Arvind Panagariya**.

GOODS AND SERVICES TAX COUNCIL

- The Constitution (101st Amendment) Act, 2016 paved the way for GST in India.
- The amendment inserted a new Article 279(A) in the Constitution. This article empowered the President to constitute a GST Council. Accordingly, the President issued the order in 2016 and constituted the Council.
- The Secretariat of the Council is located at New Delhi. The Union Revenue Secretary acts as the ex-officio Secretary to the Council.

Functions of Council

- According to Article 279, the Council is meant to make recommendations to the Union and the States on important issues related to GST, like the goods and services that may be subjected or exempted from GST.
- It also decides on various rate slabs of GST.

ATTORNEY-GENERAL OF INDIA

As mentioned in Article 76 of the Constitution of India, the Attorney-General of India is the highest law officer in India. As a Chief Legal Advisor to the Government of India, he advises the Union Government on all legal matters.

Qualifications

- The Attorney-General of India must be a person qualified to be appointed as a Judge of the Supreme Court.
- Hence, ought to be the Judge of some High Court for five years or an Advocate of some High Court for ten years or an eminent jurist in the opinion of the President.

Appointment

The President of India, on the advice of the Union Cabinet of Ministers, appoints the Attorney-General of India.

Term of Office

- The term of office of the Attorney-General is not fixed by the Constitution. He holds office during pleasure of the President.
- Further, the Constitution does not contain the procedure and grounds for his removal.
- He may quit his office by submitting his resignation to the President. Also, the remuneration of the Attorney-General is not fixed by the Constitution.

Duties and Functions

As the Chief Law Officer of the Government of India, the duties of the Attorney-General are as follows :

- To give advice to the Government of India upon such legal matters, which are referred to him by the President.
- To perform such other duties of a legal character that is assigned to him/her by the President.
- To discharge the functions conferred on him/her by the Constitution or any other law.
- To appear on the behalf of the Government of India in all cases, in the Supreme Court in which the Government of India is concerned.
- To represent the Government of India in any reference made by the President to Supreme Court under Article 143 of the Constitution (power of President to consult Supreme Court).
- To appear (when required by the Government of India) in any High Court in any case, in which the Government of India is concerned.

Rights and Privileges

- Under Article 76(3), in the performance of his/her official duties, the Attorney-General has the right of audience in all courts in the Territory of India.
- He/she has the Right to Speak and to take part in the proceedings of either the Houses of Parliament or their joint sitting or any Committee of the Parliament but without a Right to Vote.
- He/she enjoys all the privileges and immunities that are available to a Member of Parliament. He/she does not fall in the category of government servant and is not debarred from private legal practices.

Solicitor General

The Solicitor General of India is the second Law Officer of the country and assists the Attorney General. The Solicitor General is further assisted by four additional Solicitor General. The Constitution does not mention about the Solicitor General. He is appointed by the government for a period of **three years**. The Solicitor General does not tender **Legal Advice** to the Government of India and its workload is confined to appearing in courts on behalf of **Union of India**.

ADVOCATE-GENERAL

- Under Article 165 of the Indian Constitution, the Advocate-General of State is appointed.
- He is known as the highest Law Officer in the State.

Qualifications and Appointment

Following are qualifications of a person to be appointed as the Advocate-General:

- He/she must be a citizen of India and must have held a judicial office for a period of 10 years or been an Advocate of a High Court for 10 years.
- The Advocate-General is appointed by the Governor of the State, who must be a person qualified to be appointed a Judge of a High Court.

Term of Office

- The Advocate-General holds office during the pleasure of the Governor of the State, which means that he/she may be removed by the Governor at any time.
- The Advocate-General can also quit the office by submitting the resignation to the Governor.
- Also, the Constitution does not fix the remuneration of the Advocate-General and he/she receives such remuneration as the Governor may determine.

Functions

- The Governor appoints Advocate-General to advice the Government of State on any legal subject matter. The Advocate-General can also play the role and duties of any legal character that the Governor assigns them.
- At the proceedings of both the Houses of the State Legislature or any Committee of the State Legislature, the Advocate-General can take part as a member without the Right to Vote. The Advocate-General can defend the State Government in front of the High Court and Supreme Court.

Rights and Privileges

- As per the official duties of the Advocate-General, they have the right of audience in any court of law of the state. It is not a full-time post and he/she can engage in private legal practice.
- The Advocate-General can also be reappointed or is eligible for any other government appointment after ceasing to hold office.
- He has the Right to Speak and to take part in the proceedings of both the Houses of the State Legislature or any Committee of the State Legislature of which he may be named a member, but without a Right to Vote.
- He enjoys all the privileges and immunities that are available to a Member of the State Legislature.

ELECTION COMMISSION

- The Election Commission is a permanent and an independent body established by the Constitution of India directly to ensure free and fair elections in the country.
- Article 324, Part-XV of the Constitution provides that the power of superintendence, direction and control of elections to Parliament, State Legislatures, the office of President of India and the office of Vice-President of India shall be vested in the election commission.
- ECI is one of the bulwarks of the Constitution.
- ECI is a unitary feature of the Indian Constitution.

Composition

Regarding the composition of the election commission, the following provisions are found in Article 324 of the Constitution :

- The Election Commission shall consist of the Chief Election Commissioner and such number of other election commissioners, if any, as the President may from time-to-time fix.
- The appointment of the Chief Election Commissioner and other election commissioners shall be made by the President.
- The Chief Election Commissioner will serve as the election commission's chairman in the case if another commissioner is chosen in this manner.
- Subject to the provisions of any law made by the Parliament, the conditions of service and tenure of office of the election commissioners and the regional commissioners shall be determined by the President.
- The Constitution does not specify the term of the members of the Election Commission. Currently the tenure is 6 years or age of 65 years whichever is earlier.
- Their salary is equal to judge of Supreme Court (SC).
- CEC and two other election commissioners have equal powers, salary, allowances.

- The Constitution has not debarred the members of ECI from further appointment.
- The Election Commission (Conditions of Service of Election Commissioners and Transaction of Business) Act, 1991 contains the following provisions:
  - The Chief Election Commissioner and the two other election commissioners shall have equal powers and receive equal salary, allowances and other perquisites, which are similar to those of a judge of the Supreme Court.
  - In case of difference of opinion amongst the Chief Election Commissioner and/or two other election commissioners, the matter is decided by the Commission by majority.
  - They hold office for a term of six years or until they attain the age of 65 years, whichever is earlier. They can also resign at any time by writing to the President.

Power and Functions

- There are three areas in which the Election Commission's responsibilities and duties with respect to elections for the President and Vice-President, state legislatures, and the Parliament might be divided :
  - Administrative
  - Advisory
  - Quasi-Judicial
- These powers and functions are :
  - To determine the territorial areas of the electoral constituencies throughout the country on the basis of the Delimitation Commission Act of Parliament.
  - To prepare and periodically revise electoral rolls and to register all eligible voters and grant recognition to political parties and allot election symbols to them.
  - To notify the dates and schedules of elections and to scrutinise nomination papers and determine the code of conduct to be observed by the parties and the candidates at the time of elections.
  - To appoint officers for enquiring into disputes relating to electoral arrangements and act as a court for settling disputes related to granting of recognition to political parties and allotment of election symbols to them.
  - To advise the President on matters relating to the disqualifications of the members of Parliament and advise the Governor on matters relating to the disqualifications of the members of State Legislature.
  - To cancel polls in the event of rigging, booth capturing, violence and other irregularities.
  - To supervise the machinery of elections throughout the country to ensure free and fair elections.
  - To advise the President whether elections can be held in a state under President's rule in order to extend the period of emergency after one year.
  - To register political parties for the purpose of elections and grant them the status of national or state parties on the basis of their poll performance.

Non-Constitutional bodies refer to entities that are not established by the Constitution of India but are created by Parliament through legislative acts or by the Executive through resolutions or orders.

Chapter Thirty Two

Non-Constitutional Bodies

Non-Constitutional bodies are those bodies which are not mentioned in the Constitution and are created either by an Act of Parliament or executive order.

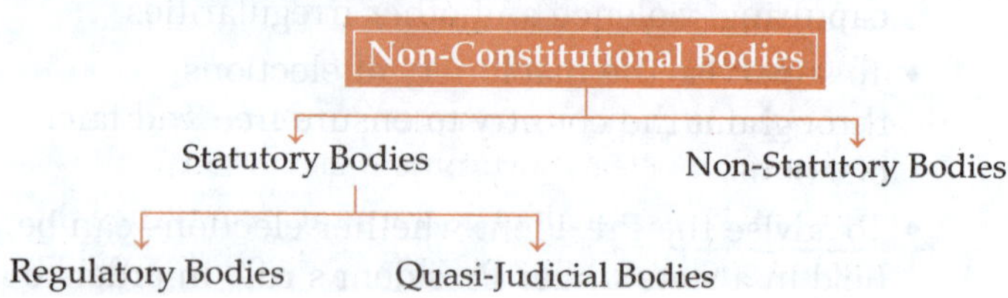

NITI AAYOG

- On 1st January, 2015, the Indian Government replaced the 1950 established outdated Planning Commission with a new organisation called NITI Aayog It operates under the leadership of the Prime Minister.
- It is also neither a constitutional body nor a statutory body. In other words, it is a non-constitutional or extra-constitutional body (i.e., not created by the Constitution) and a non-statutory body (not created by an Act of the Parliament).
- The National Institution for Transforming India or NITI Aayog, will try to offer important strategic and directional input into the development process. The co-operative federalism is its main theme.
- NITI Aayog is the premier policy Think Tank of the Government of India. It offers both directional and policy inputs.
- In addition to developing long-term, strategic plans and programmes for the Government of India, NITI Aayog also offers the Centre and States significant technical guidance.
- There are two principle offices attached to NITI Aayog are Atal Innovation Mission (AIM) and Development Monitoring and Evaluation Organisation (DMEO).
- There is also an autonomous institution called National Institute of Labour Economics Research and Development (NILERD).

Functions of NITI Aayog

The various functions performed by the NITI Aayog can be divided into four main heads :

(i) Policy and programme framework
(ii) Co-operative and competitive federalism
(iii) Monitoring and evaluation
(iv) Think-tank, Knowledge and Innovation Hub

Offices Attached to the NITI Aayog

The NITI Aayog is supported by an autonomous body i.e., the National Institute of Labour Economics Research and Development and an attached office i.e., the Development Monitoring and Evaluation Organisation. These are explained below:

1. *National Institute of Labour Economics Research and Development*

- The National Institute of Labour Economics Research and Development (NILERD) was formerly known as the Institute of Applied Manpower Research (IAMR). It is a central autonomous organisation under the NITI Aayog.
- Its primary objectives are research, data collection, education and training in all aspects of human

capital planning, human resource development and monitoring and evaluation.

- The IAMR was established in 1962 under the Societies Registration Act of 1860.
- The IAMR has been renamed as NILERD in 2014.
- The NILERD is mainly funded by grants-in-aid from the NITI Aayog (formerly Planning Commission) and supplemented by its own revenue from contracted research projects, and education and training activities.

2. Development Monitoring and Evaluation Office

- The Development Monitoring and Evaluation Office (DMEO) was established by the Government in 2015 as an attached office of the NITI Aayog by merging the erstwhile Programme Evaluation Organisation and the Independent Evaluation Office.
- The Headquarters of DMEO is in NITI Aayog, New Delhi. Till 2017, the DMEO had 15 Regional Offices known as Regional Development Monitoring and Evaluation Offices (RDMEOs).
- The RDMEOs conducted field surveys and data/information collection work for evaluation studies, and they also played an important role in promoting cooperative federalism by their interaction with the States and UT administrations.
- However, keeping in view the changed functional requirements, they were closed in 2017 and the staff were transferred to DMEO Headquarters in New Delhi.

LOKPAL

- Administrative Reforms Commissions (ARCs) under Morarji Desai submitted a report which recommended the creation of two special authorities. Lokayukta and Lokpal for the purpose of redressing citizen grievances.
- In 2002, the commission to review the working of the Constitution, chaired by Shri MN Venkatachiliah, suggested that the Prime Minister be excluded from the authority's purview.
- In 2005, the 2nd ARC, chaired by Shri Veerappa Moily, proposed that the Lokpal office be established as soon as possible. In 2011, the well-known Anna Movement for Lokpal was launched.
- These organisations carry out the duties and responsibilites of an Ombudsman, a person or body tasked with looking into complaints made by individuals against businesses or organisations, particularly governmental agency.
- In cases of alleged corruption, the Lokpal provides a mechanism for swift and unbiased investigation and prosecution. There are no limitations on who can file a complaint.

The Lokpal and Lokayuktas Act, 2013

- According to the Lokpal and Lokayuktas Act, 2013, certain categories of public employees must be investigated for corruption by a Lokpal at the national level and a Lokayuktas at the state level.
- The **Lokpal and Lokayuktas Act, 2013**, also made amendments to the Commission of Inquiry Act 1952, Delhi Police Establishment Act, 1946, Prevention of Corruption Act, 1988, Code of Criminal Procedure 1973 and Central Vigilance Commission Act, 2003.
- The Lokpal and Lokayuktas Act, 2013 created the Lokpal, the first institution of its sort in independent India, to investigate and review allegations of corruption against public officials who fall under the Act's purview.
- The Lokpal in India is committed to resolving citizen grievances and clean government aspirations.
- It must make use of all of its authority to advance the common good within its purview and end corruption in public affairs. The Lokpal offers a platform for prompt and impartial investigation and prosecution in situations of alleged corruption. No restrictions exist on who may lodge a complaint.
- The United Nations Convention against corruption has been signed by India. The government's commitment to provide clean and responsive governance is shown in the passage of legislation and the establishment of the Lokpal body to prevent and punish corruption.

LOKAYUKTAS

- Lokayuktas must be established by the states to address allegations against their own authorities.
- All members of the State Government including religious organisations, the Governor, Ministers and MLAs are under the Lokayuktas' purview.
- Even before the Lokpal and Lokayukta Act of 2013 was passed, almost all states had already established the Lokayukta as a statutory organisation with a set tenure.
- The Lokayukta can be approached directly by members of the public with allegations of corruption, nepotism or any other type of maladministration.

- States were also required to appoint a Lokayukta within a year of the Lokpal Act taking effect. However, the Lokayukta has been constituted in only 16 states.

Composition and Eligibility

- After consulting with the Chief Justice of the High Court, the Speaker of the Legislative Assembly, the Chairman of the Legislative Council and the Leader of the Opposition in both Houses of the State Legislature, the Chief Minister chooses a candidate to serve as the Lokayukta.
- The Governor will then make the appointment. Once appointed, the government cannot remove Lokpal or Lokayukta and the only way to do so is by passing an impeachment resolution.
- A former Chief Justice of the High Court or a former Supreme Court Judge normally serves as the Lokayukta.

Term of Office of the Members of Lokpal and Lokayukta

- The President of India appoints the Chairperson and members by warrant under his hand and seal.
- They serve for a period of five years from the date of their appointment or until they reach the age of 70, whichever is earlier.

Functions and Jurisdiction of Lokpal and Lokayukta

- Anyone who is or has been Prime Minister, a Minister in the Union Government or a Member of Parliament, as well as officers of the Union Government in Groups A, B, C and D, are eligible to be investigated by the Lokpal.
- If an investigation into the Prime Minister is underway, it should be conducted in secret. If the Lokpal decides that the complaint should be rejected, the investigation's documents are not to be published or made available to the public.
- Lokpal is also applied to the Chairpersons, members, executives and directors of any board, corporation, society, trust or autonomous organisation created by an Act of Parliament and supported entirely or partially by the Union or State Governments.
- It also applies to any society, trust or body that accepts a foreign gift of more than ₹ 10 lakh.
- The Lokpal has the authority to recommend the transfer or suspension of a public official who has been accused of corruption.
- Lokpal has the authority to issue orders prohibiting the destruction of records during the preliminary investigation.
- The Lokpal has the authority of search and seizure, as well as powers under the Civil Procedure Code to undertake preliminary inquiries and investigations, as well as the power to attach assets and take other measures to combat corruption.
- The Lokpal will have the authority to supervise and instruct any central investigating agency, including the CBI.
- The Lokayauktas will look after the cases submitted to them by the Lokpal.

NATIONAL HUMAN RIGHTS COMMISSION

- The Parliament enacted the Protection of Human Rights Act in 1993 resulting in the establishment of the National Human Rights Commission (NHRC).
- The commission is an autonomous statutory institution and the watchdog of the human rights in the country.
- It includes those rights related to life, liberty, equality and individual dignity that are guaranteed by the Constitution or reflected in the international agreements that are upholdable in Indian courts.

Objectives of National Human Rights Commission (NHRC)

- The specific objectives of the establishment of the commission are :
  - To strengthen the institutional arrangements through which Human Rights issues could be addressed in their entirety in a more focussed manner;
  - To look into allegations of excesses, independently of the government, in a manner that would underline the government's commitment to protect Human Rights; and

- To complement and strengthen the efforts that have already been made in this direction.

Composition

- **Chairperson** is a retired Chief Justice of India or a Judge of the Supreme Court.
- **One member** who is or has been, a Judge of the Supreme Court of India and one member who is or has been, the Chief Justice of a High Court.
- **Three members**, out of which atleast one shall be a woman to be appointed from amongst persons having knowledge of or practical experience in, matters relating to human rights.
- **Seven ex-officio members**, the Chairpersons of the National Commission for Minorities, the National Commission for SCs, the National Commission for STs, the National Commission for Women, the National Commission for OBCs and the National Commission for Protection of Child Rights and the Chief Commissioner for Persons with Disabilities.

Appointment

- The Chairperson and members of the commission are appointed by the President on the basis of recommendations of the committee comprising the Prime Minister, the Speaker of the Lok Sabha, the Home Minister, the Leaders of the Opposition in the Lok Sabha and the Rajya Sabha and the Deputy Chairman of the Rajya Sabha.
- The Chairperson and members shall hold office for a term of three years or till they attain the age of 70 years whichever is earlier. They are eligible for re-appointment.

Removal

- President can remove the Chairperson or any member
  - If he/she is adjudged an insolvent.
  - If he/she is engaged in paid employment outside his duties.
  - If he/she Unfit to continue due to infirmity of mind or body.
  - If he/she is declared of unsound mind by a court.
  - Convicted and sentenced to imprisonment.
  - President can also remove him/her on the ground of proved misbehaviour or incapacity.
  - Salaries, allowances and other conditions of service of the Chairperson or a member are determined by the Central Government cannot be varied to his disadvantage.

Protection of Human Rights (Amendment) Act, 2019

- Amendment provides that beside Chief Justice of India (CJI), even a Judge of the Supreme Court can be the Chairperson of the NHRC. Similarly, a change has been made in State Human Rights Commission (SHRC).
- The strength of members in SHRC has been increased 2 to 3, one women member is mandatory.
- The Act reduced the term of Chairperson and members from five years to three years. They shall also be eligible for re-appointment.
- The Act provides for including the Chairpersons of the National Commission for Backward Classes, National Commission for the Protection of Child Rights and the Chief Commissioners for Persons with Disabilities as the Members of NHRC.
- The Act reduces the term of office to three years or till the age of 70 years whichever is earlier.
- The Act allowed the Secretary-General to exercise all the administrative and financial powers (except judicial functions) subject to Chairperson's control.

Functions

- Inquire, on its own initiative or on a petition presented to it by a victim or any person on his behalf, into complaint of violation of human rights or abetment or negligence in the prevention of such violation, by a public servant.
- Intervene in any proceeding involving any allegation of violation of human rights pending before a court with the approval of such court.
- Visit jail or any other institution under the control of the State Government, where persons are detained or lodged for purposes of treatment, reformation or protection. It study the living condition of the inmates and make recommendations thereon.
- Review the safeguards by or under the Constitution or any law for the time being in force for the protection of human rights and recommend measures for their effective implementation.
- Spread human rights literacy among various sections of society and promote awareness of the safeguards available for the protection of these rights through publications, the media and seminars.
- The commission is vested with the power to regulate its own affairs. It has all the powers of a civil court and its proceedings have a judicial character. It may call for information from any State Government or any subordinate authority.

- Review the factors, including acts of terrorism that inhibit the enjoyment of human rights and recommend appropriate remedial measures.
- Study treaties and other international instruments on human rights and make recommendations for their effective implementation undertake and promote research in the field of human rights. Encourage the efforts of non-governmental organisations and institutions working in the field of Human Rights.

STATE HUMAN RIGHTS COMMISSION

- The Protection of Human Rights Act of 1993 provides for the establishment of a State Human Rights Commission in addition to the National Human Rights Commission.
- In line with this, 26 states have constituted the State Human Rights Commissions by notifications in the official gazette.
- A State Human Rights Commission can inquire into violation of human rights only in respect of subjects mentioned in the Concurrent List (List-III) and State List (List-II) of the Seventh Constitutional Schedule. But, if there is already a situation where NHRC is taking into its consideration violation of rights then SHRC doesn't look into that matter.

Composition

- The State Human Rights Commission consists of three members, a Chairperson and two other members.
- The Chairperson is a High Court Judge or a retired Chief Justice of a High Court. Members can be serving or retired High Court Judges or a District Judge.

Appointment

The Chairperson is appointed by the Governor. On the other hand, the members are selected if they receive recommendations of a committee consisting of the Chief Minister as its head including the Speaker of the Legislative Assembly, State Home Minister and leader of opposition in Legislative Assembly.

> **Tenure and Salary of SHRC**
>
> - **Tenure** The Chairperson and members hold office for three years or till they attain 70 years, whichever is earlier.
> - **Salary** The salary of members is determined by the Central/State Government and cannot be varied to his disadvantage after their appointment.

Removal

- Although, the Governor appoints the Chairperson and Members of a State Human Rights Commission, they can only be removed by the President. They can be removed on grounds of bankruptcy, unsound mind, infirmity of body or mind, sentenced to imprisonment for a crime or engages in paid employment.
- He can also be removed for proved misbehaviour or incapacity if Supreme Court inquiry finds him guilty. They can resign by writing to Governor.

Functions

- To make sure that no one is violating human rights and that all the government officials are doing their duties honestly.
- To mediate the pending legal proceedings including allegations of human rights violations.
- To visit the jails which are under the control of the state and analyse the detainees' living conditions and make necessary recommendations.
- To submit its annual reports to the State Government. These reports are laid before the State Legislature.
- Devise steps to effectively implement constitutional and other legal provisions that provide a shield to human rights and conduct research on human rights issues. Spread human rights literacy and make people aware of the rights and measures that are present to protect their rights.
- Encourage non-governmental organisations and institutions that are actively working in the field of human rights and make people aware of them.

NATIONAL COMMISSION FOR MINORITIES

- With the enactment of the National Commission for Minorities Act, 1992, a statutory body as National Commission for Minorities (NCM) was established.
- The National Commission was setup on 17th May, 1993. The Government of India notified six religious communities *viz* the Muslims, Christians, Sikhs, Buddhists, Zoroastrians (Parsis) and Jains as minority communities.
- The Commission is an autonomous body. It works under the administrative control of the Ministry of Minority Affairs, Government of India.

- The Commission presents an annual report to the Central Government. It can also submit a report as and when it thinks necessary.

Composition

- The Commission is a multi-member body consisting of a Chairperson, a Vice-Chairperson and five members.
- They are nominated by the Central Government from amongst persons of eminence, ability and integrity. However, five members including the Chairperson should be from amongst the minority communities.
- The salaries, allowances and other service conditions of the Chairman and members are also prescribed by the Central Government (Ministry of Minority Affairs). Notably, members include the Vice-Chairperson.
- The chairperson and members hold office for a period of three years. However, they can relinquish their office at any time by addressing their resignation to the Central Government.

Functions and Powers

- The Commission is provided with the following nine-point mandate. To evaluate the progress of the development of minorities under the Union and States.
- To monitor the working of the safeguards for minorities provided in Constitution and in laws enacted by Parliament and the state legislatures.
- To make recommendations for the effective implementation of safeguards for the protection of the interests of minorities by the Central Government or the State Governments.
- To look into specific complaints regarding deprivation of rights and safeguards of minorities and take up such matters with the appropriate authorities.
- To cause studies to be undertaken into the problems arising out of any discrimination against minorities and recommend measures for their removal.
- To conduct studies, research and analysis on the issues relating to socio-economic and educational development of minorities.
- To suggest appropriate measures in respect of any minority to be undertaken by the Central Government or the State Governments.
- To make periodical or special reports to the Central Government on any matter pertaining to minorities and in particular the difficulties confronted by them.
- To look into any other matter referred to it by the Central Government.

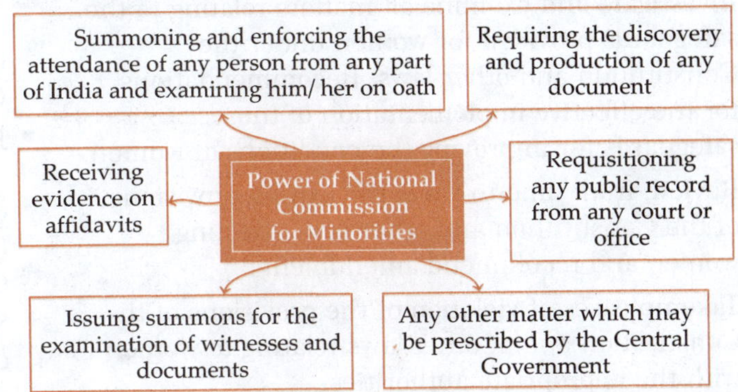

NATIONAL COMMISSION FOR WOMEN

- The National Commission for Women was setup as a statutory body in January, 1992 under the National Commission for Women Act, 1990.
- The commission established with the following objectives:
  - Review the constitutional and legal safeguards for women.
  - Recommend remedial legislative measures.
  - Facilitate redressal of grievances.
  - Advise the government on all policy matters affecting women.
- The Ministry of Women and Child Development of Government of India is the nodal ministry for the commission. The first commission was constituted on 31st January, 1992. Jayanti Patnaik was the first Chairperson of this Commission.

Composition

- A Chairperson, committed to the cause of women, to be nominated by the Central Government.
- Five Members to be nominated by the Central Government from amongst persons of ability, integrity and standing who have had experience in law or legislation, trade unionism, health, education or social welfare.
- It provides that atleast one member each shall be from amongst persons belonging to the Scheduled Castes and Scheduled Tribes respectively and a Member Secretary.
- The Chairperson and members shall hold office for a period of three years. However, they can relinguish their office at any time by addressing to the Central Government.

- The chairperson members and Member Secretary to be nominated by Central Government. He/She shall be an officer of Civil Services.

Powers and Functions

- Investigate and examine all matters relating to the safeguards provided for women under the Constitution and other laws. Recommendations for the effective implementation of those safeguards for improving the conditions of women.
- Review, from time-to-time, the exiting provisions of the Constitution and other laws affecting women and recommend amendments.
- Take up cases of violation of the provisions of the Constitution and of other laws relating to women with the appropriate authorities.
- The commission has undertaken a survey to protect the gender profile in all States and UTs to assess the status of women and their empowerment.
- It took up the issue of child marriage, sponsored legal awareness programmes, Parivarik Mahila Lok Adalats and reviewed laws such as Dowry Prohibition Act, 1961, to make them more stringent and effective.

Look into complaints and take **Suo Moto notice** of matters relating to deprivation of women's rights. Non-implementation of laws enacted to provide protection to women and also to achieve the objective of equality and development.

- It organises workshops/consultations, constituted expert committees on economic empowerment of women, conducted workshops/seminars for gender awareness and took up publicity campaign against female foeticide, violence against women, etc..
- The commission shall have the powers of a Civil Court while investigating any matter with respect to enforcing rights for women.

NATIONAL COMMISSION FOR PROTECTION OF CHILD RIGHTS

National Commission for Protection of Child Rights was set up in March, 2007 under the Commissions for Protection of Child Rights (CPCR) Act, 2005. It is a statutory body under the administrative control of the Ministry of Women and Child Development.

Powers and Functions

- The commission has the power of a Civil Court while inquiring any matter related to child rights.
- The commission has mandate to ensure that all laws, policies, programmes and administrative mechanisms are in consonance with the child rights perspective as enshrined in the Constitution of India and also the UN Convention on the Rights of the Child.
- Evaluation and assessment of the safeguards offered for the protection of children's rights in India under the current legal framework. It reports to the Central Government as and when necessary on the operation of the laws with respect to the child rights.
- Study the factors that prevent the enjoyment of rights of children impacted by terrorism, riots, natural calamities, communal violence, trafficking, HIV/AIDS, torture and exploitation, maltreatment, prostitution and pornography and suggest remedial measures for them.
- Investigate complaints and notify Suo Moto on matters relating to child rights violations and deprivations.
- By analysing international agreements and treaties, examine current laws pertaining to children's rights and protection and suggest amendments as necessary.

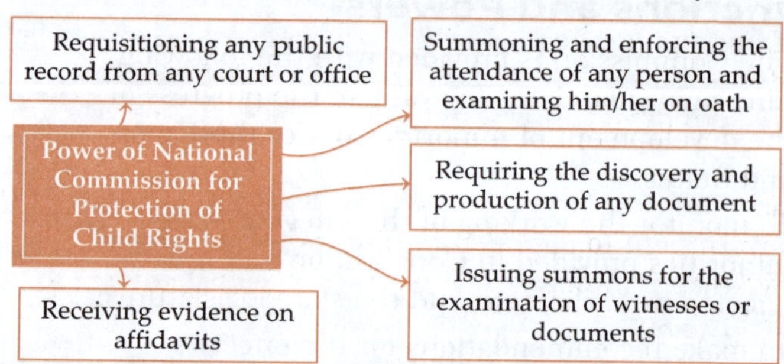

State Commission for Protection of Child Rights (SCPCR)

- The Commissions for Protection of Child Rights Act of 2005 provides for the creation of not only the National Commission for Protection of Child Rights but also a State Commission for Protection of Child Rights at the state level Accordingly, a state government may constitute a State Commission for Protection of Child Rights through an Official Gazette Notification.
- It is a multi-member body consisting of a chairperson and six members. Out of the six members, at least two should be women.
- The chairperson and other members are appointed by the state government.

NATIONAL COMMISSION FOR PERSON WITH DISABILITIES

- National Commission for Persons with Disability was set-up under Persons with Disabilities Act, 1995. It is a statutory body that functions under the Ministry of Social Justice and Empowerment.
- The commission consists of 15 persons that are persons of eminence, ability, integrity and who are concerned with the cause of the community.
- It reports to the Central Government as and when necessary on the operation of the laws with respect to the rights of persons with disability.
- It aims at ensuring inclusion and effective access to education, health, vocational training alongwith specialised rehabilitation services to children with disabilities.

CENTRAL VIGILANCE COMMISSION

- The Central Vigilance Commission was set up by the government in February, 1964 on the recommendations of the Committee on Prevention of Corruption, headed by Shri K Santhanam, to advise and guide Central Government Agencies in the field of vigilance.
- In Vineet Narain and others *v/s* Union of India case, the Supreme Court had directed the Central Government to confer statutory status to Central Vigilance Commission. It made it responsible for effective supervision of the functioning of Central Bureau of Investigation (CBI).
- The CVC is not controlled by any ministry or department. It is an independent body, which is only responsible for the Parliament.
- CVC is a multi member body comprising of a Chairperson and two vigilance commissioner members.
- The President appoints the members of CVC as per the recommendation of a three-member committee comprising of Prime Minister, the Union Minister of Home Affairs and the leader of the opposition in the Lok Sabha.

Powers and Functions

- The Central Vigilance Commission (CVC), shall have to inquire or cause an inquiry or investigation to be made on a reference made by the Central Government wherein it is alleged that a public servant has committed an offence under the Prevention of Corruption Act, 1988.
- CVC shall have to cause an inquiry or investigation to be made into any complaint against any official belonging to Group A and Group B officers of the Central Government.
- CVC reviews the progress of applications pending with the competent authorities for sanction of prosecution under the Prevention of Corruption Act, 1988.
- It exercises superintendence over the vigilance administration of the various ministries of the Central Government or corporations established by or under any Central Act, government companies, societies and local authorities owned or controlled by that government.
- The CVC is not an investigating agency. The CVC either get the investigation done through the CBI or through the Departmental Chief Vigilance Officers. The CVC orders investigation into cases of officials of Central Government Departments/Companies/ Organisations only.
- The commission is empowered to enquire or cause inquiries to be conducted in to offences alleged to have been committed under the Prevention of Corruption Act, 1988 by certain categories of public servants.
- In relation to the CBI's Delhi Special Police Establishment, it exercises supervision over and provides guidance about the investigation of offences under the Prevention of Corruption Act, 1988.
- Have all the authority of a Civil Court while conducting any investigation.
- Exercise supervision over the vigilance administrations of the various Central Government Ministries, Departments and Organisations.
- The Central Vigilance Commissioner is the Chairperson and the Vigilance Commissioners are members of the committee, on whose recommendations, the Central Government appoints the Director of Enforcement.

- The Central Vigilance Commissioner has to present annually report on its performance to the President. The President places this report before each House of Parliament.

CENTRAL BUREAU OF INVESTIGATION

- The Central Bureau of Investigation (CBI) is the premier investigating police agency in India. The Central Bureau of Investigation (CBI) is a powerful organisation that contributes significantly to upholding moral principles in society and maintaining the health of the economy.

> The establishment of the CBI was recommended by the Santhanam Committee on Prevention of Corruption (1962-1964). It was first established to look into government corruption and bribery.

- Its jurisdiction was widened in 1965 to looking into crimes involving multiple agencies, multi-state organised crime and violations of Central Legislation enforced by the Government of India.
- Additionally, it is the nodal police organisation in India that organises inquiries on behalf of Interpol member nations. It operates under Ministry of Personnel, Public Grievances and Pensions.
- It is not a statutory body; it derives its powers from the Delhi Special Police Establishment Act, 1946. It works under the supervision of the CVC (Central Vigilance Commission) in matters of the Prevention of Corruption Act, 1988.

  The CBI has the following seven divisions:
  (i) Anti-Corruption Division
  (ii) Economic Offences Division
  (iii) Special Crimes Division
  (iv) Policy and Coordination Division
  (v) Administration Division
  (vi) Directorate of Prosecution
  (vii) Central Forensic Science Laboratory

Functions

- CBI can Suo Moto take up investigation of offences only in the Union Territories.
- The assent of the State Government in question is required before the Central Government can give the CBI permission to probe a crime in a state. However, without the permission of the state, the Supreme Court and High Courts can direct CBI to look into a crime anywhere in the nation.
- Under the DSPE Act, the CBI can investigate only with notification by the Central Government.
- It investigates cases under the Prevention of Corruption Act against public officials and the employees of Central Government, Public Sector Undertakings, Corporations or Bodies owned or controlled by the Government of India.
- Investigating cases relating to infringement of fiscal and economic laws, i.e., breach of laws concerning export and import control, customs and central excise, income tax, foreign exchange regulations and so on. However, such cases are taken up either in consultation with or at the request of the department concerned.

CENTRAL INFORMATION COMMISSION

- An independent organisation called the Central Information Commission (CIC) looks into grievances and appeals about public sector organisations, financial institutions and other entities in the Union Territories.
- The Central Information Commission will investigate complaints made by those who were unable to submit information requests to a Central Public Information Officer or a State Public Information Officer.
- The Central Government established the CIC in 2005 in accordance with the stipulations of the Right to Information Act of 2005. It is not constitutional body.

Powers and Functions

- The commission has the same summoning and document-requirement authority as that of a Civil Court when conducting its investigation.
- It has the authority to order an investigation into any issue if there are sufficient grounds (Suo Moto power).
- The commission submits an annual report to the Central Government on the implementation of the provisions of this act. The Central Government places this report before each House of Parliament.
- During the inquiry of a complaint, the commission may examine any record which is under the control of the public authority and no such record may be withheld from it on any grounds. When a public authority does not confirm to the provisions of this Act, the commission may recommend steps.

- The commission has the power to secure compliance of its decisions from the public authority.

Right to Information Act

- The Right to Information (RTI) Act provides each individual with the right to seek and receive information and ideas related to any issue through any media regardless of any boundary.
- When the **Universal Declaration of Human Rights** was ratified in 1948, it went into effect. In 2005, an Amendment to the Right to Information Act was made.
- Everyone is entitled to the right to freedom of expression and the freedom to communicate ideas and information under the **1966 International Covenant on Civil and Political Rights**.
- A system was developed for Indian citizens to enable information and idea interchange as a matter of right in order to put this concept into practice.
- The Act allow the citizens of the country to question the working government and to promote transparency and answerability of the working government.

Key Provisions of the Act

- **Section 4** of the RTI Act requires Suo Moto disclosure of information by each public authority.
- **Section 8 (1)** mentions exemptions against furnishing information under RTI Act.
- **Section 8 (2)** provides for disclosure of information exempted under Official Secrets Act, 1923 if larger public interest is served.

Amendments of the RTI Act, 2005

- **Section 2(h)** This Section of the RTI Act defines 'Public Authorities'. All working organisations/bodies/ authorities falling under the Jurisdiction of Union, State or Local bodies are defined as public authorities. Additionally, civil organisations that are fundamentally funded (may be directly or indirectly) by citizens' funds also come under the RTI Act, 2005.
- **Section 4 1(b)** This section mentions that the working government should have updated information available which they are liable to share when needed.
- **Section 6** This section mentions a simple procedure for the citizens to know about fetching information under the RTI Act.

STATE INFORMATION COMMISSION

- The Right to Information Act of 2005 provides for the creation of not only the Central Information Commission but also a State Information Commission at the state level.
- All the states have constituted the State Information Commissions through Official Gazette Notifications.
- The State Information Commission is a powerful independent authority that investigates complaints and renders decisions on appeals.
- It considers grievances and appeals involving businesses, financial institutions and other public sector entities that fall within the Jurisdiction of the relevant State Government.

Powers and Functions

- The commission may examine any record under the custody of the public authority during the investigation of a complaint and no such record may be kept from it for any reason.
- The commission makes an annual report to the State Government on how the Act's provisions are being implemented.
- This report is presented to the State Legislature by the State Government.
- If there are reasonable grounds, the commission might order an investigation into any matter.
- The commission has the jurisdiction to compel the public authority to follow its conclusions.
- The commission has the power to secure compliance of its decisions from the public authority. This includes providing access to information in a particular form and directing the public authority to appoint a Public Information Officer where none exists.

NATIONAL INVESTIGATION AGENCY

- The National Investigation Agency (NIA) was constituted in 2009 under the provisions of the National Investigation Agency Act, 2008 (NIA Act). It is the central counter-terrorism law enforcement agency in the country.
- The headquarters of the NIA is in New Delhi.
  - The NIA is headed by a Director-General. He/she is appointed by the Central Government.

- His/her powers are similar to the powers exercisable by a Director-General of Police in respect of the police force in a state.
- The NIA works under the administrative control of the Ministry of Home Affairs, Government of India. The State Government extends all assistance-and cooperation to the NIA for investigation of the offences specified under the NIA Act.

Functions

The functions assigned to the NIA are as follows:

- To investigate and prosecute offences in respect of the Acts specified in the Schedule of the NIA Act.
- To provide assistance to, and seek assistance from, other intelligence and investigation agencies of the central government and state governments.
- To take other such measures which may be necessary for speedy and effective implementation of the provisions of the NIA Act.

NATIONAL GREEN TRIBUNAL

- In accordance with the National Green Tribunal Act 2010, the National Green Tribunal (NGT) was established on 18th October, 2010.
- The NGT statute instructs and grants the Central Government authority to establish an NGT to address environmental challenges. It is a specialised body created to swiftly and effectively resolve disputes affecting environmental protection, the preservation of forests and other natural resources.
- With the creation of the NGT, India became the first developing nation and third country in the world after Australia and New Zealand to establish a specialist environmental tribunal.

Powers and Jurisdiction

- All civil matters containing significant environmental questions are within the tribunal's purview (including enforcement of any legal right relating to environment).
- The National Green Tribunal (NGT) had the authority to address environmental matters nationwide as a unique forum with Suo Moto (on its own initiative) authority. The NGT's job is not just adjudicatory in nature; it must also carry out equally important preventative, compensatory or remedial roles.
- Being a statutory adjudicatory body like courts, NGT has appellate jurisdiction to hear appeals in addition to initial jurisdiction side on filing of an application.
- The tribunal is not bound by the procedure laid down under the Code of Civil Procedure 1908, but shall be guided by principles of 'natural justice'.
- NGT by an order, can provide relief and compensation to the victims of pollution and other environmental damage, for restitution of property damaged and for restitution of the environment for such area or areas, as the tribunal may think fit.
- Additionally, the NGT Act stipulates a process for a punishment for non-compliance a sentence of up to three years' imprisonment, a fine that could exceed ten crore rupees and both.
- An appeal against order/decision/award of the NGT lies to the Supreme Court, generally within ninety days from the date of communication.
- The NGT deals with civil cases under the seven laws related to the environment, these include:
  - The Water (Prevention and Control of Pollution) Act, 1974
  - The Water (Prevention and Control of Pollution) Cess Act, 1977
  - The Forest (Conservation) Act, 1980
  - The Air (Prevention and Control of Pollution) Act, 1981
  - The Environment (Protection) Act, 1986
  - The Public Liability Insurance Act, 1991
  - The Biological Diversity Act, 2002

Composition of NGT

- The tribunal comprises the Chairperson, the judicial members and expert members. They are appointed for a five year term and are not eligible for re-appointment.
- The Central Government, in collaboration with the Chief Justice of India (CJI), appoints the Chairperson. The National Government will appoint a Selection Committee to appoint the judicial and expert members.

NATIONAL DISASTER MANAGEMENT AUTHORITY

- The Disaster Management Act, 2005 provided for the creation of the National Disaster Management Authority (NDMA) to spearhead and implement a holistic and integrated approach to disaster management in the country. Initially, the NDMA was constituted in 2005 by an Executive Order of the Government of India.

- Subsequently, the NDMA was notified in 2006 under the provisions of the Act.

Functions

- To lay down policies on disaster management and to approve the National Plan.
- To approve plans prepared by the Ministries or Departments of the Government of India in accordance with the National Plan.
- To lay down guidelines to be followed by the State Disaster Management Authorities (SDMAs) in drawing up the State Plan and guidelines to be followed by the different Ministries or Departments of the Government of India for the purpose of integrating the measures for prevention of disaster or the mitigation of its effects in their development plans and projects.
- To recommend provision of funds for the purpose of mitigation and provide such support to other countries affected by major disasters as may be determined by the central government.
- To lay down broad policies and guidelines for the functioning of the National Institute of Disaster Management.

STATE DISASTER MANAGEMENT AUTHORITY

- Under the Disaster Management Act, 2005, every state government should establish a State Disaster Management Authority (SDMA) for the state.
- An SDMA consists of a chairperson and other members, not exceeding nine.
- The Chief Minister of the state is the ex-officio chairperson of the SDMA.
- The chairperson of the State Executive Committee is the ex-officio member of the SDMA. The other members, not exceeding eight, are nominated by the chairperson of the SDMA. The chairperson of the State Executive Committee acts as the ex-officio chief executive officer of the SDMA.

Functions

- To lay down the state disaster management policy and to approve the State Plan in accordance with the guidelines laid down by the NDMA.
- To approve the disaster management plans prepared by the departments of the government of the states and lay down guidelines to be followed by the departments of the government of the state for the purposes of integration of measures for the prevention of disasters and mitigation in their development plans and projects and provide necessary technical assistance there of.
- To recommend the provision of funds for mitigation and preparedness measures. To prepare an annual report on its activities and submit it to the state government. The state government causes it to be laid before the state legislature.

LAW COMMISSION OF INDIA

- The Law Commission of India is a non-statutory advisory body. It is established by the order of the Central Government from time to time for a fixed tenure.
- Its function is to recommend legislative measures for the purpose of consolidation and codification of laws. However, its recommendations are not binding on the government.
- The composition of the Commission is not fixed. It varies from one Commission to another.
- Generally, it consists of a Chairman, some full-time members, a member-secretary and some part-time members depending upon the nature of topics referred to it for consideration.

Functions

- To identify laws which are no longer needed or relevant and can be immediately repealed.
- To examine the existing laws in the light of Directive Principles of State Policy and suggest ways of improvement and reforms and also suggest such legislations as might be necessary to implement the Directive Principles and to attain the objectives set out in the Preamble of the Constitution.
- To consider and convey to the Government its views on any subject relating to law and judicial administration that may be specifically referred to it by the Government
- To revise the Central Acts of general importance so as to simplify them and remove anomalies, ambiguities and inequities.

Some Other Important Bodies

Name of Body	Main Functions
Income Tax Appellate Tribunal (ITAT)	• ITAT is a quasi judicial institution set up in **January, 1941** and specialises in dealing with appeals under the Direct Taxes Act. The orders passed by the ITAT are final; an appeal lies to the High Court only if a substantial question of law arises for determination.
Competition Commission of India (CCI)	• The Competition Commission of India (CCI) is a statutory body of the Government of India responsible for enforcing the **Competition Act of 2002**. It consists of Chairperson and six members. • The commission must eliminate practices hurting competition, promote and sustain competition, protect the interests of consumers and ensure freedom of trade in the markets of India. • The **National Company Law Appellate Tribunal** (NCLAT) constituted under **Section 410** of the Companies Act, 2013 shall be the Appellate Tribunal for this Competition Act, 2002.
Telecom Disputes Settlement and Appellate Tribunal (TDSAT)	• Telecom Disputes Settlement and Appellate Tribunal (TDSAT) were established in 2000, by amending the **Telecom Regulatory Authority of India (TRAI) Act, 1997.** • The tribunal consists of a Chairperson and two members appointed by the Central Government. The Chairperson should be or should have been a Judge of the Supreme Court or the Chief Justice of a High Court. • It adjudicates disputes and disposes of appeals regarding matters like issues of licenses. All decisions or orders of the Telecom Regulatory Authority of India (TRAI) can be challenged through appeals in TDSAT. • The orders of TDSAT can be appealed to the Supreme Court on substantial questions of law, in matters of Telecom, Broadcasting and Airport tariff matters.
Telecom Regulatory Authority of India (TRAI)	• It is a **statutory body** that governs the country's telecommunications sector and was established by an Act of Parliament called the **Telecom Regulatory Authority of India Act, 1997**. It shall consist of a Chairperson and not more than two full-time members and not more than two part-time members. • They hold office for a term not exceeding three years or until they attain the age of 65 years, whichever is earlier. • TRAI regulates telecom services including fixation/revision of tariffs for telecom services which were earlier vested in the Central Government. It is empowered to direct any of its officers or employees to inspect the books of accounts or other documents of any service provider. • The TRAI Act was Amended in 2000 which established a **Telecommunications Dispute Settlement and Appellate Tribunal** (TDSAT) to take over the adjudicatory and disputes functions from TRAI.
University Grants Commission (UGC)	• The University Grants Commission is a statutory organisation established by an **Act of Parliament in 1956**. • The commission shall consist of a **Chairman, a Vice-Chairman** and **10 other members**, to be appointed by the Central Government. • It aims to provide funds to universities and coordinate, determine and maintain the ethics in institutions of higher education. The commission upholds the universities', governments and community's interpretations. It confers recognition to Indian universities. • Recommend to any university the steps that must be taken to strengthen university education and advise the university on the steps that must be done to carry out such recommendations.
National Medical Commission	• The National Medical Commission (NMC) was founded by an Act of Parliament known as the **National Medical Commission Act, 2019.** • There will be 25 members of the National Medical Commission. The Chairperson, Presidents of Postgraduate Medical Education Boards and Presidents of Undergraduate Medical Education Boards shall make up the NMC. Director-General of Indian Council of Medical Research (ICMR) will also be a part of it. • It took the place of the Medical Council of India. The commission recognised medical qualifications, accredits medical schools and evaluates the medical infrastructure in India.
Drug Controller General of India	• Drugs Controller General of India is the head of department of the Central Drugs Standard Control Organisation of the Government of India. • It is responsible for approval of licenses of specified categories of drugs such as blood and blood products, IV fluids and vaccines in India. • It sets standards for manufacturing, sales, import and distribution of drugs in India. • It functions under the Ministry of Health and Family Welfare. It lays down the standard and quality of manufacturing, selling, import and distribution of drugs in India.
Food Safety and Standards Authority of India (FSSAI)	• The Food Safety and Standards Authority of India is a statutory body under Food Safety and Standards Act, 2006. The Ministry of Health and Family Welfare has administrative jurisdiction over the FSSAI. • The FSSAI consists of a Chairperson and 22 members, one-third of whom must be women. The Chairperson of FSSAI is appointed by the Central Government. • It is responsible for protecting and promoting public health through the regulation and supervision of food safety. • It looks into the matters related to food standards as well as compliance and Inspections.

Name of Body	Main Functions
National Consumer Disputes Redressal Commission	• The National Consumer Disputes Redressal Commission or the NCDRC is a quasi-judicial commission established as per the provisions of the Consumer Protection Act, 1986. It was established in 1988. • It addresses grievances of aggrieved consumer for goods and services having value over ₹ 1 crore. • The commission is headed by sitting or retired Judge of Supreme Court of India. • The **Consumer Protection Act of 1986** provided for a three-tier consumer dispute redressal machinery at the National (National Consumer Disputes Redressal Commission), state and district levels. • The **Consumer Protection Act, 2019** establishes the Central Consumer Protection Authority (CCPA) whose primary objective will be to promote, protect and enforce the rights of consumers.
Press Council of India	• The council functions under the **Press Council Act, 1978**. It is a statutory, quasi-judicial body that acts as a watchdog for the press, by the press and for the benefit of the press. It serves as the regulator for the print media in India, defining and disseminating professional standards. • It consists of 28 members in all, including the Chairman. The Chairman is selected by the Speaker of the Lok Sabha, the Chairman of the Rajya Sabha and a member elected by the PCI. • It may summon witnesses and take evidence under oath, demand copies of public records to be submitted, even issue warnings and admonish the newspaper, news agency, editor or journalist. • The decisions of the PCI are final and cannot be appealed before a court of law.
Bar Council of India	• The Indian Bar Council is a statutory body established by Parliament to regulate and represent the Indian legal profession. It was founded in 1961 under **Section 4** of the Advocates Act. • Each Bar Council shall have a Chairman and Vice-Chairman elected by the Council. The Attorney-General of India and the Solicitor-General of India are ex-officio members. • It aims to promote legal education and to lay down standards of legal education. This is done in consultation with the universities in India imparting legal education and the State Bar Councils.
National Highway Authority of India	• NHAI is an autonomous statutory agency of the Union Government. It was established through National **Highways Authority of India Act, 1988.** • It consists of a Chairman and not more than five full-time members and four part-time members who are appointed by the Central Government. It is a nodal agency of the Union Ministry of Road Transport and Highways. • It is responsible for the development, management, operation and maintenance of National Highways. It is responsible for management of a network of over 70,000 km of National Highways in India.
Directorate General of Civil Aviation	• It is a statutory body of the Indian Central Government to regulate civil aviation in India. It was formed under the Aircraft (Amendment) Bill, 2020. It investigates aviation accidents and incidents, maintains all regulations related to aviation and is responsible for issuance of licenses. • It is responsible for the regulation of air transport services to/from/within India and for enforcement of civil air regulations, air safety and airworthiness standards. It aims at coordination at the national level for flexi-use of air space by civil and military air traffic agencies. • Promoting indigenous design and manufacture of aircraft and aircraft components by acting as a catalytic agent.
Unique Identification Authority of India (UIDAI)	• UIDAI is a statutory authority established under the provisions of the Aadhaar Act, 2016. It comes under the Electronics and IT Ministry. • It is an agency under the Central Government of India mandated to collect demographic and biometric information of the country's residents, store the data in a central database and issue to each resident of the country a 12-digit unique identity number called Aadhaar.
Inland Waterways Authority of India (IWAI)	• IWAI is the statutory body in charge of the waterways in India. It was constituted in 1986 for the development and regulation of inland waterways for shipping and navigation. • Its main function is to build the necessary infrastructure in the inland waterways, surveying the economic feasibility of new projects and also carrying out administration and regulation.
Customs Excise and Service Tax Appellate Tribunal (CESTAT)	• CESTAT was constituted in 1982 under Customs Act, 1962. It works under the Ministry of Finance. • It is a quasi-judicial body that hears appeals against orders and decisions passed under the Customs Act, 1962 and Central Excise Act, 1944. It also has appellate jurisdiction in Anti Dumping matters. • It cannot grant compensation owing to unlawful action of revenue authorities.
Cyber Appellate Tribunal	• Cyber Appellate Tribunal has been established under the Information Technology Act under the aegis of Controller of Certifying Authorities (CCA). • The Central Government also specifies in the notification all the matters and places which fall under the jurisdiction of the tribunal.
Atomic Energy Regulatory Board	• The Atomic Energy Regulatory Board (AERB) was constituted as a statutory body on 15th November, 1983, using the powers conferred by the Atomic Energy Act of 1962. It was constituted to perform special regulatory and safety functions. The Atomic Energy Act of 1962 and the Environment Protection Act of 1986 give the AERB its jurisdiction and authority. Its headquarters is located in Mumbai. • The primary purpose of the Atomic Energy Regulatory Board is to deal with matters related to nuclear safety.

Public Services are the chief instrument for implementation of will of the state and are indispensable to the functioning of the modern state. It is also known as Civil Services or Government Services.

Chapter Thirty Three

Public Services

INDIAN CIVIL SERVICES

- Part XIV of the Indian Constitution provides for different types of classes of services for India.
- Civil Services have been categorised into three types

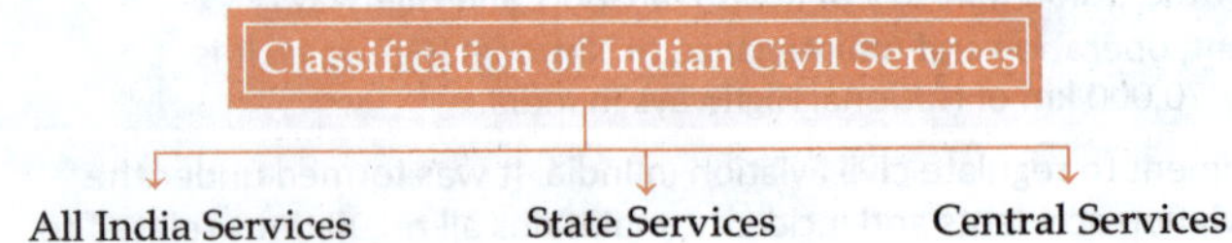

All India Services

- All India Services are common to both Centre and States. The members of these services occupy top positions (or key posts) under both the Centre and the states and serve them by turns.
- At present, there are three All India Services. They are :
  - Indian Administrative Service (IAS)
  - Indian Police Service (IPS)
  - Indian Forest Service (IFoS)
- In 1947, the Indian Civil Service (ICS) was replaced by IAS and the Indian Police (IP) was replaced by IPS, and were recognised by the Constitution as all-India services.
- In 1966, the Indian Forest Service was established as the third All India Service. Article 312 of the Constitution authorises the Parliament of India to create new All India Services based on a resolution passed by Rajya Sabha to that effect.
- Thus, a new All India Service can be created only by an act of Parliament and not by a resolution of Rajya Sabha. However, the Parliament cannot do so without the recommendation of Rajya Sabha.
- This power is given to the Rajya Sabha to protect the interests of states in the Indian federal system.
- Sardar Vallabhbhai Patel was the chief protagonist of All India Services in the Constituent Assembly. Hence, he came to be regarded as the 'Father of All India Services'.
- The All India Services Act of 1951 authorised the Central Government to make rules in consultation with the State Governments for the regulation of recruitment' and service conditions of the members of All India Services.
- The All India Services are trained and recruited by the Central Government, but they are assigned to different states for work.
- They serve State Governments and their service conditions are also governed by the states, except the disciplinary actions against them can only be taken by the Central Government.

- They also serve the Central Government on deputation and after a fixed tenure, they are expected to return to their respective states.

All the three All India Services are Class-I (Group-A) Services. The All India Services have three categories. They are :

- Super time scale
- Senior scale
- Junior scale

The three All India Services are managed and controlled by three different Ministries of the Central Government. They are :

- IAS by the Ministry of Personnel, Public Grievances and Pensions
- IPS by the Ministry of Home Affairs
- IFoS by the Ministry of Environment, Forest and Climate Change

It must be mentioned here that the All India Services are controlled jointly by the Centre land State Governments.

The ultimate control lies with the Central Government while the immediate control vests with the State Governments.

Their salaries and pensions are met by the states.

Presently, there are twenty-four states cadres in all for the All India Services.

This includes three joint cadres (i) Assam-Meghalaya and (ii) Arunachal Pradesh, Goa, Mizoram and the Union Territories (AGMUT), (iii) Manipur-Tripura.

entral Services

The personnel of Central Services work under the exclusive jurisdiction of the Central Government.

The Ministry of Personnel is the central personnel agency in the Government of India.

It must also be mentioned here that the Indian Foreign Service (IFS) is the top most Central Service in terms of prestige, status, pay and emoluments.

The Civil Services of the Union are classified into four categories :

- Central Services Class I (Group A) Indian Foreign Services, Indian Audit and Accounts Services, Indian Statistical Service, Indian Economic Service, Indian Railway Service, Central Health Service, etc.
  - Central Services Class II (Group B) Central Secretariat Service, Geographical Survey of India, Zoological Survey of India, etc.
  - Central Services Class III (Group C) Post and Telegraph Accounts Service, Central Secretariat Clerical Service, etc.
- Central Services Class IV (Group D) Peons, Sweepers, Gardeners, etc.

State Civil Services

- These are services exclusively under the jurisdiction of the State Government and primarily administer the state subjects.
- For the recruitment of state services, there are laws enacted by the State Legislature.
- Like the Central services, the state services are also classified into four categories: Class I (Group I or Group A), Class II (Group II or Group B), Class III (Group III or Group C) and Class IV (Group IV or Group D).
- Further, the state services are also classified into gazetted class and non-gazetted class.
- Usually, Class- I (Group-A) and Class-II (Group-B) Services are gazetted classes while Class-III (Group-C) and Class-IV (Group-D) services are non-gazetted classes.
- The members of the gazetted class are called Officers while those of non-gazetted are called Employees.
- The persons for the State Services are recruited through a competitive examination and process is very much similar to the competitive examination conducted by UPSC.
- Many IAS, IPS are holding positions in departments under State Governments like education, police, tourism, judicial service, medical service, etc.

Articles Related to Civil Services (Central/State)

Public Services	
Article 308	Interpretation
Article 309	Recruitment and condition of service of persons serving the Union as State.
Article 310	Tenure of office of persons.
Article 311	Dismissal, removal or reduction in rank.
Article 312	All-India Services
Article 312A	Power of Parliament to vary or revoke conditions of service of officers.
Article 313	Transitional provision.
Article 314	Provision for protection of existing officers.

Public Service Commission	
Article 315	Public Service Commission for the Union and States.
Article 316	Appointment and Terms of office of members.
Article 317	Removal and suspension of a member of Public Service Commission.
Article 318	Power to make regulations as to conditions of service of members and Staff of the Commission.
Article 319	Prohibition as to the holding of office by members of the commission on ceasing to be such members.
Article 320	Functions of Public Service Commissions.
Article 321	Power of extend functions of Public Service Commission.
Article 322	Expenses of Public Service Commission.
Article 323	Reports of Public Service Commission.

UNION PUBLIC SERVICE COMMISSION

- The UPSC is a central recruiting agency in India. It is an independent constitutional body in the sense that it has been directly created by the Constitution.
- Articles 315 to 323 in Part XIV of the Constitution of India provides for the establishment of Public Service Commission for the Union and Public Service Commission for each State.

Provisions of Union Public Service Commission as described below :

Appointment and Term of Office of Members

- The Chairman and other members of a Union Public Service Commission or a Joint Commission shall be appointed by the President under Article 316(1).
- The Constitution has not determined the strength of the commission, it is decided by the President.
- He appoints 9 to 11 members and determines their service condition under Article 318.
- According to Article 316(2), the Chairman and Members of the commission hold office for a term of six years or until they attain the age of 65 years (whichever is earlier).
- However, they have the option of resigning their positions at any moment by addressing the resignation to the President.
- One of the UPSC members may be appointed by the President to serve as a temporary Chairman in either of the following two situations:
  - When the Chairman's position becomes vacant.
  - If the Chairman is unable to carry out his duties.

Qualifications

- The Constitution does not provide for any specific qualification for its Members and Chairman.
- It mentions that one-half of the members of every Public Service Commission shall be persons who have held office for at least 10 years either under the Government of India or under the Government of a State.

Removal

- The Chairman or any other member of a Union Public Service Commission shall only be removed from his office by order of the President.
- According to Article 317, they can be removed on the ground of misbehaviour after the inquiry made by the Supreme Court.
- The Constitution's provisions provide that the advice tendered by Supreme Court in this regard is binding on the President.
- Conditions for the removal are as following:
  - If he is adjudged an insolvent.
  - If he engages, during his term of office, in any pai employment outside the duties of his office.
  - If he is unfit to continue in office by reason of infirmity of mind or body in the opinion of the President.

Independence of Union Public Service Commission

- According to Article 316, the members of the Union Public Service Commission enjoy security o tenure. They cannot be removed from the office o any other ground than specified in the Constitution.
- The Chairman of the UPSC shall be ineligible for further employment either under the Government of India or under the Government of a State.

> A member other than the Chairman of the UPSC shall be eligible for appointment as the Chairman of the UPSC or as the Chairman of a **State Public Service Commission**, but not for any other employment either under the Government of India o under the Government of a State.

- The entire expenses including the salaries, allowances and pensions of the members of UPS(are not subject to Vote of Parliament.

Functions

- According to Article 320, to conduct examinations for appointments to the services of the Union and the services of the State by UPSC.
- To advice on any matter so referred to them and on any other matter referred to by the President.
- To perform any additional functions with respect to the services of the Union or the States or any local authority constituted by law.
- Such functions may be provided in a law passed by Parliament or the State Legislature.
- Under Article 323, to present an annual report to the President on the work done by the commission.
- If requested by two or more states, it shall be the duty of the commission (UPSC) to assist them in framing and operating schemes of joint recruitment to any services requiring possession of special qualifications.
- The UPSC, if requested to do so by the Governor of a State, may with the approval of the President, agree to serve all or any needs of the states.

The Union Public Service Commission or the State Public Service Commission as the case shall be consulted on the following matters under Article 320(3).

- On all matters relating to methods of recruitment to Civil Services and for Civil Posts.
- On the principles to be followed in making appointments to Civil Services and Posts and in making promotions and transfers from one service to another and on the suitability of candidates for such appointments, promotions or transfers.
- On all disciplinary matters affecting a person serving under the Government of India or the Government of a State in a civil capacity.

UPSC vs CVC

The establishment and emergence of Central Vigilance Commission (CVC) in 1964 on the recommendation of Santhanam Committee affected the role of UPSC in disciplinary matters.

This is because both are consulted by the government while taking disciplinary action against a civil servant. The problem arises when the two bodies tender conflicting advice.

However, the UPSC, being an independent Constitutional Body has an edge over the CVC, which conferred a statutory status in October, 2003.

STATE PUBLIC SERVICE COMMISSION

Provisions of State Public Service Commission are as described below :

Appointment and Term of Office

- The Chairman and other members of a State Public Service Commission (SPSC) shall be appointed by the Governor of the State under Article 316(1).
- The Constitution has not determined the strength of the commission; it is decided by the Governor. He is also empowered to determine their service condition under Article 318.
- The Chairman and Members of the commission hold office for a term of six years or until they attain the age of 62 years. They can also be removed by writing their resignation to the Governor.
- One of the SPSC members may be appointed by the Governor to serve as a temporary Chairman in either of the following two situations :
  - When the Chairman's position becomes vacant.
  - If the Chairman is unable to carry out his duties.

Qualifications

- The Constitution does not provide any specific qualification for its Members and Chairman.
- It mentions that **one-half** of the members of every Public Service Commission shall be persons who have held office for atleast 10 years either under the Government of India or under the Government of a State.

Removal

- Under Article 317(1), the Chairman or any other member of Public Service Commission shall only be removed from his office by order of the President. They can be removed on the ground of misbehaviour after the inquiry made by the Supreme Court.
- Under Article 317(3), the Constitution's provisions provide that the advice tendered by Supreme Court in this regard is binding on the President.

Conditions for the removal are as following:

- If he is adjudged an insolvent.
- If he engages in any paid employment outside the duties of his office during his term of office.
- If he is unfit to continue in office by reason of infirmity of mind or body in the opinion of the President.

- As per Article 317(4), if the Chairman or any other member of a Public Service Commission in any way is concerned or interested in any contract or agreement made by or on behalf of the Government of India or the Government of a State, he/she shall be deemed to be guilty of misbehaviour.

Independence of State Public Service Commission

- As per Article 316, the members of the State Public Service Commission enjoy security of tenure. They cannot be removed from the office on any other ground than specified in the Constitution.
- The Chairman of a State Public Service Commission (SPSC) shall be eligible for appointment as the Chairman or any other member of the Union Public Service Commission or as the Chairman of any other State Public Service Commission, but not for any other employment either under the Government of India or under the Government of a State.
- A member other than the Chairman of a SPSC shall be eligible for appointment as the Chairman or any other member of the Union Public Service Commission or as the Chairman of that or any other State Public Service Commission, but not for any other employment either under the Government of India or under the Government of a State.
- According to the Article 322, the entire expenses including the salaries, allowances and pensions of the members of State Public Service Commission are not subject to vote of State Legislature.

Functions

- As per Article 320, to conduct examinations for appointments to the services of the state by State Public Service Commission.
- To advice on any matter so referred to them and on any other matter referred to by the Governor.
- Other powers and functions of SPSC are in congruence with that of UPSC.
- Under Article 323, to present an annual report to the Governor on the work done by the commission.

Limitations

The following issues are not included in the functional purview of a SPSC :

- The recommendations of commission are not binding on the government.
- While making reservations of appointments or posts in favour of any backward class of citizens.
- While taking into consideration the claims of Scheduled Castes and Scheduled Tribes in making appointments to services and posts.
- The Governor can exclude posts, services and matters from the purview of the SPSC.

JOINT STATE PUBLIC SERVICE COMMISSION

- It is a statutory body constituted under **Article 315**. It is not a constitutional body.
- After the creation of Haryana out of Punjab in 1966, the two states of Punjab and Haryana had a JSPSC for a short period.
- The President appoints the Chairman as well as the members of a JSPSC.
- The office is held by them for a six years term or until the age of 62 years is attained by them, whichever is earlier.
- The President can remove or suspend them. They can also submit their resignation letters to the President anytime.
- The President determines the number of members of a JSPSC and their conditions of service.
- An annual performance report is presented by a Joint State Public Service Commission to each of the concerned State Governors.
- The report is placed by the Governor in front of the State Legislature. The UPSC can also serve the needs of a state on the State Governor's request and with the President's approval.

As provided by the **Government of India Act of 1919,** a Central Public Service Commission was set up in 1926 and entrusted with the task of recruiting civil servants.

- The **Government of India Act of 1935**, provided for the establishment of not only a Federal Public Service Commission but also a Provincial Public Service Commission and Joint Public Service Commission for two or more provinces.

Language is the human capacity for acquiring and using complex systems of communication. Part XVII of the Constitution deals with the official language from Articles 343 to 351.

Chapter Thirty Four

Provision Related to Official Language

CONSTITUTIONAL DEVELOPMENT

- The Official Language Commission, appointed in the year 1955, gave priority to Hindi language in place of English, as a result of which the critics of South India opposed it.
- As a result, the Official Languages Act was presented to the Parliament in the year, 1963 itself and the Parliamentarians of South India and West Bengal debated in favour of retaining English as a language, resulting in the continuation of English without any time limit. Hindi as official language was accepted in the year 1949.
- During this time, the trilingual formula of education was brought, according to which, all the universities of the country will teach their regional language and English. In the year 1967, the Parliament amended the Official Language Bill.
- In this, provision was made that the use of English for all those official works for which it has been used till now, will continue until all the non-Hindi speaking states are ready to adopt Hindi by resolution in their Legislature.

India's Linguistic Diversity

- In the 2011 Census, people had registered more than 1300 different languages as their mother tongue.
- These languages are grouped with a few major languages; like-Bhojpuri, Magadhi, Bundelkhandi, Chhattisgarhi, Rajasthani and other such languages are added to Hindi.
- Even after such grouping, the census found 121 major languages, out of which 22 languages are placed in the Eighth Schedule of the Constitution of India and hence are called Scheduled Languages and others as Non-Scheduled Languages.
- Hindi, the largest language, is also the mother tongue of only 44% people.
- Even if the number of people who know Hindi as a second or third language is also added, in the year 2011 this number was less than 50%.
- English was reported by only 0.02% as their mother tongue and only 11% knew it as a second or third language.

OFFICIAL LANGUAGE OF THE UNION

- According to Article 343, the official language of the union shall be Hindi in Devanagari script.
- However, the President may authorise the use of English language in addition to the Hindi language.
- The form of numeral to be used for the official purpose of the union has to be the international form of Indian numerals and not Devanagari form of numerals.
- However, for a period of 15 years from the commencement of the Constitution, the English language would continue to be used for all the official purposes of the union, for which it was being used before 1950.

- Even after fifteen years, the Parliament may provide for the continued use of English language for the specified purposes.
- At the end of five years and again at the end of ten years, from the commencement of the Constitution , the President should appoint a commission to make Official Language recommendations with regard to the progressive use of the Hindi language, restrictions on the use of the English language and other related issues.
- A committee of Parliament is to be constituted to examine the recommendations of the commission and to report its views on them to the President.
- Article 344 A committee of Parliament is to be constituted to examine the recommendation of the commission and to report its views on them to the President.

Eighth Schedule of the Constitution

- The Eighth Schedule of the Constitution consists of 22 languages i.e., 1. Assamese 2. Bengali 3. Bodo 4. Dogri 5. Gujarati 6. Hindi 7. Kannada 8. Kashmiri 9. Konkani 10. Maithili 11. Malayalam 12. Manipuri 13. Marathi 14. Nepali 15. Odiya 16. Punjabi 17. Sanskrit 18. Santhali 19. Sindhi 20. Tamil 21. Telugu 22. Urdu.
- 14 languages were initially included in the Constitution. Sindhi was added in 1967 (21st Amendment).
- Thereafter three more languages *viz*., Konkani, Manipuri and Nepali were included in 1992 (71st Amendment).
- Subsequently, Bodo, Dogri, Maithili and Santhali were added in 2003 (92nd Amendment).

Commission and Committee on Official Language

- Under Article 344 (1), the President shall constitute a commission which shall consist of a Chairman and such other members representing the different languages specified in the Eighth Schedule, as the President may appoint and shall define the procedure to be followed by the commission.
- As per Article 344 (2), the Commission shall make recommendations to the President about the progressive use of Hindi language and restrictive use of English language.
- It shall be the duty of the Committee to submit a report to the President making recommendations thereon.
- The President shall cause the report to be laid before each House of Parliament and send it to all the State Governments.
- The President may, after consideration of the report, and the views, expressed by the State Governments thereon, issue directions in accordance with the whole or any part of the report.
- The Chairman of the Committee is elected by the members of the Committee.
- As a convention, the Union Home Minister has been elected as Chairman of the Committee from time-to-time. The Secretariat of the Committee is headed by the Secretary of the Committee.
- For administrative purposes, this office is subordinate office of Department of Official Language, Ministry of Home Affairs.
- In making their recommendations, the Commission shall have due regard for the industrial, cultural and scientific advancement of India.
- Official language is used for communication between one State and another or between a State and the Union.
- As per Article 344 (4), there shall be constituted a Committee consisting of 30 members of whom 20 shall be members of the House of the People and 10 shall be members of the Council of States to be elected respectively by the members of the House of People.

Recommendations of Official Language Commission

- As provided in Article 344 of the Constitution, the Official Language Commission was appointed in 1955 with Shri BG Kher as Chairman. Its report was submitted in 1956 and then examined by a Joint Parliamentary Committee.
- The recommendations of the commission were as follows :
  - English should be the principal official language and Hindi, the subsidiary official language till 1965. After 1965, when Hindi becomes the principal official language, English should continue as the subsidiary official language.
  - Considerable importance to be attached to **Article 351** in order to make Hindi that serve as a medium for expression for all elements of the composite culture of India.
- An order was issued by the President on 27th April, 1960, in which it was said that a permanent commission should be constituted to prepare terminology related to scientific, administrative and

legal literature and to translate English works into Hindi.

- In this order, it was arranged that the use of English as the medium of examinations of the Union Public Service Commission should continue and Hindi should be started as an alternative medium later.
- Parliamentary legislative work will continue to be done in English, but arrangements will be made for its official Hindi translation.
- On the basis of the report of the first Official Language Commission, the Official Language Act, 1963 was enacted by the Parliament under Article 343.

REGIONAL LANGUAGES

The Constitution does not specify the official language of different States. In this regard, the Constitutions deals some Articles for regional language. These are as follows :

- Article 345, Official language or languages of a State The Legislature of a State may adopt any one or more of the languages in the State.
- They may also adopt Hindi as the language for all or any of the official purposes of that state. Under this provision, most of the states have adopted the major regional language as their official language.
- Notably, the choice of the state is not limited to the languages enumerated in the Eighth Schedule of the Constitution.
- It has also provided that, until the Legislature of the State provides by law, the English language shall continue to be used for those official purposes within the State for which it was being used immediately before the commencement of this Constitution.

Article 346, Official Language for Communication between one State and another or between a State and the Union The language for the time being authorised for use in the union for official purposes shall be the official language for communication between one State and another State and between a State and the Union.

- As per Article 346, if two or more states agree that the Hindi language should be the official language for communication between such states, that language may be used for such communication.
- Article 347, Special Provision Relating to Language Spoken by a Section of the Population of a State Once a demand is being made the President if satisfied that a substantial proportion of the population of a state desire the use of any language spoken by them to be recognised throughout that state or any part thereof such purpose as he may specify.

Language of the Judiciary and Text of Laws

- According to Article 348(1) following provisions are to be in English language only, until Parliament provides otherwise
  - All proceedings in the Supreme Court and in every High Court.
  - The authoritative texts of all bills, acts, ordinances, orders, rules, regulations and by-laws at the Central and State level.
- As per Article 348 (2) The Governor of a State, with the previous consent of the President can authorise the use of Hindi or any other official language of the State, in the proceedings in the High Court of a State.
- However, judgements, decrees and orders of the High Court must continue to be in English only (until Parliament otherwise provides).
- Later, this provision was provided through the Official Language Act of 1963.
- Parliament has not made any provision for the use of Hindi in the Supreme Court. Hence, the Supreme Court hears only those who petition or appeal in English.
- Similarly, under Article 348 (3), a State Legislature can prescribe the use of any language (other than English) with respect to bills, acts, ordinances, orders, rules, regulations or by-laws, but a translation of the same in the English language is to be published.

Special Directives for Linguistic Minorities

- The Constitution of India contains Special Directives to protect the interests of linguistic minorities and to promote the development of Hindi language. Some articles related to this are as follows:
- Article 350, Language to be Used in Representations for Redress of Grievances Every person shall be entitled to submit a representation for the redress of any grievance to any officer or authority of the Union or a State in any of the languages used in the Union or in the State, as the case may be.
- Article 350(A), Facilities for instruction in mother tongue at Primary Stage The Article 350(A) says that

every State and other local authority within a State is directed to provide adequate facilities for instruction in the mother tongue at preliminary stage of education to children belonging to linguistic minority groups.

- In above concern, the President is authorised to issue such directions to any state as he may consider necessary for the securing of such facilities.
- Article 350(B), Facilities for instructions in Mother Tongue for Minority It say that a special officer for linguistic minorities shall be appointed by the President to investigate all matter relating to the safeguards provided by the Constitution for linguistic minorities and to report to President upon those matters.
- President lay down such reports in each House of Parliament and also before the concerned State Governments.
- Article 351, Directive for Development of the Hindi Language It shall be the duty of the union to promote the spread of the Hindi language, so that it may serve as a medium of expression for all the elements of the composite culture of India.

> In the other languages of India specified in the **Eighth Schedule** and by drawing, wherever necessary or desirable, for its vocabulary, primarily from Sanskrit and secondarily from other languages.

Official Languages Act, 1963

- It is an Act to provide for the languages which may be used for the official purpose of the Union, for transaction of business in Parliament, for Central and State Acts and for certain purpose in High Courts.
- It provides for the continuance of English language for official purposes of the Union and for use in Parliament.
- Notwithstanding the expiration of the period of 15 years from the commencement of the Constitution, the English language may, as from the appointed day continue to be used in addition to Hindi.
- For all the official purpose of the Union for which it was being used immediately before that day and for the transaction of business in Parliament.
- Some of the important provisions of Official Languages Act, 1963 were :
    - Even after the expiration of 15 years from the commencement of Constitution.
    - English may be continued to be used in addition to Hindi in Parliament and for other purposes, for which it was used earlier.
    - Translations of any Central Act or ordinance or by-laws made under a Central Act, under the authority of the President shall be deemed to be the authoritative texts thereof in Hindi.
    - The Governor of a State may with the previous consent of the President, authorise the use of Hindi or the official language of the State, in addition to the English language.
- For the purposes of any judgement, decree or order is passed or made by the High Court for that State and where any judgement, decree or order is passed or made in any such language (other than English), then it shall be accompanied with an English translation issued under the authority of court.
- English shall be used for purposes of communication between the Union and the State, which has not adopted Hindi as the official language.
- When Hindi is used for communication between one state and another which has not adopted Hindi as official language, then it shall be accompanied with an English translation.

AUTHORITATIVE TEXT : HINDI LANGUAGE

- The Acts, ordinances, orders regulations and by-laws all are deemed to be authoritative text of Constitution. Such authoritative texts of the Constitution are used in the legal process.
- The Constitution of India was adopted by the Constitution Assembly in English. In 1950, a Hindi translation of the Constitution was also published.
- Soon after that there was a demand for the publication in Hindi also incorporating all the subsequent amendments.
- It was therefore, proposed to amend the Constitution, so as the empower the President of India to publish under his authority the translation of the Constitution. Therefore, through Article 394(A) the President published an authoritative text of the Constitution in Hindi language.

Constitutional Provisions

- Originally, the Constitution of India did not make any provision with respect to an authoritative text of the Constitution in the Hindi language.

- Later, a provision in this regard was added by the 58th Constitutional Amendment Act of 1987. This amendment inserted a new Article 394(A) in the last part of the Constitution i.e., Part 22.

Provisions of Article 394(A) of the Constitution

- The President shall cause to be published under his authority :
  - The translation of the Constitution in the Hindi language with such modification as may be necessary to bring it in conformity with the language, style and terminology adopted in the authoritative texts of Central Acts in the Hindi language and incorporating therein all the amendments of this Constitution made before such publication and
  - The translation in Hindi of every amendment of the Constitution made in English.
- It states that the translation of the Constitution and of every amendment published shall be construed to have the same meaning as the original thereof.
- It further states that the translation of the Constitution and of every amendment published under this article shall be deemed to be the authoritative text.

Minority Languages

- Officially, a minority language is one that's spoken by a people of minority within a given country or territory.
- It is also including those languages which are spoken by large number of people in a State or region, but have not been accepted due to some reasons nor in educational stream neither in administration.
- Minority languages are those which a given population perceives to be minority ones or even those languages whose speaker, the linguistic minority, feel their language as threatened.

Linguistic Minority

A linguistic minority is a class of people whose tongue is different from that of the majority in the State or part of a State. The Constitution provides for the protection of the interests of linguistic minorities.

Classical Languages

- In September 2004, the Government of India declared that languages that met certain requirements could be accorded the status of a classical language in India.
- The criteria for declaring a language as classical mandates high antiquity of its early text/recorded history over a period of 1500 to 2000 years, a body of ancient literature/texts which is considered a valuable heritage by generations of speakers and a literary tradition that is original.
- Once a language is declared classical, it gets financial assistance for setting up a centre of excellence for the study of that language and also opens up an avenue for two major awards for scholars of eminence.
- Six languages thus, far declared to be classical languages are Tamil (2004), Sanskrit (2005), Telugu (2008), Kannada (2008), Malayalam (2013) and Odia (2014).

PROTECTION OF ENDANGERED LANGUAGES IN INDIA

- UNESCO has recognised India as one of the most linguistically diverse country. As per Census 2011, more than 19,500 languages or dialects are spoken in India as mother tongues while only 121 languages are spoken by 10,000 or more people.
- The Government of India has initiated a Scheme known as Scheme for Protection and Preservation of Endangered Languages of India (SPPEL).
- Central Institute of Indian Languages was established in 1969 under the administrative control of the Ministry of Human Resources (now Ministry of Education). It advises and assists Central as well as State Governments in the matters of language. It also protects and documents minority and tribal languages.

Articles Related to Official Languages

Articles	Description
Article 343	Official language of the Union
Article 344	Commission and Committee of Parliament on official language
Article 345	Official language or languages of a State
Article 346	Official language for communication between one State and another or between a State and the Union
Article 347	Special provision relating to language spoken by a section of the population of a State
Article 348	Language to be used in the Supreme Court and in the High Courts and for Acts, Bills, etc
Article 349	Special procedure for enactment of certain laws relating to language
Article 350	Language to be used in representation for redress of grievances
Article 351	Directive for development of the Hindi Language

Co-operative Society is a voluntary association of persons, who join together with the motive of the welfare of the members.

Chapter Thirty Five

Co-operative Societies

The 97th Constitutional Amendment Act of 2011 gave a constitutional status and protection to co-operative societies. Three changes were made in the Constitution in this context given as :

(i) Right to form co-operative societies is a Fundamental Right (Article 19).

(ii) Added new DPSP on promotion of co-operative societies (Article 43B).

(iii) Added new Part IX-B in the Constitution. The Co-operative Societies (Articles 243ZH to 243ZT).

CONSTITUTIONAL PROVISIONS

Part IX-B of the Constitution contains the following provisions with respect to the co-operative societies :

Incorporation of Co-operative Societies

The State Legislature may make provisions for the incorporation, regulation and winding-up of co-operative societies based on the principles of voluntary formation, democratic member control, member-economic participation and autonomous functioning.

Number and Term of Members of Board and its Office Bearers

- The board shall consist of such number of directors as may be provided by the State Legislature.
- But, the maximum number of directors of a co-operative society shall not exceed twenty-one.
- Reservation of Seats The State Legislature shall provide for the reservation of one seat for the Scheduled Castes or the Scheduled Tribes and two seats for women on the board of every co-operative society having members from such a category of persons.
- The term of office of elected members of the board and its office bearers shall be five years from the date of election and election of a board shall be conducted before the expiry of the term of the current board (Article 243 ZK) by such body, as may be provided by the State Legislature.

Co-opted Members

- The State Legislature shall make provisions for co-option of persons having experience in banking, management, finance, etc to the board whose numbers shall not exceeds two (in addition to twenty-one directors) without any right to vote.
- Election of Members of Board The election of a board shall be conducted before the expiry of the term of the board so as to ensure that the newly elected members assume office immediately on the expiry of the term of the office of members of the outgoing board.
- The superintendence, direction and control of the preparation of electoral rolls and the conduct of elections to a co-operative society shall vest in such body, as may be provided by the State Legislature.

Supersession and Suspension of Board and Interim Management : (Article 243 ZL)

- No board shall be superseded or kept under suspension for a period exceeding six months.
- In case of co-operative banks, other than multi-state co-operative banks, this period cannot exceed one year.

- However, the board of any such co-operative society shall not be superseded or kept under suspension where there is no Government shareholding or loan or financial assistance or any guarantee by the Government.

Audit of Accounts of Co-operative Societies : (Article 243 ZM)

- State Legislature may make provisions for the maintenance and auditing of accounts of the co-operative societies (within six months of the close of the financial year) at least once in each financial year.
- It shall lay down the minimum qualifications and experience of auditors and auditing firms that shall be eligible for auditing the accounts of the co-operative societies.
- Every co-operative society shall be audited by an auditor or auditing firm, appointed by the general body of the co-operative society. The audit report of the accounts of an apex co-operative society shall be laid before the State Legislature.

Convening of General Body Meetings

- The State Legislature may provide that the annual general body meeting of every co-operative society shall be convened within a period of six months of the close of the financial year.
- The State Legislature may provide for access to every member of a co-operative society to the books, information and accounts of the co-operative society.
- It may also make provisions to ensure the participation of members in the management of the co-operative society.

OFFENCES AND PENALTIES

The State Legislature may make provisions, for the offences relating to the co-operative societies and penalties for such offences. Such a law shall include the commission or omission of the following acts as offences :

- A co-operative society willfully makes a false return or furnishes false information.
- Any person willfully disobeys any summon, requisition or order issued under the State Act.
- Any employer who, without sufficient cause, fails to pay to a co-operative society the amount deducted from its employee within a period of fourteen days.
- Any officer who willfully fails to handover custody of books, accounts, documents, records, cash, security and other property belonging to a co-operative society to an authorised person.
- Any person who adopts corrupt practices before, during or after the election of members of the board or office bearers.

APPLICATION TO MULTI-STATE CO-OPERATIVE SOCIETIES

The provisions of this part shall apply to the multi-state co-operative societies and these will come under the ambit of the Central Government.

Application to Union Territories

The provisions of this part shall apply to the UTs. The President may direct that the provisions of this part shall not apply to any Union territory or part thereof as he may specify in a notification (Article 243 ZS).

Continuance of Existing Laws

Any provision of any law relating to co-operative societies in force in a state immediately before the commencement of the Constitution (97th Amendment) Act, 2011, which is inconsistent with the provisions of this part, shall continue to be in force until amended or repealed or until the expiration of one year from such commencement, whichever is less.

Articles Related to Co-operative Societies

Articles	Description
Article 243 ZH	Definitions
Article 243 ZI	Incorporation of Co-operative Societies
Article 243 ZJ	Number and Term of Members of Board and its Office Bearers
Article 243 ZK	Election of Members of Board
Article 243 ZL	Supersession and Suspension of Board and Interim Management
Article 243 ZM	Audit of Accounts of Co-operative Societies
Article 243 ZN	Convening of General Body Meetings
Article 243 ZO	Right of a Member to Get Information
Article 243 ZP	Returns
Article 243 ZQ	Offences and Penalties
Article 243 ZR	Application to Multi-state Co-operative Societies
Article 243 ZS	Application to Union Territories
Article 243 ZT	Continuance of Existing Laws

In order to realise the objective of equality the Constitution makes special provisions for Scheduled Castes (SCs), Scheduled Tribes (STs) and the Other Backward Classes (OBCs).

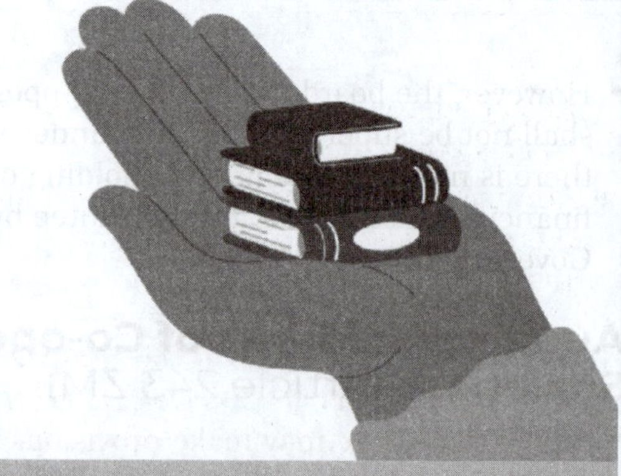

Chapter Thirty Six

Special Provisions for Certain Classes

CONSTITUTIONAL PROVISIONS

- These special provisions and privileges are contained in Part XVI of the Indian Constitution from Articles 330 to 342(A).
- They are related to the followings :
  - Reservation in Legislatures
  - Special Representation in Legislatures
  - Reservation in Services and Posts
  - Educational Grants
  - Appointment of National Commissions
  - Appointment of Commissions of Investigation
- All these provisions suggest that India is a welfare state, committed to the welfare and development of its people in general and vulnerable sections in particular.

Special Provisions can be classified into the following broad categories :

Special Provisions

Permanent and Temporary

Some of them are a permanent feature of the Constitution, while some others continue to operate only for a specified period.

Protective and Developmental

Some of them aim at protecting these classes from all forms of injustice and exploitation, while some others aim at promoting their socio-economic interests.

- The vulnerable sections in India includes Scheduled Castes, Scheduled Tribes, Other Backward Classes, Women, Minorities, Disabled and Children.
- The mere Right to equality or the guarantee of Universal Adult Franchise is not sufficient for the welfare of these people or groups.
- Social and economic democracy is also necessary for the ideal of political democracy, so there should not only be a powerful constitutional machinery to protect the interests and rights of the weaker sections of the society, but special schemes and programmes should also be implemented for their welfare, development and empowerment.

Scheduled Castes

- Scheduled Castes (SCs) are people belonging to those castes, races which have been or may in future be specified in a list in accordance with Article 341 of the Constitution.
- In traditional terms, these are the people who were considered outcastes are categorised as untouchables.
- They have remained extremely marginalised and poor on socio-economic parameters.

Scheduled Tribes

- Scheduled Tribes (STs) are people belonging to tribes or tribal communities specified in the list of such tribes as per Article 342 of the Constitution.
- The term Adivasis or Scheduled Tribes literally means original inhabitants.
- There are communities which lived and often continue to live in close association with forests.

According to Census 2011, around 8% of India's population is Adivasi.

- Adivasis are not a homogeneous population, there are over 500 different Adivasi groups in India.

Measures and Safeguards to Uplift the Condition of SCs and STs

The Constitution of India prescribes certain protective measures, safeguards and welfare measures for Scheduled Castes.

Constitutional Provisions

- In Part-XVI of the Indian Constitution, from Article 330 to Article 342A, special provisions has been made for some classes like Scheduled Castes, Scheduled Tribes, Backward Classes and other Indians.
- These provisions include reservation of seats in the Lok Sabha and State Assemblies, reservation in jobs and posts, Constitution of National Commissions, educational grants.
- The Constitution safeguards their interests with the objective of promoting their educational interests and removing social disabilities.
- The Untouchability (Offences) Act was passed in 1955. Its provisions were made more stringent and its scope was enlarged by amending it in 1976. The new Act was named as Protection of Civil Rights Act.
- In 1989, another Act called Scheduled Castes and Scheduled Tribes Prevention of Atrocities was passed.

Reservations and Affirmative Action

- The Constitution of India provides for reservation in educational institutions and public employment to Scheduled Castes and Scheduled Tribes in proportion of their population.
- The Constitution of India provides for reservation in Lok Sabha, (Article 330) State Assemblies (Article 332) and Local self-government institutions in proportion of their population.
- 15% for SCs and 7% for STs in Centre, percentage of reserved seats in states vary with the population of SCs and STs in the state.
- Originally, this provision of reservation was to operate for ten years (i.e., up to 1960) only.
- But this duration has been extended continuously since then by ten years each time.
- Now, under the 104th Amendment Act of 2019, this provision of reservation is to last until 2030.
- In Part XVI of the Indian Constitution, special provisions has been made in relation to Scheduled Castes and Tribes and Other Backward Classes in Sections 330 to 342A.

Fundamental Rights Provisions

- Article 14 proclaims equality before law and equal protection of law for all.
- Article 15 (1) prohibits discrimination on grounds of race, caste, sex, religion or place of birth.
- Article 17 of the Constitution abolishes untouchability and forbids its practice in any form.

Directive Principles of State Policy Provisions

- Article 38 and Article 46 (Directive Principles of State Policy) specifically aim at securing social justice to the deprived sections of the population.
- According to the 82nd Constitutional Amendment Act, 2000, arrangements have been made to reduce the minimum marks for SC or ST persons in any examination for appointment to Central or State Government posts or to reduce the criteria of evaluation in promotion.

NATIONAL COMMISSION FOR SCs AND STs

- With a view to provide safeguards against the exploitation of SCs and STs and to promote and protect their social, educational, economic and cultural interests, special provisions were made in the Constitution.
- For effective implementation of various safeguards provided in the Constitution for the SCs and STs and various other protective legislations, the Constitution provided for appointment of a Special Officer under Article 338 of the Constitution.
- The functions of the Commission for SCs and STs broadly corresponded with those of the Commissioner for SCs and STs.
- The functions of the Multi-Member Commission set-up in 1978 were modified by Ministry of Welfare's Resolution and the Commission for SCs and STs was renamed as the National Commission for Scheduled Castes and Scheduled Tribes.
- In 1978, a proposal was moved for Amendment of Article 338 of the Constitution (46th Amendment) for replacing the arrangement of one member system with a multi-member system.

- Therefore, the first Commission for SCs and STs was set-up as a National level advisory body to advise the government on broad policy issues and levels of development of Scheduled Castes and Scheduled Tribes in 1978.
- 65th Constitutional Amendment Act, 1990 provided for the establishment of a high level multi-member National Commission for SCs and STs and this constitutional body report to the Commissioner for SCs and STs set-up under the resolution of 1987.
- Again the 89th Amendment Act, 2003 bifurcated the combined National Commission for SCs under Article 338 and National Commission for STs under Article 338(A).

National Commission for SCs

- The separate National Commission for SCs came into existence in 2004. According to Article 338 (2), it consists of a Chairperson, a Vice-Chairperson and three other members.
- They are appointed by the President and their conditions of service and tenure of office are also determined by the President.
- The Chairman of Commission enjoy the status of a Union Cabinet Minister.

Functions and Duties of the Commission

- Clause (5) of Article 338 holds that following shall be the duty of the Commission.
  - To investigate and monitor all matters relating to the safeguards provided for the Scheduled Castes under the Constitution or under any other law and to evaluate the working of such safeguards.
  - To inquire into specific complaints with respect to the deprivation of rights and safeguards of the Scheduled Castes.
  - To participate and advise on the planning process of socio-economic development of the Scheduled Castes and to evaluate the progress of their development.
  - To present reports on the working of those safeguards to the President annually and at such other times as the Commission may deem fit.
  - To make recommendations mentioning measures that should be taken by the Union or any States for the protection, welfare and socio-economic development of the Scheduled Castes.
  - To discharge such other functions in relation to the protection, welfare and development and advancement of the Scheduled Castes as the President may subject to the provisions of any law made by Parliament by rule specify.

Report of the Commission

- The Commission can present its annual report to the President whenever it thinks fit. The President also sends this report to the Governors of the respective states.
- Which shall be laid on the table of the Legislature of the State and shall be accompanied by a memorandum explaining the action taken or proposed to be taken on the recommendations relating to the State and if any such recommendation has been rejected, the reasons for the rejection.

Powers of the Commission

The Commission has all the powers of a civil court trying a suit while, inquiring into any complaint and in particular in respect of the following matters, namely

- summoning and enforcing the attendance of any person from any part of India and examining him on oath.
- requiring the discovery and production of any documents.
- receiving evidence on **affidavits**.
- requisitioning any public record or copy thereof from any court or office.
- issuing commissions for the examination of witnesses and documents.
- any other matter which the President may by rule, determine.

National Commission for STs

- The National Commission for Scheduled Tribes (NCST) was established by amending Article 338 and inserting a new Article 338(A) in the Constitution through the 89th Constitutional Amendment Act, 2003.
- The tenure of Chairperson, Vice-Chairperson and Members of the Commission is three years from the date of assumption of the charge by each of them.

Functions of the Commission

- To investigate and monitor matters relating to safeguards provided for Scheduled Tribes, under the Constitution or under other laws or under government order, to evaluate the working of such safeguards.
- To inquire into specific complaints relating to rights and safeguards of Scheduled Tribes.

- To participate and advise in the planning process relating to socio-economic development of Scheduled Tribes and to evaluate the progress of their development under the Union and any state.
- To submit report to the President about working of safeguards and measures required for effective implementation of programmes/schemes relating to welfare and socio-economic development of Scheduled Tribes.
- To discharge such other functions in relation to Scheduled Tribes as the President may subject to the provisions of any law made by Parliament, by rule specify.

Report of the Commission

- The Commission presents an annual report to the President. It can also submit a report as and when it thinks necessary.
- The President place all such reports before the Parliament alongwith a Memorandum, explaining the action taken or the reasons for the non-acceptance of the recommendations made by the Commission.
- The report pertaining to State Government may also be forwarded by the President to the State Governor, who shall place it before the State Legislature alongwith a Memorandum explaining actions taken or reasons for non-acceptance of its recommendations.

Constitutional Provisions

- Provisions were made in the Constitution for all-round development and cultural and political security of Scheduled Tribes like- Article 15(4), 15 (5), 17, 23, 24, 25 (2) (29), under Fundamental Rights and 330, 332, 334 (regarding reservation) and under Article 371.
- In order to implement the Constitutional protection mentioned in the Constitution through rules and laws, some legal protection acts were made, in which provisions were made for Scheduled Castes and Scheduled Tribes, which are as follows :
  - Minimum Wages Act, 1948
  - Protection of Civil Rights Act, 1955
  - Bonded Labour System Act, 1976
  - Scheduled Castes and Scheduled Tribes (Prevention of Atrocities) Act, 1989
  - Extension of Panchayats to Scheduled Areas (PESA) Act, 1996
  - Forest Rights Act, 2006, etc.

Scheduled Castes and the Scheduled Tribes (Prevention of Atrocities) Act, 1989

- The Act distinguishes several levels of crimes against Scheduled Castes and Scheduled Tribes and make them punishable offence.
- It lists types of humiliation that are both physically and morally shameful and seek to punish those who
  - force a member of a Scheduled Caste or a Scheduled Tribe to drink or eat any inedible or distasteful substance.
  - forcibly removes clothes from the person of a Member of a Scheduled Caste or a Scheduled Tribe or parades him/her naked or with painted face or body or commits any similar act, which is derogatory to human dignity.
- It lists actions that dispossess Dalits and Adivasis of their limited resources or which force them into performing slave labour.
- Thus, the Act sets out to punish anyone who :
  - wrongfully occupies or cultivates any land allotted to, a Member of a Scheduled Caste or a Scheduled Tribe.
  - gets the land allotted to him transferred.
- It recognises that crimes against Dalit and tribal women are of a specific kind and therefore, seeks to penalise anyone who:
  - assaults or uses force on any woman belonging to a Scheduled Caste.
  - intent to dishonour her.

Tribal Rights and the 1989 Act

- The 1989 Act defends tribe's right to occupy land that was traditionally their own.
- Adivasis are often unwilling to move from their land and are forcibly displaced.
- Activists have asked that those who have forcibly encroached upon tribal land should be punished under this law.
- The Act confirms what has already been promised to tribal people in the **Constitution**, that land belonging to tribal people cannot be sold to or bought by non-tribal people.
- In cases, where this happened, the Constitution guarantees the **Right of Tribal People to** repossess their land.

Special Schemes and Programmes

- In accordance with the constitutional provisions and directives of the Government of India and all states have been formulating and implementing various schemes and programmes for upliftment of SCs and STs.
- These programmes are related to education, skill formation, creating job opportunities and development of the areas in which these people are concentrated.

Special Schemes in Education

- Seats in educational institutions are reserved for SCs and STs in percentage of their respective population.
- A Book Bank Scheme has been launched to provide text books required for the students pursuing medical and engineering degrees, agricultural, veterinary and polytechnic courses.
- Girls Hostel Scheme was started for the purpose of providing residential facilities to tribal girls in pursuit of education.
- Various Scholarship Schemes for students including pre-matric, post-matric and higher education.

Special Schemes in Employment

- Seats for SCs and STs are reserved in public employment in proportion of their population.
- Coaching and allied scheme for various competitive examinations for recruitment in Union Public Service Commission (UPSC), State Public Service Commission (SPSC), Public Undertakings, Banking Service, etc.
- State Scheduled Castes Development Corporation to uplift the SCs/STs population living below poverty line.

Tribal Cooperative Marketing Development Federation of India

- It was set-up in 1987 with the prime objective of providing marketing assistance and remunerative prices to ST communities.
- It protects these communities from private traders, who exploit their minor forest produce and surplus agricultural produce.

Baba Saheb Ambedkar Foundation

- This foundation was set-up in 1992. It has been entrusted with the responsibility to manage, administer and carry on schemes and programmes identified during the centenary birth celebrations of Dr. BR Ambedkar.
- Some of the awards under this scheme are :
    - Dr Ambedkar National Award for social understanding and upliftment of weaker section.
    - Dr Ambedkar International Award for social change, harmony, equity, justice and human dignity for the exploited and the under privileged.

OTHER BACKWARD CLASSES

- The Constitution of India uses the word Backward Class. It refers to a group of people having general characteristics of backwardness.
- Article 340 of the Constitution empowers the government to appoint a commission to investigate into conditions of Other Backward Classes (OBCs) and make recommendations for their development.
- The Constitution of India does not specify which groups constitute Backward Classes.
- The Government of India appointed two Backward Classes Commissions for deciding the criteria to identify Backward Classes on the basis of communities or castes.

Kaka Kalelkar Commission

- The First Backward Classes Commission was appointed in 1953 under the Chairmanship of Kaka Saheb Kalelkar. The Commission used four criteria for identifying the Backward Classes :
    - Low social position in the traditional caste hierarchy of Hindu society.
    - Lack of general educational advancement among the majority of a caste/community.
    - Inadequate or lack of representation in government services lack of representation in trade, commerce and industry.
- The Kalelkar Commission on above basis identified 2399 castes and communities as Backward Classes. The government did not accept the recommendations of this Commission.

Mandal Commission

- The Second Backward Classes Commission was appointed in 1978 under the Chairmanship of BP Mandal.
- The Commission formulated 11 indicators i.e., four on caste based social backwardness, three on educational backwardness and four on economic backwardness.

- The Commission stated that the backwardness of these groups was related to caste. It identified 3,743 castes as backward on the basis of decided indicators.
- These castes came to be known as Other Backward Castes (OBCs). The Commission recommended reservation of 27% of jobs for OBCs in central services, public sector undertakings, nationalised banks, universities and affiliated colleges and government aided firms in the private sector.
- The Commission also recommended for economic and occupational development of the OBCs. In August 1990, Government of India announced the acceptance of Mandal Commission's recommendations.

93rd Amendment Act, 2006

Through the 93rd Amendment Act of the Constitution, 2006, provision for reservation was made for socially and educationally backward classes for admission in private and non-government aided educational institutions.

National Commission for Backward Classes (NCBC)

- 102nd Constitutional Amendment Act, 2018 provides constitutional status to the National Commission for Backward Classes (NCBC).
- 102nd Constitutional Amendment Act inserted two new Articles in the Constitution of India i.e., Articles 338(B) and 342(A).
- The Amendment also brings the changes in Article 366.
- Article 338(B) provides authority to NCBC to examine complaints and welfare measures regarding socially and educationally Backward Classes.
- Article 342(A) empowers President to specify socially and educationally Backward Classes in various States and Union Territories.

Composition of the Commission

- It is a multi-member body consisting of five members i.e., Chairperson who is or has been a Judge of Supreme Court or High Court or a social scientist.
- Two persons having special knowledge in matters relating to Backward Classes and a Member-Secretary who is or has been an officer of the Central Government in the rank of a Secretary.
- All are nominated by Central Government and hold office for a term of three years.

Functions of the Commission

- To examine requests for inclusion of any class of citizens as a Backward Class in the Central lists of Backward Classes.
- To hear complaints of over inclusion or under inclusion advise to the Central Government.
- To advise the Central Government in revision of list of Backward Communities.

Schemes/Programmes for the Welfare of Other Backward Classes

Government of India has launched several schemes for welfare and development of Other Backward Classes which are :

- 27% reservation in educational institutions and public employment.
- Pre-Examination Coaching to coach candidates belonging to OBCs whose parent's/guardians annual income less than ₹ 1 lakh.
- Hostels Schemes for OBC boys and girls
- Pre-metric Scholarships
- Post-metric scholarships
- Assistance to Voluntary Organisations The scheme involves the voluntary sector to improve the educational and socio-economic conditions of the OBCs to get them gainfully employed.

Special Representation for Anglo-Indians in Legislatures

- Before 2020, the President nominated two members from the Anglo-Indian community to the Lok Sabha, if the community was not adequately represented.
- Similarly, before 2020, the Governor of a state also nominated one member from the Anglo-Indian community to the State Legislature Assembly, if the community was not adequately represented.
- Originally, this provision of special representation was to operate for ten years (i.e., up to 1960) only. But this duration has been extended continuously since then by ten years each time. The last extension up to 2020 was made by the 95th Amendment Act, 2009.
- However, the 104th Amendment Act, 2019, has not extended further the operation of this provision.

Economically Weaker Section (EWS)

- The Parliament amended the Constitution of India (103rd Amendment) Act, 2019 to provide for a 10% reservation in education and government jobs in India for a section of the General category candidates.

- Qualifying criteria for 10% quota:
  - All members of whose family together earn less than ₹ 8 lakh per annum.
  - Have less than 5 acres of agricultural land.
  - Do not possess a residential flat of area 1000 sq. ft or larger.
  - Do not possess a residential plot of area 100 yards or more in notified Municipalities and 200 yards or more in areas other than notified Municipalities.

Introduction of Article 15 (6) and Article 16 (6)

- The amendment introduced economic reservation by amending **Articles 15** and **16**.
- It inserted **Article 15 (6)** and **Article 16 (6)** in the Constitution to allow reservation for the economically backward in the unreserved category.
  - **Article 15(6)** Up to 10% of seats may be reserved for EWS for admission in educational institutions. Such reservations will not apply to minority educational institutions.
  - **Article 16(6)** It permits the government to reserve up to 10% of all government posts for the EWS.
- It was enacted to promote the welfare of the poor not covered by the 50% reservation policy for Scheduled Castes (SCs), Scheduled Tribes (STs) and Socially and Educationally Backward Classes (SEBC).
- It enables both the Centre and the States to provide reservations to the EWS of society.

MINORITIES

- The Indian Constitution recognised that the culture of the majority influences the way in which society and government might express themselves.
- In such cases, size can be a disadvantage and led to the marginalisation of the relatively smaller communities.
- Thus, safeguards are needed to protect minority communities against the possibility of being culturally dominated by the majority.

National Minority Commission

It is a statutory body set-up in 1993 under the National Commission for Minorities Act, 1992. It is under the Ministry of Minority Affairs.

Composition of the Commission

- The commission consists of Chairperson, Vice-Chairperson and five members.
- Total of seven persons to be nominated by the Central Government from amongst persons of eminence, ability and integrity.
- Each member holds office for a period of three years from the date of assumption of office.

Powers and Functions of the Commission

- The commission shall, while performing any of the functions is vested with powers to regulate its own affairs. It has all the powers of a civil court in respect of the following matters :
  - summoning and enforcing the attendance of any person from any part of India and examining him on oath.
  - requiring the discovery and production of any document.
  - receiving evidence on affidavits.
  - requisitioning any public record or copy thereof from any court or office.
  - issuing commissions for the examination of witnesses and documents.
  - any other matter may be prescribed.
- The commission shall perform all or any of the following functions :
  - To evaluate the progress of the development of minorities under the Union and States.
  - To monitor the working of the safeguards provided in the Constitution and in laws enacted by Parliament and the State Legislatures.
  - To make recommendations for the effective implementation of safeguards for the protection of the interests of minorities by the Central Government or the State Governments.
  - To look into specific complaints regarding deprivation of rights and safeguards of the minorities and take up such matters with the appropriate authorities.
  - To make case studies to be undertaken into problems arising out of any discrimination.
  - To conduct studies, research and analysis on the issues relating to socio-economic and educational development of minorities.
  - To suggest appropriate measures in respect of any minority to be undertaken by the Central Government or the State Governments.

- To make periodical or special reports to the Central Government on any matter pertaining to minorities and in particular difficulties confronted by them.

Sachar Committee

- The Sachar Committee was a seven-member High Level Committee in India established in March 2005.
- Aim of the committee is to examine the socio-economic and educational status of the Muslim community in India. The availability of data on religion was useful in highlighting the relative deprivation of minorities.
- Main recommendations of the committee The Committee made a number of recommendations to address the status of the Muslim community in India, including
  - Set up an Equal Opportunity Commission to look into grievances of deprived groups like minorities.
  - Create a nomination procedure to increase the participation of minorities in public bodies.
  - Establish a delimitation procedure that does not reserve constituencies with a high minority population for SCs.
  - Increase employment share of Muslims, particularly where there is a great deal of public dealing.
  - Work out mechanisms to link madrasas with the higher secondary school boards.

Linguistic Minority

A linguistic minority is a group of people whose mother tongue differs from that of the states or part-majority states. The Constitution ensures that the rights of linguistic minorities are protected.

Appointment of the Special Officer for Linguistic Minorities

- Initially, there was no provision in the Indian Constitution for a Special Officer for Linguistic Minorities. The States Reorganisation Commission (1955-1955) issued a suggestion in this regard later on.
- As a result, in Part XVII of the Constitution, the Seventh Constitutional Amendment Act of 1956 added a new Article 350-B. The following provisions are included in this article :
  - He or she will be appointed by India's President.
  - The Special Officer's job would be to look into any and all issues relating to the Constitution's protections for linguistic minorities.

Powers, Functions and Responsibilities

- In pursuance of the provision of Article 350-B of the Constitution, the office of the Special Officer for Linguistic Minorities was created in 1957. He/she is designated as the Commissioner for Linguistic Minorities.
- The Commissioner has his headquarters at New Delhi. He/she has four regional offices at Belgaum (Karnataka), Chennai (Tamil Nadu), Kolkata (West Bengal) and Prayagraj (Uttar Pradesh). Each is headed by an Assistant Commissioner.
- The Commissioner is assisted at headquarters by Deputy Commissioner and an Assistant Commissioner.
- He/she maintains liaison with the State Governments and Union Territories through nodal officers appointed by them.
- At the Central level, the Commissioner falls under the Ministry of Minority Affairs.
- Hence, he/she submits the annual reports or other reports to the President through the Union Minority Affairs Minister.

Articles related to Special Provisions for Certain Classes

Article	Subject-Matter
Article 330	Reservation of seats for Scheduled Castes and Scheduled Tribes in the House of People
Article 331	Representation of Anglo-Indian community in the house of the people
Article 332	Reservation of seats for SCs and STs in the Legislative Assemblies of the states
Article 333	Representation of Anglo-Indian Community in the Legislative Assemblies of the states
Article 334	Reservation of seats and special representation to cease after seventy years
Article 335	Claims of SCs and STs to services and posts
Article 336	Special Provision for Anglo-Indian Community in certain services
Article 337	Special Provision with respect to educational grants for the benefit of Anglo-Indian Community
Article 338	National Commission for Scheduled Castes
Article 338A	National Commission for Scheduled Tribes
Article 338B	National Commission for Backward Classes
Article 339	Control of the Union over the administration of Scheduled Areas and the welfare of STs
Article 340	Appointment of a commission to investigate the conditions of Backward Classes
Article 341	Scheduled Castes
Article 342	Scheduled Tribes
Article 342A	Socially and educationally Backward Classes

There are special provisions for eleven states in India. These provisions were not existed in original Constitution but incorporated subsequently by various amendments.

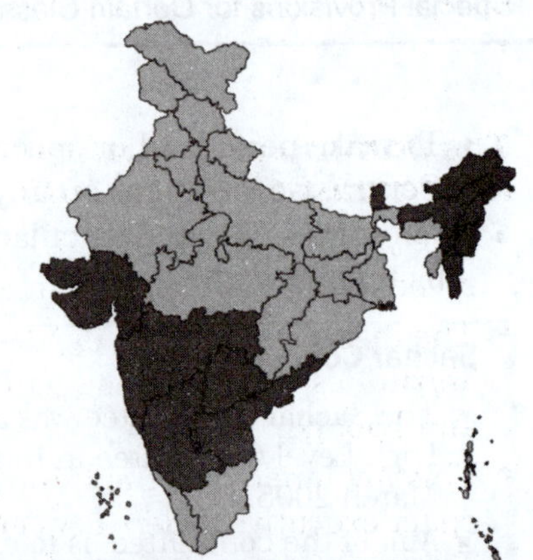

Chapter Thirty Seven

Special Provisions for Certain States

Articles 371 to 371(J) in Part XXI of the Constitution contain special provisions for twelve states *viz*, Maharashtra, Gujarat, Nagaland, Assam, Manipur, Andhra Pradesh, Telangana, Sikkim, Mizoram, Arunachal Pradesh, Goa and Karnataka. The intention behind them is to meet the aspirations of the people of backward regions of the states or to protect the cultural and economic interests of the tribal people of the states or to deal with the disturbed law and other condition.

Articles Related to Special Provisions for States

Article	Subject-Matters
Article 370	Provisions related to Jammu and Kashmir (abolished now).
Article 371	Special Provisions with Respect to Maharashtra and Gujarat.
Article 371 (A)	Special Provisions with Respect to Nagaland.
Article 371 (B)	Special Provisions with Respect to Assam.
Article 371 (C)	Special Provisions with Respect to Manipur.
Article 371 (D)	Special Provision with Respect to Andhra Pradesh and Telangana.
Article 371 (E)	Establishment of Central University in Andhra Pradesh.
Article 371 (F)	Special Provisions with Respect to the State of Sikkim.
Article 371 (G)	Special Provisions with Respect to the State of Mizoram.
Article 371 (H)	Special Provisions with Respect to the State of Arunachal Pradesh.
Article 371 (I)	Special Provisions with Respect to the State of Goa.
Article 371 (J)	Special Provisions with Respect to the State of Karnataka.

Provisions for Jammu and Kashmir

- Article 370 of the Constitution of India was described as a 'temporary provision' that granted Jammu and Kashmir a special autonomous status within India.
- The Amendment of Article 370 on 5th August, 2019, which effectively nullified the special status of Jammu and Kashmir.

Removal of Article 370 and Article 35(A)

- In accordance with the authority afforded by Clause (1) of Article 370 of the Indian Constitution, the President of India issued the Constitution (Implementation to Jammu and Kashmir) order 2019 on 5th August, 2019.
- Article 370 has been abolished and Jammu and Kashmir is fully covered by the Indian Constitution.

Article 370

- The instrument of Accession, which Maharaja Hari Singh signed in 1947 gave rise to Article 370.
- Jammu and Kashmir was exempted from the Indian Constitution by Article 370 of the Indian Constitution, which was enacted on 17th October, 1949.

Article 35(A)

- Article 35(A), which derives from Article 370 is distinctive in that it only appears in Appendix I and not in the main body of the Constitution.
- Permanent residents of Jammu and Kashmir were given exceptional privileges and rights under Article 35(A).

The Jammu and Kashmir Reorganisation Act, 2019

- The Jammu and Kashmir Reorganisation Act 2019, reconstitute the state of Jammu and Kashmir.
- The disputed region is divided into two Union Territories (UTs), namely Jammu and Kashmir and Ladakh.
- This Act empowers the Central Government to enact executive orders concerning both the Union Territories.

Current Status of Jammu and Kashmir

- The Union Territory of Jammu and Kashmir is administered under Article 239 of the Constitution of India.
- Article 239(A) originally formulated for the Union Territory of Puducherry will also apply to Jammu and Kashmir.

Provisions for Maharashtra and Gujarat

- Under Article 371, the President is authorised to provide that the Governor of Maharashtra and that of Gujarat would have special responsibility for
    - the establishment of separate development boards for
      (i) Vidarbha, Marathwada and the rest of Maharashtra,
      (ii) Saurashtra, Kachchh and rest of Gujarat,
    - making a provision that a report on the working of these boards would be placed every year before the State Legislative Assembly,
    - the equitable allocation of funds for developmental expenditure in these areas,
    - an equitable arrangement providing adequate facilities for technical education and vocational training and adequate employment opportunities in the state services in these areas.

Provisions for Nagaland

- The State of Nagaland was formed after passing of State of Nagaland Act, 1962 by Parliament.
- Article 371(A) makes the following special provisions for Nagaland.
- The Governor of Nagaland shall have special responsibility for law and order in the state so long as internal disturbances caused by the hostile Nagas continue.
- In the discharge of this responsibility, the Governor, after consulting the Council of Ministers, exercises his individual judgement and his decision is final.
- This special responsibility of the Governor shall cease when the President so directs.
- The Governor has to ensure that the money provided by the Central Government for any specific purpose is included in the demand for a grant relating to that purpose and not in any other demand moved in the State Legislative Assembly.
- A Regional Council consisting of 35 members should be established for the Tuensang district of the State.
- The Governor should make rules for the composition of the council, manner of choosing its members, their qualification, term, salaries and allowances, the procedure and conduct of business of the council, the appointment of officers and staff of the council.
- These provisions will be applicabe for a period of 10 years from the formation of Nagaland or for such further period as the Governor may specify on the recommendation of the Regional Council, the following provisions would be operative for the Tuensang district.
    - The administration of the Tuensang district shall be carried on by the Governor.
    - The Governor shall in his discretion arrange for equitable distribution of money provided by the Centre between Tuensang district and the rest of Nagaland.
    - Any Act of Nagaland Legislature shall not apply to Tuensang district unless the Governor so directs on the recommendation of the regional council.
    - The Governor can make regulations for the peace, progress and good government of the Tuensang district.
    - The Legislative Assembly can have 46 members and therefore provisions of Article 170 are not applicable in case of Nagaland.
    - A Minister to be appointed from amongst the members representing Tuensang district in the Nagaland Legislative Assembly for Tuensang affairs in the State Council of Ministers.
    - The final decision on all matters relating to Tuensang district shall be made by Governor in his discretion.

Provisions for Assam

- By 22nd Constitution Amendment Act, 1969, Article 371(B) was included. It provides for the special provisions for the State of Assam.
- Under Article 371(B), the President is empowered to provide for the creation of a committee of the Assam Legislative Assembly consisting of the members elected from the tribal areas of the state and such other members as he may specify.
- He may also direct Governor to look after the functions and responsibility of the committee as well.

Provisions for Manipur

- The 27th Amendment Act of Constitution added Article 371(C). This provides special provisions for the State of Manipur that was given statehood in 1971.
- Article 371(C) makes the following special provisions for Manipur.
  - The President is authorised to provide for the creation of a committee of the Manipur Legislative Assembly consisting of the members elected from the hill areas of the State.
  - The President can also direct that the Governor shall have special responsibility to secure the proper functioning of that committee.
  - The Governor should submit an annual report to thesubject to the jurisdiction of the tribunal.
  - The President may abolish the tribunal when he is satisfied that its continued existence is President regarding the administration of the hill areas.
  - The Central Government can give directions to the State Government as to the administration of the hill areas.

Ethnic Communities in Manipur

- The people of Manipur are grouped into three main ethnic communities -Meiteis those inhabiting the valley and **29 major tribes** in the hills dividing into two main ethno- denominations, namely **Nagas** and **Kuki-Chins**.
- The Naga group consists of Zeliangrong, Tangkhul, Mao, Maram, Maring and Tarao.
- The Chin-Kuki group consists of Gangte, Hmar, Paite, Koireng, Kom, Anal, Chothe, Lamgang, Koirao, Thangal, Moyon and Monsang.

Provisions for Andhra Pradesh and Telangana

- Articles 371(D) and 371(E) were inserted by the 32nd Constitutional Amendment Act, 1973.
- These articles deals with the special provisions with respect to Andhra Pradesh.
- In 2014, by the Andhra Pradesh Reorganisation Act, 2014, these provisions were extended to Telangana.
- Under the Article 371 (D), the following provisions are mentioned.
  - The President is empowered to provide for equitable opportunities and facilities for the people belonging to different parts of the state in the matter of public employment and education and different provisions can be for various parts of the state.
  - The President may order the State Government to establish civil posts in local cadres for various sections of the state.
  - The President may create an Administrative Tribunal in the state to deal with certain disputes and grievances relating to appointment, allotment or promotion to civil posts in the state.
  - The tribunal is to function outside the purview of the State High Court.
  - No court (other than the Supreme Court) is to exercise any jurisdiction in respect of any matter not necessary.
- Article 371 (E) empowers the Parliament to provide for the establishment of a Central University in the state.

Provisions for Sikkim

- The 36th Constitutional Amendment Act of 1975, made Sikkim a full-fledged State of the Indian Union. It included a new Article 371(F) containing special provisions with respect to Sikkim.
- The major provisions are as follows :
  - The Sikkim Legislative Assembly is to consist of not less than 30 members. One seat is allotted to Sikkim in the Lok Sabha and Sikkim forms one Parliamentary Constituency.
  - For the purpose of protecting the rights and interests of the different sections of the Sikkim population, the Parliament is empowered to provide for the number of seats in the Sikkim Legislative Assembly which may be filled by candidates belonging to such sections and

- Delimitation of the Assembly Constituencies from which candidates belonging to such sections alone may stand for election to the assembly.
- The Governor shall have special responsibility for peace and for an equitable arrangement for ensuring the social and economic advancement of the different sections of the Sikkim population.
- In the discharge of this responsibility, the Governor shall act in his discretion, subject to the directions issued by the President.

Status of Sikkim after Independence

- After independence, Sikkim joined India as a subsidiary state in 1974 by the 35th Amendment Act of the Constitution.
- The Government of India was responsible for the defense and foreign affairs of Sikkim, while the internal administration of Sikkim was conducted by the King Chogyal.
- A large proportion of Sikkim's population was Nepalese, the population of Nepali origin sought and received the support of the Indian Government in protest against Chogyal's hostility towards the rule of the minority elite group Lepcha-Bhutia.
- After this, in the year 1974, the first democratic election was held for the Sikkim Legislative Assembly and Congress succeeded.

Provisions for Mizoram

- Article 371 (G) was added to the Constitution of India by 53rd Amendment Act, 1986. It provides for special provisions for Manipur on the basis of North-East Region (Reorganisation) Act, 1971 that was carved out of Assam.
- Article 371 (G) specifies the following special provisions for Mizoram.
  - The Acts of Parliament relating to the following matters would not apply to Mizoram unless the State Legislative Assembly so decides
    - Religious or social practices of the Mizos,
    - Mizo customary law and procedure,
    - Administration of civil and criminal justice involving decisions according to Mizo customary law, and
    - Ownership and transfer of land.
    - The Mizoram Legislative Assembly is to consist of not less than 40 members.
  - Mizoram was included under Sixth Schedule areas and known as Mizo Autonomous Districts (Chakma, Mara and Lai).

Provisions for Arunachal Pradesh

- It was earlier known as North-East Frontier Agency (NEFA). The 55th Constitutional Amendment Act, 1986 added Article 371 (H). It made special provisions for the State of Arunachal Pradesh. It received statehood in the year 1987.
- Under Article 371 (H), the following special provisions are made for Arunachal Pradesh.
  - The Governor for Arunachal Pradesh shall have special responsibility for law and order in the State.
  - In the discharge of this responsibility, the Governor, after consulting the Council of Ministers, exercises his/her individual judgement and his decision is final.
  - This special responsibility of the Governor shall cease when the President so directs.
  - The Arunachal Pradesh Legislative Assembly is to consist of not less than 30 members.

Provisions for Goa

- Goa was initially given the status of a Union Territory after annexing it from Portuguese. Goa received statehood in 1987. A special provision was added through 56th Constitutional Amendment Act, 1987.
- It included Article 371(I) that contains special provisions for Goa.
- Article 371(I) provides that the Goa Legislative Assembly is to consist of not less than 30 members.

Provisions for Karnataka

- By 98th Amendment Act, 2012, Article 371 (J) was included in the Constitution.
- Article 371 (J) of the Constitution empowers the Governor of Karnataka to take steps to develop the Hyderabad-Karnataka region.
- This region includes the districts of Gulbarga, Bibar, Raichur, Koppal, Yadgir and Bellary.

Election is an inherent feature of the democratic political system in India. The elections are conducted by the Election Commission of India.

Chapter Thirty Eight

Electoral Process and Political Dynamics

ELECTION

- An election is a contest between political parties for getting people's support.
- The party which gets the support of largest number of people comes to power and forms the government.
- In democratic countries, almost all adult citizens irrespective of property, education, race, religion, gender or other differences have been given right to vote which is popularly known as Universal Adult Franchise/Suffrage.
- India is a Parliamentary democracy and its governance draws its ultimate legitimacy from the will of the people which they exercise by participating in elections.
- Article 326 of the Indian Constitution provides that the Election to the House of People and to the Legislative Assembly of every state shall be on the basis of adult suffrage. In India, every person who is not less than 18 years of age (earlier upto 1989 it was 21 years) has right to vote.

The Electoral System

- In India, different electoral systems are adopted for elections to the Lok Sabha and State Assemblies, Offices of President, Vice-President and to the Council of States and Legislative Councils.
- Part XV of the Indian Constitution (Articles 324 to 329) outlines provisions related to the country's electoral system.

Plurality System *(First Past the Post)*

- In this system, the country is divided into single member territorial constituencies, usually of equal size.
- Under this system, voters select a single candidate, usually by marking against the candidate's name.
- The voter who receives the highest number of votes, may be less than even half the votes polled, is declared the winner.
- This system is popular in United Kingdom and India.
- This system is easy to operate. It established a clear link between representatives and constituencies.

Majority System

- The majority system requires that a person declared winner in a single member constituency wins by a clear majority that is getting more than 50% votes. This can be obtained by two methods:
  - Second Ballot System In this system, there are single candidate constituencies and single choice voting as in first past the post system. In this system, to win the first ballot, a candidate requires an overall majority of votes cast. If no candidate gains a first ballot majority, a second run off ballot is held between the leading two candidates. This system is popular in France.
  - Alternative Voting System In this system, there are single member constituencies. There is preferential voting in this system. Voters rank the candidates in order of preference and winning candidate must gain minimum 50% of all votes cast. If no

candidate secures 50% in first preference, the candidate with least number of votes is eliminated and his votes are redistributed according to preferences. This continues until one candidate has a majority.

Proportional Representation System

- According to this system, the parties should be represented in an assembly or Parliament in direct proportion to their overall electoral strength.
- In this system, any party or group would secure representation in proportion to the support it has among the electors.
- This is achieved by two systems :

Single Transferable Vote System

- In this system, there are multi-member constituencies. Party may put forward as many candidates as there are seats to fill in each constituency.
- Electors vote preferentially, as in alternative voting system and candidates are elected if they achieve a quota.
- Quota is the minimum number of votes needed to elect, the stipulated number of candidates calculated according to the following formula :

$$\text{Quota} = \frac{\text{Total number of votes polled} + 1}{\text{Total number of seats to be filled up} + 1} + 1$$

- The votes are counted according to first preference. If not all the seats are filled, the candidate securing least number of votes is eliminated and the votes are redistributed according to second preference and so on, until all seats are filled.
- This system is used to elect members of Rajya Sabha and Legislative Councils in India.

Party List System

- In this system, either the entire country is treated as a single constituency or it is divided into a number of large multi-member constituencies. Parties compile lists of candidates in descending order of preference and the list is presented to voters.
- Electors vote for parties, not for candidates in this system.
- Parties are allocated seats in direct proportion to the votes they gain in the election. They fill these seats from the party list.
- A minimum percentage can be fixed to exclude small parties. This is the only potentially pure system of proportional representation and therefore is fair to all parties.

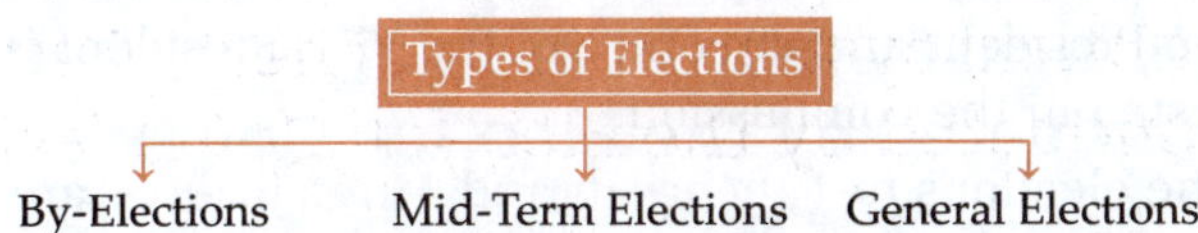

- By-Elections An election which is held out of normal schedule is called by-election. By-election takes place, if a representative from a constituency dies while in office and if the office falls vacant because of any other reason like resignation.
- Mid-term Elections If the Lok Sabha or any of the State Assemblies is dissolved before the expiry of its full term and elections are held to constitute a new house, it is called mid-term elections.
- General Elections A general election is a political voting election where generally all or most members a given political body are chosen. These are usually held for a nation, state or territory's primary legislative body. First general elections for Lok Sabha were held in the year 1951.
- In general elections of Kerala in 1982, Electronic Voting Machines (EVMs) were used for the first time in Indian elections. In the year 2004, EVMs were used in general elections of India in all 543 seats.

Conditions for Disqualification of Voter

Constitution prescribes certain conditions under which a citizen becomes disqualified to be a voter :

- A citizen with unsound mind
- A citizen punished for election related offences
- A person is not a citizen of India

ELECTION COMMISSION

- The elections are governed by Part XV from Articles 324 to 329. Besides, the Representation of People Act, 1950 governs the provisions related to the preparation of electoral rolls and voter registration.
- The RPA 1951 and Delimitation Commission, 1952 in India also govern the elections.
- The Election Commission of India is a permanent, independent and constitutional body to ensure free and fair elections in the country.
- Elections are held regularly at all three tiers of political structure i.e., Union, States and Local bodies. The Election Commission was established in accordance with the Constitution on 25th January, 1950.

- Under Article 324(1), the power of the superintendence, direction and conduct of elections to the Parliament, the State Legislatures, the office of the President and the office of the Vice-President is vested in the commission.
- The elections to Panchayats and Municipalities are vested in the State Election Commission as given in Articles 243(K) and 243(Z)(A) respectively.

Composition and Appointment

- As per Article 324 of Indian Constitution, Chief Election Commissioner shall be appointed by the President.
- Under Article 324(2), the Election Commission shall consist of the Chief Election Commission and such number of other Election Commission if any, as the President may from time to time fix.
- The appointment of the Chief Election Commissioners and other Election Commissioners shall subject to the provisions of any law made in that behalf of Parliament.
- The President may also appoint after consultation with the Election Commission such Regional Commissioners under Article 324(4) as he/she may consider necessary to assist the Election Commission in the performance of its functions.
- The Election Commission at present has Chief Election Commissioner and two Election Commissioners appointed by the President.

Removal from Office

- The Chief Election Commissioner shall not be removed from his office except in like manner and on the like grounds as a Judge of the Supreme Court.
- Any other Election Commissioner or a Regional Commissioner shall not be removed from office except on the recommendation of the Chief Election Commissioner.
- They may also resign from their office by addressing resignation to the President.

Chief Election Commissioners Till Date

Chief Election Commissioners	Tenures
Sukumar Sen	21st March, 1950 to 19th December, 1958
KVK Sundaram	20th December, 1958 to 30th September, 1967
SP Sen Verma	1st October, 1967 to 30th September, 1972
Nagendra Singh	1st October, 1972 to 6th February, 1973
T Swaminathan	7th February, 1973 to 17th June, 1977
SL Shakdhar	18th June, 1977 to 17th June, 1982
RK Trivedi	18th June, 1982 to 31st December, 1985
RVS Peri Sastri	1st January, 1986 to 25th November, 1990
VS Ramadevi	26th November, 1990 to 11th December, 1990
TN Seshan	12th December, 1990 to 11th December, 1996
MS Gill	12th December, 1996 to 13th June, 2001
JM Lyngdoh	14th June, 2001 to 7th February, 2004
TS Krishnamurthy	8th February, 2004 to 15th May, 2005
BB Tandon	16th May, 2005 to 29th June, 2006
N Gopalaswami	30th June, 2006 to 20th April, 2009
Navin Chawla	21st April, 2009 to 29th July, 2010
SY Quraishi	30th July, 2010 to 10th June, 2012
VS Sampath	11th June, 2012 to 15th January, 2015
HS Brahma	16th January, 2015 to 18th April, 2015
Nasim Zaidi	19th April, 2015 to 5th July, 2017
Achal Kumar Jyoti	6th July, 2017 to 22nd January, 2018
Om Prakash Rawat	23rd January, 2018 to 1st December, 2018
Sunil Arora	2nd December, 2018 to 12th April, 2021
Sushil Chandra	13th April, 2021 to 12th May, 2022
Rajiv Kumar	13th May, 2022 to Till Date

***As on March, 2023**

Term of Office

- The Chief Election Commissioner or an Election Commissioner holds office for a term of six years or until they attain the age of 65 years, whichever is earlier from the date on which he assumes his office.
- They enjoy and receive similar salary and perks as that of a Judge of Supreme Court.
- In case of difference of opinion amongst the Chief Election Commissioner and two other Election Commissioners, the matter is decided by the commission by majority.

Independence of Election Commission

- The Chief Election Commissioner is provided with the security of tenure. He cannot be removed from his office except in same manner and on the same grounds as a Judge of the Supreme Court. Thus, he does not hold the office till the pleasure of President, though he is appointed by him.
- The service conditions of the Chief Election Commissioner cannot be varied to his disadvantage after his appointment.

- Any other Election Commissioner or Regional Election Commissioners cannot be removed from office except on the recommendation of the Chief Election Commissioner.
- The Constitution has not prescribed term and qualification of the Members of Election Commission.
- The Election Commissioners are not prohibited from further employment under Union or the State Governments.

Powers and Functions of Elections Commission

The powers and functions of the Election Commission can be classified into following three categories:

Administrative

- To determine the electoral constituencies throughout the country on the basis of the Delimitation Commission Act of Parliament.
- To prepare and periodically revise electoral rolls and to register all eligible voters.
- To notify the dates and schedules of elections and to scrutinise nomination papers. To grant recognition to political parties and allot election symbols to them.
- To appoint officers for inquiring into disputes relating to electoral arrangements.
- To determine the code of conduct to be observed by the political parties and the candidates at the time of elections.
- To cancel polls in the event of rigging, booth capturing, violence and other irregularities.

Advisory

- Under the Constitution, the commission also has Advisory Jurisdiction in the matter of post election disqualification of sitting members of Parliament and State Legislatures.
- It advises the President and the Governor on matters relating to disqualification of Members of Parliament and the State Legislature.
- The opinion of the commission in all such matters is binding.
- To advise the President whether the elections can be held in a state under the President's rule.

Quasi-Judicial

- To act as a court for settling disputes related to granting of recognition to political parties and allotment of election symbols to them.
- The commission has the power to disqualify a candidate who has failed to lodge an account of his election expenses within the time limit and in a manner as prescribed by the law.
- The commission also has the power for removing or reducing the period of such disqualification as also other disqualification under the law.
- In the cases of persons found guilty of corrupt practices at elections which come before the Supreme Court and High Courts are also referred to the commission for its opinion.
- The opinion of the commission in all such matters is binding on the President or the Governor.

Judicial Scrutiny

- The election to either House of Parliament or to both House of State Legislatures shall be called in question only by means of an **election petition**.
- This can be filed before the High Court in respect to elections to the **Parliament** and **State Legislature**.
- The validity of any law relating to the delimitation of constituencies or the allotment of seats to such constituencies, made or purporting to be made under Article 327 or Article 328 shall not be called in question in any court.
- According to Article 329, bar to interference by courts in electoral matters not withstanding anything in this Constitution.

ELECTION PROCEDURE

- India has adopted a single member constituency system under the political territory of the country. It is divided into such number of constituencies that each constituency has approximately similar base of population.
- Every constituency elects only one representative on the basis of one person one vote.
- The winner is decided by the maximum number of votes won amongst the contestants.

Timing of Elections

- Elections for the Lok Sabha and State Legislative Assemblies are held every five years unless called earlier.
- The President can dissolve the Lok Sabha and call for elections before the five-year term ends if the government loses the confidence of the Lok Sabha, and no alternative government can be formed.

Election Schedule

- Once the five-year term is complete, or the legislature is dissolved, the Election Commission initiates the process for holding elections.
- The Constitution mandates that elections must be concluded within six months of the last session of the dissolved Lok Sabha.
- The Election Commission typically announces the election schedule through a press conference weeks before the formal process begins.
- At this point, the Model Code of Conduct comes into effect, providing guidelines for candidates and political parties.

Formal Process

- The election process officially begins with the issuance of notifications calling for the electorate to elect members.
- Candidates have a week to submit their nominations after the notification is issued.
- Returning Officers carefully examine each nomination. Any nomination that does not meet the required criteria may be rejected after a brief hearing is conducted.
- Candidates who have been validly nominated can withdraw within two days after scrutiny.

Selection of Candidates

- Political parties field and support their candidates and organise their campaigns.
- Every political party announces specific programmes and promises to implement these programmes in case it comes to power. In case of an independent candidate, since, there is no political party to support him, the candidate has to organise her/his election campaign independently.

Nomination

- After selection, the candidates have to file their nominations to the election offices, which are appointed by the Election Commission. There is a last date for filing the nomination papers. After all nominations have been filed, there is a process called scrutiny.
- Scrutiny is done to check whether the information given in the nomination papers is correct or not.
- If there is a doubt in the information filed or it is found that the candidate is not eligible, her/ his nomination paper is rejected.
- Once the scrutiny is over, candidates are given a date for withdrawal to ensure that there is as little wastage of votes as possible.

Universal Adult Suffrage

- According to **Article 326**, the elections to the House of the People and to the Legislative Assembly of every states shall be on the basis of adult suffrage.
- Every person who is a citizen of India and who is not less than **18 years** of age and is not disqualified under this Constitution or any law shall be entitled to be registered as a voter at any such election.
- Originally, the minimum age for voting was **21 years** but by the **61st Constitutional Amendment Act**, it was reduced to **18 years**.

General Electoral Roll

- According to Article 325, there shall be one General Electoral Roll for every territorial constituency for election to either House of Parliament or to the either House of the Legislature of a State.
- No person shall be ineligible for inclusion in any such roll for any such constituency on grounds only of religion, race, caste, sex or any of them.
- The electoral roll is a list of all people in the constituency who are registered to vote in Indian Elections.
- Only those people with their names on the electoral roll are allowed to vote.
- The electoral roll is normally revised every year to include the names of those who have attained 18 years of age.
- It is also updated to remove the names of those who have died or moved out of a constituency.

Allotment of Symbols

- The Election Commission allots symbols to each political party and makes sure that they are not similar to avoid the confusion among voters.
- These symbols become well-known that people easily recognise the political party.

Process of Polling and Counting of Votes

- A schedule for the election is created by the Election Commission of India.
- In a certain constituency, a specific day has been set aside for voting.
- Currently, votes are cast using Electronic Voting Machines (EVMs), which display candidate's names and party emblems.
- After voting is completed, all EVMs are sealed and transported to a single location where they are stored until the results are tabulated.
- In India, an Electronic Voting Machine was introduced to address the ballot box issue.

> **Electronic Voting Machine**
>
> An Electronic Voting Machine (EVM) is a simple electronic device used to record votes in place of ballot papers and boxes which were used earlier in conventional voting system. The advantages of the EVM over the traditional ballot paper/ ballot box system are given here :
>
> - It eliminates the possibility of invalid and doubtful votes which, in many cases, are the root causes of controversies and election petitions.
> - It makes the process of counting of votes much faster than the conventional system.
> - It reduces to a great extent the quantity of paper used thus saving a large number of trees making the process eco-friendly.
> - It reduces cost of printing (almost nil) as only one sheet of ballot paper is required for each Polling Station.

Campaigning

- It is the process by which a candidate tries to persuade (To convince someone to do or believe something by using logic, reasoning or conversation) the voters to vote for her/ him rather than others.
- It is done through various channels, which include meetings, podcasts, speeches, processions, etc. Campaigning stops 48 hours before the close of polling time.

Media Coverage

- In order to make the electoral process as transparent as feasible, the media are encouraged and provided with facilities to cover the election, although subject to maintaining the secrecy of the vote.
- The media personnel receive special access passes at polling stations to cover the election's voting and counting procedures.

Election Petition

- The procedure for challenging the result of a Parliamentary election is known as an election petition.
- According to Section 80(A) of the Representation of the People Act, 1951, the High Court shall have the competence to hear petitions for elections brought under Article 329(b) of the Constitution.
- An election petition can be filed on one or more of the following grounds :
  - A returned candidate (a candidate who has been declared elected) was not qualified on election day.
  - That a returned candidate or his election representative engaged in unethical behaviour.
  - The High Court where the petition was filed declares the returned candidate's election to be invalid if any of these are true. Within 45 days of the declaration of the results, any candidate or elector may submit a petition.

Election Machinery

- The Election Commission is assisted by Deputy Election Commissioners. They are drawn from the civil service and appointed by the commission with tenure system.
- At the state level, the Election Commission is assisted by the Chief Electoral Officer who is appointed by the Chief Election Commissioner in consultation with the State Government.

Officers Appointed by the Election Commission of India

The Chief Electoral Officer (CEO)

- The Chief Electoral Officer of a State/Union Territory is authorised to supervise the election work in the State/Union Territory subject to the overall superintendence, direction and control of the Election Commission.
- The Election Commission of India nominates an officer of the Government of the State/Union Territory as the Chief Electoral Officer in consultation with that State Government/Union Territory Administration.

Returning Officer (RO)

- The Returning Officer of a Parliamentary or Assembly Constituency is responsible for the conduct of elections in the Parliamentary or Assembly constituency concerned as per Representation of the People Act, 1951.
- The Election Commission of India nominates or designates an officer of the government or a local authority as the Returning Officer for each of the Assembly and Parliamentary Constituencies in consultation with the State Government/Union Territory Administration.

The Electoral Registration Officer

- The Electoral Registration Officer (ERO) is responsible for the preparation of electoral rolls for a Parliamentary/Assembly Constituency.
- The Election Commission of India, in consultation with the State/Union Territory Government, appoints an officer of the government or the local authorities as the Electoral Registration Officer.

The District Election Officer (DEO)

- The District Election Officer supervises the election work of a district and he is committed to make the election process free and fair.
- The Election Commission of India nominates or designates an officer of the State Government as the District Election Officer in consultation with the state.

Presiding Officer (DEO)

- The District Election Officer appoints the Presiding Officers and the Polling Officers.
- The Presiding Officer with the assistance of Polling Officers conducts the poll at a polling station.

Observers

- The Election Commission of India nominates officers of government as observer for Parliamentary and Assembly Constituencies.
- They perform such functions as are entrusted to them by the commission. Earlier, the appointment of observers was made under the plenary powers of the commission.

Constitutional Provisions Related to Elections

Article No.	Subject-Matter
Article 324	Superintendence, direction and control of elections to be vested in an Election Commission.
Article 325	No person to be ineligible for inclusion in or to claim to be included in a special, electoral roll on grounds of religion, race, caste or sex.
Article 326	Elections to the House of the People and to the Legislative Assemblies of states to be on the basis of adult suffrage.
Article 327	Power of Parliament to make provisions with respect to elections to Legislatures.
Article 328	Power of Legislature of a state to make provision with respect to elections to such Legislature.
Article 329	Bar to interference by courts in electoral matters.
Article329(A)	Special provision as to elections to Parliament in the case of Prime Minister and Speaker (Repealed).

Major Electoral Reforms in India

- Lowering of Voting Age The 61st Constitutional Amendment Act (1988) reduced the voting age from 21 years to 18 years for the Lok Sabha and Assembly Elections.
- Electronic Voting Machines (EVM) The use of EVMs in elections was enabled by a provision in 1989. The EVMs were used for the first time in the general elections (entire state) to the Assembly of Goa in 1999.
- Elector's Photo Identity Card (EPIC) The use of Electors' Photo Identity Cards by the Election Commission made the electoral process simple, smoother and quicker. A decision was taken by the Election Commission in 1993 to issue photo identity cards to electors throughout the country to check bogus voting and impersonation of electors at elections.
- Prohibition on Sale of Liquor No liquor or other intoxicants shall be sold or given or distributed at any shop, eating place or any other place, whether private or public, within a polling area during the period of 48 hours ending with the hour fixed for the conclusion of poll.
- Disqualification on Conviction for Violating the National Honours Act, 1971 This shall lead to disqualification of the person for six years from contesting to the Parliament and the State Legislatures.
- Time Limit for By-Elections Now, by-elections are to be held within six months of occurrence of the vacancy in any House of Parliament or a State Legislature.

- The Ceiling on Election Expenditure The commission has put a cap on spending of individual candidates'. For the Lok Sabha elections, the amount is ₹ 50-70 lakh (depending on the state they are contesting the Lok Sabha seat from) and ₹ 20-28 lakh for an Assembly Election.
- Contestants Restricted to Two Constituencies A candidate would not be eligible to contest from more than two Parliamentary or Assembly Constituencies at a general election or at the by-elections which are held simultaneously.
- Restriction on Exit Polls The Election Commission issued a statement before the Lok Sabha saying that exit poll results could be broadcast only after the final phase of the elections were over. This was done to avoid prospective voters from being misguided or prejudiced in any manner.
- Voting through Postal Ballot In 2013, the Election Commission decided to expand the ambit of postal ballot voting in the country. Previously, only Indian staff in missions abroad and defence personnel in a limited way, could vote *via* postal ballots.
- Now, there are six categories of voters who can use the postal ballot i.e., service voters, special voters, wives of service voters and special voters; voters subjected to preventive detention, voters on election duty and notified voters.
- Facility to Opt to vote through Proxy In 2003, this facility was provided to the service voters belonging to the armed forces and members belonging to a force to which provisions of the Army Act apply.
- Such service voters who opt to vote through proxy have to appoint a proxy in a prescribed format and intimate the Returning Officer of the constituency.
- Declaration of Criminal Antecedents, Assets, etc., by Candidates In 2003, the Election Commission issued an order directing every candidate seeking election to the Parliament or a State Legislature to furnish on his nomination paper the information on the following matters :
  - Whether the candidate has been convicted or acquitted or discharged in any criminal offence in the past.
  - Prior to six months of filing nomination, whether the candidate is accused in any pending case or any offence punishable with imprisonment for two years or more.
  - The assets (immovable, movable, bank balances, etc.,) of a candidate and his/her spouse and that of dependants.
  - The educational qualifications of the candidate and furnishing of any false information in the affidavit is now an electoral offence punishable with imprisonment upto six months or fine or both.

NOTA

- None Of The Above (NOTA) is a ballot option designed to allow the voter to indicate disapproval of all of the candidates in a voting system.
- It was introduced in India following the 2013 Supreme Court directive in the People's Union for Civil Liberties *v/s* Union of India judgement.
- However, NOTA in India does not provide for a Right to Reject, the candidate with the maximum votes wins the election irrespective of the number of NOTA votes polled.

- Introduction of VVPAT Voter Verifiable Paper Audit Trail (VVPAT) is a method of providing feedback to voters using EVMs. A VVPAT is intended as an independent verification system for voting machines designed to allow voters to verify that their vote was cast correctly and to provide a means to audit the stored electronic results.
- It contains the name of the candidate for whom vote has been cast and symbol of the party/ individual candidate.
  - The EVM, fitted with VVPAT, field-tested for the first time in September, 2013 by election in the Noksen Assembly Constituency in Nagaland. VVPAT system is introduced in 8 of 543 Parliamentary Constituencies as a Pilot Project in Indian General Election, 2014.
  - Transparency in Election Funding Government introduced an Electoral Bond Scheme in January 2018, purportedly with a view to cleansing the prevailing culture of political sponsorship.

Electoral Bond

- An electoral bond is type of promissory note that can be bought by any Indian citizen or company incorporated in India from the select branches of State Bank of India.
- The government notified it on 29th January, 2019. A donour with a KYC complaint account can purchase the bond which are issued in multiple of 1000 upto one crore.
- Any party that is registered under Section 29(A) of the Representation of Peoples Act, 1951 and has secured atleast one per cent of the votes polled in the most

recent General or Assembly Elections is eligible to receive electoral bonds.

- These electoral bonds will not bear the name of the donour and will be valid only for fifteen days.
- An electoral bond is designed to be a bearer instrument like a promissory note, it will be similar to a bank note that is payable to the bearer on demand and free of interest.

Committees on Electoral Reforms

Committees	Descriptions
Jayaprakash Narayan Committee	• The committee recommended that the voting age be reduced from **21** to **18 years**. • Procedure of selecting the Chief Election Commissioner should be reformed.
Tarkunde Committee	• The committee recommended that the Election Commission should be a **three member** body and minimum age for voting should be **18 years**.
Dinesh Goswami Committee	• The committee recommended that the question of disqualification of members should not be decided by the **Speaker** or the **Chairman** of the concerned House. It suggested for the changes in the voting pattern and shift to proportional representation of the list system. The suggestions are : — There should be fresh delimitation on the basis of 1981 Census and there should be a provision for rotation of reserved seats for **Scheduled Castes** and **Scheduled Tribes**. — The age of candidates for assembly seats should be reduced to **21 years** and for the Council it is **25 years**.
Vohra Committee, 1993	• It pointed out the Nexus between criminals, politicians and bureaucrats in India. • Agencies like CBI, IB and RAW expressed that this **criminal network** virtually runs a parallel government.
Indrajit Gupta Committee	• The committee recommended that the state funding should be in kind i.e., no financial support is to be given to parties and part of financial burden of the parties is to be initially borne by the states. • Only the recognised political parties should be given state support. The political parties should compulsory submit their annual accounts to the Income Tax Department.
Jeevan Reddy Committee	• The commission advocated a total ban on splits and mergers of political parties during the term of the Lok Sabha or Legislative Assembly. Once a member has been elected on a ticket of a particular recognised party, then he should remain in that party till the dissolution of the House or till the end of his membership by resignation or otherwise. • To curb the criminalisation of politics, the commission has suggested that a person should be disqualified from contesting elections to the Lok Sabha or an Assembly if a court has ordered framing of charges in respect of offences listed in the Representation of the People Act, 1951.

POLITICAL PARTIES

- Political parties are voluntary organisations or group of people who have common views and who try to get political power to advance the nation.
- Political parties maintain a continuous connection between the people and those who represent them either in government or in the opposition.
- Political parties in India are essential to the functioning of the political system.

Political Party System

- Generally, there are three kinds of party system in the world, i.e., **one-party system, two-party system and multi-party system**.
- There are many countries in the world where there is one-party system. Erstwhile Soviet Union and Yugoslavia had single party system. Similarly, China has one-party system.
- The United Kingdom (UK), the United States of America (USA), Australia and New Zealand have two-party system. There may exist other parties, but their role is generally insignificant. e.g., in UK, there are two main parties, the Conservative Party and the Labour Party. In the USA, the two main parties are the Republican Party and the Democratic Party.
- In a multi-party system, many parties participates in the competition for gaining power.
- India, Japan, France, Germany and Switzerland have multi-party system. On the basis of ideologies, political parties can be classified as left, right and centre. Left parties have radical ideologies, right parties have reactionary and conservative ideologies and centre parties have liberal ideologies.

Functions of Political Parties

- Parties select candidates to contest elections for public office. The choice offered to voters is thus, the choice offered by parties.
- Since, the parties provide the candidates for election, it follows that parties also provide the nation's political leaders. In the Parliamentary area, political parties provide the government and opposition.
- The party or coalition which wins a majority of seats in the lower house (i.e., Lok Sabha in India), forms the government.
- The party or parties which win the second largest number of seats becomes the opposition.

- Parties articulate philosophies and develop policies.
- All parties have methods of debating issues and formulating policies to be presented to the electorate during election campaigns.
- In government or opposition, parties utilise these policy-making processes to determine their attitude to legislation and issues of the day.
- Parties are ultimately responsible for the structure of the machinery of government.

Recognition of Political Parties

- Based on their poll results, the Election Commission recognises political parties as National or State parties and registers them for electoral use.
- The remaining parties are merely designated as registered unrecognised parties.
- A party's eligibility for certain privileges, including as the distribution of party emblems, the allotment of time for political broadcasts on state-owned television and radio stations and access to electoral registers is determined by the commission's recognition of the party.
- The recognised parties also just need one proposer to file the nomination.
- Each national party is granted a unique symbol that it uses exclusively across the nation.
- Similar to this, each state party is given a symbol that can only be used in the state or states where it has been recognised.
- On the other hand, a registered-unrecognised party has the option of selecting a free symbol from a list.
- In other words, the commission classifies some symbols as free symbols for other candidates and others as reserved symbols for candidates supported by recognised parties.

Recognition as a National Party

A party is recognised as a national party, if one or more of the following requirements are fulfilled :

- If it wins four Lok Sabha seats from any state or states and receives **6%** of the valid votes cast in atleast four states in a general election for the Lok Sabha or Legislative Assembly.
- If it gains **2%** of Lok Sabha seats in a general election, with candidates elected from three states and if it is recognised as a state party in four states.

National Parties as on March, 2023

Political Parties	Symbol (Image)	Years	Founder's Name
Indian National Congress		1885	AO Hume
Communist Party of India (Marxist)		1964	AK Gopalan
Bharatiya Janata Party		1980	Atal Bihari Vajpayee
Bahujan Samaj Party		1984	Kanshi Ram
Aam Aadmi Party (AAP)		2012	Arvind Kejriwal
National People's Party		2013	PA Sangma

Recognition as a State Party

- A party is recognised as a state party in a state, if one or more of the following conditions are met :
  - If it secures two seats in the State Assembly and 6% of the valid votes cast in the state during a general election for the Legislative Assembly of the state in question.
  - If it wins 3% of the Legislative Assembly seats or three seats in the Assembly, whichever is greater.
  - If it wins one seat in the Lok Sabha for every 25 seats or any fraction, thereof allotted to the state at a general election to the Lok Sabha from the state concerned.
  - if it wins 6% of the valid votes cast in the state in a general election to the Lok Sabha from the state concerned.
  - If it secures 8% of the total valid votes polled in the state at a general election to the Lok Sabha from the state or to the Legislative Assembly of the state.

Classification of Regional Parties

- The various regional parties in India can be classified into the following three categories :
  - Those regional parties that are founded on the local ethnicity or culture. Shiromani Akali Dal, the National Conference, the Dravida Munnetra

Kazhagam (DMK) and All India Anna Dravida Munnetra Kazhagam (AIADMK), Telugu Desam, Shiv Sena, the Mizo National Front, Jharkhand Mukti Morcha and others are among them.

- Regional parties without a strong national electoral base but with an all Indian perspective. Examples include the Nationalist Congress Party, Revolutionary Socialist Party, Samajwadi Party, All-India Forward Bloc and Indian National Lok Dal.
- Those regional parties which have been formed by a split in national parties. For example, Bangla Congress, Bharatiya Kranti Dal, Utkal Congress, Kerala Congress, Telangana Praja Samithi, Biju Janata Dal, Rashtriya Janata Dal, Janata Party and so on.

COALITION POLITICS IN INDIA

- In a democratic Parliament, a coalition is created when no single political party can win a majority of votes.
- If two or more parties can come to an agreement on a common programme that does not require too many extreme compromises with their own policies and have enough elected representatives to form a majority, then they can continue to form a government.
- The term coalition refers to the process of joining different components to form a larger entity. A coalition in politics is an alliance of several political parties.
- For nearly 20 years, Congress Party had a majority for a long time and used to win about 45% of the popular vote.
- The accommodative attitude of a several non-Congress groups helped in the formation of coalition government. It was the first time that the Centre got coalition government under the Prime Ministership of Morarji Desai during 1977 phase.

Reasons Behind the Coalition Politics in India

- Growth of Regional Political Parties. Regional parties ability provide credible alternatives to the national party in the states.
- Inability of national parties to give a feeling to the diverse population in India that they are able to adequately represent their differential needs.
- The tendency of the national parties to speak of national level issues and to force coherence in the politics and views on issues, is at odds with our extremely diverse population.

ELECTION LAWS

- Articles 324 to 329 Part XV of the Constitution deals with our country's electoral system.
- The Constitution gives Parliament the authority to establish rules for elections to the Parliament and State Legislatures.
- Parliament passed the Representation of the People Act of 1950, the Representation of the People Act of 1951 and the Delimitation Commission Act of 2002 to provide a legal framework for the conduct of elections.

Representation of People Act, 1950

- The Representation of the People Act of 1950 was enacted to provide for the distribution of seats in the House of People, as well as Members of Legislative Assemblies and Legislative Councils of States.
- The Act is divided into 32 Sections and 8 Parts.

The following **election provisions** are part of the Representation of the People Act of 1950 :

- Allocation of seats in the House of Representatives, **State Legislatures** and State Legislature Councils.
- Delimitation of Parliamentary, Assembly and the Council Constituencies.
- It provides for the electoral rolls for the Parliament, the Assembly and the Council.
- Local government for the purpose of State Legislative Council Elections. Limiting the ability of civil courts to exercise their authority.
- Procedure for filling seats in the Council of States by representatives from **Union Territories**.
- Election officials include Chief Electoral Officers, District Election Officers and Electoral Registration Officers, among others.

Delimiting Constituencies

- Only after consulting the ECI, the President of India may change orders defining constituencies. Seats in the Lok Sabha are reserved for Scheduled Castes (SCs) and Scheduled Tribes (STs).
- The ECI has the power to choose which constituencies in Meghalaya, Mizoram, Nagaland, and Tripura shall be reserved for Scheduled Tribes.

Allocation of Seats

- Articles 81 and 170 of the Constitution of India lay down the maximum number of seats in Parliament and in Legislative Assemblies of States.
- Article 171 of the Constitution of India lays down the maximum and minimum number of seats in the Legislative Council of a State and also specify the various methods in which the seats shall be filled, but the actual number of seats to be filled by each such method has been left to be provided by law.
- Each state is represented in the Lok Sabha to the greatest extent possible in proportion to its population, as determined by census data.

Electoral Rolls

- The 1950 Act allows for the registration on electoral rolls of persons who are ordinarily resident in a constituency.
- This also includes the following:
  - A service requirement, such as being a Member of the Armed Forces, serving outside of their state as an Armed Police Officer or being a Central Government employee stationed outside of India.
  - Certain offices in India as declared by the President in consultation with the ECI. Their wives are also considered to be ordinarily residing in India.

Authority to Enact Laws

- The Act grants the Central Government the authority, which it may then use after consulting with the ECI.
- Additionally, the civil courts are not permitted to contest the validity of any Electoral Registration Officers action relating to electoral roll revision.
- Voting Rights were granted to Indian nationals residing overseas in 2010. They shall be entitled to get their names registered in the electoral roll in Parliament/Assembly Constituencies.

Representation of People Act, 1951

Representation of People Act, 1951 is an Act enacted by the Parliament before first general elections.

The People's Representation Act provides for the actual conduct of elections in India.

- The Act also deals with details like qualification and disqualification of members of both Houses of Parliament and the State Legislatures.
- Rules for the mode of conduct of elections are also highlighted in detail. Salient features of the Act are :
  - Qualifications of Elected Representatives in Parliament and Assembly In addition to the Constitutional requirements, which are outlined in Articles 84 and 173 for the Parliament and Assembly, respectively, the RPA, 1951 also outlines the requirements for representatives.
    - Section 3 of the RPA, 1951 an individual must be an elector in order to be eligible to be chosen as a representative in the Council of States.
    - In accordance with Section 4 of the RPA, 1951, a member of the House of People must be a member of a Scheduled Caste or Scheduled Tribe and a voter in a Parliamentary Constituency, if the seat is reserved for one of those groups.
    - Section 5 of RPA, 1951 deals with the qualification of a member to the Legislative Assembly.
    - The minimum age for becoming MLA/MPs (Lok Sabha) is 25 years.
  - Disqualifications of Elected Representatives in Parliament and Assembly The Constitution's Articles 102 and 191 discuss disqualification, but in addition, the RPA of 1951 stipulated some additional disqualifications that were laid by the Parliament.
  - Section 8 of RPA, 1951 Disqualification on conviction of certain offenses which are mentioned in the Act.
    - Any form of gratification for electors to vote or to refrain from voting.
    - Practices of untouchability, sati, domestic violence, dowry, etc.
    - Promotion of feelings of enmity or hatred between communities.
    - Obtaining any form of assistance from any person who is in service of the government.
    - The offence of bribery or involved in importing or exporting prohibited goods.

◆ According to Section 8 (3) of the Act, if an MP or MLA is convicted of any other crime and sentenced to two years or more in prison, he or she will be disqualified for six years from the date of release.

Election Petitions The RPA of 1951 also addresses election related problems and stipulates how election petitions should be presented. No election may be challenged without an election petition submitted in accordance with the guidelines outlined in **Section 80** of the RPA, 1951. In certain cases, the High Court of the relevant state has Original Jurisdiction.

- **Registering Political Parties** The Election Commission of India is given the authority to register political parties, organisations and bodies in Section 29(A), Part IV (A) of the Representation of People Act. According to specific criteria, RPA 1951, also divides parties into national and state parties.
- **Decriminalising Indian Politics** By forbidding the entry of people with a criminal background into the electoral process, the RPA, 1951 plays a significant role in breaking the politicians, police and criminal nexus (which is one of the greatest threats to the rule of law in India). This decriminalises Indian politics.
- **Accountability** and **Transparency** The RPA, 1951, has an expenditure monitoring mechanism that guarantees the candidate's **transparency** and accountability when using public resources or abusing their position of authority for personal gain.

The Model Code of Conduct

- It is the Election Commission's do's and dont's for political parties and candidates for the period after polls are announced. It has instructions on holding meetings, organising processions and the conduct of parties on polling days. It comes into force immediately after election announcement.
- Main features of code of conduct are :
  - ◆ The Code prohibits parties and candidates from indulging in activities that can cause tension between people of different regions, castes, communities or religions.
  - ◆ Mosques, churches, temples or other places of worship should not be used for election propaganda.
  - ◆ Parties must ensure their supporters do not obstruct functions that other parties organise.
  - ◆ It disallows comments on private lives of leaders or workers of other parties.
  - ◆ No party or candidate is permitted to use any individual's land, building, compound wall, etc, without permission to erect flag-staffs, suspend banners, paste notices, write slogans, etc.
  - ◆ Voters are not to be intimidated or bribed to vote for a party or candidate.
  - ◆ Mandatory for every party and candidate to inform police and local authorities before organising any procession to ensure security measures are taken and steps needed to control traffic and maintain law and order.
  - ◆ Party must provide procession route map. No deviation from route is allowed.

The Restrictions on Ruling Party

- The Code ensures a party in power, at Centre or in State, cannot use official machinery or personnel for electioneering.
- Poll-related advertisement at the cost of public money and misuse of official mass media for coverage of political news and publicity is not allowed.
- The Code ensures other parties get equal opportunity to hold election meetings at public places and use public infrastructure like helipads and government guest house for election.
- From the day an election is announced, the Code prohibits ministers from sanctioning grants and related payments out of discretionary funds.
- Ministers and politicians are barred from laying foundation stones of new projects.
- Adhoc appointments in government or Public Service Undertakings (PSUs) disallowed.

The Code for Polling Day

- Every party must issue badges and I-cards to authorised workers. Unnecessary crowd outside candidate's camp is prohibited, as it can lead to a clash between contesting parties.
- No food or refreshment can be served to voters. The Code mandates no distribution of liquor on polling day or 24 hours before the polls.

Delimitation Act, 2002

- According to Articles 82 and 170 of the Indian Constitution, each state shall be readjusted and shall be divided into Territorial Constituencies (Parliamentary and Assembly Constituencies) on the basis of the 2001 Census, by such authority and in such manner as may be prescribed by law of the Parliament.

- Additionally, according to Articles 330 and 332 of the Indian Constitution, the number of seats set aside for members of the Scheduled Castes and Scheduled Tribes in the House of the People and State Legislative Assemblies would be adjusted in light of the 2001 Census.
- The present delimitation of constituencies has been done on the basis of 2001 Census figures under the provisions of Delimitation Act, 2002.
- Thus, the present constituencies carved out on the basis of 2001 Census shall continue to be in operation till the first Census after 2026.
- Delimitation is the redrawing of the boundaries of Parliamentary or Assembly Constituencies to make sure that there are, as near as practicable, the same number of people in each constituency.

Delimitation Commission

- After coming into force and commencement of the Act, the Central Government constitutes a Delimitation Commission.
- This Delimitation Commission demarcates the boundaries of the Parliamentary Constituencies as per the provisions of the Delimitation Act, 2002.
- The Delimitation Commission is appointed by the President of India and works in collaboration with the Election Commission of India.

It is led by a retired Judge of Supreme Court and includes members from the Election Commission of India and State Election Commissions.

Anti-Defection Law

The Tenth Schedule popularly known as the Anti- Defection Act which was included in the Constitution of India by the 52nd Amendment Act, 1985.

The main aim of this Schedule was to prevent the political defections and to strengthen democracy by bringing stability in politics and make Members of Parliament more responsible and loyal to their parties.

Anti-defection sets the provisions for disqualification of elected members on the grounds of defection to another political party. It was a response to the toppling of multiple State Governments by party hopping MLAs after the general elections of 1967.

Provisions under Anti-Defection Law

The Tenth Schedule includes the following provisions with regards to the disqualification of **MPs** and **MLAs** on the grounds of defection. Grounds for disqualification are :

- If an elected member gives up his membership of a political party voluntarily.
- If he votes or abstains from voting in the House, contrary to any direction issued by his political party without obtaining prior permission of such party and such act has not been condoned by the party within 15 days. If any member who is **independently elected**, joins any party. If any nominated member joins any political party after the end of six months.
- The decision on disqualification questions on the ground of defection is referred to the Speaker or the **Chairman** of the House, and his/her decision is final.
- All proceedings in relation to disqualification under this Schedule are considered to be proceedings in Parliament or the **Legislature of a State** as is the case.

Ground for Defection

- As per the 1985 Act, a defection by one-third of the elected members of a political party was considered a merger.
- But the 91st Constitutional Amendment Act, 2003 changed this and now atleast two-third of the members of a party must be in favour for it to have validity in the eyes of the law.
- The members disqualified under the law can stand for elections from any political party for a seat in the same House.
- The decisions on questions as to disqualification on ground of defection are referred to the Chairman or the Speaker of such House, which is subject to Judicial review.
- The Presiding Officer of a House is empowered to make rules to give effect to the provisions of the Tenth Schedule. All such rules must be placed before the House for 30 days.
- The Presiding Officer can only take up a defection matter in accordance with the established norms after receiving a complaint from a member of the House.

PRESSURE GROUPS

- Pressure Groups are the interest groups which try to secure their interests by influencing the formulation and administration of public policy.
- They are non-partisan organisation which attempt to influence some phases of public life. The role of pressure group is indirect, ordinarily invisible and intermittent yet very important part of administrative system.

- In order to influence legislations, they frequently used techniques that were legal and legitimate, such as lobbying, correspondence, publicity, propagandising, petitioning, public arguing and maintaining contacts.
- Institutional Pressure Group These groups are formally organised which constitutes professionally employed persons. They are part of government machinery and raises its protests with constitutional means. e.g., Bureaucracy, Army, Central Election Committee, etc.
- Anomic Pressure Group These are the group that have analogy with individual self-representation. They may be constitutional or unconstitutional, e.g., ULFA, Naxalites, Kashmir Liberal Front, etc.
- Associational Pressure Group These are organised specialised groups formed for interest articulation but to pursue limited goal, e.g., Trade Union, Student Association, Teachers Association, etc.
- Non-Associational Pressure Group These are the informal groups that include Caste Group, Language Group, Syndicate, Gandhian Group, etc.

Functions and Roles of Pressure Groups

- Pressure Groups bring the interests of the people to the attention of the policy makers and aid in political socialisation.
- They engage in lobbying with the lawmakers for attaining favourable laws or changes into the laws and policies of the state.
- They also try to use the legal system to advance their objectives. They frequently go before the court to have their grievances against the state and other parties resolved.
- Their efforts lead to effective participation of all sections of society in decision making.
- The pressure organisations assist opposition parties in developing constructive criticism of policies taken by the administration.
- The pressure groups are frequently involved in influencing any essential laws, rules, judgements and policies that may be related to their interests.

Major Pressure Groups in India

- The Business Group are independent of political parties and influence planning licensing bodies and economic ministers.
- They help in budget formulation. e.g., Conference of Indian Industries (CII), Association Chamber of Commerce (ACC), Federation of Indian Chamber of Commerce Industry (FICCI).
- Peasant's Organisations It gained power in 1960's. At Central level only one All India Kisan Congress exists. On Territorial basis All Kisan Kamgar, Akil Bharatiya Kisan Sangh. The Bharatiya Kisan Union (BKU) in Western Uttar Pradesh is most significant.
- Student's Organisations They pressurise the government on educational issues and various critical issues. e.g., All Bengal Student Association formed in 1928, The All India Student Federation (AISF) in 1936, Student's Federation of India, National Student Union of India, The Akhil Bharatiya Vidhyarti Parishad, etc.
- Community Associations They are in context to safeguard respective religion. e.g., Schedule Caste Federation, Backward Caste Federation, Vishwa Hindu Parishad, etc.
- Linguistic Groups These pressure groups promote certain languages. e.g. Tamil Sangh, Hindi Protection Parishad, Punjabi Sahit Sabhas, etc.

Difference between Political Parties and Pressure Groups

Political Parties	Pressure Groups
Political parties constitute government and entitled to frame policies and take decisions.	The pressure groups will not constitute government and operate outside the government.
Political parties are formed with the motive to get political power and improve the nation with their policies and practices.	The pressure groups are formed with the motive to fulfill a certain specific need. Accordingly, they emerge and dissolve based on the need only.
The membership of the political party will be open and have a transparent organisational structure.	The membership of the pressure groups has exclusive or selective membership.
Political parties, in general, bring coordination between the Executive, Legislature and Judiciary.	The pressure groups put excess pressure on the Executive, Legislature and to some extent Judiciary to change their opinion.
Political parties generally use constitutional methods to get their desired change.	Pressure groups may use conventional and non-conventional methods (corruption, strike, etc) to get the desired change.
The political parties receive donations from the general public.	The pressure groups receive donations from the local community or from persons having vested interests.

Political concepts and theories introduces political theory by focusing on enduring disputes about the nature of freedom, power, equality, justice, democracy and authority.

Chapter Thirty Nine

Political Concepts and Theories

POLITICAL CONCEPTS

- The state is one of the most fundamental political concepts. It refers to a political organisation with a defined territory, a permanent population, a government, and the capacity to enter into relations with other states.
- In simpler terms, it is the highest form of political authority, often synonymous with the term country.

The concept of the state was explored by multiple political thinkers.

- **Thomas Hobbes** (1588-1679) In his book Leviathan, Hobbes describes the state as a necessary institution to prevent the 'war of all against all'. He argues for a powerful sovereign to maintain peace and order.
- **John Locke** (1632-1704) In Two Treatises of Government, Locke envisions the state as a protector of natural rights (life, liberty and property). His vision of the state is more limited than Hobbes, advocating for a government that serves the people's consent.
- **Jean-Jacques Rousseau** (1712-1778) In 'The Social Contract, Rousseau' discusses the state as an entity created by a social contract to ensure collective freedom. His view of the state focuses on the 'general will' of the people.

- Sovereignty The state possesses absolute authority over its affairs, both domestically (internal sovereignty) and externally (external sovereignty).
- Territory The state controls a specific geographic area with established borders.
- Government The institutions and officials responsible for the administration of public policy and governance.
- Population The people who reside within the territory of the state.

Sovereignty

Sovereignty is the ultimate authority a state has over its territory and the people within it. It can be understood in two ways :

- Internal sovereignty refers to the state's ability to maintain control and order within its own borders.
- External sovereignty concerns the recognition of the state's authority by other states and its freedom from external domination.

Sovereignty refers to the authority of the state over its affairs, with no higher authority :

- Jean Bodin (1530–1596) One of the earliest thinkers to conceptualise sovereignty, Bodin argued for the absolute and indivisible power of the state in his work Six Books of the Commonwealth.
- Hobbes In Leviathan, Hobbes also argues that sovereignty must be absolute to maintain order and prevent chaos, giving full power to the sovereign.
- Rousseau Rousseau has a different take on sovereignty, believing in popular sovereignty where the people, as a collective body, hold supreme authority.

Types of Sovereignty

Absolute Sovereignty
A form of total control by the state, which is not subject to any legal limitations.

Popular Sovereignty
The notion that the people are the ultimate source of authority, and governments are created by the consent of the governed (as seen in democracies).

Democracy

- Democracy is a political system in which the people hold the ruling power, either directly or through elected representatives.
- The word 'democracy' comes from the Greek words demos (people) and kratos (rule).

Democracy is a system of government in which the power lies with the people.

- **John Locke** Locke is considered one of the founding thinkers of modern democracy. His idea of the government as a social contract and the importance of consent from the governed are essential democratic principles.
- **Jean-Jacques Rousseau** Rousseau's idea of direct democracy and the 'general will' is a central aspect of his political philosophy in 'The Social Contract'. He advocated for a form of government where all citizens could participate in law-making.
- **John Stuart Mill** (1806–1873) Mill, in his work On Liberty, argued for individual freedoms and the role of democracy in protecting these freedoms. He was a proponent of representative democracy.

Types of Democracy

- Direct Democracy A system where citizens directly participate in decision-making. This is rare in modern politics but can be seen in referendums.
- Representative Democracy In most modern democracies, citizens elect representatives to make laws and decisions on their behalf (e.g., USA, India).

Power

- Power refers to the ability of an individual or group to influence or control the actions of others.
- In political theory, power can be legitimate (as in a democratic government) or illegitimate (as in a dictatorship or oligarchy).

Types of Power

- **Legitimate Power** Power that is recognised and accepted by the people (e.g., elected officials).
- **Coercive Power** Power exercised through force or threats, often seen in authoritarian regimes.
- **Soft Power** Coined by Joseph Nye, it refers to the ability to influence others through cultural or ideological means, rather than force (e.g., diplomacy, popular culture).

Power in political terms refers to the ability of one actor to influence or control the actions of others.

- **Max Weber** (1864–1920) Weber's theory of power is central to political sociology. He distinguishes between three types of authority (traditional, **charismatic** and legal-rational), emphasising that legitimate power is essential for a stable society.
- **Michel Foucault** (1926-1984) Foucault explored how power is exercised not just by governments but in everyday interactions. His concept of **biopower** discusses how states control populations through institutions and practices.

Authority

Authority is the recognised right to exercise power. While power is the ability to make people do things, authority is the legitimacy that allows individuals or institutions to use that power.

Types of Authority (According to Max Weber)

- **Traditional Authority** Authority based on long-established customs or traditions (e.g., monarchies).
- **Charismatic Authority** Authority based on the personal qualities or charisma of a leader (e.g., revolutionary leaders like Nelson Mandela or Mahatma Gandhi).
- **Legal-Rational Authority** Authority based on legal norms and rules, as seen in modern bureaucratic governments (e.g., elected officials, presidents).
- **Hobbes** In Leviathan, discusses the authority of the sovereign as derived from the social contract. Withou this authority, society would collapse into chaos.

Legitimacy

- Legitimacy is the acceptance of the authority of a governing body by the governed. It means that the people believe their government has the right to rule.

- Legitimacy refers to the general acceptance of the authority of a government or institution.
    - John Locke Locke's concept of legitimacy is based on the consent of the governed. A government is legitimate only if it protects the natural rights of its citizens and governs with their consent.
    - Max Weber Weber's theory of legitimacy revolves around the acceptance of authority by the populace. He argued that legitimacy could come from tradition, charisma, or rational-legal systems.

Sources of Legitimacy

- Tradition Based on long-standing practices and customs (e.g., monarchy).
- Charisma Based on the personal appeal and leadership qualities of a ruler (e.g., charismatic leaders like Martin Luther King Jr.).
- Legal-Rational Based on a system of laws and procedures, such as Constitutions, elections, and representative democracy.

Ideologies

- Political ideologies are comprehensive sets of beliefs about how politics and society should be organised.
- They guide individuals and groups in understanding political processes and shaping policies.

Key Political Ideologies

- Liberalism It emphasises individual freedoms, democracy, and equality before the law. Liberals support free markets but advocate for government intervention in areas like healthcare and education.
- John Locke is a central figure in liberal ideology, advocating for individual rights and limited government intervention.
- John Stuart Mill Mill's work On Liberty supports the liberal notion of protecting individual freedoms, particularly against government intrusion.
- Conservatism Advocates for preserving traditional institutions and values, emphasising stability, authority, and a limited role for government in economic affairs.
- Edmund Burke (1729-1797) Considered the father of conservatism, Burke argued for the preservation of traditions and institutions in Reflections on the Revolution in France.
- Socialism Advocates for public or collective ownership of resources and means of production, seeking to reduce inequality and promote social welfare.
- Karl Marx (1818-1883) Marx, in works like The Communist Manifesto, advocates for the working class to rise against capitalist systems to create a classless society.
- Friedrich Engels (1820-1895) Co-authored The Communist Manifesto with Marx, contributing significantly to socialist ideology.
- Communism A more extreme version of socialism, where private property is abolished, and all economic resources are controlled by the state. The goal is to achieve a classless society.
- Fascism A totalitarian ideology characterised by dictatorial leadership, extreme nationalism, and the suppression of political opposition.
- Benito Mussolini (1883-1945) Mussolini's writings and speeches are central to understanding the ideology of fascism, which promotes nationalism, authoritarianism, and totalitarian control.

Separation of Powers

- The separation of powers is a key principle in democratic governance that divides government responsibilities into distinct branches to prevent any one branch from gaining too much power.
- Baron de Montesquieu (1689-1755) Montesquieu is credited with formulating the theory of separation of powers in The Spirit of the Laws. He argued for dividing government into three branches–legislative, executive, and judiciary–to avoid tyranny.

Three Branches of Government

- **Legislative** Makes the laws (e.g., Parliament or Congress).
- **Executive** Enforces and implements the laws (e.g., President, Prime Minister, Cabinet).
- **Judiciary** Interprets the laws and ensures justice (e.g., Courts).

POLITICAL THEORIES

Realism (International Relations)

- Realism is a dominant theory in international relations that emphasises the competitive and conflictual nature of international politics.
- It posits that states are primarily motivated by self-interest and the desire for power.
- Thucydides Often considered the father of realism, Thucydides analysed the Peloponnesian War, emphasising human nature and power politics.

- Niccolò Machiavelli In The Prince, Machiavelli argued for pragmatic, often ruthless approaches to political leadership and statecraft.
- Hans Morgenthau A 20th-century realist, Morgenthau articulated principles of political realism in Politics Among Nations, arguing that politics is governed by objective laws rooted in human nature.

Liberalism (International Relations)

- Liberalism is a theory that emphasises cooperation, democracy, and the role of international institutions in fostering peace and stability.
- It contrasts sharply with the realism that prioritises power over cooperation.
- Immanuel Kant In Perpetual Peace, Kant argued for a federation of free states that would ensure peace through cooperation and shared democratic principles.
- Woodrow Wilson As US President, Wilson championed liberal internationalism and the League of Nations, emphasising collective security and self-determination.

Marxism

- Marxism is a socio-economic and political theory that analyses class relations and societal conflict. It critiques capitalism and advocates for a classless society where the means of production are communally owned.
- Karl Marx The principal figure behind Marxist theory, Marx co-authored The Communist Manifesto and wrote Das Kapital, where he analysed the capitalist system and its internal contradictions.
- Friedrich Engels Collaborated with Marx and provided significant contributions to Marxist thought, particularly in discussing the role of the state in perpetuating class interests.

Constructivism

- Constructivism is a theory in international relations that emphasises the social construction of reality.
- It posits that the identities and interests of states are shaped by historical and social contexts, rather than simply material factors.
- Alexander Wendt In Social Theory of International Politics, Wendt argues that anarchy is what states make of it, meaning that state behaviour is shaped by social interactions and shared beliefs.
- John Ruggie Ruggie's work on embedded liberalism emphasised how domestic norms and values shape international relations.

Social Contract Theory

- Social contract theory posits that individuals consent to form governments for the protection of their rights and to maintain social order. It explores the legitimacy of governmental authority based on this hypothetical contract.
- Thomas Hobbes In Leviathan, Hobbes argued that in the state of nature, life is "solitary, poor, nasty, brutish, and short", leading individuals to surrender their rights to a sovereign in exchange for security.
- John Locke's Two Treatises of Government argued for a government that is responsible to the people and can be overthrown if it fails to protect natural rights (life, liberty, and property).
- Jean-Jacques Rousseau In The Social Contract, Rousseau argued that true freedom is found in the collective will of the people, which can be expressed through a general will.

Authoritarianism

- Authoritarianism is a form of governance where political power is concentrated in the hands of a single leader or a small elite, with limited political pluralism, individual freedoms, or democratic processes.
- Hannah Arendt In The Origins of Totalitarianism, Arendt explored how authoritarian regimes, particularly Nazi Germany and Stalinist Russia, use ideology and terror to control populations.
- Carl Schmitt A critic of liberal democracy, Schmitt argued that in times of crisis, authoritarian rule is necessary to maintain order and protect the state.

Socialism

- Socialism is a political and economic theory advocating for collective or state ownership of the means of production, distribution, and exchange. It seeks to reduce inequality and provide social welfare through wealth redistribution.
- Karl Marx and Friedrich Engels Their Communist Manifesto argued that history is driven by class struggle, and capitalism would eventually be replaced by a classless, stateless society–communism.
- Rosa Luxemburg Advocated for democratic socialism and critiqued authoritarian tendencies within socialist movements, emphasising the need for democratic freedoms and participatory governance.

Foreign Policy, also known as external policy, is the set of strategies and actions a state employs in its interactions with other states, unions and international entities.

Chapter Forty

Foreign Policy

INDIAN FOREIGN POLICY

The foreign policy of India governs its relations with other countries to promote national interests. It is shaped by various factors such as geography, history, social structure, political organisation, economic conditions, military strength, public opinion and leadership.

Key Principles of Indian Foreign Policy

1. ***Promotion of World Peace***

- India's foreign policy focuses on promoting international peace and security.
- Article 51 of the Indian Constitution directs the state to foster respect for international law, maintain just and honourable relations and encourage the settlement of disputes through arbitration. India believes that peace is essential for global economic development.

2. ***Anti-Colonialism***

- India strongly opposes colonialism and imperialism, viewing them as exploitative systems that hinder global peace.
- India has historically supported liberation movements in Afro-Asian countries like Indonesia, Algeria and Ghana.
- The country continues to oppose new forms of colonialism and imperialism in modern times.

3. ***Anti-Racialism***

- India's foreign policy is committed to opposing all forms of racial discrimination.
- India condemned apartheid in South Africa and cut diplomatic ties with the nation in 1954. The country played a vital role in the liberation movements in Zimbabwe and Namibia.

4. ***Non-Alignment***

- During the Cold War, India chose not to align with either the capitalist group led by the USA or the communist group led by the USSR.
- India's non-alignment policy emphasises an independent approach to foreign policy, without military alliances, while maintaining friendly relations with all countries. Jawaharlal Nehru believed that non-alignment allowed India to play a vital role in avoiding global conflicts.

5. ***Panchsheel***

- Panchsheel refers to the five principles of peaceful co-existence in international relations, which were outlined in the 1954 Indo-China Treaty on Tibet.
- These five principles are :
  - Mutual respect for territorial integrity and sovereignty.
  - Non-aggression.
  - Non-interference in internal affairs.
  - Equality and mutual benefit.
  - Peaceful co-existence
- Panchsheel became widely adopted by several nations and remains a cornerstone of India's diplomatic relations.

6. ***Afro-Asian Bias***

- India has consistently shown a special inclination toward promoting unity and cooperation among Afro-Asian nations.
- India has supported these nations in international organisations and provided assistance for their economic development.
- India's involvement in key Afro-Asian conferences, such as the Bandung Conference (1955), highlights its leadership role in this region.

7. ***Links with Commonwealth***

- India remains a member of the Commonwealth, a voluntary association of former British colonies.
- Despite this, India maintains full sovereignty and independence, with no allegiance to the British Crown.
- India's Commonwealth membership helps foster economic, political and cultural cooperation with other member nations.

8. ***Support to the United Nations*** (UNO)

- India became a member of the UNO in 1945 and has since actively supported its programs and activities.
- India has played a critical role in combating colonialism, imperialism and racial discrimination through the UNO.
- India has also participated in UN peacekeeping missions and continues to advocate for a permanent seat on the UN Security Council.

9. ***Disarmament***

- India supports global disarmament to promote peace and security.
- India has advocated for nuclear disarmament through various international platforms, including the UNO.
- India has refused to sign the Nuclear Non-proliferation Treaty (NPT) and Comprehensive Test Ban Treaty (CTBT), as it views them as discriminatory.
- These treaties allow only a few countries to possess nuclear weapons, which India opposes.

GUJRAL DOCTRINE

- The Gujral Doctrine was a significant milestone in India's foreign policy, proposed by IK Gujral, the then Foreign Minister of India, in 1996.
- The doctrine emphasised India's leadership role in South Asia and suggested a non-reciprocal approach to relations with its smaller neighbours.
- The main idea was that India, as the largest country in the region, should take the initiative to offer unilateral concessions to foster better relations without expecting immediate returns from smaller nations.
- Gujral explained that the doctrine aimed to ensure peaceful relations with India's immediate neighbours, particularly because India had hostile relations with two significant neighbours, Pakistan and China.
- The doctrine is based on five principles for guiding India's foreign relations with its immediate neighbours :
  - (i) Unilateral Concessions India should not demand reciprocity from smaller neighbours like Bangladesh, Bhutan, Maldives, Nepal, and Sri Lanka. It should offer what it can in good faith to maintain good relations.
  - (ii) Non-Use of Territory Against Others No South Asian country should allow its territory to be used for activities harmful to the interests of another country in the region.
  - (iii) Non-Interference Countries should respect each other's internal affairs and not interfere in them.
  - (iv) Respect for Sovereignty South Asian nations must respect each other's territorial integrity and sovereignty.
  - (v) Peaceful Resolution of Disputes All disputes between South Asian countries should be settled through peaceful bilateral negotiations.

NUCLEAR DOCTRINE OF INDIA

- India's Nuclear Doctrine outlines its policy on the use and control of nuclear weapons.
- The doctrine was designed to ensure credible deterrence while maintaining responsible control over the nuclear arsenal.

Key Elements of India's Nuclear Doctrine

- Credible Minimum Deterrent India will maintain a credible and effective nuclear deterrent, but it will be of a minimum size necessary to ensure defence.
- No First Use India pledges not to use nuclear weapons unless first attacked by an adversary using nuclear weapons.

- **Massive Retaliation** In the event of a nuclear attack, India's retaliation will be massive and designed to inflict unacceptable damage on the aggressor.
- **Civilian Control** The use of nuclear weapons can only be authorised by India's civilian leadership, specifically through the Nuclear Command Authority.
- **No Use Against Non-Nuclear States** India will not use nuclear weapons against countries that do not possess nuclear weapons.
- **Response to Biological or Chemical Attacks** India retains the option of using nuclear weapons if attacked with biological or chemical weapons.
- **Export Control and Non-Proliferation** India supports strict controls on the export of nuclear and missile-related materials and remains committed to negotiations on the Fissile Material Cut-off Treaty. India has also maintained a moratorium on nuclear tests.
- **Commitment to Nuclear Disarmament** India continues to support the global goal of nuclear disarmament through verifiable and non-discriminatory treaties.

India's **Nuclear Command Authority** (NCA) is responsible for overseeing nuclear weapons. It consists of two bodies :

- **Political Council** Chaired by the Prime Minister, it is the sole authority that can authorise the use of nuclear weapons.
- **Executive Council** Chaired by the National Security Advisor, it provides inputs and executes the decisions of the Political Council.

CONNECT CENTRAL ASIA POLICY OF INDIA

India launched the **Connect Central Asia Policy** in 2012 to strengthen and deepen its relationship with the Central Asian countries—Kazakhstan, Kyrgyzstan, Tajikistan, Turkmenistan and Uzbekistan. This policy includes political, economic, security and cultural engagement with the region.

Key Features of the Connect Central Asia Policy Include

- **Political Relations** India aims to build strong political ties through regular high-level exchanges and diplomatic engagements.
- **Security Cooperation** India seeks to enhance security cooperation, with a focus on military training, joint research and counter-terrorism efforts.
- **Multilateral Engagement** India plans to work closely with Central Asia through regional forums like the Shanghai Cooperation Organisation (SCO), Eurasian Economic Community, and the Custom Union.
- **Energy Partnership** Central Asia is seen as a long-term partner in energy and natural resources for India.
- **Medical Cooperation** India sees the medical field as an area with great potential for collaboration, particularly in healthcare services and medical education.
- **Education Cooperation** India offers affordable higher education compared to Western countries and is working to establish a Central Asian University in Bishkek, Kyrgyzstan.
- **Tele-education and Tele-medicine** India is setting up a Central Asian e-network to provide tele-education and tele-medicine services, linking all five Central Asian countries.
- **Construction and Infrastructure** Indian companies are expected to showcase their expertise in construction by building world-class structures at competitive rates.
- **Transport and Connectivity** India is working on reactivating the International North-South Transport Corridor (INSTC) to enhance land connectivity.
- **Banking Infrastructure** India hopes to encourage its banks to expand in Central Asia if a favourable environment is established.
- **Air Connectivity** Efforts are underway to improve air connectivity between India and Central Asia.
- **Cultural and People-to-People Ties** India aims to promote regular exchanges between scholars, academics, civil society and youth to strengthen cultural ties.

ACT EAST POLICY OF INDIA

India's Act East Policy was launched in 2014 as an upgraded version of the Look East Policy, first initiated in 1992 by Prime Minister PV Narasimha Rao. The Act East Policy focuses on deepening ties with the Asia-Pacific region through economic, political, and strategic engagements.

Key Elements of the Act East Policy

- Focus on Asia-Pacific The policy primarily targets the Asia-Pacific region and seeks to enhance India's engagement beyond South Asia.
- Economic and Strategic Dimensions Originally conceived as an economic initiative, it now includes political, strategic and cultural dimensions, along with institutional mechanisms for dialogue and cooperation.
- India-ASEAN Cooperation A strong focus is placed on cooperation with the Association of South-East Asian Nations (ASEAN), aligning it with domestic initiatives like infrastructure development, trade, skills development and smart cities.
- North-East India The policy emphasises developing the North-East region of India, with Arunachal Pradesh as a vital interface with ASEAN countries.
- Civilisational Links The policy leverages ancient Buddhist and Hindu ties to strengthen cultural and historical connections with South-East Asia.
- Connectivity India is focusing on improving connectivity, particularly by linking North-East India with ASEAN countries.
- Economic Engagement India has increased economic cooperation with ASEAN. The ASEAN-India Agreement on Trade in Services and Investments came into effect for India and seven ASEAN countries in 2015.
- Strategic Cooperation India seeks convergence on security interests, with cooperation in combating terrorism, promoting peace and stability, and ensuring maritime security based on international norms.

NEIGHBOURHOOD FIRST POLICY

- India's Neighbourhood First Policy is a strategic initiative that places significant emphasis on fostering strong, cooperative, and friendly relations with its neighbouring countries in South Asia.
- It reflects India's commitment to enhancing regional cooperation, stability, and prosperity by prioritising diplomatic and economic engagement with its immediate neighbours.
- The key countries under this policy include Nepal, Bhutan, Bangladesh, Sri Lanka, Maldives, Myanmar, and Afghanistan. Pakistan is technically part of the neighbourhood but presents unique challenges due to longstanding tensions.

This policy has multiple dimensions, including diplomatic engagement, economic assistance, infrastructure development, security cooperation, and cultural exchanges. The primary objectives are:

- Promoting Regional Cooperation India aims to build stronger regional cooperation through mechanisms such as the South Asian Association for Regional Cooperation (SAARC) and the Bay of Bengal Initiative for Multi-Sectoral Technical and Economic Cooperation (BIMSTEC).
- Economic Partnerships and Development Assistance Through the Neighbourhood First Policy, India provides economic assistance to its neighbours in the form of grants, loans and technical expertise. This includes infrastructure projects like building roads, railways, power plants and ports.
- Connectivity and Infrastructure Development One of the main priorities of the policy is improving connectivity, both physical and digital, with neighbouring countries. This includes the development of cross-border roads, railways, ports, and inland waterways, aimed at enhancing trade, investment, and people-to-people ties.
- Security Cooperation India works closely with its neighbours to combat regional security challenges such as terrorism, drug trafficking and human trafficking. Security collaboration is also aimed at addressing non-traditional threats like natural disasters, piracy and climate change.
- Disaster Relief and Humanitarian Assistance India has actively assisted its neighbours during times of natural disasters.
- People-to-People Ties and Cultural Diplomacy To strengthen cultural and historical bonds, India encourages people-to-people connections through cultural exchanges, educational scholarships, tourism promotion and civil society interactions. India shares deep cultural, linguistic, and religious links with countries like Nepal, Bhutan and Sri Lanka, which further bolster mutual understanding.
- Peace-building Efforts The Neighbourhood First Policy also involves helping countries in post-conflict recovery and peace-building. In Sri Lanka, for example, India played an important role in the rehabilitation of displaced Tamils and the reconstruction of war-damaged areas after the civil war.

PRELIMS FACTS

1. CONSTITUTIONAL DEVELOPMENT OF INDIA

- The provision for the establishment of Supreme Court at Calcutta under ***– Regulating Act, 1773*** *[UPPSC (Mains) 2010, APSC (Pre) 2016]*
- Under which Act, the 'Board of Control' was established? ***– Pitt's India Act, 1784*** *[UPPSC (Mains) 2015]*
- By which Act did the British East India Company's trading monopoly in India end? ***– Charter Act, 1833*** *[UPPSC (Pre) 2018]*
- In which Act, yearly ₹ 1 lakh was allotted for the education of Indians? ***– Charter Renewal Act, 1813*** *[WBCS (Pre) 2020]*
- The foundation of English education in India was laid by which Act? ***– Charter Act, 1813*** *[IAS (Pre) 2018]*
- According to which Act, the Governor-General of Bengal designated as the Governor-General of India? ***– The Charter Act of 1833*** *[IAS (Pre) 2023, APPSC (Pre) 2024]*
- The British Act that envisaged the parliamentary system of Government in India ***– Charter Act of 1853*** *[WBCS (Pre) 2023]*
- The Act which had created the office of the Secretary of State for India ***– Government of India Act, 1858*** *[UPPSC (Pre) 2017]*
- High Courts were established in Bombay, Madras and Calcutta in the year ***–1861*** *[UP UDA/LDA (Pre) 2010, UPPSC (Pre) 2013]*
- The Act which introduced separate electorate system in India? ***– The Indian Council Act, 1909*** *[MPSC (Pre) 2017]*
- Which Act introduced dyarchy in the executive government of the provinces? ***– Government of India Act, 1919*** *[UPPSC (Pre) 2012, HPPSC (Pre) 2024]*
- The Act which replaced Indian Legislative Council by a bicameral legislature consisting of an upper house (Council of State) and a lower house (Legislative Assembly) ***– Government of India Act, 1919*** *[MPPSC (Pre) 2017, WBCS (Pre) 2023]*
- In the federation established by the Government of India Act of 1935, residuary powers were given to ***– Governor-General*** *[RAS (Pre) 2016, IAS (Pre) 2018]*
- The Act that provided for the establishment of an All India Federation based on the union of the British Indian Provinces and Princely States ***– Government of India Act, 1935*** *[IAS (Pre) 2024]*
- Jawaharlal Nehru said that "we were given a car which had breaks but no engine" about the ***– Act of 1935*** *[BPSC (Pre) 2020]*
- The Constitutional Assembly was made fully sovereign body by the ***– Independence of India Act, 1947*** *[MPSC (Pre) 2019]*
- The Indian Independence Act was passed by the British Parliament on ***– 18th July, 1947*** *[NPSC (Pre) 2013, WBCS (Pre) 2017, 2020]*

2. MAKING OF THE INDIAN CONSTITUTION

- The Fifth Schedule of Indian Constitution deals with ***– Administration and Control of Scheduled Areas and Scheduled Tribes*** *[MPPSC (Pre) 2023, HPSC (Pre) 2024]*
- The proposal for framing of the Constitution of India by an elected Constituent Assembly was made by ***– Cabinet Mission, 194*** *[UPPSC (Mains) 2008]*
- The Constitution of India was enacted by a Constituent Assembly set-up under ***– Cabinet Mission, 1946*** *[MPPSC (Pre) 2011]*
- The first meeting of Constituent Assembly was held on ***– 9th December, 1946*** *[UPPSC (Pre) 2011, APSC (Pre) 2013, BPSC (Pre) 2020]*
- How many women members were there in the Constituent Assembly? ***– 15*** *[UPPSC (Pre) 2014]*
- Members of the Constituent Assembly were ***– elected by the Provincial Assemblies*** *[WBCS (Pre) 2023]*
- Constituent Assembly was elected on the basis of ***– Universal Adult Fanchise*** *[MPPSC (Pre) 2012]*
- Its electoral process was based on the Sixth Schedule of the Act of ***– 1935*** *[MPPSC (Pre) 2012]*
- Provisional President of the Constituent Assembly before Dr. Rajendra Prasad took over ***– Dr. Sachchidananda Sinha*** *[IAS (Pre) 2024]*
- The non-Congress party members of the Indian Constituent Assembly were ***– Sardar Hukum Singh*** *[UPPSC (Pre) 2011, BPSC (Pre) 2020]*
- The third reading of the Indian Constitution begin in the Constituent Assembly on ***– 14th November, 1949*** *[UPPSC (Pre) 2014]*
- Who talked about suspending adult suffrage for 15 years of Constituent Assembly ? ***– Maulana Abul Kalam Azad*** *[MPPSC (Pre) 2010]*
- The Constitution of India came into force on ***– 26th January, 1950*** *[CGPSC (Pre) 2023]*
- Sessions of the Indian Constituent Assembly were conducted for the formulation of Indian Constitution ***– 11 Sessions*** *[UPPSC (Mains) 2005]*

- The Chairman of the Drafting Committee of the Indian Constitution was *– Dr. BR Ambedkar* [CGPSC (Pre) 2003, IAS (Pre) 2009, Manipur PSC (Pre) 2016]
- The Chairman of the States Committee of the Constituent Assembly was *– Jawaharlal Nehru* [Odisha PSC (Pre) 2011]
- The Chairman of the Advisory Committee on Fundamental Rights and Minorities Constituted by the Constituent Assembly *– Sardar Vallabhbhai Patel* [MPSC (Pre) 2014]
- Part IV of the Constitution deals with *– Directive Principles of State Policy* (Articles 36-51) [UP Lower Sub. (Pre) 2004, UPPSC (Mains) 2007]
- Second Schedule of the Indian Constitution deals with *– Salaries and Emoluments* [HPSC (Pre) 2024]
- Third Schedule of the Constitution deals with *– forms of an oath and affirmations* [Assam PSC (Pre) 2024]
- Fourth Schedule of the Constitution of India deals with *– Allocation of seats in Rajya Sabha for the Council of States* [UPPSC (Mains) 2015, MPPSC (Pre) 2023, Assam PSC (Pre) 2024]
- Powers of the municipalities are given in which part of Constitution *– Part IX A* [IAS (Pre) 2024]
- The part of Constitution containing emergency provisions *– Part XVIII* [IAS (Pre) 2024]
- Provisions related to the Amendment of the Constitution are given in *– Part XX* [IAS (Pre) 2024]
- Which part of the Indian Constitution deals with the relations between the Union and the States? *– Part XI* [UKPSC (Pre) 2024]

3. SALIENT FEATURES OF THE INDIAN CONSTITUTION

- In Indian Polity, which is supreme? *– The Constitution* [BPSC (Mains) 2002, UPPSC (Mains) 2013]
- The States and the Central Government derive power from *– The Constitution of India* [MPPSC (Pre) 2017]
- In which country was the first Parliamentary Government started? *– Great Britain* [UPPSC (Pre) 2018]
- The feature of 'Office of the Governor' was borrowed form the *– Government of India Act, 1935* [IAS (Pre) 2003, UPPSC (Pre) 2010, MPPSC (Pre) 2013]
- The most essential feature of the Parliamentary form of Government is the *– Sovereignty of the Parliament* [APSC (Pre) 2015]
- The main advantage of Parliamentary form of government is that *– the executive remains responsible to the legislature* [IAS (Pre) 2017, APSC (Pre) 2018]
- The system of Indian Democracy is *– multiparty and parliamentary in nature* [WBCS (Pre) 2015]
- "The Constitution has not been molded into a tight framework of federalism", stated by *– Dr. BR Ambedkar* [UPPSC (Mains) 2008]
- A unitary feature of the Indian Constitution *– Emergency Powers of President, Strong Centre, Single Citizenship,* [Mizoram PSC (Pre) 2016]
- Who called Indian federalism as the cooperative federalism? *– G. Austin* [CGPSC (Pre) 2008]
- The system of Judicial Review exists in *– India and USA* [UPPSC (Pre) 2008, 2012]
- India is an example of *– Quasi-Federal* [Mizoram PSC (Pre) 2023]
- Appointment of Governor, President's approval on State Bills and constitutional crises are elements found in *– Indian Federal System* [CGPSC (Pre) 2017]
- The states do not have the right to secede from the Union *– in Indian Federalism* [UPPSC (Pre) 2018]
- A Parliamentary System of Government is one in which the government is responsible to *– the Parliament* [IAS (Pre) 2020]
- The Fundamental Rights of the Indian Constitution were borrowed with the inspiration from *– Constitution of USA* [UP UDA/LDA (Pre) 2014, NPSC (Pre) 2016, UPPSC (Pre) 2017]
- What does 'Due process of law' mean? *– The Principle of Natural Justice* [IAS (Pre) 2023]
- The concept of 'Directive Principles State Policy in Indian Constitution was borrowed from the Constitution of *– Ireland* [UPPSC (Pre) 1998, Manipur PSC (Pre) 2016]
- Provision for Concurrent List in the Indian Constitution is borrowed from the Constitution of *– Australia* [JPSC (Pre) 2003, UPPSC (Pre) 2014, 2016, Manipur PSC (Pre) 2016]

4. THE PREAMBLE

- The mind of the makers of the Constitution of India is reflected in *– Preamble* [IAS (Pre) 2017, UKPSC (Pre) 2024]
- The words 'We, The people of India' have been used in the *– Preamble of the Constitution* [MPPSC (Pre) 2016]
- Which part of the Indian Constitution has been described as the 'Soul' of the Constitution? *– Preamble* [UKPSC (Pre) 2012, UPPSC (Mains) 2015]
- How many types of justice, liberty, equality and fraternity in that order have been mentioned in the Preamble of Indian Constitution? *– 3, 5, 2, 1* [UPPSC (Pre) 2018]
- The correct sequence of the words given in the Preamble as mentioned in the Constitution. *– Sovereign, Socialist, Secular, Democratic and Republic* [BPSC (Pre) 2008, UP RO/ARO (Pre) 2024]
- Words present in the Preamble of the Indian Constitution as adopted on 26th November, 1949 *– Republic* [UKPSC (Pre) 2024]
- The words 'Secular' and 'Socialist' were added to the Preamble of the Indian Constitution by *– 42nd Amendment Act, 1976* [MPPSC (Pre) 2013, BPSC (Pre) 2016]
- Which is not a philosophy of the Indian Constitution? *– Communist State* [UKPSC (Pre) 2024]

- The legal nature of the Preamble of the Constitution *– it is not enforceable [UPPSC (Pre) 2019]*
- The Preamble of Indian Constitution is a *– part of Constitution but has no legal effect independently of other parts [IAS (Pre) 2020]*
- The term 'Political Justice' is mentioned in the Indian Constitution under *– Preamble of the Constitution and Fundamental Rights [WBCS (Pre) 2023]*
- What was the exact constitutional statue of India on 26th January, 1950? *– Sovereign, Democratic, Republic [IAS (Pre) 2021]*
- Due of the implications of equality in society is the absence of *– Privileges [IAS (Pre) 2017]*
- The most appropriate relationship between law and liberty *– if there are no laws there is no liberty [IAS (Pre) 2016, 2018]*
- The idea of Preamble has been borrowed in Indian Constitution from the Constitution of *– USA [UPPSC (Pre) 2015]*
- The objectives embodied in the Preamble to the Constitution of India *– Liberty of thought, expression and belief [IAS (Pre) 2017]*

5. THE UNION AND ITS TERRITORIES

- The number of States and Union Territories in India are *– 28 States and 8 Union Territories [CGPSC (Pre) 2023]*
- Article 1 of the Indian Constitution describes India, as a *– Union of States [MPSC (Pre) 2016, WBCS (Pre) 2021, HPSC (Pre) 2021]*
- Indian Parliament has the power to create a new state under the Constitutional Provision *– Article 3 [CGPSC (Pre) 2014, UPPSC (Mains) 2013, 2015]*
- Constitutional Provisions for the creation of new states are *– increasing the area of a state, decreasing the area of a state, renaming a state [UPPSC (Pre) 2013]*
- Formation of new states, alteration of areas of states and alteration of boundaries of states are possible by the law of Parliament under *– Article 3 of the Constitution [UPPSC (Pre) 2020]*
- Bihar as an Indian state was formed in *– 1936 [BPSC (Pre) 2018]*
- Indian Constitution empowers the Parliament (with the prior recommendation of President) to create new states, after their boundaries and even their names under *– Article 3 [MPSC (Pre) 2015]*
- A bill for the purpose of creating a new state in India must be passed by *– simple majority in Parliament [CGPSC (Pre) 2014, BPSC (Pre) 2016, UPPSC (Pre) 2016, IAS (Pre) 2021]*
- States and Union Territories were established by the 1956, State Restructuring Act *– 14 States, 6 Union Territories [MPPSC (Pre) 2004, 2021]*
- Himachal Pradesh was formed in *– 1971 [UP RO/ARO (Mains) 2013]*
- The correct sequence of the formation of the following states in descending order is *– Haryana, Maharashtra, Rajasthan [UPPSC (Mains) 2013]*
- The first state in India to be formed on the basis of language *– Andhra Pradesh [UPPSC (Pre) 2018]*
- The North-Eastern Areas (Reorganisation) Act was passed in the year *– 1971 [APSC (Pre) 2018]*
- The state of Jharkhand came into existence in the year *– 2000 [BPSC (Pre) 2018]*
- The state of Bombay was split and divided into two separate states of Gujarat and Maharashtra in the year *– 1960 [RAS/RTS (Pre) 2016]*
- Which state joined the Indian union after the conduct of Special Opinion Poll in 1975? *– Sikkim [Punjab PSC (Pre) 2014]*
- The state which has never been granted special category status by the Central Government *– Bihar [BPSC (Pre) 2019]*
- Uttarakhand state was created on *– 9th November, 2000 [UPPSC (Mains) 2014]*
- Uttaranchal (change of name) Act came into existence in the year *– 2006 [UKPSC (Pre) 2016]*
- Year and Chairman of the linguistic provinces commission appointed to report on creation of provinces of Andhra, Karnataka, Kerala and Maharashtra *- 1948, Justice SK Dhar [APPSC (Pre) 2024]*
- The commission had given preference to administrative convenience rather language for Reorganisation of states *– SK Dhar Commission 1948 [UPPSC (Mains) 2008]*
- A three member commission was made to address to questions of state reorganisation, under *– Chairmanship of Fazl Ali [CGPSC (Pre) 2022]*
- Commission submitted its report in 1955 and accepted language as basis of reorganisation of states, but rejected the theory of 'one language one state' under *– KM Panikkar and HN Kunzru [CGPSC (Pre) 2022]*
- In which year Goa was acquired in India as Union Territory ? *– 1962 [UPPSC (Mains) 2013]*
- By which Constitutional Amendment, Delhi was given the status of National Capital Region (NCR)? *– 69th Constitutional Amendment, 1991 [UPPSC (Pre) 2014, 2022]*
- The President has the power to make regulations for peace, progress and good governance of Dadra and Nagar Haveli *– under Article 240 (1)(c) [RAS/RTS (Pre) 2018]*

6. CITIZENSHIP

- Articles of Indian Constitution are related to citizenship are *– Articles 5 to 11 [UPPSC (Pre) 2020]*
- In which part of the Constitution of India, we find provisions related to citizenship? *– Part II [UPPSC (Pre) 2018]*
- The first citizen of the Republic of India is *– the President of India [WBCS (Pre) 2017]*

- A British citizen staying in cannot claim right to *– Freedom of trade and profession* [UKPSC (Pre) 2024]
- Legislation provided the rule regarding conferment of citizenship in India by *– Citizenship Act* [JPSC (Pre) 2012]
- According to the Citizenship Act, 1955, citizenship can be acquired in five ways *– on the basis of birth, Based on registration on the Basis of lineage, By naturalisation and By the merger of the territories* [BPSC (Pre) 1996, MPSC (Pre) 2017]
- The Constitution of India which came into force on 26th January, 1950 provides for *– Single citizenship* [Nagaland PSC (Pre) 2012, UPPSC (Pre) 2015]
- Which article explains that at the commencement of the Constitution, every person shall be a citizen of India ? *– Article 5* [MPSC (Pre) 2013]
- The Citizenship Act, 1955 prescribes three ways of losing citizenship i.e. *– Renunciation, Termination and Deprivation* [CGPSC (Pre) 2016, UPPSC (Pre) 2017]
- Which is competent to prescribe conditions for acquisition of citizenship? *– Parliament* [UPPSC (Pre) 2013]
- Who has the exclusive power to determine the issue of citizenship in India ? *– The Parliament* [CGPSC (Pre) 2013]
- Within how many days, it is legally mandatory to register the birth and death event in India under the civil registration system? *– 21 days* [UPPSC (Pre) 2019]
- Which Article of the Indian Constitution has empowered the Parliament to regulate the citizenship matters? *– Article 11* [APSC (Pre) 2013]
- An Indian is not eligible for registering as overseas citizen of India cardholder under the Citizenship Amendment Act, 2015 *– Indian who migrated to Pakistan after partition* [IAS (Pre) 2016]
- Which country accepted the policy of dual citizenship ? *– USA* [MPPSC (Pre) 2016]
- The Citizenship (Amendment) Bill 2019 passed by Parliament on *– 11th December, 2019* [UP RO/ARO (Pre) 2016, BPSC (Pre) 2020]

7. FUNDAMENTAL RIGHTS

- Part III on Fundamental Rights of the Constitution is based upon *– the Bill of Rights of the USA* [UP RO/ARO (Pre) 2024]
- The protector of the Fundamental Rights of citizens is *– Judiciary* [WBCS (Pre) 2022]
- 'Fundamental Rights' are *– Justifiable* [MPPSC (Pre) 2013]
- In India, who is competent to amend Fundamental Rights of the citizens? *– Parliament* [UPPSC (Pre) 2016]
- In the Indian Constitution, the Right to Equality is granted by five articles. They are *– Articles 14 to 18* [UPPSC (Pre) 2002, 2009, APSC (Pre) 2018]
- Which Article of the Indian Constitution advocates equality before law? *– Article 14* [Nagaland PSC (Pre) 2012, CGPSC (Pre) 2018]
- The 'Rule of Law' means *– one act for all and one Judiciary for all* [UPPSC (Pre) 2018, BPSC (Pre) 2020]
- Prohibition of discrimination on ground of religion etc. (Article 15 of the Constitution of India) is a Fundamental Right classifiable under *– Right to Equality* [Manipur PSC (Pre) 2014]
- Amendment Act under which the reservation in promotion for the SC's and ST's ensured by inserting Clause '4(A)' in Article 16? *– 77th Amendment Act, 1995* [JPSC (Pre) 2024]
- Which Article ensures abolition of untouchability? *– Article 17* [UKPSC (Pre) 2005, MPPSC (Pre) 2013, CGPSC (Pre) 2017, UPPSC (Pre) 2022]
- The Government of India instituted Bharat Ratna and Padma Shri Awards under *– Article 18 of the Indian Constitution* [Tripura PSC (Pre) 2017]
- In the Indian Constitution, the 'Right to Freedom is granted by four Articles which are *– Articles 19 to 22* [UPPSC (Mains) 2016]
- Reasonable restrictions on 'Exercise of freedom of speech and expression' under Article 19(2) are justified in the interest of *– Security of state, defamation, Sedition, Public order* [JPSC (Pre) 2024]
- An accused of any offence cannot be completed to be a witness against himself. Under the article *– Article 20(3)* [UP UDA / LDA (Pre) 2010, UKPSC (Pre) 2010]
- Which Article of the Constitution of Indian Republic relates to the 'protection of life and personal liberty? *– Article 21* [UKPSC (Pre) 2016, IAS (Pre) 2024]
- 'Right to die' is a Fundamental Right under *– Article 21* [UP RO/ARO (Pre) 2024]
- Right to Privacy' is protected under which Article of the Constitution of India? *– Article 21* [IAS (Pre) 2021]
- Which right is a Human Right as well as a Fundamental Right under the Constitution of India ? *– Right to Education* [BPSC (Pre) 2011, UPPSC (Mains) 2016]
- Which guarantees Right to Freedom of religion to all persons in all its aspects? *– Articles 25- 28* [Tripura PSC (Pre) 2011]
- Under provisions of the Act of 1992, which religious communities have been recognised as minorities by the National Minority Commissions ? *– Muslims, Christians, Sikhs, Parsis and Buddhists* [MPSC (Pre) 2013]
- Which writ can be issued by a High Court to secure the liberty of the individual ? *– Habeas Corpus* [MPPSC (Pre) 1993, UPPSC (Pre) 2015]
- A Writ of Prohibition is an order issued by the Supreme Court or High Court to *– the lower court prohibiting continuation of proceedings in a case.* [IAS (Pre) 2024]
- Under which Article of the Constitution, can an individual move to the Supreme Court directly in case of any violation of a Fundamental Right ? *– Article 32* [Manipur PSC (Pre) 2010]

8. DIRECTIVE PRINCIPLES OF STATE POLICY

- Directive Principles of State Policy are not enforceable by any court
*– **Article 37** [JPSC (Pre) 2024]*
- The Directive Principles are enshrined in the Constitution in
*– **Part IV** [Manipur PSC (Pre) 2010]*
- In Indian Constitution, the idea of the Directive Principles of State Policy has been taken from the Constitution of
*– **Ireland** [UPPSC (Mains) 2005, 2008, UP Lower (Pre) 2015]*
- The ideal of 'Welfare State' in the Indian Constitution is enshrined in its *– **Directive Principles of State Policy** [UKPSC (Pre) 2002, UPPSC (Pre) 2004, IAS (Pre) 2015, 2016, 2020]*
- Who said that the Directive Principles of the State Policy are just like "a blank cheque on bank payable at the convenience of the bank"?
*– **Professor KT Shah** [UPPSC (Mains) 2007, MPSC (Pre) 2012]*
- The purpose of the inclusion of the Directive Principles of the State Policy in the Indian Constitution is to establish
*– **social and economic democracy** [IAS (Pre) 2002]*
- According to the Constitution of India, which is fundamental for the governance of the country?
*– **Directive Principles of State Policy** [IAS (Pre) 2013]*
- Directive Principles of State Policy related to cooperative society (Article 43) is taken from
*– **Nehru's Objective Resolution 1946** [MPPSC (Pre) 2023]*
- Directive Principles of State Policy are classified into
*– **Socialist, Gandhian and Liberal-Intellectual Principles** [MPPSC (Pre) 2023]*
- Equal justice and free legal aid *– **Article 39(A)** [HPSC (Pre) 2024]*
- Right to adequate means of livelihood
*– **Article 39(a)** [HPSC (Pre) 2024]*
- Equal pay for equal work for both men and women
*– **Article 39(d)** [HPSC (Pre) 2024]*
- Right to work, education and public assistance
*– **Article 41** [HPSC (Pre) 2024]*
- Promotion of cooperative societies
*– **Article 43(B)** [HPSC (Pre) 2024]*
- Participation of workers in management of industries
*– **Article 43(A)** [HPSC (Pre) 2024]*
- Under the Constitution of India, organisation of Village Panchayat is a
*– **Directive Principle** [UPPSC (Pre) 2010, 2014, 2015, BPSC (Pre) 2018]*
- Educational and economic interest of weaker sections
*– **Article 46** [HPSC (Pre) 2024]*
- Educational and economic interest of SCs and STs
*– **Article 46** [HPSC (Pre) 2024]*
- Article of the Constitution that talks about the Uniform Civil Code *– **Article 44** [JPSC (Pre) 2024]*
- The provisions for the protection and improvement of environment and safeguarding of forests and wildlife are found in the Constitution of India.
*– **Directive Principles of State Policy and Fundamental Duties** [UPPSC (Pre) 2019]*
- Constitutional Amendment Act relates to the protection and improvement of the environment and safeguarding of forests and wildlife *– **42nd Amendment Act, 1976** [UKPSC (Pre) 2024]*
- Organisation of agriculture and animal husbandry
*– **Article 48** [HPSC (Pre) 2024]*
- In India, Separation of Judiciary from the executive is enjoined by *– **the Directive Principle of State Policy** [IAS (Pre) 2020]*
- Under the Indian Constitution concentration of wealth is the violation of *– **Directive Principles of State Policy** [IAS (Pre) 2021]*
- 'The State is everywhere, it hardly leaves any gaps'. This statement explains *– **Welfare state** [JPSC (Pre) 2016]*
- The Constitution is silent in the Directive Principles about
*– **Adult education** [UP Lower Sub (Pre) 2008, Manipur PSC (Pre) 2016]*
- In the Constitution of India, promotion of international peace and security is included in
*– **the Directive Principles of State Policy** [IAS (Pre) 2014]*
- The DPSP may be classified into three parts per the sake of convenient study, those are
*– **Socialist, Gandhian and Liberal** [UPPSC (Pre) 2018]*
- Which article directs State Government to organise Village Panchayat? *– **Article 40** [BPSC (Pre) 2018]*
- Case in which the Supreme Court of India declare the prevalence of Fundamental Rights over Directive Principles of the State Policy in case of conflict between the two
*– **Minerva Mills v/s the Union of India (1980)** [MPPSC (Pre) 2024]*

9. FUNDAMENTAL DUTIES

- Fundamental Duties of Indian citizens are enumerated in
*– **Part IV of the Constitution** [UPPSC (Mains) 2006, 2011, 2012, UPPSC (Pre) 2010]*
- Fundamental Duties were appended to the Constitution of India by the 42nd Amendment on the recommendation of
*– **Swaran Singh Committee** [APSC (Pre) 2013, RAS/RTS (Pre) 2021]*
- When were the Fundamental Duties incorporated in the Constitution?
*– **In 1976** [UKPSC (Mains) 2006, RAS/RTS (Pre) 2016]*
- Fundamental Duties under Indian Constitution
*– **to protect monuments of national importance, to develop scientific temper, to uphold unity and integrity of the nation** [WBCS (Pre) 2023]*
- It shall be the duty of every citizen of India to protect and improve the natural environment and to have compassion for living creatures is mention under the
*– **Article 51 A (g)** [UPPSC (Pre) 2019]*

- To uphold and protect the Sovereignty, Unity and Integrity of India' is a provision made in the *– Fundamental Duties* *[IAS (Pre) 2015, HPSC (Pre) 2021]*
- To respect National Flag (Article 51(A)(a) to promote spirit of brotherhood among all people of India Article 51 (A) (e) are parts of *– Fundamental Duties* *[UPPSC (Mains) 2014]*
- Which Article says, It shall be duty of every citizen to protect and improve the natural environment including forests lakes, rivers and wildlife and to have compassion for living creatures? *– Under Article 51 A (g) (Fundamental Duty) [UP Lower (Pre) 2008]*
- Protection of wildlife comes under *– Fundamental Duties, Directive Principles and Seventh Schedule [Assam PSC (Pre) 2024]*
- In the context of India, which is the correct relationship between rights and duties? *– Rights are correlative with duties [IAS (Pre) 2017]*

11. AMENDMENTS OF THE CONSTITUTION

- The procedure for the Amendment of the Indian Constitution is given in *– Article 368 [UPPSC (Pre) 2010, Manipur PSC (Pre) 2016]*
- Parliament may amend any provision of the Constitution by way of *– Addition, Variation and Repeal [IAS (Pre) 2024]*
- In India, who is competent to amend Fundamental Rights of the citizens? *– Parliament [UPPSC (Pre) 2016]*
- Constitutional Amendment Bill *– Introduced in any House of the Parliament [HPPSC (Pre) 2024]*
- Which parts of the Constitution cannot be amended by a simple majority? *– Process of the election of President [CGPSC (Pre) 2012]*
- Amendment in the Seventh Schedule requires *– Ratification by the legislatures of not less than half of the states. [HPPSC (Pre) 2024]*
- Which majority required to amend the provisions of Constitution for the Formation of new state in the Indian union? *– Simple majority [HPSC (Pre) 2024]*
- Which majority required to amend DPSPs? *– Special majority of Parliament [HPSC (Pre) 2024]*
- Amendment that seeks to make changes in Article 279 (A) *– Requires ratification of not less than one-half of the states [MPPSC (Pre) 2024]*
- Which bill must be passed by each House of the Indian Parliament separated by the special majority? *– Constitution Amendment Bill [UPPSC (Mains) 2004, UPPSC (Pre) 2003, 2007]*
- Which Constitutional Amendments are related with the inclusion of new territories into the Union? *– 10th, 12th and 14th Constitutional Amendment [MPPSC (Pre) 2015]*
- According to which amendment of the Constitution, Governor can appoint one member of Anglo-Indian community in the Legislative Assembly, if it is necessary? *– 23rd Constitutional Amendment [MPSC (Pre) 2016]*
- 26th Constitutional Amendment *– Abolition of privy purse [HPSC (Pre) 2024]*
- 52nd Constitutional Amendment *– Anti-defection law [HPSC (Pre) 2024]*
- The authoritative text of the Indian Constitution in Hindi was authorised to be published by which Constitutional Amendments? *– 58th Amendment, 1987 [UP RO/ARO (Pre) 2016]*
- Which amendment reduced the voting age from 21 to 18 years for the Lok Sabha and State Legislative Assembly elections? *– 61st Amendment Act, 1989 [MPPSC (Pre) 2014, (UPPSC (Pre) 2021]*
- 103rd Constitutional Amendment *– Reservation for EWS [HPSC (Pre) 2024]*
- Which amendment to the Constitution inserted a new Article 21 A in the Constitution providing Right to Education? *– 86th Constitutional Amendment Act [UPPSC (Mains) 2006, UKPSC (Pre) 2012]*
- Which Constitutional Amendment bifurcated the combined National Commission for Scheduled Castes and Scheduled Tribes into two separate bodies? *– 89th Amendment [JPSC (Pre) 2016]*
- Under which Constitutional Amendments acts four language were added to the language under the 8th Schedule of the Constitution of India there by raising their number to 22? *– 92nd Constitutional Amendment Act [IAS (Pre) 2008]*
- The First Constitutional Amendment Bill passed in 1951 was related to *– Protection of agrarian reforms [UPPSC (Pre) 2009]*
- Which Constitutional Amendment Act deleted the Right to Property from the list of Fundamental Rights? *– 44th Constitutional Amendment Act [MPPSC (Pre) 2020]*
- Which Constitutional Amendment Act introduced the anti-defection provision in the Constitution for the first time? *– 52nd Amendment Act [MPPSC (Pre) 2015]*
- The 97th Constitutional Amendment Act 2012 is concerned with *– Organisation and Working of Co-operative Societies [RAS/RTS (Pre) 2012]*
- The Constitution Bill (123rd Amendment 2017) deals with *– National Commission on Backward Classes [WBCS (Pre) 2019]*

14. CENTRE-STATE RELATIONS

- In which part of the Indian Constitution, legislative relations between the centre and states are given ? *– Part XI [UP RO/ARO (Pre) 2014, UKPSC (Pre) 2024*
- Inter-state quarantine is a *– Union subject under the Union List [IAS (Pre) 2024*
- Socio-economic planning is a part of the *– Concurrent List [WBCS (Pre) 2023*

- Subject not included in the three lists of the 7th Schedule of the Constitution *– Residuary subject* [HPSC (Pre) 2024]
- Space technology is an example of *– Residuary subject* [HPSC (Pre) 2024]
- Article under which the Rajya Sabha authorise the Parliament to legislate on a state subject by two-third majority? *– Article 249* [JPSC (Pre) 2024]
- The Parliament can make any law for whole or any part of India for implementing international treaties *– without the consent of any state* [MPSC (Pre) 2016]
- A resolution passed by the Rajya Sabha under Article 249 of the Constitution empowering Parliament to legislate on a state subject in national interest remains in force for a period *– not exceeding one year* [UPPSC (Pre) 2017]
- Which part of the Constitution of India describes the financial relations between centre and states? *– Part XII* [UPPSC (Pre) 2019]
- The financial relations between the Union Government and states have been discussed under *– Articles 268 to 293* [UPPSC (Pre) 2014]
- Under which article of the Constitution of India, taxes are levied and collected by the centre but distributed between the centre and the states? *– Article 270* [JPSC (Pre) 2016]
- Who recommends to the President, the distribution between the Central and State Governments of net proceeds of taxes collected by the centre? *– Finance Commission* [Nagaland PSC (Pre) 2014]
- The recommendation of the Sarkaria Commission are related to *– Centre- State relations* [JPSC (Pre) 2003, UP RO/ARO (Pre) 2014, UPPSC (Pre) 2018]

16. EMERGENCY PROVISIONS

- How many types of emergencies have been envisaged under the Indian Constitution? *– Three* [UPPSC (Mains) 2009, 2014, Karnataka PSC (Pre) 2014]
- According to Article 352, National Emergency in India can be declared on which grounds? *– War, External Aggression or Armed Rebellion* [HPSC (Pre) 2023]
- President of India declares emergency under Article 352 on the advice of *– Union Cabinet* [MPPSC (Pre) 2024]
- When a proclamation of emergency is in operation, the right to move a court for the enforcement of all Fundamental Rights remains suspended, except *– Articles 20 and 21* [UPPSC (Mains) 2009, UPPSC (Pre) 2015]
- During National Emergency, the term of the house of people can be extended till emergency last but only by *– One year at a time* [UPPSC (Pre) 2010]
- The term of a State Legislative Assembly can be extended during Emergency by *– Parliament* [UK UDA/LDA (Pre) 2007]
- Under which article of the Indian Constitution President's Rule can be imposed in a state? *– Article 356* [UPPSC (Mains) 2016, APSC (Pre) 2018]
- Article 356 of the Constitution has generated lots of debate because it deals with *– President's Rule in a State* [MPPSC (Pre) 2013]
- Under Article 356 of the Constitution of India President's Rule was imposed for the first time in *– PEPSU* [CGPSC (Pre) 2020]
- As of October 2022, in Manipur the President's Rule has been imposed for *– 10 times* [CGPSC (Pre) 2020]
- Under which article our Constitution provides for imposition of Financial Emergency? *– Article 360* [UP Lower Sub (Pre) 2015]
- A proclamation of Financial Emergency issued shall cease to operate at the expiration of *– Two months* [UPPSC (Pre) 2007]
- Which is not a ground for proclamation of emergency under the Constitution of India? *– Internal disturbances* [UPPSC (Pre) 2016]
- Which article of the Indian Constitution has never been implemented into action? *– Article 360* [UPPSC (Mains) 2016]

17. THE PRESIDENT

- According to the Constitution of India , the Head of the State is *– President* [UKPSC (Pre) 2024]
- The Constitutional Head of the State is *– the President of India* [UP RO/ARO (Pre) 2024]
- Name the article of the Indian Constitution that deals with the impeachment of President of India. *– Article 61* [HPSC (Pre) 2023]
- The Constitution of India vests executive power of the Union in the *– President of India* [UP RO/ARO (Pre) 2024]
- Article 123 of Indian Constitution deals with which provision? *– Ordinance making power of the President* [HPSC (Pre) 2023]
- Which article of Indian Constitution deals with the appointment of Attorney-General by the President? *– Article 76* [HPSC (Pre) 2023]
- Name the article that describes the pardoning powers of the President? *– Article 72* [HPSC (Pre) 2023]
- Who is empowered to establish the Inter-State Council ? *– President of India* [UPPSC (Pre) 2017]
- The election to the office of the President is conducted by *– Election Commission* [Nagaland PSC (Pre) 2016]
- President of India is elected by *– both the Houses of Parliament along with the members of the State Assemblies.* [MPSC (Pre) 2004, WBCS (Pre) 2021]
- Electors cannot use this provision in the election of a President *– NOTA* (HPSC (Pre) 2024)
- The provisions of this law is not applicable in Presidential elections *– Anti-defection Law* (HPSC (Pre) 2024)
- The impeachment of the President of India can be initiated in *– either House of the Parliament* [APSC (Pre) 2015, WBCS (Pre) 2019]

- Which Article empowers the President to nominate not more than two members of the Anglo-Indian Community to the Lok Sabha? *– Article 331* [BPSC (Pre) 2007, APSC (Pre) 2015]
- According to the Constitution of India, the President can exercise his power either directly or by Sub-ordinate authority under *– Article 53* [BPSC (Pre) 2016]
- The Joint Sitting of the House of People and the council of states is summoned by *– the President* [UPPSC (Pre) 2012, MPSC (Pre) 2021]
- The Union President can directly disallow a State Legislation *– in case of bills reserved by Governor for President's assent* [Nagaland PSC (Pre) 2014]
- The President has power to make regulations regarding *– Dadra and Nagar Haveli, Daman and Diu and Puducherry* [UKPSC (Pre) 2024]
- The President of India does not deny his consent to a Money Bill because *– it is initiated by the Finance Minister on the recommendation of the President* [APSC (Pre) 2013]
- Under which Article of Indian Constitution President of India enjoys power to withhold his assent on any bill? *– Article 111* [UP Lower (Pre) 2004, UPPSC (Pre) 2015]
- Not correct regarding the issuance of Ordinance by the President *– President can never repeal it* [UKPSC (Pre) 2024]
- Who has the power to issue ordinances under Article 123 ? *– President of India* [IAS (Pre) 2015]
- The power of the President to withholding the assent to the bill passed by the legislature *– Absolute Veto* [MPSC (Pre) 2016]
- The President can withhold the assent, but it can be overridden by the Legislature with a higher majority *– Qualified Veto* [MPSC (Pre) 2016]
- Under which article of the Constitution, the President in empowers to grant pardons to persons who have been tried and convicted of any offence? *– Article 72* [CGPSC (Pre) 2016]
- Under which article of the Constitution the President can take over the administration of a state in his own hand? *– Article 356* [WBCS (Pre) 2022]
- Controller and Auditor-General of India submits its reports relating to accounts of the union to *– President* [MPPSC (Pre) 2021]

18. VICE-PRESIDENT

- The Vice-President of India *– Article 63* [HPSC (Pre) 2024]
- Election of the Vice-President *– Article 66* [HPSC (Pre) 2024]
- The Ex-Officio Chairman of the Rajya Sabha is *– Vice-President* [CGPSC (Pre) 2023]
- Who acts as the presiding officer of the House of Commons (Rajya Sabha) without being its member? *– Vice-President of India* [Nagaland PSC (Pre) 2010]
- The Vice-President of India is elected by an electoral college consisting of *– members of both the Houses of Parliament* [APSC (Pre) 2014, Punjab PSC (Pre) 2014, CGPSC (Pre) 2023]
- Vice-President of India is also Ex-Officio Chairman of *– Rajya Sabha* [WBCS (Pre) 2017]
- The person contesting for the post of the Vice-President should not be a member of either House of Parliament of State Legislature. *– Under Article 66 of the Constitution* [MPPSC (Pre) 2015]
- The Vice-President of India can be removed from office by *– Rajya Sabha and Lok Sabha* [Nagaland PSC (Pre) 2015]
- The Vice-President of India is elected by *– an Electoral College constituted by members of the two Houses of the Parliament* [WBCS (Pre) 2022]
- Under Article 67 of the Constitution, the Vice-President is elected for a terms of *– 5 years* [MPSC (Pre) 2010]
- The resolution for removing Vice-President of India can be moved in *– Rajya Sabha only* [IAS (Pre) 2014]

19. PRIME MINISTER AND COUNCIL OF MINISTERS

- Under which Article, the Prime Minister shall be appointed by the President? *– Article 75* [JPSC (Pre) 2011, CGPSC (Pre) 2013
- The Reorganisation of Union Cabinet is based on the report of *– Gopalaswami Ayyangar* [UPPSC (Pre) 2010
- 'He represents the nation but does not lead the nation'. This dictum applies to whom? *– President* [UPPSC (Mains) 2007
- Prime Minister's Office (PMO) came into existence in 1977. Earlier it was known as *– Prime Minister's Secretariat* [UPPSC (Pre) 2019
- Who communicates all the decisions of the Council of Ministers to the President in India? *– Prime Minister* [Nagaland PSC (Pre) 2012
- Who allocates and reshuffles various portfolios among the Ministers? *– Prime Minister* [Nagaland PSC (Pre) 2016
- Who is the President of the Council of Scientific and Industrial Research? *– Prime Minister of India* [UPPSC (Pre) 2006 UK Lower Sub (Pre) 201
- The office of the Deputy Prime Minister is an *– extra constitutional growth* [UPPSC (Mains) 200
- The Policy of Liberalisation, Privatisation and Globalisation wa announced as New Economic Policy by Prime Minister *– PV Narasimha Rao* [UP Lower Sub (Pre) 201
- Department of Border Management of which Union Ministry *– Ministry of Home Affairs* [IAS (Pre) 200
- Which is the highest decisions-making authority in Indian Political Administrative System? *– Cabinet* [Manipur PSC (Pre) 201
- What does the Council of Ministers include? *– Cabinet Ministers, State Ministers and Deputy Ministe* [APSC (Pre) 201

- The Council of Ministers is collectively responsible to whom? *– Lok Sabha* [UKPSC (Pre) 2014]
- Council of Ministers's size has been restricted to 15% of membership of Lok Sabha by the *–91st Amendment Act, 2003* [HPPSC (Pre) 2024]
- The number of Lok Sabha members required to table a 'No-Confidence Motion' against the Council of Minister is *– 50 members* [UPPSC (Mains) 2013]
- It is the duty of the Prime Minister to communicate all decisions of Council of Ministers to the President relating to the administration of the affairs of Union and proposal for legislation. *– Under Article 78* [IAS (Pre) 2013]
- A system of Governance of a State where the executive is responsible to the legislature and is accountable to it. *– Parliamentary System* [UPPSC (Pre) 2015]
- After resigning whose permission does a Minister require to given a statement in Lok Sabha? *– Speaker* [CGPSC (Pre) 2015]
- Which article provides for Council of Ministers headed by Prime Minister who is the head of the government ? *– Article 74* [IAS (Pre) 2013]
- Who was the Law Minister in the first Cabinet post-independence India? *– Dr. BR Ambedkar* [JPSC (Pre) 2013]
- The Cabinet Secretariat functions directly under the *– Prime Minister* [CGPSC (Pre) 2023]
- The Administrative Head of the Cabinet Secretariat as well as the Ex-Officio Chairman of the civil services board is *– Cabinet Secretary* [CGPSC (Pre) 2023]

20. PARLIAMENT

- According to Article 79 of the Indian Constitution, the Union Parliament consists of *– the President, Lok Sabha and Rajya Sabha* [UP Lower (Pre) 2002, BPSC (Pre) 2018]
- The Union Territories are the administrative division in India get representation in *– both Houses of the Parliament* [UPPSC (Mains) 2015]
- Who have the power to increase the number of judges in the Supreme Court of India? *– Parliament* [WBCS (Pre) 2019]
- Who have the Right to Vote in the election of both the Lok Sabha and the Rajya Sabha? *– Elected members of lower house of State Legislature* [JPSC (Pre) 2010]
- In which year was the Rajya Sabha first formed ? *– In the year 1952* [UPPSC (Pre) 2017]
- In the representation of talent, experience and service in the formation of the Rajya Sabha, the makers of the Indian Constitution were influenced by *– Irish Republic* [UPPSC (Pre) 2017]
- The Council of States (Rajya Sabha) shall not be subject to dissolution it is a *– Permanent body* [WBCS (Pre) 2010]
- Who is the longest serving Chairman of the Rajya Sabha? *– Hamid Ansari* [APPSC (Pre) 2013]
- Name the bill which cannot be first introduced in Rajya Sabha ? *– Money Bill* [IAS (Pre) 2021]
- The Rajya Sabha can authorise to legislate a state subject by *– 2/3rd of the majority* [Nagaland PSC (Pre) 2015]
- Under which Article of the Indian Constitution can Rajya Sabha authorise the Parliament to legislate on a state subject by 2/3rd majority? *– Article 249* [JPSC (Pre) 2024]
- When was the first general election to the Lok Sabha held? *– In the year 1952* [BPSC (Pre) 1997, UKPSC (Pre) 2005, MPPSC (Pre) 2015]
- The provision of representation for the Anglo Indian Community in the Lok Sabha has been made in the Constitution of India by *– Article 331* [UPPSC (Mains) 2015]
- In which year for the first time in Rajya Sabha the Leader of opposition was given official recognition? *– In 1969* [IAS (Pre) 2018]
- How many Lok Sabha members are elected from Uttarakhand? *– 5 members* [UKPSC (Pre) 2021]
- Under which Article of the Indian Constitution, the provision for reservation of Scheduled Castes was made in the Lok Sabha? *– Article 330* [BPSC (Pre) 2018]
- What is the number of seats reserved for Scheduled Castes in the Lok Sabha? *– 84* [MPPSC (Pre) 2018]
- In order to be chosen a member of the Lok Sabha, a person must not been less than the age of *– 25 years* [BPSC (Pre) 2018]
- Rajya Sabha and Lok Sabha enjoy equal power in *– Amendment of Constitution* [WBCS (Pre) 2023]
- Who fixes the date of election of the Speaker of the Lok Sabha? *– President of India* [IAS (Pre) 2022]
- When a bill is referred to a joint sitting of both the Houses of Parliament it has to be passed by *– Simple majority of the members present and voting* [IAS (Pre) 2015]
- A Motion of No-Confidence against the government can be introduced by? *– Lok Sabha* [MPSC (Pre) 2010]
- What is the function of the Protem Speaker? *– Administer oath to new members* [UPPSC (Pre) 2010]
- What refers to the last session of the existing Lok Sabha, after a new Lok Sabha elected? *– 'Lame Duck Session'* [MPSC (Pre) 2016]
- The speaker can ask a member of the House to stop speaking and let another member speak. This phenomenon is known as *– yielding the floor* [Manipur PSC (Pre) 2014]
- The leader of the opposition in the Lok Sabha enjoys the rank of a *– Central Minister* [WBCS (Pre) 2015]
- President cannot return this bill to the Lok Sabha for reconsideration *– Money bill* [HPPSC (Pre) 2024]
- Any Money bill cannot be introduced in the Parliament without the consent of the *– President of India* [UPPSC (Pre) 2019, WBCS (Pre) 2022]
- Final authority to decide whether a bill is a Money bill or not *– Speaker of the Lok Sabha* [HPPSC (Pre) 2024]

- Bills other than Money bills are introduced for being passed by the Parliament in *– any House of the Parliament* [WBCS (Pre) 2022]
- What is the maximum permissible time gap between two sessions of the Parliament? *– 6 months* [APSC (Pre) 2015]
- What will happen if the President summons for the joint session of Parliament and in the meantime Lok Sabha dissolved? *– Joint session will be held in scheduled time* [CGPSC (Pre) 2018]
- What is the meaning of Guillotine in Parliamentary Procedure? *– To stop the debate on the bill* [CGPSC (Pre) 2017]

21. THE GOVERNOR

- Executive Power of the State is bestowed on the Governor by which Article of the Indian Constitution? *– Article 154* [WBCS (Pre) 2019]
- The appointment of a Governor in a State is made as per the provision in the Constitution under *– Article 155* [UPPSC (Pre) 2015]
- Who administers the oath of office and secrecy to the Governor? *– Chief Justice of High Court* [UKPSC (Pre) 2012, UP Lower Sub. (Pre) 2013, IAS (Pre) 2014]
- Under which Article, it is mentioned that the Governor shall hold office during the pleasure of the President? *– Article 156* [UPPSC (Pre) 2009]
- No criminal proceeding shall be instituted against the President and the Governor of a State in any court during his term of office under the *– Article 361* [IAS (Pre) 2018]
- When the same person is appointed as a Governor of two or more states, the emoluments and allowances payable to the Governor shall be *– allocated among the state in such proportion as determined by President.* [UPPSC (Pre) 2016]
- The commission suggested that the Governor should be an eminent person from outside the state and should be a detached figure without political links *– Sarkaria Commission* [IAS (Pre) 2019]

22. CHIEF MINISTER AND COUNCIL OF MINISTERS

- Who acts as a bridge between the Governor and the Council of Ministers? *– Chief Minister* [MPSC (Pre) 2012]
- According to which Article of the Constitution of India, the Chief Minister is appointed by the Governor of a State? *– Article 164* [UKPSC (Pre) 2016]
- Article 154 states that the Governor can exercise his executive authority either directly or through officers sub-ordinate to him. The word sub-ordinates include *– all Ministers and Chief Minister* [Nagaland PSC (Pre) 2012]
- A Bill of a State Legislature becomes an act, when it is signed by the *– Governor* [WBCS (Pre) 2015]
- Under which Article of Indian Constitution, the Governor may reserve a bill for the consideration of the President? *– Article 200* [UP Lower Sub. (Pre) 2004, CGPSC (Pre) 2015]
- The State Chief Election Commissioner is appointed by *– Governor* [MPPSC (Pre) 2022]
- Emergency in a state can be imposed by the President on the recommendation of the Governor under *– Article 356* [Nagaland PSC (Pre) 2016]
- The main force forming the principles of the procedure for the work of State Government is *– Secretariat* [CGPSC (Pre) 2022]
- The minimum strength of Council of Ministers including Chief Minister in the state *– 12 (Article 75 (1) (A)* [UPPSC (Pre) 2020]
- The Advocate-General of a State is appointed by *– Governor* [WBCS (Pre) 2020]
- It is duty of whom to give advice to the government of the state upon legal matters? *– Advocate-General* [MPPSC (Pre) 2024]

23. STATE LEGISLATURE

- The Upper House of the State Legislature is called *– Vidhan Parishad* [BPSC (Pre) 2000, RAS/RTS (Pre) 2016]
- Which Article of the Indian Constitution provides the provision of Vidhan Parishad in the state? *– Article 171* [MPPSC (Pre) 2014]
- The procedure of creation of Legislative Councils in states has been described in which Article of the Constitution? *– Article 169* [IAS (Mains) 2007]
- What is the tenure of a member of State Legislative Council? *– 6 years* [UKPSC (Pre) 2022]
- The number of nominated members in the Legislative Council is *– One-sixth of the total strength* [UPPSC (Mains) 2014]
- How many members are nominated in the Legislative Council of Uttar Pradesh by the State Governor ? *– 10* [CGPSC (Pre) 2011]
- Which state is an exception to the provision of Article 170, which says that State Legislative Assembly of a state shall consist of not less than sixty members? *– Sikkim* [UPPSC (Mains) 2015]
- What can be the maximum number of members in the Legislative Assembly of a state in India? *– 500* [IAS (Pre) 2008, UPPSC (Mains) 2014]
- The duration of State Legislative Assembly may be extended by Parliament for a period of *– One year at a time* [Telangana PSC (Pre) 2023]
- The maximum permissible period between two sessions of a State Legislative Assembly is *– 6 months* [APSC (Pre) 2016]
- For how much period/time the Legislative Council can hold the ordinary bill? *– 4 months* [IAS (Pre) 2005]
- No money bill can be introduced in assembly of a state, except on the recommendation of *– the Governor of the State* [UPPSC (Pre) 2012]

- The final authority to decide any question relating to disqualification of members of the legislature of a state is *– Governor [CGPSC (Pre) 2011]*
- Who conducts the State Assembly Elections? *– Election Commission of India [UPPSC (Mains) 2008]*
- Pay and allowances of the Ministers of a State Government are determined by the *– State Legislature Assembly [UPPSC (Mains) 2008]*
- Under which Article, the provisions for vote on account, vote of credit and exceptional grants mentioned? *– Article 206 [MPSC (Pre) 2015]*

24. SUPREME COURT

- Original jurisdiction of the Supreme Court includes *– a dispute between the governance of India and one or more states, a dispute between two or more states [HPPSC (Pre) 2024]*
- By which act the Federal Court in India was created? *– Under Government of India Act 1935 [UPPSC (Pre) 2014]*
- Under the Constitution of India, who is the guardian of Fundamental Rights? *– Judiciary [CGPSC (Pre) 2014]*
- Who is the custodian of the Constitution of India? *– The Supreme Court of India [MPPSC (Pre) 2010, 2015 IAS (Pre) 2015, UPPSC (Pre) 2022]*
- Article 124 *– establishment and composition of the Supreme Court of India [UP RO/ARO (Pre) 2024]*
- The supremacy of the Indian Constitution is upheld by *– the Supreme Court [Mizoram PSC (Pre) 2016]*
- The minimum number of judges of Supreme Court required for hearing any case involving interpretation of the Constitution *– Five [UPPSC (Pre) 2012]*
- The power to increase the number of judges in the Supreme Court of India is vested in *– the Parliament [BPSC (Pre) 2000, 2001, IAS (Pre) 2014]*
- The Supreme Court of India is different from its counterpart in the USA *– in its advisory role [IAS (Pre) 2016]*
- When was the Supreme Court inaugurated in India? *– 28th January, 1950 [MPPSC (Pre) 2013]*
- In India, 'Collegium System' was first introduced in relation to *– Judiciary [Odisha PSC (Pre) 2015, UKPSC (Pre) 2016]*
- The convention of appointing the seniormost judge of the Supreme Court as Chief Justice of India was broken in the appointment of *– Justice AN Ray [Nagaland PSC (Pre) 2015]*
- The Indian Constitution provides for the appointment of 'Ad-Hoc Judges' in *– Supreme Court [UPPSC (Mains) 2004, UPPSC (Pre) 2010]*
- The age of retirement of the Supreme Court judge is *– 65 years [WBCS (Pre) 2014]*
- A judge of the Supreme Court may resign his office by writing a letter to *– the President [UPPSC (Pre) 2014, BPSC (Pre) 2018]*
- This court can issue writs only for the enforcement of Fundamental Rights *– Supreme Court [Assam PSC (Pre) 2024]*
- Under which Article of the Constitution of India, Supreme Court safeguards the Fundamental Rights of the Indian citizens? *– Article 32 [WBCS (Pre) 2014]*
- Curative Petition in India be filed in Supreme Court under which Article? *– Article 137 [UPPSC (Mains) 2014]*
- The power of the Supreme Court of India to decide disputes between the Centre and the States falls under its *– Original jurisdiction [IAS (Pre) 1996, 2014, Odisha PSC (Pre) 2016]*
- Which Article of Constitution permits the Supreme Court to review its own judgement or order? *– Article 137 [JPSC (Pre) 2013]*
- All the cases regarding interpretation of the Constitution can be brought to the Supreme Court under its *– Original Jurisdiction [UPPSC (Pre) 2013]*
- The writ jurisdiction of the Supreme Court of India extends to *– the enforcement of the Fundamental Rights only [JPSC (Pre) 2009]*
- Which order is issued by the court to prevent a person from holding office to which he is not entitled? *– Quo-Warranto [Manipur PSC (Pre) 2008]*
- A legal action initiated in a court of law for the enforcement of public interest *– Public Interest Litigation [HPSC (Pre) 2024]*
- Supreme Court and High Court can entertain PIL under which Articles? *– Article 32 and Article 226 respectively [HPSC (Pre) 2024]*
- Where the Public Interest Litigation (PIL) can be filed? *– Both in High Court and Supreme Court [UKPSC (Pre) 2014]*
- Judicial Review in the Indian Constitution is based on *– procedure established by law [Nagaland PSC (Pre) 2014, CGPSC (Pre) 2015]*
- The system of Judicial Review is prevalent in *– both in India and USA [UPPSC (Mains) 2013]*
- The constitutional principle of the 'basic structure' was invented by the *– Judiciary [IAS (Pre) 2001]*
- In which case, Supreme Court held that 'Fundamental Rights enable a man to chalk out his own life in the manner he likes best'? *– Golaknath v/s State of Punjab [IAS (Pre) 2012]*
- The second largest bench constituted by the Supreme Court till date was in the *– 1976 Golaknath Case [UPPSC (Mains) 2004]*

28. LOCAL GOVERNMENT (PANCHAYATS AND MUNICIPALITIES)

- The Panchayati Raj System was introduced in the year *– 1959 [Mizoram PSC (Pre) 2016]*
- Which Constitutional Amendment given a constitutional status to the Panchayati Raj institution? *– 73rd Constitutional Amendment [WBCS (Pre) 2022]*

- The nomenclature of local government as 'Panchayati Raj' was the result of the suggestion of which Indian leader?
  – Mahatma Gandhi [UP RO/ARO (Pre) 2017]
- In which part of the Constitution, Panchayati Raj related Provisions have been implemented?
  – Part 9 [MPPSC (Pre) 2019]
- Feature of Panchayati Raj System
  – Three-tier structure, Direct election, reservation of seats [BPSC (Pre) 1992, WBCS (Pre) 2017, APSC (Pre) 2018]
- The system of Panchayati Raj is mentioned in *– State list* [BPSC (Pre) 2005, UKPSC (Pre) 2016, MPPSC (Pre) 2019]
- Panchayati Raj in India represents
  – decentralisation of powers [BPSC (Pre) 2000, 2014]
- Which is related to theme of Grass Root Democracy'?
  – Panchyati Raj System [UPPSC (Mains) 2013]
- Who is authorised to make provisions with respect to the composition of Panchayat?
  – Legislature of State [UPPSC (Pre) 2016]
- Panchayat is dissolved, elections are to be held within
  – 6 months [UPPSC (Pre) 2009, UKPSC (Pre) 2022]
- The Superintendence, direction and control of all elections to the Panchayats are vested in *– the State Election Commission* [UPPSC (Pre) 2020]
- Who is considered as the Architect of Panchayati Raj in India?
  – BR Mehta [BPSC (Pre) 2005, UK UDA/LDA (Mains) 2006, 2007, UPPSC (Pre) 2016, JPSC (Pre) 2024]
- The first state to implement 73rd Constitutional Amendment is
  – Madhya Pradesh [MPPSC (Pre) 2010]
- In which article the provision of reservation of Scheduled Castes and Scheduled Tribes to Panchayat has been given?
  – Article 243 (D) [CGPSC (Pre) 2016]
- Which article directs State Government to organise Village Panchayats? *– Article 40* [UPPSC (Pre) 2014, BPSC (Pre) 2014]
- Who works as a Chief Administrative officer and Secretary of the Panchayat Samiti?
  – Block Development Officer [MPPSC (Pre) 2011]
- In India, the first Municipal Corporation was set up in which state? *– Madras* [IAS (Pre) 2009]
- 74th Constitutional Amendment of India is related to
  – Urban local bodies [Punjab PSC (Pre) 2010]
- Which article deals with the power, authority and responsibilities of Municipalities?
  – Article 243 (W) [MPPSC (Pre) 2017]
- Which committee prepares the draft development plans for Metropolitan area? *– A Metropolitan Planning Committee* [UPPSC (Pre) 2011, MPSC (Pre) 2021, CGPSC (Pre) 2022]
- Under which article of the Indian Constitution is the District Planning Committee Constituted?
  – Article 243 (ZD) [JPSC (Pre) 2016]
- Which is the only link between the 73rd and 74th Constitutional Amendments?
  – District Planning Committee [MPPSC (Pre) 2017]
- The second Administrative Reforms Commissions has subtitled its report on Local Government as
  – An inspiring Journey into the future [MPPSC (Pre) 2015]
- According to Article 243 (ZJ) of Indian Constitution the maximum number of directors of a cooperative society may be
  – 21 [UPPSC (Pre) 2016]

29. CONSTITUTIONAL PROVISIONS OF UNION TERRITORIES

- How many states and Union Territories are there in India?
  – 28 States and 8 Union Territories [CGPSC (Pre) 2023]
- According to Article 239 (1), every Union Territory shall be administered by the *– President* [UPPSC (Pre) 1995]
- If a new state/Union Territory is to be formed, which schedule of the Constitution will need to be amended?
  – First Schedule [UP Lower Sub (Pre) 2008]
- How many states and Union Territories did the States Reorganisation Commission create in 1956?
  – 14 States and 6 Union Territories [MPPSC (Pre) 2004]
- The President has power to make regulations regarding which of the following?
  – Andaman and Nicobar Islands, Lakshadweep, Dadra and Nagar Haveli, Daman and Diu, and Puducherry [UKPSC (Pre) 2024]
- By which Constitutional Amendment, Delhi was given the status of National Capital Region (NCR)?
  – 69th Amendment Act, 1991 [UPPSC (Pre) 2014]
- The power of the President of India to make regulation for certain Union Territories under which article?
  – Article 240 [RAS/RTS (Pre) 2018]
- In 1961, which Union Territory became part of India and was annexed by 10th Amendment of the Indian Constitution?
  – Dadra and Nagar Haveli [CGPSC (Pre) 2022]
- Which Union Territory has a High Court of its own
  – Delhi [CGPSC (Pre) 2011]
- The Jurisdiction of the Union Territory of Lakshadweep is
  – Kerala High Court [MPPSC (Pre) 2014]

31. CONSTITUTIONAL BODIES

- Under which article of the Indian Constitution is the Comptroller and Auditor-General of India appointed?
  – Article 148 [UP Lower Sub (Pre) 2015]
- In which article of the Indian Constitution, the position and functions of the Comptroller and Auditor-General of India is explained? *– Articles 148 to 151* [Nagaland PSC (Pre) 2012, UP Lower Sub (Pre) 2015]
- The ultimate responsibility of taking due action on the comments of the Comptroller and Auditor-General vests with
  – President of India [UP RO/ARO (Mains) 2010]

- Comptroller and Auditor-General (CAG) of India acts as *– the Guardian of Public Finance [UK UDA/LDA (Mains) 2007]*
- The CAG of India is a friend and guide of *– Public Accounts Committee [UPPSC (Pre) 2006]*
- The Comptroller and Auditor-General of India can be removed from his office in like manner as *– Judge of the Supreme Court [RAS/RTS (Pre) 2018]*
- At the Centre and States the audit report of the CAG is handed over to the *– Public Accounts [MPPSC (Pre) 2017]*
- Which is considered as a 'think tank' in audit accounting and accountability matters? *– Institute of Public Auditors of India [MPSC (Pre) 2017]*
- Who called the CAG a toothless paper tiger? *– ER Subramaniam [MPSC (Pre) 2017]*
- Provision for appointment of National Commission for SCs and STs has been made in the Constitution under *– Article 338 and 338(A) [UPPSC (Pre) 2013]*
- Which Constitutional Amendment bifurcated the Combined National Commission to Scheduled Castes and Scheduled Tribes into 2 separate bodies? *– 89th Constitutional Amendment [JPSC (Pre) 2016]*
- The authority to specify as to which castes shall be deemed to be Scheduled Castes rests with the *– President [UPPSC (Mains) 2006]*
- How many sections are there under the Scheduled Castes and Scheduled Tribes (Prevention of Atrocities) Act, 1989? *– 23 [MPPSC (Pre) 2018]*
- Under which section of the 'Scheduled Tribes Rules, 1995 has 'Material for Annual Report' been provided? *– Section 18 [MPPSC (Pre) 2018]*
- The administrative head of the Secretariat who is also the Ex-officio Chairman of the Civil Services Board, is the *– Cabinet Secretary [CGPSC (Pre) 2023]*
- Under which article is the formation of Finance Commission laid down? *– Article 280 [BPSC (Pre) 2018, HPSC (Pre) 2024]*
- The State Finance Commission is a *– Constitutional Body [UPPSC (Pre) 2015, 2016, 2018]*
- Who appoints the Chairman of the Finance Commission? *– President [MPSC (Pre) 2010]*
- Who shall cause every recommendation made by the Finance Commission to be laid before each house of the Parliament? *– President of India [IAS (Pre) 2010]*
- Which constitutional mechanism is adopted for the distribution of resources between the Centre and the States? *– Indian Finance Commission [IAS (Pre) 2002, CGPSC (Pre) 2003, UPPSC (Pre) 2008, WBCS (Pre) 2012]*
- Who recommends to the Governor the principles which should govern the distribution between the state and the Panchayats of the net proceeds of the taxes and fees leviable by the state? *– State Finance Commission [CGPSC (Pre) 2019]*
- Under which article of the Constitution of India provides for a Finance Commission as a quasi- Judicial body? *– Article 280 [MPSC (Pre) 2015]*
- GST is a successor to VAT used in India on the Supply of goods and services. It came into effect from *– 1st July, 2017 [Assam PSC (Pre) 2024]*
- In case of differences of opinion among the Chief Election Commissioner and other Election Commissioner, the matter is decided by the *– The Election Commission decides the matter by the majority of opinions [MPPSC (Pre) 2024]*
- As per Article 76 of the Indian Constitution, the President shall appoint a person to be Attorney-General for India who is qualified to be *– appointed a judge of the Supreme Court [MPPSC (Pre) 2024]*

32. NON-CONSTITUTIONAL BODIES

- Mandal Commission, whose proposals created massive dispute was set-up by *– Morarji Desai [UPPSC (Pre) 2008]*
- The Planning Commission was set-up in the year *– 1950 [BPSC (Pre) 2005, Nagaland PSC (Pre) 2014]*
- Who works as the Chairman of the Planning Commission? *– Prime Minister [MPPSC (Pre) 2004, UK UDA/LDA (Pre) 2006, 2007]*
- Who was the First Chairman of the Planning Commission? *– Jawaharlal Nehru [UKPSC (Pre) 2006, Nagaland PSC (Pre) 2014]*
- NITI Aayog is a *– Non-Constitutional Body [Assam PSC (Pre) 2024]*
- The first Indian state to pass the Lokayukta Bill in 2011 is *– Uttarakhand [UPPSC (Pre) 2012]*
- The Lokayukta of Uttar Pradesh submits its report to *– Governor [UPPSC (Mains) 2017]*
- India model of Ombudsman is *– Lokpal [UPPSC (Mains) 2014]*
- Who has been appointed as the Chairperson of Lokpal of India in 2024? *– Shri Justice Ajay Manikrao Khanwilkar [MPPSC (Pre) 2024]*
- The National Commission for women was set-up as statutory body is January 1992, under the *– National Commission for Women Act, 1990 [UPPSC (Pre) 2014]*
- The tenure of the Chairman of the National Human Rights Commission is *– 3 years [MPPSC (Pre) 2017]*
- Chairperson and members of State Human Rights Commission are appointed by *– Governor [MPPSC (Pre) 2014, 2019]*
- According to National Human Rights Commission Act, 1993, its chairman can only *– a retired Chief Justice of India or a retired or serving Judge of the Supreme Court [UPPSC (Pre) 2004, 2007]*
- Who was the first Indian to join as a member of the UN Human Rights Commission constituted in 1946? *– Smt. Hansa Mehta [UKPSC (Pre) 2014]*

- In which year the Central Information Commission was established? *–2005* [UKPSC (Pre) 2022]
- Which act repealed the Official Secret Act, 1923 and replaced the Freedom of Information Act, 2002? *– RTI* [HPPSC (Pre) 2024]
- Who administered the oath of office of Chief Information Commission under the Right to Information Act, 2005? *– The President of India* [MPPSC (Pre) 2016]
- Central Vigilance Commission was set-up on the recommendation of *– Santhanam Committee Report* [Odisha PSC (Pre) 2015]
- Which legislation is extended to the whole of India and also applies to government servants and citizens of India residing outside India? *– Indian official Secrets Act, 1923* [MPSC (Pre) 2012]
- The creation of the institutions of the Lokpal was first recommended by *– Administrative Reforms Commission* [RAS/RTS (Pre) 2016]

33. PUBLIC SERVICES

- The chairman of the Union Public Service Commission holds office for a period of *– 6 years or till age of 65 years, whichever is earlier* [MPSC (Pre) 2013]
- The Union Public Service Commission submits its annual report to the *– President* [UPPSC (Pre) 2013]
- The Personnel system of local authority, corporate body or public institutions can be placed within the jurisdiction of the UPSC by *– Parliament* [MPPSC (Pre) 2017]
- Indian Administrative Service, Indian Police Service and Indian Forest Service are included in the *– All India Service* [MPPSC (Pre) 2012]
- Committee on recruitment policy and selection methods under the chairmanship of *– DS Kothari in 1976* [MPPSC (Pre) 2014]
- Which Article deals with recruitment and conditions of service of persons serving the Union or a State? *– Article 309* [MPPSC (Pre) 2015]
- The Chairman of a Joint Public Service Commission for Two or more states is appointed by *– President of India* [RAS/RTS (Pre) 2016]
- Who appoints the members of the State Public Service Commission? *– Governor* [UPPSC (Pre) 2022]
- Who can form Joint State Public Service Commission? *– Parliament of India* [MPPSC (Pre) 2012, UPPSC (Pre) 2022]
- Member of State Public Service Commission can be removed by *– President after the inquiry of the Supreme Court* [UPPSC (Pre) 2019]
- On which fund the expenditure of Uttar Pradesh Public Service Commission is charged? *– On the Consolidated Fund of the State* [UPPSC (Pre) 2010]
- Who can remove the Chairman of the State Public Service Commission? *– President on the recommendation of the Supreme Court* [MPSC (Pre) 2013]
- Rajasthan Public Service Commission presents its annual report to *– Governor of Rajasthan* [RAS/RTS (Pre) 2021]
- A Public Service Commission was established in India for the first time by *– the Government of India Act, 1919* [WBCS (Pre) 2023]

34. PROVISION RELATED TO OFFICIAL LANGUAGES

- The number of official languages recognised under Eighth Schedule of the Indian Constitution is *– 22* [UKPSC (Pre) 2006, BPSC (Pre) 2008, UPPSC (Pre) 2010]
- Which article of Indian Constitution provides the procedure for adoption of official language of the state? *– Article 345* [RAS/RTS (Pre) 2013]
- The provisions related to official language of India can be amended by *– Simple majority* [UPPSC (Mains) 2005]
- Which three languages have been added to the Eighth Schedule of the Constitution by 71st Amendment? *– Nepali, Konkani, Manipuri* [MPPSC (Pre) 1993, IAS (Pre) 2024]
- In which year the Maithili language was included in the Eighth Schedule of the Indian Constitution? *– 2003* [BPSC (Pre) 2014, IAS (Pre) 2017]
- Which state has given the Sanskrit language the status of second official language? *– Uttarakhand* [UPPSC (Pre) 2011]
- Which Article provides that every state shall endeavour to provide an adequate facility for instruction in mother tongue at primary stage of education? *– Article 350 (A)* [UP Lower Sub (Pre) 2002, UPPSC (Pre) 2003]
- Bodo is recognised as an official language under the Eighth Schedule by *– 92nd Constitutional Amendment Act of 2003* [UPPSC (Mains) 2016]

36. SPECIAL PROVISIONS FOR CERTAIN CLASSES

- The Part 16 of the Indian Constitution is related to the *– Special provisions for certain classes* [UP RO/ARO (Mains) 2017]
- The provisions of National Commission for Scheduled Tribes is given in which article of the Constitution? *– Article 338 A* [CGPSC (Pre) 2005, IAS (Pre) 2013, UKPSC (Pre) 2016]
- Which article provides reservation of seats for the Scheduled Castes and Scheduled Tribes in the Panchayats? *– Article 243 (D)* [UKPSC (Pre) 2016]
- The authority to specify as to which castes shall be deemed to be Scheduled Castes rests with the *– President* [UPPSC (Mains) 2006, UPPSC (Pre) 2016]

- Under which section of the Scheduled Castes and Scheduled Tribes (Prevention of Atrocities) Act, 1989, 'Economic boycott' is defined? *– Section 2 (b, c)* [MPPSC (Pre) 2018]
- Under the Scheduled Castes and Scheduled Tribes (Prevention of Atrocities) Act, 1989 in which section there is a provision for the arrangement of a special court? *– Section 14* [MPPSC (Pre) 2017]
- Who was the first chairman of the Backward Classes Commission? *– Kaka Saheb Kalelkar* [BPSC (Pre) 2018]
- In which year National Commission for Backward Classes was given constitutional states? *– 2018* [CGPSC (Pre) 2019]
- The Scheduled Castes and Scheduled Tribes (Prevention of Atrocities) Act, 1989 came into force on *– 30th January, 1990* [MPPSC (Pre) 2020]
- How many sections are there under the Scheduled Tribes and Scheduled Castes (Prevention of Atrocities) Act, 1989? *– 23* [MPPSC (Pre) 2018]
- Which Constitutional Amendment provides Reservation for EWS? *– 103rd Constitutional Amendment* [HPSC (Pre) (2024)]
- In which case is it alleged that the verdict of the Supreme Court of India diluted the stringent provisions of the Scheduled Castes and Scheduled Tribes (Prevention of Atrocities) Act, 1989? *– Subhash Kashinath Mahajan vs State of Maharashtra* [APPSC, (Pre) 2024]
- Under which Amendment Act was the reservation in promotion for the Scheduled Castes and Scheduled Tribes ensured by inserting Clause '4A' in Article 16? *– 77th Amendment Act, 1995* [JPSC (Pre) 2024]

37. SPECIAL PROVISIONS FOR CERTAIN STATES

- Which state was never granted the Special Category States (SCS) by Central Government? *– Bihar* [BPSC (Pre) 2019]
- Which article under the Indian Constitution pertains to special status of Jammu and Kashmir? *– Article 370* [UKPSC (Pre) 2016, Odisha PSC (Pre) 2018]
- Article 371 (B) of the Constitution of India makes special provisions for which state? *– Assam* [UPPSC (Mains) 2010]
- Which region of the country conferred special status under Article 371-J of the Constitution of the India? *– Hyderabad and Karnataka* [UPPSC (Pre) 2020]
- There is no separate citizenship for states as the Constitution of India provides for *– Single Citizenship* [IAS (Pre) 2005]
- Which part of the Constitution of India contains temporary, transitional and special provisions for states in Indian Constitution? *– 21st* [MPPSC (Pre) 2008]
- Article 371 of the Constitution makes special provisions for which states? *– Maharashtra and Gujarat* [UPPSC (Pre) 2010]
- Article 371C of the Constitution provides for the special provisions for which State ? *– Manipur* [Assam PSC, (Pre) 2024]

38. ELECTORAL PROCESS AND POLITICAL DYNAMICS

- The State Election Commission is constituted under the provisions of *– Article 243 (K) and 243 (ZA)* [UPPSC (Pre) 2015]
- Why the Tarkunde Committee was constituted? *– For elections reforms* [MPSC (Pre) 2015]
- One of the main defects of the single member constituencies is *– people choice regarding representative is narrowed* [MPSC (Pre) 2013]
- Every candidate is required to present which informations along with an affidavit while filling nomination paper in an election? *– Punishment of crime and certificate of age* [MPPSC (Pre) 2017]
- An essential and vital tool for the conduct of free and fair elections in our country *– the Model code of conduct for elections* [MPPSC (Pre) 2016]
- Where was the Votes Verifiable Paper Audit Trail (VVPAT) system first used by the Election Commission of India? *– Noksen Assembly Constituency (Nagaland)* [IAS (Pre) 2019]
- Which Article in the Indian Constitution is related with the establishment of the Election Commission of India? *– Article 324* [UPPSC (Pre) 2016, BPSC (Pre) 2020]
- The Chief Election Commissioner of India is appointed by *– by President* [UKPSC (Pre) 2010, UK UDA/LDA (Pre) 2017]
- Right to vote and to be elected in India is a *– Constitutional Right* [UP UDA/LDA (Pre) 2013, UPPSC (Pre) 2017]
- To be recognised as a National party, a political party must be a recognised party in at least *– 6 % vote + share + 4 states* [APSC (Pre) 2015]
- The Finance Commission is reconstituted *– every five years* [Assam PSC (Pre) 2024]
- In case of differences of opinion among the Chief Election Commissioner and other Election Commissioner, the matter is decided by the *– Law Commission* [MPPSC (Pre) 2024]
- In which of the seven phases announced by the Election Commission of India for the General Elections 2024, the elections were held in Uttarakhand? *– First* [UKPSC (Pre) 2024]
- Which political party is based on the support of a single religions community? *– Shiromani Akali Dal* [MPPSC (Pre) 2017]
- The first delimitation exercise in post-independent India was held in *– 1952 as per the 1951 Census* [Assam PSC (Pre) 2024]
- How many Delimitation Commissions have been constituted by the Government of India till December 2023? *– Four* [IAS (Pre) 2024]
- The Delimitation Commission is appointed by the President of India and works in collaboration with the *– Election Commission of India* [Assam PSC (Pre) 2024]

PRACTICE QUESTIONS

1. CONSTITUTIONAL DEVELOPMENT OF INDIA

1. Which one of the following statements best reflects the chief purpose of the 'Constitution' of a country? **IAS (Pre) 2023**

(a) It determines the objective for the making of necessary laws.
(b) It enables the creation of political offices and a government.
(c) It defines and limits the powers of government.
(d) It secures social justice, social equality and social security.

2. The first modern Court of India presided over by Elijah Impey was set up in **OPSC (Pre) 2024**

(a) Murshidabad (b) Patna
(c) Kolkata (d) Dhaka

3. Who among the following laid the foundation of English Education in India? **IAS (Pre) 2018**

1. Charter Act of 1813
2. General Committee of Public Instruction, 1823
3. Orientalist and Anglicist controversy

Select the correct answer by using the codes given below.

(a) Only 2 (b) 1 and 2
(c) 1 and 3 (d) 1, 2 and 3

4. Consider the following statements about the Charter Act of 1813. **UKPSC (Pre) 2016, UPPSC (Pre) 2019**

1. It ended the trade monopoly of East India Company in India except for trade in tea and trade with China.
2. It asserted the sovereignty of the British Crown over the Indian Territories held by the Company.
3. The revenues of India were not controlled by the British Parliament.

Which of the statements given above are correct?

(a) 1 and 2 (b) 2 and 3
(c) 1 and 3 (d) 1, 2 and 3

5. Which one of the following Acts of British India strengthened the Viceroy's authority over his Executive Council by substituting 'portfolio' or departmental system for corporate functioning? **UPPSC (Pre) 2002, 2021**

(a) Indian Councils Act, 1861
(b) Government of India Act, 1858
(c) Indian Councils Act, 1892
(d) Indian Councils Act, 1909

6. A Public Service Commission was established in India for the first time by **WBCS (Pre) 2023**

(a) The Indian Council Act, 1982
(b) The Act of 1909
(c) The Government of India Act, 1919
(d) The Government of India Act, 1935

7. Consider the following statements. **UPPSC (Pre) 2021**

1. The Montague-Chelmsford Reforms of 1919 recommended granting voting rights to all the women above the age of 21.
2. The Government of India Act of 1935 gave women reserved seats in Legislature.

Which of the statement(s) given above is/are correct?

(a) Only 1 (b) Only 2
(c) Both 1 and 2 (d) Neither 1 nor 2

8. The distribution of powers between the Centre and the States in the Indian Constitution is based on the scheme provide in the **IAS (Pre) 2012**

(a) Morley-Minto Reforms, 1909
(b) Montague Chelmsford Act, 1919
(c) Government of India Act, 1935
(d) Indian Independence Act, 1947

9. With reference to the Government of India Act, 1935, consider the following statements. **IAS (Pre) 2024**

1. It provided for the establishment of an All India Federation based on the union of the British Indian Provinces and Princely States.
2. Defence and Foreign Affairs were kept under the control of the federal legislature.

Which of the statement(s) given above is/are correct?

(a) Only 1 (b) Only 2
(c) Both 1 and 2 (d) Neither 1 nor 2

10. Consider the following statements. **HPPSC (Pre) 2024**

Statement 1 Finance Minister is final authority to decide whether a bill is Money Bill or not.

Statement 2 In Indian system of 'dyarchy' was introduced by the Government of India Act, 1935 during British period.

Which of the statement(s) given above is/are correct?

(a) Both Statement 1 and Statement 2 are correct.
(b) Both Statement 1 and Statement 2 are incorrect.
(c) Statement 1 is correct and statement 2 is incorrect.
(d) Statement 1 is incorrect and statement 2 is correct.

11. Which of the following terms were not the terms of August Offer? **OPSC (Pre) 2024**

1. A nominated India body would be framed after the war to frame the Constitution.
2. Dominion status was not the objective of India.
3. More Indian representation in Viceroy's Executive Council.
4. An Advisory War Council was to be established.

Codes

(a) 2 and 3 (b) 3 and 4
(c) 1 and 2 (d) and 4

12. Which Act was sanctioned by British Parliament on 18th July, 1947? **MPSC (Pre) 2022**

1. Indian Partition Act
2. Indian Independence Act
3. Draft Constitution Act
4. Constitutional Amendment Act

Codes
(a) 1 and 3 (b) 1 and 4
(c) Only 1 (d) Only 2

2. MAKING OF THE INDIAN CONSTITUTION

13. Statement I The first meeting of the Constituent Assembly was held on 9th December, 1946 in New Delhi.
Statement II Jawaharlal Nehru was not invited to the Constituent Assembly. **MPPSC (Pre) 2025**
Which of the following option is correct?
(a) Both Statement I and II are true.
(b) Both Statement I and II are false.
(c) Statement I is true, but Statement II is false.
(d) Statement I is false, but Statement II is true.

14. Who was the Provisional President of the Constituent Assembly before Dr. Rajendra Prasad took over?
(a) C. Rajagopalachari **IAS (Pre) 2024**
(b) Dr. BR Ambedkar
(c) TT Krishnamachari
(d) Dr. Sachchidananda Sinha

15. What was the exact Constitutional Status of India on 26th January, 1950?
(a) A Democratic Republic **IAS (Pre) 2021**
(b) A Sovereign Democratic Republic
(c) A Sovereign Secular Democratic Republic
(d) A Sovereign Socialist Secular Democratic Republic

16. Consider the following statements. **Manipur PSC (Pre) 2015**
1. Dr. Rajendra Prasad was the Chairman of the Rules Committee.
2. Maulana Abul Kalam Azad was a member of this Committee.

Which of the statement(s) given above is/are correct?
(a) Only 2 (b) Only 1
(c) Both 1 and 2 (d) Neither 1 nor 2

17. Which of the following statements are not correct in respect of Constituent Assembly'? **OPSC (Pre) 2024**
1. Elections to the Constituent Assembly were held in July-August, 1946.
2. The Indian National Congress won 208 Seats.
3. Muslim League won 73 Seats.
4. Princely States won 93 Seats.

Codes
(a) 1, 2, and 3 (b) 2, 3 and 4
(c) 1, 3 and 4 (d) 1, 2 and 4

18. Consider the following statements in respect of the Constitution Day. **IAS (Pre) 2023**
Statement 1 The Constitution Day is celebrated on 26th November every year to promote constitutional values among citizens.
Statement 2 On 26th November, 1949, the Constituent Assembly of India set-up a Drafting Committee under the Chairmanship of Dr. BR Ambedkar to prepare a Draft Constitution of India.
Which one of the following is correct in respect of the above statements?
(a) Both Statement 1 and Statement 2 are correct and Statement 2 is the correct explanation for Statement 1.
(b) Both Statement 1 and Statement 2 are correct and Statement 2 is not the correct explanation for Statement 1.
(c) Statement 1 is correct, but Statement 2 is incorrect.
(d) Statement 1 is incorrect, but Statement 2 is correct.

19. Which one of the following pairs (Schedule-Subjects) is not correctly matched? **IAS (Pre) 2023**

(a) Ninth Schedule	:	Allocation of seats in the Council of states.
(b) Third Schedule	:	Forms of Oaths or affirmations
(c) Eighth Schedule	:	Languages
(d) Tenth Schedule	:	Provisions as to disqualification on ground of defection.

20. Which of the following matchings are not correct in respect of Schedules and Subjects in Indian Constitution? **OPSC (Pre) 2024**

Schedules		Subjects
1. II	:	Emoluments for C&AG of India
2. III	:	Allocation of Seats in Council of States
3. VI	:	Administration and Control of Scheduled Areas,
4. IX	:	First Amendment of Indian Constitution

Codes
(a) 1 and 2 (b) 2 and 3
(c) 2 and 4 (d) 3 and 4

21. Match the following Schedules of the Indian Constitution List-I with their subject matters List-II. **Assam PSC (Pre) 2024**

List-I	List-II
A. Fourth Schedule	1. Forms of oath and affirmations
B. Eleventh Schedule	2. Languages
C. Eighth Schedule	3. Powers of Panchayats
D. Third Schedule	4. Allocation of seats in the Council of states

Codes

	A	B	C	D		A	B	C	D
(a)	1	3	2	4	(b)	4	3	2	1
(c)	2	3	4	1	(d)	1	2	4	3

22. Match List-I with List-II. **HPSC (Pre) 2024**

List-I	List-II
A. Second Schedule of Indian Constitution	1. Administration of Scheduled Areas
B. Fifth Schedule of Indian Constitution	2. Comptroller and Auditor- General
C. Ninth Schedule of Indian Constitution	3. Anti-Defection Laws
D. Tenth Schedule of Indian Constitution	4. Land Reform Laws

Codes

	A	B	C	D		A	B	C	D
(a)	3	1	4	2	(b)	1	2	3	4
(c)	2	1	4	3	(d)	4	3	2	1

(e) Question not attempted

23. Which of the following statements are correct about the Constitution of India? **IAS (Pre) 2024**
1. Powers of the Municipalities are given in Part IX A of the Constitution.
2. Emergency provisions are given in Part XVIII of the Constitution.
3. Provisions related to the Amendment of the Constitution are given in Part XX of the Constitution.

Codes
(a) 1 and 2
(b) 2 and 3
(c) 1 and 3
(d) 1, 2 and 3

3. SALIENT FEATURES OF THE INDIAN CONSTITUTION

24. The doctrine of 'basic structure' in the context of Indian Constitution was propounded in which of the following cases for the first time? **MPPSC (Pre) 2025**

(a) Sankari Prasad V. Union of India
(b) Champakan Dorairajan V. State of Madras
(c) Golaknath V. State of Punjab
(d) Keshavnanda Bharati V. State of Kerala

25. India borrowed the idea of Federal System with a strong centre from **JPSC (Pre) 2013, UPPSC (Pre) 2017**

(a) USA (b) Canada
(c) Australia (d) New Zealand

26. Consider the following statements. A constitutional government is one which **IAS (Pre) 2014**

1. places effective restrictions on individual liberty in the interest of state authority.
2. places effective restrictions on the authority of the state in the interest of individual liberty.

Which of the statements(s) given above is/are correct?

(a) Only 1 (b) Only 2
(c) Both 1 and 2 (d) Neither 1 nor 2

27. The cardinal features of political system in India are **IAS (Pre) 2009**

1. it is a democratic republic.
2. it has a parliamentary form of government.
3. the supreme power vests in the people of India.
4. it provides for a unified authority.

Select the correct answer by using the codes given below.

(a) 1 and 2 (b) 1, 2 and 3
(c) 2, 3 and 4 (d) All of these

28. Which one of the following pairs is not correctly matched? **UPPSC (Pre) 2021**

	Provisions		Sources
(a)	Fundamental Rights	:	USA
(b)	Directive Principles of State Policy	:	Ireland
(c)	Residual Powers of Centre	:	Australia
(d)	Emergency Powers	:	Germany

29. Match the features of Indian Constitution with the sources borrowed from different Constitutions of the world. **IAS (Pre) 2003, UPPSC (Pre) 2010, MPPSC (Pre) 2013**

	List-I (Features)		List-II (Sources)
A.	Office of the Governor	1.	Government of India Act, 1935
B.	Judicial Review	2.	British Constitution
C.	Directive Principles of State Policy	3.	Ireland Constitution
D.	Parliamentary System of Government	4.	American Constitution

Codes

	A	B	C	D		A	B	C	D
(a)	1	4	3	2	(b)	4	3	1	2
(c)	3	1	4	2	(d)	1	3	4	2

30. From which Constitution 'Suspension of Fundamental Rights during Emergency' was borrowed to Indian Constitution? **Odisha PSC (Pre) 2023**

(a) Soviet Constitution, USSR
(b) Weimar Constitution of Germany
(c) French Constitution
(d) Swiss Constitution

31. Consider the following pairs in respect of 'Sources of Indian Constitution' and pick up the right matchings. **Odisha PSC (Pre) 2023**

	Items		Sources
1.	Office of Governor	:	England
2.	Public Service Commission	:	Government of India Act, 1935
3.	Freedom of Trade and Commerce	:	USA
4.	The Language of Preamble of Constitution	:	Australia

Codes

(a) 1 and 2 (b) 2 and 3
(c) 2 and 4 (d) 3 and 4

32. The concept of five year plans in the Indian Constitution is borrowed from **WBCS (Pre) 2023**

(a) Russia
(b) England
(c) The United States
(d) Germany

33. Which one of the following statements best reflects the chief purpose of the 'Constitution' of a country? **IAS (Pre) 2023**

(a) It determines the objective for the making of necessary laws.
(b) It enables the creation of political offices and a government.
(c) It defines and limits the powers of government.
(d) It secures social justice, social equality and social security.

34. In essence, what does 'Due Process of Law' mean? **IAS (Pre) 2023**

(a) The principle of natural justice
(b) The procedure established by law
(c) Fair application of law
(d) Equality before law

4. THE PREAMBLE

35. The Preamble to the Constitution of India is **IAS (Pre) 2020**

(a) a part of the Constitution but has no legal effect.
(b) not a part of the Constitution and has no legal effect either.
(c) a part of the Constitution and has the same legal effect as any other part.
(d) a part of the Constitution but has no legal effect independently of other parts.

36. Which among the following is the correct order mentioned in Preamble of the Indian Constitution? **UP RO/ARO (Pre) 2024**

(a) Sovereign, Socialist, Secular, Democratic
(b) Secular, Socialist, Sovereign, Democratic
(c) Socialist, Secular, Sovereign, Democratic
(d) Sovereign, Secular, Socialist, Democratic

37. Which of the following words were not present in the Preamble of the Indian Constitution adopted on 26th November, 1949? **UKPSC (Pre) 2024**

1. Republic 2. Reliable
3. Socialist 4. Non-religious

Codes

(a) 1, 2, 3 (b) 2, 3, 4
(c) 1, 2, 4 (d) 3, 4

38. The term 'Political Justice' is mentioned in the Indian Constitution under which of these? **WBCS (Pre) 2023**

(a) Only under the Preamble to the Constitution of India
(b) Under both Preamble and Directive Principles
(c) Under Fundamental Rights and Directive Principles
(d) Under Preamble of the Constitution and Fundamental Rights

39. 'Economic Justice' as one of the objectives of Indian Constitution has been provided in **IAS (Pre) 2013**
(a) the Preamble and Fundamental Rights.
(b) the Preamble and the Directive Principles of State Policy.
(c) the Fundamental Rights and the Directive Principles of State Policy.
(d) None of the above

40. In the context of polity, which one of the following would you accept as the most appropriate definition of liberty? **IAS (Pre) 2019**
(a) Protection against the tyranny of political rulers.
(b) Absence of restraint.
(c) Opportunity to do whatever one likes.
(d) Opportunity to develop oneself fully.

41. Consider the following statements. **Telangana PSC (Pre) 2023**
1. The Constitution commands Justice, Liberty, Equality and Fraternity as supreme values to usher in the egalitarian social, economic and political democracy.
2. To establish an egalitarian social order, the trinity, the Preamble, the Fundamental Rights and the Directive Principles of State Policy delineate the path for socio-economic justice.

Which of the statements given above is/are correct?
(a) Only 1 (b) Only 2
(c) Both 1 and 2 (d) Neither 1 nor 2

42. Consider the following statements. **Andhra Pradesh PSC (Pre) 2023**
1. The Preamble was enacted before the enactment of the entire Constitution.
2. The Preamble is a part of the Constitution but has no legal effect independently of other parts.
3. It is enforceable through Courts of Law.
4. The Objective Resolution by Jawaharlal Nehru finally became the foundation for the Preamble.

Which of the statements given above are incorrect?
(a) 1 and 2 (b) 2 and 4
(c) 1 and 3 (d) 1, 2 and 3

43. Which the words have been incorporated in the Preamble by 42nd Amendment? **BPSC (Pre) 2024**
(a) Democratic and Socialist
(b) Republic and Secular
(c) Socialist and Sovereign
(d) Secular and Socialist

5. THE UNION AND ITS TERRITORIES

44. Consider the following statements about Union and its Territory. **CGPSC (Pre) 2023**
1. India comprises 28 States and 8 Union Territories.
2. India, a union of states, is a Sovereign, Socialist, Secular, Democratic, Republic with a Parliamentary System of Government.

Which of the statements given above is/are correct?
(a) Only 1
(b) Only 2
(c) Both 1 and 2
(d) Neither 1 nor 2

45. Given below are two statements, one is labelled as Assertion(A) and other as Reason (R).
Assertion (A) The President can recommend to the Parliament to change the boundary of any state after seeking views of the concerned Legislature of that state on the subject with in specified period.
Reason (R)It is not mandatory for the President to accept the proposal of the concerned State Legislature. **UPPSC (Pre) 2023**
Select the correct answer by using the codes given below.
(a) Both A and R are true, but R is not the correct explanation of A.
(b) A is false, but R is true.
(c) Both A and R are true and R is the correct explanation of A.
(d) A is true, but R is false.

46. Under the pressure of groups interested in linguistic regionalism, the President of the Constituent Assembly of India has appointed the Linguistic Provinces Commission to report on creation of provinces of Andhra, Karnataka, Kerala and Maharashtra. In which year was this Commission appointed and who was it chaired by? **APPSC (Pre) 2024**
(a) 1948, Justice Fazal Ali
(b) 1949, Pattabhi Sitaramayya
(c) 1950, Sardar Vallabhbhai Patel
(d) 1948, Justice SK Dhar

47. How many States and Union Territories were created according to the States Reorganisation Act, 1956? **MPPSC (Pre) 2025**
(a) 11 States and 6 Union Territories
(b) 12 States and 7 Union Territories
(c) 13 States and 7 Union Territories
(d) 14 States and 6 Union Territories

48. Which of the following is not a generally accepted parameter for granting special status to a state in India? **MPPSC (Pre) 2025**
(a) Hilly and difficult terrain
(b) Low population density
(c) Sizeable SC and ST population
(d) Strategic location along international border

49. A bill for the purpose of creating a new state in India must be passed by **IAS (Pre) 2021**
(a) a simple majority in Parliament and ratification by not less than two-third of states.
(b) a simple majority in Parliament.
(c) a two-third majority in Parliament and ratification by not less than two-third of the states.
(d) None of the above

50. Read the following statements with reference to State Reorganisation Commission, 1953. **CGPSC (Pre) 2022**
1. Justice Fazl Ali, KM Panikkar and Hridyanath Kunzru were its member.
2. Commission supported the splitting of Bombay and Punjab.
3. As per State Re-organisation Act, 1956 passed by Parliament, 14 states and 6 centrally administered states were made.

Which of the following statements given above is/are correct?
(a) 1, 2 and 3 (b) 1 and 2
(c) Only 1 (d) 1 and 3

6. CITIZENSHIP

51. The Constitution of India which came into force on 26th January, 1950 provides for **Nagaland PSC (Pre) 2012, UPPSC (Pre) 2015**

(a) Double Citizenship
(b) Single Citizenship
(c) Triple Citizenship
(d) None of these

52. With reference to India, consider the following statements **UPPSC (Pre) 2021**

1. There is only one citizenship and one domicile.
2. A citizen by birth only can become the Head of State.
3. A foreigner once granted the citizenship cannot be deprived of it under any circumstances.

Which of the statements given above is/are correct?

(a) Only 1
(b) Only 2
(c) 1 and 3
(d) 2 and 3

53. Which of the following rights is not enjoyed by a British citizen residing in India? **UKPSC (Pre) 2024**

(a) Freedom of Trade and Profession
(b) Equality Before Law
(c) Freedom of Life and Liberty
(d) Religious Freedom (Faith)

54. With reference to the latest notification in March, 2021 on Overseas Citizen of India (OCI) scheme, consider the following statements. **HPSC (Pre) 2021**

1. OCI can purchase agricultural land.
2. OCI can pursue the profession of doctor, advocates, architects and chartered accountants.
3. OCI needs special permit to visit any area in India notified as protected, restricted or prohibited by the Central Government or competent authority.
4. OCI can undertake any 'research', undertake any 'missionary' or 'journalistic' activities.

Which of the statements given above is/ are correct?

(a) 1 and 2
(b) Only 2
(c) 2 and 3
(d) Only 4

55. Which Articles of Indian Constitution are related to citizenship? **UPPSC (Pre) 2020**

(a) Articles 3 to 10 (b) Articles 4 to 11
(c) Articles 5 to 11 (d) Articles 6 to 11

56. Indian citizenship of a person can be terminated if **MPSC (Pre) 2023**

1. A person voluntarily acquires the citizenship of some other country.
2. A person who has become a citizen through registration is sentenced to imprisonment for 18 months within five years of his registration.
3. The Government of India is satisfied that citizenship was obtained by fraud.
4. A person has shown disloyalty to the Constitution of India.

Codes

(a) 1, 2 and 3 (b) 1, 3 and 4
(c) 2 and 3 (d) All of these

57. What is the purpose of the Citizenship (Amendment) Act, 2019? **BPSC (Pre) 2022**

(a) To remove Bangladeshi illegal immigrants.
(b) To identify genuine Indian citizens.
(c) To check border infiltration by foreigners.
(d) To grant citizenship to persecuted minority groups of Afghanistan, Bangladesh and Pakistan.
(e) None of the above/More than one of the above

58. In a Modern Democratic State, citizenship is a **Tamil Nadu PSC (Pre) 2022**

(a) Natural Right (b) Legal Right
(c) Statutory Right (d) Fundamental Right
(e) Answer not known

7. FUNDAMENTAL RIGHTS

59. In present times, Right to Property has been accepted in the Indian Constitution in which of the following forms? **MPPSC (Pre) 2025**

(a) Fundamental Right
(b) Directive Principles of State Policy
(c) Human Right
(d) Legal Right

60. Who is the protector of the Fundamental Rights of citizens? **WBCS (Pre) 2022**

(a) Legislature (b) Judiciary
(c) Executive (d) None of these

61. Match List-I with List-II and select the correct answer by using the codes given below the lists. **MPSC (Pre) 2017**

	List-I		List-II
A.	Right to elementary education	1.	Article 16
B.	Freedom to manage religious affairs	2.	Article 17
C.	Equality of opportunity in matters of public employment	3.	Article 21 (A)
D.	Protection of life and personal liberty	4.	Article 26
		5.	Article 21

Codes

	A	B	C	D
(a)	3	4	1	5
(b)	3	1	2	4
(c)	5	4	3	1
(d)	5	1	2	3

62. Consider the following statements. **MPSC (Pre) 2015**

1. Fundamental Rights are individual oriented but Directive Principles are community oriented.
2. Fundamental Rights seek to establish political democracy. Directive Principles seek to establish social democracy.
3. In a way Fundamental Rights are negative while the Directive Principles are positive.

Which of the statements given above are correct?

(a) 1 and 2
(b) 2 and 3
(c) 1 and 3
(d) 1, 2 and 3

63. Which of the following rights is not enjoyed by a British citizen residing in India? **UKPSC (Pre) 2024**

(a) Freedom of Trade and Profession
(b) Equality Before Law
(c) Freedom of Life and Liberty
(d) Religious Freedom (Faith)

64. Match List-I (Articles of the Constitution of India) with List-II (Provision) and select the correct answer using the codes given below the lists. **UPPSC (Pre) 2004**

List-I (Articles of the Constitution of India)	List-II (Provisions)
A. Article 14	1. The state shall not deny to any person equality before the law or the equal protection of laws within the territory of India.
B. Article 15	2. The state shall not discriminate against any citizen on grounds of religion, race, caste, sex, place of birth or any of them.
C. Article 16	3. There shall be equality of opportunity for all citizens in matters relating to employment or appointment to any office under the state.
D. Article 17	4. 'Untouchability' is abolished and its practice in any form is forbidden.

Codes

	A	B	C	D		A	B	C	D
(a)	2	4	1	3	(b)	3	1	4	2
(c)	1	2	3	4	(d)	3	4	1	2

65. Which of the following freedoms is not guaranteed by the Indian Constitution under Article 19? **UPPSC (Pre) 2024**

(a) Freedom to own, acquire and dispose of property
(b) Freedom to assembly peacefully and without arms
(c) Freedom to practice any trade or profession
(d) Freedom to move freely throughout the country

66. Reasonable restrictions on 'Exercise of Freedom of Speech and Expression' under Article 19(2) are justified in the interest of which of the following conditions? **JPSC (Pre) 2024**

1. Security of State 2. Defamation
3. Sedition 4. Public order

Codes

(a) 1 and 2 (b) 2 and 3
(c) 1, 2 and 4 (d) All of these

67. Which of the following is not a part of the Article 20 of the Constitution of India? **IAS (Pre) 2023**

(a) Double Jeopardy Clause
(b) Prohibition Against self-incrimination
(c) Prohibition Against Torture
(d) Ex-post Facto Law Torture

68. Right to Privacy is protected as an intrinsic part of Right to Life and Personal Liberty. Which of the following in the Constitution of India correctly and appropriately imply the above statement? **IAS (Pre) 2018**

(a) Article 14 and the provisions under the 42nd Amendment to the Constitution.
(b) Article 17 and the Directive Principles of State Policy in Part IV.
(c) Article 21 and the freedoms guaranteed in Part III.
(d) Article 24 and the provisions under the 44th Amendment to the Constitution.

69. Under which of the following Articles of the Constitution of India, the Supreme Court of India placed the Right to Privacy? **IAS (Pre) 2024**

(a) Article 15 (b) Article 16
(c) Article 19 (d) Article 21

70. In the context of Right to Freedom of Religion, which of the following provisions are constitutionally tenable under Indian Constitution? **MPSC (Pre) 2013**

1. Right to Freedom of Religion can be enjoyed only by the citizen of India.
2. State can make a law restricting any economic, financial or political activities associated with the religious practices.
3. State can make a law for throwing open Hindu religious institutions of public character to all the Indian citizens.
4. Carrying of Kripans shall be deemed to be profession of Sikh religion under Constitution.

Codes

(a) 2 and 4 (b) All of these
(c) 1, 2 and 3 (d) None of these

71. Which of the following are envisaged by the Right against Exploitation in the Constitution of India? **UPPSC (Pre) 2024**

1. Abolition of untouchability
2. Prohibition of human trafficking and forced labour
3. Prohibition of employment of children in factories and mines
4. Protection of interests of minorities

Select the correct answer from the codes given below.

(a) 3 and 4 (b) 2 and 3
(c) 1 and 4 (d) 1 and 2

72. Match List-I with List-II. **HPPSC (Pre) 2024**

List-I	List-II
A. Habeas Corpus Writ	1. Re-examining Lower court records by Superior court
B. Mandamus Writ	2. Exercising power under which authority
C. Certiorari Writ	3. Restricting officials to act
D. Quo Warranto Writ	4. To produce in person

Codes

	A	B	C	D		A	B	C	D
(a)	1	2	4	3	(b)	3	1	2	4
(c)	4	3	1	2	(d)	2	4	1	3

73. Consider the following statements. **HPSC (Pre) 2024**

1. The Writ, Mandamus can be issued against both public authorities and private individuals.
2. Mandamus can be issued to enforce a contractual obligation.
3. Mandamus cannot be issued against the Governor of a State.
4. Mandamus can be issued against a state to refund the tax collected unlawfully.

How many of the statement(s) given above is/are correct?

(a) Only one statement
(b) Two statements
(c) Three statements
(d) All four statements
(e) Question not attempted

74. In which of the following cases did the Supreme Court of India declare the prevalence of Fundamental Rights over Directive Principles of the State Policy in case of conflict between the two? **MPPSC (Pre) 2024**

(a) Golaknath *v/s* State of Punjab 1967
(b) The State of Madras *v/s* Champakam Dorairajan 1951
(c) Kesavananda Bharati *v/s* the State of Kerala 1973
(d) Minerva Mills *v/s* the Union of India 1980

75. Consider the following statements. **HPSC (Pre) 2024**

1. Privy Purse referred to a specific sum of money that was payable annually to rulers of former Princely States that signed the Instrument of Accession.

2. The payment of Privy Purse was a Constitutional obligation before the 42nd Amendment.
3. The abolition of Privy Purse was justified on the ground that it stood against the principle of egalitarianism enshrined in the Constitution.

How many of the statements given above is/are correct?
(a) Only one statement is correct
(b) Only two statements are correct
(c) All three statements are correct
(d) None of the statements is correct
(e) Question not attempted

8. DIRECTIVE PRINCIPLES OF STATE POLICY

76. Which Article of the Indian Constitution says that Directive Principles of State Policy are not enforceable by any court? **JPSC (Pre) 2024**
(a) Article 39 (b) Article 38
(c) Article 36 (d) Article 37

77. Which constitutional amendment has added Fundamental right to free and compulsory education of children between the age of 6 to 14 years? **MPPSC (Pre) 2025**
(a) By 68th Amendment
(b) By 85th Amendment
(c) By 86th Amendment
(d) By 87th Amendment

78. Consider the following statements with respect to Directive Principles of State Policy. **UP RO/ARO (Pre) 2024**
1. They are not enforceable by the courts.
2. It shall be the duty of the state to apply these principles in making laws.

Select the correct answer using the codes given below.
(a) Only 2 (b) Both 1 and 2
(c) Neither 1 nor 2 (d) Only 1

79. Consider the following provisions under the Directive Principles of State Policy as enshrined in the Constitution of India. **IAS (Pre) 2012**
1. Securing for citizens of India a Uniform Civil Code.
2. Organising Village Panchayats.
3. Promoting cottage industries in rural areas.
4. Securing for all the workers reasonable leisure and cultural opportunities.

Which of the above are the Gandhian Principles that are reflected in the Directive Principles of State Policy?
(a) 1, 2 and 4 (b) 2 and 3
(c) 1, 3 and 4 (d) All of these

80. Consider the following pairs. **HPSC (Pre) 2024**
1. Equal Justice and Free Legal Aid: Article 36 of Constitution
2. Promotion of Cooperative Societies: Article 43(B) of Constitution
3. Participation of Workers in Management of Industries: Article 43(A) of Constitution

How many of the pairs given above is/are correctly matched?
(a) Only one pair
(b) Only two pairs
(c) All three pairs
(d) None of the above
(e) Question not attempted

81. Consider the following pairs. **HPSC (Pre) 2024**
1. Educational and economic interest of weaker sections: Article 45 of Constitution
2. Educational and economic interest of SCs and STs : Article 46 to the Constitution
3. Organisation of agriculture and animal husbandry : Article 47 of the Constitution

How many of the pairs given above are correctly matched?
(a) Only one pair (b) Only two pairs
(c) All three paris (d) None of the pairs
(e) Question not attempted

82. Which of the following Articles of the Constitution of India talks about the Uniform Civil Code (UCC)? **JPSC (Pre) 2024**
(a) Article 43 (b) Article 44
(c) Article 45 (d) Article 46

83. Which of the following Provision is a part of both Directive Principles of State Policy and Fundamental Duties? **UPPSC (Pre) 2023**
(a) Participation of workers in managements of Industries
(b) Uniform Civil Code
(c) Guardians to provide opportunity for education to children
(d) Protection of environment

84. Which Constitutional Amendment Act relates to the protection and improvement of the environment and safeguarding of forests and wildlife? **UKPSC (Pre) 2024**
(a) 1972
(b) 1974
(c) 1976
(d) 1978

85. In which of the following cases did the Supreme Court of India declare the prevalence of Fundamental Rights over Directive Principles of the State Policy in case of conflict between the two? **MPPSC (Pre) 2024**
(a) Golaknath *v/s* State of Punjab (1967)
(b) The State of Madras *v/s* Champakam Dorairajan (1951)
(c) Kesavananda Bharati *v/s* the State of Kerala (1973)
(d) Minerva Mills *v/s* the Union of India (1980)

9. FUNDAMENTAL DUTIES

86. Fundamental Duties were appended to the Constitution of India by the 42nd Amendment on the recommendation of **IAS (Pre) 2001, 2012 APSC (Pre) 2013, RAS/RTS (Pre) 2021**
(a) Swaran Singh Committee
(b) Dr BR Ambedkar Committee
(c) KC Pant Committee
(d) CD Deshmukh Committee

87. Which of the following committee suggested incorporating Fundamental Duties in the Indian Constitution? **IAS (Pre) 2001, 2012, APSC (Pre) 2013**
(a) Malhotra Committee
(b) Raghavan Committee
(c) Swaran Singh Committee
(d) Narasimha Committee

88. Which of the following is/are among the Fundamental Duties of citizens laid down in the Indian Constitution? **IAS (Pre) 2012, Manipur PSC (Pre) 2014**
1. To preserve the rich heritage of our composite culture.
2. To protect the weaker sections from social injustice.
3. To develop the scientific temper and spirit of inquiry.
4. To strive towards excellence in all spheres of individual and collective activity.

Codes
(a) 1 and 2 (b) Only 2
(c) 1, 3 and 4 (d) All of these

89. In the context of India, which one of the following is the correct relationship between Rights and Duties? **IAS (Pre) 2017**
(a) Rights are correlative with Duties.
(b) Rights are personal and hence independent of society and Duties.
(c) Rights, not Duties, are important for the advancement of the personality of the citizen.
(d) Duties, not Rights are important for the stability to the state.

90. Protection of wildlife comes under which of the following in the Constitution of India? **Assam PSC (Pre) 2024**
1. Fundamental Duties
2. Directive Principles
3. Seventh Schedule
4. Fundamental Rights

Codes
(a) 1 and 2 (b) 2 and 4
(c) 1 and 3 (d) 1, 2 and 3

91. "To uphold and protect the Sovereignty, Unity and Integrity of India" is a provision made in the **IAS (Pre) 2015, HPSC (Pre) 2021**
(a) Preamble of the Constitution
(b) Directive Principles of State Policy
(c) Fundamental Rights
(d) Fundamental Duties

10. BASIC STRUCTURE OF THE CONSTITUTION

92. Identify the correct chronological sequence of the following. **UPPSC (Pre) 2024**
1. Shankari Prasad *v/s* Union of India
2. Sajjan Singh *v/s* State of Rajasthan
3. Golaknath *v/s* State of Punjab
4. Kesavananda Bharati *v/s* State of Kerala

Select the correct answer form the codes given below.
(a) 3, 2, 1, 4 (b) 1, 4, 3, 2
(c) 3, 4, 2, 1 (d) 1, 2, 3, 4

93. The concept of 'Basic Structure of the Constitution' is propounded by the Supreme Court in the case of **UPPSC (Pre) 2022**
(a) Yusuf *v/s* State of Bombay – 1954
(b) Golaknath *v/s* State of Punjab – 1967
(c) Chitralekha *v/s* State of Mysore – 1964
(d) Kesavananda Bharati *v/s* State of Kerala – 1973

94. Which of the following is a consequence of the basic structure doctrine?
(a) Parliament's power to amend the Constitution is unlimited.
(b) The Supreme Court's power to review constitutional amendments is limited.
(c) Fundamental Rights are absolute and cannot be amended.
(d) Constitutional amendments can be struck down for violating the basic structure.

95. Which case held that laws protected by the Ninth Schedule can be subject to judicial review?
(a) IR Coelho *v/s* State of Tamil Nadu (2007)
(b) Kesavananda Bharati Case (1973)
(c) Minerva Mills Case (1980)
(d) Waman Rao Case (1980)

96. The Doctrine of Fundamental Rights cannot be amended under Article 368 was propounded by the Supreme Court of India in **Tripura PSC(Pre) 2011**
(a) Gopalan *v/s* State of Madras
(b) Kesavananda Bharati *v/s* State of Kerala
(c) Golaknath *v/s* State of Punjab
(d) Menaka *v/s* Union of India

97. The Doctrine of Basic Structure has been propounded by
(a) Ajay Hasia Case **MPPSC (Pre) 2023**
(b) RD Shetty Case
(c) Kesavananda Bharati Case
(d) Valsama Case

11. AMENDMENTS OF THE CONSTITUTION

98. As per Article 368 of the Constitution of India, the Parliament may amend any provision of the Constitution by way of **IAS (Pre) 2024**
1. Addition
2. Variation
3. Repeal

Select the correct answer by using the codes given below.
(a) 1 and 2
(b) 2 and 3
(c) 1 and 3
(d) 1, 2 and 3

99. Consider the following statements. **HPPSC (Pre) 2024**
1. A Constitution Amendment Bill can be introduced in any House of the Parliament.
2. The Centre and States have equal power to amend the Constitution.
3. Amendment in the Seventh Schedule requires the ratification by the legislatures of not less than half of the states.
4. Basic structure of the Constitution can also be amended.

Choose the correct answer from the options given below.
(a) 1 and 3 (b) 2 and 3
(c) 4 and 1 (d) 2 and 4

100. Consider the following statements. **HPSC (Pre) 2024**
1. In order to form a new state in the Indian union, the Parliament can amend the provisions of the Constitution with a simple majority.
2. To amend the provisions of Directive Principles of State Policy, the Parliament requires a special majority.
3. To amend Article 368 of the Constitution, the Parliament requires special majority along with the consent of half of the State Legislatures.

How many of the statements given above is/are correct?
(a) Only one statement is correct
(b) Only two statements are correct
(c) All three statements are correct
(d) None of the statements are correct
(e) Question not attempted

101. What is the position of representation of Anglo-Indian Community in Lok Sabha? **BPSC (Pre) 2024**
(a) Nomination of them has been done away with by 104th Constitutional Amendment.
(b) Two Anglo-Indians are nominated by the President.
(c) They are nominated as per their population.
(d) One Anglo-Indian is nominated by the President.

102. Consider the following statements. **IAS (Pre) 2022**
1. A bill amending the Constitution requires a prior recommendation of the President of India.

2. When a Constitution Amendment Bill is presented to the President of India, it is obligatory for the President of India to give his/her assent.
3. A Constitution Amendment Bill must be passed by both the Lok Sabha and the Rajya Sabha by a special majority and there is no provision for joint sitting.

Which of the statements given above are correct?
(a) 1 and 2
(b) 2 and 3
(c) 1 and 3
(d) 1, 2 and 3

103. Which of the following Constitutional Amendments provided rights for making provisions in favour of the SCs and STs for relaxation of qualifying marks in any examination (or) lowering the standards of evaluation and for reservation in the matter of promotions to the public services of the Centre and the State?
APPSC (Pre) 2024

(a) 80th Constitutional Amendment
(b) 82nd Constitutional Amendment
(c) 89th Constitutional Amendment
(d) 93rd Constitutional Amendment

104. Match List-I Amendments with List-II their year of implementation.
UPPSC (Pre) 2024

	List-I		List-II
A.	42nd Amendment	1.	1985
B.	52nd Amendment	2.	2011
C.	86th Amendment	3.	1976
D.	96th Amendment	4.	2002

Codes

	A	B	C	D		A	B	C	D
(a)	4	3	2	1	(b)	2	1	3	4
(c)	3	1	4	2	(d)	1	2	3	4

105. Match List I with List II.
HPSC (Pre) 2024

	List-I		List-II
A.	26th Constitutional Amendment	1.	Reservation for EWS
B.	52nd Constitutional Amendment	2.	Education as Fundamental Right
C.	86th Constitutional Amendment	3.	Abolition of Privy Purse
D.	103rd Constitutional Amendment	4.	Anti-Defection Law

Choose the correct answer from the options given below.

	A	B	C	D		A	B	C	D
(a)	3	4	2	1	(b)	1	3	2	4
(c)	2	1	4	3	(d)	4	3	2	1

(e) Question not attempted

106. Consider the following statements.
RAS/RTS (Pre) 2013, IAS (Pre) 2019

1. The 44th Amendment to the Constitution of India introduced an Article placing the election of the Prime Minister beyond judicial review.
2. The Supreme Court of India struck down the 99th Amendment to the Constitution of India as being violative of the independence of judiciary.

Which of the statements given above is/are correct?
(a) Only 1 (b) Only 2
(c) Both 1 and 2 (d) Neither 1 nor 2

107. The 91st Constitutional Amendment Act, 2003 made a specific provision that, the total number of Minister, including Prime Minister in no case can exceed of the total number of Lok Sabha members.
IAS (Pre) 2007, UPPSC (Pre) 2015, Manipur PSC (Pre) 2016

(a) 10% (b) 15%
(c) 20% (d) 25%

12. PARLIAMENTARY FORM OF GOVERNMENT

108. Which of the following is a characteristic of the parliamentary system of government?
(a) Separation of powers between the executive and legislative branches.
(b) The executive is accountable to the legislature.
(c) The President is the head of both state and government.
(d) The Prime Minister is the ceremonial head of state.

109. Which of the following is/are stated in the Consitution of India?
UPPSC (Pre) 2024

1. The President shall not be a member of either of the Houses of the Parliament.
2. The Parliament shall consists of the President and both Houses.

Select the correct answer form the codes given below.
(a) Only 2 (b) Both 1 and 2
(c) Only 1 (d) Neither 1 nor 2

110. The presidential system of government follows the doctrine of separation of powers.
Which of the following is a consequence of this?
(a) Concentration of power in a single individual.
(b) Cooperative relationship between legislature and executive.
(c) Uncertainty in the continuity of long-term policies.
(d) Independence of the executive from the legislature.

111. In a parliamentary system, the executive is accountable to the legislature.
Which of the following is a consequence of this?
(a) Separation of powers between the executive and legislative branches.
(b) Concentration of power in a single individual.
(c) Uncertainty in the continuity of long-term policies.
(d) Cooperative relationship between legislature and executive.

112. Which of the following statements is true about the Parliamentary System in India?
(a) The President is the head of both state and government.
(b) The Prime Minister is the ceremonial head of state.
(c) The Council of Ministers is responsible only to the President.
(d) The Parliament is not sovereign.

13. FEDERALISM AND FEDERAL STRUCTURE

113. Which type of government concentrates all power in the hands of the National Government, with regional governments deriving authority from the National Government?
(a) Federal Government
(b) Unitary Government
(c) Confederate Government
(d) Republican Government

114. Consider the nature of Indian federal structure and identify the most accurate description.
(a) Federal in form and unitary in spirit, with equal state representation
(b) Quasi-federal, with a strong unitary bias during emergencies
(c) Unitary, with no federal features
(d) Confederate, with absolute state autonomy

115. **Assertion** (A) The primary objective of India's Federal design was to weave a nation out of its many diverse parts and protect national integration.
Reason (R) Accommodation of diversities has built a stronger not weaker, Indian Nationhood.
Codes **RAS/RTS (Pre) 2013**
(a) Both A and R are true and R is the correct explanation of A.
(b) Both A and R are true, but R is not the correct explanation of A.
(c) A is true, but R is false.
(d) A is false, but R is true.

116. Which one of the following in Indian polity is an essential feature that indicates that it is federal in character? **IAS (Pre) 2017, 2021**
(a) The independence of judiciary is safeguarded.
(b) The Union Legislature has elected representatives from constituent units.
(c) The Union Cabinet can have elected representatives from regional parties.
(d) The Fundamental Rights are enforceable by Courts of Law.

117. Which one of the following statement is false? **MPSC (Pre) 2016**
1. Our Constitution distributes between the Union and the States not only the legislative power but also the executive power.
2. The President may, without any legislative sanction, entrust any executive function to state.
3. With the consent of the Government of India, the Governor of a State may entrust on the Union Government or its officers functions related to a state subject.

Codes
(a) Only 1
(b) Only 2
(c) Only 3
(d) None of the above

118. Which of the following statements regarding the residuary powers under the Constitution of India is/are correct?
1. Residuary powers have been given to the Union Parliament.
2. In the matter of the residuary power, the Constitution of India follows the Constitution of Australia.
3. Seventh Schedule of the Constitution of India provides a list of residuary powers.
4. The Government of India Act, 1935 placed residuary powers in the hands of the Governor-General.

Select the correct answer using the codes given below.
(a) 1 and 3 (b) 2 and 3
(c) 1 and 4 (d) Only 4

119. Which of the following is a unitary elements in Indian Federal System? **CGPSC (Pre) 2017**
1. Decentralisation of Powers
2. Appointment of Governors
3. Unequal representation in Rajya Sabha
4. Judicial Review
5. All India Services
6. Bicameral Legislature

Codes
(a) 1, 2 and 4 (b) 2, 3 and 5
(c) 3, 5 and 6 (d) 2, 4 and 5

120. Given below are two statements, one is labelled as Assertion (A) and the other as Reason (R). **MPPSC (Pre) 2008**
Assertion (A) Constitution of India is basically federal in nature.
Reason (R) Article 352 has provisions to deal with the failure of constitutional machinery in a state.
Select the correct answer from the codes given below.
(a) Both A and R are true and R is the correct explanation of A.
(b) Both A and R are true, but R is not the correct explanation of A.
(c) A is true, but R is false.
(d) A is false, but R is true.

14. CENTRE-STATE RELATIONS

121. Consider the following statements. **HPSC (Pre) 2024**
1. Parliament can legislate on matters enumerated in the State List if two or more State Legislatures pass resolutions requesting the Parliament to enact such laws.
2. A law so enacted will be equally applicable to all the states, irrespective of whether they passed such a resolution or not.
3. Such a law can be amended or repealed only by the Parliament.

How many of the statements given above is/are correct?
(a) Only one statement is correct
(b) Only two statements are correct
(c) All three statements are correct
(d) None of the statements is correct
(e) Question not attempted

122. Consider the following pairs. **HPSC (Pre) 2024**
1. Establishment of standards of weight and measures : Union List
2. Adoption and succession : State List
3. Betting and gambling : Concurrent List

How many of the following pairs is/are correct?
(a) Only one pair (b) Only two pairs
(c) All three pairs (d) None of the pairs
(e) Question not attempted

123. Consider the following statements. **HPSC (Pre) 2024**
1. Residuary subjects are the subjects that are not included in the three lists of the 7th Schedule of the Constitution.
2. According to Article 248, both the Union Parliament and State Legislatures can make laws on these subjects.
3. Space technology is an example of a residuary subject.

How many of the statements given above is/are correct?
(a) Only one statement is correct
(b) Only two statements are correct
(c) All three statements are correct
(d) None of the statements is correct
(e) Question not attempted

124. Under which Article of the Indian Constitution, can the Rajya Sabha authorise the Parliament to legislate on a state subject by 2/3rd majority ? **JPSC (Pre) 2024**
(a) Article 249
(b) Article 243
(c) Article 259
(d) Article 250

125. The North Eastern Council (NEC) was established by the North Eastern Council Act, 1971 Subsequent to the Amendment of NEC Act in 2002, the Council comprises which of the following members? **IAS (Pre) 2024**

1. Governor of the Constituent State
2. Chief Minister of the Constituent State
3. Three Members to be nominated by the President of India
4. The Home Minister of India

Select the correct answer by using the codes given below.

(a) 1, 2 and 3 (b) 1, 3 and 4
(c) 2 and 4 (d) 1, 2, 3 and 4

126. Which of the following statements are correct regarding the Legal relationship between the Central and State Government in India? **MPSC (Pre) 2023**

1. The Subject of transfer of property other than Agricultural Land is included in the Concurrent List.
2. The Subject of Wealth Tax on property other than Agricultural Land is included in the Union List.
3. The Subject of Entertainment Tax is included in the Concurrent List.
4. The Subject of 'Antiquities Museum' is included in the State List.

Select the correct answer by using the codes given below.

(a) 1, 2 and 3 (b) 2, 3 and 4
(c) 1, 2 and 4 (d) 1, 3 and 4

15. INTER-STATE RELATIONS

127. Under which of the following Articles of the Constitution, Inter-State Council has been constituted? **UKPSC (Pre) 2024**

(a) Article 360 (b) Article 263
(c) Article 365 (d) Article 368

128. Article 301 of the Indian Constitution guarantees freedom from restrictions on trade, commerce and intercourse, but with certain exceptions. Which of the following is not an exception to Article 301?

(a) Parliament's power to regulate trade in public interest.
(b) State legislature's power to impose reasonable restrictions with President's approval.
(c) Imposition of discriminatory taxes on goods imported from other states.
(d) Nationalisation laws for government monopolies.

129. Which one of the following matters stands excluded from the jurisdiction of Inter-State Council in India? **MPSC (Pre) 2020**

(a) Enquiring into and advice upon disputes which may have arisen between the States.
(b) Adjudication of any dispute with respect to the use, distribution or control of water of any inter-state river.
(c) Investigation and discussion of subjects in which some or all of the states or the union and one or more states, have common interest.
(d) Making recommendation on any such subject and in particular, recommendations for the better coordination of policy and action with respect to the subject.

130. Consider the following statements.

1. Zonal Councils have been established under an article of the Constitution.
2. The Constitution provides for setting up of an Inter-State Council by the Parliament.
3. Union Home Minister is the common Chairman of all the Zonal Councils.

Select the correct answer by using the codes given below.

(a) 1 and 2 (b) Only 3
(c) Only 2 (d) 2 and 3

131. Which of the following statements about the Zonal Councils are not correct? **MPSC (Pre) 2017, UPPSC (Pre) 2017**

1. The Zonal Councils are the constitutional bodies.
2. They are established by the States Re-organisation Act of 1956.
3. Home Minister of the Central Government is the Chairman of the Zonal Councils.
4. India is divided into seven zones and provides a Zonal Council for each zone.

Codes

(a) 1 and 3
(b) 1 and 4
(c) 1, 3 and 4
(d) All of the above

16. EMERGENCY PROVISIONS

132. Under whose advice can the President of India declare Emergency under Article 352? **MPPSC (Pre) 2024**

(a) Chief Ministers of all States
(b) Prime Minister
(c) Union Cabinet
(d) Council of Ministers

133. In case of proclamation of emergency on the grounds of war or external aggression, which of the following is incorrect?

1. All Fundamental Rights will be automatically suspended.
2. The right to move a court for enforcement of any Fundamental Right is suspended.
3. The President may order the suspension of enforcement of any Fundamental Right except Articles 20-21.
4. The Parliament may authorise suspension of all Fundamental Rights.

Select the correct answer by using the codes given below.

(a) 1, 3 and 4 (b) 1, 2 and 4
(c) 2, 3 and 4 (d) All of these

134. Which one of the following extraordinary powers, the Indian Constitution provides to the Centre to deal with an emergency arising out war, external aggression or armed rebellion? **MPSC (Pre) 2013**

1. Centre can modify the provisions relating to the distribution of revenue between the Centre and the States.
2. Centre can give directions to any State as to the manner in which its executive powers are to be exercised.
3. Parliament can make laws with respect to any matter enumerated in the State List.
4. Centre can order the reduction of salaries of state employees, including the Judges of High Court.

Select the correct answer by using the codes given below.

(a) 1, 3 and 4 (b) 1, 2 and 4
(c) 1, 2 and 3 (d) 2, 3 and 4

135. What is correct about External Emergency as per Article 352 ? **CGPSC (Pre) 2017**

1. It is proclaimed by the President.

2. It should be approved by Parliament within two months.
3. It should be approved by Parliament within one month.
4. It should be approved by Parliament by simple majority.
5. It should be approved by two-third majority of Parliament.
6. It can be revoked by simple majority of Parliament.
7. It can be revoked by two-third majority of Parliament.
8. It can be approved in joint session of Parliament.

Codes

(a) 1, 2, 3 and 8 (b) 1, 3, 6 and 8
(c) 1, 3, 5 and 6 (d) 1, 4, 7 and 8
(e) None of these

136. Consider the following statements regarding the proclamation of emergency under Article 352. **MPSC (Pre) 2017**

1. It automatically comes to an end on the expiry of one month from its issue, unless it is approved by a resolution of the Lok Sabha before the expiry of that period.
2. The President is empowered to proclaim emergency only if the Council of Ministers recommends to him in writing that such a proclamation should be issued.

Which of the statements given above is/are correct?

(a) Only 1 (b) Only 2
(c) Both 1 and 2 (d) Neither 1 nor 2

137. Given below are two statements, one is labelled as Assertion (A) and the other as Reason (R). **UPPSC (Pre) 2024**

Assertion (A) Article 352 of the Indian Constitution deals with the declaration of an emergency.

Reason (R) An emergency may take place at any time

Select the correct answer by using the codes given below.

(a) A is false, but R is true.
(b) Both A and R are true, but R is not the correct explanation of A.
(c) A is true, but R is false.
(d) Both A and R are true and R is the correct explanation of A.

138. Which of the following are not necessarily the consequences of the proclamation of the President's Rule in a state? **IAS (Pre) 2017**

1. Dissolution of the State Legislative Assembly
2. Removal of the Council of Ministers in the state
3. Dissolution of the local bodies

Codes

(a) 1 and 2 (b) 1 and 3
(c) 2 and 3 (d) All of these

139. Consider the following statements regarding Article 356 of the Constitution. **RAS/RTS (Pre) 2013**

1. Failure of constitutional machinery in states is an objective reality.
2. A proclamation under this Article can be reviewed by Supreme Court.
3. Alongwith this proclamation, State Legislative Assembly can be dissolved.
4. This proclamation has to be approved by each House of Parliament within two months.

Which of the statements given above are correct?

(a) 1, 2 and 4 (b) 1, 2 and 3
(c) 3 and 4 (d) 2, 3 and 4

17. THE PRESIDENT

140. According to the Constitution of India, who among the following is the Head of the State? **UKPSC (Pre) 2024**

(a) Prime Minister
(b) President
(c) Home Minister
(d) Vice-President

141. Consider the following statements. **HPSC (Pre) 2024**

1. The election to the office of the President of India is held in accordance with the system of proportional representation by means of single non-transferable vote.
2. The value of the vote of each Member of Parliament from Uttar Pradesh is greater than the value of the vote of the MP from Goa.
3. Electors cannot use the provision of NOTA in the election of a President.
4. The provisions of Anti-defection law are not applicable in Presidential elections.

How many of the statements given above are correct?

(a) 1 and 2
(b) 2 and 3
(c) 3 and 4
(d) 1, 2 and 4
(e) Question not attempted

142. Consider the following statements. **IAS (Pre) 2023**

1. If the election of the President of India is declared void by the Supreme Court of India, all acts done by him/her in the performance of duties of his/her office of President before the date of decision become invalid.
2. Election for the post of the President of India can be postponed on the ground that some Legislative Assemblies have been dissolved and elections are yet to take place.
3. When a Bill is presented to the President of India, the Constitution prescribes time limits within which he/she has to declare his/her assent.

How many of the statements given above are correct?

(a) Only one (b) Only two
(c) All three (d) None of these

143. Which of the following do not participate in the process of election of President of India? **KAS (Pre) 2022**

1. Nominated members of both the houses of Parliament.
2. Nominated members of Legislative Assemblies.
3. Elected members of Legislative Council.
4. Elected members of UT Legislative Assemblies.

How many statements given above is/are correct?

(a) Only one (b) Only two
(c) Only three (d) All four

144. Consider the following statements.

1. The President of India can summon a session of the Parliament at such place as he/she thinks fit.
2. The Constitution of India provides for three sessions of the Parliament in a year, but it is not mandatory to conduct all three sessions.
3. There is no minimum number of days that the Parliament is required to meet in a year. **IAS (Pre) 2020**

Which of the statements given above is/are correct?

(a) Only 1 (b) Only 2
(c) 1 and 3 (d) 2 and 3

145. Given below are two statements, one is labelled as Assertion (A) and other as Reason (R).

Assertion (A) The President is a part of the Parliament.

Reason (R) A bill passed by the two Houses of the Parliament cannot become a law without the assent of the President. **UPPSC (Pre) 2023**

Select the correct answer by using the codes given below.

(a) A is true, but R is false.
(b) Both A and R are true and R is the correct explanation of A.
(c) Both A and R are true, but R is not the correct explanation of A.
(d) A is false, but R is true.

146. According to the Constitution of India, it is the duty of the President to present which of the following on the desk of the Parliament? **WBCS (Pre) 2019, IAS (Pre) 2012**

1. Recommendations of Union Finance Commission.
2. Report of the Public Accounts Committee.
3. Report of the Comptroller and Auditor-General.
4. Report of the National Scheduled Caste Commission.

Which of the statements given above is/are correct?

(a) Only 1 (b) 2 and 4
(c) 1, 3 and 4 (d) All of these

147. The President has power to make regulations regarding which of the following? **UKPSC (Pre) 2024**

1. Dadra and Nagar Haveli
2. Daman and Diu
3. Goa, Daman and Diu
4. Puducherry

Codes

(a) 1, 2, 3, 4 (b) 1, 2, 3
(c) 1, 3, 4 (d) 1, 2, 4

148. Which of the following statements is not correct regarding the issuance of Ordinance by the President? **UKPSC (Pre) 2024**

(a) It is linked to the legislative powers of Parliament.
(b) Article 123 deals with it.
(c) It ceases to exist after six weeks of Parliament session.
(d) President can never repeal it.

149. Which of the following are the discretionary powers of President? **CGPSC (Pre) 2017**

1. To appoint Prime Minister to the leader of majority party.
2. To summon the Parliament.
3. To return a bill to Parliament with objections.
4. To appoint the Members of Council of Ministers.
5. To assent the bill referred by Governor.
6. To detain a bill.
7. To ask the Prime Minister for such information related to any advice.
8. To say the Council of Ministers for reconsideration on any advice.

Codes

(a) 1, 2, 4, 7 (b) 2, 5, 6, 8
(c) 1, 3, 6, 8 (d) 2, 5, 7, 8

18. VICE-PRESIDENT

150. Consider the following pairs. **HPSC (Pre) 2024**

1. The Vice-President of India: Article 62 of Constitution
2. Election of Vice-President: Article 65 of Constitution
3. Terms of office of President: Article 59 of Constitution

How many of the pairs given above is/are correctly matched?

(a) Only one pair (b) Only two pairs
(c) All three pairs (d) None of the pairs
(e) Question not attempted

151. The Vice-President of India **UPPSC (Pre) 2013**

1. is the second highest dignitary of India.
2. has no formal function attached to his office.
3. discharges the functions of the President during his absence.
4. acts as the President if the President resigns or is removed or dies.

Select the correct answer by using the codes given below.

(a) 1 and 2 (b) 1, 2 and 3
(c) 1, 3 and 4 (d) All of these

152. Consider the following statements about the Vice-President of India. **CGPSC (Pre) 2024**

1. He is an Ex-officio Chairman of the Rajya Sabha.
2. He is elected by members of an electoral college consisting of members of both Houses of Parliament.

Which of the statements given above is/are correct?

(a) Only 1 (b) Only 2
(c) Both 1 and 2 (d) None of these

153. With reference of the election of the Vice-President of India, which is declared void by the Supreme Court of India, which of the following statements is/are correct? **UPPSC (Pre) 2023**

1. The acts done by him as Vice-President before such declaration are considered valid.
2. The acts done by him as Vice-President on the day of such declaration are not considered valid.

Select the correct answer by using the codes given below.

(a) Both 1 and 2 (b) Only 1
(c) Only 2 (d) Neither 1 nor 2

154. Which one of the following statements is correct? **MPPSC (Pre) 2015**

1. A member of the State Legislature cannot contest for the post of Vice-President.
2. The Vice-President can be removed by a resolution of the Council of States passed by a simple majority of the members with the house of people having nothing to do with it.

Codes

(a) Only 1 (b) Only 2
(c) Both 1 and 2 (d) Neither 1 nor 2

19. PRIME MINISTER AND COUNCIL OF MINISTERS

155. The Prime Minister of India, at the time of his/her appointment **IAS (Pre) 2012**

(a) need not necessarily be a member of one of the Houses of the Parliament, but must become a member of one of the Houses within six months.
(b) need not necessarily be a member of one of the House within six months of the Parliament, but must become a member of the Lok Sabha within six months.
(c) must be a member of one of the Houses of the Parliament.
(d) must be a member of the Lok Sabha.

156. Which one of the following statements is correct?

The Prime Minister of India **Manipur PSC (Pre) 2014**

(a) is free to choose his Minister only from among those who are members of either House of Parliament.
(b) can choose his Cabinet colleagues after due counselling by the President of India in this regard.

(c) has full discretion in the choice of persons who are to serve as Ministers in his cabinet.
(d) has only limited powers in the choice of his cabinet colleagues because of the discretionary powers vested with the President of India.

157. Consider the following statements. **IAS (Pre) 2015**

1. The Executive Power of the Union of India is vested in the Prime Minister.
2. The Prime Minister is the Ex-officio Chairman of the Civil Services Board.

Which of the statements given above is/are correct?
(a) Only 1 (b) Only 2
(c) Both 1 and 2 (d) Neither 1 nor 2

158. Which one of the following powers of the Prime Minister in relation to the Council of Ministers has been wrongly listed?
(a) He can dismiss any Minister if he finds that the Minister is not co-operating with him. **Karnataka PSC (Pre) 2014**
(b) The members of the Council of Ministers are appointed by the President on the recommendation of the Prime Minister.
(c) He allocates portfolios among the members of the Council of Ministers.
(d) He presides over the meeting of the Council of Ministers.

159. Council of Ministers' size has been restricted to 15% of membership of Lok Sabha by which Constitutional amendment? **HPPSC (Pre) 2024, BPSC (Pre) 2024**
(a) 91st Amendment
(b) 92nd Amendment
(c) 95th Amendment
(d) 103rd Amendment

160. With reference to Union Government, consider the following statements. **IAS (Pre) 2009**

1. The number of ministries at the Centre on 15th August, 1947 was 18.
2. The number of Ministries at the Centre at present is 36.

Which of the statements given above is/are correct ?
(a) Only 1 (b) Only 2
(c) Both 1 and 2 (d) Neither 1 nor 2

161. The following statements about the Cabinet Secretariat. **CGPSC (Pre) 2023**

1. The Cabinet Secretariat functions directly under the Vice-President of India.
2. The administrative head of the Secretariat is the Cabinet Secretary who is also the Ex-Officio Chairman of the Civil Services Board.

Which of the statements given above is/are correct?
(a) Only 1 (b) Only 2
(c) Both 1 and 2 (d) None of these

20. PARLIAMENT

162. Which pair is incorrect regarding the appointment of chairpersons of Parliamentary Committee constituted by the speaker of 18th Lok Sabha for the year 2024-25? **MPPSC (Pre) 2025**
(a) Public Account Committee – KC Venugopal
(b) Estimates Committee – Baijayant Panda
(c) Committee on Welfare of Scheduled Castes and Scheduled Tribes – Faggan Singh Kulaste
(d) Committee on Welfare of Other Backward Classes – Ganesh Singh

163. Consider the following statements.

1. Parliament can legislate on matters enumerated in the State list if two or more State Legislatures pass resolutions requesting the Parliament to enact such laws.
2. A law so enacted will be equally applicable to all the states, irrespective of whether they passed such a resolution or not.
3. Such a law can be amended or repealed only by the Parliament.

How many of the statements given above is/are correct? **HPSC (Pre) 2024**
(a) Only one statement is correct
(b) Only two statements are correct
(c) All three statements are correct
(d) None of the statements is correct
(e) Question not attempted

164. Under which Article of the Indian Constitution, can the Rajya Sabha authorise the Parliament to legislate on a state subject by 2/3rd majority? **JPSC (Pre) 2024**
(a) Article 249 (b) Article 243
(c) Article 259 (d) Article 250

165. Consider the following statements. **IAS (Pre) 2025**

I. On the dissolution of the House of the People, the Speaker shall not vacate his/her office until immediately before the first meeting of the House of the People after the dissolution.
II. According to the provisions of the Constitution of India, a Member of the House of the Peaple on being elected as Speaker shall resign from his/her political party immediately.
III. The Speaker of the House of the People may he removed from his/her office by a resolution of the House of the People passed by a majority of all the then Members of the House, provided that no resolution shall be moved unless at least fourteen days, notice has been given of the intention to move the resolution

Which of the statements given above are correct?
(a) I and II only (b) II and III only
(c) I and III only (d) I, II and III

166. Consider the following statements regarding the position of the Speaker of Lok Sabha. **MPSC (Pre) 2020**

1. His/her salary and allowances are charged on the Consolidated Fund of India.
2. He/she has no vote except in case of a tie.
3. He/she can be removed by a resolution passed by a majority of the members present and voting in the House.
4. He/she has a higher rank than Deputy Prime Minister.

Which of the statements given above are correct?
(a) 1, 2 and 3 (b) 2, 3 and 4
(c) 1 and 2 (d) All of these

167. What is the object of 'cut motion' in Parliament? **BPSC (Pre) 2024**
(a) To move a proposal to reduce expenditure in the budget proposals.
(b) To restrict day to day financial expenditure of the government.
(c) To restrict grants from consolidated fund of India.
(d) To restrict the grants of the government.

168. With reference to Deputy Speaker of Lok Sabha, consider the following statements. **IAS (Pre) 2022**

1. As per the Rules of Procedure and Conduct of Business in Lok Sabha, the election of Deputy Speaker shall be held on such date as the Speaker may fix.

2. There is a mandatory provision that the election of a candidate as Deputy Speaker of Lok Sabha shall be from either the principal opposition party or the ruling party.
3. The Deputy Speaker has the same power as of the Speaker when presiding over the sitting of the House and so appeal lies against his rulings.
4. The well-established Parliamentary practice regarding the appointment of the Deputy Speaker is that the motion is moved by the Speaker and duty seconded by the Prime Minister.

Which of the statements given above are correct?
(a) 1 and 3 (b) 1, 2 and 3
(c) 3 and 4 (d) 2 and 4

169. Which of the following pairs are not correctly matched? **MPSC (Pre) 2020**

1. Calling attention Motion	To draw attention of the Minister on matters of urgent public importance.
2. Adjournment Motion	To adjourn the house before the expiry of the time.
3. Privilege Motion	To draw attention of the Speaker.
4. Point of Order	To draw attention of the Speaker towards incorrect/incomplete answer by a Minister.

Codes
(a) 1 and 2 (b) 1 and 3
(c) 2 ,3 and 4 (d) 1 and 4

170. Which of the following statement(s) is/are true in reference to the joint sitting of Parliament for passage of bill? **CGPSC (Pre) 2022**

1. Provision for joint sitting is applicable for ordinary bills, Financial bills and Constitutional Amendment Bills.
2. In no situation, Deputy Chairman of Rajya Sabha can preside over the joint sitting.
3. Quorum of one-sixth of the total number of members of both Houses to be maintained for joint sitting.

Codes
(a) 1, 2 and 3 (b) 1 and 2
(c) 1 and 3 (d) None of these

171. Consider the following statements. **IAS (Pre) 2022**

1. A bill amending the Constitution requires a prior recommendation of the President of India.
2. When a Constitution Amendment bill is presented to the President of India, it is obligatory for the President of India to give his/her assent.
3. A Constitution Amendment bill must be passed by both the Lok Sabha and the Rajya Sabha by a special majority and there is no provision for joint sitting.

Which of the statements given above are correct?
(a) 1 and 2 (b) 2 and 3
(c) 1 and 3 (d) All of these

172. With reference to the joint sitting of Parliament, which statements is/are correct? **UPPSC (Pre) 2023**

1. Article 109 provides for the joint sitting of both Houses in certain cases.
2. The Speaker presides the joint sitting of the two Houses of Parliament.

Select the correct answer by using the codes given below.
(a) Neither 1 nor 2 (b) Both 1 and 2
(c) Only 2 (d) Only 1

173. Given below are two statements. **HPPSC (Pre) 2024**

Statement 1 Finance Minister is the final authority to decide whether a bill is a Money bill or not.
Statement 2 In the Indian system of 'dyarchy' was introduced by the Government of India Act, 1935 during the British period.
In the light of the above statements, choose the most appropriate answer from the options given below.
(a) Both Statement 1 and Statement 2 are correct.
(b) Both Statement 1 and Statement 2 are incorrect.
(c) Statement 1 is correct and Statement 2 is incorrect.
(d) Statement 1 is incorrect and Statement 2 is correct.

174. Consider the following pairs. **HPSC (Pre) 2024**

1. Consolidated fund of India: Payment from the fund can be made without Parliamentary appropriation.
2. Contigency Fund of India: Held by Finance Secretary on behalf of the President of India.
3. Public Account of India: Executive requires Parliamentary approval to withdraw money from this account.

How many of the pairs given above is/are correctly matched?
(a) Only one pair (c) All three pairs
(b) Only two pairs (d) None of the pairs
(e) Question not attempted

175. All revenues received by the Union government by way of direct and indirect taxes, money borrowed and receipts from loans given by the government flow into **WBCS (Pre) 2023**
(a) the Public Accounts of India.
(b) the Consolidated Fund of India.
(c) the Contingency Fund of India.
(d) None of the above

176. Which of the following committees contains representatives of both the Houses of the Parliament? **MPSC (Pre) 2022**

1. Committee on Welfare of Scheduled Castes and Scheduled Tribes
2. Committee on Empowerment of Women
3. Business Advisory Committee
4. Committee on Privileges
5. Estimates Committee

Codes
(a) 1, 2 and 4 (b) 2 and 3
(c) 3, 4 and 5 (d) 1 and 2

177. With reference to the post's in Secretariat of the Parliament, which of the following statements is/are correct? **UPPSC (Pre) 2023**

1. Common posts may be created for the Secretariate of each House of Parliament.
2. The Parliament has right to regulate the service conditions of Secretariate staff of either House of it.

Select the correct answer by using the codes given below.
(a) Neither 1 nor 2
(b) Only 2
(c) Only 1
(d) Both 1 and 2

21. THE GOVERNOR

178. The Governor of a State is an integral part of the **APSC (Pre) 2014**
(a) State Cabinet
(b) Parliament
(c) State Legislature
(d) State Public Service Commission

179. When the same person is appointed as a Governor of two or more states, the emoluments and allowances payable to the Governor shall be **UPPSC (Pre) 2016**

(a) as expressed wish of the Governor.
(b) as decided by the President.
(c) as decided by the Home Ministry.
(d) it shall be allocated among the states in such proportion as the President may be order determine.

180. Which one of the following statements is correct? **IAS (Pre) 2013**

(a) In India, the same person cannot be appointed as Governor for two or more states at the same time.
(b) The Judges of the High Court of the States in India are appointed by the Governor of the State just as the Judges of the Supreme Court are appointed by the President.
(c) No procedure has been laid down in the Constitution of India for the removal of a Governor from his/her post.
(d) In the case of the Union Territory having a legislative set-up, the Chief Minister is appointed by the limited Governor on the basis of majority support.

181. Under which of the following Articles of Indian Constitution, the Governor may reserve a bill for the consideration of the President? **CGPSC (Pre) 2015**

(a) Article 169 (b) Article 200
(c) Article 201 (d) Article 202

182. Which one of the following suggested that the Governor should be an eminent person from outside the state and should be a detached figure without intense political links or should not have taken part in politics in the recent past? **IAS (Pre) 2019**

(a) First Administrative Reforms Commission in 1966
(b) Rajamannar Committee in 1969
(c) Sarkaria Commission in 1983
(d) National Commission to review the working of the Constitution in 2000

183. Which of the following statements are correct? **MPPSC (Pre) 2017**

1. Articles from 153 to 167 of the Constitution deal with the State Executive.
2. Under Article 153, Governor is appointed by the President.
3. The Supreme Court held in 1978 that the office of the Governor of a State is a constitutional office.
4. The 6th Constitutional Amendment Act of 1956 facilitated the appointment of the same person as a Governor for two or more states.

Codes

(a) Statements 1, 2 and 3 are true and Statement 4 is false.
(b) Statement 1 is true and Statements 2, 3 and 4 are false.
(c) Statements 1, 3 are true and Statements 2, 4 are false.
(d) Statements 3, 4 are true and Statements 1, 2 are false.

184. Consider the following statements. **IAS (Pre) 2024**

1. It is the Governor of the State who recognises and declares any community of that states as a Scheduled Tribe.
2. A Community declared as a Scheduled Tribe in a state need not be so in another state.

Which of the statemens given above is/are correct?

(a) Only 1 (b) Only 2
(c) Both 1 and 2 (d) Neither 1 nor 2

22. CHIEF MINISTER AND COUNCIL OF MINISTERS

185. Select the correct statements. **MPPSC (Pre) 2016**

1. The number of Ministers, including the Chief Minister, in state shall not be less than 12.
2. According to the Article 168, the Governor is a part of the State Legislature.

Codes

(a) Statement 1 is true.
(b) Statement 2 is true.
(c) Statements 1 and 2 are true.
(d) Statements 1 and 2 are false.

186. Which one of the following statements is accurate in terms of the Constitution of India? **MPPSC (Pre) 2016**

(a) The Chief Minister decides the allocation of portfolios among the Ministers.
(b) When the Chief Minister resigns, the Council of Ministers gets dissolved
(c) All the principal policy announcements of the State Government are made by the Chief Minister.
(d) It shall be the duty of the Chief Minister to communicate to the Governor of the State all the decisions of the Council of Ministers relating to the administration of the affairs of the State and proposals for legislation.

187. Who among the following Chief Ministers of Madhya Pradesh has not held the office of the leader of the house in Madhya Pradesh Legislative Assembly during his tenure? **MPPSC (Pre) 2022**

(a) Prakash Chandra Sethi
(b) Govind Narayan Singh
(c) Babulal Gaur
(d) Kailash Joshi

188. Consider the following statements. **MPPSC (Pre) 2024**

1. It shall be the duty of the Advocate-General to give advice to the Government of the State upon legal matters.
2. The Advocate-General shall hold office during the pleasure of the Cabinet.

Which of the statements given above is/are correct?

(a) Only 1 (b) Only 2
(c) Both 1 and 2 (d) Neither 1 nor 2

23. STATE LEGISLATURE

189. In which article of the Indian Constitution is there a provision of reservation of seats for Scheduled Tribes in State Assembly? **MPPSC (Pre) 2025**

(a) Article 339 (b) Article 332
(c) Article 334 (d) Article 293 B

190. Consider the following in relation to the Legislative Council. **Telangana PSC (Pre) 2023**

1. The Council is a permanent house and one-third of the members retire in two years.
2. Members of local bodies elect one-third of the total number of members of the Legislative Council.
3. One-twelfth shall be elected by electorates consisting of graduates of three years standing, residing in the state.

Which of the statements given above are correct?

(a) 1, 2 and 3 (b) 1 and 2
(c) 1 and 3 (d) 2 and 3

191. With reference to the composition of the Legislative Council in a State of India, which of the following statements is/are correct? **UPPSC (Pre) 2023**

1. In the Legislative Council, there may not be more than one-third members of the total membership of the Legislative Assembly of the state.
2. The Legislative Council of a state must have at least fourty members in it.

Select the correct answer by using the codes given below.

(a) Both 1 and 2 (b) Only 2
(c) Neither 1 nor 2 (d) Only 1

192. With reference to the Legislative Assembly of a State in India, consider the following statements. **IAS (Pre) 2019**

1. The Governor makes a customary address to Members of the House at the commencement of the first session of the year.
2. When a State Legislature does not have a rule on a particular matter, it follows the Lok Sabha rule on that matter.

Which of the statements given above is/are correct?

(a) Only 1 (b) Only 2
(c) Both 1 and 2 (d) Neither 1 nor 2

193. Consider the following statements. **IAS (Pre) 2018**

1. The Speaker of the Legislative Assembly shall vacate his/her office if he/she ceases to be a member of the Assembly.
2. Whenever the Legislative Assembly is dissolved, the Speaker shall vacate his/her office immediately.

Which of the statements given above is/are correct?

(a) Only 1 (b) Only 2
(c) Both 1 and 2 (d) Neither 1 nor 2

194. With reference to the Indian polity, consider the following statements. **IAS (Pre) 2025**

I. The Governor of a State is not answerable to any court for the exercise and performance of the powers and duties of his/her office.
II. No criminal proceedings shall be instituted or continued against the Governor during his/her term of office.
III. Members of a State Legislature are not liable to any proceedings in any court in respect of anything said within the House.

Which of the statements given above are correct?

(a) I and II only (b) II and III only
(c) I and III only (d) I, II and III

195. If in an election to a State Legislative Assembly, the candidate who is declared elected loses his deposit, it means that **APSC (Pre) 2015**

(a) the polling was very poor.
(b) the election was for a multi-member constituency.
(c) the elected candidate's victory over his nearest rival was very marginal.
(d) a very large number of candidates contested the election.

196. Consider the following statements. **HPSC (Pre) 2023**

1. A Bill pending in the legislature of state shall lapse by reason of the prorogation of the house or Houses thereof.
2. A Bill pending in the Legislative Council of a state which has been passed by the Legislative Assembly shall lapse on a dissolution of the assembly.
3. A Bill which is pending in the Legislative Assembly of a state or which have been passed by the Legislative Assembly is pending in the Legislative Council shall not lapse on a dissolution of the assembly.

Which of the statements given above is/are correct?

(a) 1 and 2 (b) 2 and 3
(c) 1 and 3 (d) Only 2

24. SUPREME COURT

197. The provision relating to the appointment of Supreme Court and High Court judges in the Indian Constitution were incorporated on the basis of published recommendations given by .... committee. **MPPSC (Pre) 2025**

(a) Harendra Kumar
(b) Sen (Usha Nath Sen)
(c) Varadachari (S. Varadachari)
(d) Sapru (Sir Tej Bahadur Sapru)

198. Which of the following are included in the Original Jurisdiction of the Supreme Court? **IAS (Pre) 2012, HPPSC (Pre) 2024**

1. Dispute between the Government of India and one or more states.
2. A dispute regarding elections to either House of the Parliament or that of Legislature of a State.
3. A dispute between the Government of India and Union Territory.
4. A disputes between two or more states.

Select the correct answer by using the codes given below.

(a) 1 and 2 (b) 2 and 3
(c) 1 and 4 (d) 3 and 4

199. Consider the following pairs. **HPSC (Pre) 2024**

1. Enlargement of Jurisdiction of the Supreme Court : Article 138(A) of Constitution of India
2. Conferment on the Supreme Court of powers to issue certain writs : Article 139(A) of Constitution of India
3. Civil and judicial authority to act in aid of the Supreme Court: Article 144(A) of the Constitution of India

How many of the above pairs is/are correctly matched?

(a) Only one pair (b) Only two pairs
(c) All three pairs (d) None of the pairs
(e) Question not attempted

200. Which Constitutional Amendment Act dealing with National Judicial Appointments Commission, was declared unconstitutional by the Constitution Bench of the Supreme Court? **RAS/RTS (Pre) 2021**

(a) 98th Constitutional Amendment Act
(b) 99th Constitutional Amendment Act
(c) 97th Constitutional Amendment Act
(d) 100th Constitutional Amendment Act

201. With reference to the writs issued by the courts in India, consider the following statements. **IAS (Pre) 2022**

1. Mandamus will not lie against a private organisation unless it is entrusted with a public duty.
2. Mandamus will not lie against a company even though it may be a government company.
3. Any public minded person can be a petitioner to move the court to obtain the writ of Quo-Warranto.

Which of the statements given above are correct?

(a) 1 and 2 (b) 2 and 3
(c) 1 and 3 (d) All of these

202. Consider the following statements. **IAS (Pre) 2022**

1. Pursuant to the report of HN Sanyal Committee, the Contempt of Courts Act, 1971 was passed.
2. The Constitution of India empowers the Supreme Court and the High Courts to punish for contempt of themselves.
3. The Constitution of India defines civil contempt and criminal contempt.
4. In India, the Parliament is vested with the powers to make laws on contempt of court.

Which of the statements given above is/are correct?
(a) 1 and 2 (b) 1, 2 and 4
(c) 3 and 4 (d) Only 3

203. Consider the following statements. **HPSC (Pre) 2024**

1. Public Interest Litigation is a legal action initiated in a court of law for the enforcement of public interest.
2. PIL has reinforced the principle of locus standi.
3. Both citizens and organisations can file a PIL.
4. The Supreme Court under Article 32 and High Courts under Article 226 of the Constitution of India can entertain PIL's.

How many of the statements given above are correct?
(a) 1 and 2 only (b) 2 and 3 only
(c) 3 and 4 only (d) 1, 3 and 4 only
(e) Question not attempted

204. In India, Judicial Review implies **UPPSC (Pre) 2017, IAS (Pre) 2017**
(a) the power of the judiciary to pronounce upon the constitutionality of laws and executive orders.
(b) the power of the judiciary to question the wisdom of the laws enacted by the legislatures.
(c) the power of the judiciary to review all the legislative enactments before they are assented to by the President.
(d) the power of the judiciary to review its own judgements given earlier in similar or different cases.

25. HIGH COURT AND SUB-ORDINATE COURTS

205. Consider the following statements. **MPPSC (Pre) 2017**

1. The retired permanent Judge of a High Court can plead or act before the Supreme Court and the other High Courts.
2. Conduct of High Court Judges can be discussed in Parliament or in a State Legislature at the time of an impeachment motion is under consideration of the Parliament.

Which of the statement(s) given above is/are correct?
(a) Only 1 (b) Only 2
(c) Both 1 and 2 (d) Neither 1 nor 2

206. Consider the following statements. **IAS (Pre) 2006**

1. A person who has held office as a permanent Judge of a High Court cannot plead or act in any court or before any authority in India except the Supreme Court.
2. A person is not qualified for appointment as a Judge of a High Court in India unless he has for atleast five years held a judicial office in the Territory of India.

Which of the statements given above is/are correct?
(a) Only 1 (b) Only 2
(c) Both 1 and 2 (d) Neither 1 nor 2

207. Consider the following statements regarding Articles 226 of the Constitution of India. **Assam PSC (Pre) 2024**

1. Article 226 of the Constitution of India empowers a High Court to issue writs including Habeas Corpus, Mandamus, Certiorari, Prohibition and Quo-Warranto for the enforcement of the Fundamental Rights of the citizens and for any other purpose.
2. The phrase 'for any other purpose' refers to the enforcement of an ordinary Legal Right. This implies that the writ jurisdiction of the High Court is wider than that of the Supreme Court.
3. The Supreme Court can issue writs only for the enforcement of the Fundamental Rights and not for any other purpose, i.e., it does not extend to a case where the breach of an ordinary Legal Right is alleged.
4. The High Court can issue writs to any person, authority and government not only within its territorial jurisdiction but also outside its territorial jurisdiction if the cause of action arise within its territorial jurisdiction.

Select the correct statements by using the codes given below.
(a) 1, 2 and 3 only (b) 3 and 4 only
(c) 1 and 3 only (d) 1, 2, 3 and 4

208. **Assertion** (A) The Governor of the State appoints District Judges in consultation with the High Court.
Reason (R) The Governor has absolute power over judicial appointments.
Select the correct answer by using the codes given below.
(a) Both A and R are true, and R is the correct explanation of A.
(b) Both A and R are true, but R is not the correct explanation of A.
(c) A is true, but R is false.
(d) A is false, but R is true.

209. Consider the following statements.
Statement 1 The Board of Revenue is the highest revenue court in the district.
Statement 2 The Board of Revenue hears final appeals against lower revenue courts.
Select the correct answer by using the codes given below.
(a) Only Statement 1 is correct
(b) Only Statement 2 is correct
(c) Both Statements are correct
(d) Neither Statement is correct

26. LOK ADALAT AND OTHER COURTS

210. **Assertion** (A) Lok Adalats are an alternative dispute resolution mechanism.
Reason (R) Lok Adalats are a type of mobile court.
Select the correct answer by using the codes given below.
(a) Both A and R are true and R is the correct explanation of A.
(b) Both A and R are true, but R is not the correct explanation of A.
(c) A is true, but R is false.
(d) A is false, but R is true.

211. **Assertion** (A) The first Lok Adalat was held on 14th March, 1982.
Reason (R) It was established to provide alternative dispute resolution.
Select the correct answer by using the codes given below.

(a) Both A and R are true and R is the correct explanation of A.
(b) Both A and R are true, but R is not the correct explanation of A.
(c) A is true, but R is false.
(d) A is false, but R is true.

212. Consider the following statements.
Statement 1 Fast Track Special Courts (FTSC's) aim to dispose of pending cases of rape.
Statement 2 FTSC's were set-up in 2019.
Which of the statements given above is/are correct?
(a) Only Statement 1 is correct
(b) Only Statement 2 is correct
(c) Both Statements are correct
(d) Neither Statement is correct

213. Consider the following statements.
Statement 1 Arbitration is more formal than mediation.
Statement 2 Arbitration is less flexible than litigation.
Which of the statements given above is/are correct?
(a) Only Statement 1 is correct
(b) Only Statement 2 is correct
(c) Both Statements are correct
(d) Neither Statement is correct

214. With reference to National Legal Services Authority, consider the following statements. **IAS (Pre) 2013**
1. Its objective is to ensure free and competent legal services to the weaker sections of the society on the basis of equal opportunity.
2. It issues guidelines to the State Legal Services authorities to implement the legal programmes and schemes throughout the country.

Which of the statements given above is/are correct?
(a) Only 1 (b) Only 2
(c) Both 1 and 2 (d) Neither 1 nor 2

27. VARIOUS TRIBUNALS AND AUTHORITIES

215. Assertion (A) The Central Administrative Tribunal (CAT) was established in 1985.
Reason (R) It was established to provide speedy and inexpensive justice to aggrieved civil servants.
Which of the statements given above is/are correct?
(a) Both A and R are true, and R is the correct explanation of A.
(b) Both A and R are true, but R is not the correct explanation of A.
(c) A is true, but R is false.
(d) A is false, but R is true.

216. What is the term of the Chairman and Vice-Chairman of the Central Administrative Tribunal?
(a) 3 years or until they attain 60 years
(b) 5 years or until they attain 65 years
(c) 4 years or until they attain 70 years
(d) 10 years or until they attain 75 years

217. Consider the following statements.
Statement 1 Article 323(A) empowers the Parliament to establish administrative tribunals.
Statement 2 Article 323(B) empowers the State Legislature to establish tribunals.
Which of the statements given above is/are correct?
(a) Only Statement 1 is correct
(b) Only Statement 2 is correct
(c) Both Statements are correct
(d) Neither Statement is correct

218. Assertion (A) The Central Administrative Tribunal is a statutory body.
Reason (R) It was established under the Administrative Tribunals Act, 1985.
Select the correct answer using the codes given below.
(a) Both A and R are true, and R is the correct explanation of A.
(b) Both A and R are true, but R is not the correct explanation of A.
(c) A is true, but R is false.
(d) A is false, but R is true.

219. What is the difference between Articles 323(A) and 323(B)?
(a) 323(A) establishes tribunals for public service matters, while 323(B) establishes tribunals for other matters.
(b) 323(A) establishes tribunals for taxation, while 323(B) establishes tribunals for labour disputes.
(c) 323(A) establishes tribunals for the Centre, while 323(B) establishes tribunals for states.
(d) 323(A) establishes tribunals for civil courts, while 323(B) establishes tribunals for High Courts.

28. LOCAL GOVERNMENT (PANCHAYATS AND MUNICIPALITIES)

220. Consider the following statements. **IAS (Pre) 2025**
I. Panchayats at the intermediate level exist in all States.
II. To be eligible to be a Member of a Panchayat at the intermediate level, a person should attain the age of thirty years.
III. The Chief Minister of a State constitutes a commission to review the financial position of Panchayats at the intermediate levels and to make recommendations regarding the distribution of net proceeds of taxes and duties, leviable by the state, between the State and Panchayats at the intermediate level.

Which of the statements given above are not correct?
(a) I and II only (b) II and III only
(c) I and III only (d) 1, II and III

221. Match the List-I with List-II and select the correct answer using the codes given below the lists. **UPPSC (Pre) 202**

	List-I (Committees)		List-II (Years of Appointment)
A.	Balwant Rai Mehta Committee	1.	1957
B.	Ashok Mehta Committee	2.	1977
C.	LM Singhvi Committee	3.	1986
D.	PK Thungun Committee	4.	1988

Codes

	A	B	C	D		A	B	C	D
(a)	3	4	2	1	(b)	1	2	3	4
(c)	2	3	1	4	(d)	4	1	2	3

222. Which of the following committees were appointed to in quire into the working of Panchayati Raj Institution in India? **JPSC (Pre) 202**
1. LM Singhvi Committee
2. GVK Rao Committee
3. Ashok Mehta Committee
4. Balwant Rai Mehta Committee

Select the correct answer by using the codes given below.
(a) Only 1, 2 and 3 (b) Only 3 and 4
(c) Only 2, 3 and 4 (d) All of these

223. Which Committee's report paved the way for the Panchayats (Extension to Scheduled Areas) Act, (PESA) 1996 for ensuring tribal self–rule for people living in Scheduled Areas of India?
(a) Ashok Mehta Committee **JPSC (Pre) 2024**
(b) GVK Rao Committee
(c) Bhuria Committee
(d) Balwant Rai Mehta Committee

224. With reference to the recommendations of the Ashok Mehta Committee 1977 on Panchayati Raj, which of the following statement(s) is/are correct? **UPPSC (Pre) 2023**
1. The three-tier system of Panchayti Raj should be replaced by the two tier system.
2. A block should be the first point for decentralisation under popular supervision below the state level.

Select the correct answer by using the codes given below.
(a) Both 1 and 2 (b) Only 1
(c) Neither 1 nor 2 (d) Only 2

225. Which of the following statements is not true regarding Gram Sabha? **UPPSC (Pre) 2023**
(a) It has the powers and functions at the village level, like State Legislature has at the state level.
(b) Its powers are determined by the Central Government.
(c) It is a Village Assembly consisting of all registered voters in the area of Panchayat.
(d) Both a and c

226. Consider the following statements. **IAS (Pre) 2016**
1. The minimum age prescribed for any person to be a member of Panchayat is 25 years.
2. A Panchayat reconstruction after premature dissolution continues only for the remainder period.

Which of the statement(s) given above is/are correct?
(a) Only 1 (b) Only 2
(c) Both 1 and 2 (d) Neither 1 nor 2

227. In the areas covered under the Panchayat (Extension to the Scheduled Areas) Act, 1996, what is the role/power of Gram Sabha? **IAS (Pre) 2012**
1. Gram Sabha has the power to prevent alienation of land in the Scheduled Areas.
2. Gram Sabha has the ownership of minor forest produce.
3. Recommendation of Gram Sabha is required for granting prospecting licence or mining lease for any mineral in the Scheduled Areas.

Which of the statement(s) given above is/are correct?
(a) Only 1
(b) 1 and 2
(c) 2 and 3
(d) All of the above

228. Consider the following statements regarding Panchayati Raj System in Himachal Pradesh. **HPPSC (Pre) 2024**

Statement I In 1949, the Punjab Village Panchayat Act of 1939 was enforced and 132 Panchayats were established in Himachal.
Statement II By the end of 1956, there were 466 Gram Panchayats and 26 Tehsil Panchayats in Himachal.

Choose the correct option from the following.
(a) Both statements are correct
(b) Only statement I is correct
(c) Only statement II is correct
(d) Both statements are incorrect

229. Which of the following statements are correct about the Constitution of India? **IAS (Pre) 2024**
1. Powers of the Municipalities are given in Part IX (A) of the Constitution.
2. Emergency provisions are given in Part XVIII of the Constitution.
3. Provisions related to the amendment of the Constitution are given in Part XX of the Constitution.

Select the correct answer by using the codes given below.
(a) 1 and 2 (b) 2 and 3
(c) 1 and 3 (d) 1, 2 and 3

230. Which one of the following pairs is not correctly matched? **UPPSC (Pre) 2024**

(a)	Dantwala Committee	-	Rural Credit
(b)	GVK Rao Committee	-	Planning at the Block Level
(c)	Ashok Mehta Committee	-	Panchayati Raj Institutions
(d)	Santhanam Committee	-	Panchayati Raj Finances

29. CONSTITUTIONAL PROVISIONS OF UNION TERRITORIES

231. Consider the following statements about Union and its Territory. **CGPSC (Pre) 2023**
1. India comprises 28 States and 8 Union Territories.
2. India, a Union of States, is a Sovereign Socialist Secular Democratic Republic with a parliamentary system of government.

Which of the statements given above is/are correct?
(a) Only 1 (b) Only 2
(c) Both 1 and 2 (d) Neither 1 nor 2

232. Match the following List-I (Union Territories) with their List II (Years of Creation). **CGPSC (Pre) 2022**

List -I (Union Territories)	List-II (Years of Creation)
A. Lakshadweep	1. 1961
B. Daman and Diu	2. 1966
C. Chandigarh	3. 1962
D. Dadra and Nagar Haveli	4. 1956

Codes

	A	B	C	D		A	B	C	D
(a)	1	2	3	4	(b)	4	3	2	1
(c)	4	2	3	1	(d)	1	3	2	4

233. Which one of the following pairs is not correctly matched in terms of power of President to make regulation for certain Union Territories under Article 240 of Indian Constitution? **RAS/RTS (Pre) 2018**
(a) 240 (1) : Andaman and Nicobar Islands
(b) 240 (1) : Lakshadweep
(c) 240 (1) : Puducherry
(d) 240 (1) : Daman and Diu

234. The President has power to make regulations regarding which of the following? **UKPSC (Pre) 2024**
1. Dadra and Nagar Haveli
2. Daman and Diu
3. Goa, Daman and Diu
4. Puducherry

Select the correct answer by using the codes given below.
(a) 1, 2, 3 and 4 (b) 1, 2 and 3
(c) 1, 3 and 4 (d) 1, 2 and 4

235. Which of the following statements are correct about the Women's Reservation Bill, 2023?
Assam PSC (Pre) 2024

1. The Women's Reservation Bill, 2023 proposes 33% reservation for women in the Lok Sabha and the Assemblies of States and National Capital Territory of Delhi.
2. Similar reservation will also be provided within the seats reserved for SC and ST.
3. The Bill proposes that the reservation will continue for 25 years.
4. The Bill which reserves 33% of the seats for women in the Lok Sabha and State Assemblies includes the quota for women from the OBCs.

Select the correct answer by using the codes given below,
(a) 1 and 2 (b) 1 and 3
(c) 1, 2 and 3 (d) 1, 2, 3 and 4

30. ADMINISTRATION OF SCHEDULED AND TRIBAL AREAS

236. The authority to specify as to which castes shall be deemed to be Scheduled Castes rests with the
UPPSC (Mains) 2006, UPPSC (Pre) 2016

(a) Commission of Scheduled Castes and Tribes
(b) Prime Minister
(c) Governor of the State
(d) President

237. If a particular area was brought under the Fifth Schedule of the Constitution of India, which one of the following statements best reflects the consequence of it? **IAS (Pre) 2022**

(a) This would prevent the transfer of land of tribal people to non-tribal people.
(b) This would create a local self-governing body in that area.
(c) This would convert that area into a Union Territory.
(d) The state having such areas would be declared a special category state.

238. With reference to 'Scheduled Areas' in India, consider the following statements. **IAS (Pre) 2023**

1. Within a state, the notification of an area as Scheduled Area takes place through an order of the President.
2. The largest administrative unit forming the Scheduled Area is the District and the lowest is the cluster of villages in the Block.
3. The Chief Ministers of the concerned states are required to submit annual reports to the Union Home Ministry on the administration of Scheduled Areas in the states.

How many of the statements given above is/are correct?
(a) Only one (b) Only two
(c) All three (d) None of these

239. Consider the following statements. **IAS (Pre) 2023**

Statement I The Supreme Court of India has held in some judgements that the reservation policies made under Article 16(4) of the Constitution of India would be limited by Article 335 for maintenance of efficiency of administration.

Statement II Article 335 of the Constitution of India defines the term 'efficiency of administration'.

Which one of the following is correct in respect of the above statements?

(a) Both Statement I and Statement II are correct and Statement II is the correct explanation for Statement I.
(b) Both Statement I and Statement II are correct and Statement II is not the correct explanation for Statement I.
(c) Statement I is correct, but Statement II is incorrect.
(d) Statement I is incorrect, but Statement II is correct.

240. Match the following Particularly Vulnerable Tribal Groups (PVTGs) (List-I) with the States /Union Territories they belong to (List-II).
Assam PSC (Pre) 2024

List-I	List-II
A. Maram	1. Andaman and Nicobar Islands
B. Jarawa	2. Tripura
C. Birhor	3. Manipur
D. Reang	4. Odisha

Select the correct answer by using the codes given below.

	A	B	C	D
(a)	1	2	3	4
(b)	3	1	4	2
(c)	2	1	4	3
(d)	3	4	1	2

31. CONSTITUTIONAL BODIES

241. Article 338 of the Indian Constitution mandates formation of which of the following commissions?
MPPSC (Pre) 2025

(a) National Commission for Women
(b) National Commission for Minorities
(c) National Human Rights Commission
(d) National Commission for Scheduled Castes

242. Match List-I with list-II.
HPSC (Pre) 2023

List-I	List-II
A. Second Schedule of Indian Constitution	1. Administration of Scheduled Areas
B. Fifth Schedule of Indian Constitution	2. Comptroller and Auditor General
C. Ninth Schedule of Indian Constitution	3. Anti-defection laws
D. Tenth Schedule of Indian Constitution	4. Land Reform Laws

Codes

	A	B	C	D		A	B	C	D
(a)	3	2	4	2	(b)	1	2	3	4
(c)	2	1	4	3	(d)	4	3	2	1

243. Consider the following statements with reference to Special Officer for Linguistic Minorities.
UPPSC (Pre) 202

1. In the Constitution, there is a provision for the post of Special Officer for Linguistic Minorities for every state.
2. A new Article 350B was added for this by the 9th Constitution Amendment Act.

Which of the above statements is/are correct?
(a) Neither 1 nor 2 (b) Only 2
(c) Both 1 and 2 (d) Only 1

244. As per Article 76 of the Indian Constitution, the President shall appoint a person to be Attorney-General for India **MPPSC (Pre) 202**

(a) who is qualified to be appointed a judge of the High Court.
(b) who has been an advocate of the Supreme Court for at least seven years.
(c) who is qualified to be appointed a judge of the Supreme Court.
(d) who has been an advocate of the High Court for at least seven years.

245. Consider the following statements regarding the Election Commission of India. **Assam PSC (Pre) 2024**

1. The Election Commission of India is a body constitutionally empowered to conduct free and fair elections to the National and State Legislatures including the Panchayats.
2. The power of the Election Commission of India is derived from Article 324 of the Constitution of India.
3. Rajiv Kumar is the present Chief Election Commissioner who joined his office on 15th May, 2022.
4. The Election Commission is reconstituted every five years.

Which of the following statements given above is/are incorrect?

(a) 1 and 2 (b) 2, and 3
(c) 1 and 4 (d) Only 3

246. Which one of the following pairs is correctly matched? **MPPSC (Pre) 2024**

	Constitutional Body		Constitutional Article
(a)	National Commission for Scheduled Castes	-	148
(b)	Election Commission	-	165
(c)	National Commission for Backward Classes	-	340
(d)	Finance Commission	-	263

32. NON-CONSTITUTIONAL BODIES

247. Which of the following pairs is/are incorrectly matched? **Assam PSC (Pre) 2024**

1. Finance Commission of India : Constitutional Body
2. Securities and Exchange Board of India : Statutory Body
3. NITI Aayog : Constitutional Body
4. Reserve Bank of India : Statutory Body

Select the correct answer by using the codes given below.

(a) 1 and 3 only (b) 2 and 4 only
(c) Only 3 (d) Only 4

248. Match List-I with List-II and select the correct answer by using the codes given below the lists. **HPPSC (Pre) 2024**

	List-I (Commissions)		List-II (Years of Establishment)
A.	National Commission for Women	1.	1953
B.	National Human Rights Commission	2.	1992
C.	Kaka Kalelkar Commission	3.	2005
D.	National Commission for Protection of Child Rights	4.	1993

Choose the correct answer from the options given below.

	A	B	C	D		A	B	C	D
(a)	2	4	1	3	(b)	1	2	3	4
(c)	3	2	4	1	(d)	4	3	1	2

249. Who is not the Ex-officio member of the National Human Rights Commission? **IAS (Pre) 1999, MPPSC (Pre) 2014, 2018, 2019**

(a) The Chairperson of the National Commission of Minorities
(b) The Chairperson of the Law Commission of India
(c) The Chairperson of the National Commission for the Scheduled Castes and Scheduled Tribes
(d) The Chairperson of the National Commission of Women

250. Consider the following organisations/bodies in India.

1. The National Commission for Backward Classes
2. The National Human Rights Commission
3. The National Law Commission
4. The National Consumer Disputes Redressal Commission **IAS (Pre) 2023**

How many of the above are constitutional bodies?

(a) Only one (b) Only two
(c) Only three (d) All four

251. Match List-I with List-II and select the correct answer by using the codes given below the lists. **UPPSC (Pre) 2023**

	List-I		List-II
A.	Article 324	1.	National Commission for Scheduled Castes
B.	Article 315	2.	Finance Commission
C.	Article 280	3.	Public Service Commission
D.	Article 338	4.	Election Commission

Codes

	A	B	C	D		A	B	C	D
(a)	3	2	1	4	(b)	1	3	4	2
(c)	3	2	4	1	(d)	4	3	2	1

252. Which of the following statements are correct in relation to Right to Information Act? **HPPSC (Pre) 2024**

1. This act came into force on 12th October, 2005.
2. It repealed the Official Secret Act, 1923.
3. It replaced the Freedom of Information Act,2002.
4. It does not protect freedom of expression and speech under Article 19

Choose the correct answer from the options given below.

(a) 2, 3 and 4 (b) 1, 2 and 3
(c) 3, 4 and 1 (d) 1 and 2

33. PUBLIC SERVICES

253. Which of the following statements is/are correct? **MPSC (Pre) 2017**

1. Articles from 308 to 314 in Part XIV of the Constitution contain provisions with regard to Central Services and State Services.
2. Article 311 provides safeguards of Civil Servants with regard to tenure of office.

Codes

(a) Only 1 (b) Only 2
(c) Both 1 and 2 (d) Neither 1 nor 2

254. Match List I with List II and select the correct answer by using the codes given below. **MPSC (Pre) 2015**

	List I (Article)		List II (Provision)
A.	309	1.	Recruitment and service conditions of the Central Services
B.	311	2.	Claims of Scheduled Castes and Scheduled Tribes
C.	323 (A)	3.	Dismissal and removal of a member of the All India Services and Central Services
D.	335	4.	Setting up an Administrative Tribunal

Codes

	A	B	C	D		A	B	C	D
(a)	1	2	3	4	(b)	3	4	2	1
(c)	4	3	2	1	(d)	2	4	1	3

255. Which among the following are included in the All India Services? **MPSC (Pre) 2012**

1. Indian Administrative Service
2. Indian Police Service
3. Indian Foreign Service
4. Indian Forest Service

Select the correct answer by using the codes given below.

(a) 1 and 2 (b) 1, 2 and 3
(c) 1, 2 and 4 (d) All of the above

256. In which of the following matters, the State Public Service Commission is not consulted? **RAS/RTS (Pre) 2013**

(a) On the method of recruitment of Civil Services.
(b) On the principles to be followed in making appointments to Civil Services.
(c) On the principles of the followed in making promotions in Civil Services and transfers from one service to another.
(d) On making transfers of Civil Servants.

257. A Public Service Commission was established in India for the first time by **WBCS (Pre) 2023**

(a) The Indian Council Act, 1982
(b) The Act of 1909
(c) The Government of India Act, 1919
(d) The Government of India Act, 1935

34. PROVISION RELATED TO OFFICIAL LANGUAGES

258. Consider the following statements about the Committee of Parliament on official language.

1. Article 344 (4) say that there shall be constituted a Committee of Parliament on official language.
2. It consist of 30 members of whom 20 from Lok Sabha and 10 from Rajya Sabha.
3. The duty of the Committee is to examine the recommendation of official language Commission.

Which of the statements given above are correct?

(a) 1 and 2 (b) 2 and 3
(c) 1 and 3 (d) All of these

259. Under which one of the following Constitution Amendment Acts, four languages were added to the languages under the Eighth Schedule of the Constitution of India, thereby raising their number to 22? **IAS (Pre) 2008**

(a) Constitution (90th Amendment) Act
(b) Constitution (91st Amendment) Act
(c) Constitution (92nd Amendment) Act
(d) Constitution (93rd Amendment) Act

260. The Constitution (71st Amendment) Act, 1992 amends the Eighth Schedule to the Constitution to include which of the following languages? **IAS (Pre) 2024**

1. Konkani 2. Manipuri
3. Nepali 4. Maithili

Select the correct answer by using the codes given below.

(a) 1,2, and 3 (b) 1, 2 and 4
(c) 1, 3 and 4 (d) 2, 3 and 4

261. Consider the following statements regarding the provisions of official languages in India. **Assam PSC (Pre) 2024**

1. Article 343 of the Constitution of India has made Hindi in Devanagari script as the National Language of India.
2. The Legislature of a State may by-law adopt any one or more of the languages in use in the states as the official language/ languages of the states as per Article 345 of the Constitution of India.
3. The Assam Official Language Act, 1960 has been legislated as per Article 345 of the Constitution of India.

Select the correct statement/ statements using the codes given below.

(a) 1 and 2 only (b) 2 and 3 only
(c) 1 and 3 only (d) 1, 2 and 3

35. CO-OPERATIVE SOCIETIES

262. Consider the following statements regarding Co-operative societies in India.

1. Co-operatives are enterprises which are owned, controlled and run by its members.
2. The co-operative societies emerged only after Independence in India.
3. In India, the majority of the co-operative Societies are governed by laws in their respective states.

Which of the above statements is/are correct?

(a) Only 1 (b) 1 and 2
(c) 1 and 3 (d) All of these

263. With reference to 'Co-operative Societies in India', consider the following statements.

1. The subject of Co-operative Societies falls under concurrent list in Seventh Schedule of Indian Constitution.
2. The Constitution directs the state to promote voluntary formation and autonomous functioning of co-operative societies.
3. Right to form Co-operative Societies is a Fundamental Right under the Constitution of India.

How many of the statements given above is/ are correct?

(a) Only one
(b) Only two
(c) Only three
(d) All four

264. Which article contains the provision related with the supersession and suspension of Board and Interim Management?

(a) 243 ZL (b) 243 ZK
(c) 243 ZT (d) 243 ZM

36. SPECIAL PROVISIONS FOR CERTAIN CLASSES

265. The authority to specify as to which castes shall be deemed to be Scheduled Castes rests with the **UPPSC (Pre) 2016, UPPSC (Mains) 2016,**

(a) Commission of SCs and STs
(b) Prime Minister
(c) Governor of the State
(d) President

266. The purpose of specifying the Court of Session as a Special Court to try offenses under the Scheduled Castes and Scheduled Tribes (Prevention of Atrocities) Act. **MPPSC (Pre) 201**

(a) Speedy trial
(b) Time bound trial
(c) Special protection for the victim
(d) All of the above

267. Match the List-I with List-II and select the correct answer by using the codes given below the lists. **RAS/RTS (Pre) 201**

List-I (Human Rights Documents)	List-II (Years)
A. The National Commission for Minorities Act	1. 1993
B. Persons with Disabilities (Equal Opportunities, Protection of Rights and full Participation) Act	2. 1986
C. Child Labour (Prohibition and Regulation) Act	3. 1995
D. The National Commission for Backward Classes Act	4. 1992

Codes

	A	B	C	D		A	B	C	D
(a)	2	1	3	4	(b)	4	3	2	1
(c)	3	1	2	4	(d)	3	1	4	2

268. Match List-I with List-II and select the correct answer by using the codes given below the lists.

List-I	List-II
A. 26th Constitutional Amendment	1. Reservation for EWS
B. 52nd Constitutional Amendment	2. Education as fundamental right
C. 86th Constitutional Amendment	3. Abolition of Privy Purse
D. 103rd Constitutional Amendment	4. Anti-defection law

Choose the correct answer from the options given below. **HPSC (Pre) 2024**

	A	B	C	D		A	B	C	D
(a)	3	4	2	1	(b)	1	3	2	4
(c)	2	1	4	3	(d)	4	3	2	1

269. Consider the following statements with reference to Scheduled Areas. **UP RO/ARO (Pre) 2024**

1. The President of India notifies Scheduled Areas.
2. States with Scheduled Areas need to constitute a Tribal Advisory Council.

Select the correct answer from the codes given below.

(a) Neither 1 nor 2 (b) Both 1 and 2
(c) Only 1 (d) Only 2

270. As per Article 164(1) of the Constitution of India, a Minister in charge of tribal welfare who may in addition be in charge of the Scheduled Castes and Backward Classes is compulsory for which of the following states? **APPSC (Pre) 2024**

1. Madhya Pradesh 2. Punjab
3. Uttar Pradesh 4. Jharkhand
5. Odisha

Codes

(a) 1, 2 and 4 (b) 2, 3 and 4
(c) 1, 4 and 5 (d) 2, 3 and 5

37. SPECIAL PROVISIONS FOR CERTAIN STATES

271. Which Article of the Indian Constitution deals with special provisions with respect to different states? **UPPSC (Pre) 1997, MPSC (Pre) 2013**

(a) Article 369 (b) Article 370
(c) Article 371 (d) Article 372

272. Article 371, the President is authorised to provide that the Governor of Maharashtra and that of Gujarat would have special responsibility, for

1. making a provision that a report on the working of these boards would be placed every year before the State Legislative Assembly.
2. the equitable allocation of funds for development expenditure over the Vidarbha, Marathwada, Saurashtra and Kachchh.

Which of the statement(s) given above is/are correct?

(a) Only 1 (b) Only 2
(c) Both 1 and 2 (d) Neither 1 nor 2

273. Consider the following statements.

1. Articles 371 (A) to 371 (J) were inserted in the Constitution of India to meet regional demands of Nagaland, Assam, Manipur, Andhra Pradesh, Sikkim, Mizoram, Arunachal Pradesh and Goa.
2. Constitution of India and the United States of America envisage a dual policy (the Union and the States) but a single citizenship.
3. A naturalised citizen of the India can never be deprived of his citizenship.

Which of the statement(s) given above is/are correct? **IAS (Pre) 2005**

(a) All of these (b) 1 and 3
(c) Only 3 (d) Only 1

274. Consider the following statements regarding the special provisions to some of the States of India made by the Constitution. **Assam PSC, (Pre) 2024**

1. Article 371C provides for the special provisions for the State of Assam. Under this Article, the President of India is empowered to provide for the creation of committee of the Assam Legislative Assembly consisting of members elected from Tribal Areas of the State and such other members as he/she may specify.
2. Article 371C was added by the 22nd Amendment Act of 1969.
3. Article 371D deals with special provisions with respect to the State of Andhra Pradesh and Article 371E deals with the establishment of Central University in Andhra Pradesh.
4. 32nd Constitutional Amendment Act, which was made in 1973, inserted Articles 371D and 371E into the Constitution of India.

Select the incorrect statement/statements using the codes given below.

(a) 1 only (b) 3 and 4 only
(c) 1 and 2 only (d) 1 and 3 only

38. ELECTORAL PROCESS AND POLITICAL DYNAMICS

275. Consider the following statements regarding Election Commission of India. **HPSC (Pre) 2021**

1. The Election Commission of India is a five member body.
2. The Election Commission decides the election schedule for the conduct of both general elections and by elections.
3. The Election Commission resolves the disputes relating to splits/mergers of recognised political parties.
4. The Election Commission of India provides election symbols for newly registered parties.

Which of the statements given above is/are not correct?

(a) 1 and 3 (b) 2 and 4
(c) Only 1 (d) 1, 2 and 3

276. Consider the following statements. **MPPSC (Pre) 2022**

1. The Chief Election Commissioner of the Election Commission of India is paid a salary equal to the salary of the Judge of the Supreme Court.
2. The term of Chief Election Commissioner of India shall be for a period of six years from the date of assuming office or till the age of 65 years whichever comes first.

3. An Election Commissioner may at any time by writing under his hand addressed to the Chief Election Commissioner, resign his office.

Codes
(a) 1 and 2 (b) 1 and 3
(c) 1, 2 and 3 (d) Only 3

277. Which of the following are the functions of the Election Commissioner of India? **UPPSC (Pre) 2024**
1. Conduct of elections for the post of the Speaker and the Deputy Speaker of the Lok Sabha and Deputy Chairman of the Rajya Sabha.
2. Conduct of elections of the Municipal corporations and Municipalities.
3. Deciding on all doubts and disputes arising out of the above elections.

Select the correct answer from the codes given below.
(a) 1 and 3 (b) 2 and 3
(c) 1 and 2 (d) None of these

278. Consider the following statements. **MPSC (Pre) 2015**
1. In 1952, the first delimitation of constituencies was done in India.
2. The fourth delimitation was done under the Delimitation Act, 2002.
3. The last delimitation was done in India using the figures of the population Census 1971.

Which of the following statements given above is/are true?
(a) 1 and 2 (b) Only 2
(c) 1 and 3 (d) Only 3

279. What is the eligibility age, after the changes made in March 2024, for senior citizens to vote by postal ballot? **BPSC (Pre) 2024**
(a) 85 years (b) 80 years
(c) 82 years (d) 90 years

280. Consider the following pairs. **IAS (Pre) 2024**

	Party		Its Leaders
1.	Bharatiya Jana Sangh	:	Dr. Shyama Prasad Mukherjee
2.	Socialist party	:	C. Rajagopalachari
3.	Congress for Democracy	:	Jagjivan Ram
4.	Swatantra Party	:	Acharya Narendra Dev

How many of the pairs given above is/are correctly matched?
(a) Only one (b) Only two
(c) Only three (d) All four

281. Consider the following statements regarding the Delimitation Commission of India. **Assam PSC (Pre) 2024**
1. The Delimitation Commission is appointed by the President of India and works in collaboration with the Election Commission of India.
2. Article 82 of the Constitution of India states that the Parliament is required by law to enact a Delimitation Act following each Census.
3. The first delimitation exercise in post-independent India was held in 1952 as per the 1951 Census.
4. The present delimitation of parliamentary constituencies has been done on the basis of the 2001 Census figures under the provision of the Delimitation Act, 2002.

Which of the statement given above is/are correct?
(a) Only 1
(b) 1 and 2
(c) 1, 2 and 3
(d) 1, 2, 3 and 4

282. Consider the following statements regarding the Election Commission of India. **Assam PSC (Pre) 2024**
1. The Election Commission of India is a body constitutionally empowered to conduct free and fair elections to the National and State Legislatures including the Panchayats.
2. The power of the Election Commission of India is derived from Article 324 of the Constitution of India.
3. Rajiv Kumar is the present Chief Election Commissioner who joined his office on 15th May, 2022.
4. The Election Commission is reconstituted every five years.

Which of the statements given above is/are incorrect?
(a) 1 and 2 (b) 2 and 3
(c) 1 and 4 (d) Only 3

283. Which one of the following statements is not correct? **MPPSC (Pre) 2024**
(a) In case of differences of opinion among the Chief Election Commissioner and other Election Commissioner, the matter is decided by the Law Commission.
(b) The Election Commissioners cannot be removed from their office except on the recommendation of the Chief Election Commissioner.
(c) The Chief Election Commissioner and other Election Commissioners enjoy equal powers.
(d) The term of office of Election Commissioners is six years from the date they assume office or till the day they attain the age of 65 years, whichever is earlier.

39. POLITICAL CONCEPTS AND THEORIES

284. Who among the following argued that the state exists to protect natural rights such as life, liberty and property?
(a) Thomas Hobbes
(b) John Locke
(c) Jean-Jacques Rousseau
(d) Jean Bodin

285. Which of the following is an example of direct democracy?
(a) Election of Members of Parliament in India.
(b) A referendum where citizens vote directly on a policy issue.
(c) The appointment of the President of the United States.
(d) Election of a local mayor through representatives.

286. What does Constructivism in international relations primarily focus on?
(a) Economic interdependence between states.
(b) The social construction of state identities and interests.
(c) The concentration of political power in authoritarian regimes.
(d) The balance of military power among rival states.

287. Which of the following is a feature of Democratic Socialism?
(a) Complete state control over the economy and private property.
(b) A mix of democratic governance with socialist economic policies.
(c) Totalitarian leadership with extreme nationalism.
(d) A focus on military power and authoritarian governance.

40. FOREIGN POLICY

288. Which of the following articles in the Indian Constitution directs the state to promote international peace and security?

(a) Article 50 (b) Article 51
(c) Article 52 (d) Article 53

289. Which of the following principles is not a part of the Panchsheel doctrine?
(a) Mutual respect for territorial integrity and sovereignty
(b) Non-aggression
(c) Promotion of military alliances for regional stability
(d) Peaceful coexistence

290. Which of the following initiatives is part of India's efforts to improve connectivity with Central Asia under the Connect Central Asia Policy?
(a) International North-South Transport Corridor (INSTC)
(b) Kaladan Multi-Modal Transit Transport Project
(c) Sagarmala Project
(d) India-Japan Maritime Security Cooperation

291. Choose the incorrect statement about India's Neighbourhood First Policy.
(a) India is involved in post-conflict peace-building efforts in Sri Lanka.
(b) India launched Operation Maitri to assist Myanmar after an earthquake.
(c) India has assisted Bhutan in hydropower development.
(d) India prioritises regional cooperation through SAARC and BIMSTEC.

Answers

1. (c)	2. (c)	3. (d)	4. (a)	5. (a)	6. (c)	7. (b)	8. (c)	9. (a)	10. (b)
11. (c)	12. (d)	13. (b)	14. (d)	15. (b)	16. (b)	17. (a)	18. (c)	19. (a)	20. (b)
21. (b)	22. (c)	23. (d)	24. (d)	25. (b)	26. (b)	27. (d)	28. (c)	29. (a)	30. (b)
31. (c)	32. (a)	33. (c)	34. (a)	35. (d)	36. (a)	37. (b)	38. (d)	39. (b)	40. (d)
41. (c)	42. (c)	43. (d)	44. (c)	45. (a)	46. (d)	47. (d)	48. (c)	49. (b)	50. (d)
51. (b)	52. (a)	53. (a)	54. (c)	55. (c)	56. (b)	57. (d)	58. (b)	59. (d)	60. (b)
61. (a)	62. (d)	63. (a)	64. (c)	65. (a)	66. (d)	67. (c)	68. (c)	69. (d)	70. (a)
71. (d)	72. (c)	73. (b)	74. (d)	75. (b)	76. (d)	77. (c)	78. (b)	79. (b)	80. (a)
81. (a)	82. (b)	83. (d)	84. (c)	85. (d)	86. (a)	87. (c)	88. (c)	89. (a)	90. (d)
91. (d)	92. (d)	93. (d)	94. (d)	95. (a)	96. (c)	97. (c)	98. (d)	99. (a)	100. (c)
101. (a)	102. (b)	103. (b)	104. (c)	105. (a)	106. (b)	107. (b)	108. (b)	109. (b)	110. (d)
111. (d)	112. (d)	113. (b)	114. (b)	115. (a)	116. (a)	117. (c)	118. (c)	119. (b)	120. (c)
121. (d)	122. (a)	123. (b)	124. (a)	125. (a)	126. (d)	127. (b)	128. (c)	129. (b)	130. (b)
131. (b)	132. (c)	133. (b)	134. (c)	135. (c)	136. (c)	137. (c)	138. (b)	139. (d)	140. (b)
141. (c)	142. (d)	143. (b)	144. (c)	145. (b)	146. (c)	147. (d)	148. (d)	149. (a)	150. (d)
151. (c)	152. (c)	153. (b)	154. (a)	155. (a)	156. (c)	157. (d)	158. (a)	159. (a)	160. (a)
161. (b)	162. (b)	163. (b)	164. (a)	165. (c)	166. (c)	167. (a)	168. (a)	169. (c)	170. (d)
171. (b)	172. (c)	173. (b)	174. (a)	175. (b)	176. (d)	177. (d)	178. (c)	179. (d)	180. (c)
181. (b)	182. (c)	183. (a)	184. (b)	185. (c)	186. (d)	187. (b)	188. (a)	189. (b)	190. (a)
191. (a)	192. (c)	193. (a)	194. (d)	195. (d)	196. (d)	197. (d)	198. (c)	199. (d)	200. (b)
201. (c)	202. (b)	203. (d)	204. (a)	205. (c)	206. (d)	207. (d)	208. (d)	209. (c)	210. (a)
211. (b)	212. (c)	213. (a)	214. (c)	215. (a)	216. (b)	217. (c)	218. (a)	219. (a)	220. (d)
221. (b)	222. (d)	223. (c)	224. (b)	225. (b)	226. (b)	227. (b)	228. (a)	229. (d)	230. (b)
231. (c)	232. (b)	233. (c)	234. (d)	235. (a)	236. (d)	237. (a)	238. (b)	239. (c)	240. (b)
241. (d)	242. (c)	243. (a)	244. (c)	245. (c)	246. (c)	247. (c)	248. (a)	249. (b)	250. (a)
251. (d)	252. (b)	253. (c)	254. (b)	255. (c)	256. (d)	257. (c)	258. (d)	259. (c)	260. (a)
261. (d)	262. (c)	263. (b)	264. (a)	265. (d)	266. (d)	267. (b)	268. (a)	269. (b)	270. (c)
271. (c)	272. (c)	273. (d)	274. (c)	275. (c)	276. (a)	277. (d)	278. (a)	279. (b)	280. (b)
281. (d)	282. (c)	283. (a)	284. (b)	285. (b)	286. (b)	287. (b)	288. (b)	289. (c)	290. (a)
291. (b)									

SELF CHECK **FOR PRELIMS PRACTICE**
Scan QR Code & Attempt MCQs

UPSC Mains Exams Questions
(2024-2015)

Indian Constitution Historical Under Pinning, Evolution, Features, Amendments, Significant Provisions and Basic Structure.

1. Right to privacy is intrinsic to life and personal liberty and is inherently protected under Article 21 of the Constitution. Explain. In this reference discuss the law relating to DNA testing of child in the womb to establish its paternity. *UPSC 2024 (250 words; 15 marks)*
2. Discuss India as a secular state and compare with the secular principles of the US Constitution. *UPSC 2024 (250 words; 15 marks)*
3. Who are entitled to receive Free Legal Aid? Assess the role of the National Legal Services Authority (NALSA) in rendering Free Legal Aid in India? *UPSC 2023 (150 words; 10 marks)*
4. "Constitutionally guaranteed judicial independence is a prerequisite of democracy." Comment. *UPSC 2023 (150 words; 10 marks)*
5. "The Constitution of India is a living instrument with capabilities of enormous dynamism. It is a Constitution made for a progressive society." Illustrate with special reference to the expanding horizons of the right to life and personal liberty. *UPSC 2023 (250 words; 15 marks)*
6. Explain the constitutional perspectives of Gender Justice with the help of relevant Constitutional Provisions and case laws. *UPSC 2023 (250 words; 15 marks)*
7. 'Right of movement and residence throughout the Territory of India are freely available to the Indian citizens, but these rights are not absolute.' Comment. *UPSC 2022 (150 words; 10 marks)*
8. 'Constitutional Morality' is rooted in the Constitution itself and is founded on its essential facts. Explain the doctrine of 'Constitutional Morality' with the help of relevant judicial decisions. *UPSC 2021(150 words; 10 marks)*
9. 'Recent amendments to the Right to Information Act will have profound impact on the autonomy and independence of the Information Commission'. Discuss. *UPSC 2020 (150 words; 10 marks)*
10. Indian Constitution exhibits centralising tendencies to maintain unity and integrity of the nation. Elucidate in the perspective of the Epidemic Diseases Act, 1897, The Disaster Management Act, 2005 and recently passed Farm Acts. *UPSC 2020 (250 words; 15 marks)*
11. Do you think that Constitution of India does not accept principle of strict separation of powers rather it is based on the principle of 'checks and balance'? Explain. *UPSC 2019 (150 words; 10 marks)*
12. 'Parliament's power to amend the Constitution is a limited power and it cannot be enlarged into absolute power.' In the light of this statement, explain whether Parliament under Article 368 of the Constitution can destroy the basic structure of the Constitution by expanding its amending power? *UPSC 2019 (250 words; 15 marks)*
13. Explain the salient features of the Constitution (One Hundred and First Amendment) Act, 2016. Do you think it is efficacious enough 'to remove cascading effect of taxes and provide for common national market for goods and services'? *UPSC 2017 (250 words; 15 marks)*
14. Discuss each adjective attached to the word 'Republic' in the 'Preamble'. Are they defendable in the present circumstances? *UPSC 2016 (200 words; 12(½) marks)*
15. Discuss the possible factors that inhibit India from enacting for its citizens a Uniform Civil Code as provided for in the Directive Principles of State Policy. *UPSC 2015 (200 words, 12(½) marks)*

Functions and Responsibilities of the Union and the States, Issues and Challenges Pertaining to the Federal Structure, Devolution of Powers and Finances up to Local Levels and Challenges Therein.

1. How have the recommendations of the 14th Finance Commission of India enabled the states to improve their fiscal position? *UPSC 2021 (150 words; 10 marks)*
2. The Jurisdiction of the Central Bureau of Investigation (CBI) regarding lodging an FIR and conducting probe within a particular state is being questioned by various states. However, the power of the states to withold consent to the CBI is not absolute. Explain with special reference to the federal character of India. *UPSC 2021 (250 words; 15 marks)*
3. How far do you think cooperation, competition and confrontation have shaped the nature of federation in India? Cite some recent examples to validate your answer. *UPSC 2020 (150 words; 10 marks*

4. The strength and sustenance of local institutions in India has shifted from their formative phase of 'Functions, Functionaries and Funds' to the contemporary stage of 'Functionality'. Highlight the critical challenges faced by local institutions in terms of their functionality in recent times.
UPSC 2020 (250 words; 15 marks)

5. 'The reservation of seats for women in the institutions of local self-government has had a limited impact on the patriarchal character of the Indian Political Process.' Comment. *UPSC 2019 (250 words; 15 marks)*

6. Assess the importance of the Panchayat System in India as a part of local government. Apart from government grants, what sources the Panchayats can look out for financing developmental projects?
UPSC 2018 (250 words; 15 marks)

7. 'The local self-government system in India has not proved to be effective instrument of governance.' Critically examine the statement and give your views to improve the situation. *UPSC 2017 (150 words; 10 marks)*

8. Did the Government of India Act, 1935 lay down a Federal Constitution? Discuss. *UPSC 2016 (200 words; 12(½) marks)*

9. To what extent is Article 370 of the Indian Constitution, bearing marginal note 'Temporary provision with respect to the state of Jammu and Kashmir'; temporary? Discuss the future prospects of this provision in the context of Indian Polity.
UPSC 2016 (200 words; 12(½) marks)

10. Discuss the essentials of the 69th Constitutional Amendment Act and anomalies, if any, that have led to recent reported conflicts between the elected representatives and the institution of the Lieutenant Governor in the administration of Delhi. Do you think that this will give rise to a new trend in the functioning of the Indian Federal Politics? *UPSC 2016 (200 words; 12(½) marks)*

11. Khap Panchayats have been in the news for functioning as extra-constitutional authorities, often delivering pronouncements amounting to Human Rights violations. Discuss critically the actions taken by the Legislative, Executive and the Judiciary to set the things right in this regard. *UPSC 2015 (200 words; 12(½) marks)*

12. The concept of cooperative federalism has been increasingly emphasised in recent years. Highlight the drawbacks in the existing structure and the extent to which cooperative federalism would answer the shortcomings. *UPSC 2015 (200 words; 12(½) marks)*

13. In absence of a well-educated and organised local-level government system, 'Panchayats' and 'Samitis' have remained mainly political institutions and not effective instruments of governance. Critically discuss.
UPSC 2015 (200 words; 12(½) marks)

Separation of Powers Between Various Organs Dispute Redressal Mechanisms and Institutions.

1. Explain and distinguish between Lok Adalats and Arbitration Tribunals. Whether they entertain civil as well as criminal cases? *UPSC 2024 (150 words; 10 marks)*

2. "The growth of cabinet system has practically resulted in the marginalisation of the parliamentary supremacy." Elucidate. *UPSC 2024 (150 words; 10 marks)*

3. Analyse the role of local bodies in providing good governance at local level and bring out the pros and cons merging the rural local bodies with the urban local bodies. *UPSC 2024 (150 words; 10 marks)*

4. "The states in India seem reluctant to empower urban local bodies both functionally as well as financially." Comment. *UPSC 2023 (150 words; 10 marks)*

5. Compare and contrast the British and Indian approaches to Parliamentary sovereignty.
UPSC 2023 (150 words; 10 marks)

6. E-governance, as a critical tool of governance, has ushered in effectiveness, transparency and accountability in governments. What inadequacies hamper the enhancement of these features?
UPSC 2023 (150 words; 10 marks)

7. Explain the significance of the 101st Constitutional Amendment Act. To what extent does it reflect the accommodative spirit of federalism?
UPSC 2023 (250 words; 15 marks)

8. Explain the structure of the Parliamentary Committee System. How far have the financial committees helped in the institutionalisation of Indian Parliament?
UPSC 2023 (250 words; 15 marks)

9. To what extent, in your opinion, has the decentralisation of power in India changed the Governance landscape at the grassroots?
UPSC 2022 (150 words; 10 marks)

10. Judicial Legislation is antithetical to the doctrine of separation of powers as envisaged in the Indian Constitution. In this context justify the filing of large number of public interest petitions praying for issuing guidelines to executive authorities.
UPSC 2020 (250 words; 15 marks)

Comparison of the Indian Constitutional Assemblies with that of Other Countries.

1. Critically examine the procedures through which the Presidents of India and France are elected.
UPSC 2022 (250 words; 15 marks)

2. Analyse the distinguishing features of the nation of Right to Equality in the Constitutions of the USA and India. *UPSC 2021 (250 words; 15 marks)*

3. The Judicial System in India and UK seem to be converging as well as diverging in recent times. Highlight the key points of convergence and divergence between the two nations in terms of their judicial practices. *UPSC 2020 (150 words; 10 marks)*
4. What can France learn from the Indian Constitution's approach to secularism? *UPSC 2019 (150 words; 10 marks)*
5. India and USA are two large democracies. Examine the basic tenets on which the two political systems are based. *UPSC 2018 (250 words; 15 marks)*

Parliament and State Legislatures Structure, Functioning, Conduct of Business, Powers and Privileges and Issues Arising out of these.

1. "The duty of the Comptroller and Auditor-General is not merely to ensure the legality of expenditure but also its propriety." Comment. *UPSC 2024 (150 words; 10 marks)*
2. Discuss the role of Presiding Officers of State Legislatures in maintaining order and impartiality in conducting legislative work and in facilitating best democratic practices. *UPSC 2023 (150 words; 10 marks)*
3. Account for the legal and political factors responsible for the reduced frequency of using Article 356 by the Union Governments since mid-1990's. *UPSC 2023 (250 words; 15 marks)*
4. Discuss the role of the Vice-President of India as the Chairman of the Rajya Sabha. *UPSC 2022 (150 words; 10 marks)*
5. Discuss the essential conditions for exercise of the Legislative Powers by the Governor. Discuss the legality of re-promulgation of ordinances by the Governor without placing them before the Legislature. *UPSC 2022 (250 words; 15 marks)*
6. Explain the constitutional provisions under which Legislative Councils are established. Review the working and current status of Legislative Councils with suitable illustrations. *UPSC 2021 (250 words; 15 marks)*
7. Do Department-related Parliamentary Standing Committees keep the administration on its toes and inspire reverence for parliamentary control? Evaluate the working of such committees with suitable examples. *UPSC 2021 (250 words; 15 marks)*
8. Rajya Sabha has been transformed from a 'Useless stepney tyre' to the most useful supporting organ in past few decades. Highlight the factors as well as the areas in which this transformation could be visible. *UPSC 2020 (250 words; 15 marks)*
9. 'Once a Speaker, Always a Speaker'! Do you think this practice should be adopted to impart objectivity to the office of the Speaker of Lok Sabha? What could be its implications for the robust functioning of parliamentary business in India? *UPSC 2020 (150 words; 10 marks)*
10. Individual Parliamentarian's role as the national law maker is on a decline, which in turn, has adversely impacted the quality of debates and their outcome. Discuss. *UPSC 2019 (250 words; 15 marks)*
11. Why do you think the committees are considered to be useful for parliamentary work? Discuss in this context, the role of the Estimates Committee. *UPSC 2018 (150 words; 10 marks)*
12. The Indian Constitution has provisions for holding joint session of the two Houses of the Parliament. Enumerate the occasions when this would normally happen and also the occasions when it cannot, with reason thereof. *UPSC 2017 (250 words; 15 marks)*
13. "Simultaneous election to the Lok Sabha and the State Assemblies will limit the amount of time and money spent in electioneering but it will reduce the government's accountability to the people." Discuss. *UPSC 2017 (150 words; 10 marks)*
14. Resorting to ordinances has always raised concern on violation of the spirit of separation of powers doctrine. While noting the rationales justifying the power to promulgate ordinances, analyse whether the decisions of the Supreme Court on the issue have further facilitated resorting to this power. Should the power to promulgate ordinances be repealed? *UPSC 2015 (200 words; 12(½) marks)*
15. What are the major changes brought in the Arbitration and Conciliation Act, 1996 through the recent ordinance promulgated by the President? How far will it improve India's dispute resolution mechanism? Discuss. *UPSC 2015 (200 words; $12\frac{1}{2}$ marks)*
16. Examine critically the recent changes in the rules governing Foreign funding of NGO's under the Foreign Contribution (Regulation) Act (FCRA), 1976. *UPSC 2015 (250 words; 12(½) marks)*

Structure, Organisation and Functioning of the Executive and the Judiciary–Ministries and Departments of the Government; Pressure Groups and Formal/Informal Associations and their Role in the Polity.

1. 'The most significant achievement of modern law in India is the constitutionalisation of environmental problems by the Supreme Court.' Discuss this statement with the help of relevant case laws. *UPSC 2022 (150 words; 10 marks)*
2. To what extent, in your view, the Parliament is able to ensure accountability of the Executive in India? *UPSC 2021 (150 words; 10 marks)*
3. 'Pressure groups play a vital role in influencing public policy making in India.' Explain how the business associations contribute to public policies. *UPSC 2021 (150 words; 10 marks)*

4. Discuss the desirability of greater representation to women in the higher judiciary to ensure diversity, equity and inclusiveness. *UPSC 2021 (150 words; 10 marks)*

5. What are the methods used by the farmers' organisations to influence the policy makers in India and how effective are these methods? *UPSC 2019 (150 words; 10 marks)*

6. From the resolution of contentious issues regarding distribution of Legislative Powers by the courts, 'Principle of Federal Supremacy' and 'Harmonious Construction' have emerged. Explain. *UPSC 2019 (150 words; 10 marks)*

7. Under what circumstances can the Financial Emergency be proclaimed by the President of India? What consequences follow when such a declaration remains in force? *UPSC 2018 (150 words; 10 marks)*

8. Whether the Supreme Court Judgement (July 2018) can settle the political tussle between the Lieutenant Governor and Elected Government of Delhi? Examine. *UPSC 2018 (250 words; 15 marks)*

9. Examine the scope of Fundamental Rights in the light of the latest judgement of the Supreme Court on Right to Privacy. *UPSC 2017 (250 words; 15 marks)*

10. How do pressure groups influence Indian political process? Do you agree with this view that informal pressure groups have emerged as more powerful than formal pressure groups in recent years? *UPSC 2017 (150 words; 10 marks)*

11. Critically examine the Supreme Court's judgement on 'National Judicial Appointments Commission Act, 2014' with reference to appointment of Judges of Higher Judiciary in India. *UPSC 2017 (150 words; 10 marks)*

12. What was held in the Coelho Case? In this context, can you say that Judicial Review is of key importance amongst the basic features of the Constitution? *UPSC 2016 (200 words; 12(½) marks)*

13. Does the right to clean environment entail legal regulations on burning crackers during Diwali? Discuss in the light of Article 21 of the Indian Constitution and Judgement(s) of the Apex Court in this regard. *UPSC 2015 (200 words; 12(½) marks)*

Salient Features of the Representation of People's Act.

1. Discuss the procedures to decide the disputes arising out of the election of a Member of the Parliament or State Legislature under the Representation of the People Act, 1951. What are the grounds on which the election of any returned candidate may be declared void? What remedy is available to the aggrieved party against the decision? Refer to the case laws. *UPSC 2022 (250 words; 15 marks)*

2. 'While the National Political Parties (NPP) in India favour centralisation, the regional parties are in favour of state autonomy.' Comment. *UPSC 2022 (250 words; 15 marks)*

3. 'There is a need for simplification of procedure for disqualification of persons found guilty of corrupt practices under the Representation of Peoples' Act'. Comment. *UPSC (150 words; 10 marks)*

4. On what grounds, a peoples' representative can be disqualified under the Representation of Peoples' Act, 1951? Also mention the remedies available to such person against his disqualification. *UPSC 2019 (250 words; 15 marks)*

5. 'The Indian Party System is passing through a phase of transition which looks to be full of contradictions and paradoxes.' Discuss. *UPSC 2016 (200 words; 12(½) marks)*

Appointment to Various Constitutional Posts, Powers, Functions and Responsibilities of Various Constitutional Bodies.

1. Examine the need for electoral reforms as suggested by various committees with particular reference to "one nation one election" principle. *UPSC 2024 (150 words; 10 marks)*

2. Discuss the role of the National Commission for Backward Classes in the wake of its transformation from a statutory body to a constitutional body. *UPSC 2022 (150 words; 10 marks)*

3. Discuss the role of the Election Commission of India in the light of the evolution of the Model Code of Conduct. *UPSC 2022 (250 words; 15 marks)*

4. 'The Attorney-General is the Chief Legal Advisor and Lawyer of the Government of India.' Discuss. *UPSC 2019 (250 words; 15 marks)*

5. Whether National Commission for Scheduled Castes (NCSC) can enforce the implementation of constitutional reservation for the Scheduled Castes in the religious minority institutions? Examine. *UPSC 2018 (150 words; 10 marks)*

6. In the light of recent controversy regarding the use of Electronic Voting Machines (EVM), what are the challenges before the Election Commission of India to ensure the trustworthiness of elections in India? *UPSC 2018 (150 words; 10 marks)*

7. 'The Comptroller and Auditor-General (CAG) has a very vital role to play.' Explain how this is reflected in the method and terms of his appointment as well as the range of powers he can exercise. *UPSC 2018 (150 words; 10 marks)*

8. How is the Finance Commission of India constituted? What do you know about the terms of reference of the recently constituted Finance Commission? Discuss. *UPSC 2018 (250 words; 15 marks)*

9. To enhance the quality of democracy in India, the Election Commission of India has proposed electoral reforms in 2016. What are suggested reforms and how far are they significant to make democracy successful? *UPSC 2017 (250 words; 15 marks)*

10. Exercise of CAG's powers in relation to the accounts of the Union and the States is derived from Article 149 of the Indian Constitution. Discuss whether Audit of the government's policy implementation could amount to overstepping its own Comptroller and Auditor-General (CAG) jurisdiction. *UPSC 2016 (200 words; 12(½) marks)*

Statutory, Regulatory and Various Quasi-Judicial Bodies.

1. Explain the reasons for the growth of public interest litigation in India. As a result of it, has the Indian Supreme Court emerged as the world's most powerful judiciary? *UPSC 2024 (250 words; 15 marks)*
2. Discuss the role of the Competition Commission of India in containing the abuse of dominant position by the Multi-National Corporations in India. Refer to the recent decisions. *UPSC 2023 (150 words; 10 marks)*
3. Though the Human Rights Commissions have contributed immensely to the protection of Human Rights in India, yet they have failed to assert themselves against the mighty and powerful. Analysing their structural and practical limitations, suggest remedial measures. *UPSC 2021 (250 words; 15 marks)*
4. Which steps are required for constitutionalisation of a commission? Do you think imparting constitutionality to the National Commission for Women would ensure greater gender justice and empowerment in India? Give reasons. *UPSC 2020 (250 words; 15 marks)*
5. 'The Central Administrative Tribunal which was established for redressal of grievances and complaints by or against Central Government employees, nowadays is exercising its powers as an independent judicial authority.' Explain. *UPSC 2019 (150 words; 10 marks)*
6. How far do you agree with the view that tribunals curtail the jurisdiction of Ordinary Courts? In view of the above, discuss the constitutional validity and competency of the tribunals in India. *UPSC 2018 (250 words; 15 marks)*
7. Multiplicity of various commissions for the vulnerable sections of the society leads to problems of overlapping jurisdiction and duplication of functions. Is it better to merge all commissions into an Umbrella Human Rights Commission? Argue your case. *UPSC 2018 (250 words; 15 marks)*
8. What is a quasi-judicial body? Explain with the help of concrete examples. *UPSC 2016 (200 words; 12(½) marks)*

Important Aspects of Governance, Transparency and Accountability, E-governance Applications, Models, Successes, Limitations and Potential, Citizens Charters, Transparency and Accountability and Institutional and Other Measures.

1. The Doctrine of Democratic Governance makes it necessary that the public perception of the integrity and commitment of civil servants becomes absolutely positive. Discuss. *UPSC 2023 (150 words; 10 marks)*
2. What changes has the Union Government recently introduced in the domain of Centre-State relations? Suggest measures to be adopted to build the trust between the Centre and the States and for strengthening federalism. *UPSC 2024 (250 words; 15 marks)*
3. The Right of Persons with Disabilities Act, 2016 remains only a legal document without intense sensitisation of government functionaries and citizens regarding disability. Comment. *UPSC 2022 (150 words; 10 marks)*
4. Can Civil Society and Non-Governmental Organisations (NGOs) present an alternative model of public service delivery to benefit the common citizen? Discuss the challenges of this alternative model. *UPSC 2021 (250 words; 15 marks)*
5. 'The emergence of Fourth Industrial Revolution (Digital Revolution) has initiated e-governance as an integral part of government'. Discuss. *UPSC 2020 (150 words; 10 marks)*
6. E-governance is not only about utilisation of the power of new technology, but also much about critical importance of the 'use value' of information. Explain. *UPSC 2018 (150 words; 10 marks)*
7. The citizens' charter is an ideal instrument of organisational transparency and accountability, but it has its own limitations. Identify the limitations and suggest measures for greater effectiveness of the citizens' charter. *UPSC 2018 (250 words; 15 marks)*
8. Initially Civil Services in India were designed to achieve the goals of neutrality and effectiveness, which seems to be lacking in the present context. Do you agree with the view that drastic reforms are required in Civil Services? Comment. *UPSC 2017 (250 words; 15 marks)*
9. Discuss the role of Public Accounts Committee in establishing accountability of the government to the people. *UPSC 2017 (150 words; 10 marks)*
10. 'Traditional bureaucratic structure and culture have hampered the process of socio-economic development in India.' Comment. *UPSC 2016 (200 words; 12(½) marks)*

11. Has the Indian Governmental System responded adequately to the demands of Liberalisation, Privatisation and Globalisation started in 1991? What can the government do to be responsive to this important change? *UPSC 2016 (200 words; 12(½) marks)*

12. In the integrity index of Transparency International, India stands very low. Discuss briefly the legal, political, economic, social and cultural factors that have caused the decline of public morality in India. *UPSC 2016 (200 words; 12(½) marks)*

13. 'Effectiveness of the government system at various levels and people's participation in the governance system are interdependent.' Discuss their relationship in the context of India. *UPSC 2016 (200 words; 12(½) marks)*

14. In the light of the Satyam Scandal (2009), discuss the changes brought in corporate governance to ensure transparency, accountability. *UPSC 2015 (200 words; 12(½) marks)*

15. 'In the Indian Governance System, the role of non-state actors has been only marginal.' Critically examine this statement. *UPSC 2016 (200 words; 12(½) marks)*

Role of Civil Services in a Democracy.

1. 'Institutional quality is a crucial driver of economic performance.' In this context, suggest reforms in Civil Service for strengthening democracy. *UPSC 2020 (150 words; 10 marks)*

India and its Neighbourhood Relations.

1. "The West is fostering India as an alternative to reduce dependence on China's supply chain and as a strategic ally to counter China's political and economic dominance." Explain this statement with examples. *UPSC 2024 (150 words; 10 marks)*

2. Critically analyse India's evolving diplomatic, economic and strategic relations with the Central Asian Republics (CAR's) highlighting their increasing significance in regional and global geopolitics. *UPSC 2024 (150 words; 10 marks)*

3. What are the aims and objects of recently passed and enforced, The Public Examination (Prevention of Unfair Means) Act, 2024? Whether University/State Education Board examinations, too, are covered under the Act? *UPSC 2024 (250 words; 15 marks)*

4. 'Terrorism has become a significant threat to global peace and security. Evaluate the effectiveness of the United Nations Security Council's Counter Terrorism Committee (CTC) and its associated bodies in addressing and mitigating this threat at the international level. *UPSC 2024 (250 words; 15 marks)*

5. Discuss the geopolitical and geostrategic importance of Maldives for India with a focus on global trade and energy flows. Further also discuss how this relationship affects India's maritime security and regional stability amidst international competition? *UPSC 2024 (250 words; 15 marks)*

6. 'Virus of Conflict is affecting the functioning of the SCO' In the light of the above statement point out the role of India in mitigating the problems. *UPSC 2023 (150 words; 10 marks)*

7. Indian diaspora has scaled new heights in the West. Describe its economic and political benefits for India. *UPSC 2023 (150 words; 10 marks)*

8. 'The expansion and strengthening of NATO and a stronger US-Europe strategic partnership works well for India.' What is your opinion about this statement? Give reasons and examples to support your answer. *UPSC 2023 (250 words; 15 marks)*

9. 'India is an age-old friend of Sri Lanka'. Discuss India's role in the recent crisis in Sri Lanka in the light of the preceding statement. *UPSC 2022 (150 words; 10 marks)*

10. The question of India's Energy Security constitutes the most important part of India's economic progress. Analyse India's energy policy cooperation with West Asian countries. *UPSC 2017 (250 words; 15 marks)*

11. 'China is using its economic relations and positive trade surplus as tools to develop potential military power status in Asia.' In the light of this statement, discuss its impact on India as her neighbour. *UPSC 2017 (150 words; 10 marks)*

12. Project 'Mausam' is considered a unique Foreign policy initiative of the Indian Government to improve relationship with its neighbours. Does the project have a strategic dimension? Discuss. *UPSC 2015 (200 words; 12(½) marks)*

13. Terrorist activities and mutual distrust have clouded India-Pakistan relations. To what extent the use of soft power like sports and cultural exchanges could help generate goodwill between the two countries? Discuss with suitable examples. *UPSC 2015 (200 words; 12 marks)*